From The Bronx to Oxford
and Not Quite Back

Books by Norman Birnbaum

Editor (With Gertrud Lenzer), *Sociology and Religion: A Book of Readings* (Prentice-Hall, 1969).

The Crisis of Industrial Society (Oxford University Press, 1969).

Toward a Critical Sociology (Oxford University Press, 1971).

Editor, *Beyond the Crisis* (Oxford University Press, 1977).

Social Structure and the German Reformation (Arno Press, 1980).

The Radical Renewal: The Politics of Ideas in Modern America (Pantheon, 1988).

Searching for the Light: Essays on Thought and Culture (Oxford University Press, 1993).

After Progress: American Social Reform and European Socialism in the Twentieth Century (Oxford University Press, 2001).

From The Bronx to Oxford and Not Quite Back

Norman Birnbaum

Washington DC

Copyright © 2017 by Norman Birnbaum
New Academia Publishing, 2018

All rights reserved. No part of this book may be reproduced or transmitted in any form or by any means, electronic or mechanical, including photocopying, recording, or by any information storage and retrieval system.

Printed in the United States of America

Library of Congress Control Number: 2017946197
ISBN 978-0-9986433-4-2 paperback (alk. paper)
ISBN 978-0-9986433-5-9 hardcover (alk. paper)

 An imprint of New Academia Publishing

 4401-A Connecticut Ave., NW #236 - Washington DC 20008
info@newacademia.com - www.newacademia.com

In loving memory of Anna.
In gratitude for Antonia's creative and loving spirit.
In loving hope of Jonathan.

Contents

Acknowledgements	ix
PART I	1
1. The Bronx	3
2. Williams College—And a Different New York	45
3. Return to Williams	83
4. Harvard in Various Forms	101
5. Revision Germany	141
6. London, Part I	163
7. London, Part II	209
8. Oxford, Part I	253
9. Interim I: The Beginning of a Long Farewell to Europe	293
10. The Long Farewell to Europe	327
PART II	361
11. Return to New York	363
12. Amherst	405
13. The US Again	453
14. Transatlantic Politics	501
15. Germans to a Different Front	561
Appendix to Chapter 15. My DDR Adventure: Walled Out—Or, Why I Could Not Visit Stalinism by Subway	593

16. A Routine-ization of History 611
17. Georgetown Law Center: A Welcoming Academic
    Home 645
18. The End of a Century 669
Conclusion 699

About the Author 701
Index of Names 702

Acknowledgements

The Hans-Böckler-Stiftung, the Heinrich-Böll-Stiftung, The Sally and Dick Roberts Coyote Foundation, The Nathan Cummings Foundation, The Wissenschaftskolleg zu Berlin, Reinhard Bütikofer, Member of the European Parliament, Kenneth McNeil, J.D., and the Office of the President at Georgetown University supported this project. Earlier work which initiated the memoir was backed by the BMW Center for German and European Studies of Georgetown University, The Friedrich-Ebert-Stiftung, the German Marshall Fund of the US, and Nuffield College, Oxford. I trust that the text clears the books. I thank as well deans and faculty and students at Georgetown University Law Center for exemplary patience in listening to this tale, often told more than once. The Law Center provided a setting at once stimulating and humane, in fact, a home. I am indebted to editors and fellow writers and readers of *The Nation* for decades of comradeship. My colleagues on The Committee For The Republic have been both friends and teachers. Carolyn and Sally Guthrie gave much (not entirely uncritical) support. Carole Sargent, Georgetown University's Director of the Office of Scholarly Publications, was prodigal with her large energies and talents in bringing the text to publication. Rick Massimo has been an editor of critical acumen. I am grateful to each. Anna Selden of Georgetown University Law Center was very helpful with the manuscript and has my thanks.

Many with whom I would have dearly loved to share these memories are gone. I hope that I have done justice to them. There remains a contingent of the living. I would be very glad were they to find the text worthy of our intersecting lives.

I met John DeGioia when he was an effective and lively assistant to our beloved friend President Timothy Healy–and a lively and effective member of a seminar. As our university President, he has provided unstinting support over the years. I trust that this book, which he did so much to bring to publication, will strike him as partial recompense for his friendship and our decades together.

I cannot recollect many occasions upon which I was at a loss for words. However, it is difficult to express the several ways Terry Flood has enriched my life and work. I leave it at that.

Washington D.C., April 2017

Part I

1

The Bronx

Student picture from Townsend Harris High School, part of City College, age 15 1/2.

DURING the late 1960s, I attempted an autobiographical essay. The first line was easy: Was I too old, at forty-five, to be of interest? One of the self-styled heroes of the sixties had published, to respectful reviews, an autobiography at nineteen. A relative Methuselah, my friend Norman Podhoretz, published *Making It* at thirty-seven. I begin this text a few days before reaching seventy-nine years and six months.

I am sure that the recent past does interest some potential readers: my personal past might be instructive for those trying to understand the last century in order to grasp this one. Where the personal ends and history begins is an answerable question, no doubt, but my struggle for an answer has cost a great deal of effort and has stretched my capacity for dealing with difficult truths about myself—a capacity that, for long periods, was exceedingly underdeveloped. Writing this memoir is an attempt to gain clarity about matters which, for long periods, I preferred to leave in a fog. I first read *Ulysses* at seventeen and was much struck by Stephen Dedalus's words: "History is a nightmare from which I am trying to awake." My own version of it might have been "History is a reality to which I flee from the nightmare of my life." Looked at now, my life was not all that bad, although for long periods I felt badly about it, or rather, about myself. In any case, now I realize my flight was unsuccessful, and standing one's ground is the only way to understand both oneself and the world around one.

History sets the conditions for personal development. Suppose, however, that history becomes part of the self, perhaps the essential part. Freud thought so, depicting history in very long terms and allowing no escape from it. He was thinking of the permanent psychological effects of the lives of our ancestors, immediate and distant. I recollect my first analyst, when I complained that returning to the Bronx from Williamstown depressed me, declaring that I was suffering from two thousand years of history. I have struggled in and with psychoanalysis for much of my life, a secular Jacob confronting the very ambivalent angels of his nature. Perhaps that is what is left to me of the Jewish idea of God—an unstilled argument with an inner voice. Perhaps there are several of them trying to outshout each other, many of them harsh. Perhaps, however, some of my troubles had more personal and proximate causes.

I did not allow myself much inwardness as a child—building up a great deal of character armor with considerable precociousness in intellectual pursuits and accomplishments. In this way, I protected myself, as best as I could, from outer and inner dangers. I look back on a long stillness of feeling, but the silence does have echoes.

My sister, in 2005, shortly before her death, described her impression of our childhood—a joyless family, parsimonious of delight and generosity. I am convinced that this was not entirely so, that there were infrequent episodes of gaiety and gratification—but these prove the hardest to remember. Inwardly blocked, I moved in unacknowledged despair to an outer battlefield. I regarded the Bronx as a prison, once I caught a glimpse of the world beyond it—but it was the Bronx, and my family, with all of our failings, that gave me the strength to leave it.

I was not in fact born in the Bronx but in Manhattan—in Harlem, where in 1926 there was a Jewish enclave, before its residents, who had moved uptown from the Lower East Side, ventured to the one New York City borough on the American mainland. There my parents lived, and my earliest memory of landscape is strikingly rural—of what were then the open fields and woods of the northeast Bronx. Years later, reading a history of the American Communist Party by Lewis Coser and Irving Howe, I was delighted to find their reference to a pamphlet addressed to "the workers and peasants of the Bronx." I do not remember any farms, much less American Kulaks, but do recall the Bronx Zoo. We moved again when I was very little to the west Bronx, and there we remained. That was New York of the thirties and forties, apartment houses, ethnic neighborhoods, minute gradations of status and income within each—and awareness, subliminal, dim or acute, of other worlds not many blocks away, as well as of the United States, which began somewhere north of the city line or across the Hudson River. Of course, one could always visit the United States without a visa: there were the movies.

My father was a school teacher, though he was previously a violinist in the orchestra of the Capitol Theater when ornate major cinemas had orchestras to accompany silent films. Before that, he had graduated in 1922 from City College, where one of his classmates was Sidney Hook. They studied philosophy with Morris Raphael Cohen, and my father intimated that that legendary figure—a stern professor and role model to several generations of students—had advised him not to attempt a career in philosophy. Some texts in the bookcase were evidence for his interests, which ran heavily to discussions of evolution and ethics, with a decidedly progressivist cast. I found Charles Beard and Vernon Parrington at home and recall Claude Bowers's biography of Jefferson. Bowers was Franklin Roosevelt's ambassador to the embattled Spanish Republic, which Roosevelt, on account of his dependence upon Catholic voters, was

My father, Silas Jacob Birnbaum

unable to help. When I came to awareness of these things at twelve, I did not imagine that I would become friendly with the Spanish socialists and write regularly for the post-Franco Madrid newspaper, *El País*.

Behind my father were not generations of Talmudic scholars, as far as I know, but a family of Jewish artisans. My paternal grandfather came from Radom, southwest of Warsaw, and had served in the army of His Imperial Majesty, the Tsar. We had a large sepia photograph of him in full uniform with a sabre. Fortunately for all of us, he left Russian Poland in 1898, stopped briefly with cousins in Manchester, and came to New York.

He told me when I was very young that in Manchester, he had been assaulted by a thug, had defended himself by felling him, and then had been told by a sympathetic policeman to move on. The entire family's benign image of Her Britannic Majesty's realm stems from that story: we were admiring but not surprised when Britain refused to make peace after the fall of France. I wonder what effect it had on me, in combination with Freud's remark about his lifelong dismay at his father having given way when ordered off the sidewalk by a Gentile in Brno. Freud was a rebel and never gave way, and declared that psychoanalysis would have encountered less resistance had his name been Huber. I never felled an anti-Semite, but wreaked plenty of political havoc, in the best of cases, on authority—but as we shall see, I refused to allow myself to feel that I was an outsider in an anti-Semitic world. To be sure, much of the world I later inhabited was, if anything, philo-Semitic.

As a school teacher, my father obviously had contacts with colleagues who were not Jewish. The old Protestant ascendancy in the Board of Education had given way to an uneasy equilibrium in which Catholics and Jews were seeking their places. My father must have gotten on well with his Gentile colleagues. The principal of his junior high school was Irish; the principal of Benjamin Franklin, the high school in which he taught from 1934 onward, was Italian. I later went to that junior high school and recall the principal, an outsized Thomas Donahue. The Italian, Leonard Covello, was short and thin, spoke English with the precision of someone whose first language it was not.

I recall my father running up the apartment house stairs with excitement to tell us that he had received a letter with news of his appointment to Benjamin Franklin, a school built in 1933-34 with New Deal money obtained by Mayor Fiorello La Guardia and Congressman Vito Marcantonio. At the time, there was a large southern Italian population in East Harlem. My father's license was in music, but he was promoted rather soon to the post of administrative assistant, the principal's *factotum*, with considerable delegated power. Covello had done a doctoral dissertation at Teacher's College of Columbia University on the *contadino*, the southern Italian peasant, and on Italian peasant communities in the emigration to the US. He lent it to me to read, much later, when I was in graduate school. That pleased my father very much. I had become as a graduate student at Harvard *ex officio*—a person to be respected.

The student population of Benjamin Franklin changed from Italian and Irish to Puerto Rican and Black, with a certain amount of tension, over the next decades. Once, Frank Sinatra visited the school to sing and lecture the students on the value of ethnic and racial harmony. Daniel Patrick Moynihan graduated from Benjamin Franklin and was encouraged by his teachers, including my father, whom he recalled, to go to City College and not to work full time on the docks.

My father's school, briefly, was for him—and indirectly for myself—a way of envisaging a society other than family, friends, neighborhood. My family's relationship to Judaism and Jewishness was complex. My parents were not observant, belonged to no synagogue. There were some standard histories of Jews and Judaism in the house. I recollect finding one on Jews in Medieval Europe interesting, but was much more drawn to reading about American history or world politics.

My grandfather did belong to a synagogue, more or less Orthodox—but my memory about it is that there was a near-permanent quarrel in the congregation, involving perpetual conflicts between officers and the rabbi, or more accurately the rabbis, since these succeeded one another with some rapidity. My father belonged to a lodge, of which he became president at one point—amidst interminable squabbles recounted at our nightly supper table. The group was named after the British Sephardic figure, Moses Montefiore,

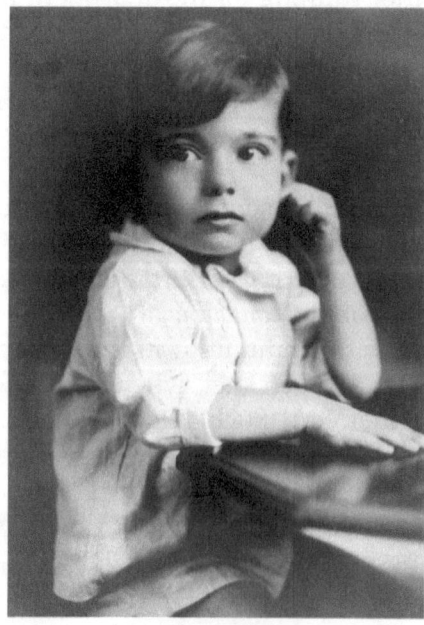

Future member of *The Partisan Review* editorial board.

legendary for his wealth and charity. I had only the dimmest idea of the Sephardic journey, but Montefiore's Britishness reinforced my early curiosity—no, fascination—with the United Kingdom. (When I finally got there, one of my friends at Oxford was a teacher of philosophy at Balliol College who was the heir apparent to headship of the family, Alan Montefiore. I spent some days in Jerusalem at Mishkenot Sha'ananim, the city's center for cultural visitors between the King David Hotel and the Old City. Upon returning home, I hastened to send their library my books. The building was in fact the hospital Montefiore had given to the Jerusalem Jewish community under the Ottomans, in the late nineteenth century.)

Jerusalem seemed, when I was young, impossibly far away, more remote than Berlin, London, Paris, Rome, as we saw these in the newsreels. I knew of the anti-Semitism of the Nazis, but the Arab-Jewish conflicts in the Holy Land in the thirties had my attention only fleetingly. Families with active Zionist sympathies did follow events in the Holy Land closely, and the fact that we did not suggested distance from the cause.

My father certainly did not run from the fact that he was Jewish, and referred occasionally to the anti-Semitism of the larger society. He repeatedly took the examination to be made eligible for an assistant principalship, and repeatedly failed the oral part. I heard him discussing one day the fact that his pronunciation of English was held against him, intimating that the examiners' judgment was unfair, very possibly anti-Semitic. My father spoke a grammatically impeccable and well-articulated English, in deep monotone—with nothing of the Yiddish cadences audible in the English of many Jewish New Yorkers. He was born, to be sure, in Irkutsk, when my grandfather was there on garrison duty, but came to the US when he was two. I did not sense in him, despite the discussion of the disappointing judgment of the examiner, an obsession with anti-Semitism, or indeed, perpetual resentment at it. He treated it as a fact of life, seemed to believe that with human progress it could be surmounted, and as a reverent admirer of Franklin Roosevelt, obviously had great hopes for the American future.

The moral forces Roosevelt sought to mobilize did after the war render the US more hospitable to Jews (and everyone else). Father certainly had no conviction that the Gentile world was unremittingly hostile—or he would not have suggested that I consider going to a quintessential fortress of elite white Protestantism such as Williams College when I was thinking about college choices.

I do now see and perhaps sensed then that there was a certain dutifulness to Grandfather's Judaism. At that time, no one used the term "identity," which came into general usage from psychoanalytic ego psychology and the work of Erik Erikson in the fifties and sixties, but certainly belonging to a synagogue was part of my grandfather's sense of self. There was another and possibly more important part, however: he read *Forverts*, the Yiddish daily with a social democratic cast. As I recall it, he was very interested in world politics, and an active member of the painter's union. He had a good friend and business partner, Morris, and they talked about world events. What they could not do was paint our apartment: my mother did not think that they were up to her standards.

I'm struck now by a direct line of political heredity. My father, too, was concerned with the larger world. He read *The New York Times* and, much to the left of it, the afternoon newspaper, the *New York Post*. (The family that then owned it, the Backers, as well as its editors, writers, and readers, would have been shocked by Murdoch's present *Post* and its vulgar apologists for Israel, seething with resentment. The spiritual achievements of the people of the Old Testament were indeed very great: they deserve contemporary defenders with rather more class.) Unfortunately, those spiritual achievements were not communicated directly to me when I was a child. As a compensation, Grandfather brought with him from Europe a sense that the world was different and multitudinous, that it and its people could be enjoyed and that one did not have to think of them as entirely hostile, actually or potentially. My father, in college and in his teaching, entered that world and brought to it the same attitude.

Father was, I now realize, ambivalent in his attitude to Judaism. He accepted his Jewishness, although as I write these words I'm reminded of Carlyle's celebrated response to Margaret Fuller's declaration that she accepted the universe ("She had better"). Jewishness was fate; the United States, Americanness was choice. Grandfather was secure in the culture he brought with him from Russian Poland, was delighted to enjoy the United States, worried about the new Haman in the distance (Hitler), and was glad that his children would carry on. Father, the eldest of seven children (five boys and two girls), had a sense of mission—or burden. He acted like a man confronting difficult challenges. John Dewey's books were in the house (I struggled early with *Human Nature and Conduct*)—and so were Mark Twain's. I now understand that these were evidence for his attempt to include himself in the nation—and of intellectual ambitions which had to be subordinated to the task of making a living on a rather difficult cultural frontier.

Mother's major preoccupation was herself. She seemed to avoid confronting the process of assimilation. I have only the dimmest memory of my maternal grandparents, both of whom died when I was very young. Mother had two sisters and two brothers, all in Philadelphia, where she grew up. I guess that her family was rather more proletarian in its European origins than my father's, based only on the memory that there were many fewer books around their houses, and their horizons seemed somewhat narrower. They were cousins of the New York Birnbaums, although I could not draw a kinship diagram today. Mother was a middle child, spent a year at Temple University and then worked as a secretary before marrying Father just about the time he joined the school system.

There was a family story to the effect that at the wedding, the rabbi refused the envelope with his fee, which he deemed insufficient, forcing my father to add to it. My father was a very generous man, so the rabbi might well have been abusing his limited tie to God. My mother told me this story, ostensibly complaining about the rabbi, but actually about Father. Mother had an extremely developed sense of entitlement and—as many of their friends were in business and somewhat wealthier— regret that we did not have more money.

That wasn't the worst of it, as far as I was concerned. My mother thought of herself as the representative of convention—or what passed for such in her mind. She wanted me to be much more familially oriented, more conventional. She didn't know what to do with me. I had the impression that she found my curiosity and independence disturbing, my disinclination to accept our world as the center of the universe (or, rather, my increasingly vocal rejection of that idea as I approached adolescence) as a rejection. I wonder now if I wasn't the surrogate for her discontent with Father—who was a good deal less critical, even approving, of the independence she despaired of. What did that consist of, if not a refusal to join the other children on the street, my immersion in books, my pointing out that I was made to undergo the ordeal of a Bar Mitzvah when they were so conspicuously distant from the synagogue?

Was my sister, Ruth, right in saying that our life was joyless, without a sense of comfort or togetherness? She complained of a sense of restriction, of the notion that any expenditure at all was an impermissible indulgence. Ruth had good reason to be bitter: she had wanted to attend the University of Wisconsin when she graduated from high school in 1948, and my parents would not hear of it. I was at graduate school then—well supported by Williams, and about to become a teaching fellow at Harvard—and was not a burden on the family. That, however, was the excuse conveyed to Ruth—who, to her enormous credit, did not bear me a lifelong grudge. Perhaps it explained why, shortly after graduating from Hunter College (its uptown Bronx campus) in 1952, she married Ed Greenbaum, an extremely amiable schoolteacher himself. Ruth subsequently had three children, and I think she was, to them, the mother she felt she lacked.

She did have conflicts with her eldest daughter, Joanne, who became a much-exhibited painter. Joanne and Ruth disagreed on Joanne's giving up a well-paying job as a photo archivist to concentrate on her painting—but I am sure there was more to it. Ruth was a particularly attentive grandmother to the children of her middle daughter, Susan, who lived near her in Westchester. Susan married an Israeli she had met when studying in Israel, and lived with him in Jerusalem for a while. Eventually they returned to the US, where he became a prosperous businessman—all the while worrying about Israel's fate, entrusted by him to those who remained. Ruth was especially delighted with her grandsons' very attractive girlfriends, one of Italian and the other of Korean descent, since her son-in-law's aggressive ethnocentricity irritated her.

Ruth once told me that, wherever she was and whatever she was doing, she began toward the end of the day to feel that she should be at home. She thought that this was an active remnant of the sense of duty inflicted upon her as a child. She certainly acted it out. She and her husband joined my parents in a summer camp they owned and managed together for some years. After my father's death in 1973, Ruth assumed responsibility for Mother—who lived very near her. I was a very infrequent visitor, despite passing through Westchester regularly on my way to stay at a surrogate family, the Fishers, in Manhattan. I suppose one could summarize the situation as a paradox. She did her duty—or what she thought of as such—despite considerable inner protest at it. I took my freedom, and ignored the inner voices of reproach. Perhaps that accounted for my curious lack of memory of feeling when I think of childhood: the memories are mainly intellectual and visual. The one feeling I do have is of loneliness punctuated by anger and dread. I have carried that with me for a very long time.

The anger was directed at my family. It spared Grandfather, if encompassing Father, who was actually benign and supportive in many ways. I recollect one period of going habitually to the subway station to meet him when he returned uptown from teaching: perhaps I resented his leaving me, unprotected, with Mother.

What I cannot grasp is why I was so angry with Mother. She gave the impression of being angry, tight-lippedly so, herself. A few times I thought inchoately that she provoked tradesmen by arguing about the quality and price of services. (I recall an angry dispute with a laundry driver in Upstate New York at a summer house we rented.) She carried a charge of resentment that was difficult to ignore.

Part of this is explicable by the conflicting demands of a difficult historical location. Her parents were emigrants from the Eastern European ghetto; her siblings were willing to settle for life in an ethnic enclave with few pretensions. She had married, however, someone more educated and had a certain sense of her responsibility for representation.

I had the impression of someone who interpreted many things as importunities. My father was no sooner home from school, than supper was prepared—very early, as if to get it over and done with. I have no memory that my mother took particular pride in directing an efficient household, though it was certainly that.

Children are not without resources. My attitude to my father was certainly ambivalent (the Oedipus complex is real, although my own attraction to my mother was exceedingly well-repressed). If ours was a more ethnically Jewish household than a religiously Jewish one, it was more Jewish for the emphasis on learning.

Somehow, the notion that the path to identity, success, was through some kind of intellectual activity, was hardly concealed. I didn't feel right about myself; I was curious about this larger world, and how to get into it. And the way to get into it, at first, seemed to be through omnivorous reading. So I picked up things.

I do recall discussing world affairs with him, and with very great pleasure a few occasions when we went by ourselves on the town. One was to La Champlain, a French restaurant on the West Side of Manhattan, where he reproached a waiter for insufficient courtesy. Another was to a Philharmonic concert conducted by Bruno Walter; we sat in a front row, and I heard the great conductor singing Mozart as he went along. We also went to a play (*Flight to the West*, by Eugene Rice). It entailed an anti-Nazi travelling from Lisbon to New York on one of the great flying boats of Pan-American, and a German diplomat on the plane who was beside himself when the pilot put in at Bermuda, where the German faced internment. There was some shooting by someone else, a victim of the Nazis, striking back. I was already reading books and weeklies and newspapers and so the play, like Hitchcock's political films and the newsreels, was history live. I knew no German but certainly knew Hitler's voice from broadcasts during the Sudeten crisis in 1938 and at the outbreak of the war in 1939. My father and I listened together.

I had become aware of the civil war in Spain. It began when I was ten, but by the time I was twelve, I was reading books about it. I have a memory of a rally for the Spanish Republic, at the old Madison Square Garden on Eighth Avenue at 50th Street.

André Malraux and Thomas Mann were among the speakers, and I already knew who they were. Later, in 1940, I joined a group of protesters at a meeting of the America First Committee at the Garden; we were met with anti-Semitic insults. I'd gone often to the Garden with Father, since his high school was a powerful competitor in the public high school sports league (there was another league for private and mainly Catholic schools).We went occasionally for college basketball, in which City College was a nationally ranked team playing against visitors from improbably distant places in the Midwest and South. I heard the memorable match between Joe Louis and the German Max Schmeling on radio; my father took me to baseball, basketball, football, but not boxing.

Jewish New York was thrilled when the Detroit outfielder Hank Greenberg sat out a World Series game on Yom Kippur—which, we hoped, earned him and the Jews respect from the rest of the country. I was aware of the persecutions of Jews happening in Europe at the time, but my reaction to Greenberg's stance revealed a defiant pride in my Jewishness that I hadn't realized was there.

Sport was very much part of public life in New York, and for me the connection of the Garden with politics as well as sport was not at all odd. Franklin Roosevelt in 1936 and in 1940 (I went to that one) spoke at presidential campaign rallies at the Garden. Attending these events attested the reality of a public world I only knew otherwise from radio and reading. I also recall being taken by an uncle in 1936 to visit the carrier Saratoga at a Hudson River dock. The bi-planes were on the hangar decks. I was impressed by the colorful insignia of a Top Hat squadron and by the stenciled names of the pilots on the fuselages under the open cockpits. Six years later, these were the squadrons that fought at the Coral Sea and Midway—and many of those men died in the attacks on the Japanese carriers at Midway. Until the war, our segment of New York society sent no one to the Navy, much less to the Navy's officer corps. That was part of America that seemed at once impossibly distant and omnipresent—in film.

When I was about twelve, I read Dos Passos's great *U.S.A.* trilogy, as well as some of the novels of Sinclair Lewis and Upton Sinclair. It was Dos Passos who made the most profound impression, perhaps because of the striking literary technique he adopted from film and newspaper (the segments marked "Newsreel" stick in memory). I recall the characters, people I could not imagine meeting, and the sense of the relentless demands of money and power. These books certainly kept me from idealizing the nation I knew was next door, or on the other side of the Hudson—but made it seem, also, a place of excitement and opportunity for adventures I could not name or even specify.

I must then have very early posed to myself the question how to encounter history—which appeared to come effortlessly to the heroes, even the anti-heroes, of the books I read. They were immersed in it, even when the books as I recall them (like Aldous Huxley's *Point Counter Point*) were not explicitly political. I overlooked, or rather under-estimated, my own immersion. I've mentioned Grandfather's and Father's interests in politics, the books in the house; *The New Republic*, then very much at the left of the Democratic Party and published in New York, and *The Nation* came, too. The newspapers were easier to deal with, on account of the straightforward narrative of events, even distant ones. The weeklies were problematic. They offered interpretations, sketches of events, movements, persons who did not quite fit the newspapers' serial stories, and in the book reviews and cultural columns, different narratives and references to matters I did not grasp.

What I did not realize at the time was how much we were immersed in history ourselves. That was due to our realization that we were living at the edge of the nation. We would have preferred it to be otherwise, but the reminders were all around us. The New Deal and progressivism generally offered an account of the nation which gave us a place—but we were quite aware that it was not a vision everyone shared.

We, or rather I, certainly identified the Republicans as far worse than Midwestern provincials or Eastern Seaboard snobs—as hateful and certainly anti-Semitic. There was a difficulty, however. Clearly, the New York Irish were part of the New Deal coalition: Al Smith had been a predecessor of Franklin Roosevelt in making New York State a small welfare state, and James Farley was the chair of the Democratic Party. But years later, my Jesuit friend Tim Healy was to express his astonishment at the anti-Semitism of the Irish who, unlike the Poles before 1939, did not have many Jews sharing their country. New Deal beliefs portrayed a nation in which these distinctions were subordinated to a common calling. In reality, we feared the power of the distinctions—and the fear was reinforced not only by the elder generation's memories of Europe but by the conquest of Germany by the Nazis and the expansion of the Third Reich.

November 9 is a singular date in German history: in 1918 it was the day of the Kaiser's abdication, his ignoble flight to the Netherlands, and the proclamation of the Republic; in 1989 it was the opening of the Wall. In 1938, it was Kristallnacht, the night of smashed glass, in which a state-organized Pogrom was retaliation for the shooting of a German diplomat in Paris by a Jewish emigrant. I was aware of the shooting and of its dreadful sequel, and intuited that worse would follow. The next day, I went to our neighborhood public library. That entailed walking a few blocks away, past a parochial school and a church. There were some boys in front of the Church and one of them taunted me: "Hey, you, the Jews in Germany had their balls cut off yesterday."

I hurried on, leaving for years later the reflection that he must have had his own fears of extreme impotence. That gang's school and church were administered by Jesuits—what would they have thought of my teaching at Georgetown? I appreciate the large changes in the nation that advanced the integration of Jews—but also the lesson in reality that the episode taught me. Murder was an omnipresent possibility.

That event made real what I was learning of the world, then, from books, film, magazines, newspapers. There were also, though, the lessons imparted directly as instruction by Grandfather and Father, and by my aunts and uncles, too. I surely learned of the world from my father's siblings, immersed in the ordinary roughness of the commercial world, contrasted with my father's choice of another sphere. As a group, they managed. One uncle worked as a clerk for Columbia Pictures at its New York office; another was in Hollywood as a sound technician; another was, like Grandfather, a painter, but sold old clocks on the side. The youngest, Bernard, abandoned rabbinical studies and could not find a job until after his wartime service as an officer in the Air Corps. He then became a prosperous department store executive. One aunt taught art in school before her premature death and another was preparing for a school teaching career before marrying. Grandfather's sister worked in the garment industry but, more importantly, was the one family member who was in or close to the Communist Party.

My mother's family in Philadelphia surmounted the Depression in its own way. One uncle worked as a manager for a fruit wholesaler. Another was an investor or middleman and had a rather large house in a prosperous North Philadelphia neighborhood. Two of my mother's sisters worked as bookkeepers or secretaries; a third kept house for her husband, a very friendly milkman. He once gave me a ride on his cart and later, alas, was thrown and fatally injured when his horse bolted. There was also an entrepreneurial brother-in-law who dealt in real estate. He was the counterweight to the communist aunt in New York, as I recall his tirades against the New Deal (and, inevitably, against blacks).

My parents had to deal with me. My aunts and uncles had a certain amount of choice, and I am grateful now for their attention and warmth. Through them, I learned just a bit about the struggles of ordinariness, about everyday existence. My prosperous maternal uncle actually provided a great treat, taking me once to the race track at Havre de Grace, Maryland. He and friends were preparing a betting coup, placing a horse in a New York race at long odds. The animal did his best but finished second. I recall visiting the barn in Maryland and actually seeing the equine protagonist. The same uncle, Ben, bought me my first airplane ride, in an open cockpit plane from an airport in North Philadelphia. The other aunts in Philadelphia were distressed to learn of the adventure. Ben was himself an adventurous sort and had shocked the family by marrying a Catholic French woman, Lucille, who was very hospitable to me.

These aunts and uncles were not preoccupied with understanding history, with the revolutions and counter-revolutions of our time. They had tasks hard enough in surviving. Whatever early skepticism I had (and it was not much) about the absolute value of the abstractions I acquired from reading, I owe to them. I also owe it to school and neighborhood. The difficulty for a long time was that I felt more at ease with abstractions.

I began at a neighborhood school, Public School Ninety. My chief memory of it is how well scrubbed the children were, how benign and encouraging the teachers. The classes were organized on a tracking principle, and I was in a very fast track, with one cohort of students who skipped an entire year. The school was largely Jewish in its student body and in the fast track; many of the students came from the prosperous business and professional families who lived in the apartment buildings on the Grand Concourse itself.

It was not entirely idyllic. I recollect a few schoolyard bullies and a couple of teachers supervising the schoolyard whose lung power was their most evident quality. The students were eager to please, and our work must have gratified the teachers, as we progressed from grade to grade with good report cards. What I cannot remember, surprisingly, is what precisely we learned. At any rate, I moved easily from whatever we did in the classroom to the education I obtained on my own.

I had much more inner tension when I went to junior high school at Prospect—Junior High School Forty, two streetcar rides away in the east Bronx. My father had taught there and was insistent on my going there. He expected me to do well—indeed, to excel, and that was the problem. I was eleven when I entered and beginning a phase of heightened rebelliousness. I cannot recollect discussions of the decision to enroll at Prospect—in itself evidence for a certain inner strain. There was no particular reason to go there; I could have remained at PS 90 until high school. I suppose that my father, proud of my academic skills, expected that these would impress his former colleagues, some of whom he was still in close touch with. One, a Mr. Solomon, was, I think, a published poet, and I recollect discussions at our home and his of his unsuccessful search for a college teaching post (with explicit reference to the barrier of anti-Semitism). It was he who declared that he would expect me to have the best notebook in the class.

Again, my memory is blurred, but I recollect uneasy, even tense, relations with two teachers of English—usually a field in which I was very good. One was a former colleague of my father's, possibly one he was not on exceptionally friendly terms with. The other was a younger man named Phillips, apparently determined not to be impressed by a scion of the old guard. I think that I thought the older man arrogant and judgmental, the younger one actually anxious to teach us something. As with primary school, I can remember almost nothing of the actual instructional material: what texts did we read? Phillips clearly thought that he was conveying method as well as content, and I showed some respect for him.

Prospect was different in another way. That part of the east Bronx had once been pre-dominantly Jewish (there was a legend that Trotsky had worked at a tailoring shop in the neighborhood). By my arrival, the student body was mixed (the student president at one point was Greek), including blacks. I recall a certain schoolyard roughness, even a couple of confrontations in which I was rescued by larger students or teachers. When I went to purchase lunch at a local delicatessen, I was occasionally the butt of aggression (from other Jewish students): my books were taken off the chair I sought to reserve and hidden. In short, it was a neighborhood inhabited by the undeserving poor—who were difficult to live with.

Paradoxically, this was a period in which my reading outside of school frequently dealt with class and political struggle—and found me invariably on the side of the exploited and oppressed. I identified with them at a distance. The American union movement had just achieved great triumphs, particularly in the industrial Midwest; the Austrian, German and Italian ones had suffered great defeats. I knew of the failure of the British General Strike of 1926, and John Strachey's *The Coming Struggle for Power* promised revenge. A copy of Edgar Snow's *Red Star Over China* found its way to our bookshelves. All I knew of China beforehand came from Pearl Buck's *The Good Earth*. Snow's Chinese peasants were much more to my liking.

It was in this period, too, that I read a letter that made an indelible impression. Father had a book with notable letters, and one was written by Thomas Mann to the Rector of the University of Bonn, who had revoked his honorary degree because his anti-Nazism in exile "harmed German culture." Mann's letter was eloquent in many ways, but I was especially struck by its conclusion. He could not have harmed German culture, he said, because German culture was to be found where he stood. The combination of political defiance and enormous pride was superb. There were books about the Third Reich in the house, Mowrer's *Germany Puts the Clock Back* among them. We occasionally met German Jews who had come to New York. The least that can be said is that they seemed very different from us in their distance and formality.

I read a bit about German Jewish history (in English) and assimilated their tragedy to that of the Spanish Jews in 1492. Could this curse be visited upon us?

I discussed some of this with my father. He had a complex, even ambivalent attitude, his response to his cultural and generational position. He had integrated himself into American society and knew a good deal about it—beyond the boundaries of our borough and city. Of course, he was aware of our family's very recent immigration and emergence from precariousness. He was skeptical of living a life entirely within the boundaries of Jewishness and was neither a Zionist nor a synagogue member, nor attached to Hebrew or Yiddish culture. He was certainly aware of anti-Semitism in American life, but less obsessed by it than some of his contemporaries and friends with similar biographies. I mentioned a Mr. Solomon (Izzy Solomon) who thought his career misfortunes due to anti-Semitism. He may have been right, and my father had indeed evoked the possibility that some of his troubles in passing the assistant principal's examination were due to prejudice. He showed admirable persistence, and years later, when I was in Europe, he did pass the examination and was appointed an assistant principal at a Bronx junior high school.

All of his friends who were teachers followed events in Europe very closely. No one mentioned the German battleship building program, or the long-range planes being test flown there. However, we tied the Nazi anti-Semitic project to German expansionism. There was an argument to the effect that avoiding war with Germany would in the end protect the Jews since it would allow a measure of international influence on the Nazi regime. Neither my father nor his friends took it seriously. (The date of the Wannsee Conference, which decided upon the extermination of European Jewry, was January of 1942, after the US finally entered the war. Perhaps total war allowed Hitler and his inner circle to drop their last inhibitions.) We knew of the very great difficulties of German Jews who sought to immigrate to the US. We knew equally that the isolationists who shortly thereafter united in the America First movement often were anti-Semitic. Events in Europe, and what we considered the inadequate American response, cast a shadow over us. This strengthened my father's loyalty (and that of his friends) to Franklin Roosevelt and the New Deal. We could be saved only by America's better spirits.

What impression did I have of the Soviet Union? The American Communist Party and the organizations it sponsored, and especially its very effective cadres in the cultural industry and the trade union movement, were most influential in the period of the Popular Front. I saw the usual Soviet films (*Battleship Potemkin* and others) and read some novels and *Ten Days That Shook the World*.

The corrective supplied by Trotsky and his followers did not, at first, reach me.in the form of alternative and critical Marxist analyses of world events. I first encountered these in 1941 when I began to read *Partisan Review* and became aware of the Marxist sects that lent such color and variety to New York's ideological garden. What I did read early, since my father had it, was the report of the John Dewey Commission investigating the Soviet case against the defendants in the various treason trials, among them (in absentia) Trotsky. The commission went to Mexico to question Trotsky and published its report in 1937.

Many of the references in it were arcane and bewildered me, but the conclusion was clear: Trotsky had been slandered, the Bolsheviks found guilty by Soviet courts of counter-revolutionary activity were victims of systematic injustice, and Stalin was a tyrant. Whatever else could be said for and against the Soviet Union, it was not the moral counterweight to capitalism and fascism that its sympathizers believed it to be. I think that I read the report in 1938. When a year later, in August 1939, the world was shocked by the Nazi-Soviet Pact, I experienced astonishment but not disappointment. I was astonished since I had expected war between Germany and the USSR (in the event, only delayed twenty-two months). I was not disappointed in the USSR, since I had begun, however dimly, to understand the world as a series of struggles for power in which dark historical forces rendered much of human purpose and will null.

My understanding was dim because I could not free myself of a certain Manicheanism which divided the world into progressive and reactionary forces and allowed almost no complexity or nuance. When I encountered historical events or commentaries which defied simple categorization, I avoided confronting these, since I lacked the intellectual resources to resolve the dilemmas they entailed. The USSR had issued from (I had thought) a glorious revolution: if it was now corrupted or deformed, what could explain this and set it right? In the meantime, what could replace the USSR of progressivist fantasy as an anti-fascist force? I could hardly, at twelve, proceed to Orwell's conclusion (at the end of *1984*) that much of history would now consist of a boot in a human face. Another problem was posed by thinkers such as Charles Beard or

Robert Hutchins, undoubtedly critical and generally on the right (which was to say, left) side of things—but who sided with the isolationists in the debate on possible US war on Germany, Japan and Italy.

Maturation takes time, and after decades in which I struggled with these issues, it would be unduly harsh to condemn an early adolescent struggling to comprehend a world which bewildered many of his much older contemporaries. The source of a good deal of my lack of clarity and resolution, however, was an inner conflict.

Once, at the Wellfleet Psychohistory group which he founded with Robert Lifton, I disagreed with Erik Erikson on the saliency of the search for identity in contemporary Western culture. I said that I thought that many persons were not looking for identities, but seeking to discard identities they had and which they did not like. Some of my enduring inner tension to this day involves a struggle over Jewishness, incompletely resolved by the thought that I remain a secular Jew. The secular part absolves me of an overt expression of ethnic responsibility; the Jewish part frees me from the (inner) reproach of deserting in the face of the enemy, having preferred a general struggle for democracy rather than a specific struggle against anti-Semitism. I am struck by the fact that the persons I know who seem closest to Old Testament ideals were Protestants who were able to take the moral content of the Old Testament and let the tribal history go—women, like my wife Nina Apel or friends Terry Flood, Sally Guthrie, Faythe Turner, Helga Soto, Abigail Trafford; active Protestants such as Harvey Cox, Erhard Eppler, Helmut Gollwitzer, Wolfgang Huber, Thomas Hughes, Wolf-Dieter Marsch, Roger Mehl, and Lewis Mudge. I learned more about the ethical imperatives of the Old Testament from them than from my Jewish friends. They were struggling, as was I, to find some distance from tradition, the Protestants to keep what seemed best in theirs. All differences of personality apart, the Protestants struck me as more certain of where they belonged, even—despite the commonplaces about the Jewish affinity for modernism—more open to experiment in their lives.

In my own case, tribal history in the form of family history was impossible to escape. I responded to preparations for my Bar Mitzvah and the event itself with unfocused anger. My parents neither kept a Kosher household (the bacon was hastily pushed to the back of the refrigerator when my grandfather was in the kitchen, to his amusement) nor communicated anything of Jewish ritual or tradition. They spoke Yiddish to keep things from the children—possibly a source of my later fluency in German. I was aware of my father's belief in and practice of assimilation, of my mother's narrow concept of Jewishness as convention. I was given Hebrew tutoring at first my by Uncle Bernard, and then sent to a grim neighborhood Hebrew school where the instruction was rote. I recollect no effort to convey anything of the history of the ritual: its importance was taken for granted. I was powerless to refuse to turn up, but do sympathize now with the officiating Rabbi who asked me quietly to look as if I were interested. I hardly remember my reaction.

My response to Jewishness was an expression of a larger inner crisis of which I was only dimly aware—or which I could not openly face. I felt rebellious—and impotent to do anything about it except develop profound hostility to authority of any kind. The sense of impotence was all the greater since there seemed to be no relief, no way out. I was too realistic to lose myself in fantasies of another family, did not know how to join a different world, did not know where it could be found. What I did know was that, gradually and then with increasing intensity, I wished that I were someplace else.

Perhaps, however, the real wish was that I could become someone else. When I graduated from junior high school, shortly before the Bar Mitzvah, my father was exceedingly angry. I had won no medals, and in the taxi taking the family to the graduation ceremony, he vented his disappointment. Neither Mother nor Ruth defended me, I wished to stop the taxi and flee. To this day I recall with asperity that the fellow student who did win medals I met later at City College, where he was a decent if ordinary chap studying engineering, whereas I went on in the end to other pursuits.

It was, I think, the loneliness and then a constant burden of internalized criticism that contributed to a persistent depression. I struggled against it, sought contacts, could never arrive at a different shore. The sharp edges, the soft depths, of experience were inaccessible: inner poetry was killed, and I had little ear for the outer kind. Certainly, my perpetually nagging ambition (which grew more demanding with anything that could be construed as success) had its origins in the wish to convert my father's disapproval into its opposite. My loneliness was heightened by the conviction that I had to flee, find another setting in which I would be welcome. When, four years later, I left college to seek psychoanalytic help, a physician to whom I had shown notes from a journal commented: "You want to look down on your father from Olympus." I wish that I had been able to confront that earlier; it would have freed my energies for the things I desperately wanted to do—and in which I usually ended up blocking or even defeating myself.

Home, then, gave me a lot, even if I did not recognize it at the time and denied it for decades thereafter. Children learn a lot from listening. When my father and his colleagues spoke of "59th Street," it was not about the commercial and cultural life of that street, its great hotels and residences facing the park; it was a reference to the Board of Education, then situated at 59th and Park. Their tones were those I heard much later from the dissidents in communist Germany speaking of "Pankow," where the party bosses resided: an implacable instance, invariably distant, unresponsive and wrong. I gathered that authority was fallible, and recall my father's refusal to participate in preparing a citywide high school orchestra for a concert, without pay. Most of all, I was helped by the fact that I did not have to swim from an island of Yiddish familial culture to the nearest promontory of the American mainland. My father had already gone ashore. The high school teacher's bookshelves made the university professor's work appreciably easier.

That is what I think now, but then it was different. It is a mistake to suppose that those from privileged backgrounds are protected against inner doubt, competitive anxiety and the pervasive uncertainty of existence. I do not think that I ever, inwardly, believed that my problems were due to being from the Bronx, or lacking wealth. I was aware of a great deficiency of *savoir faire*, and it took years for me to see that it was relatively easily overcome: the problem was *savoir vivre*. There I had lessons at home I could not appreciate until much, much later. My father was empathic, generous, and anxious to do the right thing—even if this last was frequently difficult to discern. Much of my early defiance was misplaced. Years later, when I learned to read German, I was struck by Goethe's phrase, among the many treasures of *Faust*: "What you have inherited from your fathers, you must earn to really possess." My father would gladly have given his qualities as a gift, but my own compulsion to revolt precluded my seeing that.

In a deepening crisis, and without much awareness of it, I entered Townsend Harris High School in the fall of 1939. It was unique in that it was administered by the Board of Higher Education, which supervised the city's colleges, graduated students in three and not four years, and gave them automatic admission to the colleges. I was in the next-to-last class to be graduated (in January 1942), and it was decades before the school was revived—as co-educational, to the retroactive envy of the aging alumni of what was the Jewish lower middle-class equivalent of a cloister school. Some of my fellow students actually wore jackets and ties to class, came from more prosperous families and were already embarked on careers. Most were from modest or difficult circumstances, ambitious without clear maps of the larger society and certainly little contact with it.

A few were part of the German Jewish exodus and much appreciated by our teachers because of their diligence and seriousness. Many of our teachers a decade later would have been in college or university posts. Some were quite striking personalities, whose quirks we talked about: we had, after all, hardly met people like them. Their distinctions were a source of pride. Even those of us made uneasy by the rigors of natural science were gratified that one of the younger physicists had been at the Institute for Advanced Study with Einstein.

To get to school, I exchanged the rattling trolleys of the Bronx for the grimy cars of the Lexington Avenue Subway. I used the station at 161st Street and River Avenue, three blocks west of the Bronx County Courthouse immortalized by Tom Wolfe. From the downtown platform, one could peer into the adjacent Yankee Stadium.

A change of trains at 42nd Street, Grand Central Station, put one on the local and our stop was at 23rd Street, at the Metropolitan Life Building. It was a fortress of capitalism but I recollect a chalked inscription on the stairs of the station: "Defend Trotsky!"

The school occupied four floors of what was the City College branch organized around Business Administration, now the Bernard Baruch College. Two blocks down the street was the Gramercy

Park Hotel, and the fenced and locked beauties of Gramercy Park, open only to the residents of the town houses in the square around it. On lunch breaks, we walked past these and the American Arts Club. We knew no one who inhabited these remote worlds. I was already a reader of *The Nation*. For some years its offices have been on Irving Place, down the street from Gramercy Park, and I re-visit the neighborhood for meetings of the Editorial Board. I cannot say that I hoped one day to belong to it. It was only a couple of years later that larger ambitions obsessed me. School, in my thirteenth year, was challenge enough.

I did not, at first, find the class work difficult. In English and history, I rather enjoyed it—and when I began to take Latin, its regularity appealed. I struggled with mathematics and physics. It was, however, the first time I found myself among fellow students of abilities not less than mine—and under the rigorous eye of teachers who made it a pedagogic principle to make clear that they were much unimpressed with our talent. They wanted to see what we did with it. Many graded answers to questions they posed in class, so oral recitation was hardly relaxed. Roy Begg, a Latin teacher who favored flowing bow ties (often red), adjusted the class seating weekly to reflect the students' standing. The better performers sat in front, although logic might have required them to sit in the rear and the laggards to fall under closer scrutiny.

Our French teacher had a World War I corporal's moustache, and was said to have brought a bottle of wine every day with his packed lunch. He chided us incessantly on our lack of performance. When, for my application to Williams College as a senior, I had to ask him to fill out a report form, he was in his fashion enthusiastic— denouncing to the entire class the student who barely passed but had the effrontery to apply for a scholarship to a good college. Had he learned that twenty-three years later I was teaching in French at the University of Strasbourg his indignation would have been immense. I recollect my shock at a very low grade in an English class: I had made a mistake in sentence structure.

One class was enjoyable because of its political jousting. Our young teacher was a doctoral student in American history at Columbia, an Irish Catholic Democrat. In exasperation one day he asked, "When will you Stalinists learn?" and was met with a definitive answer: "What about Trotsky, Mr. Emery?" It was also enjoyable because he treated us with good humor and even comradeship. I recall his very warm congratulations when I told him that I was going to Williams. He later taught history and was dean of social sciences at Queens College of the City University: I regret that I never visited him. Another history teacher, older and austere, bet on the races. I followed horse racing in the newspapers, and when I read that a Derby outsider had had a fast workout, I called that to his attention. The horse finished second, and the teacher, who had placed a bet on him, thanked me and rewarded me with a twenty-dollar bill. One person I recall as exceedingly sympathetic taught physical education. When I told him that I was going that afternoon for my interview with the Williams College admissions officer, he instructed me to turn up "dressed impeccably." One difficulty was that I only dimly knew what that meant.

Our teachers were, then, remarkable. They also were very diverse in age, social background, ethnicity. The Irish ones were especially exacting: they must have had Jesuit educations. What I cannot now discern is any explicit sense of cultural mission, although there was an implicit one, deeply embedded in the curriculum. We were to become civilized by adhering to subject matter, by learning rules of intellectual comportment in language and thought.

Our teachers were intent on domesticating our raw curiosity, our potentially savage passions. They called our attention to form and sequence. David Goldway was one of our English teachers, before he was dismissed for membership in the Communist Party. I recall his telling us about Coleridge and Wordsworth, but nothing on the French Revolution. Townsend Harris may well have mirrored the larger currents in American education, and especially higher education, of the thirties and early forties: a fixed ascendancy of an Anglicized American culture, a triumphalist reading of American history with Roosevelt and the New Deal as the apotheosis of progress. When my fellow students moved on, they had little to learn—intellectually—from the descendants of the seventeenth-century immigrants. We had already been taught their language.

The question, however, was one of translation. Perhaps if we had been given more of modernism, we would have had less distance remaining between us and the rest of the United States. In English,

Frost and Jeffers were about as modern as we got: I do not recollect being assigned anything else from the twentieth century. We occasionally talked about the books we read out of school. I found other enthusiasts for Dos Passos's *U.S.A.*, for Lewis and Steinbeck, and an older student had read Joyce and Mann, and somehow, I was pointed at the end of my high school career to Edmund Wilson and read his *To the Finland Station*, with its description of the nineteenth century that read like a novel, peopled by figures like Bakunin I had difficulty imagining. The primary passion that moved many of us, however, was not cultural, it was political.

New York was the intellectual capital of the New Deal. Our cultural and social circumstances, generally, meant that even if our school was ten blocks away from the border of Greenwich Village (Fourteenth Street), it was unknown, mythic territory. The midtown world of publishing was unapproachable: no one knew any of the Ivy-educated editors of the great houses. Sometimes guided by hints and more from our teachers, but mostly on our own, we struggled to appropriate the ideas of the New Deal. That entailed encounters with the Communist Party and its loud adversaries, the Marxist sects who took Trotsky as their leader. Their hero, however, was obviously skeptical of his followers' immediate prospects. Murdered by a Stalinist agent in Mexico City in 1941, he had willed his papers to an institution not quite revolutionary in purpose—Harvard University. There, he thought, they would be protected.

Our contact with society was direct. Many of the students came from homes struggling with the economic consequences of the Depression, with such mitigation as the New Deal provided. Some came from families which had trade unionists, and the unions at the time were often quite active in educating their members and families. Much of the union movement was distinctly not in Communist control; it belonged to the Jewish labor movement of Eastern Europe and was social democratic. Conflicts were endemic in the union movement, and they divided families as well. Some of this was touched upon in *The New York Times* and the *New York Post*, but not its impact on daily life. Even those of us not directly connected to these movements sensed that there was a segment of history not conventionally reported. We learned, as well, from films, from experimental theater, from newsreels. The stars of what had been the Group Theater (the playwright Clifford Odets, actors John Garfield and Edward Robinson) went to Hollywood, but a living theater legacy in New York attested their enduring influence.

The German-Russian Pact, the war, even the persecutions of the Jews, took place in a Europe which was both near and far—near in our spirits, far in actuality and texture, so that we had to imagine it. The Pact provided the occasion for a large offensive of the right against the influence of the Communist Party in the cultural industry and education. At the national level, it was entrusted to the House Un-American Activities Commission. In New York, a committee of the State Senate headed by Senators Coudert and Rapp began investigations in 1939, held hearings in 1940 and 1941, and instigated the dismissal of a number of teachers in the city's colleges. Since Townsend Harris was under the jurisdiction of the Board of Higher Education, its faculty and administration were also implicated and a number of persons were investigated, heard and then fired.

I recall my English teacher David Goldway and the school registrar as being among them. The committee's motivations were clear: the Communist Party, especially in New York City, functioned as the left wing of the New Deal—even if many of the Democrats, across ethnic lines, reviled it. The old and dishonorable American tradition of using xenophobia to delegitimize projects of social reform was revived, if it indeed had ever been dormant. What better way to attack the New Deal as alien than to demonstrate its connections to a party subservient to a foreign nation? The Communist Party's temporary adoption of the absurd slogan, "Communism Is Twentieth Century Americanism," the placarding of its meetings with iconic portraits of the founders of the republic and Jackson and Lincoln, made no impression on its enemies.

What did we know of the party? It had a large structure of organizations, used to convey the party's message and to recruit supporters for its causes without obliging them to incur the risks of membership. One of these was The American Student Union, strong on the University campuses which were traditional sites of dissent (the great state universities, above all). With its precocious students, Townsend Harris was one of the New York high schools which had a very active chapter, and I joined it upon entering school in September 1939. The fact that neither the chapter nor the national organization were autonomous, that the group was steered by a cadre of the committed, did not become clear to me for some time. One of the reasons was the efficacy of the party's strategy in deploying its forces in front organizations. Lowest common denominators of policy were chosen and emphasized: the struggle against fascism, against domestic repression and the enemies of continuing the reforms of the New Deal. The sort of emphasis on campus and educational issues which marked the protests of the sixties was missing. Apparently, it had been decided that compliant campus citizenship was a precondition of implantation.

I had a mentor, who remained a friend throughout my high school career and a bit beyond it, Channing Dichter. Channing was older than I, and we remained in touch after he left to go to college. I think that he was in the Young Communist League, and recall hints at asking me to proceed to consider membership. He dropped these when I manifested a silent but considerable reluctance. I have written of the condition of intellectual fog in which I lived, despite giving the external impression of conviction and decisiveness, even aggressive self-confidence. My inner state found a perfect external match: the American Student Union obfuscated awkward questions by insisting on the primacy of commitment. The old American labor song "Which Side Are You On?" was an intellectual refrain. You sought the triumph of progress, justice, peace? Then how could you align yourself with their malign enemies, whose tactic it was to slander the forces of progress, justice and peace? The difficulty, of which I caught glimpses through the fog, was that one was supposed to accept that the Soviet Union was the defender, the incarnation of these forces. I knew of the purges, the trials, the one-party state. Now the difficulty was even greater: the great champion of progress had entered into a pact, indeed an alliance, with Nazi Germany. I was haunted by the David Low cartoon of the day after the announcement of the pact, showing Hitler and Stalin bowing to one another: "The Scum of the Earth, I presume?" "The bloody assassin of the workers, I believe."

Then came the Soviet invasion of Finland, justified by some apologists as strengthening the nation's frontiers against eventual attack—by the very same Germany to which it was allied. The conspicuously defective military performance of the Red Army was no doubt due to the purge of the generals, but that was a connection I did not see. Inwardly disheartened or dismayed, many stilled their doubts and refused to criticize the Soviet Union for fear of siding with the miscellany of forces termed "reaction." Since the sympathizers of the Soviet Union in the period of the Popular Front had depicted it as the one reliable antagonist of fascism, the pact with Nazi Germany was especially difficult to countenance—in a city in which the Jewish presence and social progressivism were so closely connected. Matters were not improved by the cretinous slogan used by the Communists to describe the Soviet Union's world political role. With the United States and China, it was depicted as part of a "Peace Front." The fact that China was at war with Japan, and that after the Pact there was no particular closeness in relations between the US and the USSR, did not disturb the sloganeers.

Elsewhere in New York and the nation, determined groups of Marxist, socialist and social democratic critics of the Soviet Union were insisting that the Pact showed its real nature. About what that was, they disagreed. Trotsky himself held that the USSR was a decayed workers' state, but that as a workers' state it could be and should be defended against its capitalist and fascist enemies (which he conjoined). Other Marxists were struggling toward other formulations: the USSR was bureaucratized tyranny, or state capitalism of an authoritarian kind. They and the social democrats, attached to institutional pluralism, anticipated the idea of totalitarianism. A couple of fellow students discussed some of these ideas, and there certainly was plenty of polemical literature available. Somehow, I did not enter into the discussion. For one thing, I was fixated on the need to fight fascism, and to that extent still possessed of the belief that the USSR was indispensable to that effort. A notion of progressive direction in history made it too hard to accept of the terrible regression that was the failed Soviet Revolution. My growing skepticism about the USSR was frightening: I saw no alternatives, did not imagine Roosevelt managing within two years to bring us into the war.

Actually, it was my father who impelled me to leave the American Student Union. I cannot recall the exact content of our discussions, which were agitated enough. He was afraid that I would be entangled in something I could not get out of, but his anxiety was palpable and explicable only by an additional worry, that somehow my membership in the ASU would bring him to the attention of the Rapp-Coudert investigators. My father was not without courage or independence of judgement—but the persecution of the Communists reminded educated New York Jewry of its hard-won and very recent rise from marginalized precarity.

I left the ASU in the winter of 1940, having been a member only for some months. In fact, most of my extra-curricular activity at school had been taken up by working on the yearbook. I was especially drawn by its editor, a graduating senior named Sheldon Zitner. He combined efficacy, a certain inner authority, and an elegance of manners in ways I had not previously met. He was also very encouraging. I very much regret that I had no subsequent contact with him. He was in the Pacific war; took a doctorate in English literature; taught at Hampton, the black university in Virginia; and then at Grinnell College and the University of Toronto. He was, I read in his obituary, a distinguished Elizabethan scholar and an accomplished poet. He left for Canada in 1969, and I wonder if it was because of disgust with Nixon.

I made other friends at Townsend Harris, and recall a boy from Germany, Isidore Ausubel, whose deliberate and methodical manner was evidence of a culture quite unlike that of east European Jewry, with its intense volatility. It was an impression, with many others, stored for future reflection: I did not have the inner tranquility or sense of self to work through these encounters with difference. I was too laden with burdens, a devastating combination of a desire for experience and an overwhelming conviction that I could not enter new worlds—especially if they promised delight.

I must have been both singularly limited in my capacity to reciprocate friendship and needful of it. That makes me, now, very grateful to those who gave of themselves. I like to think that they recognized not only the need but some promise in return—however miserly I was with feeling. There were some common adventures: I recall accompanying, in a small band of supporters, our basketball team uptown by subway to play the Bronx High School of Science. A New York Jewish taxi driver of a vanished vintage asked us where we were going. "To play Bronx Science, we are from Townsend Harris." "What—in chess?" On the day after Pearl Harbor, New York had an air raid alarm and we were told to walk down ten flights to the street. One of the students protested to the teacher, correctly, "The Japanese are too far away and the Germans do not have planes that can reach New York." The answer was something like, "Goldstein, when General Marshall needs your advice I am sure he will ask for it. In the meantime—downstairs!"

In fact, my closest friend and I shared a certain sense of distance, a melancholic view of the life we yearned to live more fully—if only we knew how to do so in a different world we hoped to enter, through doors difficult to open.

That friend was Stanley Halperin, who left school sometime after I entered to go to City College, where I rejoined him in the spring of 1942. Stanley lived a few blocks away, across Joyce Kilmer Park. He had, even when young, a somewhat sardonic sense of human nature, a clearer view than I of the limits on human idealism, but we shared a common disdain for cant and false piety. We were especially alert to the excessive ambition of others, since we had so much of it ourselves. We were aware of the advantages others had and between ourselves derided "white Jews" as pretentious—while wondering what life would have been like had our families been wealthier and more assimilated. (When, nearly two decades later, my friend Norman Podhoretz incurred severe criticism for acknowledging his ambition in his book *Making It*, I thought his critics were unjust. *Making It* was the autobiography of at least two generations, and its virtue was its honesty.)

The difficulty with our ambition was that it was so insatiable that it blocked our enjoyment of life—or, rather, substituted for it. We had sexual fantasies, of course, but were totally defective as boys in doing anything about them. A cloud of joylessness engulfed us, and our pleasures were deferred as we concentrated our energies on getting to a future that would bring us ease and renown. Years later, again, the idea of "deferred gratification" (a thinner version of Weber's Protestant Ethic) served as part explanation, part justification, of a supposedly central American character—explaining why we were so much better organized and wealthier than others. No one, then, dreamed of buying Japanese cars, and it was before the Volkswagen Beetle arrived. Stanley and I, and many like us, anticipated the thesis without knowing anything about it. The Protestant Americans we knew only from novels and film seemed, then, to be having a lot more fun.

I had problems with friendship, just as I had with family—since I had such a large problem appreciating myself, I could not fully appreciate others. The French phrase *il n'est pas bien dans sa peau* ("he isn't at ease in his own skin") certainly applied: inwardly, I writhed all the time. I regret that I did not give more generously of myself to those friends who were certainly generous with me, take some consolation from the thought that they found compensations in our being together which at the time I could not envisage. Stanley was invariably supportive, and I appreciated the support all the more because of his undertone of severe judgement: if I passed that test, others could be surmounted as well. We recognized, I now see, our deep need for reassurance, for simple companionship, in a world which was avaricious of sympathy and warmth, of comprehension of what we were trying to do. None of the adults we knew seemed able to offer that—and in my case, I wasn't able to or willing to take advantage of the generosity of feeling and sympathy of my father. Stanley's family struck me as less well placed, culturally, than mine. In this situation, sometimes, teachers step in. My own unreflective suspicion of authority, combined with very great fear and respect of it, made it impossible to cast any of the Townsend Harris teachers in a special role—and they did not, as a group, seem willing to assume it. Stanley was in a line of friends older than myself who were, for better or for worse, elder brothers. Even before I went to Townsend Harris, I had one in the neighborhood, an extremely warm person named Daniel Greenberg. I wish, as I think of surrogate elder brothers, that I had been a better elder brother to my sister. From what she told me much later, she appreciated and was encouraged by my independence. Fate, clearly, doesn't follow a straight line and humans are sometimes good at converting losses into gains. My very distance was something she could use as an advantage.

I cannot say that I enjoyed Townsend Harris, since I could not enjoy anything very much.

After the engagement in the American Student Union ended, and Stanley and my good friend at the yearbook both left, I endured it more than anything else. I was disappointed in my academic work and did not know how to find other gratifications. That set a pattern to be repeated, with varying sorts of camouflage and in ways subtle and less so, for decades.

Unable to reach a great goal directly, in this case success and recognition at school, I could not devise alternative strategies and withdrew into sullen anger. From that I broke out, repeatedly, by moving in other directions.

The world in 1940 hardly allowed total self-absorption. What was termed the "phony war" became all too real for the people of Denmark and Norway and then Belgium, the Netherlands and France. The shock of the occupation of Denmark and Norway, the uninspiring allied response, was followed by terrifying events: the turning of the Maginot Line, the German breakthrough into France, Dunkirk and the French capitulation. We followed it in newspapers, on the radio, and in the newsreel films. Suddenly, Europe—always close to New York—seemed just over the horizon. Churchill's voice became as familiar as Hitler's. David Low's drawing of a British soldier on the Cliffs of Dover, shaking his fist at a black cloud moving in from the Continent ("Very well, alone.") summed it up: only the British stood between us and the Nazis. That was the view in New York—but not, of course, in all of New York and decidedly not elsewhere in the nation.

Franklin Roosevelt, having decided to run again, promised not to send Americans into "foreign wars." He then assiduously set about making this war ours: he sent the US Navy to protect the convoys to Great Britain and to fight the German submarines.

Much, however, had to occur before that was possible. The nation depicted by Philip Roth in *The Plot Against America* actually existed—and it was entirely audible and visible in New York. The German-American Bund, who identified explicitly with the Nazis, was active not many subway stops away; Father Coughlin's newspaper, *Social Justice*, with its own anti-Semitic message, was sold on street corners. There were some, but not many, voices in the Congress raised to ask for fuller support for Great Britain and the press was on the whole exceedingly cautious. I hardly knew that there was a group in the government (Harold Ickes, Henry Morgenthau, Henry Stimson) pressing for ever-more determined action against

Germany, knew nothing of the debates on policy toward Japan. In fact, after consultation with the British, the strategy that was to be followed in the war of priority for the war in Europe was already in place and determined military procurement and training. We hardly got beyond the surface of events, which were both bleak and tumultuous. When Yugoslavia—shortly before being attacked in the spring of 1941—signed a non-aggression pact with the Soviet Union, it did seem that it was not far from a break with Germany.

We (family, fellow students, friends, the New York Eastern European Jewish milieu) were beset by fears that much of the rest of the nation not only did not share our anti-fascism but was purposefully indifferent to the fate of its victims. Isolationism was for us a euphemism not only for provincialism and xenophobia, but for a larger charge of anti-Semitism. Our America did not wait for Roth's end-of-century portrait of it: we had Sinclair Lewis and his novel *It Can't Happen Here*. Yet the conversion of industry to arms production had begun, as had the training of a greatly enlarged conscript army, and the Congress passed the Lend-Lease Bill, which guaranteed Great Britain a steady supply of weapons. Moreover, Roosevelt had been re-elected convincingly in November 1940 despite the Washingtonian precedent that no President should serve more than two terms. Indeed, he had imposed on the party as his vice president the former Secretary of Agriculture Henry Wallace, a New Deal internationalist with roots in American prairie radicalism.

What were we afraid of? Our culture was made of memories of life in Eastern Europe, with all the hatred and meanness with which Jews were treated. To that was added Hitler, who was certainly not just a painful memory. Given the incompleteness of the process of assimilation in the US, the single color of the dense ethnic province we inhabited, anxiety produced a black-and-white picture of the nation in which the darker shades predominated. Our attitude to Franklin Roosevelt was rather like that attributed to Franz Josef II by Jews in his empire: he was the great protector. What we overlooked was that the very word had been used by Oliver Cromwell (he was Lord Protector)—who invited the Jews to return to the England from which they had been banned. Many Americans were his spiritual descendants, and their politics often showed it. I encountered it in the form of progressivism and learned only later, by going to New England, of its religious roots. My father was a very well educated person, but he would have been hard put to describe the difference between Calvinists and Lutherans, much less explain why the Lutheran Reinhold Niebuhr was a theologian of the New Deal. Come to think of it, I did once hear a historian friend of his talk about the Puritans. It was about their bitter quarrels and their intolerance—but somehow, Roger Williams emerged as a hero. Rhode Island remained very far away.

I had an inchoate conviction that there was more to the story than the standard beliefs in our milieu. After all, we went to the movies, and there met a very different America. I'm aware of two related if different objections. Much of Hollywood was the work of Eastern European Jews forging an image of the nation designed to please. The New Deal and the American Communist Party had plenty of adherents among directors and screenwriters: the nation they projected on our screens was a product of their political imagination. Still, Fitzgerald and Faulkner were no less typical Hollywood figures—and I had good reason to think that the country of Dos Passos's trilogy was real. The problem was: how to get there?

The Communist Party and its front organizations, which resorted (with shameless lack of embarrassment) to bravado after the German attack on the USSR and the de facto UK-US-USSR alliance, were of no help. Their capacity for intellectual gyration was evident, and their grotesque sloganeering continued. (The New York edition of *The Daily Worker* for Sunday, June 22, prepared before the news of the German attack, carried a strenuous Soviet denunciation of reports of tension with Germany as "provocation." The next day, however, the paper described how "Soviet falcons" rose from their airfields to destroy the invaders' planes—a considerable feat of reportorial fantasy, since much of the Soviet air force was caught on the ground in their version of Pearl Harbor.) There was little of the rest of the US in the Communist milieu in New York, even if it did include figures like Congressman Vito Marcantonio and the black City Councilor Ben Davis and the unionist Elizabeth Gurley Flynn. Most of the Communists and their sympathizers were familiarly Jewish—if, often, boring in their lack of panache and dogged lack of reflectiveness. They struck me as just a bit too stupid.

Sometime in the spring of 1941, a not-quite-accidental accident provided me with a portal into a larger world. I do not recall exactly how, but I had attached myself to a group of students who were working with the newly formed Union for Democratic Action, the predecessor of Americans for Democratic Action, and also with the Committee to Defend America by Aiding the Allies. This last, an all-star assemblage of prominent figures in business, culture and religion as well as politics, had been formed in 1940 to support Roosevelt in his struggle to overcome the restrictions of the Neutrality Act. They were themselves divided on how far the US should go, but their temper was clear: the US was directly threatened by Germany and Italy and, in addition, its democratic obligations were not limited to citizens within our borders. Many of those who formed and led the organization were descendants of the American Revolution, had ancestors who eighty years before had fought under Lincoln and Grant. The group included Midwesterners as well as Easterners, persons from the great state universities as well as the Ivy colleges. I was initially aware of its activities from the newspapers—in which they conducted a campaign of advertisements and statements.

The Union for Democratic Action was led by trade unionists, by public figures like Reinhold Niebuhr (its president) and organized by James Loeb, who taught Spanish at Townsend Harris. Later, after serving as general secretary to Americans for Democratic Action, he joined the Truman administration. I do not recollect that we formed a student group at school, but like the bi-partisan (and much more patrician) Committee, it was a presence in New York. It was formed in May 1941 and represented the social democratic part of the New Deal spectrum, for which the Hitler-Stalin pact and the casuistry of the American Communist Party were so many proofs of the deformed and tyrannical nature of the Soviet Union.

The work with the Union for Democratic Action led me to an office on 40th Street, opposite the Public Library, where their youth group worked. It was the office of the International Student Service, which formally helped refugee students find places and support at American institutions. The ISS counted among its sponsors Eleanor Roosevelt and was a stronghold of internationalist New Dealers. Its office was used as a foyer by any number of younger people from the New York colleges and schools who were student activists unwilling to work with the Communist Party.

I was very glad to make new friends there, the more so as my academic and organizational career at school itself were so disappointing. Some of the persons I met told me that they were struck by how much I knew, by the forcefulness of my opinions—and by how young I was. I must have put up a very good front to compensate for a great deal of inner uncertainty. What moved me was certainly not only the historical burden of fighting fascism. If "No paserán," the motto of the defeated Spanish Republicans, still echoed—I was looking for what I would have termed in French *la passerelle*, had I had the French to do it: the gangway or footbridge across a social chasm.

There is another way of looking at it. The American Student Union was a reservoir of student talent upon which the Communist Party attempted to draw. The ISS office made the rest of us welcome as a practical matter: it was recruiting future leaders for its political sponsors. In making it possible for some of us to move out of family, neighborhood, school to a wider world, the adults we met were issuing the moral equivalent of student loans—to be repaid in political steadiness in the years and even decades ahead.

As far as I could see, most of the contemporaries I met at ISS had no need of being introduced into a wider world; they were already in it. I was especially struck by two new friends from Fieldston School in the northwest Bronx (in the area which preferred to name itself Riverdale). Fieldston was sponsored by the Ethical Culture Society, sent its graduates to the better known colleges, and was itself conducted like a college. Its students wrote essays, did their own research papers, and made full use of their advantages: they came from prosperous business and professional families and took for granted what we in Townsend Harris worried about—their integration in a cosmopolitan America.

One of my new friends was George Fischer, who had actually grown up in Moscow and was the son of Louis Fischer, correspondent there for *The Nation*. George had gone to school with Markus Wolf, the later Communist German espionage figure.

George's mother was a Soviet citizen and when his father decided in 1940 to return to the US, she and the children were denied permission to leave. Mrs. Roosevelt persuaded the President to write to Stalin and the exit visas followed. George, who spoke with a marked and musical Russian accent, was warm, expansive, with a contagious enthusiasm for much of life. We met again, years later, at Harvard Graduate School, where he studied history and for a while was a determined adherent of the Cold War. That changed, and when I returned to the US from Europe in 1966, he was a prominent figure in the American academic new left and brought the Socialist Scholars Conference into being. When I talked with George in 1941, he was clearly an eyewitness to the things I had only read about. Mostly, I was impressed by his *joie de vivre*.

Another friend was Ralph Colp, who was far more cerebral—and sardonic. He lived in a penthouse apartment on Central Park West, and his own room looked out at the city. Moreover, his mother had artistic and literary interests and actually knew people who wrote for *The New Republic*. It was Ralph who showed me *Partisan Review*, a journal I had never heard of. In it, Clement Greenberg and Dwight Macdonald argued that the war could not be won unless conducted with the social revolution Roosevelt and Churchill were manifestly unwilling to undertake. The journal's correspondent in London, George Orwell, took a similar view. I had not encountered ideas of this sort, so different from the progressivist pieties I was accustomed to. Neither had I ever heard of the literary works so closely analyzed in the same pages—by Eliot and Kafka. *Partisan Review* was struggling with an irreconcilable conflict: its literary modernism was difficult to join to its revolutionary socialism.

I knew little, still, of either—and I can say that reading it was the start of a liberal education well before I entered college. Nothing was more educative, however, than talking with Ralph. He was intensely interested in history, let me read a term paper of his on Ireland and the Irish revolution, and struck me as being in command of great resources of understanding. He had considerable detachment, and some irony, unusual in a seventeen-year-old. He later followed his father and became a physician, specialized in psychiatry and did a great deal of history. He sent me a paper challenging the familiar assertion that Marx had sought to dedicate *Capital* to Darwin, and he expressed his surprise that the philosopher Lewis Feuer had repeated this conventional untruth but refused to correct it. Even later, he did not quite grasp that intellectual conflict for some was a matter of self-realization, not an argument about an external reality. What I admired—no, envied—about Ralph when I met him was his capacity to take self and position in the world for granted, his freedom to explore that reality.

In that period, I met some of the patricians who thought the US should enter the war. Meeting them was reassuring. They were indisputably Americans of classic vintage, and yet they were as attached to the New Deal, as opposed to Hitler, as my father and his friends. Moreover, they were in their way welcoming—matter of fact, sometimes interested and encouraging, invariably polite. The British public school Winchester, exceptionally intellectual, had as its motto: "Manners Maketh the Man." Other people's manners can do so, too, in their exemplary effects.

One of the persons I met worked in advertising, at McCann Erickson—and even then, the manipulative and soul-destroying effects of advertising were a staple of the liberal imagination. Those effects were, of course, often woefully exaggerated. I thought my new friend, Max Berking, initially as a prisoner of fate—or as assiduously boring from within to subvert capitalism. I did not realize that in their eagerness to consume, the citizens going back to work after the Depression and the new re-armament stimulus needed no external stimulus. The advertising agencies had to run hard to keep up with them. Contrary to my self-righteous repugnance for anything to do with ordinariness, the advertising executives were often poets of the everyday (later celebrated as such by Andy Warhol), and often too brilliantly creative. In any case, in a world in which not everyone could afford to treat asceticism as noble, a considerable number of critical and intelligent persons found employment in advertising.

Max was a devoted reader of *The Nation* and *The New Republic*, had studied at Williams College with its New Deal faculty. Max Berking was one of those morally generous persons one rarely meets and never forgets. In his case, generosity was substantial: he arranged for me to make my way to Williams. First, what he told me of it made it seem to be an interesting, even exciting place. Then he brought me to see Max Lerner, at the editorial offices of *The New Republic*. Of course I had read Max: everyone with left-liberal literacy had done so. He was a Williams professor who commuted to New York and Washington, a famous figure now become flesh. He was friendly, if brief, and the brevity carried a message, or so I thought. ("I'll be glad to help but then let us see what you can do"—not unlike the reserve of my teachers at Townsend Harris.) The visit had a bonus, since the weekly's movie reviewer, Otis Ferguson, whose work I read with fascination, was there. I remember his bemused and kindly informality.

Max was determined that I should get to Williams, recommended me to the admissions staff and assured me that my chances of admission, with a scholarship, were very good.

That was not on the face of it obvious. My grades were mixed—and my sense of self decidedly so. The extreme energy of my attempt to enter a different world was a compensatory activity—and the recognition I won there a substitute for the rewards I could not win at home, which Townsend Harris was. One of my sharpest memories of school, one etched in psychological acid, is of sitting through the award of honors to my classmates as we concluded our junior year. Our faculty advisor addressed the rest of us and said that honors mattered less than one's own judgment: had one been just to one's own talents? The answer I had to give myself was entirely black. Forty years later, we had a class reunion, and I told the teacher that his words had remained with me. He was appreciative—and rather surprised.

I remain grateful to my father for supporting, indeed encouraging, the Williams project. Even with a scholarship award, he would have to dispense appreciably more than if I followed his path to City College. He had originally mentioned Williams to me, and was aware of the advantages going there would bring. My mother reacted with resigned irritation, taking it as yet more evidence of the complications I visited upon the family—but not openly challenging my father.

I sent in the application form and was summoned to an interview—in the bar of the Williams Club on 39th Street. (It was long used for breakfast by the guests of the club, and I occasionally stay there.) The room seemed somewhat larger, its wood paneling more impressive, then. One of the other applicants waiting for an interview was surprised when I asked him what interested him in

Williams. His family had gone there, he said—and in any event he liked skiing. The interviewer was the director of admissions himself, Tom Wood, who also taught political science. He was decidedly friendly; we talked about the book I carried (something on the First World War or the nation's war-making proclivity by Beard) and he mentioned another critic of our world role, Sidney Fay, of whom I had not heard. My Williams education had begun, even if I could not quite believe it.

In the meantime, the world was turning ever faster. The intensity of the nation's argument over whether to join the war increased as it became clear that international conflicts would overwhelm whatever capacities our political system had to avoid it. I was bewildered by the fact that there was an enlightened opposition to the war; Beard and Robert Hutchins advanced plausible grounds for staying out. Beard declared that war would strengthen the very domestic forces the New Deal was seeking to defeat or restrain—large-scale capital. Hutchins had a somewhat subtler point—that the US by entering the war would intensify the chaos and destructiveness already dominating the world. I knew little, reading in *Partisan Review* apart, of the anti-imperial arguments of Trotsky and the various Marxist sects. I was frightened by the nativism and quite open anti-Semitism of the America First movement, and could not then (it is difficult even now) think of history in the long term.

In the short term, I remember Pearl Harbor. It was a Sunday; I was studying for my graduation examinations, the New York State Regents' exams. I was doing mathematics, in which I had difficulty, all the more reason to listen to the afternoon concert of the New York Philharmonic. Shortly before it was due to begin, at 2:30, Columbia Broadcasting interrupted its regular program to carry the White House announcement of the attack. I went to the living room, where my father had not yet turned on the radio, and we took down our atlas to see where the Japanese planes might have come from. We were puzzled by the distance from the nearest Japanese territory, the Marianas Islands. Neither of us realized how prodigiously effective industrial Japan was, and we did not think of Japan's aircraft carriers—but rather of the cheap goods to be found Woolworth's. Even in the Bronx, one could share in the nation's illusions. We were not, however, surprised that war had come: we were close enough to history to have expected it, somehow, somewhere.

2

Williams College— And a Different New York

I CANNOT say that the outbreak of war coincided with the end of boyhood: I was fifteen and five months. I developed so unevenly, both emotionally and intellectually, that the usual categories were difficult to apply. The war coincided with new experiences and new challenges, well and badly met.

When Germany and Italy spared Roosevelt from having to ask Congress to initiate war on them by declaring war themselves (on 11 December), the feeling in family and among friends was exactly that of Maxim Litvinov. Dismissed as Soviet foreign minister in May of 1939 as a preliminary to Stalin's bargain with Hitler (he was Jewish), he was sent to the US as ambassador on the last American commercial flight from Japan to the US. Arriving in San Francisco after the attack on Pearl Harbor, he said, "We are now all in it together." (His son was arrested in Red Square in August 1968 for demonstrating against the occupation which ended the Prague Spring—a gesture greatly appreciated by those who thought of his father as an authentic anti-fascist.) Litvinov's phrase did mark the beginning of a period in which, if temporarily, abhorrence for Stalinism gave way for many to admiration for the Soviet Union's struggle against Germany. The successful defense of Moscow in December and the obvious difficulties of the German army in the Russian winter, contrasted with the Japanese advance in Asia— and, indeed, with Germany's triumphs elsewhere.

We were more than dimly aware of matters not emphasized in *The New York Times*: the beginning of the extirpation of European Jewry by Germany and the nations allied with it—with the complicity, and sometimes voluntary participation, of their Gentile neighbors.

The Jewish organizations knew of this and the Jewish community newspapers reported it.

It was not, at the end of 1941, recent news. The pogrom had commenced with the beginning of the German occupation of Poland in September 1939. The terrible Wannsee Conference of January 1942, in which German civil servants (most with doctoral degrees in law) and the SS leadership planned the "final solution" to the Jewish problem in Europe, coordinated and formalized a process rather than beginning it. That event raises questions about the usual assertion that war was the only way to stop the Nazis. It is probably true—but had there been no war, had Germany maintained a normal set of diplomatic and other relations with the Western European nations and the US, would the regime have had the freedom to institute genocide?

Genocide, rather than persecution, was taking place. I could deal with it only with very great difficulty, avoided dwelling on it inwardly and certainly outwardly, and sometimes but only rarely discussed it with my father. I preferred to submerge the issue in my general repugnance for fascism as authoritarian, brutal, inhumane—and, of course, exploitative. I did not ask whether there was an irreducible destructive component in human nature and, if I had vague notions of Freud's work, certainly had not read *Civilization and Its Discontents* with its iron refusal of a benign view of humanity, actually and potentially. I could not even claim possession of the rather shallow view, even if true, that people behaved badly if mistreated. When I arrived at Harvard to begin doctoral work in the social sciences in 1947, I was confronted with this in the form of the hypothesis that frustration generated aggression. Wilhelm Reich's work on fascism presupposed serious knowledge of psychoanalysis and was in case a piece of arcane knowledge to which I had no access.

Faute de mieux, I resorted to rather traditional explanations—which had considerable value to them. There were Christian sources of anti-Semitism; Jews had been a pariah people, and there was a reservoir of enmity in Christian or recently Christian populations which could be mobilized by distress, imaginary or real—and, of course, manipulated by ruling classes anxious to divert attention from their own acts. I had read some in the Marxist or vulgar

Marxist analysis of fascism as devised by the ruling class to destroy working-class organizations—which overlooked what Mussolini learned from his socialist past, or the self-designation of the Nazis as the National Socialist German Workers' Party. It served, however, for better or for worse (intellectually, for worse), to explain the anti-Semitic component of fascism. It also had the advantage of bridging the ocean and explaining why the American anti-Semites, Republicans, anti-metropolitans, were not immediate candidates for accession to the status of the enlightened. The opportunity to vent anti-Semitism was a form of compensation—like the encouragement of racial discrimination and prejudice.

The intellectual incompleteness, if not impoverishment, of these notions wasn't entirely explained by the fact that I was not quite yet sixteen. There are scholars who, from very early on, devote themselves to one or another aspect of Jewishness. I accepted the fact that I was Jewish, would have regarded attempts to flee that as contemptible—but refused to accept that as a complete definition of myself. I was also an American, a New Yorker, an aspiring intellectual, a citizen of the world (without papers, to be sure). My uncertainty about how to explain anti-Semitism reflected my refusal to let either Jews or anti-Semites dictate the limits of my life. It remained only to live it: that, however, was not simple.

The war brought me a sense of relief: the nation had a rendezvous with history, which I understood in exceedingly simple terms. The United States, however hesitantly and imperfectly, had to redeem a fallen world. I was very dimly aware that much of the world did not view matters in this way, did not seek redemption in terms I understood or found congenial, but I preferred not to dwell on these complications. That was what kept me from exploring the intellectual world of the naysayers, the dissident Marxists and assorted meta-historians whose books and articles were within reach. In one sense, they might have been on the other side of the moon. In another, they were openly publishing texts which could have endangered my precarious intellectual and moral stability. History (or more prosaically, circumstance) had its own way of exacting a price. When three years later, in 1944, Dwight Macdonald made available, in his journal *Politics*, any number of thinkers with views far more complex than the liberal and progressivist pieties I had mastered, I was quite unprepared to profit immediately from the encounter. I intuited that Hannah Arendt, Meyer Schapiro, C. Wright Mills, Macdonald himself, had profound things to say and did not know how to connect these to my own earlier experience. Eventually, I managed—but it has taken a half-century.

The explanation wasn't intellectual deficiency; it was a matter of social ambition. By the time the war came, I had had a firsthand glimpse of the liberal elite. Applying to Williams and reading *The Nation* and *The* (old) *New Republic* weren't contradictory; they were inextricably connected. In fact, during the Christmas vacation period of December, I made my first visit to Cambridge and Harvard—to attend the organizing meeting of a new national student organization clearly intended by its senior sponsors to challenge the Communists' American Student Union.

A group of friends took me by car. The trip was organized by Adam Yarmolinsky, who was a Harvard student who had been at Fieldston School. He had a reserved demeanor, short stature and a capacity for impressive *obiter dicta* suggesting vast experience of the world and profound reflection on it. I enjoyed meeting his parents. His father was curator of Slavic languages at the New York Public Library and the author of a book on Dostoevsky I read much later with considerable profit. His mother was the poetess Babette Deutsch. The father had been a younger Menshevik, a Social Democrat, in Russia and left that country as a young man. In the winter of 1941 I was bewildered by the conflicts in the socialist camp but immensely impressed by meeting persons who not only knew about them but had taken part in them. I was also impressed during the trip when, during our stop at the inn at Sturbridge, Adam ordered apple pie with cheese and declared it an old New England dish. I was prepared to believe that it was not original to the Menshevik emigration.

During the meeting, we were housed at Harvard's student residential college, Adams House, where I was later to become a resident tutor. Some students had not gone home for the vacation. Tweed jackets, button-down shirts and flannel pants were much in evidence and there were student waiters. One of the Harvard participants, Edward Ames, invited some of us to an evening at his family home, a Georgian house on one of the Cambridge streets. It was spacious in several senses; I recall the warmth of his parents.

I also recall the different accents, the absence of New York combativeness, of some of the delegates from other places in the nation—their directness, friendliness and earnestness. The Harvard friends of Adam I met seemed much concerned with matters at Harvard, their teachers, their academic prospects. Adam had recently changed majors (termed "fields of concentration" at Harvard) from economics to American literature. His reason was that with the war, he wished to acquire as much general culture as possible before turning to the serious business of life. That was already an intimation of the imperial Harvard I was to enter as a graduate student six years later, in which the humanities and reflectiveness in general were either ornamental or ancillary to technocratic governance. At the time, however, I was much impressed by his shelf full of American classics. F. O. Matthiessen and Perry Miller were the great figures of American studies at Harvard then, and it is impossible to believe that they would have subscribed to Adam's implicitly instrumental reading of culture.

I cannot recollect much argument or ideological controversy at the meeting itself. I did not recognize that we were being both rewarded and recruited. The reward was a glimpse of power and prosperity—and style. One did not have to come from the Bronx— the Midwestern suburbs would do—to see that Cambridge, or Harvard's Cambridge, was at the apex of the nation. The recruiting for membership in the elite, or in the top ranks of its placemen, was simple: we recruited ourselves. Adam later became a lawyer, worked in Dean Acheson's firm in Washington, and helped form the Kennedy government, in which he worked for Robert McNamara. He was with Sargent Shriver in the Johnson administration's war on poverty. He later took up administrative posts in academic institutions, remained a steadfast New Dealer as the newer segments of the liberal elite abandoned .larger projects of reform and retreated to the minimalist incrementalism and maximalist careerism of Clintonism. (Despite my lack of enthusiasm for Clinton's works, I rather liked the person. When I read in the most vivid pages of his autobiography of his move from Arkansas to Georgetown, I was reminded of my own struggles: I wasn't the only one.) In early 1942, I did not realize that I was enacting an American archetype that spanned class, ethnicity, even race: the journey from province to metropolis. The rest of the US thought of the Bronx as metropolitan, but those of us who lived there knew of the distance to Manhattan.

I had taken the SAT examinations required by Williams, completed my application, and had to await the decision, scheduled for April. At the SAT examinations, I was surrounded by well-dressed contemporaries, mainly from private schools, who seemed not to doubt that they would enter the colleges of their choice. Were I not to be awarded a scholarship by Williams, I would go to City College. The sensible thing, in January, was to enroll there—exceedingly simple for a graduate of its high school. I took a different subway to the campus at 138th Street and Amsterdam Heights, occasionally with Stanley Halperin, whom I rejoined there.

City College has been so much the subject of myth that my own recollection of it as rather tranquil may be surprising. I arrived after the events of December 1941 rendered the debate on whether the US should join the war moot. Many of the students were expecting to be drafted; others had already gone. One legacy of the agitation of the years of ideological division was the story, possibly apocryphal, recounted by Stanley. Its protagonist was one "Booby" Sachs, who was a vocal student follower of Leon Trotsky and a fervid antagonist of the war as irredeemably imperialist. Sachs, drafted, visited the campus as a uniformed Private, First Class, in the US Army. He was asked about the apparent change in his position and replied with contempt: "You don't understand: now the workers have arms." Later, he taught political science at Brandeis University and drafted the Vietnam Constitution—whose protections of civil rights were no doubt at least as effective as those enjoyed by Soviet citizens under Stalin's Constitution. Actually, Sachs's progression from the margins to social integration was, precisely, what most of the City College students sought.

The teachers understood that, and treated us with a benign paternalism. That contrasted with what I intuited a half-year later at Williams. There, the teachers felt, with their cultural and political preoccupations, that they were on the margins of the class to which their students belonged. Their scrupulous politeness and friendly distance had an undertone of irony.

My teachers at City College seemed contented with themselves—not always true of the men I had met at Townsend Harris. Some came from the American mainland. One, Michael Kraus, was an accomplished historian who had been a classmate of my father's and who was especially encouraging. I experienced the atmosphere as far more open, less censorious than that of the classrooms at Townsend Harris. Certainly, the freer form of classroom dialogue—especially in history and literature—was a relief. When I told the teachers that I had been admitted to Williams, they were warmly congratulatory.

My fellow City College students were as intelligent as those at Townsend Harris, less driven, and somewhat more diverse in ethnic origin. I recollect bright black students from Harlem and rhetorically gifted Irish ones from Hell's Kitchen—but it was later, at Protestant Williams, that I first read Joyce. I liked Mordecai Chertoff, who studied English literature and was about to enter Jewish Theological Seminary to become a rabbi: his apparent achievement in synthesizing traditions seemed well beyond my reach. He later became a Zionist writer. The other students liked me, or admired my energy. I was elected to be one of the two representatives of the incoming class on the Student Council. The other was Joseph Flom, whom I later met when he was at Harvard Law School and I in the graduate school. He was later much in demand as a legal adviser on mergers, and President Clinton recognized his services to the Democrats (which were surely not exclusively pecuniary) by appointing him chairman of the board of the Woodrow Wilson Center. I met some of the other student leaders later, in the academy and Washington.

The meetings of the Student Council were interesting not least because for a time we discussed college problems with some of the members of the Board of Higher Education. Some of them had gone to Princeton and Yale, and I was struck by their civic commitment. City College was important to them on grounds of equity. Like Max Berking and the other well-situated Americans I had met, they wished to live in a society with enlarged opportunities. There was nothing patronizing about them: they treated us rather more respectfully than some of the *nouveaux riches* on the Amherst Board of Trustees treated their faculty.

For all of the differences between City College and the Ivy

League, the City curriculum and formal pedagogic ethos when I was there in the spring of 1942 were remarkably similar to what I encountered in the fall at Williams. Continuity with Townsend Harris High School was pronounced as well. In literature courses, whether English or French, in history, in political science, the teachers thought of themselves as custodians of a tradition. We were the fortunate beneficiaries of European experience, and if it was depicted as different (more anguished and bloodier, less fair and above all less promising) than ours—we in the United States were the better Europeans. My father's college classmate Mike Kraus in his writings anticipated the Atlanticism that was an ideological fundament of the Cold War. I knew nothing at the time of the Council on Foreign Relations and its inter-war studies on "War and Peace"— and I was thoroughly confused on a major issue: did the American elite support the British one in its struggle against Germany or did it intend to supplant it? The answer was—both. What I did grasp, step by step, was that there was a transatlantic community of reform, sympathetic to social revolution where it was needed. These were the connections Daniel Rodgers was later to describe in his book *Atlantic Crossings*. My academic experience at City College reinforced the progressivism I had learned from the books on my father's shelves. After all, he had graduated but twenty years earlier.

Walter Benjamin wrote of art that it was the music of hidden spheres. I do not recollect much of modernist art in the curriculum. Rather, there were careful textual analyses intended to teach us to read. We were not encouraged to move into hidden realms of experience or feeling, but to acquire a decent acquaintance with Matthew Arnold's "the best that has been thought and said." I had begun to visit the Museum of Modern Art, with its exhibits describing the enticing but bewildering ties between painting and sculpture and literature, philosophy and politics. I did not stand before doors either ajar or shut. Rather I faced a series of boxes, each of which had to be unpacked, only to turn out to contain another box. I'd also begun to read *Partisan Review*, in which I found the linear analyses of history and politics, however much they disdained the progressivist pieties, easier to understand than the writing on art and literature. I do not think that the future member of *PR*'s editorial board was, aesthetically, tone deaf. I was reliant on intellect rather than intuition to seize the world, more at home with narrative than montage, very much rooted in the epoch of black-and-white film and not able to envisage its multimedia sequel.

Perhaps adolescence, for some, was free of thought of the future—an exploration of the possibilities of a newly discovered present. That was what I found in the aura of books such as *A Portrait of the Artist as a Young Man* or *Point Counter Point* or even *U.S.A.*, which I read as a guide to the world. The difficulty was that I found it in the books but not in life. I did not consider that I had very much time to enjoy the present, since I was fixated on the future—my future. The fixation was so great that I talked about it as well as dwelling inwardly on it. I sought out one of the City College deans, known to my father, introduced myself—and when he asked me what I envisaged after college, I did not hesitate: I wished to study and teach at the London School of Economics and Oxford. His answer was skeptical but accurate: one had to be very good to do that. I took it as both a rebuke for excessive ambition and a challenge.

The contentious sectarianism of the Marxists did not dominate City's life. The onset of the war confronted the protagonists of endless debates on the capitalist state with the immediate prospect of becoming uniformed servants of it. There was another reason: with La Guardia, an ally of Franklin Roosevelt, as mayor, and with New York's political elites committed to the New Deal, City was hardly a marginal institution. Depression and the international turbulence of the thirties of course brought the issues that so troubled the Marxists to the forefront. It was the occupation of large stretches of ideological terrain by the reformers that made adjacent ground available to the radicals.

I did glimpse some of the activities of these groups, which provided a social setting and support for their members, gave them a sense of connection and purpose—exactly what any religious or secular social movement did. I occasionally read the publications of the groups with which they were affiliated. I cannot recall any student in their orbit who had much more to say than some of my high school acquaintances. I met no teacher who spoke for them. What I knew of the larger ideas of the independent Marxist tradition came from reading, mainly the essays in *Partisan Review*—and, some time in this period, Edmund Wilson's *To the Finland Station*. I was quite unable, intellectually and psychologically, to confront the major contradiction of that period. No doubt, the war was an imperialist venture and Churchill and Roosevelt (and, even more, Stalin) were bearers of their own national versions of imperialism—especially when in Stalin's case he railed against it. Still, German and Japanese imperialisms were worse, and not just marginally so. Any hope for a more humane, more just, world order had as a precondition their defeat. I concentrated on that conclusion, and let the rest slide. I wasn't wrong, just shallow.

Early April, I went to our mailbox and found a thick envelope from Williams College: I had been admitted with a scholarship and would I please fill out the necessary forms and return them with a check to secure my place. I had not only hoped but half expected the good news, after the admissions director had written positively to Townsend Harris. Now it had come true, and I was quite aware of what it meant as an opportunity. There was little I could do to prepare myself for college except to finish the term at City. One of my teachers there recommended that I read *And Gladly Teach*, by Bliss Perry, a former Williams teacher.

It was a faint intimation of my initiation into a pedagogic fraternity. For the moment, the one student I wished to see advance was myself.

The war, with its images of combat and destruction in the newsreels, daily bulletins on the radio, the concerns of family and neighbors about their drafted sons, was a constant presence. Downtown gradually filled with young men in uniform. The city experienced the arrival of a new ethnic group, the Puerto Ricans. In New York, as everywhere else in the nation, war production and the draft had generated large demand for labor and the Puerto Ricans arrived to take advantage of it.

My position on the City College Student Council, and my assiduous visits to the International Student Service office on West 40th Street, brought me a considerable step further in my search for experience of America. The International Student Service that summer organized two camps for student leaders, one in the south and one in the north. This last was at the Roosevelt family home on Campobello Island, just north of the border with Maine in Canada—donated for the summer by the family. I was selected to attend the Campobello session. I owed that to the kindness of Trude Pratt, a striking German lady of strong anti-Nazi convictions who was a searching if stern judge of talent. She was a close friend of Eleanor Roosevelt, and had an immensely long career in civic service in New York. She married the former student leader and later Roosevelt biographer Joseph Lash. I recall Joe telling me in the mid-'40s that of all his experiences, fatherhood was the most exhilarating: I had to experience it to believe him.

I met the others, all of them already in college, one day late in June at Grand Central Station for the trip north. That involved an overnight rail journey through Maine. One of the students was black, from the South. His presence in our group excited the disapproval of a white soldier on the train, who declared that he was not fighting for racial equality: "All you will get from me is a losing battle." The ideology of wartime national unity had its limits and shortly thereafter, the black leaders by threatening a march on Washington compelled the President to issue a directive to firms with government contracts to employ blacks. My own awareness of racism in our history and society was extensive but shallow. It did not, alas, lead me to question the schematism of simple notions of class domination.

We took a boat to the island from Maine. The tidal movement in the Bay of Fundy was considerable, and I still recall the trepidation with which I descended the slippery steps from the dock. Despite my bravado, the trepidation had to do with taking on yet another challenge far from home—after enjoying the familiarity of City College as a secure first step to independence. Now, as before in my seeking new friends of different ages in Manhattan (and in my imminent enrollment at Williams), I was ahead of my chronological age, rushing it.

The Campobello summer was, after all, another step not only into a wider world but up in it.

Of that, a group of younger Americans being trained at a Civilian Conservation Corps camp in Maine across from the island had no doubt. When Mrs. Roosevelt came for a few days, she was true to her legend. I knew the splendid *New Yorker* cartoon depicting two miners at a pit face, one of them staring astonished down the dark shaft: "My God, here comes Mrs. Roosevelt!" She was indeed

At Campobello Island Youth Leadership Camp. Me and Stanley Halperin (right) swearing in Chinese Ambassador Hu Shih to what we called our Bronx Philosophical Society.

the President's eyes and ears, no group, occupation, place in the nation remained unvisited. The time with the aspirants to the elite had to be balanced, so she spent some hours with the young men at the camp—none of whom, in those days, would have dreamed of college. We were taken along, and I recall talking with the CCC recruits, who were friendly, open and welcoming—but who made clear that they knew that we had fortune on our side.

The students at Campobello (there were twenty of us) did come from across the country. I recall David Hsiu, who was a pre-medical student friendly with the Chinese ambassador, who was one of a procession of interesting dignitaries who came to talk with us. He most definitely did not return to the People's Republic. Virginia Smith, from Washington State, was later president of Vassar. Wilson Dizard was from Fordham, and gave me my first idea of the self-consciousness and sense of being threatened of the educated Catholics. Townsend Harris and City College were for men only and I was bound for Williams with its version of a cult of masculinity. Campobello was a co-educational experience I could not even repeat later at graduate school, given the attitudes and practices of the forties and early fifties at Harvard. It was well before Mary McCarthy wrote *The Group,* but the women were shy neither about their political views or their judgements of persons, which I remember as being a good deal more insightful and sympathetic, too, than those of the men. One of the students decidedly caught my fancy—the extremely attractive and intelligent and rebellious daughter of a Reform rabbi (his congregation were decidedly not recent immigrants) from San Francisco. We became friends and I learned of her problem: her parents were opposed to her attachment to a young man of Armenian descent. Common origins in the Mideast did not interest San Francisco's well-situated German Jews. It seemed that she came to the camp because her father, thinking the transcontinental trip a very good idea, had arranged it with Mrs. Roosevelt. The rabbis I knew of in the Bronx were not that influential.

The academic program was exciting, if strenuous. Intellectual and political dignitaries succeeded one another with considerable rapidity. I recall two New Deal officials who were the first bureaucrats I'd met—and they turned out to be gratifyingly interested in changing the world. One I now recall because he was Thomas Remington, sent to prison in the late forties for having denied a supposed connection to the Communist Party—and murdered in a federal facility by a fellow prisoner. There were economists, historians, sociologists. These included Robert Merton, whose detached coolness and sparse verbal elegance conveyed authority in a way I had not encountered before. I cannot, however, remember what he said; perhaps he dwelled on the studies of primary group influence he embarked on after his earlier work on science and society in seventeenth-century England. The academic director was a large figure, Robert MacIver, and talking with him was itself an education. MacIver was Scottish, had come to Columbia from Canada after writing *Community*, a book that was both political philosophy and sociology. He brought to the summer a sense of the weight of history and embodied the learning and sensibility one needed to understand it. He and his wife clearly enjoyed the company of the young, and made us feel part of a larger company of the civilized which was somehow disinterested and reflective—good for the long term.

That was in rather sharp contrast to the emphasis on immediate politics the ISS resident director, Molly Yard, brought. Mrs. Roosevelt herself, with her account of what she had heard from White House visitors Churchill and Molotov, reminded us of the headlines even if the newspapers arrived late. So did the German submarines operating off shore: we saw one ship being chased. Mrs. Roosevelt as I recall her was both impersonal and gracious, with an evident purposiveness and sobriety: there was no problem in the world she was prepared to overlook, no situation that could not be bettered. She treated everyone alike, and I wonder now whether this considerable achievement of egalitarianism was the result of an economic decision. The world being her responsibility, its single dwellers could hardly be attended to one by one. Yet she obviously had a devoted group of friends (Molly among them), and the biography I read decades later by Blanche Wiesen Cook depicted a person of considerable vulnerability, which is to say, humanity.

Williams College 59

Eleanor Roosevelt on the Campobello dock, summer 1942.

The group at Campobello, photo taken from the house.

Mrs. Roosevelt's visit, like that of other political people (including James Wechsler of *PM*, New York's leftmost daily), heightened a dilemma of which I was sublimely unaware at the time: was I an intellectual, attempting to develop critical distance from current events in order to understand them—or a very committed activist, who grasped the great imperatives of the moment and sought to meet them? At the time, I saw no conflict; I had read in and of intellectuals like Laski and Strachey who combined both roles in one persona. The disappointments of Dos Passos and Wilson (or Trotsky) had not touched me as disappointments, and the opposition to much of American politics by Charles Beard struck me as an interesting footnote to the triumphs of the New Deal and not as something more fundamental. Wasn't he, like John Dewey, so present in public argument that he could not be dismissed as an iconoclastic naysayer?

These musings apart, the dilemma (and even more my own lack of manners and tact) led me to asinine behavior. Jacques Barzun came and spoke on a theme from intellectual history. I asked a question which intimated that his preoccupations were a large waste of time in a moment of crisis. Barzun was imperturbable, undoubtedly the most stinging of reproaches.

It would take time, too much of it, before I developed sufficient insight and reflectiveness to recognize how indispensable thought was to politics. That, in turn, entailed recognizing a necessary division of labor in the public sphere, in which thinkers and scholars ostensibly remote from politics were often, by intellectual adventurousness and independence, contributing the most to an enlarged consciousness. Twenty years later, when Iris Murdoch and I gave a seminar on "The Concept of Alienation" at Oxford, we both thought of it as a political act as well as a philosophical inquiry. Perhaps it was, but it hardly involved much immediate revolutionary mobilization.

The summer at Campobello was thoroughly educational, even if I was unable at the time to enjoy all of its pedagogic benefits. It was de-provincializing: I met a striking array of persons, older and younger, of very different backgrounds. The visiting lecturers came from France, Weimar Germany, Czarist Russia and the Chinese National Republic and also included a very distinguished

American black scholar, Alain Locke. The New Deal bureaucrats who came made the trip to Maine's northeast rewarding: out of Washington, they were prepared to speak more freely of what had brought them to the capital. Mainly, however, I made the acquaintance of a number of accomplished younger persons further along than I was in their quests for a vocation—who spoke American in their own accents. For them, New York was interesting, perhaps exciting, but not the center of the world. They came to the public sphere, additionally, with very different motives and perspectives than my local contemporaries: some had been influenced, in church and family, by the Christian Social Gospel movement. They also had good manners. En route home to California, one of them after coming to our home for dinner, wrote to my mother praising her potato salad. It was not a response she was accustomed to.

The Campobello summer over, I made my first visit to Washington for an International Student Assembly. It was also sponsored by the International Student Service, with backing (one suspects) from the New Dealers in the State Department. The USSR sent a woman soldier who was acclaimed not for what she said but for what she had done as an effective sniper—and a youth leader of about thirty-five years old who promptly got down to business: agitating for the "Second Front" (Stalin's demand that the Western allies attack in Western Europe to relieve the pressure on the Red Army, a demand obsessively echoed by his western sympathizers). The message of unity in the face of fascism could survive that, but not the anti-colonial and anti-imperial agitation of a number of Asian, African and Latin American students, backed by some African-Americans who also evoked race relations in the US. One of the British delegates was a decorated Scottish officer in kilts who defended British control of India as an exercise in benevolence. I was surprised by the vehemence with which the themes emerged and could not deal intellectually with these anticipations of the conflicts of the post-war world. Those Americans present who struck me as close to the Communist party did not emphasize matters such as poverty, race, or labor in the US and were insistent only on the Soviet Union's immediate priorities. That was an echo of what I had already experienced in high school with the American Student Union.

Sympathy for the underdogs, for the exploited and the oppressed, was clearly not enough—especially as very opposing groups claimed to practice it. In a speech to the Assembly, Franklin Roosevelt made one of his early statements about the four freedoms: freedom of speech, freedom of religion, freedom from want, and freedom from fear. He spoke of a new "world civilization" which would unite Asia, Europe, and the Americas in a common project— and criticized the well-financed domestic antagonists who declared his project unrealizable. It was a proposal for a global social democracy. What would Roosevelt, had he lived, thought of the post-war American substitute for the welfare state, organized in the market by cooperation between the large firms and the unions? What would he have thought about the inextricable connection between the post-war social compromise and the readiness of the nation to support the Cold War? What, indeed, would he have thought of the inertia of the Cold War, the inability and unwillingness of those who started it to stop it—and their exploitation of the repressive brutality of Stalinism to discredit American progressivism? In the thirties and early forties, the United States was identified in Europe as the nation which in the New Deal had found an answer to the moral brutality of capitalism. Willy Brandt seriously considered emigrating to the US—and social reformers such as William Beveridge in Great Britain and the technocratic planners of France's post-war welfare state (in London with de Gaulle) looked to the US for inspiration and social technique. This was the United States which was host to the meeting. It was also the nation espoused by many of the men I was shortly to meet as teachers at Williams, even if a lot of my fellow students thought differently.

The Assembly was nothing if not colorful, since the play of personality among the speakers and in the delegates was remarkable. The delegates were often delegated by no one, selected by their governments, chosen by the International Student Service, or there on their own. In a rough and quite unintended way, that made for pluralism. I recall the American black leader Pauli Murray, then a student at Howard, and a British physician in the Royal Army Medical Corps whom I later encountered in London at the Tavistock Clinic.

Another more senior figure, Sir Norman Angell, who had won a Nobel Peace Prize, was one of the speakers: I was struck by what

I thought of as the excessively rational view of human nature he propounded, a liberal utopia. To that I opposed a world view in three parts. One was Marxist class theory, another was the view that elites were invariably rapacious, the third was a belief that humans would unite to better themselves and emerge with a higher community, but only with more revolutionary action. In authentic and original Marxism, an exploited class would recognize its own hidden and latent strength, and in a perfect synthesis of absolute constraint and total freedom, liberate itself and everyone else.

In fact, at the time I looked for liberation to the newer political and intellectual elites in charge of the New Deal coalition—who attracted me precisely because they were on top rather than on the bottom or even in the middle. As for a sacred union in pursuit of human betterment, that was imaginary compensation for the very real fears I had of some form of universal fascism, tinged by anti-Semitism. The inner contradictions of my world view were indeed a response to the world's conflicts, with their roots in historical and psycho-cultural processes I could hardly grasp, much less name. Every major and many minor contemporary event, every book I read, every person I met from another milieu, made the world seem more complex.

The intellectual structure held together because its substratum had to do not with the historians' history but with my own. I depicted the world as open to a resolution of its most profound conflicts, as capable of achieving a condition of grace which would enable its inhabitants to walk in dignity and freedom. That future social world would provide me with relief from my own conflicts, open the warm home I lacked. The authoritarian, brutal and exploitative elites who so strenuously opposed its achievement deserved all the hostility I reserved for them. I displaced onto history a set of inner conflicts I could not articulate, much less master. The process led to my own version of soteriology: salvation lay on the horizon. The difficulty was that the horizons kept receding. A goal no sooner attained than the next and more difficult one replaced it. In crossing cultural and social boundaries, I set myself tasks someone with more inner equanimity and self-respect would have found difficult enough.

Plunging into tasks dictated by ambition, I sought escape from the dreadful lack of equanimity and self-respect that plagued me. The concentration of my energies on that ambition, of my attention on a chaotic outer world, was all the greater for my having so much inner turmoil to flee. I was very dimly aware of this as I prepared to leave for college, so much so that I invariably turned away from discussions of the inner world, of character, of sensibility: the territory was dangerous. I was anxious to make friends and win respect in the world, but I neglected to start with myself.

I left for Williamstown in the fall, then, inwardly and outwardly confused—and armored with a considerable amount of bravado to reinforce my denial of that condition. There were enough immediate challenges. In those days, there were three railway routes to Williamstown from New York. I traveled the eastern Hudson shoreline to Troy, a journey I was familiar with from our summer vacations in towns on the other side of the river, then took the Boston and Maine train to Williamstown. It stopped at towns with names such as Hoosick Falls and Eagle Bridge and North Pownal, and I had the impression of visiting a different country, with its farmhouses and fields and bright foliage (it was late September). Some months later, back home, some of my friends asked me what Williamstown was really like: the notion of a place without apartment houses struck them intrinsically improbable. As I have mentioned, when I first took the Lexington Avenue subway to 23rd Street to begin classes at Townsend Harris, there was a chalked inscription in the primal grime of the station: "Defend Trotsky!" The Williamstown train station had its inscription, too: "Beat Amherst!"

There were orientation and registration proceedings that I do not recall. My first contact with faculty was in the classroom. I do have a memory of being struck by the bearing of my fellow students, a certain deliberateness in mode of address and restraint in rhetoric. They were as much on trial as I was, I realized only much later, but they knew how to conceal it and so acted as if coming to Williams was their due—which in most cases, it was. A good many had gone to private schools and knew each other, or what to expect of each other. I was given a room in Sage Hall, at the top of the staircase. One of my neighbors was Bob Coye, who would become a loyal and understanding friend. He was the son of a physician, headed for medical school—but had to make a detour through the army as an infantry officer in combat in France, Belgium, and Germany. Bob seemed intuitively to grasp that I needed simple friendship more than anything else, and was glad to listen to what I told him of growing up in New York (he came from suburban Rochester). Some of the others I met were rather distant, mostly because they could not place me and wished to avoid a faux pas. They were already attentive to the conventions of upper middle-class life (above all, this was true of those on scholarship). For a while, using an entirely unreflective set of notions I derived from the novelists John Marquand and Sinclair Lewis and from figures such as the literary critic Malcom Cowley, I thought of my classmates as complacent and obdurate philistines. After they returned from the war, I realized that I had seriously underestimated them. So far from resisting experimentation and modernity, they were trying to find their ways through it.

The pattern of undergraduate life, even in wartime, did not differ much from what it had been before. New students were screened by the fraternities, and those who either did not wish to join one or were deemed not suitable (most Jewish students) became members of the Garfield Club, which had its own dining hall. Like everyone else, I participated (while rather bewildered) in the screening process, groups of students being invited in turn to meet with the brethren at the fraternity houses on campus. What I recall is the atmosphere of good manners, despite the certainty on everyone's part that I would not be invited back. Edgar Bronfman, whom I hardly talked with, was in my class and did join a fraternity. He was later asked to leave the college for systematic inattention to his studies, which so shocked the family that (after he was readmitted and graduated) they gave millions to the college. When I was at Amherst I asked a Williams dean whether the same process could be repeated with Edgar's son, then an undergraduate, but the colleague was regretful: "No such luck; this Bronfman is a good student."

The Garfield Club had an interesting mixture of students and a faculty advisor who was a former diplomat of the Spanish Republic. At some point dining arrangements in the college were altered, as a Navy training course took over our dining hall, and we were distributed throughout the fraternity houses, Garfield reconstituting itself after the war. It was at Garfield that I met the students who would be close friends and intellectual companions, but some of the campus intellectuals (Leston Havens and Cushing Strout) were at fraternities and it did not harm them—may even have profited them. Before John Sawyer became president in 1961, he made the abolition of the fraternities a condition of his accepting the appointment. Were they strongholds of militant anti-intellectualism to which students retreated to recover after being exposed to the withering fire of faculty thought in the classroom? In the wartime and immediate post-war years that wasn't the case, and afterward, to judge by my own experience at Amherst, the source of campus attitudes was not in local structures but in the larger texture of the culture. The notion of the American academy as an intellectual Mont Saint Michel rising above the tides of philistinism off the coast of the mainland by is absurdly simplified.

I had a job as a student waiter along with some of the other scholarship students. (I would have preferred the job given at the time to a football player from Michigan, which required him to wind the university's clocks—an assignment facilitated by the fact that they were electric.) The others anticipated some of the diversity which was later to be a theme of the American academy. One of my fellow waiters was the son of a black postal worker in Harlem—Wayne Calloway, whose self-possession and humor in a difficult position were evident. A certain number were offspring of educators, and some came from the Massachusetts mill towns (and played on the college teams). Bringing the deserving poor to Williams served to recruit members to the elite, or at least calm potential opposition. A majority of my fellow workers did exhibit considerable class consciousness—they wanted to join the prosperous as quickly as possible and had little or no concern for redistribution or equality. Some became more open to reforming society once they'd integrated themselves in it, and perhaps in that sense contact with students (and above all teachers) of a critical disposition may have given them a latent sense of alternatives. The one overt encounter I had with anti-Semitism at Williams I endured from a fellow waiter, who most definitely came from the Massachusetts working class.

That that event was an exception is evidence for an attractive quality of life at Williams, whatever the exclusions institutionalized in the fraternity system. Once one was there, one was a member of a club—and was entitled, despite all differences, to a reasonable minimum of civility. A majority of the students I met when I first came to Williams had no aspirations to climb into the highest reaches of culture and intellect, but they were quite explicitly respectful of fellow students who seemed to be heading there. Many did not volunteer or participate very much in class, but they were usually quite willing to learn something from those who did. There was a minority which occasionally gave vocal disapproval when a fellow student appeared too eager to answer a teacher's question—or, worse yet, had an answer of which the teacher approved. That was, clearly, not something I had experienced at City College. The practice disappeared after the war, when the veteran's B replaced the gentleman's C.

What about the teachers? Williams was turbulent in the late '30s, when President Tyler Dennett and the trustees clashed. Dennett wanted to increase the number of public school graduates in the student body. The trustees, of course, won.

Dennett's successor, James Phinney Baxter, had taught naval history at Harvard, later took leave as official chronicler of the scientific segment of the war effort, and was an old-fashioned liberal. He and Dennett brought to Williams a number of scholars who were New Dealers and early Keynesians, one, Alan Sweezy, having been dismissed by Harvard as an economist at about the same time as John Kenneth Galbraith. Some of the alumni were disturbed when a group of faculty supported strikers at a factory in the desolate neighboring town of North Adams. Later, a teacher in economics showed me a copy of a letter to Baxter from a trustee. It was 1946; the US had entered a period of sustained growth, due to consumer demand and full employment, and the trustee was profoundly disturbed. The young men, he told Baxter, were coming to Wall Street with Keynesian notions they had acquired in college. Against these imbecilities, Baxter held firm. He thought Williams should be a place of intellectual quality. It was impossible to have a faculty which was entirely conservative and totally intelligent. There were obdurate economic conservatives at Williams, including an elderly economist who frequently wrote to *The New York Times* denouncing the trade unions as conspiracies in restraint of trade. There were cultural and social conservatives defending the values of New England gentility. Most of the social science faculty, however, favored the New Deal. Amongst those teaching the humanities, the modernists decidedly outnumbered the traditionalists. If there had been a struggle between the avant-garde and the rest, by 1942 the avant-garde had won. The faculty's deep regret, however, was that the students did not side with them, or worse yet, did not quite know that there was an argument.

The teachers I first encountered were of both camps. The historians were prudent, preferring precise narratives to great interpretations. Had I listened more closely to them, no doubt I would have acquired a sense of complexity earlier than I did. They did give me the impression that for them the "old country" was the United Kingdom, that the rest of the US would do well to keep colonial Boston in reverence, that revolution and turbulence were matters that affected other peoples. The political scientists were younger, and had in their ranks a national star, Max Lerner. Max was friendly, invited me to his house, and was a stern paternal figure who pointed out that my prose was distinctive only for its lack of style. He cited the New York Post columnist Sam Grafton as a model. Given my great interest in politics, however, something unexpected happened: my education was most deepened by the teachers of English.

They were avid readers of Eliot and conveyed, even when they did not state it, Eliot's dictum that a classic is a work which alters our reading of the past. Reading the classics with them, I was put on new paths to the present, a different understanding of its historicity. The fog that had enveloped my earlier reading of literature, my perplexity at what I found in *Partisan Review*, in Edmund Wilson's texts, lifted somewhat. I could not entirely or explicitly describe what I was learning, had the conviction of an opening. Some of my fellow students helped. Claudio Guillen came from a Spanish background (his father, a poet, had gone to Cuba to escape Franco), Roger Jospe came from a French-speaking one, and George Walsh, from an Irish family in Pittsfield, had a particular affinity for Joyce. I read and re-read *A Portrait of the Artist as a Young Man*, equating Joyce's fictionalized account of his break with Irish Catholic convention with my own story. That was stretching it more than a bit, since Joyce found University College in Dublin, the Jesuit institution he attended, stifling—and I found that Williams offered the prospect of liberation. One difficulty, however, was that I did not have any clear feeling or idea or sense (the choice of three imprecise terms to describe a very vague conception is appropriate) of what liberation meant.

Other friends, chief among them Cushing Strout, seemed to have a better grasp of the concept, perhaps because they felt that American society was theirs - they didn't seem to need to be liberated from anything. Liberation clearly had something to do with achieving a stable inner position in life, which would enable me to experience it as a real and not imaginary progression.

Meanwhile, the teachers served as role models. They lived in pleasant houses, had attractive women as their wives, and obviously enjoyed what they were doing. I especially admired Hallett Smith. He was outspoken, and had periodic arguments with the student newspaper, *The Williams Record*. Once he declared the average Williams student dead from the neck up, and the paper responded (its editors no doubt thought, triumphantly) by reporting that he had said the same thing ten years ago. Hallett later became dean of humanities at the California Institute of Technology, invited me to speak in Pasadena when in 1962 I traveled cross country before returning to Oxford. He was elegant and ironic, approached the Elizabethan age with what I later identified as an anthropologist's eye—and measured our America with acerbic distance.

I also had a freshman advisor from the English department, the amiable and sympathetic Fred Stocking. Fred once visited us in London and was extremely pleased to see that I had come some distance from the confusions of freshman term. Those confusions, inner and outer, were large and painful, and some weeks after arriving I did ask my father to visit. He did so, as I recall was benign, reassuring and sovereign, talked with Fred and my resident dormitory and junior class advisors .Williams, clearly, offered its students social support of the sort prescribed a generation later for students struggling against poverty. The dormitory advisor was Derek Brinkerhoff, who advised me to talk more often with my father—good advice I unfortunately did not take. The junior advisor was Richard King, whose father taught chemistry at Williams, and himself became an assistant Williams dean and an educator. Richard, unlike Derek, was a New Englander and very reserved, helped by intimating a general empathy—which was, in fact, enough. I survived for three semesters at Williams, despite much inner turmoil, because of the empathy and encouragement of faculty and my friends.

They knew that I was struggling behind an aggressive façade—but my own awareness was limited. Alternatively, it took the form of ever more grandiose ambition.

The friends I had were intellectual—without the cerebral and frenetic manners of the New Yorkers. Most seemed to think they had time to take, rather than worlds to conquer. I'd eschewed a Jewish heritage and was in search of not, as the historians put it, a usable past but a usable future. My friends knew where they stood, and were (or so I thought) far less worried about their destinations. I most closely identified, I think, with George Walsh—who had rejected the Catholicism in which he grew up. He later became an Anglican, and I suppose my enthusiasm for the church of progressivism was something similar. I once heard the great German intellectual Franz Borkenau say of György Lukács, whom he knew, that he had a Jewish sense of moral problems. My contemporaries Les Havens and Cushing Strout did not at the time go to church or profess an active Protestantism—but they certainly dealt with questions of biography and culture as matters of moral decision. Claudio Guillen and Roger Jospe were the Europeans I knew. Claudio had an aesthetic approach that struck me as out of touch with the harsh realities of history—but which evoked my envy when he described his adventures with the girls he knew. Roger Jospe would have been speechless had anyone declared that harshness was not the essential characteristic of existence. He conceived of life as a struggle to gain a small measure of respite from its severity. The person with the largest sense of humor, alternately benign and sardonic, and the deepest understanding, was Bob Coye. As a medical educator, he must have been a gift to his students.

I mentioned Claudio's amorous adventures, real or otherwise. My friends were not visibly active in this regard, whatever they said or hinted at. I certainly was totally abstemious. I did go to Bennington and liked the girls I met there, who were older by two or three years or more.

If I really could get to know one of them, I imagined, I'd be introduced to an entire cosmos of experience I knew only from novels. The cosmos remained in the novels or in the movies. I felt stuck in awkwardness. My friends, whom I saw through most of the days, and the faculty (whom I met intermittently) certainly had hints or intimations of my inner turbulence, without having an opening to address it directly. I think that we spoke in code, talking about characters in novels, ideas in books—and meaning ourselves.

Withal, my joining the larger Williams family by becoming a member of our smaller circle had positive effects—I felt that I was to some degree esteemed, even (more improbably, as I then thought) liked. This small measure of social integration allowed a bit of inner freedom.

The spring of 1943 was especially beautiful, and I awoke to the fact that I was living in a Yankee Garden of Eden. Some of my inhibitions on feeling, which generated my compulsive intellectualism, loosened. I even began to sense strong feelings, sometimes a general and vague desire for experience, sometimes a totally unfamiliar sense of connection. I had entered a new realm, rather like the one described by the novelists I so devotedly read. Our group did not resemble the friends who gathered in the tower in *Ulysses*, and if Jewish I certainly wasn't Solomon Bloom—I identified, of course, with Stephen Dedalus.

Still, I had the conviction that I had taken a large, even giant, step, even if I could not explain or even describe much of it. I talked of it with George Walsh and found the word "vision" to characterize my new experience. I think that I may have derived this from reading Jacob Burckhardt's *The Civilization of the Renaissance in Italy*, which he began by declaring that his starting point was a vision and that without it, he could do nothing with the manifold aspects of history. George was much attached to Christian ritual, and this made him receptive to Jewish neurosis. I had begun to read Freud and found at the very beginning of his *The Future of an Illusion* his discussion with Romain Rolland on the "oceanic feeling" the writer had asked Freud to explain. It seemed close to my new sense of oneness with things, although I could not accept Freud's explanation that it was a reminiscence of the child's attachment to his mother. My own attachment to my mother was buried, and I lacked the archaeological courage to dig it out. A lifetime later, I think my own case was somewhat more complicated and, at any rate, I was under the impression my new feelings were connected with moving away from dependence. Whatever the causes of my enlarged emotive capacity, and however ephemeral, it was a trip to a psychological promised land. The trip was, alas, very short.

The spring passed, a new term begun, I became depressed. Grayness enveloped me, as the contours of experience lost their sharpness. I recollect no great sadness, no external disappointments of a disturbing kind. I simply felt that something essential was missing, that I was imprisoned in a narrowing cell. I had read enough and heard enough to sense that I needed help, and arranged to see the college's consultant psychiatrist, who came up periodically from the Riggs Foundation in Stockbridge. His name was Edgerton Howard, and he mostly listened but did say that he thought that my separating from home was causing, inevitably, some guilt. I concluded that I needed more help, and gradually decided that I would have to leave college to obtain it. Howard had, as I now see it, a certain authority.

I suppose that I could have remained, gone down to Stockbridge several times a week by bus for treatment. The college, however, was shrinking visibly; some friends, such as Cushing, Leston, and Roger, followed Bob Coye into the army. I did not like the institution's loss of vitality, and the sense of being even further apart from history added to my inner desolation.

I do not think that I discussed my decision to leave college with anyone, certainly not with my father or teachers—possibly with George Walsh. I was clear that I needed psychiatric help, had an imprecise sense that psychoanalysis was the treatment of choice—but I had no friends who had been analyzed; I knew of it through some reading in Freud and others and from novels. I traveled home, but first went to Boston and visited with Morton Bader at Harvard Medical School. Mort and his twin, Richard (who went to Columbia Medical School), was a friend from the Bronx. I suppose that my stopping off there, rather than going right home, had something to do with seeking advice, but I cannot recollect what we talked about. I do recollect that I went to Boston the day Italy capitulated. When I did arrive at home, my father was bewildered as well as vexed: what did I intend and how did I propose to deal with the rest of my life? If he had any advice to give at that point, he was very sparing with it, put off by my own sullen independence. Now that independence took the form of a feeling of isolation, but I knew where to turn to break out of it.

One of the sponsors of the International Student Service was an elegant lady I had met, Mrs. David Levy. I knew that her husband was a psychiatrist of some distinction, and I contacted him, introduced myself, and obtained an appointment. I gave him some of my journal writings to read; he administered a Rorschach test, we talked and he agreed that I could profit from treatment. He had glanced at the journal for only a few minutes while I sat there before reaching the aforementioned conclusion that my problem was my consuming ambition: "You want to look down on your father from Olympus." He undertook to find a suitable colleague, and I cannot recall why he did not suggest himself. He certainly had an interest in the things that preoccupied me: he published case studies of anti-Nazis, had worked on maternal over-protection and childhood hypochondria, and by the time I saw him was clearly a younger elder statesman in American psychoanalysis. I was impressed by his calm and his combination of directness and reserve. I had no doubts that he would give good advice.

He sent me to a neurologist who was at the beginning of a psychoanalytic career, David Beres. He was as old as my father (his son was later a contemporary at Williams) and paternal, even patriarchal, in manner. Treating adolescents or young adults remains problematical for psychoanalysts, and many who begin doing so in the end move to dealing with adults, where failure and success are more easily measurable. It is now my impression that Beres's primary aim was not to provide total insight and help me to a major characterological change. He studied with the American scions of Freud's ego psychology (Hartmann, Kris, Loewenstein) but I have the impression that he experimented with patterns of interpretation, trying to find a repertory which would enable me to engage more fully in the process. I certainly wished to do so, but had had little experience of self-confrontation, and little direct social support for the process. Beres was at times admonitory, intervened more than once to provide judgement and guidance in life situations, and alternated this with straightforward listening. At one point, he told me that I was the sort of person who would be in and out of psychoanalysis throughout his life—an entirely correct prediction. That allowed him to assign himself a very specific initial task—getting me to the point at which I could return to college and resume my career.

I'd sought out Dr. Levy and begun with Dr. Beres without consulting my parents or bringing them into the process. There was no familial experience with psychotherapy and very little if any in their social milieu. They were, initially, shocked by my decision. My mother added it to her unending list of grievances with a world which did her insufficient honor. My father voiced worries about the wisdom of my choice: how could I know that the physician wasn't a charlatan? Their indignation at not being consulted refracted their bitterness: I was repudiating their parenting. Who, my father wanted to know, would pay the bill?

I had an answer, which did not noticeably decrease their distress. I'd found a job—and one which turned out to be interesting. The government's agency for propaganda abroad, the Office of War Information, had a large broadcasting studio and editorial office in New York—in a building on 57th Street, just a block west of Carnegie Hall. I was hired as a clerical assistant (in a newsroom, I would have been termed a "copy boy") in the OWI's Cable and Wireless department. When I reported for work, I was delighted to find that the editors and journalists working there, an exceedingly colorful lot, were friendly. In a very short time, they realized that the seventeen-year-old in their midst not only followed the news but knew modern history. Many of them were supporters of the New Deal; some had been active in the American Newspaper Guild.

In recollection, some stand out. John Day was from Kansas and had written on that state's small civil war, which preceded the national one. Some years later, when I was at Harvard, he arrived there as a Nieman Fellow. Eugene and Maria Jolas had lived in Paris, where they were deeply immersed in artistic and literary modernism, edited a magazine called *transition*, and were friends of James Joyce. I was so struck by their cosmopolitan bearing and arcane presence that I waited months to talk with them. Robert Bendiner had been La Guardia's press spokesman and declared that the stresses of dealing with the war were comparatively relaxing. One of the men writing in German was from Vienna, described in terrible detail the Pogroms that followed the German invasion—by Austrian Nazis. I was especially impressed by the self-confident and capable women journalists who had seized the opportunity to use their talents in areas generally not open to them. The cast changed frequently, as the journalists worked there for some months and then went off to the United Kingdom to prepare for the invasion, or to the Mediterranean.

I was soon given writing assignments. The office was another one of those doors which, when I pushed, opened into a larger world.

One of the writers at the OWI was Seymour Krim, and through him, I met persons I previously knew about from books, who lived in Greenwich Village, and were authentic bohemians. They were artists, musicians, and writers, or lived otherwise by their wits, did not with some rare exceptions (the persons in question were quick to apologize for it) have steady employment, came from all over the nation but could not be situated in the class system. What united them was a disdain for routine so pervasive that they did not think it worth articulating; they contented themselves with living it out. Of course, they kept no regular hours and smoked what was called tea (marijuana) in imitation of the jazz musicians among them. My own friends were more literary: Constance Smith was something of an elder sister to me. The especially gifted Milton Klonsky was another, and I recall Chandler Brossard, who later wrote a superbly funny article for *Commentary* on being a Gentile intellectual in New York. There were inter-connected circles and I became friendly, briefly, with the gentle and intelligent Isaac Rosenfeld. I also knew David Bazelon, intelligent but hardly gentle, bursting with moral passion: in a world ruled by lies and stupidity, he pursued honesty in permanent anger. All these persons were older than I, but still only in their twenties and thirties. The older residents of the Village, the custodians of its artistic and intellectual traditions, the *Partisan Review* editors and writers, the artists who were forming the School of New York, were but steps away—but I did not meet them. I went to museums, to the movies, but my imagination was historical and political. I envied my new friends their freedom from dogmatic fixation on career, their seeming ability to live in the interstices and margins of society.

That envy had something sexual about it, or rather, reflected my sexual frustration. I imagined their lives as highly eroticized and indeed, attractive women were very much part of the scene. Not very much different in their behavior than many women as depicted in Hollywood films, many of them were demonstratively attached to their men and said very little. I experienced a frustration which was sexual in a very broad sense: I felt the need for warmth and had no sustained source of it.

That accounted for my wandering in and out of very different groups (a pattern which has continued) looking for what they were in the end unable to provide. Perhaps my bitter rejection of imposed identities of any kind was due to the conviction that in the end I would be abandoned to my fate—a parody of familial relations. Psychoanalysis did not reach these depths, even if it touched upon them. Instead, as I recall it, there was discussion of my being inhibited, in work and play. That was certainly true, as my experience of the larger society consisted of forays into different areas followed by retreats, and never accompanied by a great sense of adventure or freedom. There was something driven about it, something never-ending. Ostensibly engaged in growing up, I kept repeating myself: whatever breakthrough I sought was always over the next horizon.

Despite that, I did make some modest progress in sexuality. I recollect two very agreeable ladies with whom (one at a time, to be sure) I had my early experience of intercourse. The first one was older, an actress from the South, encouraging. The second was my age and a New Yorker, too, more matter-of-fact. What I did not do was to develop these encounters into more than temporary relationships.

I had already been in love. Joy was a Californian, a few years older than myself, working at the office. There was something inwardly illuminated about her, she had come to New York after studying at Berkeley. There, she told me, she had had a lot of contact with the professors and students at the university's international house. She knew Haakon Chevalier, Malraux's translator and the friend of Robert Oppenheimer who perhaps asked him for information about the Manhattan Project to pass on to the USSR. Joy did not mention Oppenheimer; I had never heard of him and knew nothing of the project. Joy's international interests were cultural rather than political: she was looking for experience not available in her home town of Modesto. Joy had an American Protestant clarity about her, a clearness of definition and directness of response. Her being, her capacity for feeling, were infinitely appealing. She certainly liked me, which I could not quite believe. We spent time together, even visited Williamstown, but I was too hesitant and we did not become lovers. There was a door ajar which I lacked the capacity to open, even though I knew that on the other side of it was a realm of feeling which I longed to enter.

I reproached myself bitterly for this failure, realized that I had no one to blame but myself, but it took years before I could understand that hidden beneath my ambition, bravado, desire, was the conviction that I was entitled to very little. That sort of insight belonged to character analysis, which delineated the patient's ego and then sought to strengthen it. Character analysis, in the United States, was just beginning in those years. In any event, Dr. Beres evidently thought that his task was less the lengthy reconstruction of my character than helping me to find one to begin with, to enable me to recover from the overwhelming depression that lay like a pall over much that I did.

I was quite able to function in the office, where the work of writing up the news was not an insurmountable intellectual challenge. The difficult challenge was to understand the larger and shifting historical patterns made visible by the war. There, I was aware of ideas strikingly different from the amalgam of American triumphalism and New Deal progressivism which (with varying degrees of certitude) most people I knew voiced. Most of the Bohemians did not talk much about politics, but some did. David Bazelon and Isaac Rosenfeld were fiercely critical of the current clichés. I read *Partisan Review* as well as *The Nation* and *The New Republic*, and in late 1944, Dwight Macdonald began to publish *Politics*, its editor's and authors' criticisms of the reigning pieties etched in acid. I particularly recall Macdonald's bitter comments on the morality of the atomic bombing of Hiroshima and Nagasaki.

There were events that caused me to think. The Greek Civil War marked the beginnings of the Cold War. It started with the revolt of parts of the Greek Navy in Alexandria in 1943 and continued with the fighting between Greek resistance forces on the one side and the British and Royalist forces on the other in 1944. I had immense difficulty in situating this, went off and read some in modern Greek history. I must have read of the sense of affinity of Eastern Orthodox Greeks for Russia, of the fact that nations which defined themselves as churches were often open to the appeal of Communism as a secular religion. I was quite far from understanding this, and so thought of the Communist and radical democratic Greek left as a party of secular liberation from ecclesiastical tyranny, an extreme simplification. I was bewildered, too, by the BBC broadcasts to Germany by Patrick Gordon Walker, the Oxford historian and later Labour Party politician and minister. He addressed a German public which he supposed to be not entirely Nazi, and I did not know who these Germans were. The 20 July 1944 rising increased my perplexity: were the anti-Nazi officers (I was ignorant of the civilians involved) opportunists, or did they have motives I could hardly imagine? The liberation of Paris occasioned questions about the French resistance movement: who were these persons, precisely, and what position did de Gaulle have in the political spectrum? When, some months later, Malraux became his Minister for Information, my puzzlement increased. I knew that he had broken with the Communist Party, may by then have heard his famous words to the effect that in the end, there would only be the Communists and "ourselves" (the nationalist followers, as I thought of them, of de Gaulle). Yet the Communists were in many places very much in evidence, and I had heard of Togliatti's return from Moscow to join the Italian government. The failure of the Soviet Army to come to the aid of the Polish Home Army in 1944 reinforced my conviction that I was missing a great deal, but the conviction was subliminal. In those months, I postponed doubt rather than confront the obvious need to begin from the beginning and learn about the world anew.

Toward the end of 1945 Sartre himself, enveloped by the aura of the resistance and of existentialism—in New York an advertising slogan for quick and vicarious trips to an entirely fictional Paris—came to give a talk on the French theatre I listened, entirely ignorant of what he was talking about and disappointed that he did not speak of French politics. Years later, I learned that he did speak of French politics, with his hosts from *Partisan Review*. Clement Greenberg and William Phillips, especially, (as I reconstruct from conversations with them over the years) wanted assurances from Sartre that he definitely did not give, of prophylactic distance from the French Communist Party. Whatever was true of the Party in the US in the months immediately following the war, it was not a mass movement. It had members and sympathizers in important positions in the cultural industry and the trade union movement; the Soviet Union had a large amount of prestige on account of the military victory over Germany; there was a benevolent curiosity about the Chinese Communists. Domestically, the party took positions quite aligned with the trade-union Democrats, perhaps less determined ones since the party's aim was to insert itself in the American political process, and was quite prepared to seek the benefits of compromise and conciliation with the class enemy (which for a while it did not describe as such). The French Party at the high point of its electoral success (1946) had twenty-eight percent of the vote, ministers in government until 1947, and was firmly implanted in working-class neighborhoods, in the French educational system, and among the intelligentsia. There, the Communists were not seen as representing a backward foreign state but as modern descendants of the Jacobins, as custodians of France's own vanguard traditions.

Moreover, Marxist thought with its ostensible historical concreteness was conceived as a corrective to the abstractions of the French philosophic tradition and its emphasis on the subject. There was no French John Dewey in the decades before the war to provide a home-grown canon of politics. Sartre spoke for an entire generation in supposing that no democratic politics in France could exclude the Communists, and the cohorts of the disillusioned who later left the Party to seek an independent course were in 1945 still in alliance with it, or actually members.

In the United States, for a variety of reasons (conviction, fear, opportunism) the beginnings of Cold War conflicts between the new imperial apparatus of the nation and the Soviet Union led to a new thinking, much of which upon examination was not new at all.

What was new was a familial reconciliation: many of the intellectuals concluded that instead of looking elsewhere, or to the future, for an achieved revolution they had only to recognize the one outside their front doors. Mary McCarthy gave it perfect expression by pronouncing the new housing estates such as Levittown evidence for the authentic social revolution wrought by American prosperity. The trade unions thought the same, despite two severe defeats. One was the failure of an organizing drive in the South—which meant that investment was exported across state lines from unionized regions to low-wage areas, a domestic anticipation of what we know as globalization.

The other was Walter Reuther's failure to obtain for the United Auto Workers a share in the governance of the large firms. The unions turned to a strategy that entailed high benefits and wages—autonomous welfare states in the private sector. Meanwhile the Democratic Party in the Congress, federal and state governments, and the judiciary protected these arrangements, and sought against considerable resistance to extend the public welfare state.

Truman's 1948 re-election campaign, under the slogan "Don't let them take it away!" defined American progressivism as the defense of the achievements of the New Deal. It also defined it as indispensable to the defense of the national interest, the domestic political component of an enlarged global role. Alliances, access to raw materials, markets, had to be assured. The American people, however, could be mobilized for the nascent Cold War only if they were guaranteed a fair share of the nation's prosperity: the warfare state was also a welfare state.

The tensions within the wartime alliance could not be hidden, and their multiplication as the war ended set the old antagonism between the Communists and the Social Democrats in a global framework. I struggled with, or rather against, the realization that an interlude had ended—since I sensed that the new definition of American politics would require domestic and international political realignments which would seriously challenge progressivism I lacked the knowledge, and even more the perspectives, with which to treat the years 1933-1945 as history.

That was an incentive to finish, or suspend, psychoanalysis and return to Williamstown. I had overcome the paralysis of depression and I expected to be able to meet the academic demands of college. I talked over the matter with Dr. Beres and (to his pleased surprise) with my father.

The physician held that I had about exhausted the therapeutic possibilities of a situation in which I had removed myself from college. My father was glad that he could catch a glimpse of normality in me. None of us reckoned with an inconvenient fact.

Williams, at first, did not want me back. The campus physician told the Dean that I would constitute a problem, on account of my past psychiatric history. After corresponding with the college I went to Williamstown to make my case in person. What moved the college to relent was not my new or improved persona or my argument that I was being penalized for doing what others often did not do, confronting inner problems directly. A new medical officer was appointed and he was a psychoanalytic psychiatrist, just returned from naval service, who also took a personal liking to me. His name was Dana Farnsworth and he did not remain at Williams very long, since he shortly departed for MIT to serve as dean of students. Dana's revision of the college's codes of normality was part of the large cultural change experienced by middle-class America in those years. The assumptions and habits once largely confined to a few metropolitan areas, worship of the secular gods of rationality and self-fulfillment, skepticism about the rigidities of a life that denied expansiveness to the self, a certain experimentalism in morals, replaced a more limited version of Protestantism. True, faculty and some of the students at pre-war Williams were already metropolitans. Now, their war with the suburbs ceased as the suburbanites proclaimed their urban identities. Faculty, derided in pre-war Williams by a certain number of alumni and students because none of them "ever met a payroll," found themselves the intellectual chief executive officers of the post-war college.

The returning veterans had experienced a complicated and larger world and were open in their acknowledgement that they had not entirely understood it. The normality to which the veterans returned, they knew, had large elements of permanent uncertainty about it. By pre-war standards, it wasn't normal at all. It was, then, to a very changed Williams that I returned, veteran only of my inner battles.

3

Return to Williams

THE WILLIAMS COLLEGE I had entered in the fall of 1942 was of course affected by the war, but the college was defined by the class and cultural conflicts of the thirties. A New Deal faculty struggled with a largely Republican student body. Once in the late thirties, alumni and trustees were troubled (and many indignant) that faculty joined workers in the nearby town of North Adams on a picket line.

These divisions were deeper than political cleavages. The faculty looked to the urbane academic communities at which they had studied, to New York and to Boston, and to London and Paris, for their models of comportment, their ideas of the good life. Many Williams teachers thought of themselves as bringing Greenwich Village to Berkshire County. Those who were made uncomfortable by the modernism, the experimentalism in values, of many of their colleagues, represented a Protestant New England culture which thought the modern world redeemable. John Dewey, after all, was a Vermonter. Williams's Brahmins were especially devoted pedagogues, since they supposed that they were saving their students from the sins of spiritual idleness.

When I returned in October 1945, post-war Williams was a place transformed. The gentlemanly C of the pre-war epoch was replaced by the veteran's B: the returned students no longer regarded classes and term papers as burdens to be endured to get to the revelries of the weekend. Of course, they wished to get on with their lives, to get to the business, law and medical schools (and in some cases, the graduate schools) or to start working. The new purposiveness was not, however, entirely utilitarian. They had experienced things undreamed of in the undergraduate philosophy of the pre-war years. I recollect Sam Hunter, the art historian, recounting a kamikaze attack on his navy oiler. They had been in very different countries, encountered other civilizations. They'd also lived, in the armed forces, with fellow citizens who had never heard of Williams—the American majority. The GI Bill of Rights enabled veterans who had never envisaged attending Williams to do so, and so gave us classmates such as Al Kernan, whose splendid account of his years at post-war Williams is entertainingly true.

Faculty, too, had changed. Some returned from governmental and military service, newer sorts of teachers appeared (a very intelligent woman teaching in economics among them). With the older veterans dominating the student body, what had been a distant and wary relationship between students and teachers was replaced by a more direct, more open, connection. Our classes, frequently, were joined by women. Some of the returning veterans were married, and their wives took Williams courses to accumulate credit for degrees in other places.

Two things bothered me in this new setting. I returned with a residual uncertainty as to my academic capacity, but that was overcome rather rapidly. What remained was the larger question: how and where did I fit in? I discounted, excessively, what I had learned in the past two years—about myself and the larger society. The role of apprentice, perhaps perpetual apprentice, seemed easier to assume. The friends who returned from the war, energetically glad to be alive, seemed to have far fewer doubts. The profusion of intellectual opportunity around me was an additional problem: what, precisely, should I study? I already sensed that I was headed for graduate school in the social sciences. Indeed, I foreclosed other possibilities by hardly considering them. Years later, before I went to Georgetown University's law faculty, I realized that the study of American constitutional law was a pathway to much that was essential in our history. Its practice, moreover, was a form of social engagement often rather more effective than a certain number of my literary activities. These insights escaped me when I was younger, partly because I did not think that I had the luxury of choice, partly because other themes seemed more compelling.

Exactitude and system in thought were not, at the time, my

strong points. When I read Jacob Burckhardt declaring that his starting point had to be a vision, otherwise he could do nothing, I felt relieved—and legitimated. Williams College at the time had two masters of generality. One was William Miller, the senior philosopher at the college.

Much of philosophy in the nation was at the time dominated by analytic philosophy, by models of thought which privileged the method of the natural science. Miller stuck to an older tradition and was Emersonian in his scope—and his lack of fear of being thought eccentric or out of touch or up to date was his badge of authenticity, rather prominently worn. He was given to speaking in aphorisms, and ostensibly preferred the wisdom of rural and small-town America to the sophistry (as he depicted it) of the academic vanguard. His self-presentation was all the more effective because he believed it. Actually, Miller was a very learned man, with a very lyrical prose style and a large sense of humor. He had clearly decided that he would beat the academic game by his refusal to play it. That wasn't entirely true: he delighted to recount how, in his view, he had won an appointment at Williams. He had been summoned to town for an interview with the president, and sent in his visiting card—which, he suggested, marked him as a gentleman, an adherent of the right forms. Miller was a John Dewey who never made it to the big city—and whose aura consisted largely of exuding doubt that the journey was worth making.

I had taken a course with him before leaving for New York in 1943 and visited him when I returned once to Williamstown with my friend Joy, but find it difficult now to describe what drew me to him—or to philosophy, for that matter. I suspect it had something to do with the impression he generated of independence, paternal reserve and strength. I'm not sure that the impression rested on something genuine. As to philosophy, perhaps its vagueness (as he conceived it) was an attraction. Still suffering from plenty of inner confusion, unsure of what to think of a world emerging from the torments of war to different problems, I was incapable of developing much complexity or differentiation of mind.

Miller solved the problem for me. I took an independent study course with him, a tutorial, and found that he preferred to set the themes and the questions in ways that left me little scope for intellectual exploration. I believe that we dealt with some major texts, but he was less interested in the texts than in his own message. Then, one week he cancelled our tutorial: his son was visiting from college. Fair enough, but he objected rather strenuously when the next week or the one after that I asked to be excused so that I could go home for the Jewish New Year. I do not think he was anti-Semitic; the idea just didn't strike him as consonant with my academic duties. I ignored his irritation and went, and then set about looking for another field of study: the episode had made me aware of something tyrannical in him. I think, also, that his expressed hostility to psychoanalysis had something to do with my re-evaluation of Miller.

The other great Williams generalist was Frederick Schuman, who had come to Williams from the University of Chicago and taught political science. He was a specialist in international relations, but mastered s good deal of the social sciences. He was a German-American (Catholic), and had obviously profited from the very cosmopolitan atmosphere of his university, which in the thirties was very open to the European emigrants. I first made his acquaintance when I returned from my absence and was taken with the way he combined historical narrative, political drama and the play of ideas. It was he who introduced me to thinkers such as Karl Mannheim and Georges Sorel, even the obscure and ponderous Pareto. Fred was generous with his time, encouraged students to take their distance from the reigning political clichés, and made it quite clear that his view of American democracy was like Gandhi's of Western civilization: it would be a very good thing. Fred was exceedingly skeptical of the Cold War, disinclined to treat the Soviet Union as anything but a flawed revolutionary power.

I did not, however, enroll in the political science department. I thought, rightly, that with the reading I had done and my wartime experience, much of the material would be familiar. In any event, it was exceedingly clear that I would be studying social science in graduate school. Why not do something different?

That opportunity was provided by Lane Faison and the Department of Art. Lane had left the college to serve in a military unit in Europe charged with protecting artistic monuments, and later, with recovering looted art. He was immersed in the enjoyment of human creation, and he combined sensuous appreciation of the works he discussed with knowledge of the artists' biographies and historical settings. He knew that the world was a vale of tears and devoted himself to extracting from it what pleasures the spirit could devise. I enrolled in his department and had the benefit (which I counted upon) of a first-rate education in European cultural history, too. Lane allowed me to blunder through an honors thesis on Masaccio, although much of the reading about that great fifteenth-century innovator was in German and Italian. My German was rudimentary and I used Latin to get to Italian. I did learn a great deal about the evolution of forms, read in the social history of Renaissance Florence and above all profited from Lane's pedagogic rigor. He insisted that I write and rewrite to make clear statements about defined objects. About forty years later, I was in Florence as guest of the Italian Communist Party at a national Congress, and met the regional head of the party—a younger university teacher. When I told him what I had studied he was unequivocal in his praise for the obvious superiority of American higher education.

The campus was, intellectually, very alive in those years. The social changes that brought different sorts of people to Williams (and challenged those who thought that being at Williams was their birthright) led to a search for new definitions of the nation's culture: just one would not do. The earlier assumption of the superiority of a New England fusion of piety and power gave way, or rather was nationalized. Much of the rest of the nation was accepted as New England's heir, finally come into its estate. The country's beginning mobilization for the Cold War contest with the Soviet Union, the world wide extension of US power, surely had a major role in this transformation. The Williams teachers in economics and political science who had returned from governmental service knew people who remained to direct the expanded or new agencies of the executive branch. Some went back and forth to Washington with its imperial tasks themselves, such as Vincent Barnet, who later directed the Marshall Plan in Italy. For part of the college, patrician gentility gave way to technocratic rigor.

I struck up a friendship with a group of economists new to the college. I'd known Alan Sweezy before: he was one of the pre-war faculty recruited from Harvard, which deemed his Keynesianism unacceptable. Now there were Emile Despres and Kermit Gordon. Emile was of French Jewish origin, and with his vivacious wife, Joanna, presided over a continuous salon. He'd been at the Office of Strategic Services, the predecessor to the CIA, and had a major role in designing post-war economic policy for Germany. He was an economist's economist, with an enormous reputation among his peers and who later taught at Stanford. He had an acute eye for the political theater's chaotic backstage. I wondered, later, why this brilliant figure, so keenly interested in the governance of the world, was content to remain in the academy. Perhaps it was because he had seen enough of the world outside (he'd also worked for the Federal Reserve in New York) to realize that success in it had a moral price he was not prepared to pay. Of that, his attitude and bearing said little or nothing. I was too young, or just unempathetic, and could not interpret his jaunty cynicism as the expression of deep regret that the world being the way it was, it could not be otherwise.

Kermit was rather more sober, but conveyed an elegant amusement at the foibles of academic and social pretense. He came some years later to Adams House at Harvard when I was a tutor there, to finish a much-delayed doctorate. He joined the government in the Kennedy years, was Lyndon Johnson's Director of the Office of Management and Budget and was listened to by the President (a shrewd expert on human frailty) with very great respect. He became the President of the Brookings Institution, and I would have liked to have talked with him, but he left our world before I came to Washington. One of his children later published a memoir on domestic distress in his family; perhaps his detachment had its negative aspects.

What I experienced at college was not a slow initiation into the human subtexts of academic rhetoric: that had to wait until graduate school and the beginning of my own career in London. It was more like schoolboy gratification at being noticed by my teachers. My own work in economics was barely mediocre, but the economists seemed to forgive me that on account of other qualities, a certain knowingness—or at least, a plausible claim to it. My own development as a person did not come to a stop when I returned to college, but I was living off the accumulated emotional capital of relatively successful therapy. Economically, I had to concentrate my energies on getting back to work and the rest had to be postponed for a while. I cultivated my intellectual precociousness and did not wait for the rest to catch up.

I was just nineteen, my fellow students usually older, and the faculty older still. There were familial accents to my friendships. In some cases, I was viewed as a younger sibling, in others as a son. The familial resemblance was made more real by the invitations I had to take meals with the Despres or the Faisons, who lived on campus and actually welcomed my dropping in on them. One other family deserves mention—my freshman-year friend Bob Coye returned from his harrowing service as an infantry officer in Northern Europe and married Janet Loper, who was at Bennington. They promptly had a child, so I could act and feel like an uncle. It did not occur to me, however, that I was entering a period in which marriage and paternity were not just remote possibilities.

I could not conceive of myself as grown up. No doubt the self-assessment was dismally accurate—but it had the sad consequence of reinforcing my sense of unhappy separateness.

I knew some attractive and interesting young women, mainly at Bennington, but had no very large passion for any one. The exception was a student at Smith whom I decidedly liked very much. Her interest in me was initially encouraging, until it became clear that she was primarily intent on recruiting me to the Communist Party. To make matters worse, she introduced me to her friend, a printer from Springfield. It was, despite my theoretic solidarity with the working class, not an encounter I enjoyed. I appreciated one thing: she sensed how I felt and apologized for not being able to reciprocate. I wondered, later, how she fared in the years immediately thereafter, when party membership brought substantial disadvantages. The young lady was from an old New England family and obviously took Smith's injunction to its students to think of socially useful careers more seriously than did her contemporary Barbara Bush.

One social engagement in this period brought unexpected rewards. I met a young woman who had come with her parents from Austria. She was studying at Bard College, and I arranged to call for her on a weekend night in the fall of 1946. When I arrived at her family's apartment in a West Side brownstone, I was much impressed—she was talking with her parents in German. Her father was obviously an intellectual, with heavy texts on economics piled on a work table. We could have been in one of those black-and-white films of the European thirties, except that the colors I recall are brown and grey. I was introduced and sensed a mildly patronizing if friendly tone: it was unusual for me to be thought of as a representative of American culture. My partner for the evening voiced a certain amount of regretful consternation. She had not been able to reach me, but her writing teacher at Bard, Mary McCarthy, had invited her to an evening at Peggy Guggenheim's house on the East Side. The *Partisan Review* intellectuals would be there, in full force. She, the Bard student, did not know if I would be at my ease. I admired the Old World approach. Instead of telling me that it was unlikely that I would fit in, she gave me an opening for a discreet and gentlemanly withdrawal—an opening I refused. I'd be delighted to come, I said—pretending to ignore the implicit message. After all, I continued, I'd been reading *Partisan Review* ever since I'd attained serious literacy and was of course, an unremitting admirer of Ms. McCarthy. I kept one argument in reserve but did not need to deploy it: I had even submitted something to *PR*. It was true: I once wrote a letter to the editors on some point of world politics, unpublished and indeed unacknowledged. My own version of Old World finesse worked, and half-resignedly, half-amusedly, the young lady suggested that we put on our coats and take the bus across town.

The party was upstairs in Ms. Guggenheim's house, and coming in, we encountered Mary. (I later met her again through William Phillips and saw her last at Mitterrand's cultural conference in 1983 in Paris, where she was her usual self: good manners, directness of address, and ferocious energies just beneath the surface.) She was exceedingly gracious, encouraged me to tell her about myself, and then introduced us to her *PR* friends. Philip Rahv gave the impression that he was being imposed upon; Dwight Macdonald was a bit tentative, as if he needed a good argument to find his footing; William Phillips seemed preoccupied with unspoken or unspeakable problems. We moved upstairs, our hostess received us, and it was clear that the party was becoming rather large. One guest who made a considerable impression on me was the *New Yorker* artist Saul Steinberg: he looked like one of his own drawings. The crowd included others from *The New Yorker*, and some artists whose names I recognized. Mary kept with us, a gesture of a maternal sort, and then waved to a friend to join us. He was Clement Greenberg, and that was for me an important encounter.

Clem was already on his way to fame and influence as the herald—no, the prophet—of the New York School of painting. (Years later, in the fifties, after the philistines had ceased describing the abstract expressionists as enemies of the spirit, comprehensively if vaguely subversive, covert CIA funding subsidized a travelling exhibition of their works. I saw it at Basel, where the museum guard told me in Swiss German, "These guys have something"—*Die Kerle haben etwas.*) I knew his cultural and political writings in *Partisan Review*, as well as his art criticism in *The Nation*.

Clem spoke with a singular mixture of New York and Southern accents, had a hesitancy in address that was nicely calculated to convey consideration for his interlocutor, and discretion as his major principle. In fact, it allowed him to size up situations into which he then charged with a prizefighter's pugnacity. Clem was very interested in what I told him about my studies and wished to hear about Lane Faison. More, he asked about my views on politics and was especially curious as to how I fared, culturally and socially, at Williams. I recall little pugnacity that evening—and the implicit promise of a continuing relationship. There was also an implicit bargain entailed: I was to listen to Clem's advice in a tutorial that had no boundaries, encompassing art, culture, manners, politics and everything else. Clem had a son, Dan, who lived with his mother and gave his father no end of trouble. I was not entirely a substitute son, perhaps more like a younger brother. I was certainly treated as family, in that Clem freely discussed some of his problems—and was devastatingly frank about colleagues and friends. Clem did have a brother, Martin, who later also worked (as Clem did) as an editor at *Commentary*. I met him, however, much later.

I saw quite a lot of Clem in the years that followed, and we corresponded regularly when I moved to Europe, especially in the early years. Clem lived in a cramped apartment on Bleecker Street in the West Village. He occasionally took me with him to social gatherings, and to art galleries. He preferred to maximize his opportunity for imparting advice, and so we often met by ourselves. The advice he proffered ranged from matters of decorum to comment on my career. I recall two major themes. One was that I had to think of myself, always, as a "highbrow." He made no concessions to the democratization of culture, which he thought unachieved. Clem's virulent antagonism to Stalinism and implacable defense of the US in the Cold War was for him entirely compatible with severe views of the culture and character of his fellow citizens. The second theme was Jewishness, or how to deal with it in the Gentile-dominated world of culture. The post-war opening of cultural institutions, including the Ivy universities, was a process he was slow to recognize. Yet many of his friends were not Jewish, and some of his antagonists were. He did not think that Jews were uniformly gifted in the spheres of culture, and was unmoved by Zionism. Jewishness was one's fate: it could not be denied but need not dominate.

The remains of his earlier socialist convictions expressed themselves in his transposition of social historical progressivism to the realm of art. The evolution of forms struck him, now, as clear and as inevitable as the inner laws of capitalism were for a Marxist purist. There was very little trace of respect for the people in his thought (Dwight Macdonald was a fellow traveler). Historical development had stranded the people in a permanent Sinai of the spirit, the milk and honey of true culture inaccessible or on the other side of a very distant horizon. What he did worry about was the defense of high culture in the territory it occupied. He thought of the Village as a modern Concord. The barbarian badlands began at 14th Street. The editors, writers and readers of *The New Yorker* were cast as philistines, those of *Time* and *Life* depicted as in outer darkness. Clem was especially upset when *Life* published a denunciation of Jean Dubuffet as an enemy of humanism, written by William Henry Chamberlain, an ex-socialist himself. Clem thought that the article violated something like a cultural non-aggression pact negotiated between the editors of *Partisan Review* and those of *Time-Life*. The *Partisan Review* group thought of itself as in charge of their own state—a conviction William Phillips never abandoned. He would simply not see, later, that the influence of the journal in the thirties, forties and fifties was due to cultural and political circumstances which were bound to change.

Clem, then, brought me into a world I had occasionally encountered in New York in the years 1943-1945. It was very different from the political universe of Williams's more worldly professors—and provided a view of culture and intellect not found in their Williams curriculum. Still, it was territory for occasional excursions, the more prized for their rarity. Most of the time I spent at college and with friends. My recollection is exceedingly schematic, but we did talk about four themes. First, we talked about ourselves, our struggles to situate ourselves—and to move on. Those who had been in the war had more equanimity: they'd survived worse things than the uncertainties of the educated elite. Everyone in my circle was guarded about relations with the other sex, a reticence not always conspicuous at the college. Individually and collectively, we apparently thought that the other burdens of life were enough without devoting major portions of our lives to learning to live with the other sex, It might have been different had Williams been co-educational, but, the veterans' wives apart, it was not.

Of course, we talked about our studies—a good deal more about the strengths and weaknesses of our teachers than about what they taught in formal terms. We talked about books about ideas—and I recall a certain amount of abstract ethical puzzlement. We wished to live good lives in a moral sense, and did not quite know how to combine this with psychological fulfilment. We thought of ourselves as if the wooden dormitory we shared were that tower in James Joyce's *Ulysses*—but the US was not the Ireland Dedalus and his friends struggled to escape. Our personal attachments to our teachers were important, evidence for the human usefulness of the collegiate model. There were paths to adulthood, even if we did not always know where they were or how to tread them. The teachers had taken them; we could follow.

Finally, we (and the rest of the college) talked about politics. The Cold War was breaking out, but those who had returned from fighting against the Germans and the Japanese did not imagine how soon the defeated nations would become American allies.

More than a few of our teachers did, across the political spectrum. Fred Schuman was conspicuous in depicting the nascent Cold War as an exercise in the extension of American power, in his pitiless analysis of the domestic forces interested in resisting "Communism."

There was precious little "Communism" visible in Williamstown. I surmised that a couple of fellow students sympathized with the American Communist Party: their political vocabulary was liturgically rigid and their positions coincided with those of the party—much talk of "peace" and references to the Soviet-occupied nations as enthusiastically engaged in socialist reconstruction. Fred Schuman's arguments were substantially different, dealing with the international system, and he gave the problem of Germany much attention as one in its own right.

The Greek civil war was evoked by a student from Greece in luridly simplistic terms in the college newspaper, and I challenged that. Most students interested in politics (unburdened with much knowledge of modern Greek history) sided with our visitor. It was the official position of our government that the revolt of the Greek left against the return of the monarchy (in which the army and the church, allied to merchant capital in an archaic and familialistic culture, imposed authoritarianism on the nation) was a threat to the United States. Confident in the nation's moral credentials after the victory of 1945, my fellow students were disinclined to question the ideology of the nascent Cold War. Those teachers who had their doubts were quite discreet, or were realists with a large sense of historical complexity. I do not recollect any retrospective criticism of the bombing of enemy cities, or of the morality of using atomic weapons against Japan. Neither can I recall much discussion of the Holocaust or of fascism in general. The only scholar at Williams who approached the Soviet Union as a distinctive social formation was the one unjustly accused of excessive sympathy for it, Fred Schuman.

We lived in present and future, which clearly entailed problems enough. The similarity to my own approach to life I now find striking. Despite two years of therapy, I had a great deal of difficulty confronting my past and preferred to concentrate on matters before me.

Senator Vandenberg's advice to Truman on mobilizing support for the Cold War was entirely apt: "Scare the hell out of them, Harry!" The US had survived the Great Depression, the war had brought full employment, and many citizens considered that they had much to lose. The Soviet Union was a power which did not accept our rules, an alternative church. I knew a little, then, of the conflict between Eastern and Latin Christendom but could not quite connect it with the events on the front page of *The New York Times*, or the ever-more-alarmed editorial notes of *The Nation*. Intellectually and personally, I suffered from a deficiency of historical reflection. I read Dwight Macdonald's journal, *Politics*, with its cosmopolitan authors and Macdonald's own corrosive contempt for the replacement of thought by slogans—and, of course, John Hershey's disturbing *New Yorker* article on Hiroshima. What I could not do was to use my own distrust of authority to take some distance from the intellectual clamor around me: I kept reacting to the noise.

Williams had a tradition of student-organized conferences on national politics held in the spring. We renewed it in 1947. I was co-chair with my classmate Norman Redlich, who later was the chief legal officer of the City of New York, deputy counsel to the Warren Commission investigating the Kennedy murder, and dean at New York University Law School. For years whenever we met, Norman, without my saying anything about it, would vehemently insist on the rightness of the Commission's finding that the Kennedy assassin Oswald acted alone. He was right to suspect me of considerable skepticism as to the conventional account of the murder. To this day, more than half of the public is also skeptical. Norman was exceedingly intelligent and greatly attached to conventional categories of thought, a firm Democrat. I favored unconventional thought, but was encumbered by my inability to say what that might be and what politics were appropriate to it.

I invited Clem Greenberg to the conference to discuss culture, and the psychiatrist Frederick Wertheim as well. The analytic theorist Wilhelm Reich was already in trouble with the government, and I did not know the Marxist Freudians in psychoanalysis—and had no knowledge, either, of Erikson, who adhered to these ideas in somewhat modulated and less explicit form. The liberal Democratic technocrats returned from war held center stage: John Kenneth Galbraith, for one. I was much impressed by the self-assured presence of George Kennan, who had already written the famous paper on containment for *Foreign Affairs* under the name "X." What particularly impressed me was Kennan's assertion that the US could and should work with social democratic governments in Europe, and his assertion of an intellectually compelling world view—combined with the fact that he was officially a person of great influence. My distant and hostile view of the apparatus of power was already strong, and Kennan's prominence challenged it. The conviction that intellectual and personal integrity could be had only by remaining an outsider had its uses, but I certainly exaggerated: the fact is, I lacked real knowledge of how differently people dealt with these situations. Kennan's doctrine of containment, to his own dismay, was turned into an argument for a total offensive against the Soviet bloc. Kennan finished his life as an outsider—on his own terms.

As the panelists discussed domestic issues, they certainly reflected what was then the Washington consensus—among Democrats. The nation had begun the most sustained period of economic growth in its history, government programs of all sorts and tax incentives having started the process, it was government which steered it. That did not prevent a senior Williams trustee from writing to the president of the college (one of the economists showed me the letter) to express the deepest of disquiet. The recent Williams graduates who had joined his investment bank were infected with a very dangerous virus—Keynesianism. That the economist's ideas, accompanied by a considerable amount of governmental control of markets, were also responsible for the beginnings of recovery in the world economy had escaped the trustee's notice. It was, perhaps, too much to expect a dispassionate scrutiny of the world from someone who did not grasp what was going on in his own country.

I wonder, now, at his militant stupidity. Significant sectors of the American elite did catch on rather rapidly in those years, colonized the government of Harry Truman and, in accepting the legacy of the New Deal, remodeled it to their liking. A good deal of social conflict did occur, as the unions and the militant heirs of the New Deal rejected compromise. The unions failed to penetrate the South. The United Auto Workers did not obtain a share of corporate governance in the large firms. Meanwhile, women left their wartime jobs and returned home, and the black leadership chose a painfully incremental judicial and political strategy for more equality. Entire sectors of unionized industry had their own welfare states, written into bargains on benefits and wages, and this gradually set standards for much of the rest of the economy. The

New Deal did cross the Atlantic to Western Europe, where post-war planners of the enlarged welfare states had taken inspiration from it as well as from their own Christian social and socialist traditions. Of course, there are echoes of these processes in our mountain valley—usually not very loud ones. I read about them in *The Nation*, in a *New York Times* some of whose journalists were rather more direct than their compulsively discreet contemporary successors, and of course, caught glimpses of a very different reality when I visited New York. Faculty friends followed matters and were always available with sophisticated analysis and an entertaining measure of inside gossip. There was argument in the student body, and I recall it as thoroughly stereotyped.

There was no more assiduous purveyor of stereotypes than myself. Two decades before I wrote for *The Nation*, I could voice its editorials with untroubled fidelity. There was large justification to this, since much and at times most of what *The Nation* said was true.

The United States was a class society, and the consciousness, and political acumen, of the ruling class was rather more developed than that of much of the rest of the country. Why the citizenry did not rise to assume the powers rightly its own remained a question, but it was one I answered in shallow terms: the citizens were somnolent or manipulated.

Suppose, however, that they were as citizens undeveloped, unready and unwilling to assume the burdens of democracy? I caught sight of the problem and looked away. I could not deal with the devastating consequences of that observation for the view that progress was unfolding, some perturbations apart, in a straight line. That there was something awry was a conviction I could not deny, but voicing it too loudly seemed impious; confronting it by myself, too arduous.

The beginning of the Cold War was another complication. The historical evidence was obvious. Fascism, especially in its German version, had combined social solidarity with external aggression and domestic repression. The American New Deal was entirely compatible with imperial policy abroad, and where rhetorical reinforcement was required, plenty of intellectuals were grateful to be asked to supply it. The combination of the many benefits of empire with the material and moral satisfactions of a considerable amount of social decency at home was formidable, the more so as democratic normality appeared permanent. The ignoble conformity of anti-Communism had begun to congeal, but the period of systematic persecution lay ahead.

Nothing gave me more trouble than the question of Stalinism. I disliked the culture of the few Stalinists I knew: their addictions to sloganized views of the world, obsessively repeated incantations about "the people" which had nothing, visibly, to do with the real population—and above all, their uncritical adherence to an obvious form of group thinking. They were spiritual plebeians and to make matters worse, often social ones as well. Still, the Soviet Union and the world Communist movement were important, however impotent and repellent its American comrades. There was little doubt that the Communists in some countries had succeeded in forming alliances with authentically democratic groups, and with political formations seeking social justice. At a distance, I thought that to be the case in Greece, and on the basis of very fragmentary knowledge, intuited that it was true of Italy as well. After all, the European groups which rushed to align themselves with the United States as the Cold War began had impeccable anti-Communist credentials, in France in the years 1940-1944, in Germany 1933-1945, and in Italy 1923-1943. The central Europeans who now complained that they were being oppressed were often, as in Poland, anti-Semites and fascist thugs. I did not accept the credentials of another resolute anti-Communist, the Pope—and knew of the conflict in world Protestantism which opposed the lawyer John Foster Dulles, the American Presbyterian incarnation of self-righteousness, to the Swiss theologian, Karl Barth, accused of the sin of neutralism.

Above all, I think, the threat of a nuclear war seemed to me to outweigh the threat of Communism. I could not see what would justify destroying life on much of the planet, reducing civilization to a new barbarism, in a destructive frenzy which would certainly extirpate the ideals for the sake of which the war would be fought. I was convinced by the writings of Dwight Macdonald, by the arguments of some of the nuclear scientists—and by the casualness with which American opinion assumed our national rectitude.

That much said, there was a large deficit in my thinking. I reflected insufficiently on the universal implications of Stalinism, on the question of its origins and viability as a social formation, on the connections between Stalinism, Leninism, Marxism, and a secular eschatology. A good deal of this was due to my age: I had not had the time to sort out the dazzling light display I had been exposed to and was somewhat blinded. Some part of the difficulty owed to inner confusion, an inability to formulate questions with clear distinctions and sharp edges. That wasn't entirely negative, as it led me to holistic approaches to larger constellations of events. Indistinctness had as a compensation a wider horizon. The wider it became, however, the more inwardly lost I felt.

I stumbled toward the decision to attend graduate school at Harvard in sociology. What I knew of sociology was rather little. Perhaps it would be more accurate to say that I had an idealized and Europeanized view of it, derived largely from books Fred Schuman called to our attention. First there was Max Weber, and I read the translation of his writings in political sociology by Hans Gerth and C. Wright Mills. In fact, the thinker who impressed me the most was Karl Mannheim, and I read his *Ideology and Utopia* as well as *Man and Society in an Age of Reconstruction*. I had read the Lynds' Middletown books much earlier, but did not grasp that their politically inspired examination of Muncie, Indiana, represented a strain in American sociology which had been replaced by the claims to objectivity inspired by a (shallow) model of the natural sciences. Works like Lederer's *The State of the Masses* were also on my list, and I read the anthropologists Malinowski and Fei. The sociology that interested me dealt with the questions of historical change, of struggles for power, of the emergence of classes and the problem of elites, of the formation of belief systems, of individual fate. There was something of the large novel about it, of a description of destiny. I was looking for the excitement I sensed when reading Edmund Wilson's *To the Finland Station*, the possibility that ideas could change history. In many of these respects, the sociology and the sociologists I encountered at Harvard left me very disappointed. There were, however, some unexpected compensations.

4

Harvard in Various Forms

WHEN I entered Harvard's Graduate School in 1947 at age twenty-one I was not marching resolutely into my future. Neither was I enjoying much of the present. I had decided to seek a doctorate in sociology since I thought the field dealt with just those large questions which interested me—about social classes and movements, about historical changes, about the differences between our nation and other ones, about the interplay of character and social setting. I wanted to explore a larger intellectual world, glimpses of which I had caught in books and film, in meetings with persons who were obviously at home in it. The difficulties were that I only knew dimly how to go about it—and that the uncertainty was connected to great anxieties about my career. Could I think and write well enough to win a teaching post in a college or university? My doubt was all the greater as I took rather exceptional figures as models—not only professors who were masters of their classrooms but those with much to say to an appreciative public, veritable secular prophets. No doubt it was a distillation, of which I was hardly aware, of a rabbinical vocation—but if so, that only increased my doubts as to whether I was worthy of anointment.

My initial experience of Cambridge did not amount, then, to a continuation of my rather happy progress at Williams. I was just another provincial come to the metropolis to seek his fortune. The combination of New York and Williamstown should have been an advantage, but I could not treat it as one—perhaps because Harvard made it clear that the outside world was drearily unequal to Harvard's standards. (One day, it was said, someone dropped in to see the president, Abbott Lawrence Lowell, and was told: "The president is in Washington seeing Mr. Wilson.") Had I been more self-confident, I would have looked at Harvard with that sort of ethnographic curiosity my teachers in social anthropology insisted was the beginning of wisdom. Instead, I was intimidated by its triumphant joining of two claims—to be at the apices of the hierarchies of inherited social status and intellectual meritocracy.

So great and persistent was my anxiety that my memory of much of the summer before I went to Cambridge, and the entire first year of graduate study, are blurred. If there were audible records of inner states, a steady and barely stifled whine would describe mine. I do recollect the trip up by train from New York. I had decided that given this anxiety, it would be best to resume psychoanalysis—but there was nothing reflective about the decision. In fact, I was not uneasy; I was panicked. Finding an analyst seemed more important than settling in the room I had rented, or registering for courses, or meeting my fellow students.

Under pressure of this sort, one doesn't always make the right decisions. No doubt, I was helped by the analyst I chose—and whether I might have been helped more by someone else, I do not know, since I took almost no time and made an instant decision. After the initial panic dissipated, the pall of depression that settled over me dissolved very slowly. Throughout my five years in Cambridge, I had the impression for a good deal of the time of a bifurcation all the more difficult since I kept it to myself. To many colleagues, friends and students (I began to teach a year later), I was culturally and intellectually engaged, open and even jovial as well as witty, active in a number of social circles, someone with plenty of stories to tell already who would have much more to say later. Internally, I frequently felt vacant, unable to enjoy the many opportunities around me, hesitant about my own ambitions and afraid above all of whatever passions I had buried. Indeed, despite the social persona I presented, I often felt that I was dragging myself into combat, that there was something troubling which I could not identify or grasp—something which decades later I recognized as a pervasive sense of inauthenticity.

Certainly, Cambridge's cultural and moral climate so affected me that I internalized, uncritically, whole segments of it. It was exceedingly competitive, and the competition never ended. Those who climbed one rung of the ladder could hardly congratulate themselves or pause: they had to scramble higher. Undergraduates strove for high grades, recognition from their peers and teachers, membership in literary societies. Graduate students struggled for teaching assistantships; a few thought they might be chosen for the Society of Fellows (Harvard's academic equivalent of a sacred order); fewer still dared to seek a faculty post at the university. Those who did obtain junior appointments promptly began to worry about their chances of being made permanent, and the permanent party spent its energies and time in relentless pursuit of the inner certainty that they were entitled to their obvious privileges of rank. Many of Harvard's senior professors concentrated on their disciplines; others staffed and chaired the committees which did much of the university's academic business.

That was (and is) Harvard's meritocracy. Harvard had another face, that of the Bostonian social elite and its cousins and in-laws nationwide. *Pecunia non olet*—money doesn't smell—but older money smells sweeter. The proprietary rituals and the behavioral codes of the Brahmin and patrician part of the Harvard population (including any number of formidable women, often more gracious, insightful and intelligent than their men) were not quite hidden from view. They were not flaunted of course, but the rest of us were given to understand that we were guests in a stately home. John Marquand's Harvard was still quite visible in the university which, a decade previously, had been vexed by the presence at its tercentenary celebration of the excessively casual and dubiously loyal patrician, Franklin Roosevelt.

Harvard's political functions provided a third road to status. Many of the teachers who returned from wartime service continued to commute to Washington, and took along younger colleagues. Ambitions were satisfied in an entirely bipartisan way. John Kenneth Galbraith and Arthur M. Schlesinger Jr., as guardians of the New Deal, were ironically admiring, but admiring all the same, of the rise of Henry Kissinger. Most of those who went back and forth from the classroom to the capital were less openly ideological, announced that they were devoted to public service, and were in fact prototypical technocrats—putting their knowledge at the disposition of power. A certain number of Harvard's teachers were worried by this, but some seemed to envy the rewards available to colleagues whose work was valued as practical. Arthur Schlesinger Jr. was audibly skeptical of the claims of the systematic social sciences, and when he asked Talcott Parsons, the chair of the sociology department, what his department was doing, he was told: "We are splitting the sociological equivalent of the atom." Parsons's belief that his work was somehow equivalent to a grand theoretical advance in physics was not motivated by intellectual hubris alone. He wanted the world to need his sociology.

It took me some years to draw a map of Cambridge (a good deal more sharply outlined now, six decades after I got there). For one thing, my initial routines were quite circumscribed. I went to class, talked with my fellow students, saw the psychoanalyst, and had little initial contact with even a wider university milieu. What I had to deal with was, to be sure, unfamiliar and trying enough.

I was enrolled in a doctoral program in sociology, but the previous Department of Sociology had been absorbed into a new Department of Social Relations which had four tracks: clinical psychology, social anthropology, social psychology, and sociology.

Our first year was largely taken in common, and the department talked incessantly of its inter-disciplinary approach—and of the rigor of the methods its scholars employed in ways we, their apprentices, would do well to imitate. I had thought of sociology as a larger sort of historical interpretation, bur was now instructed that the development of an abstract science of society required an intellectual sacrifice: one had to study matters small, even trivial, for the sake of advancing (if with painful slowness) to larger vistas.

Obvious anomalies were not discussed. Most members of the department thought of themselves as masons, adding bricks to the unfinished of edifice of a comprehensive science of society. Talcott Parsons thought of himself as an architect, with a master plan. Domed stadiums had not yet come to football, but he had one for society. The clinical psychologists, and the senior social anthropologist, Clyde Kluckhohn, as well as Parsons, thought that psychoanalysis was the best recourse in psychology. Gordon Allport, the senior social psychologist, did not. In fact, though modern art was not much talked about in our conversations, the department in its conceptual disunity resembled one of those self-destructing sculptures by Yves Tanguy.

It took more than a year for me to realize that intellectually, the Social Relations group was quite isolated from the more vital intellectual currents of the university. Those currents were often shallow enough, but they did enable those in different fields, even with different political perspectives, to talk with one another. The Social Relations faculty, and their most loyal students, conducted themselves as initiates of an esoteric church in possession of truths which a presently unbelieving world would in time have to acknowledge. What united them was a belief in the scientific status of their work. Morton White, the Harvard philosopher who knew a good deal about science, termed it "methodolatry." When I want instruction on science, he said, I'll go to the scientists; what I want from your department is what they do not offer—knowledge about major social processes. The complaint was repeated, if in different words, by another friend, the widely read and very gifted economist Carl Kaysen. Later, I read the early twentieth-century French mathematician and philosopher Henri Poincare, who said of his colleagues in sociology: they write about methods they are careful never to apply, so it is impossible to say whether sociology is a science or not. That was untrue of his exacting contemporary, Émile Durkheim, but Durkheim was gifted and insightful.

When speaking to the first-year students in the first week of the semester, Clyde Kluckhohn did evoke Durkheim. He told us that his *Suicide* was indeed a masterpiece, but methodologically primitive. Max Weber's *The Protestant Ethos and the Spirit of Capitalism*, he said, would be judged unacceptable if presented as a doctoral dissertation in 1947. Kluckhohn's remarks expressed a great deal of hubris, but were part of a socialization process akin to hazing. Talcott Parsons, for his part, expressed surprise that most of us expected to teach in major universities—since, given the inevitable selection process, many would end at liberal arts colleges. He'd been a student and then a teacher at Amherst—the son of a Midwestern Calvinist pastor, he was quite sure that his ascent at Harvard was evidence for the rigor of the university's selection process. The pressure on the students, then, was intense. Given the fact that we were nearly all driven by our own ambitions, it did not make for a climate in which we had energy and time for critical reflection.

I was in an especially dense fog. The primary element in it was hardly intellectual but came from the anxiety and unease that impelled me to renew psychoanalysis. The analysis itself began haltingly and proceeded thusly. The analyst was Walter Langer, who had been analyzed by Anna Freud in Vienna, was associated with the Harvard psychologist Henry Murray in the group that produced the volume *Explorations in Personality*, and had worked with the Office of Strategic Services in the war. At one point he lent me a remarkable portrait he had done of Hitler, in which he predicted his suicide. His brother was the Harvard diplomatic historian William Langer, and his other patients included fellow students and at least one faculty member. Credentials do not, alas, tell the whole story. I felt uncomfortable, on trial perhaps, in his presence—but was never able to confront this directly. He was ritually reticent, which I interpreted as passive indifference.

I must have improved somewhat during the years I was with Dr. Langer, or else I could never have completed my course work, taught with considerable success, and enjoyed a wide circle of friends. Dr. Langer came from a German-American family, and I now wonder about the role he played in my decision to write a dissertation on the social basis of the German Reformation—and to go to Germany to gather materials for it.

At the time, I took little consolation from whatever progress I made. The acute anxiety I experienced on coming to Harvard diminished appreciably—to be replaced by a pervasive sense of depression. There was one moment when I thought that I was on the verge of a positive change, a psychological leap forward. I was excited by meeting a young woman, a Radcliffe student who was actually a tutee when I began to work as a teaching fellow. In those days (1948) the university did not prohibit or even discourage relationships across the (loose) boundaries of caste. I liked her very much, was stirred by the thought of a new and certainly different life, had a sense of the imminent fall of a wall keeping me from a realm of feeling. The one analogy I had was to the period five years earlier in Williamstown, when I thought I was about to enter similarly vivid territory on my own. I was quite unable to develop and sustain a loving relationship and whatever chances there were of securing the woman's affection and loyalty dissolved. Years later, Dr. Langer told me that he too was hopeful about the experience—

but at the time, he was remarkably silent about it (or I was remarkably deaf to what he was saying).

My first friends at Harvard, a few contemporaries from Williams apart, were fellow graduate students. Misery loves company, and we huddled together in an attempt to reduce our anxieties. The others were invariably older; some had been in the war; all had studied the social sciences as undergraduates and some had master's degrees from other universities. More than a few were married; there were some women, and I was invited to homes and able to enjoy a bit of the familial support I missed—while denying to myself that I needed it. My most vivid memory is of Marc Fried, who had studied at City College and at the Sorbonne in a program for American soldiers and who was fully conversant with his field, clinical psychology. He was also very sympathetic, interested in ideas, and realistic in his refusal to idealize our teachers or the university. A medical student from Boston University, Jacqueline Zilbach, came to our seminars and she and Marc became a couple, later married and lived in a group house I often visited. That softened the effects of living in a graduate dormitory, which combined the comforts of a monastery with the aesthetics of a prison. I ate at the new Graduate Commons, and I am sure that it was a place of interesting conversation. The difficulty is, I recall none, although I do remember someone talking about an article in *Partisan Review* and a philosopher asking if it wasn't "a bit pinko." That would have disappointed his fellow if elder philosopher William Barrett, who had already expressed *Partisan Review*'s renunciation of its political distance from American power in his article "The Liberal Fifth Column."

The world, in 1947 and 1948, was immensely turbulent. The Cold War was beginning; a Republican majority in the Congress had begun its projected reversal of the New Deal; Europe was in the throes of hunger and actual or threatened civil war; the Soviet bloc was struggling with the national versions of Communism exemplified in Titoism, and national liberation movements were fighting in the Third World to stop the return of imperial rulers. The first tremors of McCarthyism were felt in Cambridge. Historians and political scientists, economists and philosophers, the academic chroniclers of literature, made the changes in the larger world their central themes.

The courses in Social Relations seemed to refer to another planet. The effort to construct a science of society was primary, what was happening in society a good deal less so. When important matters were touched upon, they were trivialized or sanitized. We trooped over to Newton High School for a research project and returned with the finding that offspring of Irish and Italian working-class families were less likely to proceed to elite colleges than the children of educated Jews or Protestants. There was much discussion of "values" as constituents of social norms, but little reference to the inquiries of cultural historians, historians of religion into specific cases. Evocations of Max Weber's work on Protestantism were frequent, but Harvard's great scholar of New England Protestantism, Perry Miller, was ignored. Some of the discussion of modernity was anticipated, with the contemporary United States depicted as at the apex of human evolution. Neither the modernist struggle in Catholicism nor the modernist movement in art and literature was mentioned. The contemporary United States itself was imagined as a suburb living in Protestant middle-class felicity, to which other groups would in due course accede.

The situation was somewhat paradoxical. Most of the faculty were liberal Democrats, if inclined to suppose that the social and especially class conflicts of the New Deal era were definitely behind us. They were, equally, cosmopolitan and horrified by the vulgarities of McCarthyism and the narrowness of a culturally isolationist Republicanism. The social psychologist Daniel Levinson was appointed and he was the one American-born author of the collaborative work *The Authoritarian Personality*, which translated the angry anti-Nazism of the Frankfurt School, with its critique of modern society as a whole, into the more mellifluous American English of liberal progressivism. Talcott Parsons, with his experience of Europe, was certainly interested in the fate of civilizations. He concluded that ours was not only there to stay, but bound to remain on top. The department had a major role in establishing the university's Russian Research Center. Its head was Clyde Kluckhohn, who in the war had analyzed Japanese culture at a distance without knowing Japanese. His ignorance of Russian and of the Soviet Union were not considered disadvantages. The center sent its researchers to Germany to construct a picture of Soviet society by interviewing former Soviet citizens who had left with the German army after collaborating with the occupation.

There were some critical voices. The sociologist Pitirim Sorokin, a very learned man, was skeptical of the project of constructing a new science of society. I recall his remark to Kluckhohn about the latter's new task. "Clyde, I read in *The New York Times* that the Carnegie Corporation gave you a half-million dollars to study Russia. Clyde, I do not bear you any malice, but if Carnegie came to me and offered me a half-million to study the Navajo Indians, modesty would make me say no." Delivered in a pronounced Russian accent in the corridor of Emerson Hall between classes, and with students all around, the remark was taken as evidence for Sorokin's eccentric attachment to outdated notions of scholarship. Barrington Moore joined the center and taught some courses, conveying an ironic distance from the project of constructing a science of society. I suspected that the distance had something to do as well with political disappointment at the course of the Soviet Revolution. Years later, when I learned how close the genteel dissident Moore, who did not find it his primary task to challenge all of the strivers of Cold War Harvard, had become to Herbert Marcuse, later perhaps the senior thinker of the international New Left, I saw that I had been right, but had underestimated Moore's distance from the reigning American political consensus.

The graduate students were struggling to find a scholarly consensus they could identify with—or more accurately, be seen to be identified with. Most put their personal cultural and political ideals in storage as they tried on apprentice professional vestments. I did so, too, but continually and anxiously re-opened the storage locker to make sure that my own possessions were still there. The anxiety was all the greater for my not knowing what to keep of the things I had brought to Harvard with me. I was dimly aware that I was being socialized into a culture. I was certainly glad to join Harvard and high academic culture in general, though doubtful that full achievement of standing as a sociologist was supremely valuable. Inadvertently, Clyde Kluckhohn's honesty helped. Talking to his large introductory class in social anthropology, he remarked that the brightest students at Harvard did not attend graduate school but went on to law school. I wasn't tempted by that, although had

I been more adventurous, I would have taken the risk of looking around for alternatives and might have discovered an affinity for constitutional law and jurisprudence. I did ask myself what I was doing in a field described by one of its more successful practitioners as secondary and indeed second-rate, the more so as its inner rationale—the eventual construction of a social science—was not entirely convincing. By that point, I had also begun to see that our department was rather cut off from the intellectual riches of the rest of the university. Something did not add up.

I did not have the inner freedom to explore other paths—a trait that years later led me to stay in several situations (human and professional) I would have done well to terminate.

In that first year at Harvard, I did realize that I would have to strike out on my own, without quite knowing how.

The problem was made both easier and more difficult by my condition as a novice in the social sciences. Concentrating on making good the gaps in my knowledge provided a respite from the question as to whether I wanted to be there at all. Concentrating on doing well provided surcease from my inner doubt: if I could indeed find a place for myself, I could swallow the criticism I could not still. The difficulty was that my inner doubt about my capacity wasn't easily assuaged. Containing that doubt exhausted the energies which a more self-confident person would have employed to think more clearly about his situation. As we began our trial runs in the race for a career, our teachers kept putting new hurdles on the track. Nearly all were individually supportive—it was their collective behavior which was problematical. I enjoyed the solidarity, the network of mutual support, that the students built: we did not dissolve in a war of each against all. We raised some objections to the program in the first year. The formal objections about content did not quite conceal deeper anxieties, a demand for more recognition. To their credit, the faculty responded rather positively. I was one of the student spokespersons. It was hardly the sort of revolutionary action I knew from history books, films and novels, but it was gratifying all the same.

As the academic year drew near to its end, I learned that my Graduate School scholarship would not be renewed; my grades were deemed too ordinary. Fortunately, the department gave a year-end examination and I placed very well in it. I was appointed to a teaching fellowship—and on that very day, attending a Nieman Fellows discussion at the Faculty Club, ran into Talcott Parsons. Would he think that I had rushed there to claim my new status—when in fact I worried that I really did not belong in so exclusive a place? I also had to take a newly instituted oath to uphold the constitution of the Commonwealth of Massachusetts, which I did despite my profound disdain for Senator McCarthy and all of his works: Cambridge *vaut une messe*.

It began to be worth a good deal more. I had begun to climb the academic ladder and the teaching fellowship opened new possibilities. At age twenty-two, not much older than my students and in some cases younger, I conducted discussion sections, did some tutoring, and was an academic advisor. The Harvard and Radcliffe undergraduates, many of them, were not only intelligent but had interesting life stories to tell, and were often quite appealing and distinctive persons. I discovered a vocation as a teacher, was in many ways never a better one than as an eager apprentice. With a new entering class of graduate students to face the doubts and torments of the uninitiated, my cohort became veterans. The air of that fall was somewhat easier to breathe. My newly won position enabled me to begin to confront the department's intellectual claims in a more critical way. It also was the beginning of a journey into the vast stretches of Harvard I did not know—which in the end was appreciably more educational than my work in sociology itself.

My idea of social science when I arrived at Harvard was shaped by my reading in the history of the United States as recounted by the Progressive historians, by a collage of Marxist theory and an anti-fascist historiography of Europe, and by psychoanalysis admixed with deep suspicions of a repressive normality. Somehow, too, I had acquired an inchoate impression of the polyvalence of religion. I'd read some of Max Weber and a bit in the German social theory of the twentieth century. At Harvard, these things were marginal, if mentioned at all. Harvard's Max Weber was depicted as an aspiring associate professor in Social Relations—or as a figure fortunate enough to have anticipated Talcott Parsons. The methodological obsession was retained, the historical passion ignored.

Parsons was puzzling. He knew European society and thought,

was anything but a provincial. He was right to suppose that our historical development was different.

Somehow, American triumphalism suffused his vision. It was a special kind of triumphalism, self-consciously meritocratic. He cited his own suburb, Belmont, as evidence for the moral efficiency of our status system. A large place in his universe, however, was reserved for the meritocracy of learning. There, he clearly regretted the incapacity of the social sciences, as yet, to achieve the certainty of the natural sciences.

He thought of his own work as a contribution to a new canon of social knowledge—not as one approach in a pluralistic, even conflicted, intellectual field but as a theoretic system which would, in the end, command universal assent.

With the other graduate students (and no small number of his colleagues), I struggled with his system. He was still writing *The Social System* (published in 1951) when our class arrived, and before finishing that put together his essays in *Essays in Sociological Theory* (1949). He did me the honor of asking me to prepare the index. The task gave me a far clearer view of his project than the difficult text *The Structure of Social Action* (1936), with his distillation of the legacy of sociological thought—and the beginning of his transformation of it into his own language. Parsons's work was divided. He analyzed family structure, the professions, gender roles in modern America, occasionally wrote some very insightful articles on Germany. His articles on modern institutions in their specific settings argued that the contradictory demands of a complex society frequently overburdened its members. The ensuing tensions were the result of socially induced psychological strains. However, the need for social cohesion was the *deus ex machina* in Parsons's dramaturgy: order was invariably restored.

Parsons termed his view of society "structural functionalism." He put the variety of human motives, ideal and material, in a social matrix which imposed conventions and norms on its human parts. He drew upon social anthropology and comparative studies (and the history of religions) for his depiction of norms, and upon psychoanalysis for his account of persons. The scheme presupposed a social rage for order, in bounded human groups. The immediacy, even desperation, of human conflict in Hobbes was left out, the jagged variety of social histories flattened, the fantasies and passions which troubled Freud domesticated. Suppose, however, that his version of the rage for order was a reflection of the value he placed on the pursuit of social stability. Suppose, too, that it expressed an intellectually unsecured loan from biology—just when biology, with genetics and microbiology, was itself entering a period of huge indeterminacy.

I could hardly have phrased my doubts that way in 1948. They took form as I wondered, stimulated by a miscellany of critics in other universities, about Parsons's insistence on consensus in the United States. Much of American history was conflict-ridden, and I was skeptical of the intellectual mobilization for the Cold War everywhere evident at Harvard, which made consensus so useful an idea. Much of history beyond our borders was certainly a record of conflict, and I knew enough of the religious history of the West, from the crusade against the Albigensians to witchcraft trials in Salem, to doubt that the church brought peace. Most tellingly, my reading of Max Weber suggested that he would have been rather doubtful about the large claims Parsons made for his theory. Weber's experience of political and social turbulence gave his sociological abstractions very different accents.

There was not much, at the time, that I could do with my doubts. I recall asking Parsons why he had translated Weber's term *stand* as "status group" rather than "estate." Parsons suggested that mine was a philological quibble, that his translation was faithful to Weber's intentions. I remain unconvinced. Weber thought of sociology as a refined commentary on history, rather than as a replacement for historiography. His analysis of the distinctiveness of the modern West described the supersession of estates by classes, and he did not favor historically disembodied categories.

There was another intellectual ancestor whose memory, I thought, was not being honored: Freud. By 1948, psychoanalysis had conquered much of American psychiatry, and considerable numbers of social scientists were working on the interaction of culture and character. Many of my fellow students and teachers were undergoing personal analyses. Whatever they were learning in their therapeutic hours—the whole body of Freudian thought, with its contradictions and discontinuities—did not interest them. Then-recent work in ego psychology did, since the depiction of the ego as mediating between biological drives and social demands was, apparently, a convenient point of entry for the social scientists. They did not, however, venture into the labyrinth partially excavated by Freud. The archaeological and historical aspects of his work embarrassed them, and they were largely ignorant of the attempts to join Marxism and psychoanalysis of earlier decades. I recall an anecdote about a senior analyst in New York declaring, "When I encounter a normal person, I begin treatment immediately."

Psychoanalysis was domesticated, banalized—it became the *via regis* to the new American normality or to understanding the pathologies of those who were adamantly different. The senior clinical psychologists at Harvard were the exceptions. Henry Murray was a psychiatrist, had led the group which produced the remarkable *Explorations in Personality* in 1938. He was also a cultivated and widely read New York patrician (his family gave its name to Murray Hill) who implied that, with all the world a stage, we could not take any one actor all that seriously—even eminent figures such as himself. The other was Robert White, who was director of the Psychological Clinic, which occupied an old house on Plimpton Street. White was a gently ironic figure. One day he brought in a puppy he had acquired and I was struck by the gentleness, which extended to his students and colleagues. For a while, I frequented the Psychological Clinic and its lunch table, prepared by an elegantly stately lady who with White was very kind to me. They sensed my vulnerability, my need for a place, as well as a certain independence on my part. I did not trust myself to proceed beyond introductory courses in personality theory, and certainly did not think of myself as capable of treating others. I did raise questions, mainly unanswered, about what Freud and Reich would have thought of the seemingly seamless integration of their work into the busy routines of a university. Most of my contemporaries simply did not understand what I was driving at (Marc Fried excepted). White welcomed the diversion. For myself, alas, it wasn't much more than that. I did read deep texts, but could not make use of them as I struggled with my own resistances to insight.

The clinic was near the Grolier Bookstore and the offices of *The Harvard Crimson*. That was a contrast in itself. The bookstore was run by an exceedingly unhurried gentleman in a tweed coat who exuded unconcern for customers and who was host to young men and women who looked like well-bred characters out of the novels they presumably aspired to write. The *Crimson* was staffed by very energetic young men with little time or use for the muses. Their eyes were on big prizes, which many of them certainly got. They were very lively, astonishingly knowing and unimpressed by the intellectual and social hierarchy of Harvard. David Halberstam was among them, and I was not surprised when his reporting from Vietnam disturbed the Pentagon and White House.

My second year at Harvard increased my sense of belonging. Teaching, and with it membership in the Board of Freshman Advisors, brought me into closer contact with the undergraduates—and with the rest of the university. My teaching duties were straightforward. As an advisor, I discussed with the students their choice of courses—and, sometimes, a great deal else in their lives. Harvard at this writing is still struggling with the duality of its ambitions. It wished to be (or to remain) the pre-eminent university in any number of fields of scholarship and science. It also wished for supreme distinction in undergraduate education. Great scholars and scientists cultivating international reputations, younger colleagues trying to scale those heights, were not always enthusiastic about teaching the very young—and many did not have pedagogic gifts.

The undergraduates to a significant extent educated one another, and were assisted by a significant number of senior and especially junior faculty with vocations as undergraduate teachers. The teaching fellows, many of whom had not been undergraduates at Harvard or any place like it, were closer to the undergraduates in age and often welcomed teaching as a respite from the competitive and intellectual rigors of their doctoral studies. However shabby our offices, or temporary our positions in front of the class, for the moment we could enjoy the authority graciously lent us by the university.

It was that authority which saved us from the unrelenting critical capacities of our gifted students. They were extraordinarily tolerant about being taught by persons not much older than themselves and clearly designated as apprentices. We were accepted as lesser links in an academic chain of being. Suppose that we were weaker links? Some of the more sophisticated of the undergraduates thought of their forbearance as their initial alumni gifts to the university: by enduring the teaching fellows, they were contributing to Harvard's larger mission. *The Harvard Crimson Guide to Freshman Courses* was distinctly harder on full-time faculty than on us. I was very glad that my own work occasioned good notices. They were justified: I taught for an additional fifty-one years but was never better than in those initial ones. I enjoyed everything about it: the direct relationships, the chance to share intellectual enthusiasms, the opportunity to occupy center stage.

I was assigned to the Department of Social Relations's introductory sequence. The first half was taught by Gordon Allport and concentrated on social psychology. Allport, a liberal Midwesterner who had worked on prejudice, had a strong bias against psychoanalysis. I appreciated his personal kindliness; he appeared less driven, less demanding than other senior faculty. Along with a couple of my contemporaries, I did not realize how much he incorporated of twentieth-century psychological thought, and did not know how morally engaged he had been in matters such as finding employment for scholars fleeing European fascism. According to the new canons of the social sciences, that was civic activity separated from professionalism; consulting with a government agency would have been more appropriate, or prestigious. Allport represented an entire strain of progressive American thought which, we were given to understand, could be considered naïve, or in any event out of date. I regret that I was not able to connect his work with the progressive historiography I had read as a schoolboy, and that I denied myself an opportunity to learn more on account of thinking of him as an amiable pastoral figure rather than as a very serious scholar.

My contrition is greater because the Cambridge defenders of psychoanalysis as the one true theory of human nature were, in many cases, busy hobbling the rough edges of Freud's work. Freud voiced profound skepticism, in the end, about the amelioration of the human condition—but did think that the psychoanalytic legacy would enrich cultural and social inquiry. He willed to future generations the intricate and unfinished complexity of his late work—and left open the ways in which it could be used by the social scientists. My Harvard contemporaries frequently acted as if they had closed the issue, by depicting psychoanalysis as a description of human adaptability rather than of our consummate destructiveness. Allport was more honest about what bothered him in Freud.

The second term's introduction to social anthropology and sociology was taught by George Homans, who was serenely untroubled by the department's inter-disciplinary charter. Homans was a direct descendant of the Adams family, had written an ethnographic account of a medieval English village, and constructed a view of society in which human idiosyncrasy and systemic purpose were precariously joined. He seemed to think of himself as a bemused survivor—but of what remained very unclear. His historical interests were pronounced—but for George, history had largely come to a stop and could be apprehended, now, by ethnographic mapping. It was history with all the drama in the past. Perhaps that was a reflection of his sense of heritage—or dispossession. He was committed to an ironic sobriety, thought in linear terms and clearly doubted that there were uncharted depths to human existence. He did me the honor of asking me to coordinate the work of the Teaching Fellows. I am sorry for apparent ingratitude, fifty-nine years later: I cannot spontaneously recall what texts and subject matter we gave the students. I cannot, indeed, recall what we taught in the first and psychological half of the course.

What I do recall is the quite extraordinary eagerness and receptivity of the students. It took different forms, some of the graduates of the preparatory schools taking care to affect a certain casualness. They were, however, as diligent as the rest in preparing their reading assignments. Perhaps it was the excellent quality and college-like content of the work they had done at school, but they were more likely—more by attitude than word—to pose the question: what is this in aid of? The graduates of the good public high schools were more unequivocally ready to treat the social sciences as good news in a theological sense, a new way of making sense of things familiar. Additionally, the difference may have been due to the cultures of class in the US. The preparatory schools taught that the world could be understood as necessary, if occasionally and regrettably unjust to those without the good fortune to have been born into the right circumstances.

The social sciences were merely adumbrating what anyone of

good sense knew: that life was often unfair. The gifted high school graduates who came to Harvard were determined, on their part, to place themselves in the right circumstances—which for the moment meant a certain suspension of disbelief when confronted with the curriculum.

The students with interests in science, I noticed, were rather more methodical and just a bit more distant, but by no means dissenting: the skepticism voiced by many of Harvard's natural scientists about the scientific status of social inquiry was not, or not yet, theirs.

The only difference I can recollect between the men and the women is that the range of responses among the women was narrower. They were nearly all good students quick to grasp the point and exceedingly likely to turn in finished, even polished, pieces of work. In matters psychological, they frequently showed more empathy. It was a period in which few planned to go on to graduate or professional schools. The women could afford, in the circumstances, a more relaxed attitude by contrast with the competitive anxieties of their male peers. In a lecture in his course on American society, Parsons voiced his sympathy for the dilemma of the Radcliffe students: they would graduate, work as teachers or secretaries or perhaps in the social services for a few years, and then marry. Could they be sure, however, that the young man of their choice would attain tenure at a prestigious university, become a partner in an eminent law firm, rise from a residency to a distinguished career in medicine, or reach the heights in business or finance?

Life, he concluded, had its uncertainties.

There were a few students from the working class and some of them trusted me enough to speak of their origins when we talked. They enjoyed being at Harvard, took it as a personal validation in most cases and not as a trial or ordeal—and were remarkably open in using their own experience of American society to make it clear to some of their more complacent peers that there were more things in our heaven and our earth than they knew.

The ethnic and religious composition of the student body imposed no overt code of sensitivity on the college. I thought that I detected a patronizing undertone in some administrators, teachers, and students from traditional Harvard Protestant families—taking the form of a wry self-congratulation on their generosity in having made room for others.

There were very, very few black students at Harvard, either as graduates or undergraduates. The Jewish students struck me as divided by class, and the same was true of the Catholic ones. What seemed more important was that attending Harvard was understood to constitute an achievement in itself, a membership card in a desirable club, and a first-class ticket to other exclusive destinations. I am sure that there were Jewish students who worried about their relationship to tradition, and Catholic ones preoccupied with reconciling ancestry and an open American destiny (the more so as many were Irish in what had been the stronghold of their self-proclaimed betters). I recollect few open discussions of the matter. Faculty were not much inclined to talk about these things, either in the social sciences or in the humanities—and the new influx of younger Jewish faculty and a much smaller number of Catholic colleagues in their cohort were at pains to cultivate generic professorial personae.

What did the university, explicitly, seek to impart to undergraduates? It was thought that a student who chose courses carefully could do rather well by reading three and only three books: Joseph Schumpeter's *Capitalism, Socialism and Democracy*, Max Weber's *The Protestant Ethic and the Spirit of Capitalism*, and Melville's *Moby Dick*. (Some would have suggested, instead of Melville, Henry James's *The Golden Bowl*.) The choices were significant. Schumpeter was actually at Harvard, but not very available to undergraduates. In a period in which there were endless professions of democratic faith, and a considerable amount of American self-congratulation, his text expressed considerable skepticism about democracy. He also argued that the intellectuals were congenitally hostile to capitalism. The eagerness of most of his colleagues in economics and politics to declare the US an achieved revolution suggested that, whatever had been true in central Europe, Cambridge was a good deal more complacent. Weber's book could also be read as a celebration of much of American life, the jeremiad at its end on the soullessness of modern capitalism as a secular equivalent of an edifying and non-binding New England sermon—rather like Schumpeter's Old World warnings on democracy. As for Melville (and James), they were supposed to convey a tragic sense of life, much talked about in English departments. It was exceedingly unclear what consequences for their lives the students were supposed to draw from these texts since they were quite committed to conventional success. Taken together, the texts were perhaps a warning, one the faculty could not or did not wish to utter directly.

In New York at the time, Lionel Trilling was calling attention to James's political text *The Princess Casamassima*, with its description of the eruption of moral despair and melancholic account of the price of culture. In its choice of texts, were his Harvard colleagues, discreetly, conveying the same message? The senior ones left out texts they had read in the thirties, by Marx—texts which had impelled Schumpeter and Weber to write as they did. There were effective reasons for the omissions, but hardly pedagogic ones: indeed, the undergraduates were cheated of a part of the Western heritage.

There wasn't much evidence of Marxist thought in Cambridge, unread books in the libraries apart. In the 1948 elections, a small group of followers of Trotsky invited the vice presidential candidate of the Socialist Workers Party to speak. I was reproached, afterward, by one of the sponsors (it may have been the mathematician Chandler Davis) for having asked a question both hostile and snobbish. My recollection is dim, but I believe that he was right—and trust that subsequently he learned to think better of me.

There were a group of supporters of Henry Wallace (not by any means all or mainly connected with the US Communist Party). Norman Thomas, the traditional leader of American socialism, made an electoral stop during his 1948 presidential campaign, and argued for his version of an alternative politics. When Truman won, a considerable number of faculty were pleasantly surprised. Some were New Dealers; others thought the Republicans too primitive (or too isolationist), while others welcomed continuity in their work in the nation's capital. The election did not much stir Harvard, which believed, correctly, that it was needed by the nation no matter who was in government.

There was a bit more evidence of anxiety caused by the anti-Communist campaign to which Senator McCarthy gave his name. Blame where blame is due: it wasn't his alone. He was preceded by the House Un-American Activities Committee, and the Truman administration and its agencies behaved with maximal odiousness. One very large difficulty was that there were very few Communists in Cambridge, although a more extended definition of the term would certainly have included many descendants of the New Deal. McCarthyism in its primitiveness confirmed Harvard in its conviction that a substantial number of our fellow citizens were beyond redemption, a belief that had been held in New England somewhat earlier.

The official and unofficial dealings of the university's administrators and intermediaries with the government only were disclosed decades later. They were a great deal more supine than the robust pronouncements of university figures, great and small, suggested.

The larger Cambridge community included MIT, and the scientists, many of them veterans of the Manhattan Project and other wartime scientific enterprises, were especial targets of the new vigilantism. I was most struck, at the time, by the fate of a very great scholar, F. O. Matthiessen. A founder of modern American studies, his work on the Concord thinkers and New England was among other things a major contribution to the delineation of what was American in the American spirit. Matthiessen did not take political instruction from philistines and time servers. He had been a visiting professor in Prague when the Communists seized power in 1948, and his book on that experience was much too uncritical of them. The new world power, was intolerant of domestic dissenting voices. It was also frightened of a domestic enemy, as it was thought, if anything, worse than political subversion, homosexuality. Matthiessen, who was homosexual, was blackmailed by the FBI and committed suicide. I knew him only slightly, had gone to talk with him in his office hours and he had expressed pleased surprise that a sociologist was as politically critical as he found me to be.

I'm now surprised at that, myself. My capacity, then, to insert what was happening in the nation and the academy into a larger historical framework was seriously underdeveloped. I knew that my personal intellectual resources were limited, but I did not know where to find more ample ones. I dimly sensed that the vulgarities of popular anti-Communism and the elegant complacency of Harvard's celebrants of our virtues were connected, but could not say how. What I did think was that the notions of social inquiry canonized in my department promised no relief for my restlessness. There were occasional moments in which, sometimes joined by others, I could laugh at the dilemma. The departmental Christmas party, and the script some of us prepared as a skit for it, ventured far more criticism than we dared to utter in seminars.

My friend Tom O'Dea was at Harvard thanks to the GI Bill of Rights, and as a true son of South Boston did not allow himself to be intimidated. In a seminar on ideas and society, Tom asked Talcott Parsons why he had not assigned the writings of Karl Mannheim. I'm not sure that he was read anywhere else at Harvard, but one would have had to been very provincial in the late forties not to have heard of him. Talcott was indignant: "The next thing you know, Tom, you'll be asking me to assign Gurvitch." Georges Gurvitch was a French sociologist who had edited a volume which I'd read in college on twentieth-century sociology, a major element in my decision to study the field. After teaching in New York during the war, he was back in Paris. Tom and I went to Widener Library and took out the uncut copies of his two recent books, *La Vocation Actuelle de la Sociologie*, and *Déterminismes Sociaux et Liberté Humaine*. They were dense, full of references I did not understand, but conveyed an intention to shape an open historical situation. I'd read something of Sartre and could imagine Gurvitch arguing with him in a café. Five or so years later, when I was beginning to teach at the London School of Economics, Gurvitch came to deliver a series of lectures. I recounted the episode, and he took it as a tribute.

I owe Parsons, however, a very great deal. He certainly sensed my disinclination to convert to the church over which he presided. He appreciated, I think, my interests in history and philosophy. In the spring of 1949, he made it possible for me to change, drastically, my life at Harvard. He introduced me to the political philosopher Sam Beer, who promptly appointed me a teaching fellow in his general education course on the social sciences. More, Parsons urged Adams House to appoint me as a resident tutor, and the house master and his head tutors agreed. In the fall of 1949, I arrived very near to the center of the university's life. My debt to Parsons is all the greater as he was quite aware of my skepticism and even rebelliousness. No doubt he and the department got something in return: I was culturally and intellectually presentable in the rest of the university. Still, it was both fair and generous of him. Not for the last time, I learned that a bit of Midwestern Calvinism goes a long way.

The Harvard house system did not entail much direct pedagogic activity, but its broader and indirect contributions to undergraduate education were very large. The three upper classes of the college were assigned to seven residential houses. Each had a master and resident tutors, and a considerable number of faculty associates. The resident tutors, mainly teaching fellows and junior faculty, were of course available for talks, formal and informal, on the students' work. They also participated in, and sometimes inspired, the programs of clubs, concerts, discussions, dramas, team sports which the students organized in their houses. The faculty associates who came from their laboratories and studies for lunch regularly, dinner occasionally, included some of Harvard's stars. They occasionally even ate with the students. The life of the houses provided support, even solidarity, to students who would otherwise have been more alone when confronted with the sometimes ruthless competitiveness of the university.

It certainly was a second home to me. The separate houses had profiles, or more accurately, tags. Adams was especially mixed in its student composition, boasted of its own kitchen (rather than the less than masterful central one), and struck me at once as hospitable. The master was David Little, who was the university secretary and neither academic or intellectual but jealous of the house's reputation. Our head tutors were John McCormick, who taught English, and Joe Palamountain, who was a political scientist. My fellow resident tutors included Bernard Bailyn, who had come to Harvard from Williams a year before I did and who was already on his way to originality as a historian of Colonial America. The more senior tutors, who came frequently for lunch and house events, included Arthur Schlesinger Jr. and Morton White, the philosopher. They were encouraging and took me along on their journeys into the intellectual and political conflicts of the period. I was but twenty-three. For the students, I was a fortunately placed and comradely elder brother. For the more senior faculty, I was an interesting and promising younger one. I wasn't their doctoral candidate: they could enjoy my critical disposition. For Parsons and the other teachers in sociology and Social Relations, I was a successful ambassador to the larger Harvard. For myself, I was delighted to be part of a lively community, and even more delighted to connect with the main currents of the university.

My good fortune was doubled by my work with Sam Beer. Sam had designed an introductory course in the social sciences, Social Science II, in the General Education Program. During the war a small group of senior Harvard figures joined President James Conant in writing *General Education in a Free Society*. They anticipated considerable democratization of access to higher education and, confident that Harvard would be expected to lead the way into the new epoch, they proposed a new charter for undergraduate education, especially. Much of it was not new, and some copied from curricular innovations at Columbia and the University of Chicago before the war. What was new was the depiction of the US as the primary spiritual heir of Western civilization, as the champion of liberalism and the incarnation of freedom—which burdened the colleges and universities with historical responsibilities to cultivate, impart and renew the Western tradition. That certainly transformed the presuppositions of our pedagogy. We weren't just talking about interesting ideas, methods of inquiry, human nature, nature entire, and history. We were forming citizens, shaping a national vocation. What had been tacitly assumed by the old elite now was matter for rigorous scrutiny. What Harvard did not doubt was its qualifications for the task, its legitimacy as national spiritual mentor.

The general education program required all Harvard students to take courses in their freshman and sophomore years in each of the major areas: humanities, natural sciences, and social sciences. In each area, alternative courses were offered—and, Harvard being what it was, a genteel but insistent competition for prominence in and through the program developed. The students were not the final arbiters, but good ratings in the Guide to Freshman Courses helped. What counted was a mixture of student enthusiasm, the propagation of an aura of knowingness to one's colleagues, and the intimation that the course was central. If the question was asked, "Central to what?" the answer was sure to refer to the Western tradition as defined by the program. Even when claiming service to tradition, Harvard kept its ineradicable narcissism.

Some departments were skeptical of the program; others sent their best teachers to it and their most talented graduate students to assist them. Some of the scientists had doubts, absurdly, about introductory science courses intended for non-scientists. Thomas Kuhn taught one of these with Conant himself, and was reproached by his teachers in physics: it was an amateurish kind of thing to do. Years later Kuhn drew upon his experience in general education to write his influential book on the structure of scientific revolutions. True, a certain amount of pretentiousness was the inevitable accompaniment of the program. When a younger teacher of literature wondered what he should title his general education course, he narrowed the choices to "God and Destiny in Western Thought" or "Divine and Human in the Western Tradition." Morton White asked him, solicitously, what the course was about and was told that it would begin with Plato, proceed through the Old and New Testaments to Augustine, Dante, Burke, Dostoevsky—the all-time best seller list. Morton was helpfulness itself: "Why don't you name it 'Reading I've Liked'?"

These inevitable intimations of human frailty apart, those of us teaching in general education did think that we were representatives of a tradition. It was something other than Matthew Arnold's "the best that has been thought and said." The best, we believed, was being thought and said, at the very moment, at Harvard, and we were not given to concessions to antiquarian pretenders. Rather, we were pious if critical descendants of large visions which had contributed to our own. Our liberal society was an ordered society and to that order belonged our capacity to situate ourselves in relation to a past whose embarrassing and troubling aspects we had overcome. We could find in that past intimations of our own aspirations to greatness, aspirations we expected to see rapidly fulfilled. In the meantime, we had a way to deal with disappointment: it was to cultivate a tragic sense of history—absent from our socially successful lives but available in Shakespeare or our own Henry James (and for those with recondite tastes, in the Greek dramatists and Racine).

As for present limitations on the extension of individual autonomy, civic liberty, and a decent but not exaggerated measure of social solidarity, these were surely due to tasks imposed on us by adversaries. Having saved freedom from the Fascists and Nazis, having defeated Japan's expansionism and instructing it in democracy, we were prepared to stop Communism. That entailed a considerable diversion of resources from tasks which otherwise would be compelling, but a sober examination of the situation yielded but one conclusion: that we were right to pay this price. No less an authority than Reinhold Niebuhr assured us, after all, that we did not have to be perfect, only better than our enemies—and since these were led by Mao and Stalin, we could congratulate ourselves on our moral superiority and adopt whatever means were fitted to the tasks at hand.

Not all of this found its way so explicitly into instruction in the humanities and social sciences at Harvard, or into our general education courses. I have sketched, however, the ideology of adaptation shared by persons of varying cultural and social preferences.

Western tradition was the substratum of our existence. The history of our nation, with its incompleteness and rawness, even brutalities, was something we would now rewrite—not by abrogating the past but by interpreting it as the precondition of a happier future. We were not educating citizens; we were educating citizens who as Harvard graduates would take their places in the nation's elite.

What I now find remarkable is the intellectual docility with which we conducted ourselves. We pursued historical and moral questions, political arguments and cultural inquiries, and of course psychological diagnoses of ourselves and others—especially others. The academic division of labor certainly explained part of our unwillingness to develop more skepticism about our ultimate purposes, but at other times and places many academics did ask rather more piercing questions than we posed. I cannot exempt myself from the charge that we should have thought harder. What I and my contemporaries were experiencing, even more intensely than our students, was a process of socialization. We were being prepared for careers as the intellectual middlemen of empire—an assignment our thesis advisors, seminar teachers, and the senior colleagues supervising our teaching had already accepted.

Much later, I visited research institutes in the Soviet Union. Czechoslovakia, the German Democratic Republic, Poland. There, often with a very heavy hand, an official line was imprinted. We had much more freedom but exhausted ourselves, often, in conflicts which never quite got out of hand. We were even allowed a large measure of dissent, expressions of distaste: few at Harvard could be accused of abuse of the privilege.

Sam Beer, who taught Social Sciences II, had gone to the University of Michigan, been at Oxford as a Rhodes Scholar, and written a book on the political implications of Alfred North Whitehead's philosophy of freedom. He'd also been in the wartime army and was a very compelling witness to American diversity, a term then not at all in use, so we spoke of class. When I first went to Britain, after three years of Sam's tutelage, I looked at things with his eyes—a very large help. Sam had a vocation as a teacher, and that came from his sympathetic interest in others. He was a born democrat, no man's servant, and a serious scholar. He was able to convey the drama of ideas, since he was enthralled by their importance—and his lectures kept the attention not only of the students but of his teaching fellows.

The course was on Western civilization, and the teaching fellows Sam recruited shared his pedagogic aims, or rather we accepted these the more eagerly since our own were largely unformed. Sam had some sympathy for discussions of method in the social sciences, but rightly held that method could not be taught apart from substance. The first thing new students at Harvard needed, he thought, was knowledge of our intellectual origins, and a large look over national boundaries. What he offered was an intellectual ethnography of the West. The students read texts in chronological order, concluded with twentieth-century classics such as *The Protestant Ethic and the Spirit of Capitalism*.

What now strikes me about Sam's reading list is, first, the matter that was not on it. Knowledge of our own national origins and thought was in the hands of the historians and those teaching American studies, and Sam judged that many students would have encountered Adams and Jefferson, Emerson and William James, elsewhere—or would shortly do so. Actually, as an acute student of Great Britain who knew its political traditions, Sam certainly grasped the significance of Bernard Bailyn's work on the British origins of the thought of the American Revolution. Bailyn, however, was doing his graduate work and about to begin a thesis on the New England merchants, and his contribution to the debate on national origins lay a decade ahead. There was nothing in the course on the American debate on slavery, none of the writing by Frederick Douglass or W.E.B. Du Bois. To be sure, Africa, Asia, the Hispanic world, and Byzantine and Slavic Europe were also left to others. What was given to the students was an introduction to an Anglo-American view of Western civilization, broader than much of what they would have had in England because the US had absorbed so much from France and Germany.

The students read Nietzsche, who was so obviously not English or even British that when I began to teach in the United Kingdom in 1953 he was in the ambivalent custody of Germanists and historians of Germany. The philosophers made it clear that they wished to have nothing to do with his thought.

Texts do not exist for themselves; they are connected and interpreted. We put our texts together to tell an ideal story of our antecedents. We went from religious passion to secular sobriety, from authoritarian rule to civic participation, from plunder to entrepreneurship—and from unhappy Europe, struggling with memories of its recent ideological fratricide, to our own optimistic country, in which liberty was used with such restraint. True, there had been a Civil War (not easily forgotten in abolitionist Boston yet decidedly not in the forefront of memory). Segregation, however, was a Southern pathology. The nearly total absence of blacks at Harvard had interesting but remote causes, about which most people at Harvard did not think—and if they did, they shrugged in resignation. Senator McCarthy was raging; the federal and state governments were prosecuting Communists, authentic or otherwise, and employers discharging them. Harvard, however, recoiled in pious horror at these excesses. Why persecute Communists when it was so much easier to demonstrate their intellectual absurdities and moral failings—and their cultural and psychological deformations as well? It was decades before the university's collaboration with the FBI became known, but it is doubtful that earlier disclosure would have altered the narrative in a fundamental way.

Recall the introduction to the *Communist Manifesto:* "A spectre is haunting Europe."

Cambridge did not fear Communism; the point was to mobilize for the American project. There were on faculty and among the elder graduate students persons who had good reason to fear difficulty on account of their pasts; they hardly insisted on public discussions of their anxieties. The spectre that haunted Cambridge was the thought that even if matters were the way they were, they could be otherwise. That accounted for the pervasive disparagement of Marxism, which often took the form of ignoring it—or asserting that history had proven it to be wrong. The achieved revolution, after all, was the American one. At one point in this period Mary McCarthy insisted in *Partisan Review* that the American suburbs were evidence for a true social revolution. That was Harvard's view, and it was of a piece with its domestication of psychoanalysis, the near-elimination of its darker and meta-historical roots, their replacement by an account of the difficulties of human adjustment.

Still, the course was liberating for the students and exciting for those who taught it. It was for most of the students an introduction to ideas and problems they had not encountered before. The world could be thought about—even critically. True to Harvard, we treated the possibility of criticism as an achievement and did not push it excessively.

Provincialism, we intimated, treated the present as absolute; we placed it in history. Our history was Eurocentric, and that was cosmopolitanism enough for the US at mid-century. I know that Sam Beer was skeptical of the idea of an American Century, of American triumphalism. Yet what our students took away with them was the conviction that they were legitimate heirs of the ages.

The course brought me into daily contact with the entire range of undergraduates at Harvard, including some going on to the natural sciences. David Binder, Richard Bushman, Eric Kandel, and Harvey Mansfield were among my students. I worked with an interesting and talented set of graduate students from the social sciences—the other teaching fellows. In my final year at Harvard, 1951-52, I coordinated the work of the fellows. We were joined by a new graduate student in government, who already had a formidable reputation: Henry Kissinger. His attitude during our staff meetings was palpably ironic. Somehow, he conveyed that the rest of us would become departmental chairs at Amherst and Berkeley, no doubt write some estimable books, but that he was destined for demanding tasks in the real world. He told me that we read the wrong Max Weber, with his melancholy reflections on Protestantism and its fate. He preferred the Weber who, fascinated by the struggles at the end of the Roman Republic, showed that he understood the essence of politics. Since I knew German, I would understand Weber's use of the term *ausmerzen* to describe the way the successful dealt with their opponents: they rubbed them out. There was, however, one person among our peers Henry accepted as an intellectual mentor. Klaus Epstein was like Kissinger from Germany, was an historian of conviction and intensity. Klaus was a vocal disbeliever: he thought most Americans naïve about democracy and everything else. That was a lesson Henry, clearly, took to heart.

I had two very close friends on the faculty to whom I owed a great deal—encouragement, stimulation (no, tutoring), and the generosity to include me in their families. The elder was Morton White, a fellow New Yorker, who had graduated very young from City College and then studied philosophy at Columbia. He had come to Harvard from a teaching post at Pennsylvania, and was rapidly recognized as a major figure. He combined knowledge of analytic philosophy with serious interest in the historical and social issues that did not lend themselves to reduction to testable empirical propositions. Morton was a youngish veteran of. New York's ideological conflicts, knew the émigrés from the Frankfurt Institute of Social Research and the *Partisan Review* group. He brought to contemporary history a large amount of lucidity, a capacity to examine his own passions as well as those of others—and a sense of humor suffused by irony. His book on Beard, Dewey, Holmes, James and Veblen (*Social Thought in America: The Revolt Against Formalism*) reshaped our reading of the immediate past. Some of these iconic figures were progressives, but Morton argued that they were all modernists, breaking dogmas as they reunited spirit and the world.

Morton was very glad to be at Harvard (his father owned a shoe store on the Lower East Side of Manhattan). He was justly proud, however, of the trait his friends admired: his independence of fashion, pretense and snobbery. I was made to feel welcome in his house on Shady Hill. His wife, Lucia (who collaborated with him on a book on intellectuals and the city), was very much a presence in her own right, her gracious manner combining with unsparingly acute judgements of ideas and persons.

Another friend was in some ways Morton's antipode. Carl Kaysen was in the Society of Fellows when we met again after a brief and exceedingly argumentative encounter in 1942 in his native Philadelphia. Carl had gone to the University of Pennsylvania, was in the armed services and attached to the Strategic Bombing Survey during and right after the war. At Harvard he deployed his immense analytical powers as a political economist. He enjoyed politics—not least in its academic variant—delighted in the oddities of human character, and cherished a set of friends from the sciences. He was especially drawn to the European émigrés in Cambridge. Like Morton, he conceived of the world as a stage, but unlike him was not content with the role of drama critic. He wanted to write the plays and act in them, too. He eventually had his chance: he was deputy national security advisor to John Kennedy and succeeded Oppenheimer as director of the Institute of Advanced Study. He arranged for Morton's appointment there, but the two later had a bitter struggle over Carl's proposal to appoint Robert Bellah to the institute.

Carl's great career lay ahead of him, but it was clear that he would have one. It was on this point that I had doubts about myself, but I must have sublimated these well enough for Carl to treat me as a valued friend who had something to say. His wife, Annette, was especially sympathetic. She liked Cambridge society but saw through it in an amused way. Carl, sure of his empirical observations of economy and society, thought the idea of a natural science of society absurd, and that, along with Morton's more philosophical doubts, reinforced my own skepticism. However, I think that Carl's large contribution to my education lay in his introducing me so very directly to those at Harvard who took for granted intellect's proximity to power. His friends in the sciences were struggling with it. Some, after Los Alamos, were actively attempting to influence arms policy. His senior sponsors in economics (and law) commuted to Washington as a matter of course. Carl somehow managed an uneasy synthesis of piety and skepticism. He implied that he wished the world were different, but since it was as it was, realism dictated that one work in-house for more rationality. As for the realm of the heart, with an audible sigh of relief, he left that to novelists and philosophers—but thought that he was doing the best that one could in circumstances no doubt far from ideal.

It was an attitude I had difficulty in identifying with. I simply could not imagine any agency of power having need of my talents. In subsequent decades, I elaborated that into a principled acceptance of the status of an outsider. Had I felt less of one on grounds far from philosophical, perhaps I would have been more open to the ordinary compromises of politics.

The pursuit of intellectual achievement was my path to engagement. The broad church of academia did ask what potential communicants believed, but above all wanted acknowledgement of its rituals. A bit of dissidence went a long way for anyone who could reasonably claim academic respectability. As the ideological anxiety of American society at the beginning of the Cold War, including the serial imbecilities of the militant philistines, took repressive forms, the academy fought back. Individuals whose employment was denied, terminated or threatened were defended, with extremely varying degrees of firmness and solidarity. An enormous amount of energy was expended on general expressions of support for academic freedom. One large diversionary movement was all the more effective since it mobilized very authentic feelings. The Cold War (and the national security state constructed to fight it) were reluctantly accepted, and issues of class and race were systematically de-emphasized. The cultural struggle occupied the center of the stage: could the nation in its new prosperity allow or encourage the development of qualities of autonomy, judgement, reflectiveness—in short, a democratic high culture? David Riesman's *The Lonely Crowd* set the agenda of discussion. The old radicals transformed themselves into new social critics—and presented my generation with models of comportment and expression which had large benefits. We could claim that we were a very loyal opposition—and since our opposition was emphatically cultural, it could be indulged. We ran into no obstacles to integration in the academy and indeed our criticism (like that of our seniors) was welcomed as proof of the spiritual largesse of the system we ever so faintly opposed.

The proclamation of a Jewish state, the Communist coup in Czechoslovakia, Tito's defection, the Soviet atomic bomb, the election of 1948, the outbreak of the Korean War, McCarthyism, the case of Alger Hiss and the travails of Oppenheimer, Eisenhower's decision to run for President in 1952—all succeeded one another. I certainly did not ignore these events, but I had no developed response to them—nor did I attempt to develop one. I joined no political group, though I did attend in 1948 meetings of a dispirited group of self-styled progressives, made the acquaintance of a serious if discreet set of Marxists who were concerned with what we should today call the world system or globalization, Trotsky rather than Stalin their inspiration. Isaac Deutscher came to Harvard to work on the Trotsky archives and gave a talk to faculty at Adams House, recalling Wordsworth's refusal to join the ideological war against France and praising it as a useful example for those who wished to back neither side in the Cold War. That shocked most of those present and left me more perplexed than ever: I did not wish to join the Cold War consensus, but what would I join? I followed all the controversies and had a deepening if mostly unarticulated conviction: the terms of American debate were skewed and shallow, and the answers were to be sought somewhere, somehow, but were not visible either at Harvard or in New York.

In New York, I saw Clement Greenberg often —every ten weeks or so. Clem at the time was enjoying his role as herald of the New York School of artists (the prophet of abstract expressionism, he was an early advocate and friend of Jackson Pollock). I went occasionally to galleries with him, and it was clear that he had celebrity status—which did not visibly displease him. Two general matters concerned him. One was the quality of American culture, which he thought abysmally low. The other was the nation's commitment to confront Stalin and all his works, of which he thought highly.

He did not consider a striking contradiction: how could a society so spiritually mediocre assume a sublime world historical task? The problem was descended from another one. A decade previously, the *Partisan Review* group simultaneously advocated social revolution and modernism. This last, however, had an aesthetic and intellectual sensibility mainly unavailable to populations expected to assume revolutionary tasks. True, Charlie Chaplin was a universal figure—but Cézanne was not and neither were Eliot and Kafka. Modern art was a realm of freedom, but the ordinary world was unable to free itself of necessity. In the late forties, the New York intellectuals discovered charms in that world they had not appreciated in the thirties. Mocking the crudities of the American version of social realism went only so far. For the rest, they were reduced to the intellectual equivalent of shrugged shoulders—or, in some cases, a knowing wink.

That wasn't true of everyone. At *Commentary*, where Clem worked, editor Eliot Cohen presided over a simultaneous rediscovery of Jewishness and American culture.

The younger editors and writers were particularly entranced by this opportunity to move into the mainstream while remaining true to their roots. Cohen had been in the Communist Party and apparently retained something of its pervasive rigidity. Clem did me a large favor and I was invited to try to review a book on personality and society. I thought it very good and said so. Cohen rejected the review. Attributing character to social milieu, he declared, was dangerously close to "Stalinoid" thought. The book was Erikson's *Childhood and Society*.

Clem and I lunched occasionally at the Jewish delicatessen opposite *Commentary*'s office on 33rd Street. The sandwiches were enormous, and so was the television screen showing the New York teams. Clem was free with recriminatory gossip about his friends, all of whom I had read but few of whom I had met. Their lives were different from those available to the academics. Whatever the difficulties and drawbacks of academic life, I sensed, it offered more prospects of a certain psychological stability than the free-floating existence of those who lived from one article or book to the next. Clem did not discourage me in this regard, although his major worry was that I might become too enamored of Cambridge's high style and lose a critical edge. Never forget, he declared, you are a highbrow and have to think of yourself as one instinctively. How one could adopt an instinctive attitude was difficult to fathom, but I saw the general point: to thine own self be true. As to what that self was, I was, despite many friendships, on my own.

My boyhood friend George Fischer, a contemporary at Harvard Graduate School, one evening in New York took me to a cavernous apartment on Riverside Drive where I met the Cosers and Dennis Wrong. The Cosers were Europeans: Rose, Belgian; Lewis, a Berliner. Son of a banker, he had first emigrated to Paris and came to the US in the early forties. He contributed to Dwight Macdonald's *Politics* under the pen name of Louis Clair and was studying for a doctorate in sociology. Unlike most of my fellow students, he was an authentic intellectual with a passionate interest in larger questions. Rose was a European feminist who defied the sexual segregation of the forties and fifties well before her American sisters woke up. They became friends for life and later I was able to persuade Lew that Germany, or parts of it, had changed and that he should visit. He did so, and established ties to a newer generation of German intellectuals. I owe the Cosers a great deal. Steadfast in their friendship, they were early models of a rare continuity in sociology, bringing to it back to the general ideas of its founders, American and European. Dennis Wrong was a Canadian, his grandfather the founder of Canadian historiography (a Canadian Frederick Turner), his father the founder of Canada's diplomatic service and ambassador to Washington, where Dennis grew up. His family thought him destined for Oxford and a Canadian career, but instead Dennis went to Columbia and became a New York intellectual. Indeed, with his surgical lucidity and sense of the absurd, he became an honorary Jewish intellectual.

All of these experiences raised an insistent question: where did I fit in, or where did I wish to fit in—and to what end? Had I been more certain of my capacity to achieve an ordinarily rewarding academic career, I might have been able to face the question more directly and forcefully. Instead, my uncertainties cast a cloud over everything. On the other hand, I might with normality have lapsed into the higher conformity. Explicit and full political engagement was blocked by my half-conscious realization that there was little I wished to engage with. I saw enough of academic sociology to think it insufficient when not deficient. I was not consciously struggling with a Jewish identity and saw in an American one any number of problems, but lacked the experience to compare it with anything else. The persistent if vague conviction that Europe had some answers to my personal puzzles grew on me, but remained inchoate. I knew Europeans in the US, and European cultural artefacts, but did not yet know Europe.

Harvard, my teacher Talcott Parsons, and my fellow teaching assistants in general education came to my assistance. Perhaps the distance between Parsons's upbringing in a Midwestern Congregationalist pastor's home and Germany was as great as that between the Bronx and Central Europe, but it was a different path and he had traversed it. My own reading in German social thought followed early acquaintance with German film and novels. Meanwhile, apart from older and younger emigrants who had fled Nazism, Harvard was host to Germans from the new Federal Republic. I recollect meeting the young political scientist Wilhelm Hennis and the historian Gerhard Stoltenberg. Harvard canonized Max Weber and above all his analysis of Calvinism as driving force of capitalism, democracy and much of Western civilization. He was a European witness to our own nation's indispensability, an all the more impeccable one in view of his apparent ability, in his reports on his visits to the US, to contain his enthusiasm for our culture and society.

I had been struck in Weber's analysis of Protestantism by his critical treatment of the Lutheranism in which he was raised—he held that it had engendered German political quietism. Weber died in 1919, and it is impossible to say how he would have responded to the rise of Nazism and the Third Reich (ambivalently, I suspect). However, I saw that that might be a critical element in an understanding of modern Germany and its political fate.

That was hardly an original thought, but I combined it with another, which allowed me to smuggle Marxism into my work at Harvard without incurring unnecessary grief. Weber insisted that his work on Protestantism dealt with only one side of the complex relationship of belief to institutions and social processes, and that it was legitimate to examine the social roots of Protestantism as well. He accompanied that by a skeptical analysis of a reductionist version of historical materialism—and proceeded in his work on the sociology of religion to a refined portrayal of the "metaphysical needs of the human spirit" in their historical settings. My reading knowledge of German served me well, and I found in the Widener Library treasures no one had told me about. I read works of German social history and social thought written in the febrile years of the late Wilhelmenian empire, the Weimar Republic and then in exile. When C. Wright Mills published *White Collar* in 1952, I saw that he had used much of the modern German sociological analysis of the new stratification of a changed capitalism.

These readings reconnected me to my own past, to a boyhood spent in New York wondering about the agonies of Europe—which seemed quite immediate at the time even if my own circumstances and experiences were so different. They also opened a new world for me: the history of Christianity. I realized that the Reformation was not the great struggle for freedom that a shallow historical progressivism would deem it, but a much more ambiguous and complex process. I acquired more knowledge of Christianity than I had of Judaism, although given the impoverishment of my own Judaism, that wasn't very difficult. Indeed, reading about Christian views of the Old Testament I learned more of Judaism than I had done at home or in preparing for my Bar Mitzvah. I did not have much help from anyone on faculty, did not contact anyone at the Divinity School and found that there was no historian of the German Reformation on the Harvard faculty, although one of the professors of German literature was helpful about the culture of the period. Somehow I had obtained the name of a professor at Hamburg, wrote to him, and received a very cordial and helpful response with lots of bibliographical material. He was Fritz Fischer, to become famous years later for his book documenting the German military's role in initiating the First World War.

The faculty had to agree to proposals for doctoral dissertations and, with Parsons's backing, mine was accepted. Sam Stouffer, the senior social researcher, expressed regret that I was not going to do an empirical thesis, but I argued that the sixteenth century had indeed taken place. I phrased the project as an inquiry into the Reformation in the German cities. The idea was stimulated by my reading on Zwingli, the reformer of Zürich, where much of Calvinism in Geneva was anticipated. Zwingli had a symbolic interpretation of the Eucharist, a more Congregationalist conception of church organization; Luther's rendition of the Eucharist was more literal, his conception of the church more hierarchical. Were the cities which, in the early divisions of doctrine and practice in the Reformation, were receptive to Zwingli's doctrines, different in economic and social organization and outlook than the ones which accepted Luther's vision? If so, perhaps there were connections between historical base and religious superstructure undreamed of by Max Weber's more literal followers—but quite readily acknowledged by Weber himself.

Beyond all this was another question: to what extent had Lutheranism contributed to the rise of Nazism? Ernst Troeltsch, the historian of Christian social thought, had argued that Lutheranism inclined adherents to respect for constituted authority, indeed, to political quietism. About Calvinism, by contrast, there was always the actuality of defiance of constituted power, and a recourse to the ascendancy of belief, of conviction. In view of my profound curiosity about Nazism, these questions seemed a key to unlock the German past.

I gave the project an academically anodyne title, "A Study of The Reformation in the German Cities," and was awarded a Social Science Research Council Grant to go to Germany to work on it there. The award was timely. My teaching fellowship was ending. David Owen, the extremely kindly and supportive historian who chaired the general education program, evoked the possibility of my returning as faculty. Parsons had said that he wanted me to move on to the "next thing" without indicating what that might be. Without a doctorate, I would be consigned to academic limbo, to worthy but small colleges, or to interstitial and tenuous posts at larger and major institutions. All would insist on productivity, sooner rather than later. How suited was I to develop the discipline and resolution required to take advantage of the opportunities that were, clearly, open to me?

On the face of it I was well suited—or at least, well dressed. I had acquired some manners and social presence in my years at Harvard, conveyed a certain vivacity and above all knowingness. I did, indeed, know a lot—but did not quite believe it. Still, I had taken an invitation from Sam Beer to give a lecture in Social Science II and used it to write an article on Marx and Weber. If a great deal of it reproduced what I had read in Karl Löwith and others, at least it could be said I knew who to copy. It was original, in any event, to so thoroughly renounce the addiction to a science of social knowledge of the sociologists—and to take my distance from the rest of Harvard by refusing to portray our own society as the culmination of history. I sent the article off to *The British Journal of Sociology* and it was published there in 1953, with the happy consequence of interesting the London School of Economics in appointing me. I had published my first scholarly article in *The Journal of General Education*, edited at the University of Chicago. It was on general education in the social sciences, about which I had spoken at a symposium at Adams House. In the discussion, I took the view that an authentic social critic would have to be an underground man of some sort—a decidedly aberrant play on Dostoevsky. That pleased one of the participants, a French natural scientist teaching in the program who must have recalled the French discussions (some of which I had read) on the vocation of intellectuals. The rest of the public gathered for the event thought it a good conceit, and was pleased not to be bored. Could I, however, do more than provide high-quality entertainment?

I doubted it. There was an abyss between my public persona and my inner view of myself. I was aware of it, of course. Even if I now consider that I could have made more progress in analysis, I was unable to deceive myself into thinking that my difficulties came solely or primarily from the stresses of apprenticeship. To this inner uncertainty about my professional competence there was added a painful vacuum in the center of my life. I had friends, even close friends—but being with them made me somewhat aware of what I lacked, an intimate and warm familial setting. I would have liked to have had a close relationship with a woman, and Cambridge was full of attractive women. However, my own romantic episodes remained that, episodes which I could not or would not deepen, including a rapidly terminated engagement. I chose partners who were not easy to live with. There was much, however, that I had to experience before I could begin the inner alterations that made me capable of a somewhat fuller life.

5

Revision Germany

GERMANY had long been an imagined place for me when in 1951 I decided to go there, ostensibly to get materials for my thesis on the German Reformation in the early sixteenth century cities. Actually, I knew that all the books and journals I needed were in Harvard's library, which was much larger than any in Germany itself. That wasn't the point.

Studying first-hand with German church historians and theologians was a more plausible reason for going. But the reality was, my teaching fellowship expired in 1952 and going to Germany was a good deal more interesting than seeking employment in the academic no man's land reserved for those who had not yet completed their theses.

There were other motives. Germany in 1952 was for me a surrogate for all of Europe, its cultural depths, its social conflicts, its murderous politics. (Harvard's anthropologists and historians did not dwell on our own practice of genocide.) Behind the inquiry into Lutheranism there was my bewilderment at Nazism: none of the then-current explanations were very convincing, and I suspected that the term "totalitarianism" obscured as much as it illuminated. I had read Arendt, was immediately skeptical of her comparison of Nazism to Stalinism, thought that the strength of her work was its dense historical description. The one book that had struck me as authentic was Lederer's *State of the Masses*, Americanized echoes of which found its way into the writings of both C. Wright Mills and Richard Hofstadter. The ideas of a rootless American middle class in Mills and one driven by anxiety at status in Hofstadter were ways of uttering the familiar warning: it could happen here. It did, however, happen there, and that was what I wanted to learn about.

Something else was more fundamental. By the age of twenty-six I had experienced something of our own nation's high culture. In the separate versions of New York and New England. I had not read much of Henry James and what I did read left me rather unsatisfied: there was no obvious reason why his fictional Americans should have been so disturbed by their encounters with Europe, since James's Europe struck me as contrived, even bloodless. He was better at talking about passion than conveying it.

From Joyce, Mann, Stendhal (as earlier from Huxley and Wells), I had a sense of very different rhythms of life—an impression especially strong when I read in and about Freud. The Europeans I knew, even the ones who had come to the US rather young, were different, spoke in different accents even when they used American English. Our supposed cultural first cousins, the visiting British, reminded us of the breadth and depth of the Atlantic by casual nods. There were other ways of being in the world—going to Europe offered a chance to encounter these.

Inner conflicts are terrible, if inevitable—but sometimes desperate efforts to overcome them have unanticipated and positive consequences. Had I been more accepting of myself, more sure of eventual success, more content with what I had achieved, I might have gone to Europe not as an anxious pilgrim but as a rather complacent tourist. After all, we Americans were on the top of the world—or so we were told. I could not identify with any group or nation except a mythic fellowship of perpetual outsiders, and so was open to European virtues many Europeans doubted were worth very much. Not so long ago, I stood with Eric Hobsbawm on the steps of the Athenaeum, and he remarked that it was built at a time of unchallenged British supremacy. Napoleon had been beaten; much of the map of the world was painted British imperial red, and the embarrassment of losing part of North America in the circumstances was easy to bear. Britain in the early twenty-first century confronted a very different world. It has not taken quite as long for US power to run down, although some compulsively deny it. I cannot now say whether in 1952 I thought that it could not last—or, convinced of its permanence, sought resources to live in a way different than most of the colleagues and friends so determinedly seeking places for themselves within our imperial city. In any case, my misery sought different company.

One connection to the past is clear. Not only Williams and Harvard but New York and the Jewish Bronx had made me aware of Europe. I was an exceedingly unlikely striver for reconciliation with the narrow world of my boyhood—but that too was there, however unacknowledged.

I obtained a pre-doctoral fellowship from the Social Science Research Council and left for Europe in September. I left on the *Liberté*, once the *Bremen*. I might have had a shipboard romance and perhaps a more enduring connection to a very attractive graduate of Barnard on her way to a job with an American firm in Paris. She certainly seemed interested in me—but it was just that I could not believe. For much of the trip, I was astonished by the French crew and the French passengers: they seemed to have come right out of French films. The whistle on the boat train from Le Havre sounded, again, like something in cinema, and when I got to Paris, I went the next day to the Porte des Lilas to see if it resembled the film of that name: it did.

I walked the streets of Paris, especially the Latin Quarter, for two days and was pleased that my passive French was useful. A friendly bus conductor spoke to me in German and explained that he had been a prisoner of war. His tone suggested that some of his memories were positive and the episode was a demonstration that I would find more things on European earth than allowed by a narrow philosophy. I also recall my first meal in a French restaurant, the Restaurant Les Ministères in the Rue du Bac, with a waiter mixing the salad in sacerdotal seriousness. (The restaurant is still there, and I enjoy its unchanged menu still.) I did not have the inner freedom to linger in Paris, and took the train to Frankfurt. The station names recalled the First World War. A countryman in the first-class part of the carriage (I traveled in third) reminded me of the outcome of the Second. His peremptory arrogance echoed down the corridor, and at Metz he paid for food from a platform vendor by proffering coins he did not bother to count: "Take a handful of these." Again, the contours of the countryside, the crowded but friendly atmosphere of the compartment, the manners of the conductor, reminded me of film.

Late afternoon, we crossed into Germany. I had a small portable typewriter, and a German lady who took a seat after the border pointed to it. "Sie sind Journalist? Sie sind gekommen um fürchterliches ueber uns zu schreiben." "Are you a journalist? You must have come to write something terrible about us." The evidence of material reconstruction was everywhere evident from the window of the train—and it was soon to become clear that Germany had already rebuilt its psychic defenses against dealing with the past. Foreigners were deemed incapable of understanding what had happened since they had not experienced it themselves. Above all, they were incapable of seeing that what crimes had been committed were not the work of the German people, largely ignorant of what was done in their name, but of a handful of persons, many themselves misled. Moreover, charges of criminality were being laid at normal or in any event inevitable acts of war. It was victors' justice, not justice—and the Allies themselves had plenty to answer for: saturation bombing of cities, and acceptance by the Western allies especially of the brutal treatment and expulsion of the German populations of central and Eastern Europe. That in turn brought matters to the possibility of reconciliation in a common front against the Soviet Union and Communism. After all, Germany and its allies had anticipated the Cold War. Moreover, it was absurd to declare all of National Socialism morally illegitimate. There were effective reasons why millions, including Germany's elites, had supported it—and some of these reasons were even good.

Had I invested a Deutschmark for every occasion on which I heard this argument during my first year in Germany, I would has profited greatly from the German post-war recovery. It was uttered with varying degrees of honesty and hypocrisy, openness and deviousness—but constituted the dominant narrative of the population of the Federal Republic. The official story was of course very different, one of new beginning, repentance and democratic conviction—assiduously propagated by many who did not believe it in a German version of the old Yiddish phrase "for the Goyim" (a blatant untruth told to naïve outsiders). Most of my casual interlocutors identified me as an American, some as Jewish: I cannot recollect much difference in the arguments. Of course, discussion was much more complex in intellectual and learned circles—but not necessarily deeper or franker.

I talked with Theodor Adorno in Frankfurt, in the new building of the returned Institut für Sozialforschung. Adorno expressed surprise that I was going on to Marburg, which he described as "brown" but gave me the name of Wolfgang Abendroth, the political scientist there. His warning did not bother me overmuch: what was the point of going somewhere very different only to cultivate one's original sensibilities? I had seen enough of Germany in twenty-four hours to sense that its past was omnipresent.

From the train as it reached Marburg I saw its castle, site of the discussion between Luther and Zwingli in which the German and Swiss Protestants failed to form an ecclesiastical and political alliance, and so unwittingly secured the survival of much of German Catholicism. In the room in which they actually met there was an inscription from the historian Ranke on Luther's refusal to make any doctrinal concessions to the Swiss: "It wasn't well considered, it wasn't shrewd—but it was great."

Apparently, Israelis are not the only peoples with Masada complexes. The German one was well hidden, at the time, by the frenzy of reconstruction. As I walked up the medieval street to the center of town from the station, the hammering and sawing were very loud. Battered leather briefcases (from which lunch was frequently extracted) abounded—and everyone was in a hurry. Even those sitting in cafes were reading or talking with systematic intensity. Some of the Harvard sociologists were doubtful about the empirical rigor of my project to study the origins of German Protestantism, but this briefest of field observations suggested that Weber was right: delight in life wasn't a primary Protestant quality. Of course, there was the great post-war problem of which Mitscherlich wrote—guilt and loss, pervasive depression. That became evident to me only slowly, and perhaps my own inner grimness accounted for an unacknowledged identification with the Germans as losers.

It was not clear that they were entirely on the losing side. In my first weeks I moved from a student house to a bourgeois pension. People of all ages and conditions talked freely about the past to their foreign interlocutor, portraying themselves as victims. Many, however, were full of projects for the future. These were invariably individualized; some very important things were not. I recall my first visit to a German post office, which functioned as a disbursement agency for the German welfare state—and for the compensation paid to victims and survivors of all sorts. Proffering an extraordinary variety of documents, much of the German population stood regularly in line to collect benefits from the state.

That did not make the early Federal Republic a nation of Social Democrats. The war had destroyed a great many milieux, and attenuated the distinctiveness of others. Germany in 1952 was marked by the simultaneity of very different epochs, each forming the mindset of different generations and of different groups within the generations. The nation was internally divided to exquisite degrees. Those over thirty-four had at least been born in the Kaiser's state; those younger, in the Weimar Republic or the Third Reich. Quite apart from the experience of historical discontinuity, class, regional and religious origins shaped their sense of self and society. I was struck by the importance of church membership, which made of Catholics and Protestants bearers of explicitly different cultures. In the US Eisenhower at the time declared that every American ought to have a religion, and he did not care which one it was. In Germany, the churches were still confronting one another—and affiliation opened (or shut) doors.

I was no less struck by the intensity of the class and national passions evident in attitudes to the Social Democrats, who were in power in some of the states, but not the national government. The party was a proud community with a large sense of embattlement. Its antagonists, or many of them, denied it any legitimacy—as if Kaiser Wilhelm's description of the Social Democrats as "vaterlandslosen gesellen" ("unpatriotic bums") was still to be taken seriously. Repugnance for the Social Democrats had little to do with the Soviet occupation of part of the country (the Social Democrats under their first post-war leader, Kurt Schumacher, were unequivocal spokesmen for national unity and democracy) but instead expressed deeper attitudes to authority and hierarchy, with the Social Democrats cast in a role which would have bewildered many of their voters, as the party of the Enlightenment in Germany. The voters understood the party as an instrument of class solidarity, and Enlightenment was the concern of the party's intellectuals. Both groups of Social Democrats were proud of the party's parliamentarians having voted against the Nazis' Enabling Act of 1933, which legitimated the end of German democracy. Each was proud, too, of its record of resistance—precisely what many of its antagonists could not stomach.

These were matters underlying the ebb and flow of the daily political tides, the debate on rearmament, the conflict on the nature of the new Federal Republic. I learned something from the daily newspapers and the weeklies (*Der Spiegel* and *Die Zeit*), from essays in the monthlies, and from books. Mostly, I learned to read Germany by listening to the recollections of friends and watching the way they were writing the current chapters of their autobiographies. That of course presupposed that they were willing to serve, however informally, as tutors.

The first of these pedagogues was Wolfgang Abendroth. His life history could have come from one of those novels of central Europe I read as a boy in New York: educated as a lawyer, he had worked with Willy Brandt in a small party—Sozialistische Arbeiterpartei, or Social Workers' Party—which situated itself between the Communists and the Social Democrats in a vain effort to bring the two together to combat Nazism. After Hitler seized power, Abendroth went to Switzerland, returned to organize resistance to the Third Reich, was arrested and sent to prison. Fortunately, it was a Prussian prison, where the warders were Social Democrats and the other prisoners soon solicited legal advice from Dr. Abendroth. That was, compared with his next stop, in a penal company of the German army, an idyll.

His company, in a secular miracle, was not sent to clear mines on the Eastern Front but to the Greek island of Lemnos. There, the commanding officer informed him that he was of course a traitor but that since he was a doctor of laws, he was to be chief clerk to the garrison. In a café, he was approached by Greeks who asked him whether he spoke French and when he said that he did, they declared: "liberté, égalité, fraternité." Those were not words, Wolfgang replied, currently very popular in Germany. The Greek resistance had identified the penal company as made up of anti-Nazis. Somehow, Wolfgang arranged for a three-way bargain in which the resistance (the radical democratic front ELAS, with strong Communist participation), the local Archbishop, and the German garrison agreed on a truce. In 1944, Wolfgang and some of his comrades joined the Greek resistance when their unit evacuated the island.

They were subsequently captured by the British forces and imprisoned in Egypt. Wolfgang was identified by British intelligence, in the person of the German Social Democrat who in 1932 had edited the first publication of the Paris manuscripts by Marx, as a dangerous person and was not allowed to return to Germany until 1946.

There, he married and started a family, began to teach law at Leipzig in the Soviet occupation zone, but fled to the West when threatened with arrest for opposing the forced merger of the Communist and Social Democratic parties. The Social Democrats found him a teaching post at a new university in Wilhelmshaven—and fate and Nazi arrogance brought him to Marburg. The US occupation authorities thought that German democracy could flourish if the universities taught political science (the subject matter of which in Germany was generally divided between modern historians and scholars in public law and jurisprudence). The idea was absurd, but had some practical justifications—above all making room in the universities for those whose belief in democracy did not date from 8 May 1945. The US offered to finance a chair of political science in Marburg's law faculty, but the lawyers, predominantly unrepentant Nazis or arch nationalists, indignantly rejected the offer. The humanists in the philosophical faculty, who did not take the occupation as a moral affront, accepted the chair and assigned Abendroth third place on the list of candidates it proposed to the government of Hesse. The lawyers promptly wrote to their colleagues denouncing Abendroth as a "Communist" and they as promptly reassigned him to first place on the list. They could understand the lawyers' political errors in the recent past, but interference in the affairs of another faculty was impermissible. The drama did not end there. When Abendroth learned of his good fortune, he asked his friend the Social Democratic Minister President of Hesse to see that the formalities of appointment were rapidly completed. The Minister President responded that his bureaucrats were masters at taking their time, but Abendroth insisted. He rode the overnight train to the Hessian capital of Wiesbaden to take possession of the document naming him a public official for life—and rendered futile the urgent warning received by the state government some hours later from the Office for the Protection of the Constitution not to appoint him.

Abendroth did not disappoint his enemies. He was unremitting in his analysis of the return of Germany's elites to power, in his criticism of the Federal Republic's integration in the American bloc, his insistence on civil liberties and pluralism. His considerable legal skills were at the disposition of the unions, especially the powerful IG Metall, which united much of the manufacturing labor force. He placed himself very much to the left in the Social Democratic Party, where not the least of his functions was to say publicly what others only thought. He had at Marburg a circle of devoted students and some faculty friends, and he and his wife, Lisa, included me in the new German state's most left-wing and relaxed of salons.

Abendroth treated me as a younger colleague. He intuited that I was searching for ideas that went much beyond the possibilities delimited by American social science. His own Marxism was curiously bifurcated. On one hand, he thought that an authentic social revolution was possible—somehow, somewhere. Like Deutscher, he thought that the Soviet Union would grow out of Stalinism. On the other hand, he was extremely aware of the limitations of human character, and in his encounters with the Third Reich and German Communism he had certainly not benefited from the moral heroism of others. He understood the ordinariness of ordinary life, the constraints of ambition and circumstance. He also was able to laugh at pomposity and vanity, and derided the rigidity of much social convention. These were qualities I was later to find in Henri Lefebvre and Herbert Marcuse. They were all three artists, constructing a possible world out of familiar everyday materials. The humanity they imagined was far different from the one whose measure they daily took.

I referred to Abendroth's salon, but perhaps the German term *Kreis*, circle, is a better description. It included colleagues, students, and visitors. The colleagues came from across the disciplines and were chosen for personal amiability and political sympathy. Given the persistent rigidities of German academic culture, the freer spirits, who had good reason to think of the university as a gloomy museum run by authoritarian and not overly bright curators, were generally in the Federal Republic's political opposition anyhow. It was a moment in German history when laughter itself was more than a bit subversive. It certainly did more for the young than any number of lectures on democracy. The visitors were academics from other universities, politicians and trade unionists, unattached publicists and writers.

I was impressed by the students, many of them veterans of the war, quite a few with families. After what they had experienced, the veterans were not very reverent in their attitudes to university conventions. Their studies were for them a path to autonomy, occupational and civic. One was very reticent, very observant. He was the son of one of the senior army plotters of 1944, General von Tresckow, who committed suicide when the plot failed. The younger von Tresckow went from Marburg to work for the metal workers' union. Some of the students envisaged academic careers, but they did not let the primitive Malthusianism of the German university deform them, or deprive them of amusement at its foibles. For that, they had Abendroth's own great sense of the absurd to thank—as well as his insistence on treating others as equals.

None had been to the US, although two had been American prisoners of war. All had met Americans, but I was the first one (or so they said) who did not attempt to impart instruction on the significance of their experience. That was due less to purposive modesty on my part than to systematic bewilderment: the Germany I was now encountering was nothing at all like the rendering of it I had acquired in the US. For one thing, it was far more complex and divided. The notion of a nation split between aggressive Nazis and passive followers doing their will was a caricature. There had been gradations and stages of compliance, a quite large spectrum of motives, and ample access to knowledge of the regime's crimes as well as self-induced blindness about these. When persons were described me to as having been Nazis, they were usually also described as anything but fanatic and mostly as corrupt and cynical.

There were histories and memoirs of the Third Reich in the bookstores, but what I found endlessly fascinating and deeply instructive were the casual personal recollections of my new friends—and the attitudes they had to past and present. One had to join them in everyday life to benefit from their spontaneity, and for a time I found myself in an indeterminate zone between friendliness and intimacy. That ended when I met Nina.

Nina Apel (Gudrun Apel) was then an assistant in the Slavic

Seminar, had studied in Berlin and Bratislava in the Slovak satellite state. Her late father had owned a factory, which had been nationalized, in Quedlinburg, the old Saxonian city in which she grew up. He came from the skilled German working class and had been a prosperous entrepreneur. Her mother, living in the family house in Quedlinburg, was from the educated middle class; her uncles were a retired Reichsbahn president and an engineer—Nina's favorite uncle, since he had taken her for rides in locomotives—and a professor of pathology at Hannover Medical School. Another uncle was an admiral who took his own life in a British prison camp shortly after the 1945 capitulation. Nina had two sisters, one a music teacher married to an architect and living on the border with Luxembourg in Bitburg, the other a physician working at the Institute for Tropical Medicine in Hamburg. Her brother, returned recently from six years of captivity in the Soviet Union, was studying architecture in Hannover, thanks to the generosity of the medical professor.

It was not a family which expected, seven years after the end of the Third Reich, to have a Jewish member. Nina insisted that not too far back in the ancestral tree, there was a Jewish branch—not at all uncommon in Germany. I was accepted with a certain degree of awkward friendliness, with my American identity as much of a puzzle to the family as my being Jewish. The uncles were unintentionally entertaining. We called on the retired railway president in his cavernous apartment in Charlottenburg, not far from the Technical University where he had taught. He addressed me as Herr Doktor, anticipating Harvard somewhat, possibly because he could not envisage his niece, herself already with a doctorate, in the company of a mere aspirant to the title. On one thing he was quite insistent, and delighted to enlighten me: the use of diesel and electricity for railroad traction, he thought, was limited. "Herr Doktor, es bleibt bei Dampf." ("Doctor, steam will survive.") The pathologist was a witness to the oddities of the Italians. He had taken a vacation in Italy, parked his Mercedes while having lunch, and then discovered that his tires had been cut—very possibly by bored ex-partisans. "Herr Doktor, sowas könnte bei Uns nicht passieren." ("Doctor, that could not happen in Germany.") He was right; there weren't any anti-Nazi partisans around.

The family members of Nina's generation were decidedly critical, without having very explicit political views. Her brother was scathingly indignant, a couple of years later, when he was asked to rejoin the German air force. The brother-in-law's war stories were mainly of the systematic corruption of the regime's fervent defenders. The sisters, with children and professional jobs, concentrated on the difficulties of daily life (easing as post-war privation ended)—and on the foibles of friends and neighbors.

Clearly, being with Nina gave me a way into German culture and society. That wasn't, however, the entire story or even the main one. Nina was encouraging and supporting, even (at the beginning) somewhat maternal or sisterly. With her, I found it much easier to overcome my residual homesickness (larger than I admitted to myself), not to feel isolated and lonely, to get on with my career despite my inner doubts. She introduced me to a more domestic and definitely lighter side of European culture. Her friends in Marburg included a charming family, economically distressed nobility—and some of the *grandes dames* hard at work restoring what could be restored of bourgeois society.

Nina and I traveled to Berlin for my first visit to the city. The descent into Tempelhof Airport at eye level with the neighboring apartment houses was right out of the newsreels. There was no wall—Soviet military patrols politely inspected the elevated railway and subway trains to the west at the last stops in their sector looking for Soviet deserters. We went to the cinema in East Berlin and saw a film about West Germany entirely unsubtle in its satire. It included scenes of American GIs making life very comfortable for imprisoned German generals as they planned another attack on the USSR. (Years later, I learned that when Konrad Adenauer was planning the new West German army, the US obliged by allowing Field Marshall Kesselring, the imprisoned Nazi commander in Italy, to visit with the Chancellor.)

East Berlin—with slogans abounding on placards, a profusion of uniforms, grimly drab shops and no visible concessions to the lightness of being (even in the cafés people seemed depressed and wary) —resembled a Hollywood image of a Communist capital.

Years later, on visits to East Berlin and other places in Communist Germany, I spoke with academics, church persons, intellectuals, and party officials, and caught glimpses of a much more complicated situation. The regime's unique contribution to Marxist political economy was the gigantic hidden public works project that was the Ministry of State Security's network of informers. The anxiety of the Stalinists was justified: when the end came it became clear how provisional and shallow the obsessively enforced consensus that substituted for politics in Communist Germany was.

Prosperity had not yet come to West Berlin, but much of the wartime rubble was gone. Still, there was something ominous in the atmosphere, as if the city's ghosts could emerge at any moment. The population was busy — and brusque. They had, after all, seen quite a lot.

In February 1953, I visited the United Kingdom for the first time, meeting colleagues at the London School of Economics and making a day trip to Oxford to visit Nuffield College.

London was busy differently than New York, the people less harassed, briefly and restrainedly voluble, as if to emphasize their self-containment. I grasped that there was much that I did not grasp. When later I lived in the country, that was still true, but for long stretches of time I resigned myself to it rather than repeatedly running into the stone wall of "Englishness." My initial impression of British academic life was that most persons were at great pains to appear understated and unimpressed with much else.

I did not, then, have the desire or the means to live well I later developed, but ordinary British asceticism was striking, especially in the light of Germany's intensifying drive for prosperity. What I did not know was that there was a line across (or, rather above) which asceticism ceased. Like much else in the country, it was not well marked — or marked at all. Years later, visiting the British Treasury, I noticed that there were no names on the doors of the senior officials: if you did not know who was behind the door, you probably did not belong in the building in the first place.

Perhaps it was no wonder that during my visit I came down with flu — perhaps a way of indicating affinity with my hosts after all. When I recovered and was walking down The Strand, I read the headline on a newspaper seller's placard: "Stalin — A Stroke." History was about to change and I wondered even more about situating myself in it. The late great leader and teacher of all progressive mankind died as I was in the Berkshire countryside, recuperating at a pleasant inn recommended to me by the Dicks family. Dr. Dicks was an analyst who had worked on psycho-cultural problems and I'd met him when he and his wife visited the Russian Research Center at Harvard. He predicted deep mourning and distress in Russia, since he thought that Stalin's authoritarianism and brutality was less Leninist than Russian. The history of the country since 1953 hasn't proved him wrong.

I would have liked to have dug beneath history's surface in that way. I'd read widely and occasionally deeply in the literature on culture and personality, and of course in Freud. I certainly intuited that the national differences I was now experiencing at first hand had a good deal to do with familial structures and child raising. I distrusted my own capacity to do more with the materials, even as in my own life I seemed to be acting out a good deal of inner conflict. Certainly, leaving the US (and then remaining abroad for so long) not only a positive adventure but a flight. Choosing to live in Britain after feeling the remoteness of its people wasn't accidental. In a land of emotional reserve, perhaps no one would force me to deal with my own feelings of permanent hurt and insecurity.

That is what I now think. Then, I had no such clarity. Psychologically, I was flying blind.

After my struggle to understand Germany, it would have been wise to return to the US to assimilate what I had learned. I did not give myself any respite. My colleagues and friends in the US were getting on with their careers, enjoying the new ethnic openness of the nation (true whatever their origin, since none profited more from the integration of American Catholics and Jews than those who allowed or invited us in), and above all profiting in ways open and subtle from participating in the rise of American power. I could not complain on that score, my fellowship dollars having allowed me to buy my first car—a Volkswagen Beetle of extremely uncertain age but commendable reliability.

My situation of relative prosperity was marred: the fellowship money was running out and I thought of the next year with considerable apprehension.

I'd been so absorbed by learning about Germany that I had not pursued my thesis work in any sustained way. Part of the trouble was perfectionism—the feeling that I had to master late medieval and Reformation history, church history and theology before writing a word. Part of it was distrust in my abilities, whatever the learning I acquired to fend off doubt.

Another part was the recklessness of youth about time. There was a compensation, even if has taken me a lifetime to appreciate it: I was experiencing Europe in a way few born in the US had done. It was my grand tour.

It was also a tour of the past. The early radical democratic critics of the Federal Republic, some liberal, some socialist, some social Christian, deplored its "restoration" of habits and institutions dominant before 1945. They all knew about the French Revolution and many regretted that Germany had not had its own early modern settlement of accounts with the Ancient Regime. However, the French Revolution also taught us that historical continuities are sometimes strongest when most opposed. I was incapable of generalizing about recent German history, but it was clear to me that there was no need to restore what never had been set aside. The German university of 1952 was far closer to the institution of 1913 than today's universities are to those of 1952.

My direct contact with German sociology began in a small house in the old part of the city, a bit uphill from the Elisabeth Church. There, the sociologists were housed. The senior figure was Graf (Count) zu Solms, who was interested in the forms of sociability.

He was a gentleman of the old school, at ease with himself and free of pretense and pomposity, who freely admitted that there was much in the world he did not understand. His message to his students was that if they learned a bit each day, they would have accomplished a very great deal. His attitude to the United States was like that of many older and cultivated Germans: he could not fathom how the society held together. Unlike them, however, he did not conclude that Europe was superior; it was simply different. Zu Solms came from a tradition of German sociology I knew from texts and history books, one concerned with human nature and its variability. He'd returned from service as an officer in the war and had about him that air of casualness of many German veterans: nothing now in their lives could equal the anguish of the years 1939 to 1945, and so they took things as they came.

Zu Solms's assistant was from a very modest social milieu in the Saarland, had been in France during the war as a soldier, knew the language and the country well, and made it clear that French attitudes during the occupation had been quite nuanced. His name was Karl-Heinz Paehler, and despite our dissimilarities of experience (he was a skeptical Catholic) we recognized that we had a bond. In our own societies, each of us was seeking upward mobility through a university career. Karl-Heinz had never been in the US, but his grasp of my situation followed from the acute powers of social observation he brought to the Marburg scene. There, discussions of the mission of the university were dutiful; gossip about the rector's wife using the official Mercedes for shopping trips was passionate.

University society was a microcosm of German bourgeois existence, the better preserved for its insulation from the frenzied economic revival around it. The retention of old forms of hierarchy in academic organization had its counterpart in the informal but rigidly delineated patterns of sociability in the town, professorial wives their relentless enforcers. Lisa Abendroth, Wolfgang's wife, was if anything more outspokenly in favor of a social revolution than he. It did not prevent her from remarking, from time to time, that this or that younger academic might find it difficult to make a career since his wife was so socially out of place. Nina came from a secure bourgeois background and had an amused eye for the foibles of this side of Marburg, as well as a good deal of empathy for its more marginal characters. Germany had lost the war, the US had won it—but the community in Cambridge was clearly more open, less stuffy, than its Marburg counterpart.

I went to one scholarly meeting, the annual conference of the German Sociological Association, held in Weinheim on the Bergstrasse, an old town of considerable charm. It greeted the assembled scholars with a banner over the main street, not something one would have seen in American cities. German sociology emerged from the war reduced in numbers, divided into schools, and more than a bit paralyzed by the tasks of explaining a bitter past and a perplexing future. An older generation of survivors had not yet brought a younger one into chairs. One of the exceptions, the extremely intelligent Helmut Schelsky, made a rather rapid transition from his earlier enthusiasm for the Third Reich, buttressed with thoughts of a new beginning for humanity, to an entirely realistic description of a sobered society. The Frankfurt School sociologists had returned and were politely received but resolutely ignored. Their earlier analyses of authoritarianism were still disturbing and their new probing of German society threatening in a different way: it demonstrated the banality of much that was depicted as a new moral order. René König returned from exile to Cologne and portrayed a world without lyricism.

I was bewildered by the rapid alternation of post-war German social thought between large meta-historical constructions and ordinary social observation. Later, as the newer generation of sociologists (Dahrendorf, von Friedeburg, Habermas) struggled with their legacy, I read their ancestors and was able to understand them. At Weinheim, matters remained a blur.

One thing was constant: the German penchant for thoroughness. I was listening to a paper on the occupational preferences of Berlin youth. The author began with the idea of a vocation and was at its Biblical origins when a friendly colleague suggested we go out for coffee. I said that I wanted to hear his findings and the (young) German was reassuring: "Don't worry; by the time we return he will have only reached Aquinas." He was entirely correct.

I also visited Bonn to meet with one of the founders of the Social Market Economy, that fusion of state steering with the market which was consensual in the early Federal Republic. I'd known Alfred Müller-Armack's work on Weber and the question of religion and capitalism, but did not know that he was in the Adenauer government as a state secretary in the Economics Ministry. It was extremely generous of him to take time to receive an unintroduced American graduate student. No one at Harvard had suggested that I read his book, and like much else that I found in the Widener Library, its pages were uncut when I took the volume off the shelf.

I also called on the Social Democratic Party, and was received by the International Secretary himself. Close to Willy Brandt, he later was ambassador to India. I remember an unpretentious younger nobleman curious about what remained of American progressivism. I was dimly aware of what, later, struck me as a large benefit of my years in Europe: a truer view of my own country.

In the spring of 1953 I left Marburg to take courses at Heidelberg. I found a room in a pleasant house on what had been a country road above the castle. The Protestant theologians and church historians at Heidelberg seemed less remote than those at Marburg. I attended a course on ethics with Edmund Schlink, whose affiliation with the Confessional Church had kept him out of the academy until the end of the Third Reich.

Schlink was presumably the prototype of the professor of philosophy and father of the uncertain hero of *The Reader*, the novel by Schlink's son, Bernhard. The philosopher in the book was decidedly more abstracted than the theologian in the classroom, who conveyed ironic sympathy for the human condition, along with the impression that it would be well not to take even theology as the ultimate ratio of that condition. Another person on that faculty who impressed me with his realism was the Luther scholar Heinrich Bornkamm. He had not been an opponent of the Nazis, expressed relief that the nightmare was over, and seemed intent on demonstrating that ordinariness had its advantages.

Of all the theologians and church historians I met, I was most impressed by the Jesuit Joseph Lortz. I'd read his book on the Reformation and Counter-Reformation at Harvard, with its view that they were inseparable parts of a larger reform process (and that Luther could not be understood as a rebel: he was too Catholic). Lortz taught at Mainz in an institute for European history funded by the French occupants of the city. When I called to ask whether I could attend his weekly seminar, he was visibly consternated. "You've read my book on the Reformation," he asked. "Have you read anything else I've written?"

I grasped his unease. "Father Lortz, do you mean, do I know that you were sympathetic to the Nazis? Yes." That cleared the air and he and I became friends. He told me a lot about the sensibilities of the Catholics in modern Germany, and implied by his reticence reservations never directly uttered about the structure and ethos of the modern Church.

He'd been born and raised in Luxembourg (his brother had become a French citizen) and he had a deep ambivalence about Europe's inner borders. As I recollect, his pro-Nazi writings bespoke a German mission in Europe, and he was now attached to a European project in Germany. There was a deep sadness in him which I now suppose was in large measure disappointment at the course taken by twentieth-century history. He expressed distant curiosity about the United States, which was clearly for him a very foreign culture. There remains (and his frankness about the past is part of it) the memory of someone both encased in and identified with his own history, anguished about large parts of it, unable and unwilling to break out and start anew. In his seminar, he exhibited tired patience with the students: they could never match his experience, since it was unique—and without it, all they had were texts very difficult to call to life.

The Catholic figure of contrast with Lortz was Eugen Kogon, who had been a political prisoner in Buchenwald, was co-editor of a journal (*Frankfurter Hefte*) very critical of the early Federal Republic's compromises with the past, and had written a remarkable book on the concentration camps, *Der SS-Staat*. Kogon radiated hope and humor. It was more than his delight at having survived (many survivors had survivor guilt and in a minor way, I had some myself when thinking about European Jewry and my family's escape). He had an inner serenity which conveyed indifference to the passing vagaries of life, and a sense of pedagogic mission which enabled him to ignore trivia. Withal, he was engagingly direct, humanly encouraging.

Kogon had a television program and was a strenuous participant in the Federal Republic's public debates: he argued that Germany had not won an empire but lost a war and a very great deal beside. I was impressed with the way in which debates entailing a good deal of national self-criticism, which in the US were limited to the educated elite, had a somewhat wider public in Germany, and included some of the politicians. Years later, the German student movement had a slogan: "*Bild* Lesen Macht Dumm." *Bild* was the mass circulation daily of the Springer chain, which read as if it had been written as illustrative material for the Frankfurt School's texts on authoritarianism and mass culture. In the Germany of 1952-1953, this parallel stream of philistinism, pseudo-information, and primitivism was not yet as broad or unashamedly open as it became with prosperity and Germany's political integration in the Western alliance.

In the spring, there was an election—and Germany's rearmament was an issue. The Social Democrats opposed it because it would prolong, indefinitely, the division of the country. A small formation called the German People's Party took the same position and was even more explicit in calling for negotiations with the USSR on the basis of the Stalin note of 1952, in which he proposed the military and political neutralization of Germany and the withdrawal of all occupation forces. It was headed by a Protestant opponent of Nazism, Gustav Heinemann, who had resigned from Adenauer's government when he learned that the Chancellor had secretly negotiated German rearmament with the allies. His party got but one and one-half percent of the vote, even if its younger supporters included Erhard Eppler, Jürgen Habermas, and Johannes Rau, all major figures in the later years of the Federal Republic. Heinemann himself became the first Social Democratic president of the German Federal Republic, in 1969, and I much admired his answer to an interviewer's question when he was elected: "Herr Heinemann, it is said that you do not love the state." He replied, "I love my wife; that is quite enough." I heard Heinemann speak in Marburg's town square, anticipating many of the arguments used later to justify the German *Ostpolitik*.

What had I learned in my year in Germany? The encounter with the Nazi legacy certainly made it impossible for me to trade for long in historical simplifications. I did succumb in subsequent years to the denigration of political adversaries, to the attribution to them of the worst possible motives—whilst I and my friends claimed all the moral nobility in the world. Whenever I did so, however, I was shortly called to account by an inner voice which reminded me not least of the surprised perplexities of that year.

I also learned something of the processes of historical accumulation, which in the end gave me a far deeper reading of society than the one I had acquired at Williams and Harvard. I did not get to Germany in what was termed "the year zero" (1945) and by the time I arrived, several new starts had been tried and some discarded. Hesitantly and unclearly, I began to realize that there are no total new beginnings in history—just the churning of old elements in an often-repaired centrifuge. Persons were formed by their antecedents, even though they had greatly different degrees of inner clarity about it. There, my interest in the German churches put me on the right path. Political structures change far faster than the cultural beliefs and rituals passed directly, one generation to another. Again, my appreciation of what I learned was not very large—but the progressivism I had brought with me to Europe could not ever again function as an unquestioned item of personal faith. There was a final lesson, and I owe much of it to Nina: character counted when all else did not—and persons with good characters, however difficult to define, had good chances of moral survival in catastrophe. They had even better chances in normal times, whatever these might be.

However unclear these intellectual gains were (many were subliminal, to move slowly to the forefront of my awareness over the years), they were as a brilliant burst of light compared with the troubled darkness that enveloped my sense of self. I could not dwell in any sustained way on my inner development, and compensated for my persistent inner unease by strained pursuit of the next thing—whatever it might be. It was a psychological parody of the idea of progress—and no doubt accounted for a large part of the social imagery implicit in my political thought. Someday, somehow, somewhere, there would be a great liberation. In the meantime, ceaseless personal activity would bring me closer to inner repose—or at least, to a plateau from which I could confidently storm new heights. Having struggled in Germany, I allowed myself no respite—and so moved on to London.

6

London, Part I

AFTER the considerable inner strain of living in Germany, it would have been sensible to return to the United States. My thesis was not completed and I could not have obtained a major university post, but I could have installed myself in a college to decide what kind of future I wanted. That would have been not only too reasonable but too comfortable for someone who regarded living with inner and outer danger as unavoidable. My response to a constant sense of threat was to convert inner fantasy into reality—by putting myself in difficult situations. I did not understand why I did this, and conducted my life in frenzied bouts of activity alternating with long periods of depressed passivity.

Great Britain occupied my imagination for many years before I ever visited it. In novels by Huxley and Wells, the ways the characters comported themselves fascinated me: they did things by indirection, unlike American literary characters who were so unmitigatedly forceful. The London I knew from reading was unlike the New York of Dos Passos or Thomas Wolfe, but no less exciting. I'd read Dickens and a fair amount of history, and knew about things such as the Peasants' revolt of 1382, the English Revolution, and Chartism. Harold Laski, John Strachey, and Roger H. Tawney were intellectual heroes. I admired the early Orwell, when he was the London correspondent of *Partisan Review* before his somewhat involuntary transformation into supreme ideologue of the Cold War. My strong interest in Great Britain was a direct derivative of my wish to ascend within American culture. I knew that our cultural elites regarded Great Britain as distant homeland and, more ambivalently, model. It was only much later that I realized that our

English-descended rulers did not allow ancestral piety to influence them: they were at least as ruthless with the United Kingdom as with any other nation.

British films had an effect. I was drawn to something very defined in the social world they depicted, by contrast with the unclear boundaries of American life. There seemed to be a time and place for everything and everyone. The class contradictions of British life did not leave me unmoved. I read Strachey and enjoyed Woodhouse, admired British anti-fascism, appreciated the ironies of the Hitchcock political films, and enjoyed the absurd pathos of the wartime films aimed at the US—like *Mrs. Miniver*. I was not, in short, very discerning about what awaited me in the United Kingdom.

I did not know many people from the United Kingdom, even at Harvard, and so saw Great Britain as reflected (or distorted) in literature—and in the recollections of Americans who had been there. There was, at Harvard, a great deal of talk about Great Britain, the British universities (above all Cambridge and Oxford), and British books. The Harvardians did not see themselves as colonials, but I detected a somewhat restive feeling that whatever had happened, perhaps we were still obliged to look from our flourishing province to Great Britain as metropolis. Many of Harvard's economists were Keynesians; the political philosophers discussed Locke and Mill rather than Rousseau and Marx, and Henry James was (at least for dissertation purposes) the English Department's favorite novelist. There was some discussion of Popper's 1945 book, *The Open Society and Its Enemies*, but it was a text sometimes referred to and not often read.

Isaiah Berlin visited Harvard and was a sought-after dinner guest—as much for his great performance as a raconteur as for his reassuringly resolute defense of the liberal traditions of the English-speaking world. Popper visited in the academic year 1951-1952 but did not make a very convincing personal impression on Harvard's opinion-makers. It was only in 1952 that Berlin published his Oxford Inaugural lecture, "Two Concepts of Liberty," but some had read his essays before that and knew of his interesting combination of exacting analytical reasoning and passionate defense of a classical idea of freedom.

Great Britain between 1947 and 1952 liberated India (if amidst terrible bloodshed), struggled elsewhere to retain imperial control, greatly extended its own welfare state, questioned its own classbound cultural conventions, and endured the traumas of loss of economic and political power. Much of that was not discussed at Harvard, and when our social scientists referred to "modernization" only the most schematic images of modern British history were invoked. Harvard's Britain was largely an ideal country, in the minds of those who had studied there, passed through or worked with the British during the war. These were the persons who decidedly enjoyed our own imperial reach. Sam Beer went from New Deal Michigan with its labor struggles to Oxford before the war: Orwell's Britain was real to him.

I went to Great Britain, in fact, in search of validation. Ambitious to join our own society at its top, I reckoned that any kind of success there could easily be converted into its American equivalent, Britain's academic currency remaining strong despite the fall of the pound. Teaching at the London School of Economics would make a fine line in my curriculum vitae. As a reader of *Partisan Review* and an aspirant to the New York intellectuals, I thought that these universal thinkers would be impressed by my crossing the Channel as well as the Atlantic. About these advantages, I was right.

The actual story of my appointment to the London School is prosaic. In my last Harvard year, the LSE sociologists began to publish a *British Journal of Sociology*.

I was much impressed by a review of Talcott Parsons's *The Social System* by an LSE sociologist, Donald Macrae, who made it clear with brutal elegance that he did not think that Parsons had succeeded in developing a convincing analysis of society. The words of his review stick in my mind: "Either Professor Parsons is in possession of some arcane truth I do not understand, or he has convinced himself of a vast tautology." Macrae appealed to my own rebelliousness, and did so with all the authority of what I thought of as an older and wiser world. Parsons, I knew, had studied for a year at the LSE before going on to Germany to obtain a Heidelberg doctorate: what better way to both confound him and impress him than by joining his critics at his *alma mater*? My first step was to submit an article: the text of the talk on Marx and Weber I had given to Social Sciences Two. In February 1953 I visited London from Marburg. Macrae and the others told me that there might be a post available in their department that fall. In due course, it was advertised in the old *Times of London* and I applied.

The invitation to come to London for an interview reached me when Nina and I stopped in Paris on our return from a splendid trip to Burgundy. French cities such as Dijon and Auxerre, the churches and old buildings, above all the beauty of the countryside, a work of art rather than of nature, made us feel as if we had entered a *Book of Hours* come to life. The United Kingdom and London, by contrast, struck me as monotone, even depressing. Later, living there, I saw that France for many of the British was the imagined embodiment of all the *joie de vivre* they did not allow themselves.

Still later, when I lived in Strasbourg myself for two depressed years, the charms of Alsace and France did nothing to help me out of misery. The Kingdom of Heaven is within you, says the Gospel—but so is the Kingdom of Hell.

The interview went well and I was offered an assistant lectureship at 500 pounds a year, rather less than I had earned as a Harvard teaching fellow. Macrae, malice in a Scots accent, later told me that I had been foolish not to insist on immediate appointment as a full lecturer, or at least on a higher salary.

He sensed my own inner hesitation and lack of self-esteem—the source of my desperate drive to scale whichever heights I feared were too high for me.

Nina accompanied me to London, having obtained a grant from the British Council. We found a grim furnished apartment in West Hampstead, on a street that would have been flattered to be termed nondescript. We did not have much money, but we had some and there were obvious ways in which I could have earned more. Being stuck at the bottom of the British middle class income scale, with a steep road ahead to climb out of it, struck me as regrettable, or worse—but as inevitable, or foreordained. My sense of deprivation was heightened by the knowledge that even in a beginning academic post in the US, I would have been economically much better off. I did not decide to make the best of it for a year or two and return, but persisted, as if to see what, in the end, would happen.

I had a sense of purpose both overly developed and constantly shrunken.

At the LSE itself, new junior teachers were politely welcomed, given to understand that they were fortunate to have joined so distinguished a place, and instructed implicitly that they had better show themselves worthy of their good fortune if they wished to be noticed. The assistant lecturer grade was the beginning one, and normally, after three or four years, promotion to lecturer followed. That was a career grade, with the British equivalent of tenure (a seven-year appointment, renewable until retirement, and invariably renewed in practice). Any number of criteria, I quickly learned, could be used to justify promotion. A doctorate or a book wasn't then required, although some evidence of scholarly competence clearly was. Two or three plausible articles would do. Presence had a good deal to do with it, as well as the ability to converse knowingly, and so did tact—understood as the avoidance of standing out too markedly. One's ability as a teacher was also considered, although no one in the United Kingdom at the time thought of asking students to evaluate their teachers—the fact that this was done in the US was held to be a less than engaging American oddity— but somehow, word about one's teaching capacity got out, which was characteristic of the entire process. It was rather like joining a club—or the trial in Lewis Carroll's *Alice in Wonderland* (Carroll taught at Cambridge and there were traces of its culture in his fictional universe). Above all, it was not a matter to be discussed between candidates for tenure and their senior colleagues—although much spoken of among the candidates and their friends.

To survive, let alone thrive, in this system one had to master its silent language. It wasn't set out in grammars but rather in a code of conventions and conduct communicated in families and schools. It rested on inflexions of speech, significant silences, gestures, a system of understanding designed to be unintelligible to those outside it—including Britons of the other social classes. They had their own codes, as one could discover in any grocery shop. I was truly in a foreign country.

Fortunately, I rapidly acquired several guides. The first was Ernest Gellner, a colleague returned from a year at Harvard. Ernest was in the sociology department as a social philosopher. He'd come with his family from Prague in 1939, served in the Czech Brigade attached to the British army, and studied at Balliol College. His first words to me, after remarking that he'd heard about me at Harvard from mutual friends, were about our students. "The best boy in every Sixth Form goes to Balliol: we get his audience." Ernest, offended by the pretentiousness of British philosophy, later turned to anthropology and studied a village in the Atlas Mountains of Morocco. I recall his amusement at a very serious American colleague who had distributed a questionnaire in the village, in French—so that when the answers came, he could not tell whether the villagers had understood his question about the school teacher to refer to the Gallicized schoolmaster or the religious Imam. What struck me at first was Ernest's enormously refined sense of irony—but that was followed by my realization that he had an equally large sense of empathy. Decades later, with a global reputation as comparativist and Islamist, he went to Cambridge as professor of social anthropology. His death of a heart attack at the Prague airport (he taught at the Central European University) had its own pathos. Ernest was an anthropologist *avant la lettre*, regarding the British, and especially the English, as a tribe—and since he was prepared not to be totally at home anywhere, was everywhere sovereign and at his ease.

When on a skiing holiday, he met Susan, whom he later married. He invited her go to Morocco with him, on rather short acquaintance, and she accepted. Susan's family, rather conventional on the surface but with a good deal of humor about it, had their own way of dealing with the situation. "But I do not see," her mother said, "what use she will be to you out there." He was an acute, even angry, critic of the absurd claim of the British academics that their systematic denial of imagination would in the end prove to be the most enduring chapter in the history of human thought. No one was more derisive about much of American culture—or more appreciative of the seriousness of our political and social thinkers. He came closer than anyone I knew to seeing humans and societies as they were. He was a loyal friend and an unfailingly frank counselor, and enriched our lives in many ways.

His friendship was all the more important on account of the less sublime aspects of life in our department. Donald Macrae was brilliant and learned, but rarely wrote and converted his disappointment about his own career into bitter sallies at others'.

Perhaps he had made his own what I later experienced at Oxford—the view that a man under forty should be too modest to write a book and one over forty too proud to need to do so. Donald was seconded in his generalized hostility by another colleague from Oxford, Julius Gould. Julius voiced an obsessive sort of anti-Communism: one would have thought Britain was neutral and not in NATO and that the small and battered British Communist Party at least as large as the French one. Something, however, held Julius back from defining himself (as some did) by unmitigated admiration for the United States. He liked the idea of a culture which respected elites, and seemed nonplussed by American energy and openness. I cannot now describe Donald and Julius as primarily intriguers, since they were so transparent. Effective intriguers do not proclaim their plans every afternoon at tea.

The senior members of the department were interestingly unalike. Morris Ginsberg came from the eastern European Jewish immigration, had been a sergeant in the First World War, and was very attached to the social evolutionary perspective of his teacher, Leonard Hobhouse. He had British reserve and irony and was Jewish in his passion for ideas which placed liberal Britain at the apex of human development. His younger colleague, David Glass, was a demographer with his own Jewish passion for utopia and a correspondingly large, indeed huge, charge of disappointment at the failure of every human institution, social movement or political party to advance unhesitatingly toward it. David carried into the fifties the ideas of progress of the Transatlantic left of the thirties—including its ambivalence about the Soviet Union. He had many friends in the US, but the Cold War with its McCarthyism convinced him that the party of progress in our nation had been sentenced to inner exile for the indefinite future. The most detached and elegant of the professors was T.H. Marshall, from the family of Cambridge gentry which had given us the father of welfare economics. He exuded critical skepticism, but once one came to know him, his own familial disdain for Olde England and its complacent prejudices stood out. Tom's book *Citizenship and Social Class* was a masterly charter statement of a democratic social policy. He had a rather unique attitude to the US, unlike Ginsberg's determination to ignore it and Glass's bitter criticism of it—we were there, he was here and quite at home in Britain and Europe (he later left to become assistant director of UNESCO for the social sciences). The US was different, and he was not particularly bothered by it, being firm in his own place. Perhaps the classical basis of the educated Britons of his generation helped. They did not think of denouncing Rome, since they thought it evident that they lived in Athens.

I shared an office with David Lockwood, who had just completed his study of the British white-collar class, *The Black-Coated Worker*. David appeared to match the profile of a taciturn Yorkshireman, but showed his disdain for fixed sociological categories by marrying a lively American graduate student, Judith Davidoff.

He was friendly with another student, Ralf Dahrendorf, who was completing a thesis with Marshall after studying with Schelsky in Hamburg. It was at the LSE that Ralf wrote a paper that caused a stir in Germany ("Gibt Es Noch Soziale Klassen?" — "Do Social Classes Still Exist?") and where he acquired the distance that enabled him later to situate modern German politics in its social historical context. I recall sitting with him when the Guyana independence leaders Forbes Burnham and Cheddi Jagan, removed from government by the British, spoke (to considerable enthusiasm) at the LSE. What was so impressive about them, Ralf said, was how little routinized they were. He later sought an un-routinized political career in Germany but stumbled when he became deputy foreign minister. When Brandt worked to achieve a modicum of co-existence with the other German state and its Soviet sponsor, a policy Ralf had strenuously advocated, he thought that the opposition of the German Cold War party made the project impossible. He left Bonn for Bruxelles and the European Commission and eventually became director of the LSE. I thought of Ralf as moving perpetually but with increasing discretion between routine and its opposite. The difficulty for all of us, of course, is to know just what that opposite might be. Ralf has settled in the UK, speaks for the Liberal Democrats in the House of Lords, and remains what he was to begin with — a cosmopolitan son of Germany's most British city, Hamburg.

A colleague I greatly admired was Tom Bottomore. He attended the Nottingham grammar school which claimed D.H. Lawrence as an alumnus. He had the illusion-less clarity of the British provinces — where the language of fact and the rhetoric of criticism were one. He abjured the small spaces which some of our colleagues preferred to inhabit. He'd been in the British army in India, had done a study of higher civil servants in France (a solid contribution to the discussion of the new class structure of the industrial societies), and, as general secretary of the International Sociological Association, had a large view of the world.

I owe to Tom among other things the enrichment brought by two sets of French friends to whom he introduced me. One consisted of cultural and social critics around Edgar Morin, a group which turned against the rigidities of the Marxism of the Communist Party in the late forties and early fifties and who were the original precursors of the revival of western Marxism and the New Left. The second were dissident Catholics, themselves in close touch with the theologians who set the agenda of the Second Vatican Council. The critical Marxists reminded me of ideas and persons I had known in New York and even in Cambridge. (In the spring of 1954, I was heartened by the appearance of the first issues of *Dissent*.) The Catholics invited me into a very different world—their own—and gave me a view of the church and of religious conviction far more complex, deeper, than any I had encountered before.

The LSE had a faculty as interesting as it was varied. The social anthropologists were first cousins, intellectually, to the sociologists and not shy about thinking in large terms of the small societies they studied. Edmund Leach was there for my first year. He asked me what my work on the Reformation was all about, and I told him that I'd established a considerable truth: what was important in its bearing on religious choice in the Reformation was not class position as such, but the ways in which a group's position was determined by the entire class structure. "One has to be a Harvard sociologist," Edmund growled, "to think that new." What I liked about the anthropologists (Raymond Firth, Maurice Freedman, Isaac Schapera, and Paul Sterling) was what my colleagues in sociology to a large extent lacked: distance, even coolness. A London upper-class scandal, the British nation's troubled sense of itself, the imperturbable assumption of the English upper middle class that the rest of the world was a regrettable exception from the norms it set, were no more surprising to the anthropologists than the fertility rites of the peoples they had lived with. They were equally rigorous about the organized peculiarities of British academic life.

One met colleagues from other departments in the Senior Common Room—for morning coffee, lunch, or tea. I struck up an acquaintance with Michael Oakeshott, whom I admired for being so thoroughly at home in the world or, at least, giving a very strong impression of being so. I recall his plopping into a chair on a Thursday, classes having begun on Tuesday, and sighing: "My, this term is dragging." I picture him opening the *Times,* noting that there was a new Archbishop of York, recalling that he knew him at Cambridge and concluding: "It does show how far a fourth-rate man can go in the Church of England." Michael's irreverence was perhaps part of his political philosophy (on the necessity of belonging)—if one was attached to the world, for better or for worse, far better to temper the inevitable with laughter. Michael enjoyed the good things of life, wine, women and horse racing among these. When he published a book entitled *A Guide to the Classics,* advance orders poured in from schools anticipating a masterful introduction to Plato and Aristotle. The work was about the Derby and England's other great races. Since Oakeshott did not believe that politics could change much in a human lifespan, why not settle into enjoying as much of it as possible? To the objection that much of the rest of the world was writhing in convulsions, I can imagine his answer: I am not writing about them. As British imperial power dissolved, its last ramparts in extreme disrepair, the national sense of being central to world history more and more a fiction, a major political philosopher declared thought itself more than a bit vain.

One of Oakeshott's younger colleagues who disagreed was Ralph Miliband. The last student of the legendary Harold Laski to join the faculty, Ralph had escaped from Belgium in 1940 and served in the Royal Navy. His family came from Eastern Europe and was part of the Jewish labor movement. Ralph immersed himself in the British Socialist tradition, wrote on Robert Owen, and was the intellectual voice of the Labour Party's left. The group, led by Anuerin Bevan, Michael Foot, and Harold Wilson in the last years of Labour's government (through 1951), was very audible when I came to Britain in 1953. It was critical of the incremental caution it attributed to Attlee and later to his successor, Hugh Gaitskell, skeptical of the alliance with the United States—and also distinctly unenthusiastic about joining a social Catholic Europe.

There was something of Puritan irredentism about them (as I saw much later), and a great deal of what was termed Little Englandism. They believed that the United Kingdom had potential for economic and political autonomy systematically ignored by the elites (including by many of their comrades in Labour) and were impatient with what some saw as the lessons of history. "Let's get on with it" was their motto. They were not given overly much to reflection on the obstacles to the unfolding of progress. There was something of earlier British Evangelicalism about them, joining a notion of the fundamental purity of the human heart to a belief in the reign of common sense—each leading directly to socialism.

Ralph had a blunt, occasionally sardonic, manner—but he did not criticize persons, despite his conviction that great ideals were threatened by diminution if not betrayal. He saw danger in an absence of clarity, in the pervasive refusal of many to wake from a near-drugged sleep. On the surface a Marxist who thought that the USSR was a failed first experiment, he was the Low Church guardian of tradition in Labour politics. His knowledge of European history and thought fortified his version of British patriotism: Labour would redeem the promise of the Enlightenment by uniting liberal ideas of freedom from constraint to socialist ones of voluntary cooperation. His favored figure was Robert Owen.

We taught some seminars together, and I recall Ralph in perpetual search of a historical destination, an end point which would reduce our present disappointments and perplexities to irrelevance. Isaac Deutscher came to one seminar as our guest, and at lunch beforehand, asked if we were or were not Marxists. He wasn't displeased when I evoked the complexities and varieties of the Marxist traditions, but took it as evidence for my success in clothing truth in academic ambiguity. Ralph was much more straightforward. The point was not whether we were Marxists; of course we were—the point was the engagement that empowered our thought.

There were plenty of other friendly and interesting colleagues at the LSE: Richard Titmuss in social policy, Lord Chorley, John Griffiths and William Wedderburn in law, and some exacting historians. (I recall John Fisher, who taught economic history, describing sociology as history with the hard work left out.) The economists were not quite dominated by the theatrical figure of Lionel Robbins, who propounded the sovereignty of the market with theological pathos. Indeed, as with much of British intellectual life, the legacy of the churches was just beneath the surface. Nineteenth-century struggles over evolution and divine descent, individual will and social causation, responsibility and solidarity resurfaced as contemporary economic and political controversy. One of the economists who made a considerable impression on me was James Meade. I occasionally listened to his conversation, gathered that he had come to economics from classical studies as one of the first Oxford economists, missed (absurdly) talking with him about his very great commitment to social reform, and mistook his modesty for standoffishness. The younger economists included a number of engaging young men about town: I envied their casualness, which put my own involuntary Puritanism in even sharper and more painful relief.

The director, the demographer Alexander Carr-Saunders, was an imposing figure—the more so as he resembled nothing so much as a senior British academic in a film. At the beginning of term, the entire faculty met under his chairmanship. (When I signed the attendance list, using my last name, I was asked by Lord Chorley how long I'd been in Britain. "Three days" was my reply. "Then I must congratulate you on an extraordinarily rapid career." He explained that in the United Kingdom, only members of the House of Lords signed with their last names.) A committee brought in a report on which it had labored for some time. My colleagues were disturbed: in the final examinations, the failure rate was in their view alarmingly high (something around three-quarters of one percent). Their report proposed a series of remedial steps. The director was not moved. "I really do not see the problem. A young person comes to us, enjoys the teaching of the distinguished men and women around this table, the company of lively fellow students, and the cultural advantages of our great metropolis. Just because the student fails an examination, it strikes me as absurd to suppose that the years must be thought of as lost. I really do not think that the faculty will wish to pursue this discussion." I do not recall anyone on the committee protesting; the director's authority was considerable and despite my innate rebelliousness, I saw that it rested on something far more substantial than his office. He had assumed responsibility for the good order of the institution, and he thought it right that in its turn, the institution accept his competence.

Some years later, at his retirement dinner, one saw how much he had enjoyed it. He told of coming to the LSE in 1937 (it was in crisis on account of conflict between its previous director, William Beveridge, and the faculty) to find that his most audible professors were Harold Laski and Friedrich Hayek. He felt, he said, like a clergyman who had arrived at a new parish to find that his curates were the Prophets Elijah and Jeremiah.

A few months after his retirement, this imperturbable figure suffered a minor stroke, evidence for how much he missed the place. Thorstein Veblen, in *The Higher Learning in America*, mocked the university presidents of the first part of the twentieth century as "captains of erudition." Carr-Saunders was not a man one could have mocked; he actually believed in education as public service, had a fine eye for the problems of his younger faculty and the students, and was traditionalist enough to prefer stewardship to entrepreneurship.

In fact, our students were worth caring about. I was given a tutorial group, and was struck by their polite if restrained curiosity about their new teacher, their good-mannered eschewal of display. A week later, when their first essays came in, I was astonished: these twenty-year-olds wrote as if they were to some literary manor born, with a clarity and even finality I envied. If, as Ernest Gellner insisted, they were the ones who did not go to Balliol, so much the worse for Oxford. One was the daughter of a Master at Eton, another from Ceylon, a third a child of the Irish emigration to England, but they had all acquired a straightforwardness that contrasted with the mixed anxiety and bravado of Harvard undergraduates. The LSE students seemed to know where they were, if remaining unclear about where they (and their country) would end. The UK in 1953 had had the experience of war and Labour's partial but definite social revolution. Mixing rather than levelling was the result. The students had somehow been prepared (perhaps by grammar school educations which gave them command of their own language and history) for a situation their parents, in the thirties, most definitely did not have to confront—a severe diminution in national possibilities in a post-imperial society.

Some, a bit older, were more bitter about it (Kingsley Amis and John Osborne), but the twenty-year-olds uncomplainingly went to work.

With a very international as well as lively British student body, the LSE cultural and political calendar was charged. The faculty, connected to the arts as well as to British politics with many ties across the Channel and overseas, extended itself to bring in speakers and visitors, and the student clubs were busy on their own. The world flowed through our crowded buildings. Mendès France came; so did Pastor Niemöller. John Kenneth Galbraith found our Senior Common Room chairs comfortable and serried rows of front bench and back bench politicians of all parties marched in and out.

It was quite fascinating, not least because of the unspoken subtexts. Great Britain was tired. More precisely, those of my colleagues who had been through the war had a lasting sleeplessness: they had not had enough rest. They were sparing of wartime anecdotes, but from time to time tales were told—not of defiant heroism but of slogging through. True, by 1953 economic recovery had begun, but on the other side of the Channel the French, the Germans, the Italians were somehow quicker, richer. The United States had clearly emerged the winner in many ways. The struggle for national survival of 1939 to 1945 had become one to accept a reduced position in the world. Much of the effort of national solidarity made by and under the Labour governments of 1945 to 1951 had its subtext, too: national loss was to be borne in equal shares.

I did not see much of this very clearly at the time. There was, however, an indirect hint of a large kind: the British social scientists and historians were very unreceptive to the theory of modernization as advanced in American universities. They preferred other historical narratives and other generalizations (frequently one that asserted generalization was impossible). They preferred to think of British parliamentary democracy as a fortunate accident of their own history rather than as an inevitable consequence of some major meta-historical current. For other societies, they were prepared to apply what was soon to be called "thick description" by the anthropologists: France was, well, French because of centuries of compounded peculiarities. By extension, the United States was also lucky—but American thinkers should not suppose they had a key to universal felicity on account of it.

The whole was conveyed, like much else in British and especially English life (the Irish, Scots and Welsh, even the northern Englanders were harsher and franker), by turns of phrase, pauses, verbal parentheses, audible semi-colons, or feigned agreement. It was never clear to me how many serious American visitors to our Senior Common Room were entirely aware of what their hosts thought. The contrast between the millennial enthusiasm of the Americans and the polite skepticism of the English was also a matter of dress and posture. I think it was Michael Oakeshott who praised the "shabby and the sly" in thought. Looking back, I now see what he meant—but it has taken some decades for the matter to sink in. That, my former colleagues would agree, is evidence for how right they were.

Wasn't the LSE, however, a stronghold of the Left? My description of a rather conservative, and certainly not millennial, attitude on the part of many of its teachers will certainly surprise those who associate the LSE with Harold Laski, R. H. Tawney, Evan Durbin, and other progenitors of the Labour Revolution of 1945. Many of my colleagues were their students or had been their junior colleagues. What was the Left I encountered in Britain? Labour in the thirties, demoralized and disunited when its Prime Minister, Ramsay MacDonald, accepted in 1931 a coalition with the Tories in a financial crisis and was in continuous conflict with the British Communists and smaller groups advocating revolution in a decidedly non-revolutionary country. A substantial minority of Labour Party members and leaders most were unmistakably not anti-Communist, but who stuck with Labour because it had the loyalties of much of the working class. British left politics in the thirties, like that of the United States and the other democracies, was riven by argument over the Soviet Union and its claim to leadership of all the movements seeking socialism, everywhere. Of course, these arguments agitated a great many students at the LSE, the more so as the student body was international.

Many faculty when I arrived were Labourites—social democratic reformists and not Marxist revolutionaries. Laski had been an inspiring figure but a somewhat wavering theorist without one coherent historical project. Tawney was a Christian socialist and moralist, nearer to the conservatives of conscience who could not abide a severely divided nation. Laski did have severe conflicts with William Beveridge, the LSE director, but with the support of other faculty drove him out in 1937. The conflicts concerned Laski's political activity. Beveridge later wrote a charter document of the post-war welfare state, the Beveridge Plan, on health and old age insurance. It was to keep order in society that he proposed what was later called a "silent social revolution."

Some at the LSE were troubled by what they thought of as its undeserved reputation for radicalism—and for appointing teachers not shy about public controversy. When I arrived, Oakeshott had replaced Laski (who died in 1950). The chair of international history had not been given to either of two prominent applicants— E. H. Carr, the historian of Russia sympathetic to the Soviet Revolution, or A.J.P. Taylor, the historian of great power conflict omnipresent in the media. It went to W. Norton Medlicott, a sober scholar content with a life in the archives. The radical clusters in the faculty consisted almost exclusively of defenders of Labour's institutional legacy, but in truth, there was not all that much of a specific threat to the welfare state. The Tories, returned to office in 1951, had not undone it.

Two matters bothered the aging veterans of the struggles of the thirties and forties—and younger colleagues, rather rare, who attached themselves to them. One was the absence of social purpose in the new prosperity. "Enrichissez-vous" was a French slogan from the mid-nineteenth century, a material antidote to the ideological frenzies of the age. Great Britain in the fifties was living through what Eric Hobsbawm called "our Belle Époque," and lots of persons across the social classes were enriching themselves, as best they could. The other problem was a challenge to the notion of social purpose itself.

The LSE had invited Isaiah Berlin to present his ideas on the two concepts of liberty at the very beginning of the decade—and Berlin's flights of rhetorical imagination had more labored philosophical reinforcement in Karl Popper's denial of the possibility of larger social purpose. Berlin insisted that the only authentic liberty was freedom from constraint. Popper thought "piecemeal social engineering" acceptable, but social reconstruction impossible. Revolution, small or large, abrupt or slow, was depicted as a long-refuted, and in any event dangerous, belief. Britain, the land of hope and glory of Tory myth, the New Jerusalem of Labour, was now a plebiscitary democracy of consumption. Muddling through might be unexciting, but it was immensely preferable to the unleashing of savagery that inevitably followed efforts to achieve total or even large-scale changes. The Israel historian Jacob Talmon, who in his book *The Origins of Totalitarian Democracy* attributed many of the crimes of the modern era to Rousseau, was widely cited—the more so as he flattered British prejudice by denigrating the French Revolution.

Norman Cohn's *The Pursuit of the Millennium*, situating revolutionary socialism in a chiliastic tradition as irrational as it was destructive, was much evoked as well. Rather little was said, historical discretion obliging, about the Putney Debates in Cromwell's army over the future constitution of Britain, and other British expressions of the same sort of Utopian belief in the seventeenth century.

These were surely specific British versions of the general debates going on in the Western societies, but they differed from those I had heard in Cambridge and New York, and the Germans had their own problems. I found it a difficult intellectual environment on two counts. For one, it wasn't obvious, for all the British books that I had read, that these were arguments which I could connect to the American progressive tradition from which I had drawn so much. Second, it was even less obvious how I could join these political arguments to my interests in social theory. If I could construct the right theory, I might be able to assimilate what I was learning to a revised progressivism—or achieve a perspective which would enable me to develop a very different historical project. There the trouble was that I had been appointed to teach social theory in an environment which was deeply skeptical of the capacity of theory to do anything.

The central moral concern of much of British sociology was social reform, and in its service a decidedly empirical social mapping was the preferred model of inquiry. The theorists might be right or wrong, entertaining or stolid—but fundamentally, in the British view, they were conversationalists. I could not defend the effort by Talcott Parsons to construct an abstract model of society, and the many histories I was encountering (and living with) could not be talked about in the same language.

I had come too far to go back: there was no way that I could return to an American sociology department and take up argument on social theory as if all the historical and human complexities I had encountered were stops on a grand tour with no serious consequences. The trouble was that after a couple of years in Britain, I saw no clear way forward.

My intellectual perplexity was matched by an inner awareness of drift. Its primary causes were surely not cultural or intellectual. I'd not returned to the United States, but, having gone away, I was burdened by my problems in ways more painful than if I had tried to master them in a more familiar setting. Behind the sense of drift was something starker yet, and very difficult to deal with. No matter what external successes I booked, I was devastated from time to time by a deep sense of inadequacy. It wasn't all-consuming—but periods of respite were brief and the experience of inner desolation recurrent. Some of it was, undoubtedly, loneliness—but that quickly merged with inner despair, the conviction that I could never set things right.

I came to London in 1953 and by 1954 had decided to resume psychoanalysis. Fortunately, I had a good contact in the London psychoanalytic group, and he introduced me to a younger analyst from South Africa who combined rigor and sympathy in a very positive union. The London analysts at the time were divided into three groups: Freudians around Anna Freud, followers of Melanie Klein about that formidable figure herself, and a bemused assortment of clinicians (mostly British) who wondered aloud whether their colleagues were not taking Continental quarrels too literally. My analyst (Walter Joffe) belonged to the Freudian camp, but had a very good ear for clinical details which spoke volumes in any theoretic language. Perhaps it was because he came from Johannesburg and could understand the situation of an outsider, but he did grasp without having to be given too much instruction the cultural and social legacy of a Bronx boyhood.

I considered that I had found a friend, if a critical one, and took heart directly from our sessions. Unfortunately, after somewhat less than two years, he had to return rather hurriedly to South Africa. He recommended that I continue with Hilda Abraham, the daughter of Freud's early friend, Karl Abraham. He considered that she would not be too rigid and that that would be positive. Half the prediction was true. Dr. Abraham proved to be excessively judgmental, giving an excellent representation of an indignant mother figure. Since I had already thoroughly internalized one, her rendition was more than superfluous: it did not allow me to gain any distance at all. I may have been very independent, fiercely radical, in my political judgements and pronouncements. In a situation in which I had to consider my most vital interest, I was incapable of acting and chose to hang on, as if an unsatisfactory analysis were—again—a consequence of fate.

Persons with problems frequently can draw support from their families and friends. In my case, I had a generally supportive environment—but I do not think that anyone in particular realized how badly I felt. That was my fault: I did not communicate it. Nina had come with me from Germany, had some difficulty in dealing with a culture so very different from the European ones she knew. She thought of me as having made the choice of an intellectual's life—and therefore, as distant from ordinary ambition and doubt. It is true that she could not quite visualize, despite meeting many of my American friends when they visited London, the situation of ambitious outsiders in the US. I do not think that was because she took at face value the absurd claims of openness which our cultural agencies, and bought foreigners, so shamelessly propagated as part of the cultural conduct of the Cold War. It was, rather, due to her likening my situation to that of the very bourgeois and very German Jewish scholars she knew or knew of: she had met plenty of them on their return visits to Germany and Marburg. Whatever the nuances and subtleties of the German-Jewish relationship in the modern epoch, and however brutal and terrible its course after 1933, it was different from our fate or fates in the US. Jewish New Yorkers on the rise were in a milieu quite different from that of Arendt, or Scholem. Our milieu did not offer cultural certainty and a certain social stolidity; it thrived on competitive innovation and immersed us in perpetual anxiety. Nina often intimated that she could not understand why I did not get on with the tasks of the day and longer projects. It was just these, however, that provoked my inner doubts.

There was another, if related, problem. Historians of thought have done a great deal of work on the cultural and scientific origins of psychoanalysis. Whatever the precise sequence of causation at issue, it is clear that the collisions and conflicts of imperial Vienna provided more than colorful background to Freud's work: he drew upon its frenzies while rising above them. Nina did not appreciate frenzy, and her notions of inwardness had more to do with Romantic poetry than with the clinical inquiries of psychoanalysis. She had difficulty, briefly, in empathizing with my efforts to come to terms with myself.

Struggling alone with these problems was neither easy nor pleasant, but relief was provided by the friends we acquired. Nina had considerable gifts for making friends, and had a set of loyal and helpful women who simply dropped by. The Bottomores were neighbors, and of course, we saw others of my colleagues. Politics and its divisions cast long shadows, and we moved in very different ideological milieux.

One reflected, in an odd way, New York. When I arrived to teach at the LSE, Irving Kristol came to London as American editor of *Encounter*. Many people sensed or suspected its CIA origins; some spoke of it, though few had any evidence except for Irving's unabashed sense of superiority. It was not, he intimated, that he spoke for a powerful and wealthy nation; it was that power and wealth were entirely deserved. In this setting, I met George Lichtheim. George kept his own anti-Stalinist (and decidedly Russophobic) views under control—not least to maintain his self-conception as custodian of the wisdom of the Old World and resigned tutor to the new one. George had grown up in Istanbul where his father, who came from the prosperous Berlin Jewish society which also produced the Scholems, Benjamin, Arendt, Marcuse, and many others, was representative of the Jewish Agency to the Ottoman Court. He'd been sent to school in England at one point, had to leave Heidelberg University in 1933, and spent the next twelve years in Jerusalem. Jewish society in Mandate Palestine was small, and so he knew the founding cultural and political elite of Israel. He returned to Europe in 1946 to cover the Nuremberg Trials for the *Jerusalem Post* and then moved to London, took British citizenship, for a while edited a journal called *The Twentieth Century*. In due course his articles and books (including an excellent treatment of Marxism) won him a reputation in Europe and the US—entirely deserved: he was in a class with figures such as Raymond Aron. He died, possibly by his own hand, in 1973.

We came to know him very well; he visited us from London in Oxford and later France. He was a self-conscious survivor of European bourgeois society in its German Jewish version who thought that the catastrophe had destroyed not only the European Jews but (morally) their murderers. In any event, he held, post-war Europe was a different, perhaps temporarily domesticated, form of mass society—and the United States, despite Harvard and the New York intellectuals, not equal to its power. He did come to respect Kennedy and after his assassination declared that it was difficult to take the US seriously. I had the impression that the more he wrote of history, the more it served him as a refuge from a present he disliked. He allowed himself the expression of his sadness after visiting Habermas in Frankfurt once: in a different world, he too would have been a professor at a German university. He did not have to cultivate distance from the socialist parties, their liberal or conservative antagonists, the generation of 1968: it came naturally to him.

Yet his historical and social writings, his political judgements, complex and ironic, were free of bathos. He did not refuse subventions from the Congress for Cultural Freedom and was the last person to think of it as disinterestedly benign, yet his anti-Communism was strikingly different from that of the ex-believers, Stalinist or Trotskyite, who were so insistent on defending "the free world." He derided these claims, depicted Stalinist and post-Stalinist Russia as the heir of Russian backwardness and tyranny and not as the material emanation of some meta-historical fall. He was cool but not especially antagonistic to figures like Carr, Deutscher, Hobsbawm, or Marcuse, and I imagine that Freud's words in *Civilization and its Discontents* must have moved him: the remark that the wildest revolutionary, like the most pious believer, wanted the consolation Freud refused to offer.

George became a British citizen rather than returning to Germany or continuing to live in Israel. He appreciated the British sense of historical continuity, the tired knowingness of the elite. He admired France (and de Gaulle) for the same reason, and had a markedly Prussian skepticism of Adenauer's Catholic Europe. He took no one at face value, and was in that sense a critical but difficult friend. He thought, correctly, that my own outspokenness made a difficult professional situation even more difficult for me—but never quite sat down with me to say so directly. He was an oddly indifferent counselor. Once Nina and I left for the US in 1966, we saw little of him: he did not come to the US very much in the turbulence of the late sixties. Before he died, I wrote for *Commentary* a very positive review of a book he did on the intellectually and politically difficult figure of Lukács. Across the ocean in London, he was appreciative, but that was all.

Others were regular visitors. One was Geoffrey Barraclough, originally an historian of medieval Germany who came to London as Arnold Toynbee's successor at the Royal Institute of International Affairs. Geoffrey was a clipped in expression, had a perpetually unlit pipe, and played the role of the dour don to perfection. He trusted no institution, or for that matter, person, and read history teleologically: it was an exponentially increasing chain of errors. When in 1956 the Soviet army crushed the Hungarian revolt and some British Communists protested, he was contemptuous: did they think they had signed on for a suburban garden party? The United States and its democratic culture might have existed on the other side of the moon—and yet in the late sixties he took a chair at Brandeis. Geoffrey perfectly expressed a strain in British life: Puritan dismay at a fallen cosmos.

Quite the opposite was Eric Hobsbawm. No one needs to be reminded of his seriousness, but he did think that enjoying life was a no less serious matter than preparing for revolution, if it could be done. Eric was, when we came to know him, jazz critic of the *New Statesman* under the pen name of Francis Newton. I had read him on British labor history, as well as his exciting venture into historical social anthropology, *Primitive Rebels*. Perhaps there was something, in the mid-fifties, in the cultural air. Just as the Western working class, from Michigan to the Midlands, from the outskirts of Paris to the Ruhr and northern Italy, joined the affluent society, those who hoped for social transformation looked afield. Eric kept a large amount of historical composure. Having never seriously thought that the Western societies would reinvent their revolutionary legacies, he asked under what conditions they could change.

That made him into a world historian, as the beginnings of his great historical series (The Age of Revolution) showed.

Eric had studied at Cambridge, and of course knew many contemporaries from the nations and societies just liberated from imperial domination. He profited from teaching at a college of the University of London which had an adult and cosmopolitan student body, Birkbeck—and from his friendship with Braudel and the inter-disciplinary group of social scientists at the Sixth Section of the École pratique des hautes études, who took all of human history as their field of study. He made early and intelligent use of what in France was called *Tiers-Mondisme* (minimally translated as sympathy for the developing nations) and was quite aware that until recently, the Western nations were epitomized by the desperate poverty of Dickens's London. The French contemporaries upon whom he drew were not only Marxist but Catholic. Eric regarded Marx's nineteenth-century scheme of inevitable historical progression with considerably nuanced reserve. He was less surprised by the jagged discontinuities of our own societies than most who so loudly insisted on the openness of history, but who meant that things would continue as before, only more so.

The year 1956 was full of surprises. Khrushchev threw the Communist world into turbulence with his denunciation of Stalin before the astonished participants at a Congress of the Soviet Communist Party. He also released tens of thousands from concentration camps. Mao declared that one hundred flowers should bloom—and then proceeded to mow down those that did. A national and revisionist alliance captured the Polish Communist Party from the Stalinists, negotiated a reconciliation with the Catholics that effectively placed Poland under a Communist-Catholic condominium—and had to convince an outraged Khrushchev not to invade the country. The Hungarian revisionists under Nagy provoked an invasion by taking Hungary out of the Warsaw Pact. The United States acknowledged the Soviet sovereignty in central Europe it otherwise so loudly denounced, and did nothing to assist the Hungarians. In our own sphere, France, Israel and the United Kingdom attacked Egypt to undo Nasser's nationalization of the Suez Canal, and were forced into humiliating withdrawal by the United States. In Algeria, the rising against France assumed ever-wider dimensions. In

Indo-China, the US refusal to accept the compromise negotiated in 1954, as well as the obdurate nationalism of the Communists, made the agonies of US intervention later inevitable.

I learned a great deal from the coincidence of living through these events and seeing them with the eyes of these older friends. Certainly, after the events in Poland and Hungary (and their reverberations in Communist Germany, which I followed), it was impossible to think of the Stalinist regimes as monolithic or effectively totalitarian. Jeane Kirkpatrick later (priority in the matter went to Peter Berger) drew a distinction between totalitarian regimes which could never change and authoritarian ones which could. That justified unyielding opposition to the former and a more flexible approach to the latter. In specific terms, it explained the case for sending money to Franco's Spain and contracting a military alliance with the regime, but for refusing to deal with Castro. The events of 1956 suggested that the distinction was untenable, even if it took some time for that to become clear. Kirkpatrick actually advanced the idea in 1976, when it was a useful rationale for US policies before and after.

What I did not fully grasp, as I struggled with the question of what could reinforce and renew the movements for reform in the Communist societies, was the extent to which our own societies were integrated about their imperial projects. The Suez crisis in Great Britain provided a good deal of evidence. The leadership of the Labour Party opposed the attack on Egypt, as did significant parts of the ruling elite: there was a revolt among the diplomats, who were otherwise passionate only about remaining imperturbable. I was beginning to see that Labour's leadership was not in fact an alien body in the British social cosmos but a considerable part of its regulatory system. Labour voters and much of the rest of the nation thought Prime Minister Eden was right, and agreed with his likening of Nasser to Hitler. In newspaper and television interviews, and in conversation in buses and shops (the usual British reserve was reduced for a few days), ordinary citizens expressed their disdain for the Egyptians. Many had been in the Mideast as soldiers: their sense of superiority was unaffected by Britain's subsequent withdrawal from Egypt. A large amount of dismay was occasioned by the way in which the US government (under Eisenhower, a president admired in the UK) forced Britain to awake from its imperial dream. Khrushchev threatened to come to the aid of the Egyptians, and Eisenhower did not propose to be drawn into nuclear war to restore European power in the Mideast. He preferred that the US, there as elsewhere, assume the dominant role.

These events made even more acute the crisis of my world view. As the Europeans developed their own version of consumerism, as the American nation gave every indication of satisfaction with the serial complacencies of the Eisenhower epoch, where were the social groups demanding a radical transformation? I wasn't inclined to another sort of emigration, spiritually, from the Northern to the Southern Hemisphere. If, as was argued frequently enough, the peoples of the Third World were now the revolutionary vanguard, the least that could be said was that the Western working classes showed no inclination to join them.

No general theory of society gave an answer, and I realized that if such a theory existed, which I doubted, it could not do so. Humans had one earth but multiple histories, and these did not resemble one another. All that theory could do was to propound generalities, but we did not live in an indeterminate society—rather, a very specific one. I was drawn to the use of the idea of industrial society, which at times was a euphemism for what in Germany was termed "late capitalism." The term implied that something would follow the capitalism we knew—an entirely unverifiable and vague belief, evidence for the enduring if shrunken power of Marxist prophecy.

Marxism had failed in several ways. The socialist revolution had occurred not in the most advanced but the most backward of capitalist nations, and had certainly not brought a new accession of human freedom. In the advanced nations, whatever the share of the working population in national income, there was no evidence for increasing immiseration. Further, social democratic and social Christian reforms notwithstanding, revolutionary possibility in the advanced nations was nil. Finally, nationalism and religion were contemporary forces stronger than international class solidarity— or, indeed, than class solidarity within the advanced nations. The secularist progression intrinsic to Marxism was as least as mythic as its earlier economic certainties.

There was plenty of evidence for profound and pervasive class differences as the most obvious aspects of the organization of the capitalist societies. The trouble was, these were morally and politically untroubling to their citizens—even, and maybe above all, when they supported one or another of the parties seeking more redistribution. Any number of thinkers, some adhering to one or another version of social conservatism, others liberal, still others social democratic, concluded that it was both more honest intellectually and useful politically to understand Marxism as a nineteenth-century doctrine which no longer applied in the twentieth. Some (the Frankfurt School's seniors) regretted the failure of its prophecy; others held that recognizing that was the pre-condition of a new sobriety. Precisely in this situation, and in direct and self-conscious opposition to those who still clung to a belief in the primary importance of the Soviet Revolution, a newer generation of social scientists formed a not quite invisible and certainly not inaudible large international college, and proclaimed itself Neo-Marxist, revisionist and above all the legitimate heir of Marx's fusion of analysis and criticism. (I originally wrote not "college" but "sect" and decided to change the term.) Our sectarian characteristics were less important than our argumentative openness, and we were certainly eclectic in that we drew upon a variety of contemporary ideas in our attempt to modernize Marxism.

We took as our beginning point the obvious fact that the Western proletariat was no longer that, but had become a culturally and politically integrated working class. We wondered if the processes of alienation had migrated from the factory (and, increasingly, the office) to the rest of social life, especially the spheres of culture. We had our troubles with church and nation, but had to admit that their very profane cultures, and not visions of future transcendence, were the common sense of our contemporaries. We acknowledged that on one point the defenders of Western pluralism were right: perhaps the populations of the Soviet-bloc states had any number of economic benefits, but free political activity was conspicuous in their societies only by its absence. We sought for our societies a culture of political conflict in which citizenship was not limited to voting in periodic elections but was a large part of active lives, but we admitted that without periodic elections, little or nothing else could follow.

We were at least as attentive to social history as to sociology, and indeed thought that in the end the distinction between the two was artificial. We accepted the socio-historical analyses of those with whom we disagreed, philosophically or meta-historically. Bell, Bendix, Galbraith, Hartz, Hofstadter, Lipset in the US, Aron in France, Bahrdt, Dahrendorf and Schelsky in Germany, Briggs and Marshall in the UK, Myrdal in Sweden, provided refined distillations of a great deal of scholarly inquiry to give us a view of the social structure of the Western democracies with which it was exceedingly difficult to disagree. We disagreed, rather, with the political consequences most of them drew from their work—which was that, the world being the way it was, it was unlikely to change into something much different.

When I say "we" I mean my British contemporaries—Halsey, Lockwood, Miliband, our French ones Morin and Touraine, our German colleagues Habermas and von Oertzen. We too had masters: C. Wright Mills, Henri Lefebvre and Pierre Naville, Wolfgang Abendroth and Herbert Marcuse. For me, joining this informal international network was a way to disengage from my position as unhappy son in American sociology and society and become a welcome member of a European family. At the time, I certainly had read much of the literature in the sociology of knowledge, but was reticent about applying it to myself. Instead, I preferred the pathos of a more personal interpretation. In fact, the two explanations complemented one another.

It wasn't only the provincial self- congratulation of American thought that I was abandoning but its political setting. There was a connection between the claims of the social scientists to the certitude of the natural sciences and politics: their descriptions of the world had legitimating functions. What had been the promise of progressivism, epitomized in books such as Robert Lynd's *Knowledge for What?* (and Dewey's *The Public and its Problems*) was changed into market research for the powerful. I was right to see this connection. I overlooked, however, the extent to which a considerable body of research did focus on the inequalities and injustices of the society. I paid far less attention than I could have to the organizations and persons who even in the Eisenhower years persisted with a New Deal agenda—many of them in government and politics in Washington. My American friends (we corresponded and some visited) in sociology were Lewis Coser and Al Gouldner, the larger group around *Dissent* (founded in 1954). There was a lively and undiscouraged current of opposition to the sterile pieties of the Eisenhower age: I was the cousin who had gone abroad—and when I did return, much, much later, I was to be surprised at how much had changed.

In the meantime, I vastly extended the range of my reading. I'd already done a sizable amount in the European literature (and in early American social criticism) when I was at Harvard. Now that I understood the historical settings rather better, I could read British, French, German, and Italian thinkers with a clearer sense of what burdened them. The essay I'd written at Harvard on Marx and Weber owed much to Karl Löwith's work—but at least I'd struggled with the original texts. In fact, the essay was far too smooth. Marx on alienation and Weber on rationalization were not describing the same process, although I said that they were. Alienation, for Marx, would drive humans to revolt to recover the potential fullness of their being. Weber did not scoff at the idea, though he considered it theologically comprehensible but historically impossible: what the world had lost in disenchantment could not be recovered.

I did not pause to ask whether he was right, and went on to read the vast literature of Marxist and Marxist-influenced social inquiry, which argued that modern capitalism was a transitional development which a more educated and more courageous humanity would overcome. Actually, some of the most acute writing on Marx at the time came from theologians. The Germans had the Marxismusstudien of the Evangelical Academy in Bad Boll, in southwest Germany. The French Jesuit Jean-Yves Calvez as a young man published in 1954 *La Pensée de Karl Marx,* which insisted on the unity of his thought, beginning with the *Economic-Philosophic Manuscripts.* The Dominican Henri Desroche in *Signification du Marxisme* emphasized the theological sub-stratum of Marx's humanism. I was impressed by the theologians who took Marx seriously. For one thing, German Protestants and French Catholics were far from the world of American progressivism—or so I thought. (Later, I learned that the Vermont Protestant John Dewey as a young man had studied Hegel. It was a roundabout way to come to Dewey, since one of the

Americans who knew him best had been a friend at Harvard—but better late than never.) The Marx I came to appreciate was a figure in a long and continuing development in European thought, and the Christians' approach to his work opened unexpected historical connections and depths. I felt rather as I did when, on a trip, I pushed open the door of a medieval church and entered an aesthetically and culturally different world.

I was taking my distance from not one but two intellectual provinces. One was the meta-historically flat landscape of British social thought, with its ostensible matter-of-factness—which ignored the disconcerting conflicts, the obduracy, of much in British life itself. The other was the unbounded flight of American fancy, with its imperial description of the US as the new master of all space and time.

At first, my writing showed little obvious trace of my new intellectual venture. I gave the German *Zeitschrift für Politik* an account of the American intellectuals in politics, anticipating later discussions of the Congress for Cultural Freedom by concentrating on mobilization for the Cold War. It was an ordinary progressivist polemic. Then, sufficiently acclimated in radical Britain to scoff at the party of conservative restoration, I published a very unfriendly commentary on a quite extraordinary performance by two colleagues. After the Coronation of Elizabeth II in 1953, Edward Shils and Michael Young (of whom one might have expected more skepticism) published a celebration of it as the ritual reflection of a harmonious society. Their refusal to acknowledge any roughness in the texture of British culture was absurd; their denunciations of those who called attention to conflicts, frenetic. I described their essay as an effort to portray deference and hierarchy as necessary virtues. I now ask myself why they published it in a purely academic journal, *The Sociological Review*, rather than giving it to *Encounter*, the Congress for Cultural Freedom monthly. It occurs to me that the *Encounter* editors, Irving Kristol and Stephen Spender, might have thought that they were laying it on too thickly. Much of *Encounter* was intended to have amusement value, and Shils and Young were lugubrious rather than entertaining.

There were several sequels to my sortie. A great many colleagues in the US read the critique and were delighted that someone had tackled Shils: intellectual and personal generosity were not his most evident attributes. In modern history, politics and sociology a large number of British scholars communicated their satisfaction. "After all," one said, "Burke in sociological jargon is no improvement on the original." Actually, Shils and Young wrote without jargon—but in a curiously flat prose that had a faint ring of obsessive insistence. Neil Smelser and Seymour Martin Lipset wrote to ask permission to re-publish my article in an anthology of the sociology of the fifties, but I did not hear from them again. The essay by Shils and Young did appear in the volume. I had first met Shils when he taught as a visitor at Harvard, and my article converted what had been a relationship of some ambivalence on his part to one of unmitigated hostility. The ambivalence wasn't entirely his, and I wasn't hesitant about reciprocating. Shils was not only a very brilliant and learned, if acerbic, academic, but very active in the Congress for Cultural Freedom, and advised the Ford Foundation's European division on the disbursement of money to individuals and institutions. Later, he edited *Minerva,* the house organ of an eminent international group of scholars united in their rejection of the movements of the sixties. He'd worked for the Office of Strategic Services with persons who later went to the Central Intelligence Agency. It is difficult to believe that he did not retain some of these ties. He played to perfection the role of former radical made very uncomfortable by younger colleagues who reminded him of his own past. Still, his insights into the primordial nature of attachments to family, church, ethnic group and nation were valuable. It was a pity that his own angry exaggeration made it so difficult to distinguish between the man and the message. It was more of a pity since he was, of all the American social theorists of his generation, the one most at home in European thought.

In the excitement of those years, and given a realistic sense of security by promotion to a tenured post at the LSE in 1955, I put off finishing my thesis. I had exalted ideas of what I wanted to accomplish. This included refuting Parsons and Weber, and devising a new interpretation of a major historical rupture—in short, producing a major work which would excite attention and admiration. That was asking a lot, so my delay was in fact a refusal of a necessary compromise. Setting down a few interesting ideas and finding some historical materials to suggest that these might not be all wrong was possible, but not exhilaratingly cosmic. I did not, despite the most grandiose of ambitions, think myself entitled to adulthood. There was an American aspect to the story, too: with a doctorate, I would be eligible to move to a potentially permanent post at a major American university. Despite having obtained tenure at the LSE, I obviously had doubts about facing this test. Add to this an undercurrent of rebelliousness: I preferred to be on the outside, looking with critical disdain at those within—since I did not trust myself to both conform outwardly and retain inner sovereignty.

However, I did in one respect use those years to very good advantage: I obtained a view of religion from the perspective of Catholic and Protestant theologians struggling with a very profane world. Tom Bottomore introduced me to a French scholar who became a close friend, and from whom I learned an immense amount. Henri Desroche had been a Dominican, wrote on Claudel, and then turned to Marx. The publication of his book, *Signification du Marxisme*, displeased the head of the order, the Spanish priest Fernandez. Desroche told me that when he was summoned to Rome to be admonished, he came to appreciate anew the portrait of the Grand Inquisitor in *The Brothers Karamazov*. The order suggested that Desroche return to literary studies, but he refused and left it, all the while keeping contact with figures such as the Dominicans Yves Congar and Marie-Dominique Chenu, whose ideas of church renewal led to the Second Vatican Council. Desroche obtained a post at the famous Sixth Section of the École pratique des hautes études, which later became École des Hautes Études en Sciences Sociales, a chair of cooperative studies. His studies of cooperative movements and experiments were part of a larger interest, in France, Europe and elsewhere, in autonomy and self-determination in a world of relentless bureaucratization and centralization. Desroche remained Catholic, giving all of his writing an irreducible pathos: the struggle to create living communities was also an effort to seize a breath of the divine.

Desroche was helped by the Dean of the Sorbonne's Faculty of Law, Gabriel Le Bras. Son of a Breton baker, he had worked on the history of Canon law and religious practice in the medieval church as a member of the original *Annales* group (Marc Bloch, Lucien Febvre and Maurice Halbwachs) at Strasbourg. He was the French Foreign Ministry's advisor in its negotiations with the Vatican on the naming of bishops. Le Bras told me that that greatly facilitated his access to Church archives. There were several lessons for me in these friendships. Le Bras, at the top of French society, lived in the Decanal apartment of the old Faculty of Law overlooking the Pantheon—an apartment cluttered with his children's model railway tracks and all the other artifacts of ordinary life. He was the director of a section of the Centre Nationale de La Recherche dedicated to sociological studies of religion, and employed any number of Church dissidents. Desroche and Le Bras made me realize how broad and complex the actual life of the Church was, how even Pius XII was unable to eradicate dissent. The Church had cellars and corners in which alternative forms of being and thought survived, their protagonists aware that they might dwell in internal exile indefinitely, but confident that no matter how much later, they would be heard.

As sophisticated as Williams and Harvard were, as cosmopolitan as my New York intellectual friends, they did not prepare me for an encounter with a French Catholicism fully integrated in the life of the republic. Certainly, there was a *Catholicisme de gauche*, studiously critical of the new society of consumption for the sake of ideas of solidarity. What impressed me even more was the effort of the Catholics to come to terms with the discontinuity and openness of modern culture. The old opposition between believers and militant secularists (*croyants et laïques*) had given way to a much more complex and nuanced relationship. The defeat of France and the agonies of the occupation, the rejection by many of the legacies of the Enlightenment and the Revolution, and much else in contemporary history had certainly shaken everyone's certainties. The Church on the eve of the war confronted its own situation as a minority in a book by Cardinal Suhard of Paris with the title *France, Pays de Mission*.

The Catholics had a sense of sense of moral density, of the inextricable connection of institution and person—and took for granted their immersion in history as they examined its antecedents and consequences. My new friends struck me as in possession of resources which did not leave them struggling against both bewilderment and isolation. Like their secular contemporaries, they were also certain of their nation: it had been there for a long time and would survive its present vicissitudes.

The French Protestants I met through them, and in other settings, were no less striking. The Lutherans of Alsace-Lorraine were about one-third of the local population. The Calvinists of the Reformed Church of France were about one percent of the nation. The Alsatians thought of themselves as bound to their local history. The Calvinists did not expend much energy on regretting Henri IV's conversion, which cost them their chance to dominate the nation. After all, they were a large presence in the higher civil service and the professions, in the universities and the economy. They had a controlled combativeness, combined with considerable self-assurance that the history of modern France could not be written without them. They had an ethos of responsibility which contrasted with that of the Catholics, who supposed that a community was in place and asked what could be done to make it more authentic, more encompassing. The Protestants insisted on the burdens individuals had to assume, lest the moral universe become inert.

Minority status is sometimes good for the spirit. In the German Federal Republic, the Protestants were not a majority of the population. They confronted a somewhat complacent Catholic majority, the nation's terrible past, and a new world which God seemed to have abandoned. Here and there, I had met morally exemplary Protestant laymen and theologians: In Great Britain, the changes wrought by Labour represented for an influential group of Anglicans the success of the social teachings of an earlier generation of theological critics of capitalism. I had the impression, in my early years in London, of meeting a group living off spiritual capital.

What I lacked was much contact, apart from reading, with American social Christianity. At Harvard, those who insisted on its legacy were historians, and the Divinity School was uninspired. There was plenty of activity in the country, but I had not encountered it. There, too, my European residence brought a change. I began to be invited to symposia at the Ecumenical Institute of the World Council of Churches, in Bossey, outside Geneva.

Its director was Hans Wulff, a German theologian descended from the Confessional Church—the Protestants who had refused total integration in the Third Reich. One of his colleagues was an American, Charles West, who was working on his book *Communism and the Theologians*, and who represented a socially engaged current in American Protestantism. The symposia were exceedingly international, brought together persons of considerable talent, and provided yet another lesson on how differently the world's torments could be confronted.

I found myself in the role of a totally unauthorized spokesman for an entirely ambivalent sort of secularism—ambivalent since I freely admitted that it was difficult to live without faith, in God or much else, while acknowledging that the theologians' critical analysis of much of modern society was in many ways identical with that of the most critical of secularists. Since the theologians I met were well versed in Marxism, American pragmatism, French existentialism and the other twentieth-century visions of a Godless world, they were not surprised by what I had to say, if often too polite to say so. They were equally polite in not asking why I had not recurred to Judaism: apparently they found the figure of Godless Jewishness familiar, perhaps a reminder of a Europe that had emigrated to New York. Privately, Wulff once raised the question with me, and so did two very unlike but honest friends, the directors of the Evangelical Academies in East and West Berlin, Gerhard Bassarak and Wolf-Dieter Marsch.

Bassarak did not spare anyone in his depiction to me of the ordinary venality of the Communist regime and its supporters—but obviously thought that in a world of bad choices, his was as good as any and better than most. Marsch had written a thesis on Lincoln's faith and so provided instruction on an American legacy. He was also, later, the first person in Germany to call my attention to a newly published novel, *Die Blechtrommel* (*The Tin Drum*). I had no answer to their pointed inquiries about Judaism, apart from a very stereotyped one: after the Holocaust, it was impossible to believe in a God of Israel—or any other.

The friendship and interest of these persons counted for a great deal. My French colleagues appointed me editorial secretary of their journal, *Archives de Sociologie des Religions*, and so provided me with regular visits to Paris—and an opening to French culture and society. The Ecumenical Institute was true to its name in respects that went beyond its official mission: it afforded a view of a world still struggling with the considerable remnants of imperialism. My European academic experience had already taken me out of the self-preoccupied provincialism of a good deal of American social science. Now I was being educated in matters even many European social scientists examined far too cursorily. The question was, what could, and did, I do with these gifts?

The question was made somewhat easier to answer by my entry into another European culture: that of the political thinkers. Often, their only connection with politics was abstract. Sometimes, they were active in one of the socialist parties—although their activity was invariably in programmatic disputes and the meta-historical arguments that underlay these. The recent émigrés from the Communist parties were usually content to confine their political activity to thinking, initially. After enduring the discipline of the parties, they felt and acted as if they were on a long vacation from routine.

In the United States, the reconciliation with the nation and its culture sought by many intellectuals was often no less abstract. Persons I hardly knew were working in government and the unions preparing for the Democratic re-conquest of the presidency in 1961. Since the Democrats in the Eisenhower years held large majorities in both houses of Congress, these were individuals who might have sympathized with a philosophical critique of our social existence, but who preferred to take specific steps to change it. I knew nothing about them, but wasn't alone. A decade later, when I had returned to the United States, Norman Podhoretz, as editor of *Commentary*, told me of his surprise in discovering how many intellectuals there were in Washington. (I think he defined an intellectual as a person who read his work.) Those who preferred the rigors of systematic criticism of our society joined what they saw as the great chain of American outsiders—descending from Tom Paine and the Anti-Federalists to the early Abolitionists to the socialist prophets of the Gilded Age. Dwight Macdonald said of the contributors to the first *Dissent* anthology that they were "professors of revolution." True, but there were more professors of counter-revolution about, so a little pluralism went a long way.

One large difference between the American dissidents and the independent European Marxists was the latter's sense of rootedness. They shared a sensibility with many citizens who, often across generations, envisaged their situation in terms of class. The intellectuals sought a situation of historical transcendence; the ordinary voters of the Left generally wanted very immediate and often material improvements. They also wanted dignity and recognition, and many thought these attainable only in a different society.

The leadership of the parties of the Left was often divided between intellectuals from the universities and unionists from the factories. Aron's *Opium of the Intellectuals* was a polemical exaggeration. It was not a self-indulgence of the intellectuals to ask how the quantitative changes brought about by the post-war welfare states could serve as a beginning point for qualitative ones. Moreover, post-war ideas of transformation came not only from the intellectuals of the Left but in substantial measure from conservative thinkers and parties seeking to give substance to the idea of the nation.

It is true that revolution was an ambiguous rhetorical figure. Disappointment at the fate of the Soviet Revolution resulted in despair but also in imaginative attempts to depict alternative paths to transformation. A number of thinkers, such as Antonio Giolitti and André Gorz, argued that major reforms could open the way to a changed setting which would make still larger steps possible. That is what Willy Brandt intended when, years later, he made "Let us dare more democracy" the theme of his chancellorship. An old figure re-emerged: the idea of the autonomous, sometimes creative, individual. Projects of economic self-government and of worker participation in the direction of workplace and firm superseded, gradually, discussions of an extension of the public sector. The answer of the New Left to the problem of bureaucratization, of concentration of power even in public enterprises, was the democratization of the economy.

There were parallel projects in the Soviet bloc, expressed in guarded language. There, the figure of the educated worker was a surrogate for open discussions of citizens' economic rights. Marx's *Grundrisse* was standard reading at the time, in Western universities and state socialist research institutes. If the essential element of a modern socialist economy was the utilization of knowledge, state bureaucrats and party officials would have to renounce their false claims to historical and sociological omniscience. This last was not stated, but the implications were clear to the more sophisticated segment of the publics in the Communist states. Natural science was progressive because self-correcting, and did not legitimate the claims of the ruling parties to possess the one true science of society.

The post-war welfare states, much investment in public infrastructure, and the joined skills of an educated labor force and of the entrepreneurs and engineers in charge of firms brought prosperity to Western Europe. Recall the daily miseries of existence evoked in pre-war novels (Hans Fallada's *Little Man, What Now?*, Sartre's ambivalently titled *The Roads to Liberty*) or in Orwell's ethnography. Immiseration was an increasingly abstract concept, as the Western European working class acquired more spacious housing and filled it with refrigerators, television sets and washing machines, while taking vacations in newly purchased automobiles. Film, television, spectator sports and the mass media filled its leisure time. Less was spent on political activity, and the administration of social services was professionalized in any case. An older form of working-class culture, based on neighborhood solidarity and a sense of a distinctive social existence, gave way to more differentiated and diffuse sensibilities.

Older proponents of class solidarity mourned the beginning of its passing. Those who thought that the fundamental Marxist concept was less exploitation than alienation portrayed the new consumerism as a refined sort of bondage—made worse, if anything, by the workers' eager embrace of it. A new generation of Marxists called for a revolution in the super-structure. Claiming that they had grasped the true nature of his thought, they stood the old Marx of class conflict on his head. No wonder we made common cause with the Christians: we each sought a new earth and a new heaven.

Two sets of Marxists inhabited parallel universes which did not touch. One group vaunted a new vanguard—the educated workers, especially scientists and technologists. Once they realized how irreplaceable they were, only a few steps (not specified) would be required before they assumed command of production and politics, too. In another world, the working class, drugged by consumption, had lost combativeness and indeed intelligence—so, far from becoming an agent of change, it had become, spiritually speaking, a huge *Lumpenproletariat*. The economic ascent of the working class made it the cultural equal of the employed middle class and many professionals, themselves dumbed down. The Marxist intellectuals who wrote about this change in the working class depicted a world which did not at all correspond to their progressive vision of history. Afloat on a vast sea of regrets, their old compasses dysfunctional, they looked desperately for land.

Such shores as were visible had been colonized, extensively, by the party of permanent counter-revolution. That party was by no means monolithic and itself contained large segments in permanent schism or sectarian separatism. All took as an ineluctable axiom that revolution, a large self-transformation of society, was not possible without throwing society into economic chaos, moral disintegration, and political tyranny. Conservatives or liberals, even radicals, advocates of the free market or of the welfare state, religious believers and secularists united in looking back to the Soviet Revolution (and some to the French Revolution) with iron conviction: never again. The convoluted dramas of the Cold War constituted a gigantic screen on which these obsessions were projected. Events in the socialist bloc, in the American client and satellite states, sometimes termed "allies," relations between the power blocs, were instantly recast into an unchanging and unending, morality play. Large parts of the world developing independently of the struggle with China and the Soviet Union were ignored, or depicted in absurdly schematic terms. The history of much of Europe and the United States was rewritten as if it were entirely a prelude to the present: the density and specificity of the past did not count.

London was a much better place to experience the deformation of Western freedom in the name of defending it than Cambridge, Massachusetts, or New York. Britain reluctantly accepted subordinate status to the US in the confrontation with the Soviet Union—the reluctance quite evident. The United Kingdom had diplomatic relations with the Chinese People's Republic when Dulles refused to shake Chou En-Lai's hand (at the 1954 Geneva conference on Vietnam). Eden as foreign minister proposed a reduction of NATO and Warsaw Pact forces in Central Europe.

A certain skepticism about the zealous millennialism of US policy and a rather open inclination to pursue friendly relations with the USSR were voiced by the elite.

There were public arguments for a more autonomous course for Great Britain—some conservative or otherwise traditional, and others quite radical (if, to be sure, in an ethnocentric British way). There were plenty of Central and Eastern European émigrés in Great Britain, but unlike the situation in the US, there were not so many employment opportunities for propagating one or another version of Manichean historiography. The large numbers of Poles who had settled in Britain visited Poland regularly and many understood Poland's ambiguous position in the Soviet bloc.

Finally, there were Christian and secular advocates of a negotiated peace with the Soviet bloc—or, at least, a considerable deepening and extension of co-existence. Some clung to a residual notion of the USSR (and China) as historically progressive; others argued that only a large dissipation of international tensions would allow the Communist regimes to diminish their repressiveness. The Channel wasn't all that broad, and French criticisms of Western Europe's integration in an American-led bloc did not evoke in London the instant rejection they incurred in the US. At the end of the fifties, de Gaulle, returned to power, enjoyed much esteem in Britain for saying what the British thought.

Before I left Harvard in 1952, I heard its president, James Bryant Conant, defend the dismissal of Communists from American university faculties by asserting that the British were doing the same. In fact, in Britain avowed Communists did not face the academic difficulties they experienced in the US. There was pressure in the social sciences exerted by some of the more vocal defenders of the free world, but it was thought to be in bad taste, even indecent, to demand someone's head for ideological non-conformity. Isaiah Berlin was at pains to conceal at least one decidedly illiberal intervention in an appointment discussion. The Cold War, then, did not cover the United Kingdom with an ideological ice pack.

Mainly however, I profited from having to live in a different country with its own sense of history. While de Gaulle would say "the world being the way it is, it is not otherwise," the way the world was constituted was very much a matter of historical and political interpretation, and that depended upon temperament and sentiment. My own rebelliousness was considerable, and after I heard many senior figures insisting that the world lent itself only to one reading, I was driven to seek an alternative one.

Just what that alternative might be, and what sort of career I could or would make with it became somewhat more clear after my initial three years in London. In my last year at Harvard, the General Education Committee was host of a dinner to consider its past, present and future. Its chairman, the historian David Owen, was a benign and helpful friend. He invited me to speak, as sole voice of the teaching fellows in the social sciences. I indulged in a certain amount of self-dramatization. A promising younger teacher and scholar on his way up Harvard's steep hill, I depicted the ideal academic intellectual as an "underground man." The senior members of the New York intelligentsia, whom I admired, could not have done better—denouncing conformity while making of the avant-garde an institution. In Europe, first in Germany and now in London and Paris, I had met large numbers of persons who thought of themselves as critical but socially indispensable outsiders. They placed themselves in the long tradition which led back to disobedient medieval clerics, stubbornly eccentric Protestants, and the free thinkers of the Enlightenment. They would have been indignant had their rejection of the social order not been taken seriously, had they been dismissed as court jesters. They thought themselves a threat to those in power and wanted from them the legitimation of unrelenting antagonism.

That is precisely what much of society denied us: they paid us little attention. The anti-Communist persecutions of the McCarthy era in the US were appreciably different. They drew inspiration from a long American tradition of suspicion of unchurched thought: the nation was the church, which demanded faith. One complication the unreflective did not anticipate was the eagerness of many intellectuals to remain in the church. For every Communist, or figure accused of harboring the wrong thoughts, there were two or three or even five strident accusers with intellectual credentials, some quite genuine. That situation wasn't entirely unknown in Western Europe in the fifties, but those who had left the Communist church had different sorts of apostasies. The intellectuals I knew and liked in Europe had a problem: they were still resolute in search of a revolution they could believe in. The larger society and those who ruled it, and their educated apologists, by and large were unafraid of a revolution they thought exceedingly unlikely.

There were national differences in the structure of the relationship of the critical intellectuals to society within Europe as well as between Europe and the US. What was constant was ambiguity: the closer they came to power, or to a party or movement with a realistic chance of exercising it, the more endangered they thought their independence. The model of a church opposing the state did not apply. The notion of a sect challenging a church was more apt. Our marginality was self-imposed, and there were plenty of intellectuals who disdained it, or did not think it necessary. Nearly every one of the possible attitudes could be found on the LSE faculty alone.

I gained a certain sense of belonging by thinking of myself as temporarily marginal, in possession of truths which one day the world might honor. If it did not, I still had the satisfaction of thinking of myself as in a vanguard: the absence of followers was then proof of integrity. Just as my academic career began to prosper, I joined to my academic persona a rather different one, that of an intellectual of the left. That the first was the economic precondition of the second was clear to me. That much of liberalism, which allowed the process, was intact should have been clearer.

The International Sociological Congress at Amsterdam in 1956 was a theater of ideas, with a colorful cast. I'd attended the 1953 meeting at Liege, mainly composed of West Europeans and scholars from the two Americas. Its tensions were contained, or confined to polite argument after the formal sessions. In 1956, colleagues from the USSR and the Soviet-bloc states appeared, and were welcomed with argument they did not all expect—from Western colleagues who thought themselves the custodians of the authentic Marxist legacy. Amongst the Western sociologists, a debate inspired by Marxism continued: what was the nature of the class structure of the Western societies, and what did it mean for culture and politics? Scholars from the Third World were there, but the themes of imperialism and under-development were not central to the debates. We met, interestingly, an Institute for Tropical Studies, which had been known as the Institute of Colonial Studies.

My own initial contact with the colleagues from the other Europe was with Czechs and Slovaks. At a reception, Nina (who spoke Slovak) met someone from the Slovak Academy of Sciences. We were joined by a Czech social philosopher, Karel Kosík, later one of the inspirations for the Prague Spring and an original thinker of considerable courage. Given the chance to leave after the extirpation of the 1968 experiment in democratic socialism, he refused. We persuaded the populace to follow us, he declared, and it would be ignoble to run from the hardships of defeat. He became a bus driver until allowed to write openly for his West German publisher. I saw him in Prague in 1990: he'd been restored to his university post, but was under constant attack as a Marxist from colleagues who had made a late discovery of the virtues of the West. In 1956, I was struck by the inner freedom of Kosík and some of his colleagues: they assumed that authoritarian constraint would dissolve at a time and in a manner no one could predict—and dwelled on the contradictions of Marxist thought as their contribution to hastening the event. What one does not do or say, Kosík told me, is at least as important as what one does.

An impressive group of Poles were also there. One was Adam Schaff, who exuded worldliness by way of anticipating our questions: he did not need Western strictures on Stalinism; he knew what it meant. Schaff was an ideologue troubled by the conscience of a philosopher—or a philosopher constrained by official ideology. He had a personality for different contexts. Another was Julian Hochfeld, who was in Parliament as deputy for Radom, my grandfather's city. He later went to UNESCO in Paris as director for the social sciences—the regime's elegant way of sending off someone unable to bow. There were others (I recall Jan Szczepański and Andrzej Wiatr) who were empirical in their emphases. Their work on social mobility under socialism made its point: if there was mobility, there was a class structure, and classlessness was a matter for the indefinite future.

The Soviet Academy of Sciences sent a delegation conspicuous for its heavy-handed defensiveness. The Khrushchev speech on the "Cult of Personality" had shaken Soviet society; they knew that we knew this. The Soviet bureaucrats who came to Amsterdam were determined to make no concessions to what they (unlike the more sophisticated Czechs and Poles) thought of as a monolithic West. Some of the more senior among them had considerable difficulty in grasping the fact that many of us did not speak for our governments or for anyone but ourselves. They were astonished when

Edgar Morin and I convened an informal—and densely attended—session on Marxism in the twentieth century. When we made it clear that we were as interested in a Marxist analysis of state socialist societies as of our own stage of capitalism, they responded with little more than slogans. I recall an acute set of contributions to the evening by some Yugoslavs. No doubt, there were critical thinkers in the USSR in 1956—but they were not yet sent abroad.

The Congress was not all politics. A lively group of sociologists of religion used their national and philosophical and religious differences to confront the theme of secularization. My French colleagues were the animating force of the meetings. It was they who insisted that we could not only focus on in one segment of social existence, that we had to regard the fate of religion as a metaphor for that of an entire civilization.

What freedom for the spirit in a world of constraint? The Catholics had considerable experience of struggling for autonomy against the administrators of tradition. The Protestants had made a tradition of autonomy, and wondered if they had lost their original passion. The secular progressives, myself included, were not free of self-criticism. Perhaps we were missing something our religious colleagues knew, or had. We studied religion, then, not to confirm our certainties about social progress but to explore our doubts.

There were philosophical implications in the entire work of the Congress. Even as schematic a distinction as the one between theorists of society and empirical students of social processes lent itself to interpretation. The theorists were seeking the fundamental codes of existence. The empiricists denied so theological an ambition, declaring it difficult enough to discern profane routines. The Marxists themselves were divided, between prophets and un-exalted philosophers, between visions of an unrealized future and depictions of an all too real present. Why, even in the Soviet bloc, were Jewish sociologists never quite free of theoretic ambition and many of the others more resigned to the world?

That world made itself known with considerable violence shortly after we all had returned home. A change of ruling group in the Polish Communist Party led to policies which even the reformers in Moscow disliked: rapprochement with the Catholic Church, more open discussion of state policy, more freedom for the intellectuals.

Poland narrowly escaped the invasion which was Hungary's fate after the Hungarian party's revisionists made common cause with the anti-Communist majority and declared the nation independent of the Soviet bloc. The attack on Egypt by France and Great Britain suggested that for all of the analysis of the industrial democracies as post-ideological, or modern, imperial residues were still at work.

I wrote an account of the Congress for *Commentary* just before events lent substance to our imaginings of the world. I titled the article "Science, Ideology and Dialogue" and took issue with Aron's view that sobriety had been achieved by renouncing large ideologies. The making of theory in the West, seriously pursued, entailed a rupture with surface images of a consensual society. In the Soviet bloc, empiricism required courage: the enumeration of a significant range of facts about social structure was subversive. As for dialogue, I implied that I and some friends—as critics of Western society—were best positioned to confront the rulers of the Soviet empire and encourage its opposition.

The *Commentary* article was the equivalent of an inaugural lecture. It marked me as a member in good standing of the New York intelligentsia, even if in London. Indeed, it was in some significant measure because I was in London and Europe that I was listened to. It was certainly true that I could not have written that article had my experience been limited to ascending the ranks in an American university—or of arguing with other New Yorkers. The response to the article confirmed something quite extraordinary in my life—an accession of self-confidence. I had, finally, won a place: entirely between worlds. (The group photograph taken of the participants in the Sociological Congress put me at the end of one line, my head slightly cocked as everyone else stared seriously at the camera.)

I used the ensuing burst of energy to complete unfinished business. Talcott Parsons had many admirable qualities, but the capacity to step outside his world was not one of them. He had expressed not pleasure but paternalistic doubt when I was given tenure at the LSE. I hadn't finished my thesis, and he took that as a reversal of the moral order of the academic universe. Not having completed the doctorate did disturb me, even if I had spent my time in altogether rewarding ways. I gathered my accumulated materials, used the riches of the library of the British Museum, and drew on the historical and philosophic sensibility I had begun to construct. In six months, I wrote a coherent narrative of the Reformation in the German cities of Lübeck. Strasbourg, Augsburg, and Nürnberg. I argued the case that the cities which had not yet achieved a fuller market capitalism, which were still ruled by a guild structure, espoused Lutheranism. The cities which were more open socially, more dynamic economically, were more pluralistic in their Protestantism and hospitable to Zwingli's doctrines. These were a more radical break with Catholic hierarchy and with the Catholic belief in God's presence in the world.

The thesis was an extended footnote to Weber and even more, to Ernst Troeltsch, who had given Weber many of his ideas. There were many things wrong with it. Much of it was indeed derived from a Marxism of the super-structure—in which larger historical conditions produce psycho-cultural tendencies which then achieve a large measure of autonomy. My description of the larger historical situation of early sixteenth-century Germany was generally accurate, although I am not sure that newer inquiry will allow a sharp demarcation between the types of cities. My account of the churches and theology, even of popular theology (well documented) was equally accurate. I am not at all sure that my analysis of the connection between social structure and religious ideas and church organization was entirely solid. It did have more historical substance than Fromm's account of Protestantism in his *Escape from Freedom*. Erik Erikson in his *Young Man Luther* deepened my analysis but did not supersede it. Perhaps (I think of my reading on the French Revolution and its consequences, and on our own revolution and Civil War) no break in historical continuity is as enduringly radical as its protagonists claim. However overly simple my framework, I did learn something of historical complexity.

Would I have written a different thesis had I been an historian and not a sociologist dealing with historical causation? Even had I been an historian of the *Annales* school, or of the British group around *Past and Present*, the answer would have been a qualified yes. Historians immerse themselves in detail, and that is why their explanations of events are often so convincing. Disciplinary boundaries should function like the open borders of the European Union, not like the Berlin Wall and its miserable imitations. My thesis was unmistakably the work of a sociologist looking not only for cause and causes in a single case but attempting to draw generalizations from it. I do recall that Talcott Parsons told me that he was surprised by my conclusion: "I do not wish to fault your historical scholarship, but as you describe it, the Reformation does not conform to my theoretic expectations." I was historian enough, it appears, to have confounded a master of grand theory.

At the time, I understood that much of modern sociological thought was an attempt to grasp the historical specificity of the industrial societies of the West. We were preempting judgements otherwise reserved for the generations that will look back on us.

Sociology appealed to the impatient who thought of themselves in more flattering terms, as profound or even visionary. My own historical studies and reading limited some of my intellectual grandiosity—but not very much of it. My contemporaries and I were intellectually ambitious. That was what united American and European, progressivist and conservative, liberal and Marxist, religious believer and convinced secularist. It may have been more important than the marginality frequently cited as a fundamental source of a sociological perspective. Who could have been more rooted in American culture than C. Wright Mills, from Texas, and Talcott Parsons, from Ohio, more British than Bottomore and Marshall, more French than Bourdieu and Touraine, more German than Habermas and von Oertzen? For many, what there was of marginality was elective.

Finishing my thesis gave me academic citizenship papers. I became a member of the international nation of the learned. It freed me of a burden, and my energies flowed into other tasks, including participation in the birth of a new political movement—and parenthood.

7

London, Part II

THE MOST personal memories of the past are the ones about which I am most ambivalent. I struggled, back then, to ward off my deepest feelings—inadequacy and loss, wounded pride, anger and envy—by perpetual psychic motion. Ambition, hope, and a search for transcendence (in the form, alternately, of revolution and religion) were also mine. I was convinced, however, that I could never achieve my ambition, that hope was illusory, transcendence a myth. A clinician would have said (and some did) that a deep depression made reconciliation with the ordinary vicissitudes of life impossible. For every step forward I took, I expected to have to take two, even three, back. I kept hoping against hope that something would change, but was perpetually disappointed.

None of this made me easy to live with. A pervasive inner joylessness, punctuated by occasional periods of relief and a miserly few moments of pleasure, did not make me a very benign or reassuringly supportive companion. Colleagues and friends often had a rather different impression: I struck them as friendly and witty (and by English standards, spontaneous and unreserved). The difference between this social persona and my self-image increased my distress.

Living in middle-class English society made the maintenance of a good front mandatory, but also reinforced my own version of a dual personality. In England, if one were asked "How do you do?" it would have been shockingly bad form to give an honest answer. That left me with two recourses. One I have already written to—a lengthy course of psychoanalysis. I struggled in mine, making very little progress, thus creating an unwelcome but inevitable confirmation of my inner pessimism. I did not, clearly, think that I deserved better. The analyst, Dr. Abraham, played her role to perfection: a relentlessly critical maternal figure disinclined to displays of sympathy with her patient.

I was so immobilized that I could not directly express my distress. I had an un-Midas-like touch, turning everything to dross. I suppose that my failure in analysis in so critical a period of my life demonstrated, in a perverse way, how authentically representative of that life analysis was.

My other recourse was family, or Nina. We married in the summer of 1955. Her visa was about to expire; Her Britannic Majesty had not empowered her Home Secretary to recognize co-habitation, and if we did not marry, Nina would have had to return to Germany. I was ambivalent about the step, but did not feel strong enough to live alone, and decided that marriage was the best solution. For a while, it was. Nina enjoyed the appreciation and loyalty of a diverse set of friends. After we moved into an attractive garden apartment in Hampstead, it became a meeting place for our British friends, visitors from Europe, and lots of itinerant Americans. It was where both C. Wright Mills and Michael Harrington met the group about to form the British New Left.

Tolstoy's remark about marriages (all happy ones are alike, unhappy ones vary) never struck me as convincing. Happy marriages have different sorts of happiness, while unhappy ones all suffer from the partners' inability to rely upon one another for anything but disappointment. I was never quite able (or so I felt) to count on Nina's full loyalty and support. She was certainly deprived of what I could not give—understanding of her need for order and tranquility, a recognition of her sacrifices for our common life. I retreated inwardly, and was ever more engaged in matters outside our home. She increased her attention to the minutiae of living. The distance between us was never bridged. Something, however, did lead us to settle for considerable imperfection, even unhappiness—our children. Once Anna was born in 1958 in London (Antonia followed a bit over two years later, in Oxford), Nina and I put aside thoughts of separation—which, to be sure, we had not voiced to one another. It might have been better had we done so.

Before the children came, there was much else. C. Wright Mills

With Nina (Gudrun Apel), in Marburg Germany, 1952. We married three years later.

was in Denmark in the academic year 1956-1957 on a Fulbright grant. I heard of this and invited him to come to talk at the LSE. When he arrived, I was his host. He was a large presence, an archetype of the frontiersman in a metropolis whose tired citizens stayed home at night. Mills told me that he had listed the LSE as his preferred destination on his application, and asked me why the LSE sociologists had told the Fulbright officials that we had no interest in his coming. That wasn't the case—no one, junior or senior, in our department had been asked about this, and the LSE administrators said that they never had been contacted. I believed them: the Fulbright office apparently thought that they could not deny the most widely read and vocal of the social critics of the Eisenhower age an appointment, but preferred to send him to Copenhagen.

Wright and I became friends and he subsequently formed a very close tie to Ralph Miliband, whose two sons were later leading British Labour politicians. What impressed me most about Wright was his directness, his absence of personal and intellectual pretension, his intellectual and moral dedication. I recall, still, with anger a crudely denigrating review of his 1958 book, *The Sociological Imagination*, in *Encounter* by Edward Shils—a large example of smallness. He was the same whether talking with the intellectual elite of London or another diner at a neighborhood restaurant about the stranger's native India. Wright had only been in Europe once before—to take factory delivery of a BMW motorcycle. He had, however, acquired by reading and by his association with Hans Gerth at the University of Wisconsin an ample map of modern European social thought, especially that of the years between the two wars. He wanted, now, to know what the new Europe thought. Wright's 1952 book, *White Collar*, was a great portrait of our nation at midcentury. Scanning the Western European bookshelves, an experience he was to repeat in Poland and even in the USSR in the more confined spaces of the research institutes, he found that the Europeans were using his work to explore their own social histories. That impelled Wright to ask whether we were joined, involuntarily, in one history. He then found himself dealing with the international struggle for power.

I was in touch with other Americans. Carl and Annette Kaysen came to London for a Fulbright year at the LSE, and Nina and I found them a grand house in Frognal. My colleagues were indeed discerning, and appreciated Carl's intelligence and wit, his intellectual ambition and curiosity. Lionel Robbins, not given to enthusiasm for other economists and sufficiently cosmopolitan to realize how provincial imperial America was, pronounced him the most interesting Fulbright visitor the LSE had had.

The US, and especially Harvard, were not impossibly far. The director of the LSE gave a dinner in honor of Sam Beer and Louis Hartz, causing Ernest Gellner to remark on how much more serious they were than their British counterparts in political philosophy, how much more grounded in the complexities of history. My Harvard teachers Talcott Parsons and George Homans each spent a year at Cambridge as the Faculty of Economics and Politics there pondered how (or whether) to introduce sociology into their curriculum. Morton and Lucia White visited us in London and I recall an amusing episode: one of our Indian friends from the LSE was writing a doctoral dissertation on John Dewey, about whom Morton had written his first book. There Nina and I were, on a street in Bloomsbury with the Whites, when we ran into my Indian colleague. When I introduced him to Morton he was delighted: could he call at his hotel and talk? Morton agreed and told me later that no one in the US had expressed an interest in the book for years. David Owen, my old patron in the General Education Program, and his wife came and were much taken with Nina: they were relieved that I had done so well.

I extended my own friendships at home beyond Harvard. David Riesman was one of the most diligent letter writers of our time, in touch with contemporaries from many countries and of many interests—and generously attentive to the young. We had already corresponded when I was still in Cambridge and he encouraged me to write him from Germany and the UK. A new dimension was added when I was asked to write an essay on his vision of politics for a series termed *Continuities in Social Research,* which was to publish a book of essays on Riesman's work. (The publisher decided to produce the book within months of his having written to me that he saw no market for the project and could not proceed with my proposal to edit such a volume.) I wrote the essay and sent the initial draft to Riesman, who replied with three letters in succession. The first said that I had depicted his views wrongly; the second, that I may have had some things right but that my conclusion lacked balance, and the third that he had indeed written as I described, but that he had changed his mind and that a package of new essays followed. When I contrast his response with that of Shils (or a later one by Isaiah Berlin), Riesman's stature as a gentleman as well as scholar stands out.

There was also an American opposition. I read *The Nation* regularly but did not yet write for it. I did know Lewis Coser, who with Irving Howe (and money contributed largely by Norman Mailer) had founded *Dissent* in 1954. I corresponded regularly with Lew, who was a Berliner from a wealthy family, had spent the thirties in Paris, had come to the US and been in the US Army, and then taken a doctorate in sociology at Columbia. He was teaching at Brandeis—indeed, I can claim a modest share in his having gained tenure there. When his excellent book, *The Functions of Social Conflict*, was published in the UK, *The Times Literary Supplement* asked me to review it. Reviews in the TLS were then anonymous, and I adopted a faintly patronizing British style ("...the most interesting contribution in sociology to have crossed the Atlantic to us in years...")

The Anglophile party at Brandeis promptly overcame their reservations about Lew's radicalism. The radicalism in *Dissent* was a fusion of the late Marxism that had developed among Trotsky's American followers and their American inheritance, our national progressivism. The *Dissent* editors and writers were, generally, younger than the founders of *Partisan Review*, more inclined to take their American roots for granted, and freer to be selective about what in American tradition they appropriated. I began to write for *Dissent* and also provided Lewis and Irving with a continuously updated map of the politics and thought of the Old World. They, in turn, gave me a sense of events in the US—as seen by intellectuals who resolutely refused to be mobilized for the Cold War, and who had no sympathy for simplifications of any sort.

Visitors, correspondence, reading and film (we saw *The Sweet Smell of Success* and *Rebel Without a Cause* in a Hampstead theater), and American students at the LSE all made the Atlantic appreciably narrower. A friend teaching at Smith told me that I was closer to Cambridge and New York than he was in western Massachusetts. Perhaps he was right, but I did not fully understand the complexity of American culture and politics behind the occasional excitements of the Eisenhower age. There were occasional glimpses of changes to come—but the horizon described by Mills and the writers of *Dissent* and *The Nation* was entirely covered by clouds gray and black.

In London, meanwhile, the sky suddenly became brighter and redder—not in the west or the east but directly overhead. In the spring term of 1957, a young man (eight years younger than I) came to my office, introduced himself as Ralph Samuel, an Oxford graduate now studying economic history at the LSE, and gave me a copy of a newly published journal, *Universities and Left Review*. It had been produced at Oxford by Ralph, with Stuart Hall, Charles Taylor and Gabriel Pearson. The first issue connected the Suez attack with the Soviet invasion of Hungary in a systematic denunciation of the older and newer imperialism. Less conventionally, it called for a recasting of Western politics. It criticized the British Labour Party for living in a past in which appeals to class solidarity would motivate citizens now actually inhabiting the very different cultural and social structures of a society of consumption. Equally, it rejected the party's assumptions that the future could be entrusted to technocrats occasionally validated by an otherwise passive citizenry at election time.

The biographies of the founders explained their readiness to take their distance from the assumptions of the thirties and forties. Ralph came from the Jewish labor movement; his family had lived through decades of argument and struggle. Stuart was a Jamaican, had come to Oxford on a Rhodes scholarship to study literature, and was especially sensitive to the cultures of modern politics. Charles was a philosopher; half his family were English Canadians and the other half French ones, and he was at home in critical Catholic thought and the ideas of what the British termed "the Continentals"—the part of Europe unfortunate enough not to be English. Gabriel, too, studied literature and drew upon a moralizing tradition in British aesthetics: Dickens was one of his heroes.

They were convinced that conventional British thought (above all of those who were in sympathy with Labour) was ossified. The older, academic Left wanted to elevate ordinary citizens, so that they could, at least, appreciate the wit of the senior common rooms. Ordinary folk, however, had long since migrated from the pubs, where the dons thought they congregated, to sit in front of television, a window on a very different social world. As for world politics, they did not believe that tyranny produced bureaucratization, but that bureaucratization produced tyranny. The usual liberal notions of freedom struck them as both out-of-date and shallow. They were attracted to a stream of political thought underground within both liberalism and Marxism, the description of the sometimes-hidden, sometimes-open, consequences of processes of emancipation which had turned or been turned into their opposites.

They knew and liked much of our own culture, saw effective social criticism in plenty that Hollywood produced, and read our own melancholy reflections on the nation as evidence of vitality. Galbraith, Marcuse, Mills, *Dissent,* and *Partisan Review* were familiar to them. They shocked our own cultural arbiters, such as Daniel Bell and William Phillips, by their enthusiasm for Macdonald and Mailer. As the older American intellectuals saw it, their view of the US was perverse. The Americans were insistent that our economic and political system was working well and would in the end do better. They took their distance from much of American culture and especially mass culture. The younger British writers reversed their American seniors' judgements. Our economic and political system, they held, had to be replaced—especially in its imperial incarnation. They discerned the first steps toward that in the youth culture abjured by those who had come of age in the twenties and thirties. It was an American epoch, after all, in which Diana Trilling went to a Beat reading at Columbia afraid that performers and public would smell.

The Americans would have found it even difficult to *talk* with an entirely different group of persons of their own age, who at the same time were founding *The Reasoner*. They were Communist intellectuals teaching in the British universities. Their leaders were John Saville and Edward Thompson, who seized upon the Khrushchev speech of 1956 to demand the de-Stalinization of the British Communist Party. It is difficult to explain, now, the attraction of the Communist Party (and the USSR) for that generation. The British Party did have an appeal to some scientists, and was implanted in some of the unions. The USSR was the land in which revolution had become permanent. The Khrushchev speech, then the turbulence in Eastern Europe and the suppression of the Hungarian revolution (led by a Communist party), brought to the surface all the doubts these historians had accumulated, and repressed, over the years. They came to the conclusion reached much earlier by critics of Stalinism: opposing it was a duty imposed by fidelity to revolutionary ideals, not a break with revolutionary tradition.

The Reasoner editors were told by the party leadership that the Central Committee sympathized with their interest in more open discussion inside the party: as soon as they agreed to cease publishing their journal, the matter could be addressed. Edward and John, and a number of others including Christopher Ifill and Rodney Hilton, left the party (Eric Hobsbawm remained but made his solidarity with the dissidents clear).

They renamed their journal *The New Reasoner*, won a wider public among those on the left of the Labour Party, and opened a current of discussion parallel to but somewhat different from that in *Universities and Left Review*. There was considerable overlap between these dissidents and the Anglo-Marxist school of history.

The Anglo-Marxist historians looked back not to the French Revolution but to an entire stream of popular movements. They did not ask why Great Britain had had no French Revolution but insisted that the British version of consensual history, in which the nation absorbed these attacks on power and moved on, was false. British history from the Norman Conquest on was made up of continuing conflicts, and these were buried only later by those who wrote history from the top downward. They set about resuscitating the memory of those who had been willfully deprived of their voices. Now persons who had spent their entire adult lives in the Communist Party abruptly left it: finally, they were finding their own voices.

The New Reasoner drew contributions and readership from far beyond the reach of the Communist Party. A good many reflective Labour supporters were interested in the editors' analysis of the new structures of international capitalism, the more so as the pre-war generation grew up still thinking of the nation as a great imperial power—not as a relatively impoverished middling one. Others were reassured by their insistence that Great Britain had not achieved a new classlessness, that older structures of domination persisted if sometimes in newer forms. Saville was an economic historian and Thompson a general one. He had written a large book on William Morris and his attempt to give new life to artisanship in the industrial age.

Thompson, with much of a great career before him, was a striking figure. His father was an Oxford don who taught Hindu studies after leaving the Indian Civil Service. A Methodist, he rejected the idea of empire after having been one of its chosen few, a member of the small group of British who gave their lives to administering

India. His mother was an American, related to Adlai Stevenson and Ambassador Philip Jessup. His brother had been a British intelligence officer killed on a mission to Bulgaria. Edward himself had driven a tank in the Eighth Army in the desert and Italy. He was rooted in the English tradition of dissent. A person of great eloquence, he was incapable of writing a letter of less than three to five single-spaced typed pages. Later, when joining in the negotiations over the fusion of *The New Reasoner* with *Universities and Left Review*, I admired his stubborn insistence that even the smallest points were matters of large concern: he had a view of the whole. His energy, talent, and outspokenness did not only bring him friends. Some of his contemporaries were shocked by the most obvious thing about him—he was honest when he said that he sought a revolution.

Edward at the time taught in the adult extension department of Cambridge University. Two contemporaries of his had similar posts—Raymond Williams at Cambridge and Richard Hoggart at Oxford. The combined cultural influence of the three was very large—their principled devotion to the education of adults who were too old to profit from the post-war opening of access to universities gave them insights into ordinary existence not always available on campus. Williams published a work, *Culture and Society*, which provided an historical background for new questions about political culture. His argument was that we could not identify a specifically political culture; all of culture is part of a larger struggle for power in society—and an attempt, equally, to create free space for those who could not win it directly. There was something familiar about the work of this scholar from the border between England and Wales, reminiscent of the moral resolve and demand for reconciliation voiced by the one-nation Tories and the Christian social reformers. They proposed changing society in response to fixed spiritual values. Williams thought these were in continuous transformation and sought to democratize the processes by which they were created.

The other book at the time which inspired the new left was by Richard Hoggart. In *The Uses of Literacy*, he asked what had happened to Matthew Arnold's project ("we must educate our future masters"). The older forms of working-class solidarity were dissolving, and far from appropriating high culture, the class (along with the descendants of Arnold's readers) was immersed in the newer patterns of consumption. They were also participants in a newer, ostensibly classless, culture—but if industrially produced and commercially marketed, this had occasional seizures of social criticism. In the US, a large group of social critics depicted the new mass culture as an ideological narcotic. In Great Britain, the guardians of cultural propriety regarded it as did the Baskin family in Forster's *Howard's End*: an intruder to be dismissed from the premises instantly. Like Williams, Hoggart sought a future in which citizens were equal in their access to art, science, and thought. More, they wanted new definitions and new forms of culture. They acknowledged the difficulty of achieving a democratic revolution in culture—the more so as much of the intellectual elite was at one with much of the citizenry in assuming that cultural stratification was here to stay. Neither was very distraught about this, which put those worried by the problem in the role of vanguard (as we saw it) or sect (as some others saw us).

The thought of the early New Left was hardly systematic, but it was not shapeless. It had as its elements the analysis of the internationalization of capitalism, the continuation of imperialism in new forms, the degradation and stagnation of state socialism, and the predominance of bureaucratization in the Western welfare states. We sought new agents of transformation and new ways to broaden the practice of citizenship, and deemed generational conflict as well as class conflict inevitable, and potentially positive, politically. The older Marxists in *The Reasoner* looked for a new wave of political mobilization in direct class confrontation, the younger group in *Universities and Left Review* asked whether unexpected modes of conflict would provide new paths to a reconceived political engagement. Both groups were disappointed and perplexed by the fate of artistic and philosophic modernity. The most telling renditions of our condition deepened our pessimism if not despair: over which horizon could we find the end of alienation?

As we were deepening these discussions, I left for a summer in the United States. I had not been home for five years; I had to defend my thesis at Harvard, and an invitation to teach at the Harvard Summer School made the trip possible. I arranged for an exchange of apartments with a Harvard philosopher. Nina and I took temporary possession of a frame town house in a friendly complex on the Charles, reserved for junior faculty and full of lively children. When we came out to say hello, some were playing with a large Samoyed. I asked whose dog it was. "Yours," was the reply. Our hosts had left it in charge of neighbors, but the dog regarded the house as home, adopted us as family, and was delighted to resume his habit of following the philosopher to classes. He did not hold my discipline against me.

The world had changed, but Harvard had simply deepened its sense that the world revolved around it. For large parts of the globe, it was right. Harvard had money to invite an eminent European to lecture for a year. I was asked by an assistant to McGeorge Bundy, then the provost, for suggestions: I suggested Sartre. My interlocutor, Michael Maccoby, objected that Sartre did not speak English. Since no one at Harvard would admit not to knowing French, I replied, his lectures would be even more crowded. Maccoby intimated that Sartre's political views might be an obstacle: he was not in the forefront of the Atlanticist party in Europe. Even better, I suggested; it would be an American gesture toward the Europeans. Maccoby, still an undergraduate and not very imposing in physical stature, drew himself upright: "Harvard doesn't make gestures."

My Harvard friends had grown more prosperous materially—and morally, too: they were well into rewarding careers. Cambridge was home not only to faculty at Harvard and MIT, but to younger professionals who crowded its restaurants and coffee shops. Student culture seemed to have escaped the vice of the V-necked jersey and the tartan skirt, but even in the pursuit of pleasure seemed organized and purposeful. Cambridge's dropouts were very visible. They were more than faintly reminiscent of the Indian student who allegedly had "B.A. Oxon (Failed)" printed on his visiting card.

I talked politics with Carl Kaysen, Arthur Schlesinger Jr. Sam Beer. They enjoyed criticizing the Eisenhower regime and gossiping about it with a certain assurance and verve: their evident premise was that they would be back in Washington sooner rather than later. Four and a half years after Stalin's death, they had some contact with Soviets, scientists especially, but they were not much concerned with the cultural and political ferment in Moscow, and Communist China was completely distant. The specialists of course paid attention to the alternating widening and constriction of space for criticism in Russia, but what they knew (a very great deal) had little impact upon the assumptions of the Cold War, which had hardened into dogma.

I was invited to lunch at the MIT Faculty Club and noticed security guards. My host explained that the building housed MIT's Center for International Studies, which had government contracts. I learned years later that the center was financed extensively by the CIA. Indeed, in an effort to obtain an independent perspective on China, Senator John F. Kennedy asked the center to prepare a report for him. It was only when he was president that he learned that it may have been independent of the State Department, but not of the government.

Some of the scientists were interested in arms control, and I met a few one could term American dissidents. The scientists were secure since they knew their estate was indispensable. The dissidents had the format to accept a certain cultural and professional marginality. Harvard and MIT were not like the European universities, where radical political views did not impair careers. I was aware of the morally tortuous problems of the recent past, but did not inquire further. Had I done so I would have learned that the acquiescence of the Cambridge academic community in American foreign policy followed some episodes in which failure to do so was costly.

I visited with the editors and some of the writers of three major journals of opinion: *Commentary, Dissent,* and *Partisan Review.* They knew each other, wrote for one another's journals, argued incessantly. Of course, the journals were products of a New York milieu. That milieu was as self-centered as ever, but by 1957 it had established colonies on the campuses across the country. It had never been exclusively Jewish, and in New York its influence extended to publishing and the higher journalism. The journals were even read in Eisenhower's Washington, although few of their editors and writers noticed. For some, that would have disturbed their self-portrayals as iconoclasts.

Commentary alternated between obsessive anti-Communism and compulsive affirmation of the openness of American life. American prosperity and a very rapid diminution of overt anti-Semitism gave a new Jewish generation professional and social chances denied to an earlier generation and *Commentary*'s founding editor, Eliot Cohen, thought that gratitude was due to the nation. *Commentary* often published political and social commentary and description, rather more irenic than cutting.

Its support for Israel was dutiful, even complacently distant: no one evoked Masada, and the editors would have excised a reference of that sort as absurdly over dramatic. What most interested its readers, mostly educated Jewish businesspeople and professionals, were questions about their place in modern America.

There was a certain ambiguity in its sense of mission. Was it a Jewish journal making a contribution to discussions of our national problems? Was it a national journal with a part of its attention given to the problems of the educated and emancipated segment of American Jewry? That is how many writers and readers, Gentile and Jewish alike, saw it. When, after returning to London, I wrote an article intimating that Eisenhower's US was not a divine commonwealth, Cohen did not want to publish it He told George Lichtheim, who had gone to New York for a year to work at *Commentary*, that he was uneasy about publishing so critical a piece by a younger Jewish writer. Lichtheim (and the other editors) convinced him to take a chance; I recollect no dire consequences. In fact, I recollect no consequences at all: the importance of the word did not always carry over from Holy Script to secular prophecy. The cumulative effect on national discussion of the ideas published in this milieu was no doubt considerable, but that did not necessarily lend importance to any one article, idea or writer. When he became editor in 1960, Norman Podhoretz grasped the political consequences of his work in more realistic and yet more subtle terms—but he represented a generation far more at ease in the US.

Partisan Review was very much in the hands of the Depression generation, in the person of its founders Phillip Rahv and William Phillips. Unlike Cohen, they preferred not to make Jewishness the core of their existence. They were acutely aware of anti-Semitism and its political and social consequences, but their way of dealing with it was to insist on their right to occupy what had been in the American universities in the twenties and thirties restricted territory for Jews: the realms of aesthetics, history, literature, philosophy. They did so in the name of the Enlightenment as they understood it: a singular mixture of old ideas of emancipation and new ones of both radical democracy and cultural freedom.

They assembled in the thirties and early forties an exceedingly mixed group of thinkers (by no means entirely Jewish) to write outside the prevailing academic canons whose relentless pursuit of both high art and revolution I'd been astonished and educated by as a teenager. By 1957, however, *Partisan Review* had itself become an institution—the quasi-official voice of the avant-garde. Revolution had been dropped, with reconciliation, after a fashion, with the United States replacing it. Rahv and Phillips were brilliant at mocking their erstwhile adversaries—even when these had become allies and patrons. They insisted that, having seen beyond their original attachment to Trotsky (their alignment with the Communist Party was not mentioned), they were better qualified than others to defend the United States. Someone, somewhere in the governmental apparatus agreed, and covert CIA subsidies (of a very modest sort) supplemented the journal's perpetually precarious budget. Meanwhile, the triumph of modernism in the universities allowed them to claim that they had been at the voice of high culture all the time: the academics described by Alfred Kazin as English-descended Protestants with three names were caretakers only of a cemetery.

Partisan Review maintained a good deal of its generalized aggressiveness and permanent sense of indignation. Capitalism was no longer the problem, and was now even praised for spreading wealth around. The trouble was that it wasn't being spent on the right sort of cultural goods. The *Partisan Review* group had moved from Trotsky to Burke without an intervening phase. No one used phrases such as "the swinish multitude" or "the unbought graces of life," but a sense of beleaguerment was obvious. Still, it was difficult to deride the reign of philistinism when officialdom arranged for an abstract expressionist exhibition to be sent abroad as evidence for American artistic creativity. *Partisan Review*'s contributors deplored the culture of the new capitalism, but did not agree on what had degraded it. Philip Rieff, reviewing Mills's *The Power Elite*, said that Mills had written of the "higher immorality" but asked why he had ignored "the lower mindlessness." In short, *Partisan Review* was still the guardian of high culture, but was unsure both of what it was guarding and who it was guarding it against.

I spoke with William Phillips, and would get to know him much better in subsequent years. He treated me as a serious contributor to intellectual debate, and evinced both curiosity and skepticism about the British New Left. Lack of knowledge of its historical setting and exact development did not inhibit his judgments. Why should he treat us any differently than he treated the matter that crossed his editorial desk? I was extremely pleased to be taken into his critical confidence: it was at least as gratifying as my return to Harvard as a respected scholar.

Dissent was the work of unreconciled American progressives, of writers connected to the labor movement, of obdurate democratic socialists. The journal's title conveyed its intention: to reject what Irving Howe in an earlier article in *Commentary* termed the American celebration, to keep alive what was left of radicalism. Its articles covered the cultural and social map, from debates on psychoanalysis to descriptions of the new American class system. The authors and editors saw no reason to depict matters as better than they were, but they kept a sense of humor. Many of the articles were written by scholars struggling to fuse serious inquiry with political passion, evoking Macdonald's later description of them as "professors of revolution."

Commentary could not escape the question, "Is it good for the Jews?" *Partisan Review* struggled desperately to keep the distance its editors saw as authenticity. *Dissent* was, in the fifties, more critical of the dogmatic rigidities of Cold War politics and yet irreducibly American in its belief that the nation could change for the better.

Discontinuities abounded. *Partisan Review* had introduced Eliot, Kafka, and Sartre to many, but published Lionel Trilling's sedulous defense of ordinariness. Norman Mailer certainly took modernism's message seriously: cultural boundaries were there to be transgressed. Yet he was a founder of *Dissent* with its nostalgia for New Deal populism. *Commentary* was pious about American life but frequently published sketches of American culture etched in acid.

In fact, many of these differences were attributable to the authors' ages, social origins and experience, and temperaments. A few weeks in New York gave me a rather clearer sense of these human complexities than long periods of reading the journals at a distance. I saw my old friend Clement Greenberg become an iconic figure as intellectual spokesman for the abstract expressionists. Clem was more strenuously critical of the quality of American life than ever, but as passionately anti-Communist as in Stalin's lifetime and suspicious of a "Europe" he accused of insufficient political conviction. His avarice had grown with success. He warned me against allowing myself to be exploited by vending articles, interviews, lectures, too cheaply. It was flattering advice: no one was attempting to exploit me in that way, since almost no one was inviting me.

It is only now, years after Clem's death, that I realize how deep was his anger, how enormous his pride, how driven his ambition, his sensitivity to slights real and imagined. He did for a while serve as a mentor and I am grateful for his recognition of my talents. He saw in me some of the ferocity of his own ambition—and attempted to help by advising me of the manners appropriate to advancing it. Perhaps I would have been helped even more by learning that there were things in life more important than ambition. I was not, at the time, very receptive to that message.

Lewis Coser taught that by example. We visited the Cosers at their rented cottage on Massachusetts Bay, near the Wellfleet dock. In the years since I had seen them in New York, they had moved to Boston, where Lew taught at Brandeis, Rose at Wellesley. They treated Nina and me as family. Lew was in touch with politics and thought on two continents, and did not see why high culture had to entail dead seriousness. His observations on colleagues and friends were saturated with sympathy. He did not consider himself free of human limitations and wished for a world in which we were free to be more generous. Rose was angry at the subordination demanded of women in the American academy at the time—and made her case by doing exemplary work in studies of American medicine, which anticipated by two decades sociological perspectives now thought of as commonplaces, but which were then deemed disturbing. Rose scorned the idea that women should be defined primarily by their maternal functions, and yet among her many gifts was a motherly strength upon which both her children and friends counted.

We spent an evening with Wright Mills and his family at their house in Nyack—built, largely, by Wright himself. He had been disappointed, but not surprised, at the conventionality of the reviews of *The Power Elite*. Claiborne Pell, then a journalist and later a Rhode Island senator with quite an enlightened record, declared in *The American Political Science Review* that it was "an insult to the American people." Mills was certainly in one tradition of populism—in which the people had first to become aware of the conventional beliefs, and the conventional ignorance, which held it down.

In the fall of 1957, Wright was preparing to go to Europe to write *The Sociological Imagination*, a settlement of accounts with academic conventions and an attempt to restore sociology to its traditions of large historical narrative, philosophical anchorage, and political commitment. He was struggling with these issues in his own life: how could he break out of the confinement of a professorial career and address a larger public? The examples of Galbraith and Schlesinger and Riesman were before him, but he wished to deliver a message at once more radical and more personal. Already the nation's best known sociologist, it was before he achieved fame far beyond our borders with *Listen, Yankee* and *The Origins of World War Three*.

Meeting Wright in the United States after having first met him in Europe deepened my admiration for him. He was interested in the vocation of the intellectual and the practice of intellectual workmanship. His curiosity was large, and his capacity to decide that there were things he ought to know, techniques he should master, larger still. Standing with Galbraith at the White House reception after the Kennedy funeral, de Gaulle looked down on Kaganovitch, and said "The world belongs to tall men." Wright, who was tall, wondered whether the world was better understood by shorter and perhaps more patient figures who had accumulated the intellectual resources needed. He interpreted his own impatience as a response to the political crisis that was upon us, and was unsure of the importance of the large resonance of his books. To what extent he already sensed that his time was cruelly limited I do not know: in less than five years he would be dead at age forty-six.

I visited, as well, the different world of New York psychoanalysis, which responded to other rhythms. In London earlier that year, I had considered undertaking psychoanalytic training—not to change professions, but to deepen my reach as a social scientist. The London Psychoanalytic Society did admit lay persons as candidates, and seemed receptive to my own interest. At first, anyway: Anna Freud was friendly, even encouraging. I had also to see a well-known theorist, Winnicott. He played the role of brusque British gentleman to perfection. Since I was an American, was the burden of what he told me, I would have to pay American rates for my training analysis. I was startled at the salience of payment in his conversation, remarked that I was after all working in the United Kingdom on a British salary, and was given to understand that the interview was over.

In fact, there was an agreement that the London group would only accept Americans approved by their institutes at home. I contacted the New York Psychoanalytic Institute and saw two members of the relevant committee.

The first was Heinz Hartmann, who came from Vienna. He had heard Max Weber lecture there, was quite receptive to the notion of a younger American joining what seemed to be a church, or a guild, or a club (it did not take him long to elicit my sense of distance from much of American social science as insufficiently historical and reflective). Hartmann impressed me as having retained a great deal of his European-ness of language and thought, a grand *seignior* visiting New York.

The second analyst was cordiality personified (I was struck by the contrast with Winnicott). He seemed very interested in my project and sympathetic to my professed motives, and we talked about the differences between Europe and America. I knew that he had done work on dreams and sleep, recalled having met him at a large party in New York at the end of the war, and we parted on good terms. His name was Charles Fisher and ten years later, we were to become very good friends. I did not, upon my return to London, pursue the matter. I cannot now recall what accounted for the decision not to proceed. It was not, certainly a lack of money: with a determined effort, I could have found it. Something held me back, and it was not the fear of dispersing my efforts. Most likely, it was a frequent if at the time subliminal sense that I wasn't entitled to this—or any other—promising venture. It could be put another way: I was enjoying a nice modicum of success: why endanger it by trying to enlarge upon it?

The summer visit also brought a return to my family. Father, who had tried for years, did succeed in the necessary examination and had become an assistant principal at a junior high school at the Bronx entrance to the Throgs Neck Bridge. He and Mother moved out of our apartment on 163rd Street in the Bronx and joined a new and irresistible Jewish exodus—to the suburbs. When I was growing up, Westchester County had enclaves of prosperous Jewish families, but was otherwise the sort of place John Cheever wrote about in *The New Yorker*. Now it had a full measure of newly built synagogues and, of course, delicatessen shops.

My parents had joined the mainstream in another, entrepreneurial, way. With my sister and her husband, Ed, they purchased an old hunting camp on a small lake in northwestern Connecticut, right at the Massachusetts border. The nearest town was New Boston, Massachusetts, on what three centuries before had been the frontier. They converted the site into a summer camp for children, and found themselves not only on the familiar terrain of education (Ed was also a teacher) but the unfamiliar one of small business.

Nina and I liked the site: one could swim across the lake or row across it (not allowed to the campers without supervision) and walk in the woods. Old stone fences were remnants of the farmers who had settled the place, and then moved westward. I did not have the impression that much pedagogic energy in the camp was invested on the New England past.

In fact, the American Jewish community was enjoying the present. Many of the baleful consequences of the pervasive anti-Semitism of a Christian society had been attenuated or disappeared. Discriminatory quotas and outright exclusion in higher education and the professions were gone or much reduced; restrictions on Jewish acquisition of residential property had been legally and politically challenged—successfully. *Commentary* had a series of articles on the new wave of inter-marriage. The generation now come to maturity and leadership of the Jewish community was fully American: many had been in the armed services during the war. There was considerable American horror at the Holocaust, and the liberal churches had frequently aided the Jewish organizations in a very intense legal and political campaign against discrimination. Moreover, in the expanding post-war economy (and in government, charged with permanent mobilization for the Cold War and the administration of a greatly enlarged regulatory and welfare state) careers were open to talents.

Two themes now dominant in American Jewish consciousness were audible, but not nearly as dominant then as they are now. One was the Holocaust, or rather, the necessity of not forgetting it. At the time, Holocaust survivors who had come to the US after the war, and their children, preferred not to talk very much about it. The study of the Holocaust in universities was not as extensive or organized as it is now, and the Holocaust Museum had not even been conceived. What discussion there was frequently moved in directions different than those now predominant (which often insist on the uniqueness of the Holocaust, as part of a claim to Jewish exceptionalism). In the fifties, the Holocaust was evidence for the imperative universalism incumbent upon Jews. A renewal genocide could be averted only if Jews joined others in pursuit of a peaceful society. Support for Israel was not the *raison d'être* of the Jewish community it has now become, and total identification with Israel was left to small conventicler of Zionists quite distinct from, and even rejected by, an avowedly assimilationist majority.

Drawing all of these threads together was difficult. I had no direct contact with actual politics, despite incessant political discussion. I did meet Michael Harrington, whose commitment to social justice was as deep as his understanding of the many obstacles to it. My encounter with European social Catholicism had made me aware, for the first time, of the importance of Catholicism in American social reform. Mike's lifelong patience was shaped by his Catholicism, as estranged as he might have been from the official Church. There are no ex-Catholics any more than there are former Jews. Indeed, lapsed Catholics were like secular Jews in that matters ecclesiastical were as important to them as matters ethnic to the Jews.

I returned on the *Queen Elizabeth*—four days in which to reflect. It was difficult to do so, since the trip had called many spirits from the deep. The trouble was, they appeared, danced enchantingly or grimaced menacingly, occasionally said something half-audible, then disappeared. The visit did not strengthen a decision to remain in Europe; it confirmed an underlying indecision I could not confront directly. I could not even be sure of what sort of expatriate I was—permanent or provisional. Was I a cultural pilgrim, even if it would have been absurd to depict the American universities and New York intellectual life as philistine landscapes (there was a great deal of European traffic in our direction, after all)? Was I a political one—even if I had not suffered in the slightest from the Cold War and had encountered signs of radical life? Could I find the resources (which I doubted) to become a transatlantic commuter, resolving the problem by never having to say farewell?

Behind the question of location was one I could not articulate, even if it shaped everything I did. I hesitate to use the phrase a problem of identity. It was years before I told a skeptical, even irritated, Erik Erikson that most persons were not searching for an identity but trying to alter the identities they had, but I was immensely dissatisfied with what I knew of myself, and sought to throw off that persona by changes of continent, country, culture, by joining now one, now another group. Perhaps a New England college town would have provided a fixed stage and allowed me to see more clearly that I was acting out a personal drama (even though Amherst failed signally to do that a decade later, when I had far more accomplishments and experience and perhaps even more insight). Upon my return to London, I constructed a maelstrom, the better to plunge into it.

In short, the visit to the United States added new dimensions to my problems and did not contribute in the short run to my solving them. I now regard the visit, however, as thoroughly positive. It threw many things into sharp relief, not least my inability to live with success, modest or less so—and by intensifying my perpetual sense of crisis, certainly prevented me from lapsing into any one pattern and becoming prisoner of it.

I kept struggling, against authentically adverse inner forces and exaggeratedly inflated outer ones. No doubt, some of the tumult was genuine: my creativity in seeking ways to maximize environmental disturbance was considerable. More of it was due to something I could not at the time imagine, much less grasp—a sense of inner emptiness, maybe loneliness.

Actual life, as distinct from inner processes, was anything but lonely. I plunged into a crowded round of activities—and kept from touching psychic depths by ever more movement on the surface. A steady stream of visitors (colleagues, political acquaintances, students and just friends) came to our home, to Nina's enjoyment as well as my own. The New Left moved off the pages of our journals and became an actual political movement. We founded a London Left Club (others followed in several cities) and in a moment of inspiration, took what was for England a revolutionary step—we opened a café in central London, in Soho Square.

The project was supposed to provide funding for *Universities and Left Review*, housed in offices above it. Alas, the café quickly proved so unprofitable that it in fact threatened the journal with financial ruin. There were lots of customers, but many ordered one cup of coffee (without the pastries we also offered) and remained for hours, talking or playing chess or checkers or reading the newspapers. We clearly needed a regime like that in French cafes ("Messieurs et Mesdames Les Clients Sont Pries De Renouveller Leurs Consummations etc."). The one regular who did renew was a gentleman in a suit and with a perpetually strained expression, as if he intended to convey a generalized sympathy but could not quite contain its opposite. We finally concluded that he was the Scotland Yard agent sent to keep track of us. His presence posed a theoretic problem. Were we actually a danger to the existing order, and therefore justified in congratulating ourselves? Alternatively, was the entire imperial apparatus so rickety that our very modest projects were a threat? The financial crisis of the café (we named it The Partisan Café, rather as the younger founders of *Partisan Review* had found a name for their journal a quarter-century earlier—to indicate our readiness for combat, without specifying for or against what) deepened. The café's backers were prosperous business persons of undiminished ideological fervor. They met with a committee of New Left intellectuals (Eric Hobsbawm, who may have been the intermediary, as well as Stuart Hall and Doris Lessing). The intellectuals proposed drastic measures to put the place on a business-like basis. The North London backers, mostly Jewish, were aghast: one could not, they insisted, run a socialist café on such deplorable principles. Somehow, we marched, or stumbled, on.

We also formed the London New Left Club. Our debt to the continent was obviously large. The café came from France and central Europe, although some insisted on reminiscences of London's eighteenth-century coffee houses. I suppose we thought of a club in terms of the Club des Jacobins. In Paris, every sort of political group from the fifties onward had distinctly non-revolutionary discussion circles, but of course they were termed clubs in deference to national tradition. The London New Left Club concentrated on talks and discussions, and attracted an interesting series of speakers and lively listeners. It was there that I met Iris Murdoch. I served frequently as chair of our evenings: I now think that my British friends thought that a New Yorker could handle occasional outbursts of raucousness. Grammar school boys and girls came, as well as older trade unionists and veterans of every one of Britain's many ideological wars. What counted as raucousness in post-war London would have been thought of in the New York I grew up in as ostentatiously courtly manners.

I retain memories of two high points of those evenings. One involved Dwight Macdonald, visiting in London from New York for a few months to replace, temporarily, Irving Kristol as editor of *Encounter*. I introduced him as one of my "boyhood heroes"—and Dwight lurched to his feet to declare "I'm not that old." I continued, undeterred, and praised him as someone who "had never sold out." This time Dwight came halfway to the podium to declare that "no one had ever offered enough to buy me." He was, clearly, in a mood to deflate, even mock, his public's expectations and that evening did conclude a bit noisily—when he praised the deference of waiters in Great Britain as contrasted with the unpolished manners of their American colleagues. Dwight had not yet, clearly, returned to radicalism.

The second memory is of a very early meeting of the club. As an unexpectedly large but also youthful crowd turned up, a great historian drew upon his stock of generalizations. Eric Hobsbawm said that the New Left was definitely on the way up. "Ascendant social movements always attract the most charming women."

We obviously met a need the Labour Party and its affiliated groups, or the Marxist sects which hung on more determinedly as they shrank, did not satisfy. One of the qualities which appealed to many, as I spoke with them at our meetings, was our openness: one needed no ideological combat medals or wounds in past political battles to apply. In fact, one did not apply at all but simply turned up. The historians of British church life termed it Latitudinarianism. It lived on, and indeed, a fair number of our new friends were social Christians and had participated in the social works of their churches—or, at least, were versed in their social doctrines. These were, also, the persons most sympathetic to the United States—in the sense that they expected great changes of us, since they were in touch with church groups whose beliefs and campaigns were unnoticed by, indeed usually unknown to, my friends in Cambridge and Manhattan.

Something was in the air in London in 1957, and we were its beneficiaries. It is hard, simple formulations apart, to say exactly what it was. A desire for something new, for a break with cultural and political routine, was evident—but what made so many think that we were not only young but had something original to offer? A newer generation had a less puritanical disposition than the older one—and hedonistic deviations from it were now definitely not reserved for the more prosperous. The young, in their experimental and mocking mode, voiced the doubts and hidden passions of the old. The national consensus on the welfare state, meanwhile, paradoxically, encouraged a desire for a large historical break.

The Conservatives, ostensibly, were worried by so much centralization and direction from above in the distribution of public goods. Nothing shocked them more, however, than the revival of older demands for participation and self-governance: if met, one could no longer say who was up and who was down, in or out. The Labour reforms of 1945-1951, and their acceptance by significant numbers of Conservatives, made possible the diminution of deference in British social organization. The New Left represented its brash sequel, a culture which began to prize youth and impulse over age and convention. In the arts, John Osborne's play *Look Back in Anger* and the Colin MacInnes novel *Absolute Beginners* expressed this mood perfectly. The characters in Iris Murdoch's early novel *Under the Net* (many lacked fixed addresses) did so as well. A jagged line divided the New Left between those who were part of this new culture and those (invariably older) who were descendants of Matthew Arnold and William Morris.

The young favored the US, its films and music—or a surrealist idea of France. The old thought of themselves as guardians of cultural propriety—and of Europe (the ancient world excepted) as a place for vacations and the US as an experiment about which it was discreet to refrain from uttering very justified doubts.

Other divisions were there, too. Anti-colonialism and anti-imperialism had a long and at times effective history in the British Left, but the emigration to the United Kingdom of an increasing number of Africans, Asians and people of color from the Caribbean posed different problems. There was a racial disturbance in Notting Hill, London, in 1958: a white gang had attacked black immigrants and the immigrant community responded with a very disorderly protest. I went with two friends (Doris Lessing and Clancy Sigal) to the site some hours later, when matters had calmed. The residents voiced their complaints about discrimination in general. The scale of immigration was still small and the debate about it was diffuse. What was hardly diffuse was the persistence of a sense of superiority among white Britons who had, after all, very living memories of empire. Wars of colonial repression had just been fought in Kenya and Malaysia (and in Europe, in Cyprus). The new immigration added to the British impression that much in the world, despite the victory of 1945, had turned worse. Somewhat later, the Tory MP Enoch Powell voiced, in straightened form, the racism and xenophobia the rougher sort began to express in the streets. Of course, there were direct connections to the fascism led by the aristocratic adventurer Oswald Mosley in the thirties. Mosley made a pathetic return to British politics in the late fifties, but his wartime sympathies for his friend Hitler had discredited him.

The Commonwealth immigration brought home issues of difference once thought settled forever by overseas domination. "Home" in British imperial language meant the homeland—even for those, such as Australians, who had never seen it. Now, home in a literal sense became the site of traditional struggles which moved out of bedrooms and breakfast tables to novels and the stage—between men and women. The British Left had always had a contingent of extremely competent women, devoid of illusions. Many had chosen to treat the problem of emancipation as part of a larger complex, although there were always advocates and exemplars of sexual equality and freedom. It was in this atmosphere that Doris

Lessing, who joined the board of *Universities and Left Review* in 1957, began to write *The Golden Notebooks*, which she published in 1962. Still, the nation was retrograde enough to ban the original version of *Lady Chatterly's Lover* until the courts struck down the prohibition in 1960. I recall a letter to the old *Times of London* mocking the pompous ass who as Crown Counsel prosecuted the case, and who had asked the Court whether the book were fit material to be given to "your maidservant." "Sir," asked the letter writer, "would it not be more appropriate to ask if it would be wise to give it to your gardener?"

The *Times* in this period published letters on specific controversies to which it assigned an identifying sub-head. As part of the argument over emancipation, an official commission had brought in a proposal to decriminalize homosexual acts between "consenting adults" and that was the heading for a long series of readers' letters. One country parson did not, obviously, countenance the commission's liberalism and posted a letter which was an exceedingly brief Biblical quotation: "And the Lord rained down fire on the cities of the plain." That was not all the newspaper was concerned with in this period, and another set of letters debated the morality and wisdom of Britain's nuclear weapons—and of its providing bases for the US airborne and undersea nuclear strike forces. The parson's sortie was promptly followed by another reader's question. "Sir, you published the letter under 'consenting adults' but would it not have been more appropriate under 'nuclear weapons'?"

It was, indeed, a matter which vexed the British—and in which we in the New Left were involved. We found ourselves partly following, partly serving as a vanguard of, a movement against nuclear weapons larger, more deeply rooted in society, and more spontaneous than we had imagined possible. Our astonishment was all the greater as, despite our incessant invocation of the necessity and value of active citizenship, we wondered—not silently—whether history, even the history of so fundamentally democratic a nation as Great Britain, had rendered improbable large popular protests.

In 1957, Bertrand Russell, the Labour journalist and parliamentarian Michael Foot, some trade unionists, and an inter-denominational group of Bishops decided that the time had come to revise British nuclear policy. They argued that with US forces operating from Britain, the country had lost a critical part of its sovereignty. They suggested that the United Kingdom could give an example to the world by renouncing nuclear weapons. They addressed the public in a conventional way, a letter to the *Times*.

Somehow, through schoolteachers and church groups, it reached persons who did not read that newspaper at breakfast daily—mainly young people. Out of sight of the prominent signers of the original statement, a national discussion began in very local circumstances—inaudibly, then quietly, and in any case under the radar screen of the BBC and the press. Then some veterans of past struggles decided to stage a march from Trafalgar Square to the British nuclear weapons factory at Aldermaston, some fifty miles to the west of London. That caught on; delegations came from abroad (the US was represented by Bayard Rustin who spoke with much eloquence in the Square), and two thousand or so marchers lined up to depart behind a band rendering "When the Saints Come Marching In."

Several thousand more assembled in the square to see them off. I was there, again, with Eric Hobsbawm, a great historian not hesitant about judging history in the making. This could take off, he said, and become much larger. Knots and swirls of people were arguing in the square. A bearded man tried to join an argument, but a middle-aged lady with a strident voice turned him away. "I do not," she announced, "talk to people who wear beards." An angular Anglican priest emerged from the crowd and posed a question: "Madam, what would you say were Jesus Christ to appear in Trafalgar Square?" I did not hear her response, but the marchers touched national nerves.

The positive response to what became the loosely organized Campaign for Nuclear Disarmament had several sources. Especially strong among the young was fear—fear that a nuclear war would deprive them of their futures. The hedonism of the new generation was Freud's old Eros put to political uses—and nowhere more determinedly than in their repudiation of what Edward Thompson later was to term "exterminism." The younger party of libido was joined by an older one, more sublimated, which envisaged a British example to the world, a moral gesture which might inspire other peoples or even governments. Nearly all of the participants distrusted the bona fides, and the very competence, of the British elite. There was a connection between the emergence of mass protest and the disaster that had preceded it—the abortive attack on Egypt and the humiliating British withdrawal under combined American and Soviet pressure.

The marchers brought the discussion of alternatives into the national media. A year later, 1959, the protest route was reversed—from Aldermaston to London. Tens of thousands took part. The Labour Party's official position had been expressed by the former leader of its internal opposition, Aneurin Bevan, in the remarkable formulation: "Do not send the British Foreign Minister naked into the conference chamber." Labour would not renounce British nuclear weapons unless something could be won in return, an argument invariably followed by descriptions of Soviet mendacity and the impossibility of serious negotiations with the USSR. Labour instructed its Members of Parliament not to participate, so quite a few of them stood silently on the streets as we passed to intimate their support. I also recollect cheers for a large banner carried by Clancy Sigal and Philip Rieff: "The University Of California Against The Bomb."

The unintended joining of the Campaign for Nuclear Development with the New Left's hopes for participatory democracy did not quite conceal the evidence. We appealed to the makers of opinion because we were the stuff of high-level gossip that lent a bit of color and novelty to political discussions which were standardized.

Those were the years of "Butskellism" in which the Tory reformer Rab Butler and the Labour leader Hugh Gaitskell, both sons of Indian civil servants, graduates of the same unsparingly intellectual public (private) school Winchester, in fact led different branches of the same party. They agreed on keeping and reinforcing the welfare state, on the alliance with the US, on distance from the Continentals and their Common Market, on the voluntary liquidation of imperial positions. Above all, perhaps, they agreed on fiscal and monetary policies which (at least in good times) would keep up the citizens' spending power. Our own appeals for a qualitative rethinking of quantitative socialism, for a renewal of the public sphere, evoked a loud silence from many, including Labour voters. In 1959, Harold Macmillan (who had been a Keynesian and an ardent anti-appeaser in the thirties as a Tory dissident) won a national election easily against Gaitskell with the motto: "We are all workers now." He was not referring to the theory of the new class that we borrowed from French neo-Marxists (or post-Marxists), but to the leveling effect of a consumer society in a Great Britain that had abandoned the rigidities of class and status and did not quite know what to make of the new situation. Whatever else the citizens sought, our advice was not wanted. We did not know it at first, but the elder and more staid elements in the Labour Party had our measure. They knew that Britain was then open to what Gaitskell termed "a modest program of social reform" and not much more.

We were but the latest in a long, and sometimes lively, succession of renewal movements in the party. What made us distinctive was that we emerged in a post-imperial period, when Britain's international position had become that of the largest satellite state of the US. We had the lack of politesse to point this out. We weren't in the long line of succession of pro-Soviet groups in Labour, since we were children (or readers) of Orwell and repelled by the grimness of the USSR even after the termination of terror. Labour's leaders, unionists or Cambridge and Oxford dons, had always managed to amuse themselves on the side. We insisted that *joie de vivre* be home grown, not just imported from France. The Labour thinker who agreed, Anthony Crosland, didn't think total upheaval was required to achieve that, and suggested that perhaps the American model of a consumerist democracy wasn't so bad.

Crosland was writing (in his *The Future of Socialism*, published in 1956) about a US society in which the unions set benefits and wages and had brought the American working class up to what were middle-class levels of consumption—and in which American cultural egalitarianism made even Labour Britain seem anachronistic.

He might have looked across the Channel at France and Germany, or over the North Sea to Scandinavia, but was attracted to our dynamism. His depiction of the US wasn't wrong, but his later critics could suggest that he read Galbraith's 1958 *The Affluent Society*, with its censure of a nation with insufficient attention to the common good.

The New Left's vision for Great Britain was as radical as that of some of the Christian revolutionaries who anticipated modern socialism in 1647, at the debates in Putney between factions in Cromwell's army. Honorable lineage, however, did not make our demands more realizable. Egalitarianism, participatory democracy in economy, politics, society, national and global redistribution, a general end to authoritarianism and repression, certainly would mark the "New Jerusalem in England's bright and shining land" evoked in the Labour anthem.

Most Labour voters, however, were far less revolutionary in their expectations—and we did not wish to think of ourselves as sectarians. Rather rapidly, it became clear to us that we were the modern successors to a long line of critical, dissident and vanguard groupings in Labour. We had lent more than a bit of color to the British scene. But we were more or less politely ushered from center stage—which we had occupied, if at all, only for the briefest moment.

We then did what many groups invested in ideas and sensibilities do when they conclude that they were no longer listened to: we turned inward.

We spent a great deal of energy and time on negotiating a merger between *The New Reasoner* and *Universities and Left Review*. Generational differences sharpened the discussions, and these were connected with opposed ideas of the autonomy of Great Britain. Those who had fought in the war and experienced as adults the Labour governments of 1945-1951—mainly, *The New Reasoner* group—sometimes took as want of seriousness the interests of the *Universities and Left Review* figures in ideas from Europe, especially France, and the US. The seniors clung to their idea of a parliamentary road to socialism; the young (or younger) asked why the road had turned become an obstacle course. Stuart Hall for *ULR* and Edward Thompson for *NR* did most of the bargaining, and we celebrated the merger in an entirely British fashion—with a country house weekend.

These differences continued when the two journals merged, finally, in 1960, and led after a brief period to Stuart Hall's departure and his replacement by Perry Anderson—and to strenuous criticism by Edward Thompson on the new editorial perspective, which he saw as too Continental, insufficiently rooted in British experience. Looking back, the change brought the generations which had originally founded the journals together in defense of the original project of somehow altering British politics. The Anderson editorship was a response to the belief the change was impossible, remote, or likely only in relatively small ways.

Our readers, the people who marched with us in the anti-nuclear weapons campaign and came to Left Club discussions up and down the country, our editors and writers, carried their experiences into their own cultural and political engagements. In the late sixties in Great Britain the embers flared up, and now we are the stuff of scholarly conferences, academic books—and memories.

I owe my friends in the New Left a great deal. Norman Podhoretz, writing about his early years in New York, described the group around *Commentary* and *Partisan Review* as "the family." It is clear that he intended the imagery of a warm family, a place one had to be taken in—even if in his book *Making It*, joining the family was a career objective he sedulously pursued. The group in London provided comradeship, support, and vindication. In a period in which I was beginning to write more, but still struggling, its members took my ideas seriously, valued my knowledge of the Europeans and Americans—and, above all, offered personal acceptance and affection. That wasn't available in the academic settings I frequented, although I had glimpses of it among my new acquaintances such as Henri Desroche and Edgar Morin in Paris. They were some distance away, and the US still further: it was not clear what primary group I belonged to there, despite a sizable network of academic and intellectual and political connections.

Indeed, it was the validation I had in the New Left that helped me begin to break what had been a writer's block. I've mentioned the article for *Commentary* on the Amsterdam sociological congress. One followed for the British historical journal, *Past and Present*, on the Zwinglian Reformation in Zurich—taken from my doctoral thesis. On one piece, I did bog down. I began an answer to the question "Is Marxism out of date?" by writing a small number of ambivalently ambiguous pages with some sketchy good ideas on them. Ralph Samuel encouraged me to amplify the text but, somehow, I did not feel that I was sufficiently in command of the theme. Ten years later, I wrote an article entitled "The Crisis of Marxist Sociology" in a few hours in a Paris hotel room—and it had no small impact in a number of milieux. One of my regrets is that I did not write every day, waited for inspiration or occasion, and only slowly learned that the one way to overcome the terror of the blank page is to begin to fill it.

What image of society did I have? It was certainly poorly articulated. On the one hand, I thought social classes, institutional constraints, decisive. On the other, I paid much attention to cultural legacies, to ideologies and religion. I incorporated the painfully acquired insight of personal analysis (reading Freud was easier and I knew the corpus of his writings as well as I knew Marx) only partially into my work. History was omnipresent. We were living in the Cold War, after all, and I had already moved through American society somewhat and lived in Germany before coming to London.

The great German sociologist Simmel was so opposed to Prussian militarism, it was said, that when the First Prussian Guards Regiment marched down Unter den Linden past his classroom, he ostentatiously covered his ears in response to the band. When the First World War broke out, however, he supported it "for methodological reasons." I was very unsure that profound changes could come, acutely feared a nuclear war, was convinced of the failure of both the liberal project of education and the socialist one of emancipation—but clung to a belief in a better world for psychological reasons. I saw no moral justification in accepting the one I lived in. Clearly, revolt against authority had become a major part of my adult persona. Existing authority and authorities did not provide convincing evidence for profound reconciliation.

It was only decades later that I realized that there were lessons to be learned from my British contemporaries which I did not, when living among them, readily grasp. I have written of their tiredness, and that was true. There was, however, something else in their adherence to time and place. The contraposition of the metahistorical flights of imagination of continental European thinkers and the dogged empiricism of the British is familiar. It animated, no doubt, the British scholar exasperated by questions as to what history meant who responded: "History? History is one damned thing after another."

Britain's Marxist historians published a journal, *Past and Pres-*

ent. The editors included Christopher Hill, Rodney Hilton, Eric Hobsbawm, and Edward Thompson. Their felt and expressed kinship was with the group in Paris around the French journal *Annales.* The French historians who had founded that journal between the wars had enlarged the prevailing academic historical enquiry to include social conflicts and their symbolic representations but were by no means Marxist. When their successors formalized a methodological canon in the seventies, it entailed studying "mentalités"— world pictures in their social settings and functions. They joined that to ideas of larger historical settings and deeper continuities on which their teachers had concentrated. The figure who connected the generations was Fernand Braudel, who assembled a large number of social scientists (and some from the humanities) across the disciplines to found the École des hautes études en sciences sociales —which had no British equivalent. The editors of *Past and Present* had struggled to reconcile different and even contradictory perspectives. As Marxists, they retained a sense of progressive direction in history as well as of the importance of class conflicts. As scholars, they knew that historical progress was usually difficult to discern and that class conflicts could take varied forms even in one nation—sometimes becoming latent.

As Britons, they were members of a society unique in its continuities and its capacity for changes. In 1958, they decided to diversify the editorial board and I became its sociological member.

The original *Past and Present* historians searched for evidence of resistance to domination and exploitation, and found it in popular custom as well as in popular rebellion. They were inclined to write the history of their own country as a history of inner resistance— and in so doing, they mirrored the Whig historians with their emphasis on the serial enlargement of liberty. What they conveyed (criticizing a book or suggesting revisions in a submitted article) was their acute sense of the intricacy and, at most times, the slowness, of processes of historical accumulation. Sometimes (I think of Hill's marvelous book *The Legacy of Defeat,* on the ways in which the brief triumph of the English Revolution became the long travail of its beleaguered but determined heirs) those processes were not clearly visible. The historians assumed the task, piece by piece, of writing a counter-history—as in their view it had been lived by generations past. They were nothing if not patient and were quite prepared to wait while demonstrating that previous epochs were not, in their deeper structures and longer consequences, what they seemed.

What they were waiting for, then, was no sudden and total transformation, the replacement of toil and trouble by a permanent festival. It was a different sort of historical periodicy—to be made possible, not least, by a changed historical consciousness. That is why thought it useful to argue with more conservative colleagues, indeed, to find much of value in their work. Compared with the angry controversialists who filled the pages of *Dissent* and *Partisan Review* (and with the moral indignation voiced by Mills and the American radical historians), they were patient. Behind and beneath that patience, however, was a very different sort of conviction, a sense of belonging to a community already formed.

One of the main historical arguments in those years concerned the gentry—the prosperous landlords, merchants and early manufacturers who were the allies of Henry VIII in his despoliation of the church—who were, in their autonomy, discipline and sobriety, largely drawn to Protestantism. British Marxists such as Christopher Hill saw in them early exemplars of the bourgeoisie, and interpreted their ideological and political choices (their alliance with Henry VIII and Elizabeth II, the Tudor monarchs who rationalized the state) as the work of a rising class. Hugh Trevor-Roper, difficult to describe ideologically and certainly no instinctive conservative, was unconvinced and argued strenuously that they were a class struggling against decline, threatened by Tudor absolutism rather than allies of it. The argument went back and forth and my colleague on the new *Past and Present* board, Lawrence Stone, published a thick defense of the view that the gentry were indeed rising—but took it out of the Marxist narrative.

Was *Past and Present* itself then, burying Marxism by complicating it? No, it was contributing in its own way to an international discussion in which simple notions of a material basis and an ideological, political and social superstructure gave way to much more complex interpretations of historical causation. In the research institutes and universities of the Soviet bloc, survivors of Stalinism and a post-Stalin generation were openly moving toward analyses of their own past and present which acknowledged that in the state socialist societies, there were phenomena strikingly similar to class formation and ideological rationalization in the capitalist ones.

I came to the meetings of the *Past and Present* board with the advantage of immersion in much of the new international literature on classes, ideologies and social movements. I was also able to connect these with my considerable knowledge of earlier twentieth-century sociology. It was a combination of impatience to claim a modern synthesis and its opposite, excessive deference, that kept me from working more directly and in a sustained way on these problems. My articles and reviews contained hints and indications, but I did not try a frontal attack—and so postponed profiting from what I was learning from my new colleagues until years after our work together. What I put together then was upon examination quite contradictory. I took the optimism about the possibility of fundamental change from American progressivism, and joined to it the sense of historical fatality of European social thought.

To the Marxist teleology I added no small amount of psychoanalytical skepticism. I was certainly aware of the contradictions, but attributed these to the task of depicting the fissures in our contemporary experience—and so reverted to the Marxist theory of alienation as the explanatory device which would unite all else. What was not now possible for humans would be within their grasp in the future, and their present limitations properly understood would mobilize their energies in a politics of both self-actualization and self-transcendence. No wonder I was so fascinated with the efforts of my Catholic and Protestant friends to appropriate modern thought and yet remain true to a message of redemption. They lived much more joyfully with disappointment than I did, were much less embittered, and could even from time to time visibly enjoy life.

Something did happen to allow a major recovery from my inner demons, my sense of incompletion tied to an incessant pursuit of a great if vague future. Nina became pregnant, and our daughter Anna was born in August 1958. Nina had spent the three months before that immobilized in University College Hospital on account of placenta previa, with an imminent threat to both the unborn child and herself. The birth was two months premature, and Anna weighed all of two pounds, twelve ounces when she emerged. It was a teaching hospital and the professor in charge came in on the weekend to supervise a very difficult delivery.

Nina remained for some weeks; we did not bring Anna home for two months. The devotion of the medical staff was exemplary, and the efficacy of British health insurance at the time no less so. I paid my normal contributions through my salary deduction, and for all that was done never had a bill.

Of course, I have mixed memories of the period. Some are of my anxiety and foreboding during Nina's long hospitalization, and the concentrated anguish of the crisis around the actual birth. Nina's stoicism helped somewhat. I recall the early morning of the birth itself, when it was still unclear whether mother or child would survive. I left the hospital and went around the corner to Eric Hobsbawm's apartment, waking him up—he generously gave me breakfast.

A happier memory is of the day we finally took Anna home to Hampstead, when she weighed all of six pounds. There followed the fascinated delights of experiencing her growth. I was, all in all, a devoted father.

That, with teaching and writing, my engagement in the New Left, and the constant and welcome stream of visitors to our home, would have been quite enough for most people. I was insatiable, and in ways large and small, had to pay for it. I can list the obvious things I did not do—returning to my thesis to make it into a book, returning to my 1952 essay on Marx and Weber to deal (using all that I had learned in the meantime) again with the related ideas of alienation and rationalization. I imagined that I was too immersed in the present, would get to these matters in good time (which came only much, much later), and did not admit to myself that the broad reach of my activities was compensation for a pervasive sense of disconnectedness. That it took the form of seeking connection in many places at once did not make matters better.

I also had considerable combativeness. I'd come to know Dwight Macdonald somewhat when he temporarily replaced Irving Kristol as American editor of *Encounter* in 1957. In 1958, returning to the US, Macdonald wrote a critical article on his re-impressions of the States, and it was scheduled for publication in *Encounter*. The Paris office of the Congress for Cultural Freedom did not think that a good idea, and publication was canceled. Macdonald published the article in the British journal *The Twentieth Century* and, with a brief note about the aborted arrangement with *Encounter*, in *Dissent*. I discussed the matter with friends from *Universities and Left Review*, and we decided to publish an open letter from myself to the Congress, criticizing the refusal of the Macdonald article and asking where the Congress obtained its funding. I was not the first to do so, and my own record was not impeccable. I had published an article in *Encounter* in 1958 on a trip to East Germany (not paid for by the magazine) and however small the fee, was a beneficiary of whatever funding the Congress had.

Internally, the question was a different one: I was not in the rather exclusive circle of recipients of *largesse* from the Congress (grants of all kinds, invitations to interesting meetings in distant places, and beyond the money the gratification of membership in a prestigious club). No doubt, a certain amount of ordinary resentment frequently motivates those who proclaim the value of moral and political purity, and I cannot claim total exemption from this ordinary failing.

Still, on the face of it, it was absurd of the Congress and its publications to insist on the value of pluralism—and yet attempt to shield the US from criticism. It was especially absurd since what attracted many to the US was not official dogma but the contentious, open and raucous nature of our culture.

The letter occasioned a tempest in a transatlantic teapot. There were public and private exchanges of all kinds, and the original refusal of the article was overshadowed in fact by the unanswered question of the funding of the Congress.

It was not until 1967 that *The New York Times* published an account of the CIA's considerable investment in the realms of culture and ideas, with the Congress and its publications an important element in the venture. Later, it was suggested that the account came from the CIA itself, which for whatever reason supposedly had reached the conclusion that its cultural activities were in several respects too expensive. For myself, I acquired the enmity of some and the admiration of others—and on balance I would say that the career advantages (appearing as a fearless critic of those with power and position) outweighed the disadvantages (exclusion by those who were already predisposed to unfriendliness).

The storm, such as it was, soon subsided, leaving me as before with a major unanswered question, which I turned into an unanswerable one: what was I going to do with the rest of my life? Another diversion presented itself: the miserable human climate in the Department of Sociology at the LSE. Having had enough of it, our most gentlemanly senior colleague, Tom Marshall, left to direct the social sciences at UNESCO. The others intensified what they had been doing before: Gould and Macrae, poor imitations of Rosencrantz and Guildenstern, went from one intrigue to another. Morris Ginsberg retired, changed his mind, and returned—leaving Ernest Gellner to remark that his retirement dinner was apparently to be an annual event. David Glass continued to bemoan the delay in the social revolution he had worked for so long. Tom Bottomore and Ernest Gellner, and David Lockwood, concentrated on their work. There were lots of interesting and sympathetic people at the LSE outside of our narrow circle, and it would have been simplicity itself to have done my teaching (quite gratifying, in view of the talents and amiability of our students) and lived my own life.

All of the metropolis was increasingly open to me—and Europe with its old and new friends was next door. Living my own life, however, appearances to the contrary, was what I found most difficult to do. I certainly had an inner core to my personality; the trouble was that it was divided. One half very much wished to deepen my independence of judgment and accumulate academic and cultural resources for the long run. The other was anxious about the world's immediate judgement of myself (even if in truth the world had other and far more pressing priorities) and did not have the steadiness required to defy or more realistically ignore it. By then, David Riesman's compelling simplifications of American middle-class experience were the stuff of everyday language. I was "inner determined" and "outer determined" in equal measure and, some appearances to the contrary notwithstanding, spun like a top in the prevailing winds. That accounted in part for the importance to me of my attachments to the New Left and to the informal international caucus of sociologists of religion: each reinforced, in distinct ways, the angels of my nature.

The demons, however, were omnipresent—and one day, they

caught sight of an advertisement by Nuffield College of Oxford University of a vacancy for a permanent appointment. Actually, in one of those odd coincidences which make the paths not taken so eternally appealing, it was the second advertisement they noticed. The first, in 1958, had been for a fellow and tutor in politics at Balliol College. I wondered whether I should apply, thought that I could indeed master the teaching of political philosophy required and that my work as a sociological theorist was certainly not a disqualification—but did not make the usual discreet inquiries. Later, someone at Balliol told me that my name had come up but that it was thought that I would hardly wish to leave London. *Sic transit gloria mundi*: I would have saved myself a great deal of toil and trouble had I been able to go to Balliol.

The two-way traffic between the ancient universities and the London School of Economics was indeed constant. Some began their careers in the colleges at Cambridge and Oxford, came down to London as junior or senior teachers, occasionally returned to chairs or headships of colleges. Others went up to the old institutions for the first time. I had visited from time to time, of course, and had lots of friends who had studied at Cambridge and Oxford. I knew something of the atmospheric difference between the two: Cambridge, Puritan and scientific; Oxford, Charles II's capital during the English Civil War and humanistic (or what it took that to be). Britain at the time was confronting the course and consequences of the social changes (I will not say revolution) begun by Labour in 1945-1951, and the role of the older universities was much discussed.

The discussion was not invariably enlightening, nor did it have, invariably, much reference to Oxbridge (as the two were summarily termed) as they were. Some thought that the older universities were strongholds of privilege, and that access should be democratized. It was true at the time that ten percent of their undergraduate bodies were students of working-class origin, as opposed to an average in England of more than twice that. Often, demands for democratization rested on highly idealized images of the qualities of Oxbridge. (No one talked of the differences in resources and faculty and student talent between the Oxford colleges.) Others depicted the ancient places as the Galapagos Islands of higher education.

That was especially so of the Cambridge physicist and novelist C.P. Snow, with a popular novel (*The Masters*) and a BBC series on the prejudice at the older places against the natural sciences—which he connected to the nation's deficits in modernizing itself.

An unintentionally comical footnote was supplied by the then-editor of the *Times of London*, who had come to the post from his position at the BBC, where he had the Gilbert-and-Sullivan-like title "Director of the Spoken Word." He kept publishing editorials the burden of which was that Cambridge and Oxford were the only true British models of higher education, the rest inferior—a position striking for an editor who had never himself attended university at all. I had followed this as a minor chapter in the ethnography of the United Kingdom, knew that the older universities were more complex than their caricatures, and occasionally wondered about the hold they had on the nation's cultural imagination. Even the Scots, who were so important in Britain's elites, paused on their way to dominating England to seize control of much of Oxbridge.

Sociology wasn't part of the undergraduate curriculum at either place. Cambridge had invited three American sociologists for a year each (Talcott Parsons, George Homans and W. Lloyd Warner) from 1953 to 1956 and nothing much had followed. Oxford had a chair in sociology (termed a readership) on its books, but had never appointed anyone to it. Economics, economic and social history, political science and political philosophy, social anthropology, flourished at the ancient universities. Why was sociology so ostentatiously unrecognized? One answer was that it was thought "Continental"—the sort of thing done by fanciful or overly ambitious Europeans (Comte and Pareto and Weber). Yet political and social philosophy at the old universities were replete with large questions—if, in the fifties, ones subjected to exacting and exhausting dissection, that is, cut down to size. Another was that it was too close to everyday realities, the sort of themes the Webbs and the others at the London School of Economics cared about. Cambridge and Oxford, however, had, and had had, a full complement of social reformers. Their economists and political scientists were not shy of occasional governmental service, and many of their students entered the Civil Service, the Foreign Office, or journalism and politics. That sociology was too American was an unconvincing hypothesis: Herbert Spencer's countrymen could hardly believe that—and many things American were held in high regard.

Oxbridge was in those days especially sensitive to charges of backwardness or remoteness. The old universities met these in two very different ways. One was to declare that their antiquarian habits were not dysfunctional evolutionary traits but entailed a great contemporary advantage: a direct line to the best of the past. The other was to insist that true contemporaneity entailed judgment as to what was significant and what was ephemeral. The Oxford version of this attitude that I later encountered was that if it isn't already taught at Oxford, it cannot be knowledge.

These disputes did not trouble most of the old universities' teachers and at times they appeared more important to those elsewhere in Britain than to the residents of Cambridge and Oxford. Still, the sorts of persons who headed colleges, chaired committees, and were in charge of what were self-governing institutions had keen instincts for discerning possible troubles. They wished to avoid parliamentary questions, press criticism, and anything else that could threaten the unimpeded flow of public monies to their coffers. Joined by some members of their universities who were actually interested in what sociologists wrote, they let it be known by very discreet public hints and some private communications that they were open to persuasion. Perish the thought that Oxbridge was backward! Sociology may have been invented by Comte early in the nineteenth century, sociological research developed by the Scots at the end of the eighteenth. The mid-twentieth century, then, was early enough for a measured approach to the subject—provided, of course, that sociology really had something to offer.

Here the two ancient universities diverged. Cambridge thought it over, collectively, and came up in the spring of 1960 with a direct solution. Two positions in sociology were advertised by its Faculty of Economics and Politics.

Oxford followed its own rule, that the shortest distance between two points is never a straight line. In the spring of 1959, the university's post-graduate college in the social sciences, Nuffield College, advertised a permanent position—discipline unspecified. The university's senior teachers in the social sciences encouraged Nuffield to cast a line: perhaps a sociologist or two would bite. The colleges, let it be said, were more autonomous and important in appointment decisions at Oxford than at Cambridge. In Oxford's terms, the proposed process made sense. If Nuffield brought a sociologist to the university, the appointee, if successful, could be moved into the vacant university chair. If not, the damage would be contained. No one, of course, worried much about what would constitute success—apart from a consensus that person and institution matched. One difficulty was that the institution was of no clear or agreed mind on what sort of sociologist was welcome. Under the best of circumstances, whoever came would be at risk.

I had some, but not much, knowledge of the situation when I read the advertisement. My discontents at LSE were absurdly exaggerated but psychologically real. Oxford had an appeal that was unique to my situation as an American in the United Kingdom. The LSE had plenty of prestige in the US, but Oxford had (as I had seen at Harvard) near-mythic standing. I was struggling with the problem of my basic capacity to do serious and sustained work, about which I had severe doubts. I certainly had made progress, and was writing articles which did quite well, but did not have the patience to sit at my desk and extend my reach. An appointment to Oxford would not only function as confirmation of my worth, which I doubted, but would surely impress colleagues in the US, and so make a triumphal return very much easier—no matter how little I wrote.

I visited Nuffield College for a friendly interview and talked with the fellows. One question put by one of the more sympathetic ones should have served as a yellow light, if not a red one: He suggested, politely, that perhaps I was not the sort of sociologist Oxford and the college needed. The College wrote to me rather quickly thereafter. They had decided not to proceed with filling the permanent position, but would be glad if I could come for a long-term (seven years) impermanent one. It would have been sensible, at that point, to write a polite note of thanks and to decline. The College might then have changed the offer, and in any event, I could have applied later for the vacant university chair without having paid Oxford the overly generous compliment of giving up a permanent post to move there.

I was deficient in two respects. One was in self-respect, which would have dictated a refusal. Instead, I traveled to Oxford again to discuss matters and this time called on Isaiah Berlin. He urged me to take the post, and promised his support for the chair, indeed his support "in every way"—quite promising, I thought, since he was on the selection committee. I think it was Berlin's urging, along with the great prospects held out by Nuffield's Warden, that convinced me that the risk was worth taking—because not very large.

The other element missing was sensitivity to others. My friend Ernest Gellner, who had been at Oxford and knew it well, was unequivocal in his warning. If you go there without tenure, he said, they will treat you with contempt. Nina did not want to leave our life in London, was very dubious about the terms of the offer, and I ignored her objections.

No doubt, there were other ways to deal with the matter. I could have suggested a year's visit, taking leave from my LSE post with the possibility of returning to it. Alternatively, I could have taken the risk but not interpreted it as a matter of personal validation. or professional life and death. Others might have gone to Oxford to experience it, with the confidence that they could move on if they had to do so. A bit of flexibility would have gone a long way—but I was so driven that I could not (or did not) step back and think.

8

Oxford, Part I

THE SENSE of being driven shaped my years at Oxford—complemented by the belief, shortly after I began my five-year stay, that I was trapped. I learned a great deal there, about academic life, Great Britain, modern history and modern thought, and certainly about myself. I also acquired a far firmer grasp of the values of family and friendship. What I did not immediately learn was that I was learning these things. The relative tranquility of recollection casts a nice light on the period, and allows laughter at its (many) amusing aspects. That was not, however, what I felt at the time.

One doesn't go to Oxford; one goes to a college or department or laboratory or research unit. The university is much more centralized now, as dons communicate by email instead of handwritten notes delivered by the university's messenger service. When I arrived, the university was its own Platonic universal: particular lives were lived in its particular places. The Oxonians had acute status sensibilities (and anxieties, of course, to match).

Places at a college were assiduously sought and zealously guarded. Those who taught or did research at Oxford without a college affiliation were thought of as outsiders, and when one came to lunch or dinner or tea at a college, confronted with their dismal station. New colleges (such as Saint Catherine's and later Wolfson) were endowed specifically to provide places for scientists, especially, lest the university's lack of hospitality become too large a charge on its public relations budget. The colleges struggled perpetually to reach the top of the internal institutional order. Much of this was entirely a matter for gossip, but it did sometimes get into novels, a very few critical university publications, and the journalism of (licensed) rebellious daughters and sons. Oxford's graduates in the larger society were, clearly, counted upon to sustain the university's fixation upon itself—better that they should write disparagingly of it than not write at all. Cambridge had a parallel existence in Britain's imaginary space, and the supposed differences between the two places (Cambridge Puritan and scientific; Oxford, Anglican and literary) were exaggerations implying that together, they exhausted the promises universities could make.

That was an obvious untruth. The United Kingdom had the Scots universities, with their own national traditions. The colleges of the University of London and Manchester were great metropolitan centers of learning. New universities such as Essex, Sussex, and Warwickshire were about to be founded as sites of academic quality and renewal. One of the very first things I learned in Oxford in 1959 was that Heathrow Airport, outside London was a stop on an air shuttle not unlike the ones flying between Boston and New York and Washington. Entire cohorts of Oxonians made their way every year to the Ivy campuses and the great state institutions—and quite a few did not come back. The continental universities had recovered, and more, from the war. The editor of the *Times* might say that the only real universities were to be found in Oxbridge—but even, or above all, there he was treated as an entertainer and not a serious figure. The scientists at Oxbridge were living testimony to the wretchedness of the fiction, since they rent the heavens with their complaints of the backwardness with which they had to struggle. The more productive social scientists (here the social anthropologists were at a great advantage) treated their colleagues' obsessions as small talk—sometimes useful, sometimes tiresome, but never important.

Why did Oxford and Cambridge insist so much on their own uniqueness? They certainly had long histories, inextricable from that of the nation.

The university reforms of the mid-nineteenth century, analyzed by the historians (to be sure, many of them Americans), had opened the institutions to the middle classes. The first generations of professional civil servants (and the men who ruled India and the rest of the empire) were all Oxbridge graduates. The modern universities (London and Manchester, especially) had been founded as competitive ventures, the Scots cultivated their own traditions—but few at the older places were caught wondering aloud whether they had something to learn from the others.

Harvard, as I knew it, was self-congratulatory on moving with the times and its official unofficial history was termed *Making Harvard Modern*. When I came to Oxford, Harvard was proud of its Nobel Prize winners in the sciences and best-selling authors in other fields and looking forward to the presidential candidacy of its Irish Catholic graduate, John Kennedy. Oxford was arguing about whether the natural sciences were innately soulless.

As for politics, that was a generally dubious business lent a patina of respectability by the fact that the better sort of politician had certainly gone to an ancient university—even if his academic performance was discreetly unmentioned. Nuffield, with its interests in public policy, had Edward Heath and James Callaghan as visiting fellows. Each later became prime minister, but as rising politicians spent Fridays and Saturdays at the College. Heath was a scholarship student at Oxford; Callaghan had not gone to university (his intelligent daughter was there as an undergraduate). The old universities' hold on the British imagination was very great.

Perhaps that was the essential point. The past become alive was what made the universities so attractive. When I asked my colleague and friend the anthropologist E. E. Evans-Pritchard where he stood on the debate at his college (All Souls) about admitting a scientist to a fellowship for the first time in its 520 years of existence, he was unequivocal: the candidate should not be appointed, he said, because traditions (even poor ones) had to be maintained. He was also disturbed that the person was an experimental physicist: "Suppose he were radio-active?" A firm adherence to tradition and a bit of irreverence shared by insiders was what warded off the shock of newness. It took a bit of time for me to learn that many at Oxford took seriously what at first I thought of as an amusing exaggeration. When in doubt about anything, or made uncomfortable by argument about it, they reverted to the dictum that nothing should ever be done for the first time. It appeared to be an academic Disneyland where rituals, gowns, Latin graces, old titles lent color, but its routine business was educating an important segment of the governing class. That education was done well or badly at different times and in different colleges, graduate education and scholarship and scientific research were tacked on in no very coherent way, and the university kept going by propagating the myth that its essence was timeless. That was its defense against interference from outside, and the university counted on its graduates and the like-minded in the political elite to protect it.

Brideshead Revisited depicted an Oxford between the wars which few Oxonians knew: most were thinking of their careers, and not of life as perpetual entertainment. The social classes did not quite mix at Oxford but neither were they very distant from one another. It was an institution of social incorporation. Unlike its offspring in the United States, however, it had more continuity to conserve and (especially after the exhausting war) less of the diminished national power to share. The trouble as seen by many there was that its imagined archaism threatened to turn real.

I had not the dimmest notion of the complexity of Oxford when I came. I did imagine that there were two universities, an old one of port-drinking dons whose motto seemed that of the British ambassador in another Waugh novel (*Surtout pas trop de zèle*, or "above all, don't be overly zealous"), and a modern one of science and scholarship. I did not see that the two depended upon each other, like partners in an unhappy marriage neither spouse felt badly enough about to end.

Nuffield College was founded in 1937, but its accession to full function awaited the end of the war; the construction of its building, the early fifties. It was the first Oxford college to be specialized in an area of research (the social sciences), to be limited to graduate students, and to admit men and women as students and fellows. The critical part of its early history is undocumented and will probably remain so. Lord Nuffield was the title chosen by the local automobile manufacturer William Morris. He developed an interest in medical and technological research—an interest said to be all the greater since he was reported not to be particularly well regarded by the royal family. That made investment in horse breeding superfluous: he was not likely, however fast his animals, to be invited to the royal enclosure at the Ascot race course. It is reported that he thought that he was giving to the university a college which would be specialized in engineering and medicine, but that although a very good businessman, he did not read the fine print. The dons had somehow outsmarted him, and he found to his dismay that he had endowed education in the social sciences—which he regarded with considerable suspicion.

Later, his foundation funded the construction of the college building. The original design was to be a modern structure, but he objected: he had been deprived of his medical and engineering college, and now he felt he couldn't be expected to give his name to something with flat roofs. He wanted a real college, and he got one: a neo-Gothic structure with a chapel tower (used to house the library's initial book collection) and crenelated moldings. When I arrived in 1959 architectural problems remained. The college's wine cellar had somehow been situated next to the heating plant, so at considerable expense a cooling system had been installed to right the balance. Tiles occasionally fell from the roof; the windows did not always close properly, and the cobblestones in the courtyard were dangerously slippery in the rain.

Still, there we were, the first college one passed if one walked from the rail station to the center of town—evidence, perhaps, for Nuffield's special relationship to the city and Westminster, even if (unlike the London School of Economics) not situated between them. I recollect one American colleague visiting from Ann Arbor who envied me my immersion in tradition. He asked what could be seen from my office (or rooms, offices not a term much favored). To the right, the town gasworks, I said; to the left, the jail. His own office was in a very pleasant green courtyard. I am glad that my sober answer did not dampen his enthusiasm.

Oxford colleges are self-governing entities, their financial and legal relationships to the university codified in hundreds of years of statutes, judicial rulings, university conventions and regulations— and purposeful obscurity. The point was (and as far as I can see, remains) to maintain a maximum of college sovereignty while seizing whatever advantages the university offered. How were colleges formed in the mid-twentieth century? They required, apart from a juridical identity and university recognition, a governing body—an initial set of fellows. The group charged by the university, in the mid-thirties, with administering Nuffield's incorporation thought it more economical to dispense with the selection of the first body of fellows—and named itself. One understands: Oxford then provided almost nothing to its scholars in the social sciences by way of research or even secretarial assistance; stipends for promising graduate students were difficult to obtain, and the intellectually profitable clustering of scholars working in the same field was blocked by the dispersal of Oxford's talents in the colleges. Nuffield in its origins would resemble nothing so much as the normal American academic department or division (and its Continental equivalents). Its unacknowledged model was surely the London School of Economics, but when I arrived two decades later the official view and unofficial attitude was that Nuffield was unique.

The fellows there in 1959 included some of the original ones, and some appointed later. Some had conjoint appointments to full-time university posts, some were on Nuffield's payroll but members of the faculties of economics or politics or (a few) history. I was in the category of research fellow, which covered a range of ages and attainments. Presiding over it all was the warden—a wily political scientist from the Midlands, Norman Chester, who had worked (with many) in the wartime government. Chester invested his considerable passions in the college, and the fellows reciprocated by backing him in the many struggles of the college within the university. Some concerned Nuffield's influence and patronage in the social sciences, and all took administrative or financial forms. The college was a good deal more richly endowed than many others and the administrative questions were usually far from fundamental. What did trouble the fellows was the question of their standing in the university's unofficial and unwritten but important league table. The older colleges were in fixed places; the newer ones had to scramble for esteem, even attention.

That set a problem for my colleagues. On one hand, they wished very much to be fully integrated in Oxford (one of the senior members, the competent and perceptive electoral scholar David Butler, kept referring to Nuffield's "traditions" as if the college had begun under the Tudors). On the other, they participated in the national and international world of scholarship, were hardly averse to being cited in the media on the issues of the day, and in some cases were open to the possibility of moving or returning to government.

They were quite sensitive, above all, to the currents of university opinion. Beneath a certain bravado, and quite understandable pride in the quality of much of the college's work, they were more than a bit anxious. In fact, most of my senior colleagues were quite conventional in opinion. Many, certainly a majority, were supporters of Labour, and some had worked in the Labour governments. Neither governmental experience nor political conviction had radicalized them: their cast of mind was technocratic, and when they thought of progress at all, it was in severely incremental terms. It was, as I described the New Left's disagreements with the leadership of the Labour Party, the era of "Butskellism"— and my colleagues claimed it as their own. They were, with the exception of our licensed political philosopher, John Plamenatz, determinedly unphilosophical, even if they had the normal European and British sense of historical intricacy. The world, to them, was very much as it appeared.

In another part of Oxford, the philosopher of everyday language J.L. Austin warned sternly of "l'ivresse de grand profondeur"—the intoxication of profundity. In this respect, my colleagues were thoroughly abstemious. Their conventionality attested a decent respect for British society's claims to considerable achievement. Great Britain had done much to win a long and painful war, and then had half pursued, half endured, a considerable social transformation. Like my colleagues at the LSE, the Nuffield group clearly thought that their nation was the better for it. Some voiced satisfaction that some barriers of class had fallen, and presumably thought themselves beneficiaries of the process. They did not talk about their own social careers, and they did not expend much thought on the possibility of an alternative society. Some, if they discussed the problem at all (most did not), thought it quite unnecessary; others simply declared it impossible. Like Austin, they were not interested in realms of being beyond routine.

In this, the warden, Norman Chester, was very much their leader. He had begun his career at Manchester, came to Oxford after government service in the war. His closest faculty ally was Hugh Clegg, who was a solid student of British industrial relations with very good ties to the unions. At my initial interview, Clegg had said that Oxford and the college were looking for a different sort of sociologist (a well-intentioned warning which I ignored). Clegg was a helpful person with a certain amount of empathy. That was not quite true of yet another influential colleague, David Butler. He was an accomplished student of British elections, and spent his academic life either looking back at the last one or ahead to the next one. He was also most worried about Nuffield's place in the university (even if Chester took care of that and the wider world of business and politics, too) and very anxious that it should be thought of as a real college. He judged everyone and everything by reference to a notion of university opinion, which became the more ephemeral the more strenuously David expressed it. The quadrumvirate was completed by Phillip Williams, who knew an enormous amount about France—whilst retaining the habits and mind of an Oxford bachelor right out a series on BBC television.

There were others with great influence on the college's decisions, such as the very reserved economist Ian Little and the more open Donald MacDougall. They took a friendly but somewhat distanced view of my presence, obviously leaving judgement to the political scientists. There were some twenty or so scholars on the actual governing board of the college, ten or so research fellows, a miscellany of visitors, and thirty students—some of them quite interesting. In my first year of residence, I commuted weekly from London, lived at the college as well as working there, and had the experience of total immersion.

No sooner had I arrived than it was clear that I had put myself in a precarious position. I was dependent upon the college for promotion to a tenured status, but the criteria were not at all clear. A mixture of rebelliousness and self-respect combined to make me wary of trying to ingratiate myself. Rebelliousness took command, compensation for the inner uncertainty that flared up under the pressure. I am very unsure that any amount of *savoir faire* would have altered matters, but that was what I lacked.

The college offered an alternating array of encouragements and discouragements, interspersed with the occasional ordeal. One encouragement was to allow me to host a conference, at college expense, of sociologists of religion. The event went off well; colleagues came from Berkeley, Berlin, Madrid, Paris. The warden was confirmed in his belief that Nuffield was at or very near the center of things. I thought of it, rather, as opening a window on the world for an institution too long too local.

I suppose that showed, somehow. Very early in the academic year, I was struck by the linearity of my colleagues' views, by the conventionality of their sense of the limits of politics, by the fact that they were so at home in the prevailing consensus that questions about it struck them as evidence of the questioners' imperfect grasp of reality. I was not asked to set aside my connection to *New Left Review*, or those views of American politics and society more likely to be found in *Dissent* than in the Harvard Yard, or my interest in the burgeoning revival of a Marxism of culture and consciousness. These were simply outside the boundaries of their everyday discourse. In their private lives, I knew, some of my colleagues took considerable account of complexity; no doubt one or two had discreetly recurred to psychoanalysis. Flights of imagination and plunges into the depths were not, however, the stuff of lunch or dinner conversation at Nuffield. I had grounds to feel estranged, and even more for what I could not admit—that perhaps I had made a large mistake.

The ordeal was a college seminar at which I was to speak, as I chose, on sociology. The warden introduced me by taking a (nineteenth-century) dictionary definition of sociology as "the master science" and—not without a certain paternal kindliness—presented me as "the master scientist." I gave a standard account of the background of the contemporary concentration of sociology on the analysis of industrial society, with a brief view across the Atlantic and another one over the Iron Curtain. There was something in it of the German debate (*Industriellegesellschaft* or *Spätkapitalismus*, in which the terms conveyed antithetical political meanings), of Parisian arguments (*l'alienation* or *la société de consummation*) and American ones (in which critics fought off conformists). The British discussion did not divide the sociologists but took explicitly political forms—in the argument between Anthony Crosland and the New Left over the possibilities of British socialism, and in the debate between the liberal philosophers and their critics on the actual enjoyment of freedom in modern societies. I see that now; then, I had an incomplete view of the problem—with a dim apprehension that those who disliked sociological analysis were defending their own view of British society and did not wish to be troubled by other ones.

What I presented was, inevitably, a mélange of historical description, theoretic condensation, and political philosophy. It was an attempt at public relations—with a somewhat resistant public, which I knew to be skeptical in other ways as well. Most of the people in the room, from Nuffield and the university social scientists, were not inclined either to take critical views of their society or sketch large historical pictures of it.

Their spokesman that afternoon was Max Beloff, who had a chair of political institutions. Beloff was a cantankerous polemicist with an especial dislike of socialist intellectuals, as well as being a talented figure. He was very skeptical that Oxford needed sociology, and said so, at some length. I replied that he had voiced three propositions. One was that sociology did not exist as a discipline; a second was that it existed but was valueless, and the third, that it existed and had something to say—but that these things were already being said in the Faculty of Politics at Oxford, so its presence at the university was unnecessary. I'd be glad to debate any of these notions, I added—with which one did he wish to start? We exchanged some other pleasantries, and the discussion moved on. Some colleagues thought I had done quite well; others were admiring of my having challenged Beloff so directly. No one made the obvious point that since he was on the committee for the university chair, perhaps I could have found a different tone. Perhaps, but he was not a person easily mollified and had behaved ungraciously toward a younger colleague. Isaiah Berlin was there, but I do not recollect his saying anything. He somehow conveyed distance from Beloff's idiosyncratic and un-Oxonian passion. They did not disagree on very much, but Berlin preferred a much lighter approach to matters important—at least, on the surface.

I wonder, now, whether my colleagues at the college had decided then and there that they had made a mistake. They had hoped for stimulation, but not the sort I favored. They were decidedly not inclined to challenge university opinion for the sake of a cause they could not make their own. Social science in their view could be ameliorative and might occasionally be interesting, but if it got too far under the surface of the society to which they were so exquisitely attuned, it became too disruptive.

On the surface of our daily relations at the college, nothing changed. One episode, however, irritated the warden immensely—and certainly, unnecessarily. To become a full member of the Oxford faculty (so that I could give seminars and lectures in the Faculty of Politics), I had to have a university Master of Arts degree. Degrees from Cambridge and Trinity (Dublin) were recognized, others not. In due course, the college obtained the MA for me (not all research fellows got it, or got it so quickly)—and I received a bill for fifty-five pounds. I thought that the college should pay it; the warden thought it an honor I should be glad to pay for myself. A sympathetic senior fellow somehow found a solution. How could I have been so ill-advised as to be so obdurate about a relatively minor, even trivial, matter?

In the meantime, the university process for filling the vacant chair in sociology had come—and gone. The committee met, interviewed the applicants (myself included) and decided to postpone decision for another two years. The college could have responded by promoting me to a tenured post at that point, but did not.

Cambridge advertised two permanent posts in sociology, I thought of applying, but was immobilized.

The three other interviewed applicants were formidable. Chelly Halsey was from the Methodist working class, had been an RAF pilot in the war, and had a great deal of both radical social conviction and self-possession. He certainly was the only one among us who was a legitimate heir of a British tradition of politically pointed social enquiry. Another was Stanislav Andreski, an acute and prolific Pole—who might have fit into one of Oxford's reserved niches for continental scholars with an un-British obsession with ideas. The third was unlucky not to get a job which by usual Oxford procedures might well have been his. Julius Gould was an Oxford graduate and my LSE colleague, and had offended no one by his writings, since there were virtually none. Given the objections on the committee to the rest of us, he might have been a compromise choice—but I gathered from Isaiah Berlin that the committee feared derision if it set aside three persons of profile for one with none.

Isaiah Berlin (and my London colleague and friend David Glass, who was on the committee) indicated that postponement was the best they could do for me. Edward Shils had seized the moment to publish an article in *Encounter* on the problem of sociology at the old universities, and advised Oxford to take someone "at home in the breadth and width" of British society—good advice, no doubt, but singular coming from an American. At the interview, Beloff did not question me on my views of sociology in the curriculum, but harassed me about a letter I'd written to the *Times* on NATO. Shils was in many public ways associated with the CIA's academic and cultural operations through the Congress for Cultural Freedom. Now, I can flatter myself that I was thought a danger by Beloff and Shils to good order in the heartland of Anglo-American empire. Really, the result might have been the same had I been ingratiatingly supple at the college and serenely broad in university discussion.

Had I had that much capacity to take my distance, I probably would not have come to Oxford under such uncertain conditions. Indeed, I would have had to have been a strikingly different person. I took the decision as a severe personal defeat, blamed myself for having come to Oxford and added all the self-reproaches I had in any circumstances about not having achieved more.

In some ways, I had not done so badly in that first year. At Oxford, classes and seminars were offered in abundance, but not always taken. I'd given classes in modern social thought and in the comparative study of industrial societies at Nuffield, and a lively set of undergraduates, graduate students, and a few foreign scholarly visitors had come. They appreciated hearing what was being argued about from Berkeley to Warsaw, my connecting British disputes to larger currents, and my irreverence about all or any authority. Some of them were quite outspokenly sympathetic about my suspended academic fate.

When some years later, teaching in sociology became part of the degree in philosophy, politics, and economics, some of my students, as tutors in history and politics at their colleges, constituted the first generation of the university's teachers of sociology.

Equally, I'd made friends among my peers. I knew the historians of *Past and Present* (Trevor Aston, Christopher Hill and Lawrence Stone) and met others across a spectrum of disciplines. They were interested in what I had to say and responded as if I had brought some fresh air into the local conversation. Still, I had the feeling of visiting the set of a film about Oxford—or turning the pages of an especially detailed novel about it. At one point, Lawrence Stone invited me to dine with him at his college "Tuesday of fourth week." Oxford told time by its own calendar, which divided the academic year into three eight-week terms.

No one was more critical of Oxford's complacency than Lawrence, who, upon concluding that his colleagues would never change the teaching of history, left for Princeton. There was a considerable dissenting party at the university, many of them constant visitors to the US and the European universities. They conserved energy by conforming to the university's rituals and usages, the better to get some free space for themselves or a like-minded few within their colleges or faculties. I am now reminded of those who called themselves the Inner Emigrants in the Third Reich. The Oxonians, when they'd had enough, went to the US or took posts in London, an emigration that was constant as well as real.

Nina and Anna had spent the academic year in our Hampstead apartment. Now we were scheduled to move to the top two floors of a college house on the Woodstock Road. Nina was very reluctant to leave London, but she agreed that we had no alternatives. I could not return to my post at the LSE and had made no other plans. To make matters more complicated, she was pregnant with Antonia, our second child. In addition to disappointing myself, I felt that I had greatly disappointed her, making me feel worse. The essential difficulty in our marriage, a lack of trust on my part in her desire to provide emotional support, deepened my despair. Since I could offer no perspective for our future but some years in a place she did not wish to live in, I now see that I felt that I was unworthy of support. I struggled with a cloud of depression.

Actually, as she had done in London, Nina managed to establish herself comfortably with a set of friends, and our house again became a place many liked to visit. We especially liked two neighboring families. John and Frances Walsh moved in directly across the street. Frances had been a research assistant at Nuffield, later told me that when she first saw me there, asked someone who that unusual person was and had received the reassuring reply: "Don't worry, all New York intellectuals look like that." John was born in India, where his father, a Methodist minister, had been a missionary. He grew up in Bradford, in the Midlands (as he later said, when the city was black and the inhabitants white), had served in

Germany in the last part of the war, and returned to Cambridge to study nineteenth-century British history. He is especially interested in the churches and has taught me a lot about the cultural texture of British history. (Frances was from Scotland, where her family's Calvinist parson was the father of Gordon Brown.)

Uniting empathy and an infallible eye for human failings, John's conversation has provided me for fifty years with an experience akin to reading Dickens. I recall his dropping in on me for lunch at college, asking for a glass of whiskey, and explaining that he'd come from tutoring. Like many colleges, his (Jesus) had its fellows tutoring in fields adjacent to their own. John did political philosophy as well as history. As he explained it that noon, "The thousandth time one hears a student beginning his essay on Hobbes by citing him on the life of man as nasty, poor, brutish and short, one begins to believe it."

Another couple we liked were Raymond and Joy Williams, who moved a couple of blocks away to a house on the towpath of the river. Raymond taught in the university's adult education department, and had personal qualities evident in his writing: a gentle willingness to accept others on their own terms and an equal determination to encourage them to remember that these were not always universal. Joy was astute and lively. Neither was bothered by Oxford's conventions since neither took them seriously.

Shortly after the university refused to invite Chelly Halsey to Oxford to initiate sociology, a permanent place was found for him as director of the Department of Administrative and Social Studies. He was given a fellowship at Nuffield, and with his wife, Margaret, and their children moved to a North Oxford house not far from ours. A splendid career unfolded, with Chelly conducting any number of serious social inquiries, writing a good deal, and exercising a large influence on public policy. Chelly never forgot his origins in the British working class, and occasionally referred to the advice given to him by Morris Ginsberg when he was a student at the LSE. Morris was pessimistic about many things, but especially about the future of sociology in the British universities, and so suggested that Chelly give up hopes of an academic career and seek one in social work. Shortly thereafter, Chelly did obtain a lectureship at Birmingham, and in the end he became Oxford's first (and for a while only) professor of sociology.

The warden of Nuffield was disturbed by Chelly's political outspokenness and reproached him in terms reminiscent of the behavior toward critical junior colleagues of the director of an institute of social studies in a Soviet bloc nation. At one point, the warden publicly recommended that Chelly impose on himself a long period of silence. Chelly narrowly missed election as the warden's successor, but over a half-century at Oxford he has never been hesitant to speak and write as he thinks best. As I recollect our time together, he was a loyal and warm friend, encouraging when circumstances were adverse. A newcomer to Oxford, even if permanent, there was little he could do institutionally to alter my situation: his support was all the more valuable for its intrinsic generosity.

We also became friendly with Iris Murdoch and her husband, John Bayley. Iris resembled nothing so much as a more colorful characters in one of her novels.

She was Anglo-Irish, and something Celtic mixed with the manners of the English public school graduate and Oxford teacher of philosophy. That she always had a corkscrew in her cavernous handbag impressed Nina and myself immensely. John was a teacher of literature, who had clearly taken to heart Goethe's dictum that there was a canon of *Weltliteratur*. At the time the English faculty at Oxford could not agree on whether anything after Keats was indeed literature: I recollect that Dickens was regarded by some with extreme reserve. John had a traveler's flair and an empathic imagination. Talking with Iris, I sensed that for all of her fine portraiture of persons and places, and her mastery of entire streams of European thought, her attention was fixed on an inner world to which she gave no one access. She struck me as a somewhat skeptical visitor in this one.

We also invited some of the students, usually the irreverent ones. When I arrived, John Torrance had returned from a year at Berkeley. John had the imperturbable air of a British officer, which he had been. I asked him whether he had read Seymour Martin Lipset's new book, and he replied—not yet, but he believed he had written a chapter of it. John advanced shortly to a politics fellowship at Hertford College, eventually wrote a large study of the ideas of Marx and had a considerable interest in the concept of alienation. He was one of the least alienated persons I could imagine. Decades later, his lovely wife fell ill with Alzheimer's, and John moved to Dorset to take care of her. His stoic sense of duty did not surprise me.

Steven Lukes was another student who went on to a college post, at Balliol—where he was Christopher Hitchens' tutor, making me Christopher's academic grandfather. Steven wrote a thesis on Durkheim, which he revised into a very good book. Durkheim had a critical distance from society, a capacity to seize the implications of apparently banal facts, which placed him in a line of descent from British nineteenth- and early twentieth-century thought—but no one in the UK had noticed this before Steven. He kept noticing the odd things ostensibly concealed by normal appearances, and spent years in Italy before moving to the US. Perhaps he was helped by his nominally poor eyesight to more acute human vision. His empathy and liveliness combined to make him very good company.

One undergraduate who was a pleasure for us to know was Angus Hone. Angus said that after hearing me on television (I occasionally did the British discussion program *Brains Trust* on the Third Program, the cultural channel of the BBC) he decided to study at Oxford. He came from a family, charming and warm, in Worcester, and after we had spent a day with them in their home, Nina observed that Angus and his brother had had childhoods of marvelous care and delight. Angus was an especial favorite of my daughters, brought us lots of fun in North Oxford's occasional grayness, and later used his considerable talents as an entrepreneur. I am sure that he was helped in business not only by his great intelligence but by intuitive gifts: he could detect, emotively and intellectually, pretense quicker than anyone I met in Oxford.

One group of undergraduates remains in memory. Led by Paul Foot, they were the editors of the undergraduate journal *Isis*. Rebels in search of a cause, they asked me for suggestions as to how to enliven their pages. Oxford's classes and lectures did not have the importance of those at Harvard, since the undergraduates were dependent on their college tutoring, which elicited very varied responses from its beneficiaries. Rating nearly 2,000 tutors was for obvious reasons awkward, and perilous. Perhaps, I suggested, they could look at what the Harvard undergraduates did in the *Crimson Guide to Freshman Courses*. It did not take them long to procure a copy of that unsparing document. Those Americans who later wrote about "soft power" included a Rhodes Scholar from Harvard, Joseph Nye, but he overlooked what was, surely, a considerable instance of our cultural influence. *Isis* began to review Oxford's wide lecture offerings. Its start was modest, with just a few lecturers scrutinized. That sufficed: the editors were confined to their colleges by order of the university proctors, and the vice-chancellor ordered the beginning of disciplinary proceedings. By evening of the same day, Paul and the other editors were giving interviews to BBC Television crews from the windows of their colleges. The next day, questions were asked of the Chancellor of the Exchequer, who funded the universities, in the House of Commons. ("Would the Right Honorable Gentleman inform the House what steps he proposes to take to improve teaching at the older universities?" "None, sir; that is in the competence of the University Grants Committee.") The vice chancellor, shocked, took to his bed, and the disciplinary charges were dropped. Isaiah Berlin told me that he suspected my hand in the matter, which for several days was the talk of both junior and senior common rooms as well as entertaining part of the nation. I insisted, affecting pained serenity, that it was a pure case of the local folklore Isaiah so enjoyed.

The outer world did, however, at times reach Oxford. In April 1961, part of the French army in Algeria revolted against President de Gaulle, because of his obvious intention of negotiating with the Algerian independence movement. He put on his army uniform and in a televised address to the nation ordered the army not to accept orders from the rebel generals. He did not add that he had arranged with President Kennedy that the US Mediterranean Fleet would prevent the Algerian forces from flying or sailing to the metropolis. Instead, he ended a great performance on a pathetic note: "Français, Françaises, aidez-moi!" The *Marseillaise* was played, and the BBC returned to the serious business of its evening, a cricket match. I heard the speech at Jesus College, where John Walsh had invited me to meet the new principal. He was described by John as a not entirely scintillating figure—a former public school headmaster who would preside elegantly at dinner, raise a bit of money from alumni, and leave the fellows free to run the college themselves. At dinner, I saw his point. As a guest, I had the honor of sitting with the principal at dinner and after the broadcast, he turned to me. "You see, Birnbaum, my father was right—he always said that the French could not govern themselves."

The same week, it was our nation's turn to draw attention to itself—with Castro and his Cuban revolution in a distinctly non-supporting role. Kennedy allowed himself to be led into ignominy at the Bay of Pigs. I was visited by a group of American students at the university (Richard Celeste and William Maynes among them, as Rhodes Scholars). They were looking for an American faculty member to sign a letter of protest to the president. They had spoken with an eminent mathematician who declared his inability to sign: he did not read the newspapers. They had also talked with Arthur Goodhart, an American lawyer who was master of University College. He had warned them against proceeding with the letter, as it could damage their career prospects. I was very glad to sign, and suggested that they make sure that the two serious British Sunday newspapers, as well as *The New York Times*, get copies. *The New York Times* did have a brief report of the protest, but the *Observer* and *Sunday Times* honored the letter with front-page headlines: "American Don and Rhodes Scholars, etc."

I suppose we were given that much attention in Great Britain because of the prevailing myth of Oxford's importance. It was, apparently, shared by John Kennedy. Some months later, I visited Arthur Schlesinger in the White House, and he told me that the President had been disturbed by the letter. Fortunately, he was also disturbed by the CIA's performance and the Joint Chiefs of Staff's unfailingly miserable advice. He dismissed Allen Dulles, and did not listen to the Chiefs later, during the Cuban missile crisis. In the end, I am unaware of any serious harm to the careers of the signatories: Bill Maynes returned to Harvard, then joined the Foreign Service, was assistant secretary of state for international organizations, then-editor of *Foreign Policy*—and continued to demonstrate that steady independence which made him so admired by his friends. Dick Celeste was governor of Ohio and President Clinton's ambassador to India, and is now president of Colorado College.

The Cuban revolution figured in another episode. Raymond Carr was an Oxford colleague at Saint Antony's College, had fought in the Spanish Civil War in the International Brigade, and was an excellent historian of Spain. He had become critical of what he regarded as the intellectuals' addiction to revolutionary illusions. The US intervention in Cuba, in the setting of the Cold War, figured prominently in the debates encouraged by David Riesman in his newsletter *Committees of Correspondence*. Some talented Harvardians were with Kennedy at the White House; others were anxious to get there. Riesman sought to reach a wider range of opinions in raising critical questions about our world role. I participated in several of the arguments, and in one suggested that the idea of "freedom" was being misused. Carr took that as a defense of dictatorship in Cuba and in a review in the *Sunday Observer*, listed me with C. Wright Mills and Jean-Paul Sartre as prominent Western apologists for Castro. I visited Harvard shortly thereafter, in 1961, and found that the readers of the *Observer* were many. My friends in Cambridge were delighted at the elevated standing I had apparently won in Europe.

The Harvard visit was to participate in a seminar organized in honor of Sam Beer by his former teaching fellows. Sam deserved our thanks and respect. Many of us spent much of the rest of our lives pursuing large themes he had opened in the course—at a time when appreciably narrower canons dominated in the social sciences, while great historical and philosophical ideas took homogenized forms. The visit gave me a chance to renew ties with friends, and brought me on Independence Day weekend to Wellfleet on the Cape. Alfred Kazin gave a large cocktail party in honor of the nation's birthday, and the Cambridge and New York intellectuals turned out in full summer strength. I found myself arguing about Cuba again, this time with Richard Goodwin of the President's staff, who dwelled emphatically and exclusively on his role as an insider. "Look, Dick," I had to say, "we have talked for forty minutes and all that you have said is to advance a proposition I do not contest, which is that you are at the White House and I am not."

Talking with Arthur Schlesinger was distinctly more rewarding. I had the impression that the intellectuals were charmed, even excited, by a sense of new national possibility they attributed to the president—but that most of them were quite remote from the everyday realities of politics in Washington, and absurdly over-optimistic on the problems of overcoming the inertia of the Cold War.

David Riesman was, not for the first time, an honorable exception: he knew how things worked, or why they did not.

I visited Washington, talked with Carl Kaysen and Arthur Schlesinger at the White House—and for political diversification called on I.F. Stone. Carl was busy with what was then the Berlin problem (shortly to be solved for Kennedy, as he said immediately thereafter, by the erection of the Berlin Wall). I had the impression that he and his colleagues from Harvard felt fully equal to their new tasks and brought with them a good deal of their old outspoken habits: They made no secret that they found Dean Rusk pedestrian. Self-critical doubt wasn't, in short, the most visible response of my friends to their burdens. I am not sure, at least in those early days, that they would have agreed that they were carrying burdens. They would have characterized it as acting on behalf of a president wise enough to have appreciated the nation's needs for their talents.

Arthur did provide a moment of honesty. The Sino-Soviet conflict had surfaced, but with tense American relations with the USSR and no embassy in Peking, reliable intelligence on what was happening and what it meant was scarce. I found Arthur reading an article on the conflict by Isaac Deutscher in an American paper. You must know Deutscher, Arthur asked: does he have good sources? I explained that his sources were excellent, since he had close contacts with former Polish Communist Party comrades now well situated in Warsaw. The question puzzled me. I asked Arthur why, with all the resources of the CIA, Pentagon, and State Department at his disposal, he needed a central European Trotskyite living in Hampstead. It is precisely because I can call on these agencies, he said, that Deutscher is so valuable.

Carl introduced me to a younger member of the then very small National Security Council staff, Marcus Raskin. A graduate in law and international relations from Chicago, and a native of Milwaukee, he had worked with Rep. Kastenmeier in organizing a small liberal caucus in the House. Early in the administration, McGeorge Bundy asked Riesman to suggest for a post as unofficial in-house dissident someone critical of the Cold War. Riesman rightly thought that Marc's familiarity with Washington, and his possession of a degree of realism not generally found in the academic Left, would be advantages, and Bundy took him on. Marc was very curious about the British and European New Left and had read my articles, and we began an enriching friendship. I learned from him that there were openings in American politics that totally negative images concentrated on its constraints did not grasp.

In fact, I'd previously talked about the political situation with Norman Podhoretz, who had become editor of *Commentary* in 1960—and promptly opened its pages to what was to become the American New Left. In his opening editorial, he declared that the time for the defense of "liberalism" (by which he meant an amalgam of the New Deal traditions of pursuing social equality and the enlargement of civic and personal freedoms) was past; the moment for renewing it had come. He published David Riesman and Michael Maccoby on what they described as the American crisis, the essays which Paul Goodman was to extend in *Growing Up Absurd,* Staughton Lynd on the Cold War, and a number of articles critical of the specific policies of the new Kennedy government. Withal, Norman had discovered that there were those in Washington who read *Commentary, Dissent,* even *Partisan Review* (as well as Harper's and *The New Yorker*). He was surprised, and gratified, that the New York intellectuals did not speak just to New Yorkers and those in college and university towns who thought of themselves as metropolitan.

Earlier than many in New York, Norman had realized that the New Deal transformation of the permanent government (and Washington generally) by close connections to the academy and the spheres of culture generally had continued. The Eisenhower Cabinet was derided as one of "ten millionaires and a plumber" (the plumber was a Republican trade unionist)—but the congressional staffs, the House and Senate themselves, and the federal agencies and departments, were all full of people with dual citizenship: they also held passports from the realm of ideas.

My Washington conversations provided ample confirmation. I spoke not only with Kaysen, Schlesinger and Raskin, but with Richard Barnet, whom I had known as a Harvard undergraduate and who was working in the new Arms Control and Disarmament Agency. I. F. Stone himself described a porous capital city: he suggested that I introduce myself to an extremely conventional Republican congressman as an American Marxist working in Europe and enrich the honorable gentleman's mind by speaking my own. By the time, eighteen years later, that I moved to Washington from New England, the Republicans had caught on. The American Enterprise Institute, the Center for Strategic and International Studies and the Heritage Foundation were new centers for a modernized, and quite intelligently conceived and conducted, intellectual campaign against the progressive legacy in American thought.

The Washington visit led me to pose questions to myself so troubling that I hardly dwelled on them. I had chosen expatriation and opposition. Now persons I knew, and admired and liked, were very much closer to history. Podhoretz and Stone, without governmental posts, were recognizable outsiders—but not quite outside. True, Raskin and Barnet would shortly depart government to found the Institute for Policy Studies—but it was barely two miles from the White House, and I was (despite the Oxford letter) thousands of miles distant. Was there some part of my own inheritance I wished to reclaim?

I pushed back the thought and returned to Europe. The second half of 1961 we spent in Strasbourg. I clung to the idea of finishing a project I never completed, turning my thesis into a book. Strasbourg was the most open of Reformation cities in allowing a variety of churches and doctrines to exist. Calvin was there first as pastor of the refugee French Protestant congregation, then again after his first period in Geneva. From Anabaptists to Catholics to Lutherans to Zwinglians, the citizens had an early anticipation of modern religious choice. Perhaps the city's archive and its libraries would rekindle my enthusiasm for the project. Four years after I had finished the thesis, I was struggling with two considerable inner obstacles to turning it into a book. The first was the realization that it was expected, and that stimulated my rebelliousness. The second was my singular inner aversion to doing the things that would bring the academic recognition and success I sought, an expression of a larger self-destructiveness. I did not see it that way at the time, preferring to think of inner processes in rather reified terms—as if I were not responsible, or much involved. My considerable theoretic grasp of psychoanalysis was, at the time, just that—theoretic. Of course, I found all kinds of alternatives and diversions: moving to Oxford as I did had been one of them.

There were perfectly plausible reasons to find Strasbourg interesting. Nina and I had first visited it in 1953, on our way to Burgundy and the south of France. The city with its mixture of German medieval houses and French Renaissance architecture, its great cathedral and smaller churches, was history come alive. I'd visited again as guest of the Faculty of Protestant Theology when its dean, Roger Mehl, in 1958 convened a meeting of European sociologists of religion, and he became a friend. (He complained that at a meeting of the World Council of Churches in Evanston, Illinois, city regulations made it difficult to get a drink.) Strasbourg was where Marc Bloch taught between the wars, and where he joined a small group of social scientists in founding *Annales*, an innovative journal of cultural and social history, and much else besides. By the time I became aware of it in the Williams College library, it had classical standing. At Harvard, I learned that the *Annales* and its interdisciplinary tradition had been moved to Paris as the sixth section of the École pratique des hautes études. Visiting Paris from London and Oxford, I actually met scholars from these intellectual heights.

Strasbourg was a free city in the Holy Roman Empire until Alsace was annexed to France in the settlement of the Treaty of Westphalia in 1648—and Alsatian Protestantism was protected by the state even when the Calvinists in *la France de l'interieur*, as the Alsatians termed it, were persecuted. The Germans reclaimed Alsace-Lorraine in 1871; the French took it back in 1918, and it was incorporated in the Third Reich from 1940 until 1944. The Alsatians spoke an Allemanic version of German at home, learned French at school, and had a sense of the discontinuity of European history as its one constant. An entire generation had been conscripted in the twenties and thirties into the French army, then been put in the German one. Some of my Alsatian friends and later colleagues had had the good fortune to face the American army, rather than being sent to die in Russia, and had taken the first opportunity to surrender. They had enjoyed US prison camps—before extricating themselves by joining the French forces under de Gaulle.

The Alsatians, and especially the Strasbourgeois, were enthusiastic about the French Revolution and then fervent about Napoleon, some of whose favorite generals were Alsatian. By the time I came to know the city, it was true to de Gaulle, whose inclusive nationalism, idea of a strong state as master of the economy and society, and reconciliation with Germany were just what they wanted. We had stopped in Marburg for a few weeks on the way to Strasbourg. We visited with the Abendroths, and noted how much had changed since we left it in 1953.

Germany had become much more prosperous and self-confident. Inwardly, however, the nation was divided. Traditionalists and modernists fought it out in the arts and culture generally as if they were in Weimar Berlin. Actually, even if they did not quite believe it, the modernists were winning. A younger generation or a significant part of it found the stiffness of older behavioral norms absurd.

Germany moved with the rest of the West with regard to a new openness about sexuality as well. These conflicts, frequently played out in larger and smaller families, mixed and even merged with conflicts over the Third Reich. The elder generation which had lived contentedly (and more) under Hitler referred to 1945 not as *Niederlage* (defeat) but as *Zusammenbruch* (collapse) — as if it were an inexplicable natural phenomenon. The passage of time did nothing to dampen the passions of and about the past. These were joined not only to cultural but to political conflicts. Adenauer as a patriarch who was himself an anti-Nazi was increasingly viewed by the ascendant generation as retrograde in his authoritarianism, as too willing to integrate former Nazis (some of them very well placed in the Third Reich) in German politics.

The anti-Communism and implacable hostility to the USSR of the earlier years of the Federal Republic were giving way to more complex views. The German Protestant Church, especially, with its discussion centers (termed academies) and later, its commissions and their reports, openly sought measures which would narrow the division between the two German states, that implied a degree of recognition of Communist Germany the Federal Republic refused in principle but would often accept in practice. The *Aggiornamento* (opening to the world) of the Catholic Church under Pope John XXIII encouraged a new ecclesiastical and lay generation of German Catholics to think in ecumenical terms — and to accept the autonomy of the secular world. Across generational and political boundaries, it was clear to many Germans that the division of Germany had its advantages for the Western powers—not least, a large army prepared to respond to any incursion with its own movement eastward. In Communist Germany, Stalinism had long outlived Stalin—but it was impossible to escape all of the ideological turmoil long evident in the other Communist states. For citizens of Communist Germany, the Western world was, in Berlin, still a subway ride distant. Familial visits, television, and Church ties did the rest. The closed society was, until it was walled in on August 8, 1961, somewhat open. In the West, the protection given by the presence of American, British, and French troops was beginning to be viewed as not entirely benign and certainly not disinterested. In the East, similar doubts about the alliance with the Soviet Union could not be expressed—but they were there, not least among just those educated strata of the population on which the regime depended.

The place where these German conflicts could not be hidden from view was Berlin. West Berlin was not legally part of the Federal Republic, and sovereignty was exercised by the three Western powers. Their formal position was that the claim by the USSR and the Communist state that East Berlin was its capital city was illegitimate. Shortly after the construction of the Berlin Wall in August 1961, American insistence on the right of American forces to enter East Berlin uncontrolled by the Communist German authorities led to a serious confrontation.

I visited Berlin frequently before the Wall went up, was friendly with Pastor Bassarak, a Protestant who directed the church academy in the eastern part of the city. His colleague in the western part of the city said that Bassarak's name had the effect on the Bishop of Berlin, Hans Dibelius, of a red cloth on a bull. The Church was institutionally united but politically and even spiritually divided, and Bassark thought that Dibelius's opposition to authoritarianism had come a bit late: it wasn't evident under the Third Reich. Bassarak was belligerently skeptical of the Communists' claim to represent a moral new order, thought that the regime was there to stay for the indefinite future and that the Church could not function in the east as an agency of the west. I found Bassarak's openness a welcome contrast with the wooden circumlocutions of the Communist academics and intellectuals I occasionally met. It was only decades later that I came to know serious dissidents, and the limited openness of the seventies among the integrated intelligentsia was limited indeed. Bassarak's frankness was a mark of trust: publicly, he was not outspoken.

West Berlin was by contrast a seething cauldron. Lots of male students had come to the Free University to register as West Berlin citizens and avoid military service. Many of their teachers were quite strenuous propagators of Cold War ideology. They included some interesting representatives of a new generation, convinced that they had a double task—consolidating democracy in West Germany and opposing the pseudo-democracy of the east. Others did not see how West German democracy could be developed if the society's energies were so consumed by the Cold War—and did not wish in any case to grant standing as democrats to many whose anti-Communism had been particularly evident in the years 1933-1945. A certain number of émigrés had returned to both parts of Berlin, adding to the general tension and the disturbed co-existence of generations.

My closest friends in Berlin at the time were Margherita von Brentano and Dietrich Goldschmidt. Margherita came from the distinguished Catholic family: her uncle was Adenauer's foreign minister, who resigned in 1955 at what he considered the untimely opening of diplomatic relations between the Federal Republic and the USSR. That followed Adenauer's realization that the Western allies were seriously adverse, whatever they said, to making German interests as defined by their client state their own. Adenauer's move, in 1955, could be thought of as the first step in what was later termed *Ostpolitik*, a rebalancing of German interests to take account of its geopolitical position between the blocs.

Margherita had studied philosophy with Heidegger, had been in Berlin during part of the war, and had a chair of philosophy at the Free University. Like many Germans of her generation, she was philo-Semitic, had friends among the returned émigrés—and eventually married Jakob Taubes. Margherita was, like many persons sure of their own social positions, free of snobbery and an amused and ironic commentator on the follies of ambition. She later became dean of the social sciences and philosophy at the university, and a great ally of the student protest movement. She had an instinct for the weakness of authority, all authority, and since authority in West

Berlin was exercised by the Social Democrats, she was extremely critical of their unique combination of protestations of civic virtue and egregious self-dealing—not least in the university.

She was relentless, as well, in her disdain for those who apologized for, or even retroactively justified, the works of the Third Reich—including some of her colleagues. She took a broad view of philosophy and was at the center of a lively circle of artists, independent politicians, and writers. The society in which she had made her way was by no means free of patriarchy, and her directness and toughness in fighting prejudice against women when she encountered it disconcerted many who were already wary of her general cultural and political attitudes. She was a dissident Catholic, with something irreducibly Catholic about her—a large suspicion of the claims to total rectitude of the Protestant Prussians who set much of the tone in Berlin.

Another of my friends, a political ally of Margherita, was a Prussian Protestant—if a half-Jewish one. Dietrich Goldschmidt had studied engineering in the Third Reich because he could not study the social sciences: his father was a Protestant pastor of Jewish origins, who had emigrated to Great Britain. Dietrich endured the dangers and discomforts of those who were, according to the Nürenberg Laws, outside the national community. (The authoritative legal commentary on the laws, for the use of the Nazi administration, was written by a figure prominent in post-war Germany: Dr. Hans Globke, chief of staff to Adenauer.) After the war, Dietrich studied sociology with Helmuth Plessner, and returned from exile in the Netherlands, at Goettingen. We met because of Dietrich's interest in the social role of religion, and his activities as an engaged Protestant. He later took a senior research post at the Berlin Institute for Educational Research. He and his extremely helpful wife and family occupied a large house with a splendid garden in Dahlem, near the university. I was often their guest; they were friendly with Nina and the family. Dietrich had a visible uprightness about him, a simple moral clarity that made him a frank and loyal colleague. Through him, I learned a lot about the healthy living tissue of German Protestantism—as well as of its pathologies.

Dietrich was friendly with Helmut Gollwitzer, who had the chair of Protestant theology at the Free University and who had returned from long captivity in the Soviet Union to write a remarkable book, *Und Führen, Wohin Du Nicht Willst* (translated into English as *The Unwilling Journey*). It was an account of captivity, of the encounter of the German prisoners with their Russian jailers—for whom Gollwitzer developed considerable sympathy. He had come from the anti-Nazi resistance and when he returned he was a vocal antagonist of German forgetfulness and the anti-Soviet obsessions which lent the Federal Republic a considerable continuity with the Germany of 1933-1945. A serious theologian, he was a contributor to the discussion between Christians and Marxists which was an indispensable element in post-war Europe's attempt to win some spiritual independence from the superpowers.

In 1963, on the day Kennedy visited Berlin, the three friends acting on behalf of an independent committee visited with Khrushchev in East Berlin to discuss the reduction of tension—to an angered official and public response in West Berlin. When I visited Gollwitzer in those days, a police van which was an undisguised electronic listening post was posted outside his house. Clearly, some Germans had profited from post-war democratization; the difficulty was that much of the rest of the society took the consensus of 1933-1945 as an enduring model. Of course, to be fair to the city government, perhaps the van was there to protect Gollwitzer. In West Berlin, with its constantly moving lights and shadows, both explanations could be true.

We made the trip to Strasbourg by train, crossing the North Sea to Hoek van Holland from Harwich on the night boat. When we presented our passports to the Netherlands border policeman, I learned that I was a public personality. He greeted me as "Professor" despite the fact that my passport was devoid of occupational identification, and then indicated that he knew that we were going first to Marburg. I asked to speak to his supervisor and inquired about their interest in me, since my only intention was to cross the country en route to Germany. The supervisor reproached his younger colleague in Dutch for talking too much, told me in English that I had clearly misinterpreted the Netherlands' wish to be hospitable—and had the policeman carry our luggage to the train. Obviously, there was a European or NATO network which conducted surveillance.

My work in Strasbourg consisted mainly of visits to the city's archives. Much of the Reformation material had been destroyed when the archives were burned in the Franco-Prussian war, but diligent local historians and pastors had used it before—and done much reconstructive history afterward. I learned quite a lot about the embeddedness of larger ecclesiastical and doctrinal conflicts in local settings, about the early European vocation of a city very sure of its own uniqueness. It was an Alsatian variant of the lessons about history as a process of cultural and social accumulation I was learning in England. Alsatian colleagues and friends carried their history with exemplary unpretentiousness. Since they were in on a secret few others appreciated as they did, that Strasbourg was a metropolis, they were open to the ideas and impulses which continually reached them from Berlin, New York, Paris and beyond—but invariably treated these with a discernible if gentle measure of skepticism. They were not traditionalists in any conventional sense; they wished to be shown that there were really new things in heaven or on earth. Meanwhile, they enjoyed what the local earth had to offer—a very great deal.

I was aware of how much I learned there later. In more centered and stable periods of my life it served me very well. What I could not do at the time was use my new knowledge to write a book on the Reformation—or abandon the project in good conscience and move on to other themes. My paralysis was at the time the most honest thing about me, but I confided in no one. I had sufficient insight and strength, or pride, to convey an impression of normalcy—but there was no energy left to deal with the several sources of my incapacity. I felt my familial burdens strongly, and met them as I now see reasonably well. I enjoyed my daughters growing up, believed strongly that Nina was an affectionate and caring mother—but could not articulate the difficulties and insufficiencies of our partnership. I suffered from a surfeit of demand for recognition, and yet a very large inner doubt that I merited it. That had sources, not obvious to me at the time, in my distant relations to my parents when I was a child. That I had expatriated myself, did not then allow myself to think of returning to the US despite the many opportunities to do so, also spoke loudly. I did not, at the time, put all of these things together. I was, rather, someone erring in a dark landscape, never able to find a clearing which led to a straight road, always on paths which promised to open only to close again, abruptly and often, apparently, inexplicably.

It wasn't accidental, then, that when I returned to Oxford for the term beginning in January 1962, I was enthusiastic about co-teaching a seminar with Iris Murdoch on the concept of alienation. Obviously, I transferred to a very large canvas some very personal problems. That did not invalidate what I painted on the canvas and certainly did not reduce the complexities of the literature on the concept to babble, or the fraudulent exteriorization of unacknowledged inner turmoil. Marx and Engels had originally thought that capitalism made humans spiritually wretched, by depriving them of autonomy, pride and productivity in the labor process. The stunted humanity engendered by capitalism was not, as were previously exploited and oppressed classes, enchained by external constraints: hunger and the sword. Under capitalism, humanity had internalized its bondage. Those students (and critics) of Marx who insisted on the religious origins and theological structure of his thought were right. Alienated humanity was portrayed as if it had been abandoned by God, and revolution was depicted as a desperate grasp for earthly transcendence.

Iris, with her profound knowledge of aesthetics and philosophical anthropology, opened the seminar by talking of the artistic path to overcoming alienation. I cannot now quite remember whether she dwelt at length on Schiller, whose work on aesthetic education surely was one source of the Marxist idea. I do recall that she referred to the idiosyncratic, occasional, eruptive nature of art—providing moments of illumination and epiphanies. Her own writings were, however, picaresque—with characters thoroughly alienated and grateful for bits of relief. She wasn't free, then, of her own contradictions. Art was a realm of fleeting and even furtive freedoms, but while waiting for liberation in a great festival, art was the best we could do. Still, it offered a glimpse of possible futures.

I do not think that my own introductory presentation matched hers in either compactness or daring. I reverted to a familiar theme: how a falsely construed empiricism had ideological functions—blocking the exploration of possibilities of change. That involved considerable reference to thinkers generally unknown at Oxford, to alternative traditions in the social sciences. Isaiah Berlin, upon learning of our intention to teach the seminar, announced with good humor that it was clearly aimed at him and his skepticism about positive freedom: he would come and defend himself. He did, as did a couple of other colleagues. What Iris and I found rewarding, however, was the participation of some very interesting students. I recall Peter Burke, Marshall Berman, Steve Lukes, Ed Nell, Oona Nell, Bertell Ollman, John Torrance. They presented one stimulating paper after another. One moment of relief was provided by a visit by the Russian violinist David Oistrakh brought by Berlin—with his escort, presumably a KGB officer.

Both expressed surprise at how much Oxford knew of Marxism. We did not try to disillusion them by insisting on our atypicality. Unfortunately, Berlin did not arrange for Oistrakh to play for us.

As I recollect the papers, Peter Burke, who was writing a thesis on the Counter-Reformation turned his attention to the literature on work; Steven Lukes gave us material from his study of Durkheim; Ed Nell criticized the failure of ordinary economic theory to deal with labor in anything but schematic terms, and John Torrance anticipated his later book on alienation in Marxist theory by establishing a connection between Marx and classical political philosophy. They had studied with me before, and I was glad that I had broadened their intellectual horizons somewhat. We were, in effect, establishing a British outpost of a Western interpretation of Marxism that extended geographically from Berkeley to Warsaw (with a large detour around Communist Germany or an underground tunnel through it).

Meanwhile, the Faculty of Politics was formally considering what to do about teaching sociology. A committee was constituted, and two sociologists were on it—myself and Peter Collison, who taught social policy in the Department of Administrative and Social Studies. Peter, rightly, insisted that a new curriculum ought to include large reference to a British tradition of empirical social inquiry.

Berlin did not think Collison convincing and seemed to fear that university opinion would regard studies of class and community, poverty and wealth, as outdated political proselytizing—an unwelcome and unnecessary reminder of the thirties. He seemed to fear that the students and younger faculty would find my own project, integrating social theory with political philosophy, all too convincing, undermining the ways certain questions had been asked at Oxford for a generation. The university's social anthropologists, absurdly, were excluded from our work.

It soon became evident to Berlin and the others that if they did not listen to Collison on the British tradition of social research, and myself on the international discussion of social theory, they would have to recommend that sociology not be taught at Oxford at all. The university's inability in 1960 to appoint someone to its vacant chair had been criticized in and out of the university, and Berlin obviously felt that he was under conflicting pressures: another firm decision to make no decision was inadvisable. It was clear to the committee that the person with a larger view and a clear pedagogic perspective was myself—and I was asked to draft a report. It was quite straightforward, proposing that two new examination papers be introduced into the degree in Politics, Philosophy, and Economics—one on the social structure of the industrial societies, the other on sociological theory from Saint-Simon onwards. It was striking how much the report did conform to Oxford's premises—or prejudices. Most of the world was left to the anthropologists and the historians of Africa, Asia, and Latin America. The United States and Western Europe were to be studied, with a restrained glance at the state socialist regimes. I succeeded in conveying the notion that this would supplement the ordinary teaching of politics and political institutions, but by no means replace it. Sociological theory was to be treated as an offspring of classical political philosophy, Marx read in the light of Rousseau and Weber to follow de Tocqueville and Mill. I was astonished at my own relative subtlety, but in fact I was following history: that is just how sociology, in general, had developed. The committee made my draft its own, with very few changes, and the Faculty accepted the report.

It remained only to fill the vacant chair, and that was done later in the spring.

I recollect being asked by the vice chancellor at the interview if I thought that I could teach to the new curriculum. After I had said, yes, he asked what made me think so—and I did say: perhaps because I had written it. Berlin later said that my response was typical of the attitudes that had caused me such difficulty. It was, however, too late for active repentance or major personality change; the post was given to Brian Wilson, who was at our house when, visibly surprised, he heard of his good fortune. One path to my future at Oxford having been barred, my Nuffield colleagues promptly closed another one: they appointed Jean Floud to a permanent fellowship in sociology. Jean was a very good scholar of the connection between education and class in Great Britain, a prewar student at LSE and a graduate of its radical tradition, and an extremely cultivated and intellectually sophisticated person. At the same time, the university decided to revitalize its marginalized Department of Social Studies by appointing Chelly Halsey to direct it. With two excellent empirical sociologists in the great British tradition (both with LSE degrees), with Brian Wilson as a very literate and perceptive reader of major European currents in sociology, with younger scholars like Steve Lukes and John Torrance about to enter its teaching ranks, Oxford had become, overnight, a center of sociology. That left me where I had begun, at the Porter's Lodge at Nuffield College—and a number of friends in and out of the university expressed regrets, condemned the powers in being, and assured me that in the end I would not suffer. They were right, but at the time, a happy ending did not appear imminent. I was left with my self-recriminations and what I imagined to be Nina's silent ones.

I have expended far too much emotion, since, on my defeat. I was not the only person, after all, to have experienced a failure—or to have brought it on myself, first by going to Oxford under dubious terms and then by not playing the game thereafter. Had my Nuffield colleagues been saints, they would have made room for me—but they made no such claims. The one person whose behavior I still resent was Isaiah Berlin. He had a major role in inducing me to come by promising to back me "in every way." It is difficult to believe that Isaiah thought me, then, a conventional American liberal. He did at one point pay me a large compliment. George Steiner had not only grievously offended Isaiah by taking the side of C.P. Snow in an unfriendly exchange between the two figures; he had evoked Isaiah's disdain by a belated attempt to conciliate him. Isaiah told me that he had instructed Steiner that he would not accept his protestations of loyalty: "One cannot serve two masters." We were walking on High Street, and Isaiah stopped and laughed. "Of course, there are persons like yourself—who can serve none."

He had reached that conclusion, apparently, on getting to know me when I came to Oxford—and left it to me to gather that he was disinclined to exert himself very greatly on my behalf. He neither said so directly nor advised me to seek my fortune elsewhere. Isaiah had a reputation as a sage, as a pronouncedly humane figure whose wisdom included moral dimensions which went well beyond his intellectual capacities and scholarly achievements. These last are certainly very large. As for his larger humanity, a certain amount of doubt strikes me as justified. He was addicted to academic and political gossip and intrigue and enjoyed making derisive remarks about colleagues and persons, including many who were less influential or powerful than himself. He was far from straightforward, or even loyal, with those he had led to believe were his friends. There were effective reasons for the contrast between the unequivocal enthusiasm for him outside Oxford and the more nuanced feelings about him within it.

He had indeed personal grounds for distancing himself. Isaiah was very sensitive on an issue I did not dwell upon in that stage of my life: Jewishness. He was a very vocal supporter of Israel, a passionate critic of the Stalinist and post-Stalinist Communist regimes for their official and unofficial anti-Semitism, and frequently in conversation (and writing, when it was relevant) declared that Marx had a charge of self-hatred. There were ways in which England (Calvinist Scotland was different) and the English elite were rather more openly and deeply anti-Semitic than was the United States. It was in precisely this England that Berlin had made his way to the heights—retaining considerable suspicions of hostility beneath the surface.

In the fall of 1960 I sketched an article for *Commentary*, published in February 1961, titled "Empiricism and British Politics." I argued that serious political debate had become attenuated or vacuous in Great Britain, where an ostensible devotion to common sense and sobriety did not quite conceal a self-congratulatory ideology. That ideology, unacknowledged as such, depicted British institutions as exceedingly well adapted to the twin exigencies of both liberty and efficacy—and so made very difficult any serious consideration of historical alternatives. It fell, in my view, to acute and intelligent European immigrants to Great Britain to formulate these beliefs, as they did in various ways. I termed them "cosmopolitans" to contrast their thought with the obdurate provincialism of many of the British themselves—above all, when thinking of their own society.

Isaiah disagreed strenuously with nearly everything I had written in the draft I sent to him, and said so in a long letter to me. He was, however, incensed at the term "cosmopolitans" to describe himself, Polanyi, and Popper—and also at pains to argue that each had very different views. (That did not prevent him from adding, curiously, that he could not read Polanyi.) Isaiah declared that this was usage borrowed from the anti-Semites, and that unless I eliminated the phrase, he would write to *Commentary* to complain of my recourse to anti-Semitism. He added that *Commentary* would publish the letter, since it delighted in "lacerating" itself—hardly flattering to the recently terminated editorial reign of Eliot Cohen.

The text as published in *Commentary* eliminated the phrase, but not the thought.

Berlin had bullied a younger colleague professionally beholden to him. At least he did not attempt to varnish his outburst by warning me of the harm that might result for my career: he proposed to inflict that injury himself.

I regret to have to write that I did eliminate the phrase, if leaving the substance of the argument intact. I wish that I had had more autonomy. (He might also have been bluffing, since he could hardly have been unaware that some readers might have thought him both over-sensitive and unduly harsh to a younger colleague.) I also regret that, after the episode, I was still rather deluded as to his support. Of course, he used my talents afterward to achieve a sociology curriculum reasonably consonant with his historical and philosophical interests—but did nothing in return.

What had I learned in three years at Oxford? Unfortunately, I learned too little at the time about myself and others—or, rather, postponed the learning experience until much later. Wordsworth's emotion recollected in tranquility was not mine in those years. John Osborne's looking back in anger, and anger principally at myself, was more like it.

I did learn quite a lot about politics and society, since Oxford offered much contact with the British elite and its effective techniques of survival. I saw something of the European academic and political elite (Nuffield had close ties to France). I was in touch with several generations of American academics and intellectuals, and so could follow the new Kennedy epoch rather closely. Great Britain's thinkers generally thought of themselves as closer to the US than to Europe, but I intuited that they were wrong: they were in mid-Atlantic between the continents.

The initial excitement of the New Left subsided; the journal *New Left Review* and its quarrels were out of daily sight in London, and the turbulence of the mid- and late sixties lay ahead. Re-reading an essay I wrote for *Partisan Review* in the summer of 1962, "The Coming End of Anti-Communism," I see that I did anticipate some of what occurred a few years later, if rather dimly. Despite my inner feeling of loneliness, even isolation, at the time in fact I had lots of friends, and Nina could have been of more help had I been able to accept it. The groups with which I kept contact, in Cambridge and New York, in Berlin and Paris, were interestingly mixed. Some were emphatically academic in their emphases, others primarily political, some Christian, the rest (including nearly all the Jews) resolutely secular. Some were obviously very much at home in their national or political or religious traditions; others (think of what Burke would have said, with his denunciations of the "astronauts" of France) purposefully or resignedly floating in historical space. All had a sense of distance, and most had eschatological hopes: someday there would be a rupture, and our old lives would cease, new ones begin. In the meantime while begrudging the present its agonizing incompleteness one could experience gratitude for the opportunity to convert disappointment into prophecy.

We, my friends and I, were neither church nor sect but had something of each.

Like a church, we were not rigidly dogmatic, and we were open to including persons coming from different and even ostensibly antagonistic political and spiritual positions. Membership in our visible college presupposed enlisting in a campaign of unspecified because unknowable duration. The point was to try to discern a more aesthetically gratifying and socially generous human future amidst the restrictions of the present—indeed, to see how those restrictions in the end would generate their own dissolution. One large problem was: who, exactly, would join us in our project? We were clear that the old industrial working class was no longer large enough, and certainly not dissatisfied enough, to serve as a major force of transformation. We drew upon the idea of a new working class, comprising the educated and technical parts of the labor force, as an alternative vanguard. Given the increasing dominance of these workers in a labor process with a greatly expanding role for knowledge, we thought that we had identified the political force of the future. Projects of workers' control were connected to a larger end: treating much of the economy as part of the public sphere, to which democracy had to be extended.

The theory of a new working class, however, was joined to a new view of politics. Older propertied elites had given way to newer ones, reproducing in the commanding positions of economy and the state the primacy of knowledge.

Some of us were skeptical about views which we thought minimized the capacity of capitalists to integrate lots of people from the new elites in its service. The new working class, like the old one, would have to face antagonists unwilling to relinquish power and privilege.

The advantage of this schematic description of modern society was, not least, that it enabled us to speak across national borders: it bridged the Atlantic and the Channel and the Rhine and the Alps. More, we found that colleagues in Poland, openly, and in the USSR and other state socialist states more discreetly, were thinking in these terms. They frequently resorted to circumlocutions and euphemisms, but they were talking about monopolies and oligopolies of power derived from command of the economy—and the possible forms of resistance to these.

Another advantage was that, as intellectuals, we did not have to depict ourselves as total outsiders. Modern society was complex and difficult to understand, and we were needed to illuminate it—if only a larger number of citizens could be persuaded of our usefulness. Some of our political antagonists asserted that we were shame-faced Leninists, seeking to legitimate our claims to leadership by inventing an indispensable social function for ourselves.

In fact, the political division between the liberal defenders of the new capitalism and its socialist critics did not rest on a very deep sociological disagreement. Industrial society as depicted by Mills was not all that different from the one sketched by Aron. The differences concerned, rather, human potentiality. The liberals argued that in the light of history, Western society had much to be said for it. The rest of us insisted on its deficiencies of participation, on its stunting the possibilities of human growth.

The argument turned on the question of the present limits of human potentiality. Figures such as Aron, Bell, Bracher, and Crosland were certainly aware of the limitations of the liberal polities and societies they so praised. They were rightly seen by many of their contemporaries as reformists and, when they chose a party, aligned themselves with the American Democrats and the European social democratic parties. (Aron kept a critical distance from all parties, but certainly approved of the post-war welfare state in France and was as accepting of Mendès France as of, later, de Gaulle.) In the US, Galbraith and Riesman occupied ground between the fronts, each in his way. Both were critical of what they thought of as the excesses of Cold War enthusiasm; each was skeptical about the bona fides of much of the American elite (while enjoying full membership in it). Each had plenty of radical insights, but neither adopted a radically oppositional position. Galbraith joined the Kennedy government; Riesman was prodigal with generally sympathetic advice to it. Niebuhr's realistic reading of the human condition was no doubt an authentic extrapolation from Protestantism. The skepticism of others about what they thought of as utopianism was grounded in a secular reading of history in which great projects of transformation were deemed derivatives of religious visions which were best kept out of politics.

There was something to that argument: we, the radicals, were to some degree believers in things unseen. Our own spiritual biographies were diverse, and if they resulted in political similarities, the original differences persisted. I was much struck by how Catholic my Catholic friends remained. They had a very acute sense of community, of historical continuity, and of the occasional wanderings of the spirit. They in turn reminded me of how Jewish they thought me, even if I declared myself not only non-observant but non-believing. To them, I was a somewhat prophetic outsider, believing in eventual redemption and return—even if I did not quite put it that way and could not say to what humanity would return, since I so resolutely looked ahead. I admired many of those with Protestant origins for their obduracy of conscience, their responsiveness to inner illumination. I thought then that a good deal of secularization was marked by the religious origins of separate paths to secularism, which retained much of the eschatology and soteriology of the several religious traditions.

I was so immersed in this Western sequence that I paid little attention to the religions of the greater part of humanity: Buddhism, Hinduism, and Islam.

In the period, there was considerable assent to the proposition that Leninism was the Calvinism of the impoverished nations. That struck me as too simple to be true, and I was aware that on the periphery of my own map of the world, politics and the religions were joined in ways both complex and profound. I occasionally read some interesting papers and texts, but did nothing with these. It was a large failure of my own historical imagination.

I did not, in matters essential to my own life, examine Judaism and Jewishness; I identified myself as what Deutscher termed the non-Jewish Jew in history, and for all of my interest in and knowledge of Germany, did not then consider very deeply the outer and inner fate of German Jewry. I recalled words by Freud to the effect that his greatest service to the Jewish people was never to have denied that he belonged to it, and was astonished decades later when I read Yerushalmi's book on Freud's Judaism. If I had been asked to write a statement of personal belief, much of it would have consisted of repetitions of then-contemporary beliefs on the critical role of intellectuals as repositories of the tradition of the Enlightenment, joined in no very coherent way to the argument that the rest of humanity would somehow catch up with us. A certain amount of psychoanalytic thought completed the collage—not the pessimism of Freud's *Civilization and its Discontents* but the rather conditional optimism of Marcuse's *Eros and Civilization*.

I am struck by how schematically abstract my meta-historical thought was. I only dimly recognized a large contradiction between my belief in the possibility of change—and my fascination with the depth, irony and rigor of Freud's thought. The phrase from *Civilization and Its Discontents* to the effect that he had no consolation to offer, followed by his assertion that that was what they all wanted, the wildest revolutionary no less than most pious believer, gave me aesthetic pleasure—but I must also have thought it true of myself. Freud had learned to live without consolation; I sought it in a process of transformation, in chiaroscuro, situated just over whatever historical horizon I was looking at.

Meta-history and my actual life, with its anxieties, burdens and occasional delights, remained unjoined.

9

Interim 1: The Beginning of a Long Farewell to Europe

LIFE in Oxford wasn't all academic strife—or devoted to the higher realms of spirit. Nina, even though she regretted our move to Oxford, made our home on the Woodstock Road comfortable—and it was open to a steady stream of visitors. There were colleagues and students, but also a contingent from London. I recall a weekend on which it snowed, despite the obdurate English belief that this did not happen, with pipes frozen all over southern England and trains stopped. It was the weekend of a visit by George Lichtheim—an enterprise that required full concentration even when the climate was mild. George had objected to my planning a cocktail party in his honor and inviting Isaiah Berlin ("Then I won't be able to dominate the conversation"). He regarded travel anywhere, except perhaps from his apartment in Hampstead to central London by taxi, as fraught with uncertainty and even danger. Now he was stranded in North Oxford which, despite its resident academics, he thought of as at best a remote outpost of civilization.

The encounter with Berlin, as I recall it, went as expected: each was elegantly polite, and only disparaging of the other in private conversation later. Their performing selves were different: George, distant and ironic, watching the response of his public from under half-closed eyebrows, while Isaiah was direct and volatile, making the point that attending to him was a unique opportunity which should not be missed.

On a different occasion, William Phillips turned up. William, like an astronaut on a spacewalk, carried his own oxygen with him. Unlike the astronaut, he was supremely indifferent to the environment. He concentrated on what was obsessing him at the moment.

Once we talked about the difficulty of maintaining a civilized style of life in Manhattan, although I had observed that any number of my British contemporaries were fleeing to the US, not least for financial reasons. Then he complained of the narrowness of New York's intellectual horizons, followed by a lament that there was very little to be learned in Europe. He did, to his credit, re-publish Iris Murdoch's call for new thought ("A House of Theory"), which was as convincing in North America as in the United Kingdom. Sometimes, William broke through his own laboriously constructed defenses: his great fear was of going off on an historical tangent, so he often preferred standing still, as if waiting out a thick fog at an unmarked crossroads.

There were other American visitors. Dan Bell came, witty and friendly but conveying, as always, the unspoken but definite intimation that he saw not into but through whatever he confronted. Jack Sawyer dropped by and found Oxford very much a world unto itself and of not much use to him in his task as reforming president of Williams College: there was little that he could bring back with him. Victor Butterfield, the reforming president of Wesleyan, had already had that experience. He came to Oxford, was invited by Maurice Bowra to dine at Bowra's college, and was asked by that considerable wit how he found "as you would say, our operation." Butterfield expressed his perplexity at Oxford's haphazard ways: as he read the lecture list in the Faculty of Modern History, he found four classes on the French Revolution taught by four different people in the same semester. "What's wrong with that?" Bowra said. "Two for, and two against."

A somewhat more serious note met Paul Lazarsfeld, who gave a talk on the history of the Bureau of Applied Social Research at Columbia. Later, at our house, he was surprised that a British colleague, Jean Floud, insisted on the connection between political perspective and the study of sociology. "I do politics after six in the evening," he declared—and added some denigrating remarks about Wright Mills. Angered, Jean left. That was unusual in someone who disciplined her passions.

Our European visitors knew that the English had passions, but had great difficulty finding immediate evidence for their presence. Artur Henkel, who taught classical German literature at Heidelberg, said that he found it easy to relate to Continental colleagues, but that it was a strain to visit Britain. As cultivated, as at home in the traditions of the West as the British were, he sensed a barrier. Artur was elegantly reserved, but more rambunctious visitors such as Ernst Bloch and Lucien Goldmann declared England impenetrable. Bloch seemed to be looking for Blake or the Fifth Monarchy men. Goldmann was astonished at the Oxford dons for dining at college and leaving their wives at home. "But won't they then have adventures on the side?" "With whom?" Nina asked. "All the other men are in college, too." Goldmann wished to visit with Isaac Deutscher and I arranged that. Lucien, however, was dreadfully afraid that Deutscher would not recognize him at his rail station near Windsor, and so an elaborate scheme was devised by which Lucien would carry a copy of *Temps Modernes*. The station was mostly used by bankers in bowler hats with furled umbrellas, and the idea that Goldmann, who looked like not one but two European intellectuals, might blend into the crowd was considerably exaggerated.

Isaac Deutscher came with his wife, Tanja, and was my guest at the college's annual dinner—full of city and industrial magnates, front-bench politicians, and cultural industry managers. Isaac had lived in the UK for many years and knew what tone to take. He was expected to play the central European so un-socialized in British culture that he could speak openly. His presence was appreciated, and he had a quite friendly conversation with the leader of the Tory Party, Lord Hailsham. Hailsham played the clown for the benefit of the press but was actually quite shrewd: He clearly thought that the Tories could manage imperial decline—but not by acknowledging the situation they were struggling with, and so offered an unending round of distractions to the public in general and imperial reassurance to his electorate in particular. He and Deutscher talked about the Soviet Union, agreed that Khrushchev should attempt reform much more energetically while he had the chance. A year later, Khrushchev was ousted and the sclerotic Brezhnev epoch began. The Cold War party which spanned blocs, the party of immobility (Moscow branch), had won again.

There was a Soviet bloc movement, or perhaps more accurately a sensibility, favoring more change, and we had visitors from it. Julian Hochfeld was a Polish socialist who had returned after the war after having had the good fortune to have survived imprisonment with the Polish army in the Soviet Union to be released with others under General Anders to join the allied army in Italy. Hochfeld had a post-war political career in which he was parliamentary deputy from Radom, the city from which my grandfather came. He met Communist rule by insisting publicly on the ethical imperatives of the socialist tradition with its demands for political freedom. The regime sent him to UNESCO as deputy director of the social sciences. He was quite clear that he had made a choice which posed larger and smaller moral dilemmas every day. He died in 1962: it is difficult to imagine that he could have remained in Poland after the anti-Semitic and anti-revisionist purges of 1968. He was someone who in his way practiced, well before the sustained protests which eventually brought down the regime, a secular form of exemplary prophecy. A visitor from the Soviet Union was Edward Arab-Ogly—who went from Moscow to work on *World Marxist Review* in Prague as a specialist for Western thought. It proved convincing enough for him to form friendships with a number of Western colleagues, myself among them. We first met at F, in 1959—when walking on the shore of Lago Maggiore, he likened Stalin to Bonaparte. I said that Bonaparte, for all of his despotism, was a more constructive figure than Stalin. Edward shrugged his shoulders: he envied me my freedom to form opinions; he had to work with colleagues socialized under Stalinism. Decades after I saw him in Oxford I met him in Moscow, where he had come out of retirement to work at the Institute of Marxism-Leninism in the early Gorbachev years. Arab-Ogly was not typical of the metropolitan Russian intelligentsia, since he came from a small Caucasian ethnic group. He could have become emphatically dogmatic, to demonstrate his integration in the Soviet version of empire. Instead, he developed an unmistakable distance, even skepticism. Arab-Ogly, clearly, was more of a conformist in his behavior than Hochfeld—but the USSR and Poland were much different. Hochfeld gave a public talk at Oxford; Arab-Ogly took the train from London for a private visit.

These were interesting and pleasant aspects of the Oxford years. They were made more than bearable, livable, for me by my children. Both were born in situations which seriously threatened

Nina's life—and the lives of the infants. Somehow, she transmitted to them her own insistence on living. Anna came to Oxford at age two; Antonia was born there. Nina was a concerned and caring mother who gave the children the conviction that they were at the center of our lives—but who also let them know that our lives encompassed much else, of which they had to take account but which they also could or would join. I'll take credit for being a good father, present in the home, delighted with their lives, attentive to their feelings. Interestingly, in recollection I condense our four years on the Woodstock Road as if it were one happy instant—and that is what they made of the time I spent with them.

For much of this period, Nina worked late afternoons and evenings, sometimes four times a week. She taught in the University of Maryland program for American servicemen on nearby bases. We had a succession of agreeable and helpful au pair girls from Austria, Germany, Switzerland. One difficulty was that a few of them were so much part of the family that the children were much saddened by their departures. I usually came back from college to be with the girls late afternoons, or if I remained for seminars (which at Oxford were taught from five to seven), came home in time to put them to bed. When they had grown a bit, they liked nothing better than to come to college for tea—where students, staff, even the stiffest of dons took it upon themselves to make them feel welcome.

They were particularly friendly with the Walshes across the street, and the attachment was fortified when they had children—giving ours a sense of belonging, as it were, to an elder generation. There was a friendly family next door with boys and girls a bit older and I recall the boys' unequivocal admiration when Antonia climbed high up on the tall tree in their garden. There were other families with children with whom we exchanged visits.

The girls grew up bilingually, Nina speaking to them in German, and I in English. It did not strain them and at one point, Anna expressed some surprise at discovering that the college family which lived downstairs in our three-storied house spoke only English. Anna spoke late but then spoke in quite finished and full phrases in both languages. Antonia spoke very early. Anna's English was quite Oxfordian, Antonia's more American in its accents.

At one point, we got them a book with the English alphabet and there under "B" was the beetle. Antonia declared the book wrong, a beetle she said was someone who—and mimicked playing the guitar. Clearly, she was with it.

The children liked nothing better than visitors, and had very high levels of toleration for the most abstruse of conversationalists. Their intuitions were, usually, unerring. They liked our French friend Éric de Dampierre with his noble irony, found the couple Perry Anderson and Juliet Mitchell amusing, were politely appreciative of all who spoke directly with them. Some of our British guests were surprised that the children were not banished to their room once company arrived, but as in other matters great and small, British fortitude triumphed and they bore the girls' presence bravely. I think that I detected a political correlation in these responses, with persons on the Left decidedly more at ease in the enlarged family circle. When I put on my academic gown to dine at my college, the girls instantly grasped what was at issue. "Are you going to a costume party?" Oxford was my costume party; they returned me to life.

The strains of spring 1962 behind us, we set off in June for the United States. We flew, in what appeared to be interesting and was certainly congenial company, the long way around—with the cut-price airline Icelandic Air. Our first stop was my parents' apartment in New Rochelle. Waiting for the elevator with our baggage, I suggested that two resident matrons take it first. As they got in, I heard one ask the other, "Where did he get that British accent?" The door closed and the car ascended before I could tell them.

I did not need to be so reticent with others, and saw Clement Greenberg, Norman Podhoretz, William Phillips, and Irving Howe. Clem and Norman and William each in his way asked me about the United Kingdom and Europe—to proceed at once to answer the questions themselves. Irving showed a melancholy curiosity about British Labour and a great deal of doubt about the political judgement and staying power of the American university Left. *Partisan Review* had published a symposium on the Cold War in which some of the contributors expressed disquiet: anti-Communism had become an end in itself; the friends of liberty were often allied with groups and thinkers they abjured; insufficient energy was being spent on the problems of the United States. A couple of contributors did note that a nuclear war would be bad for everyone's health, but no great energies were expended in writing about it. *Commentary* in that period was much more open. Norman, as editor, had a free hand—and the American Jewish Committee, which paid for the journal, had not yet made the journey from a sovereign American interpretation of Jewishness to the ethnocentrism which marked it later. Wealthy Jewish liberals were quite prepared to pay for Norman's editorial sponsorship of Paul Goodman, Staughton Lynd, William Appleman Williams, and any number of cultural and political voices critical of the liberals' friends in the Kennedy government.

Yet it was the Kennedy government which had opened space, if only by raising expectations and hopes it (or any other government) could not fulfill. I found movement in lots of places—among African-Americans (then still termed "Negroes"), in the unrelenting criticism of mass culture that united despairing conservatives and radicals, in the scientific community's opposition to mobilization for the Cold War, in a range of discussions of new needs and new possibilities among academics and intellectuals. Something was in the air, and it affected even the most hardened figures of New York's intellectual elite. Even with Galbraith and Schlesinger in the White House, the elder generation was having difficulty in dealing with a situation in which it would have been absurd to portray American politics as dominated by philistines. I sensed a generational difference, which seemed more pronounced in 1962 than during my visit in 1961. Norman Podhoretz as editor of *Commentary* had temporarily seized the leadership of the intellectual opposition to Kennedy—depicted as insufficiently willing or unable to break with the ideas and policies of the Cold War.

The writers around *Dissent* argued among themselves as to how far the Kennedy government could be moved to more decisiveness—and by whom. Michael Harrington was about to publish *The Other America*. Dwight Macdonald's eccentric independence made him acutely sensitive to changes in culture and politics, and it was he who in *The New Yorker* called attention to Harrington's book—reaching, above all, the president.

By contrast with the familial size (and feeling) of British life, the American stage was very large, marked by rapid changes of cast and scene, a limitless repertory of contrasts. The New Yorkers were made uncertain by Washington's new ascendancy, but most of them did not see the significance of the critical energies accumulating in the colleges and universities—surprising since no small number of them were themselves teachers. Undergraduates and graduate students and those studying law and medicine, as well as younger faculty, were in every way the privileged offspring of the new American prosperity. They had only to walk through open doors to rewarding careers. That, however, made them suspicious. They wanted something else, some sense of larger social engagement. They had been touched by the civil rights movement in the South. Some had inherited a domesticated, or dormant, radicalism from parents who were themselves children of the New Deal. Lionel Trilling later referred to the student movement as "modernism in the streets"—intimating that the students had taken the texts he so cherished rather too seriously by rejecting the narratives society expected them to enact in their own lives. Trilling wasn't the only one confounded by a student generation which took some of what it was taught seriously. The rebelliousness of the British and German students I had known was almost entirely extra-mural, and the episode of the attempted sanctioning of the Oxford editors who had reviewed courses was obviously preposterous.

I had as little sense of what was coming as anyone else. In 1960, Andrew Hacker published in *Commentary* an article titled "The Rebelling Young Scholars" on the American journals *Studies on The Left* and *New University Thought* as well as on *New Left Review*. The rebellion of which he wrote was vigorous dissent, intended to enlarge political debate but not to replace it by new forms of political action. (He described the editors of *New Left Review* as the sorts of persons who would not be welcome in British universities—giving me the chance as senior American of the British New Left to respond that he was, ultimately, correct but that for the time being thirty of thirty-five members of our editorial board were university teachers.)

Harvard in 1962 was certainly very much alive—in contrast with the mask of routine, even somnolence, favored at Oxford. Harvard in Washington was a central topic of conversation. The Summer School was sufficiently representative of the university to make it clear that it was as proud of its worldly connections as of its scholarship. Plenty of old friends, such as Morton and Lucia White, were around and we were made to feel very welcome. I was struck by one contrast: compared with the British reserve toward children, ours were greeted with Mediterranean warmth. We had rented Stuart Hughes's house near the Mt. Auburn cemetery—which had a garden spray that delighted Anna and Antonia. We lived near the Whites, an added advantage.

The lease included arrangements for Stuart to stay, since he could not join his family on Long Pond in Wellfleet. Public duty called: he was running for the Senate as a candidate opposing the Cold War and all of its works. His opponent was the young Edward Kennedy, making his initial claim for electoral support. Stuart's campaign manager was Martin Peretz, then a twenty-four-year-old graduate student in political science. Meanwhile, Henry Kissinger was directing a seminar for young leaders chosen from any number of countries, an enterprise financed covertly by the CIA. I met some of the participants, have no recollection of having met two of the Germans who became my friends later, and whose careers suggested that the CIA had in their case not invested wisely, Günter Gaus and Erhard Eppler. Gaus was editor of *Der Spiegel* when it was most critical of West Germany's unconditional alignment with the US and then joined Brandt in the Chancellor's office to work on Germany's autonomous policy in Central and Eastern Europe. He was the Federal Republic's first permanent representative in the Communist German state. Eppler, who was Social Democratic minister for overseas development, was the leader of the Protestant peace movement which opposed the emplacement of medium-range nuclear missiles in Germany. I am sure that Kissinger took this with a certain serenity: the point of the seminar was, after all, to advance both the national interest and his own—and he liked being connected to all the players, even if he could not always write the script. I cannot recollect that he expressed any curiosity that summer about the British New Left, or about new social thought in Europe.

Lots of others did. My interlocutors were equally divided between those concerned with European thought and those interested in politics. Harvard's Widener Library had acquired many of the most interesting European writings, but much of it had never been borrowed. Despite a steady stream of other European visitors, almost none of the European Marxists had ever been invited to Harvard. The historians, or some of them, read *Annales*—but the French and European debates that animated it were largely *terra incognita*. The younger faculty studying European literature knew about these, but the social scientists were immune to the temptation to think anew. Ideas of modernization surgically severed from the philosophical discussion of modernity still dominated their view of history. Those interested in radical politics were much impressed by the British New Left's alliance with the Campaign for Nuclear Disarmament, and quite a few had visited our meetings in London or witnessed the anti-nuclear protest marches. The stirrings in France and Germany which were challenging the stolidity of both the French Socialists and the German Social Democrats, the capacity of some European intellectuals to interest the unions on ideas of economic democracy, fascinated them. Some few understood the currents of dissent in the French and Italian Communist parties as parts of a movement which extended to Prague and Warsaw, occasionally even to Moscow. My friends struggled to grasp two very different tendencies in Europe. One was the strong beginning of generational protest; the other was a systematic rethinking of socialism (frequently connected to re-evaluations of Marxism—some returning to its humanist roots, others criticizing its economic categories and predictions). I explained to whomever would listen that the Europeans were no less perplexed about reconciling these trends than American readers of Marx, despite the difference in political surroundings.

    The rethinking of American society lay over the historical horizon. The task assigned the Kennedy government by its supporters at Harvard, enthusiasts and sceptics alike, echoed the president's own campaign words about getting the nation moving again. The Eisenhower years on this account had seriously slowed the society's march to the future. Now that Harvard and MIT had returned to the White House (which, in fact, they had never truly left) the powers of science and technology, the productivity of the economy, would be used for the public good. Upon examination, that entailed some investment in education and science, appreciably more in weaponry, and a good deal of old fashioned patronage distributed to the Democratic Party's urban and state machines in the form of infrastructure projects. The public was instructed to help itself and the nation by spending, that is, consuming, more. Galbraith had criticized private opulence and public squalor, but had decided that he would be unable to right the balance even as chair of the Council of Economic Advisors, and had gone to India as ambassador.

It was assumed that Kennedy was the heir of the progressive legacy, and the durability and solidity of that legacy were not questioned in either the White House or Harvard Yard. There were some exceptions. When the president in his inaugural address declared, "Ask not what your country can do for you; ask what you can do for your country," he clearly had in mind the internationalization of the American project. The words followed the admonition that a new generation would bear any burden to defend freedom—as we defined it. The enthusiasm of the many of all ages who volunteered for the Peace Corps was evidence for a considerable amount of idealism in parts of the society. Some considered that they did not need to go abroad to express it. The intensifying struggle of the African-Americans for civil rights in the South, the beginnings of a renewal of the discussion of poverty across racial lines, revived a view of American society which emphasized our failure to have fully enacted the progressive agenda. Meanwhile, some of the scientists who had worked on the Hiroshima and Nagasaki bombs, joined by veterans of the foreign policy and military apparatus, academic critics of empire, and Christian and secular pacifists, formed an heterogeneous skirmish line in a battle for arms control and especially superpower negotiations for limits on nuclear weapons.

The battlefront did not always run, I learned, between those inside the Kennedy government and those outside it. Himself a master of ambiguity in his moral judgements on American society, David Riesman kept two feet firmly in both camps. Marcus Raskin and Richard Barnet had by then left government to found the Institute for Policy Studies. Despite the obvious impiety of his decision to run against the president's younger brother (then hardly the lion he was to become), Stuart Hughes was discreetly encouraged by some of his Cambridge friends in Washington. There were less equivocal critics of Kennedy, such as Herbert Marcuse.

I understood the ambivalence toward the president and his government which marked the New York intellectuals. It was impossible to function as rigorous outsiders when the insiders were offering government-sponsored lecture trips abroad—or, at least, responding to critical articles as if they were being taken seriously. The New York intellectuals weren't unique: the entire national intelligentsia was in one or another way fascinated by what Christopher Lasch was later to describe as a fusion of café society and Route 128 (the Boston circumferential highway where the newer consulting and technology firms, often the work of Harvard and MIT professors, were cited).

The visit certainly made possible my return to the US four years later. Its long-term implications were, then, quite hidden from me. Indeed, the trip initially reinforced my conviction that I belonged to a cohesive international guild, marked by its equidistance from all existing regimes. Cambridge, Berkeley, Chicago, New York, Washington were—like Berlin, London, Oxford, Paris—places to which fate had assigned our spiritual brothers and sisters. The places were hardly identical or interchangeable, but we spoke the common language, an unsteady mixture of alienation, criticism, and hope.

In a definite way, however, I was recurring to American themes. Then, as now, I thought much of the theory of modernization as ahistorical and shallow. If the US to some extent was a model, more accurately, an exemplar of cultural and social development, it was because our problems represented on a larger scale what many elsewhere were experiencing. The splendid hopes of the Kennedy years, the sense of anticipation voiced by many, envisaged an open future. If that future were open, however, much of the usual sorts of social analysis was unimportant, even irrelevant. What was important was what could be created, not what followed with iron regularity from the regular functioning of the social apparatus. History and historical thinking became salient. The past had its lessons—as well as identifying comportment and ideas that were indeed past. In 1962, the reconstruction of the American past as a triumph, against recurring obstacles, of liberalism was no longer compelling. There was too much illiberalism to be found in our history; progress had been too irregular and by no means linear—and the meaning of liberalism was in any event a subject of argument.

I thought that I had been right about the historical nature of sociology, wrong to suppose that the tension between history and sociology could be contained, much less resolved. That year I published in the UNESCO-sponsored series *Contemporary Sociology* a long essay, or short monograph, on the current state of the sociological analysis of ideology. It was a period, after all, of dispute, conflict, and movement within the two superpower blocs. No one of the very intelligent and upright persons who obviously had to labor reluctantly under the constraints of state socialism believed state socialism represented the future. They left it to their own ideologues, often not especially gifted, to declare that we in the West, orphaned by history, had only our illusions. Indeed, there was a striking paradox. In the West, many who thought of themselves as critical or radical argued that the idea of an accumulative science of society on the model of the natural sciences was untenable. Empirical inquiry, they continued, made sense only when it was put into the context of an idea of the historical totality that was our society. Some sociologists took the long view, looking for inquiries which might function like the physicists' capture of the bending of light at an eclipse, to verify Einstein's theory. We had no Einstein (and Talcott Parsons, who had once studied biology, did not use models derived from physics but from bodily functioning—in a very analogical way). The Soviet bloc radicals, however, thought of empirical studies as actual or potential refutations of the ruling parties' fabrications of mythicized historical projects, in which present disorders were denied in favor of claims of progress toward total success.

Teaching that summer at Harvard, I did not find many of the undergraduate or graduate students in sociology much interested in these matters, leaving them to scholars in history and politics. Much of American history, and the history of other societies, was *terra incognita* for the sociologists. Even those in area studies (of China or the Soviet Union, for instance) concentrated on contemporary phenomena, on matters that could be ascertained by empirical inquiry or its equivalent (using informants when direct access to a society was impossible). Many scholars were debating Louis Hartz's view of the domination of American politics by a relatively monolithic liberalism, but very few sociologists were concerned with the issue. Of course, it was not susceptible to direct empirical verification—but studies of the political attitudes and behavior of a segmented American society might have cast some light on it.

Instead, most sociologists studied the segments and not the way they occasionally came together or remained apart. Survey research and a pointed sort of empirical inquiry were increasingly employed by political scientists, and historians were attempting, with some success, to capture the larger movements of culture beneath the fluctuations of opinion and politics. Parsons was a cultivated generalist who processed all kinds of data in his categories, and who was aware of the doubts of many about the utility of his model of society. Riesman was a gifted and intuitive practitioner of social commentary. He used all kinds of models and if he took anything as exemplary it might have been film or novel. His legal education and experience (as at the beginning of the New Deal the legal realists were trying to expel their more formalistic colleagues from the modern temple, the courts and the modern synagogue, the law school) had accustomed him to ambiguity and conflict. The one classical sociologist around was actually Barrington Moore (with Hughes one of two close Harvard friends of Marcuse, who taught at Brandeis nearby,) Moore was accumulating the matter he would later use in his major works, and kept his distance from much of the activity of the university's social scientists.

One set of scholars at the time under-estimated their own points of strength—economists. Economics at Harvard had come a long way since John Kenneth Galbraith was not kept on in a junior post owing to excessive attachment to both the ideas of Keynes and the politics of Franklin Roosevelt. By the time these had become respectable, the university was at equal pains to make it clear to one of the English-speaking world's most gifted Marxists, Paul Sweezy, that he could not return to the university with tenure after wartime service. A combination of the intellectual influences of Keynes and Schumpeter, and the governmental experience of many of faculty, had as a consequence the amplification of the scope of economics, beyond classical notions of the autonomy of the market.

Galbraith was in India as ambassador. I had not come to know him when at Harvard as a student and the pleasure and profit of doing so had to wait until I returned to New England in 1968 to

1968, daughter Anna on the Canal Grande in Venice.

teach at Amherst. His books with their raids, or deliberate marches, into territory guarded by other disciplines could not be ignored—not least because the educated public thought they connected with their lives.

The French have a phrase for it—*vases communicants,* communicating vessels. To what extent, in Kennedy's America, did the academic and cultural elites communicate with their fellow citizens who lived in very different settings and had other ideas of society and moral and political convictions? Of course, there was a certain amount of daily and routine contact, at service stations and shops, in offices, and in the provision of domestic services. Those in government could hardly avoid congressmen and senators speaking for constituents without Ivy degrees. My impression now (I hardly remarked on the matter then) is that the friends we visited with in 1962 were immersed in their own milieu. When, later, their students desperately sought contact with "the people," many of them promptly lost their way in social space. Of course, the American undergraduate and graduate student body was socially diverse—and different at different institutions. Later in the sixties, as a teacher at the graduate faculty of the New School for Social Research from 1966 to 1968 and at Amherst College thereafter, as well as on visits to other campuses and meetings with student groups, I saw that the linguistic and intellectual conventions of the faculty struck many of the young as oppressive. Very little of this was evident or imagined in 1962, when even or above all student protesters aspired to join the faculty in their cultural enclaves. Those who remembered the student movement of the thirties and early forties recalled it as part of the New Deal coalition, concentrating on economic and political issues in the larger society much more than on questions of academic culture and governance.

The New York intellectuals and the Harvard Brahmins (those left) were pleased to be citizens of a superpower. Their disdain for mass culture had plenty of justification in terms of a larger project for a democratic nation. Their younger readers and students were prepared to look for virtues in places their elders never visited—or from which some of them had fled. Upon reflection, my own inability to anticipate the coming turbulence had two sources. The British New Left was very concerned with cultural question, but in a very British historical idiom—and had an image of the United States, in part idealized but in part real, as much more welcoming to popular creativity. Fundamentally, too, I thought of my career as a critical intellectual as an ideal sort of social ascent: one could climb in good conscience.

Certainly, much of the visit was a return of the prodigal son. I did not burden friends with my miseries at Oxford but provided them with an ironic view of the university, with any number of anecdotes to enliven the account. They knew that the British New Left, and its Continental cousins, were closer to social movements implanted in their nations' political institutions than an American Left connected to the New Deal by legend and nostalgia. Meanwhile, the perspectives I had learned in Europe put me in their view on the frontiers of new thought in the social sciences. The combination of the piece on ideology and the political polemic in "The Coming End of Anti-Communism" (despite the fact that it was twenty-seven years too early) gave me standing among social scientists and social critics alike. I worried about the books I had not yet written;

others were glad to read what I had published. The cultivated impersonality of British middle-class culture certainly was a façade, but it effectively nullified expressive emotion. American spontaneity could be intrusive, but its warmth was very welcome: I did not have to pretend to an indifference I did not feel.

I went to two sociological meetings in Washington at the end of the summer, the annual event of the American Sociological Association and the tri-annual one of the International Sociological Association. Each was an occasion to re-connect with friendly colleagues and make new acquaintances. Thematically and politically, they entailed rather sharp contrasts. The civil rights movement was underway in the United States; the movement of protest against US nuclear weaponry was active in the universities; the trade unions were then a third of the labor force and a political grouping to be reckoned with. Michael Harrington had just published his *The Other America* and if the publication of Betty Friedan's *The Feminine Mystique* was a half year in the future (February 1963), some stirrings among women colleagues were discernible to those who cared to look. Class and race were never missing from the preoccupations of academic sociologists, but the discipline as a whole was severely segmented—so much so that some studied work and others power separately. What unified the sociologists was not, curiously, the interest in society many had—but argument on how to study it, with many of the participants, myself included, voicing very shallow versions of the work of philosophers of knowledge. Meeting in Washington generated a certain uneasiness among the Americans. Economists, historians, lawyers, and political scientists were prominent in government, the sociologists absent from the White House and not much in public view when in the permanent government.

Yet there was an assumption shared by most American sociologists with the other social scientists—that there was a distinct process of modernization, that the United States was in its vanguard, and that it provided optimal conditions of material and moral freedom. Modernization entailed the triumph of a secularized pluralism in public space, the replacement of ethnic and religious norms in that space by Universalist ones, a privileged political position for knowledge, especially scientific knowledge. That ascribed an indispensable role to the educated, although they were often portrayed as representing the educated citizenry as a whole. There were not appreciably fewer persons of academic background in the Eisenhower administration than in the Kennedy government. Bundy, Schlesinger, Galbraith, and McNamara were more adept at marketing themselves than Eisenhower's men and women, and the presidential couple lent the enterprise charm and even excitement.

By contrast Khrushchev figured as a grandfatherly figure, whose repetition of revolutionary slogans was inauthentic. (China was not much talked about and the Cultural Revolution, when it occurred, evoked widespread bewilderment.) Khrushchev himself was impressed, reportedly, by Castro and the Cubans, as embodiments of real revolutionary ardor. In fact, in the Soviet bloc, research institutes and some thinkers were developing their own version of the theory of modernization—the view that the next stage of development in the state socialist societies would consist of a very large increase in the scientific component of production. That, too, implied an indispensable role for the educated in these societies. With an increase in their numbers, as they worked with and coordinated a highly educated labor force, it also implied a creeping but unmistakable process of democratization. At the very least, the knowledge elite to function in the larger social interest would have to be relieved of the burdens of dogma imposed by a vulgar Marxist populism.

The Washington gathering of international sociologists in 1962 had a considerable presence from the Soviet Union and the other Soviet bloc nations. As at the Amsterdam meeting in 1956 and the one at Stresa in 1959, the Poles were outspoken, quite at home with their Western colleagues, and under no constraint to use Aesopian language or cumbersome circumlocutions. In 1956, the Yugoslavs with their rather free interpretation of Marx and familiarity with Western Europe mediated between the Westerners and the Soviet bloc sociologists. By 1962, some Poles assumed this role—with quite a few others either ignoring their inclusion in the Soviet bloc or using black humor to describe their own regime.

On the formal program, two themes marked the encounter of the blocs. One came from the inner conflict in Western sociology, between Western Marxists (most disdainful of Stalinism) and an extremely heterogeneous group united only by its claim to have thrown off all dogmas. The Marxists thought of their society as "late capitalism," while the others wrote of "industrial society." The borders of the groups were somewhat porous and in particular, the Marxists frequently displayed considerable imagination in interpreting the master's texts. Pluralism was not conspicuous in the politics of the state socialist nations, but some was beginning to be evident in the thinking of their intellectuals. Listening to the Western Marxists, it was often difficult to believe that they all inhabited the same time and space. On matters of class structure, the function of elites, the limits on democracy's possibilities, they frequently agreed with the secular sceptics, many of them self-consciously post-Marxist. The Western Marxists, situated across the political spectrum, had residual notions of a future socialist transformation. The others were prepared to settle for the considerable consolations of social democracy.

Many colleagues from the Soviet bloc intimated that they had more in common with the Western sociologists who were not seeking a new heaven or a new earth than with the true (or old) believers in their own camp. The arguments, across all intellectual and political boundaries, about theory and empirical inquiry made that clear. Many Westerners interested in larger historical interpretations, and in political philosophy, insisted on the ancillary nature of empirical work. Its results, indeed its questions, only made sense when set in a larger framework. The notion of a science of society as cumulative was naïve, or a dogmatization of what actually mattered in the natural sciences. (Thomas Kuhn published, in the same year, his *Structure of Scientific Revolutions*, but not many of the social scientists knew the work of the historians and philosophers of science. They depended on Robert Lynd or C. Wright Mills, sometimes on Karl Mannheim—recondite references in those days in the English-speaking world—or Adorno and Horkheimer. The French were better off, with learned and subtle antagonists such as Aron and Gurvitch.) For the critical party in the Soviet bloc, however, empirical inquiry was liberating. They could not be penalized, Stalin dead, for describing without adornment stratification, even alienation in the labor force, in their own societies.

The arguments were hardly limited to plenary sessions and

working panels. They continued over meals and at the crowded swimming pool of the old Sheraton hotel. I was experiencing, meanwhile, a large ambiguity. I was chair of the International Sociological Association's Research Committee on the Sociology of Religion—and, absurdly and erratically, running from its sessions to the discussions of Marxist eschatology and back again. Some very good scholars using comparative materials were present, and so were a set of intelligent and worldly priests from Europe and the US, as well as the inevitable contingent of very serious Protestants from northern Europe and the US. Scholem spent a life dedicated to exploring the duality in Judaism, between legalism and mysticism, Torah and Kabbalah. No such sharp contrast marked my movement between thinking about history in large terms and depicting religious belief as a primary motive. I acknowledged the continuity between socialist beliefs in emancipation and religious ones of redemption—but was unwilling, because unable, to deal fully with social thought as meta-history. Having discarded religion early, I lacked a spiritual itinerary to retrace. At the time, I had a clear and unexceptional view of what had brought me to study modern societies and their social movements: I was a child of the New Deal. Germany, and all of Europe, followed from my fascination with the thirties and forties. When it came to religion, I lapsed into (quite literally) bookish explanations: I had read Weber, or Hill on the Puritans.

Of all my colleagues and friends, one saw beyond (or through) that: Henri Desroche, the former Dominican who remained a Catholic. An intellectual companion, he never doubted that I was pursuing a spiritual vocation. I now wish that I had recurred to him more often as a confessor, or in that splendid French phrase, *directeur de l'âme*.

We had obtained some money for a two-day colloquium and meeting of the Committee at Georgetown University at the end of the larger international congress. It was very international, and the participants from the United States were quite struck by the variety and vitality of the work others were doing—and by their unashamed closeness to theology. Nietzsche had declared that German philosophy had a pastoral father, and that was certainly true of much of American sociology. (Robert Park and Robert Lynd began as theologians; Talcott Parsons' father was ordained.) Just as in the study of larger social structures, the Europeans in particular surprised the Americans with their capacity to move across intellectual boundaries. The main, even obsessive, theme was the supposed prevalence of secularization. Even those studying profoundly committed religious groups acknowledged that religion in a secular or partly secular environment differed in its continuity, substance, and texture—and therefore in the souls and actions of believers—from religion in pre-secular settings. Was this so very different from the response of religions to co-existence with other religions?

Two days, in the absence of comparativists and historians, were hardly sufficient to get to, much less beneath, the surface of events. Ideas of a linear and irresistible increase in secularization, whether Marxist or derived from notions of modernization (that is, owing much to Weber's reading of Marx), did not dominate. It was agreed that these were too simple—but what followed perplexed the participants. A response, of a sort, was given by two participants from Poland—as ever, ahead of the rest of the Soviet bloc—who collected their expense allowances and were not seen until the closing reception.

Washington was well chosen as the site of the congress. It was, after all, an imperial city—celebrating past triumphs and contemplating future battles.

One embarrassment for the American hosts was the evident indifference of the Kennedy government to the presence of so many thinkers. We never, it would appear, could escape the pages of journals read only by other scholars—and the adventures of some of the rest of us in little journals read by the international intelligentsia were of not much more interest. The guest speaker from public life was Walt Rostow—not a major Washington figure, though rather more prominent in the universities for his rather simplified defense of the theory and practice of modernization. The President himself was at Hyannisport, the House, Senate, Cabinet, and sub-Cabinet intellectuals nowhere to be seen. I still think that the arguments of 1962 were important for what they indicated of things to come in both blocs, but decoding or translating was too strenuous for those with daily tasks of governance. Yuri Zamoshkin, one of the newer generation of Soviet sociologists, got it right when he greeted some of us at the door of the Soviet embassy as we arrived for a reception. I was on my way back to New York and had a suitcase; Daniel Bell and Seymour Lipset arrived in another taxi right after mine. "You see," he told them, parodying the title of a much-read tract by an earlier defector from the Soviet Union, "Birnbaum chooses freedom." Zamoshkin was free of the vulgar scholasticism of the older Soviet ideologues, but even he could hardly have predicted what would follow in twenty-five years. For the moment, a modest dosage of irony had to do.

Perhaps I exaggerated, and did myself a slight injustice. Some of the people in the apparatus were mildly curious about the meeting. Carl Kaysen was the president's deputy national security advisor, and he and his wife, Annette, invited us to dinner at their house on Hillyer Place. Carl brought McGeorge Bundy for a drink, and Brahmin manners led him to talk with Nina. Bundy went on home; a pleasant evening was had by all, and there were even questions about Europe and the conference despite the preoccupation of the Washingtonians. On the way back to our hotel, Nina asked me who, exactly, was the arrogant young man Carl had brought for a drink. "What did you talk about," I asked. "Germany," she replied, adding that she had to tell him he knew nothing about it. She was not at all disconcerted to learn who he was, and declared that there was all the more reason to worry that the Berlin crisis would come to no good end.

At about this time, my old friend Richard Barnet and a new one, Marcus Raskin, were preparing to leave their posts in government to found the Institute for Policy Studies. I now wish that I had stayed on for a few days to meet with the congressional heirs of the New Dealers—the liberal lobbying groups, the unions. I had met persons from that milieu when they traveled to the United Kingdom, and had I experienced them at home, it might have hastened the slow, very slow, decision to return. Were I, however, to dwell on missed opportunities at the time, I would have little energy and less space for writing about what actually happened—inwardly and outwardly.

The elder New York intellectuals were prisoners of their own time warp. They interpreted the Kennedy government in the light of their New Deal years, when they approved of much of it but regretted that Roosevelt did not add Trotsky to a list of interlocutors which included Keynes. They were rendered uncomfortable by the thought that they could not maintain their independence by distance. I had taken as an ideal a very imprecise image of a critical thinker, sternly rejecting the temptations of an equally vague pattern of conformity. What I could not deal with was the conviction that I could not and did not belong anywhere in particular, even though the immediate evidence that summer was unequivocal: I was relieved and delighted to be accepted at home, in the academic and intellectual settings I frequented. I simply did not think of a career in ordinary politics as an alternative to, or extension of, my active and literary engagement.

The barrier was not one imposed from without in the Kennedy years. It had much more to do with my own sense of marginality, the strong inner suspicion (constantly denied in gestural bravado) that I could not belong anywhere because I was not wanted.

Back in New York, my French friends unintentionally added to the inner discomfort clearly not stilled by the positive sides of my visit. They asked me to accompany them on the Circle Line's boat ride around Manhattan, which they greatly enjoyed. For my part, I reflected on my inner distance from my own native city, a feeling reinforced by the sense that the French (some of them former priests and all of them dissident in one or another way in de Gaulle's nation) would not dream of questioning their own identities. Some days later, at the Museum of Modern Art, I encountered Alain Touraine—who was not only one of the most brilliant and productive of our generation of social scientists but a fierce critic exceedingly avaricious of praise. Alain found very good words about my monograph on ideology, and insisted that he was not just being polite by reminding me (unnecessarily) that he did not frequently voice enthusiasm. My own inner response was one which has dogged me for decades, the equivalent of the question: if you are so smart, how come you are not rich? If Touraine were right, why had I not done more?

My inner heaviness was lightened by the Trillings. I had asked to speak with Lionel Trilling, at the request of an Oxford colleague, to discuss a student we shared. Graciously, the Trillings invited me to dinner. Then Lionel Trilling called back: he and his wife so objected to my *Partisan Review* article "The Coming End of Anti-Communism" that they thought it best if we did not discuss it. (He didn't detail his objections.) I knew that Lionel Trilling was much concerned with the limits reality imposed on liberalism, and on moral and philosophical ideas in general. I had not imagined that he himself would enforce limits in quite so obvious a way. Days later, still, he called to express his regrets: something had come up and they were obliged to cancel the dinner. William Phillips recounted that the article caused him more trouble than any he had published recently — and noted that the Trillings had reproached him for publishing it at all. I was somewhat puzzled by the attention.

Before my article appeared, *Partisan Review* had published a symposium on the Cold War in which some of the contributors were as critical. Perhaps they were more discreet. It was, after all, the period of the 1957 BBC Reith lectures by George Kennan on the neutralization of Germany, as well as the period of much activity by scientists critical of preparations for nuclear warfare. It also preceded by less than a year John Kennedy's call for an end to the Cold War in his June 10, 1963 address at American University. I regret that I never did come to know Lionel Trilling: his book *Sincerity and Authenticity* demonstrated a rare mastery of modern culture.

Nina and the girls returned to Oxford and I embarked on a trip across the United States. The first stop was, however, the University of Toronto. My hosts said that at first their dean was reluctant to provide money for the visit, but that when he learned that I was from Oxford, volunteered more than they had asked for. I admired the quite European way in which the Canadians defended what made them different from the United States: they lived to their own rhythms, refused to cast their questions in molds provided by their southern neighbors. The university (or the dean's part of it) was an enclave of Anglo-Canadianism in a very mixed city. Even the Anglo-Canadians, however, understood themselves as part of a distinctive mosaic: the snobbery inseparable from the narrative in the Canadian novels I had read years before had become antiquarianism.

Cornell came next. I was scheduled to speak on "Marxism, East and West" and quite a substantial crowd turned up to listen. They were, clearly, not all anxious for instruction in a user's guide to Cold War ideology: something was changing.

Some things, however, were not. When I arrived in Ithaca, I was told that the campus and the town were arguing about the expulsion of a graduate student from the university. His landlady had complained that he had concealed from her the fact that he and his lady friend did not possess a marriage certificate. I could not resist beginning by saying that I had a certain reticence about dealing with Marx and his views of the existence of two classes in a university which had so much difficulty acknowledging the existence of two sexes. My host, Andrew Hacker, said, and not *sotto voce*, that I should stop right there: I had already hit a high note. For the rest, the response in Ithaca was marked mainly by curiosity and even excitement—about Europe. I reported that a revived Marxism in both parts of Europe was not just an intellectual exercise, much less nostalgia. An analysis of the class structures of the state socialist regimes could have profound political consequences, as the events of the years since Stalin's death showed. If the Soviet bloc thinkers chose to phrase their criticism of their regimes in terms which legitimated their claims to be true to socialist tradition, they were not behaving all that differently from American radicals who claimed to be standing on native ground. If, west of the Iron Curtain, younger Europeans experimented with an open Marxism consonant with much else in Western thought, they were behaving traditionally by reinventing traditions. The themes they took from early Marxism (the alienation of the psyche under domination and exploitation, enlarging participation in the control of economy and the workplace for a greatly enlarged practice of citizenship) were not immediately congruent with the other Marxist treasures they were discovering. These, from the *Grundrisse*, depicted knowledge as a revolutionary force. That, however, gave indispensable functions to knowers, and so opened the way for conflicts among elites for power—East and West. The Cornell public took all of this in, but very few thought it had direct relevance for the United States. The Europeans I talked about thought large transformations in their societies possible. The residents of Ithaca were aware of turbulence elsewhere in the nation, and especially in the South, and clearly favored an enlargement of American democracy and American prosperity, but somehow thought that the steps to this could be measured. Still, something was in the air—a pervasive sense of anticipation.

Next, at Ann Arbor, I met Tom Hayden, who was unwilling to settle for anticipation. Tom had already written the Port Huron statement, the charter document of the American New Left, and we compared protest in Western Europe and the United States. The American dissenters' attitudes to the Democrats and the unions were quite like the newer European generations' view of the established parties of the Left (including the French and Italian Communist parties as well as Labour, the French Socialists, and the German Social Democrats). It was a mixture of impatience with their deliberate slowness, and a refusal to accept that, because young, critics should be seen, but not heard. Tom and his generation thought that they had something distinct to say about the Cold War, race relations (the women's question was to come somewhat later), and the forms of politics. Was it a familiar case of generational conflict, salient when generations experience history differently, develop new sensibilities, use unfamiliar words? All of that was occurring, leaving the elders bewildered at the disrespect of the young, the young vexed at their parents and teachers for not listening.

Tom and his University of Michigan contemporaries allowed an exception. They regarded some of their elders in the United Automobile Workers as allies. They were trade union activists, often trade union intellectuals. The Port Huron call for drastic alterations in the ownership and control of American industry did not mobilize the men and women on the production lines to visible enthusiasm; it wasn't even clear that they had heard of it. When the student activism of the period entered the familial lives of union families, it frequently caused conflicts. Opposition to the war in Vietnam and support for the African-American demand for civic equality did not evoke enthusiasm in much of the organized working class. Were the well-paid automobile workers so socially integrated as to be oblivious to the nation's problems? When their immediate interests were at stake, they were ready to behave with considerable militancy. Their union leadership, meanwhile, was active in the civil rights struggle and took increasing distance from the war in Asia. My visit to Ann Arbor was two years before these problems became acute.

Neither Tom nor I read the future with any precision—but Tom was confident that major ruptures were imminent.

I went on to the University of Chicago, again gave a talk about contemporary European thought and the newer social movements. As I recollect it, the university public was at pains to convey that there was little on heaven and earth unaccounted for by its philosophy—but showed quite considerable curiosity, and more than a bit of skepticism, about the depth and staying power of the European New Left. They were both right—and wrong. Much depends upon our view of the longer and indirect influence of the New Left, and that makes summary judgements shallow. The visit to Chicago occasioned the beginning of a lifelong friendship I greatly treasure. I had read for some time the writings of Barbara Probst Solomon; now she was there in person, as her husband was teaching at the university. Barbara was the daughter of a cultivated and wealthy family, had spurned conventional paths to unconventionality, and as a young woman had had an extraordinary European education. She joined the younger Spanish resistance to fascism and lived in Paris in its most creative post-war years. Unlike many New Yorkers, she never took the city's power and wealth for centrality. She had an acute (and devastating) pen for pretense and sovereign disdain for intellectual and political fashion. Her writings showed her great gifts: ruthless observation joined to unfailing empathy. As a friend, she was invariably honest and always loyal. My life is richer because I know her.

After the highly charged University of Chicago I visited a more restful, even tranquil, place—Washington University in St. Louis. It was a very good university, with a faculty of national distinction—who were, visibly, glad to be there and intent on enjoying their lives. Their hospitality was untinged by the competitiveness of other places; they saw themselves as educators as well as scholars. It was the one place at which I was closely questioned about Oxford's curriculum and teaching arrangements. My hosts were not prepared to accept Oxford's (extremely positive) judgements about itself—which struck those at most other places as just.

California lived in its own world. Light and time and space were different—as I noticed at an appropriate place for cosmic measurement, the California Institute of Technology at Pasadena. I was the guest of a college teacher and friend, Hallett Smith, an Elizabethan scholar who was the dean of the institute's faculty of humanities and social sciences. Before I gave a talk, I was his guest at a local French restaurant—where the meal began, as it would not have in France, with coffee. The physicist Murray Gell-Mann was there and he asked about the scientific component of general education in the United Kingdom, to which the short answer was that there was no general education in the United Kingdom.

The long answer was that the British were struggling with the problem of the divisions of modern culture strenuously but extra-curricularly. Perhaps the idea of the gentleman amateur ruled: the scientists were amateurs in the humanities and the humanists were not expected to be different in the sciences. Gell-Mann objected that his British colleagues knew so much about many things. He was curious, as well, about the scientific possibilities of social knowledge, listened politely as I talked with much conviction and little specificity of the political functions of social knowledge. Years later, after he had won a Nobel Prize, he was prevented by French colleagues from giving a scheduled talk at a Parisian institute. They wanted him to explain why he had worked with the US Air Force on weaponry (the Vietnam War was on) and he did not think he owed them an explanation. No such tension disturbed our evening: I could have intimated to Hallett that I would be receptive to the offer of a job, was as befogged about the future as glad to have escaped the spring months at Oxford, yet let the opportunity like so many others pass without thinking of it.

The colleagues at the University of California, Los Angeles, were busy—with their careers in sociology. One had a long-term project, and declared that he was prepared to invest years in it to answer its central question: did the United States have social classes and could these be identified empirically? Nearly a decade after that, I met the colleague at the University of Rochester, to which he had moved—and was pleased to learn that he considered that he was making progress and that, tentatively, he could answer the question with a yes. He graciously recalled our Los Angeles conversation and even more graciously said that I had helped him. All that I recollect is that I had said something about the US being exceptional, indeed, but not extra-terrestrial. I lacked the self-critical capacity, at the time, to realize how remote I was. In a talk to the UCLA sociologists, I asked whether American and European social theory were merging—since the advanced industrial societies increasingly resembled one another. Across the ocean, there was Asia; the city itself was full of Asian immigrants and more from Latin America. No colleague challenged my assumptions about the centrality of the Euro-American model. For all of the Marxism I had absorbed and recondite literature I had read, I had not broken out of an implicit provincialism—and was much closer to the votaries of modernization dogma than I wished to admit.

Berkeley, next, conceded nothing to Harvard in self-congratulation. The universities congratulated themselves for different qualities. Max Weber said that privileged classes celebrated what they were, unprivileged ones, what they would become. Harvard honored its traditions; Berkeley lauded what it was becoming.

Harvard prided itself on connections to established elites and government; Berkeley, to a new world of international learning. The familiar line about the Unitarians believing in the fatherhood of God, the brotherhood of man, and the neighborhood of Boston had been enlarged by Harvard to encompass the more prosperous parts of New York and the more powerful ones of Washington. Berkeley dwelled on its Californian connections, but depicted California as the site of experiments in the future. Were there distinctly more immigrants, foreign visitors, socially ascendant Americans on the Berkeley faculty? I know of no data, but it would not have disheartened the university community to have its self-image as a capital of the new cosmopolitanism confirmed.

I walked around the campus with the chancellor, Clark Kerr. He explained that a new master plan for the university entailed stopping Berkeley's expansion, shifting resources to other and newer campuses. We turned a corner and there was a large building in construction. My host explained that it was a new biology laboratory: a faculty member had won a Nobel Prize in the past year, and "the least we can do for him is to give him a building." I recalled Oxford's absurd controversy of the spring, when the faculty voted against constructing a new biology laboratory to replace the forty-five-year-old structure in which its scientists struggled against leaks and (non-experimental) mice. The majority thought that it would disturb the appearance and tranquility of the parks, much favored by those who walked their dogs there. The ensuing derision and dismay in press and Parliament confirmed the naysayers: the rest of the world could not be allowed to intrude on Oxford.

Berkeley, by contrast, invited the world to come. Its arguments in the social sciences were arguments about emergent social formations. Had I known then the American history I subsequently learned, I might have recognized something of the ideology and purposiveness of the frontier. As it was, I enjoyed the quality of the energies I found there and did not have to give many justifications for what I was doing in Europe. Berkeley was always a university campus at which young, old and many in between paid great attention to politics (as the biographies of Galbraith and Oppenheimer, who were there in the thirties, show). Whatever the considerable stirrings I glimpsed there in the fall of 1962, it was impossible then to imagine what would happen in 1965. When I spoke of the European protest movements, colleagues who had strong opinions on the origins and nature of anti-nuclear protest in Britain, opposition to the Algerian war in France, and German antagonism to rearmament did not imagine that they would soon be confronted by their own students with charges of complicity in a pervasively repressive system. They still thought of themselves as the vanguard of enlightenment.

There were signs of difficulty ahead. Tom Hayden's Port Huron Statement expressed distrust in those who claimed to be working for progress in existing institutions and traditions. Wright Mills' polemical writings, as well as his larger socio-political analyses, were widely read on campuses and canonical texts for a rising generation of social scientists. The critical tone of some in journals such as *Dissent* (Marcuse, above all) was sharper. Paul Goodman had published *Growing Up Absurd* in 1960. *Commentary* under Norman Podhoretz as editor, starting in 1961, moved from an irenic view of the United States to uncompromising criticism. Where Eliot Cohen had been hesitant about taking his distance from Eisenhower, Podhoretz enjoyed casting doubt (and more) on Kennedy.

David Riesman, with characteristic flair, had sensed what lay ahead. His initiative, conveyed in the modest typography of the bulletins of his Committee of Correspondence, was not modest in aim. He intended to make permanent a dialogue, and possibly even an alliance, between radical critics of the US and progressive reformers who thought of themselves as liberal in the American sense of the term. The scientists were indispensable to the enterprise, not just because of their obvious concern with questions of nuclear arms. They fought daily over contested terrain, where public purpose, knowledge, and all the forces of institutional inertia and private avarice collided. Riesman also had few illusions about public intelligence in the nation. When the storm broke, he was not surprised that much of the nation's ignorance, hatred, and violence were mobilized against the grouping that termed itself "the movement." By so casually dismissing the elites (including their teachers) for solidarity with a (hugely hypothetical) people, they had marched resolutely into sectarian isolation.

Returning to Oxford from what had been a triumphal visit to the United States, speaking before large, attentive audiences, I was more concerned with the pressing problems of my future than the larger currents of history. At thirty-six, I had no permanent post. My college fellowship had four years to run—but rejection by my colleagues heightened my inner doubts, not small in the best of circumstances. Two rational steps, not mutually exclusive, were or should have been obvious. One would have been to clear out, take another position. No one in the US had asked for precise details of my situation at Oxford, and the friendly reception I had had suggested that a position would have come available had I seriously sought one.

The second course would have been to complete my unfinished book on the Reformation—or publish something else of a major kind. I sensed the stigma of not having written a book, and dealt with that by an absurdly self-destructive form of semi-conscious defiance: If that is what was wanted, I would not deliver it. A world which managed only imperfectly to recognize my talents was not worth joining.

The trouble was, I did wish to join it, but could not entirely acknowledge that. I was not ready to return to the United States, partly because it would have required convincing Nina that we should leave Europe, but opportunities in Europe in the best of cases were few. I told myself that I would write, but did so spasmodically.

Instead, I continued as before. I had no particular university responsibilities, continued offering lectures and seminars because I enjoyed it, and did not wish to be seen as hurt and resentful. I kept up my political activities and contacts, even if living through a paradox. As the New Left gathered adherents and intellectual and political strength on the continent and in the US, the British New Left was consolidated, staked out its own territory in the United Kingdom, but ceased to grow. No doubt, personally I would have been helped by returning to psychotherapy—but did not do so. Friends (some in the US) proffered sound advice, mostly urging me to write more substantially. I responded to these outer and inner pressures by the personal equivalent of the immobility my comrades and I were diagnosing in Western politics. I would have been better off had I left the world to its own devices for a year or so and done more for myself—but it now strikes me that I did not think that I deserved much better.

I went to one event which was both outwardly and inwardly instructive, the German Sociological Society's symposium to mark the hundredth anniversary of the birth of Max Weber. At the major plenary panel Raymond Aron, Herbert Marcuse, Paolo Rossi, and Talcott Parsons spoke. Parsons declared that there were three major philosophical-political systems contending in Weber's lifetime: conservatism, liberalism, and Marxism. Weber, he insisted, was notable for situating himself beyond any one, for constructing an illusion-less assessment of modern society, Aron expressed polite skepticism that any thinker could rise so clearly above historical circumstances and praised Weber for his ruthless clarity. Rossi echoed him. Marcuse, by contrast, took Weber's description of the free choice of values as an inspiration for Carl Schmitt's insistence that political decisions were ultimately irrational. In other words (which Marcuse also found), Weber was an ancestor of modern German authoritarianism, even Nazism.

The ensuing debate with the scholarly public present, if restrained on the surface, anticipated the conflicts which were to divide Germany shortly—a conflict of generations on the German legacy.

I spent some time with Marcuse in those days in Heidelberg. He was openly moved by this return trip to Germany, wondered whether he had made a mistake in not returning after the war. When he began his talk, he cited the inscription on the entrance to the university building housing the conference. It was dedicated to "der lebendigend Geist" ("the living spirit') and read "es gibt Wörter, die sich nicht übersetzen lassen" ("There are words which are untranslatable").

I took the Congress, and the fact that I was not invited to do more at it than participate in a discussion of the sociology of religion, as another occasion for self-rebuke. I considered that I had had chances and time, and should have done work of a more substantial kind. I was right, but my response was not useful: It was produced by the depression I could not directly confront, and which was to deepen in the next years, despite the interesting, indeed fascinating, setting I soon moved into.

10

The Long Farewell to Europe

BACK in Oxford, routine was pleasant enough. I went to the College, saw colleagues and students. I set about expanding the essay on ideology from the UNESCO series into what years later would become the short book *The Crisis of Industrial Society*. At the time, however, I was dissatisfied with what I had written, and did not continue. Converting my thesis into a book was postponed—if not daily, weekly. I wrote some interesting shorter articles, made my debut in *Der Spiegel* with an essay on Germany originally published in *Commentary*. A longish article on the United Kingdom and its culture and politics published in an American anthology had a good response among British friends. For all of my connections with others and ostensible political passions, I had ceased to develop, intellectually.

I was a prisoner of the categories of a critical sociology, taking literally if implicitly its denial to modern society of the capacity to experiment. Certainly there was little experiment in my own life.

My intellectual immobility was discerned, much to my irritation, by a student at the Free University in Berlin when I gave a talk there in 1963. He declared, with commendable forthrightness, that all I could offer to meet the current social crisis was a faithful summary of neo-Marxism—with a disembodied critical intelligence as a poor substitute for any revolutionary agency. The student referred to the forthcoming text *One-Dimensional Man*, by Herbert Marcuse. I am reminded of David Riesman's observation that in the post-war years, the Europeans proclaimed existential despair with considerable exuberance, whereas Americans treated optimistic progressivism as a heavy burden. Marcuse did not think his responsibility ended with a description of one-dimensionality but saw the description as the beginning of a struggle to end it. I was to see much of him in Germany over the next years. His native country (and especially his native Berlin) seemed to stimulate him to mix inspiration with analysis. I originally wrote that perhaps he was re-enacting his youth. He spent part of his youth in the army of the Kaiser in the First World War and then was an assistant to Heidegger before attaching himself to the Frankfurt Institute for Social Research and its desperate encounter with modern history.

Meanwhile, history made itself felt in a very pressing way: in the fall, the Cuban missile crisis was upon us. My memory is of a pervasive atmosphere of dread—and of a sense of acute passivity, a recognition that decisions affecting life and death in or of the United Kingdom were being made in the US and the USSR. The inhabitants of the United Kingdom were not being asked for advice, and Harold Macmillan apparently grasped that he was not being asked either. Kennedy sent Dean Acheson to tell the Europeans about the blockade of Cuba, and Macmillan was driven up to an American airfield north of London to meet him. Acheson went on to Paris, where he was told that President de Gaulle would receive him not that morning but at his customary hour, five in the afternoon. (Acheson passed the time by flying to Bonn to visit Adenauer.) French legend has it that when Acheson began to talk, de Gaulle interrupted him: "Are you asking me or telling me?" There is no record of Macmillan allowing himself that much irony. I recall the extraordinary crack in the voice of the otherwise imperturbable BBC news announcer when describing the Soviet freighters' advance toward the US Navy blockade line. Afterward, there was relatively little triumphalism in British commentary; rather, a large collective sigh of relief. It was only later that reports of Kennedy's resistance to the pressures of his generals were published—increasing the very large esteem in which he was held in the United Kingdom.

The missile crisis had a special incidence in Germany, There, the weekly *Der Spiegel* was jeeringly disrespectful of Germany's culturally and politically conservative elites, whose personal and political collaboration with Nazism it delighted to anathematize. The journal also had reliable informants in business, culture, government, and politics. It made life very uncomfortable for many. Shortly before the missile crisis, it published a Defense Ministry report on the German armed forces which suggested that the new German army might not in case of conflict make good the failure of its fathers: the Soviet army could stop it. One of the weekly's antagonists was the defense minister, the Bavarian Franz Josef Strauss, a man of boundless ambition and vanity, and no small talent. He was also not immune to the temptation of monetary rewards, and his position certainly gave him ample opportunity to profit from the West's struggle against (Godless) materialism. He thought of *Der Spiegel*, which enthusiastically recorded the less sublime aspects of his career, as an obstacle on his way to the Chancellorship and seized on its publication of the report, in the midst of the crisis, to retaliate. He persuaded Adenauer to agree to seizing the magazine's editorial premises and files, arresting its senior editors, and charging it with treason. The city official in charge of the police in Hamburg, Helmut Schmidt, at first demurred, and Adenauer threatened to send the armed forces to the city. In an entirely appropriate touch, the arresting officers were all Gestapo veterans. In the end, the charges were dropped and Adenauer sacrificed Strauss lest he himself have to resign.

What made the episode distinctive was the public reaction. The more liberal elements in German society did not content themselves with indignant articles in their newspapers or the hostile inquiries of the oppositional Social Democrats in Parliament. An entire student generation, in universities and the gymnasia alike, came alive and took to the streets—often with their teachers, and with large contingents of trade unionists joining them. Someone in Germany wrote of the emergence of a *Gegen-Öffentlichkeit*, a counter-public—but it was more accurate to describe it as a public. The (rare) older survivors of opposition to Nazism were conspicuous in the movement, but it was dominated by younger persons—many of them (like the arrested *Spiegel* editors) war veterans, some younger still. One element in the situation especially enraged the protesters. Strauss had arranged for the arrest of one of the accused editors, on vacation in Spain, by Franco's police. There had been Easter marchers in Germany to protest nuclear weapons, and before that a substantial movement in the mid-fifties to protest re-armament.

These groups were reanimated and joined to a much larger public in opposing what was, clearly, a reversion to the crudest sort of authoritarianism.

The colleagues and students organizing protests at the Free University of Berlin asked me to identify cultural and political figures in the United Kingdom who could send messages of solidarity. I was glad to do so, obtained some notable names, and reinforced in the process my own alliance with persons and groups in Germany who were not so long thereafter to transform life in the Federal Republic. The transformation was long prepared, as I had seen on the universities and in the study centers of the Protestant Church. German conflicts were much intensified by their historical dimensions—sometimes stated, sometimes not. Everyone seemed to be confronting, at once, a contemporary political situation, their parents and indeed their grandparents. They lived in the Federal Republic, but acted as if the Third Reich, the Weimar Republic, Imperial Germany, if not still extant, had expired only yesterday.

John Kennedy was murdered, in circumstances still obscure, a year later. The evening of his death and the days following remain unforgettable. I was giving a seminar at Nuffield College (on the structure of industrial society) at the customary Oxford time—5 to 7 p.m. When we came out (it was 1 p.m. in Dallas) we learned of the shooting. Some forty minutes later, we had gone into dinner, the college butler whispered in the warden's ear. He stood up, visibly paling, and informed us that the president was dead. No one spoke for what must have been ten minutes, then a low murmur of anguish rose in the hall. There were the usual ten or so American students and some senior academic visitors at the college for the year, a couple of occasional visitors, and of course the rest—African, Asian, from the Commonwealth and Europe, and British. Distress knew no national boundaries.

I hurried home through what seemed to be a deserted city. Nina was numbed. Anna, five, was still awake. "Pappi, something terrible: Mr. Kennedy has been killed."

I can still hear the BBC announcer, opening the nine o'clock news, "The BBC announces, with very great regret, the death of John Fitzgerald Kennedy, thirty-fifth president of the United States." There followed the prime minister, Lord Home, and a moving personal recollection from Harold Macmillan, an older man who sounded much older that night. We were too shocked to think of the future, and discussion of the assassination itself waited for some days.

John Kennedy had been in the United Kingdom with his family when his father was ambassador, was a frequent visitor as a senator, and was viewed by many as incarnating the ideal aspects of American existence: our openness, vitality, newness. 1963 was only nineteen years after several million Americans had crowded into Great Britain preparing to land in Europe, and thousands had come back to return to the US with British brides.

The President's elder brother had died in a flight from the UK. Kennedy, and the Kennedys, were adopted by the British. During the 1960 election. Isaiah Berlin was generous with gossip from his wartime friends in Georgetown. He was so voluble about the contest that I reminded him that we were only electing a President, not a Warden of All Souls. From Oxford High Table to the popular dailies, the Kennedys became family. The day after the murder, I boarded my usual bus on the Woodstock Road.

It was a very British bus. Conductor and passengers had traveled together for years. Occasionally, if someone was in an expansive mood, he would remark that it was a bright day and likely to remain so—or that an Oxfordshire drizzle would continue. Mostly, we nodded good morning to one another and left it at that. That morning the conductor paused after taking my fare. "Excuse me, sir, but aren't you the American gentleman at Nuffield?" I had done some British television and I supposed that her had heard and seen me. "May I, and also on behalf of my wife, extend my most sincere condolences?" He extended his hand. A few of the other regulars stood up, shook my hand, and wordlessly returned to their seats. I remain very, very grateful to them.

The British nation did not leave its television sets for the next days—from the murder of Oswald to the funeral. My French friend Edgar Morin later summed it up in an article: *Une Télé-Tragédie Planétaire: L'Assassinat du Président Kennedy.* Lyndon Johnson's Texan origins and manners were, at first, cause for dismay among my British colleagues and friends. Few knew enough to recall his New Deal credentials. I overlooked them myself, or rather thought of these as long since abandoned, portrayed him as an extraordinarily skilled ordinary politician. The reality was much more complex, and he may indeed have been recalled to his better self by the civil rights movement. All of that, early in 1963, lay before us.

There was a certain amount of discussion, public and private, in the United Kingdom as to who or what had killed Kennedy. When the Warren Commission presented its report in 1964, concluding that Oswald had acted alone, it met as much skepticism in Great Britain as it did in the United States. I found the view of Oswald as a solitary actor difficult to accept, but never did any of my own research on the matter—or even very wide reading. My skepticism was fortified by two later encounters: a college classmate, Norman Redlich, as one step in a very full career (he was also counsel to the City of New York with Mayor Lindsay and dean of New York University's Law School), was deputy counsel to the Warren Commission. Whenever, after my return to the US in 1966, I met Norman, he was at pains to assure me that I was wrong to be skeptical of the Commission. Perhaps—but since I had never put my doubts to paper, or uttered these to him, he was engaging in a pre-emptive strike, and perhaps protesting too much. More importantly, when I came to know the Galbraith family, I gathered from them that the Kennedy family (and especially his widow, who was very close to the senior Galbraith) had severe doubts. I believe that it would be impossible to find a public record of the Kennedys endorsing the Commission's work: they preferred silence. I would have liked to learn what de Gaulle thought (and knew) of the matter: it was certainly not the European Left alone which thought that there had been a conspiracy to remove the President.

The development of the civil rights movement and the emergence of American feminism, combined with the protest of the Vietnam War and American civil unrest, all took Europe by surprise. Those who knew American history, with our social movements and theological passions, were few—and even the most sophisticated had been convinced by the American votaries of consensus. The European welfare-state advocates, such as Anthony Crosland and many on the Continent (including Willy Brandt), were convinced that the US had struck a reasonable balance between state intervention and market freedom. The Johnson Great Society program of 1964 onward struck them as a return to the traditions of the New Deal. Those discontented with their own European versions of social democracy were quite receptive to those on the American Left who were so critical of what was then termed "corporate liberalism" in the US. One obstacle to a clear view of the American situation was posed by much of the American New Left itself. Our own analysis (at the time, I followed C. Wright Mills) taken literally would have precluded our own emergence.

I followed these developments from Oxford with a mixture of astonishment and enthusiasm, alternating with several varieties of self-reproach. Having been a consistent critic of the warfare-welfare state, should I not hurry back across the Atlantic to participate actively in its undoing? I did have a considerable role and plenty of recognition as a transatlantic cultural and political commuter, but in those years, little or nothing could compensate me for my lack of greater literary and scholarly achievement. Looked at in another way, the 1962 trip had brought me closer to a reconciliation with Kennedy's America. With Kennedy gone, Johnson was leading a country I had great difficulty in joining—even in imagination. The new prominence of ideas I had held for my entire adult life increased my sense of alienation. I could not decide on what side of the Atlantic I belonged, and in what capacity. The temporary respite afforded by my Oxford position made avoiding the problem easier, and I avoided confronting the avoidance by any number of substitute activities. I wrote and spoke; connected with colleagues, political comrades, allies, in Europe and the US; traveled quite a lot to the Continent, and had lots of visitors in Oxford itself. Much, indeed most, of what I did and experienced was interesting and intrinsically valuable, and has provided ample lessons and memories in the intervening five decades. The trouble was that at the time I lacked the inner resources to master the situation, and consigned myself to drift.

Rather than turn inward again to confront my problems (above all, my problems of self-regard) I again sought a change of environment. I arranged, not without difficulty, for a visiting appointment in sociology at the University of Strasbourg. We had been in Strasbourg, before, for six months. It provided, with its ample library and faculties of theology, as well as its archives, ample resources on the Reformation. The city itself, as a Free Imperial City, had been a very important center of Protestant activity. It was more open than many states and cities which had shifted allegiances, allowing a variety of Protestant churches and doctrines to compete. The Catholic Church and the Bishop were not suppressed but suffered a worse fate—challenged to maintain themselves in a largely Protestant setting.

Something else had drawn me to Strasbourg since I first visited it in 1953 en route to Burgundy. I knew of Marc Bloch, later learned a good deal about the *Annales* School, founded at the university in 1929. The complex, even tortured, history of the city of German-speaking Alsatians incorporated in France in 1648, struck me as evidence for the depths of Europe. I knew that the city and region had had a Jewish population, and in my imaginary search for an alternate identity, wondered what my life would have been like had I been born there instead of in New York. One obvious answer was one I did not dwell upon: in all probability, I would have shared the fate of French Jewry, been abandoned by the French government to the Germans, deported and murdered. I had by the time we went to Strasbourg in 1964 any number of French friends who were Jewish, but in fact my single closest friend in Strasbourg was the dean of the Faculty of Protestant Theology, Roger Mehl.

There was an old European adage, now seen as a quaint reminder of a distant past: every civilized man has two countries, his own and France. If anything has replaced it, it is the fascination of much of the world (including Europe) with the culture of the United States. I grew up in a world in which the culture of metropolitan France still counted for much. Why else would Fitzgerald and Hemingway and Miller have gone to Paris?

The old American ambivalence to France was expressed by Henry James. France was the country of rigid tradition, incorporated in church and family. It was also, however, the land of sensual delights which appealed immensely to the guilty imaginations of English-speaking Protestants.

France and French intellectual tradition figured little in my early education, and what I collected was a *mélange* of impressions. I read Zola and a bit about the Dreyfus case, without being able to situate it in the history of modern France, of which I knew almost nothing.

That the French Revolution was a very large event was clear, but what had caused it and what followed were matters of perplexity. I read Stendhal, took Rousseau out of context, was enthused by Malraux. I read Malraux as witness for the entire European Left, not as a figure embedded in France. Mostly, I think, France was the country of its own films. (When I first visited Paris in 1952, I took the Metro to Porte de Lilas to see whether it was like the film named after it.) These depicted segments of France (the countryside, the urban milieu) in no way I could put together. Lots of French artists and writers were in New York after the fall of France, and some very important thinkers (Gurvitch, Lévi-Strauss and Weil among these) came to the US as well. Eugene and Maria Jolas worked at the Office of War Information but I had only a vague idea of their journal and their participation in Parisian literary modernism, thought of them as indeed striking figures from a distant world. I occasionally went to exhibitions of French art at the Museum of Modern Art, understood what I experienced as part of modernism. Sartre came in 1945 and delivered a talk on the French theater, which I attended in the conviction that he was a significant figure, but I could not insert him in a coherent narrative. *Partisan Review* and Dwight Macdonald's *Politics* published Camus and Merleau-Ponty. Their work struck me as important, but I could not say why.

Harvard, with its obsessive cult of modernization, did not help. I recall a project by historians and social scientists who knew France: they concluded that France was not and could not become modern. They did so just as France had begun what the French later termed *Les Trente Glorieuses,* the thirty years of continuous and rapid postwar economic and social transformation. Harvard's debates on history sometimes involved the English Revolution; the French case stood alone and largely ignored. There was something approaching a cult of de Tocqueville, and the very unanimity with which his account of the United States was praised sufficed to move me to ignore it. There were occasional French visitors in sociology and university teachers and graduate students in the other disciplines working on France, but much of what happening there simply was outside my field of vision.

I did some reading in graduate school on the French Revolution. The historian Crane Brinton was the Harvard expert on it, but

I did not study with him, and I did not get beyond a rather simple understanding of the narrative. The transformation of revolutionary fervor into fanaticism, the fate of Catholicism, resistance to the Jacobins, and the transition from revolutionary France to Napoleon's imperial nation all remained historical puzzles I could not solve—even when I read the standard French authors, such as Aulard, Mathiez, Lefebvre. A serious debate on the Revolution was taking place in Paris, and I had hints of that from my reading, but could not profit from it. I also did some reading on Calvinism and early French Protestantism. I had a bit of knowledge of the sixteenth century in France, but the fate of Protestantism thereafter, its stubborn presence in French culture, was something I learned much later, in France. What was completely beyond my ken was the most obvious element in French history—its version of Catholicism. I interpreted French history and politics in absurdly reductionist terms, with Dreyfusards and anti-Dreyfusards identified with the resistance and the Vichyites—again, about which the available narratives were entirely one-dimensional.

Occasionally, I read novels—and Sartre's series *Les Chemins de la Liberté* conveyed something of the atmosphere of pre-war France, rather like old films. I read Sartre's political writings, bought and struggled with *L'Être et le Néant*, but had no idea of his dependence on Heidegger, or of Merleau-Ponty's on Husserl. Few in American philosophy and certainly no one at Harvard at the time bothered to read these texts, although Morton White did so a bit later.

I did read, from my graduate school days onward, some of the French sociologists. That enabled me to understand France as its own unique instance of a class society. In that respect, I dealt with France as I did with the US or the UK or even, at first, with Germany—as a concrete instance of a general idea. I did not begin to realize how shallow my ideas were until having been thoroughly challenged by living two successive years in Germany and then in Great Britain. It was, in fact, a British friend who made it possible for me to achieve serious knowledge of France. My London School of Economics colleague Tom Bottomore had lots of French friends, and he had introduced me to the Dominican Henri Desroche, who retained a very large interest in religion, and close contacts with contemporaries and teachers in the Church. Through Desroche, I met some of the worker priests, and an entire group of scholars (most former priests) who had transmuted their theological criticism of the Church by studying it as sociologists. I also met Dominicans in considerable difficulty with the Vatican, such as Fathers Marie-Dominique Chenu and Jean-Yves Congar—who emerged under Pope John XXIII as theological inspirers of Vatican II. Best of all, I came to an understanding of the complexity of Catholicism which replaced the schematic notions of it I had acquired in the United States—and with that, acquired a different view of France.

When Nina and I visited Paris from London in 1953 and 1954, we sometimes stopped at the corner of Boulevard Saint-Michel and Rue Soufflot to look at the windows of the Centre Richelieu, the Catholic student center. We were struck by the variety of offerings of talks and study groups, by an obvious opening to much of France's secular culture.

It was a French Catholicism which was certainly not a morose, angry defense of traditionalism—not fighting old battles. The new ones had to do with achieving citizenship and solidarity for the French working class, with a positive view of modernity. Evangelization was a major current in it, perhaps conversion would be a more accurate term. One key text was a book written by the Abbe Godin during the war, *La France, Pays de Mission?* The vanguard thinkers of the Church were aware that France was no longer entirely or even majority Catholic. They could, like the Protestants, now make the best of their marginality.

The forces of lay France, meanwhile, were by no means united. Marxists and former Marxists, liberals and technocrats, Communists and ex-Communists, argued strenuously about the future of France. De Gaulle had retreated to Lorraine, but a current of nationalism (some of it enlightened, some of it less so) spoke in his name. The Third World was much in view and the Algerian insurrection was about to break out. A European party held that France had to reconcile with Germany and (a project which met at least as much resistance) accept Great Britain as a full partner. The United States as transatlantic colossus loomed large, to strident arguments about our culture and power.

What the Catholics contributed to all of this, despite their own divisions (accompanied for many by a large distrust of Rome and considerable lack of enthusiasm for the person and views of Pope Pius XII) was, first, their sense of the continuity of French history. They had seen regimes come and go; agrarian France was even then being replaced by the advanced industrial nation we are accustomed to; Sartre (after an interval) had followed Voltaire. History, for the French Catholics, was shared—and interpretations of it, or lessons from it, had to be shared, too. More importantly, they also contributed their ideas of the primacy of solidarity, of the value of the human person. That kept the more naked forms of economic thinking from dominating French Catholic consciousness.

The differentiated France we see today has gone beyond the antithesis of la France *Catholique* and *croyante* and *la République indivisible*, the opposition of two churches. The belief that society is more important than the market persists.

Catholic intellectuality was, equally, new to me. I was inwardly surprised to learn that the tradition of Talmudism I had inherited (with no personal immersion in the Talmud) wasn't the only royal road to the heights of thought—a background in patristics did as well. The Catholics I met were at home in much of human thought and had an ecumenical attitude to the varieties of human culture. Sure of their own national and religious legacies, they were totally unthreatened by matters different or new.

The situation of some of the secular intellectuals I met at the same time was very different. I became friendly with Edgar Morin, who was Sephardic Jewish, at the beginning of a career which made him a figure of reference for two generations. He studied mass culture and film and inquired into the sub-stratum of modern culture: his book on *La Rumeur d'Orléans* is a study of contemporary anti-Semitism, and his depiction of the response to the murder of President Kennedy an early study of cultural globalization.

Above all, Edgar's sardonic critique of the rigidities of the French Communist Party (to which he had once belonged) was a triumph of moral intelligence. He was at the center of a group which had the same itinerary—like Robert Antelme, who had been deported as a resistant, and Denys Mascolo. I met the young Claude Lefort in this company, and learned that in addition to *Les Temps Modernes*, there was *Socialisme ou Barbarie*—which dared to imagine democratic and pluralistic forms of revolution.

Well before I went to Strasbourg in 1964, my friends from these two circles helped me to a privileged view of French culture. The Catholics taught me that, in France at least, many remained Catholic in spirit even if rejecting the substance of Catholic teaching. Having written that, I am unsure of it. They remained attached to the idea of a church, seeking it in the future since the actual church proved disappointing. They interpreted much of human history (and not only the history of religious groups, which they studied so intensely) as attempts to ground true churches—true in the sense of responding to basic human needs for solidarity and support. That is, no doubt, what accounted for my admiration and wonder (mixed with no small amount of envy) of the group: I never had so enduring an attachment. That they expected all these efforts to fall short increased my respect for them: it was evidence for a rare absence of illusion, even a good deal of spiritual heroism.

The former Communists had a distinctly similar historical progression in mind. They had served the inauthentic revolution, the untrue church—but still believed in a major social transformation. Their problem was: who would effect it, and how could it retain and deepen the democratic traditions of France? Both groups lived with hope (it was not quite expectation). There was an eschatological aura about them, an undercurrent of anticipatory excitement. I made their acquaintance in 1954 and 1955, before Raymond Aron published his mocking tract *L'Opium des Intellectuels*, in which he turned Marx's view of religion as illusory consolation against them.

I am now quite unsure that Aron, for all of his sober brilliance and vast knowledge, fortified by the closest of examinations of French and world politics, was right. In his devotion to studying ordinary and workaday politics, he was himself devoid of neither hope nor moral commitment. He had experienced at first hand the transition to Nazism in Germany—and returned from his studies to write an excellent book on German sociology and another on German philosophies of history. He made his way to London during the war to work with de Gaulle, toward whom he maintained a somewhat skeptical distance. De Gaulle apparently reciprocated, as I recall hearing Aron with some pleasure quote de Gaulle on their relationship: *Je ne peut pas lui saisir* ("I really can't grasp him"). Aron wrote several times a week for *Le Figaro* and had a very large influence, of course, in the English-speaking world and elsewhere in Western Europe.

It would be erroneous to describe him as a conservative. He did have a large measure of realistic skepticism of human motives, thought that parliamentary democracy with a considerable welfarist component was the most appealing as well as plausible of political forms, and certainly sympathized in the United States with Humphrey, Kennedy, and Stevenson, and in the United Kingdom with Attlee and Gaitskell. Yet he served as a *bête noire* of the French Left. His support for NATO and a rather sympathetic attitude to the American interpretation of the Cold War accounted for some of the antagonism to him, but his generalized skepticism, his amusicality regarding revolutionary themes may account for more of it. He did point out (in his book on classes in France, *Dix-Huit Leçons Sur La Société Industrielle*) that the transition to an industrial from an agrarian society in France, a rising standard of living, was itself a major change.

Indeed, an ascending generation of French sociologists set out to map it. They included Pierre Bourdieu, Serge Mallet, and Alain Touraine. Their work combined exacting description with historical generalization. It served the technocratic reformers in politics around Pierre Mendès France (who represented an entire segment of the French elite, installed in the ministries whatever the political colors of the governments which rather rapidly replaced one another) as a Michelin to the new France. Their work owed much to a figure in the older generation, Georges Friedmann, who was a serious student of industrial sociology—and who, politely received and as politely ignored, had visited with the Harvard sociologists when I was in Cambridge.

The large figures of French intellectual life (Aron, de Beauvoir, Sartre, Lévi-Strauss, Malraux, Merleau-Ponty, Ricœur) were so important to contemporaries abroad because they evoked universal themes. Even those working on French history, such as Furet, insisted on its larger significance. It was a culture in which learned monks (Calvez, Desroche, Lubac) wrote about Marx and a Jewish immigrant (Goldmann) about Pascal. Contrasted with what I depicted at the time, perhaps with too little nuance, as the triumphalism of American thought, they struck me as authentic seekers after the truth of our common history. The contrast with Great Britain (even with the British Marxists) could not have been greater. Confronted with my last sentence, most British colleagues would have immediately voiced distress at the vagueness of terms such as "common history" and "truth." The prominent philosopher Austin made it a point to warn against *l'ivresse de grande profondeur* (the intoxication of the pretension to great depth). He and his Oxford colleagues need not have worried: they were in no danger of intoxication.

I had the good fortune to work at Strasbourg alongside one of the most imposing thinkers of the generation which preceded Sartre's: Henri Lefebvre. From the southwest near Pau, the son of a local civil servant, he was active in the twenties when Sartre and the rest were still students. Attracted to surrealism, he later joined the Communist Party, which regarded him as an intellectual adornment and allowed him rather more philosophical liberty than usual: it had little choice. Henri was in the Resistance and after the war joined the exodus from a Communist Party which remained Stalinist until well after Stalin's death. In the meantime, he wrote (tellingly) on a great range of themes: the social life of his native region, the modern city, and contemporary culture and its political implications. His writing was inseparable from his person: it bore his *joie de vivre* as well as his amused and often sardonic, but sympathetic, view of the human situation.

Somehow, we became friends. He insisted, always, that I write more—and when I eventually overcame a long fallowness, well after I left Strasbourg, he was genuinely pleased. Henri saw no need to spare his colleagues and friends the cutting edge of his judgements. These were often right, and in any case, accompanied by a full measure of warmth. It was as if he had saved, for the colder climate of northern and eastern France, a good deal of the color and sun of Navarre. I think that he learned something from me of a more positive side of the United States: he was not surprised when I declared that for all of the rigidities of our Protestantism, we did have John Dewey. Henri was old enough to have appreciated Roosevelt, and visited New York in the thirties. He knew Italy quite well, and lots about German thought. One of his close friends, with whom he had written, was the Polish Jewish exile in France, Norbert Guterman. Together, they produced in the thirties the earliest French writings on the idea of alienation in Marx.

At Strasbourg, Henri lived with his younger companion, Nicole Beaurain. Nicole came from a working-class family, her father was a Communist trade unionist at Citroën. He and a friend had once driven to the USSR and when they crossed the border en route to Moscow could convince no one that they were Communists: their Citroën proved the opposite. Nicole was the first in her family to attend university, and the family was exceedingly distressed at her liaison with an elder teacher. Her father had some notion that Henri had had some connection to the party and when he enquired (after Henri's departure) was informed that Henri was a British agent. Eventually, the family were reconciled: the birth of Armel in the fall of 1964, just when we came to know them, helped. Nicole and Nina and Anna and Antonia became good friends. By a stroke of good fortune, they lived just around the corner from us, and the girls could visit by themselves.

We placed Antonia in a French kindergarten and arranged for Anna to go to school across the river in Kehl, the German border town. Some six weeks after, Antonia went around the corner one afternoon to visit with Nicole and the baby. Nicole came back with her and asked whether we knew: Antonia had acquired enough French to talk with her. There was also a very welcoming Alsatian family around the corner, the Ungerers, with an attractive mixture of children.

Life in Strasbourg was very agreeable. The faculty had its divisions, but there was general agreement that the visitor from Oxford had shown much discernment, intelligence and wit in choosing Strasbourg rather than obtaining a post in Paris.

(I always met colleagues when I took the morning express train to Paris and recall Roger Mehl declaring that the outer suburbs of Alsace were not, after all, that distant.) We were often invited to dine and had our own set of visitors, from Great Britain, the United States, and Germany.

In Germany in 1952, I discovered that the universities were not all that remote from their Wilhelmenian progenitors. In France in 1964, the Third Republican model of the university was dominant. The system was national but in Strasbourg, especially, local roots were cultivated. I occasionally breakfasted with deans of the several faculties on the express to Paris and they were invariably underway to extract money from the minister or the director of higher education at the ministry. Often, the matter concerned the fact that too much (or anything at all) had been given to Nancy and not enough to Strasbourg. One argument was that Nancy was a provincial university—not, to be sure, without its limited merits, but not to be compared with the great European center of learning that was Strasbourg. Another, even more effective: the minister had only to look across the Rhine at the well-financed and well equipped German universities. If he preferred that *la jeunesse Alsacienne* cross the river to pursue its studies, he had only to continue his (inexplicable) policy of restricting money for Strasbourg. Returning on the evening train, it was usually possible to enjoy a celebratory glass with a triumphant dean: he had the check in his wallet.

De Gaulle is said to have declared that of all the *Corps d'État* he found the university teachers and the scientific researchers the most difficult to deal with. He took revenge, with not much subtlety. The political philosophical tendency of his antagonists was generally some form of radicalism, occasionally in its socialist variant, sometimes joined to left Catholic social doctrine. There were plenty of Gaullists in the universities and the research institutes, convinced that the President used the traditional language of national pride to achieve a project of modernization. De Gaulle confounded friend and enemy alike by ensuring the appointment to senior university posts of any number of Communists, on the grounds that they too were part of the nation. Certainly, the Communist Party was not conspicuous in the protest movement against the Algerian war, possibly because the French working class was quite unenthusiastic about the Algerian presence in France. Meanwhile, I can testify that the presidency's intelligence services functioned to perfection. One day I spoke at a discussion of Cuba and praised French policy (de Gaulle had to be severely advised by his staff not to visit Castro) as à *la hauteur des événements et à l'honneur de la France* (responding to the demands of history). By mid-morning, I had a call from the professor dealing with higher education at the Élysée Palace in Paris, suggesting that I drop by for lunch one day.

Looking back now, I understand de Gaulle's impatience with

the professors. In the humanities and some of the social sciences (the natural sciences and technology generated different attitudes): they clung to an artisanal model of production. They were right to do so—but since the society paid for only a certain number of artisans, competition for places was intense and a guild-like closure of the system resulted.

Meanwhile, the universities were full and over-full, short of the most elementary resources, their skeletal administrative services overwhelmed. The professoriate confounded its considerable privileges with the future of culture. Most of the citizenry sought expanded life chances and increased income, and the most influential part of the elite was devoted to developing an institutional framework for a measuredly democratic society of consumption. The academics' insistence on things unseen was certainly right. The difficulty was, they thought not only that their vision was legitimate, but that alternate views were perverse. They thought of themselves as Jacobins, but the state they wished to serve had long since become Bonapartiste. The revolution, briefly, was behind them.

No doubt, their capacity for ideological obstructionism was great—and strengthened by their total sincerity, their identification of themselves with French democracy entire. I recall the day we arrived in Strasbourg. The teacher and student organizations were striking, to protest budgetary insufficiencies. There were a couple of desultory pickets in front of the old Wilhelmenian building housing the faculties of letters and the two theological faculties, and the building was dark. I started to make my way upstairs, to see whether the dean was there. A figure emerged from the gloom: Monsignor Nédoncelle, the dean of the faculty of Catholic theology. We chatted a bit and he asked me whether *messieurs les collègues* at Oxford also went on strike from time to time: not very often, I told him. He was very proud: his faculty's rate of participation in the strike was one hundred percent.

We parted and Roger Mehl, dean of the faculty of Protestant theology, appeared. He noted that I was talking to his eminent colleague and expressed skepticism about the Catholic theologians' militancy. I observed that they were, according to their dean, all on strike. Perhaps, Roger said, but they belong to the Christian teachers' union and we to the real one—of the Left.

I went on upstairs and found the dean of the faculty of letters and social sciences alone in his office. He declared that we would go out for a drink to mark my arrival. These must be difficult days for you, I observed, since I had read in *Le Monde* that the minister of education had instructed the deans to provide lists of teachers joining the strike, so that appropriate deductions could be made from their salaries. Maybe the minister has asked that, said the dean, but since the concierge is striking no mail has come to me. If this request does come, he noted, of course I will circularize the professors and all the other academic ranks, ask anyone who was striking to inform me, so that I can give their names to the minister. In the event (purely hypothetical) that no one responds, he concluded, of course I will tell the minister that I have no names to give him. A year or so later, at a discussion in the Academic Senate of university reform, one of the professors, a senior figure with the Rosette of the Légion d'Honneur in his lapel, rose to declare: "I remind everyone that we are servants of the state. It follows, that it is our duty to resist the minister to the utmost of our ability."

De Gaulle was wise to conclude that to fight with the professors would constitute an unnecessary rear-guard action. A considerable number of them supposed that they incarnated France's traditions of democracy, even if de Gaulle and his party kept winning elections. (It was a sensation when in the 1965 presidential campaign, François Mitterrand forced de Gaulle into a run-off.) De Gaulle had succeeded in dividing the live forces of the nation, drawing much of the technocratic elite to his side. The passing agitation at the University of Strasbourg left most of the students greatly unmoved. Strasbourg had a splendid faculty, and some research units of international standing. The best students in France were not, however, at the universities but at the Grandes Écoles. The Strasbourg students were predominantly from the region, anxious about careers or confident that their families would be of help, and in no case ready or willing to take to the streets for any cause whatsoever. On Thursdays (when schools were out in France) large numbers of ecclesiastics appeared. Church schools could obtain subsidies if they had qualified teachers, and these were ordered to the universities to obtain their degrees. Nothing, absolutely nothing, in the university or the city could have been interpreted as anticipating the turbulence of 1968.

Sociology attracted a very mixed set of students. It was grouped with philosophy, psychology, social anthropology in those days in what was termed the section of philosophy. Students preparing to teach philosophy at Lycée took some sociology; we had a large number of students who intended to enter the field of "communication," as they put it, and some from disciplines such as history or political science (but not very many, despite the fact that Strasbourg was the home of *Annales*). We also had a small group of students, mainly European, who were in some measure eccentric or engaged. The eccentric ones were disturbed because no one noticed their professions of anti-bourgeois faith; the engaged ones were saddened by the absence of large causes, or any cause at all.

Lefebvre of course attracted some exceptional students—a couple from the Maghreb, who came to Strasbourg specifically to study with him.

Some of *les enragés* (angry young French) did so as well, and these were especially drawn by his views of the city as a potential utopia, a place for a permanent festival. Some joined the movement termed *Situationniste*, which proclaimed its affinity with surrealism and dada, and depicted much of modern culture as an oppressive fraud—which, in turn, obliged those able to see through it to employ any and all means to replace it. What would follow? The revolution in spontaneity was program enough. These views were set down by the French writer Guy Debord, who, on a visit to our department, proposed that we make the dinner that usually follows a visitor's lecture the main and sole event.

Lefebvre objected that that would exclude quite a few persons who could not be accommodated at the restaurant from the benefits of listening to him, since he did not propose that evening to seize the restaurant. The senior Strasbourg philosopher Georges Gusdorf suggested that Debord was running from an argument. One promptly ensued, and Debord later pronounced himself entirely satisfied with the very minor disruption he had caused: more ample consequences, unspecified, would follow. We finally proceeded to dinner.

The *Situationniste* students were in fact attentive, friendly and supportive, and took what we said in our courses very seriously—in short, model students. Some of them in the fall of 1967 would be elected to run the student government, and provoked the university administration to obtain a judicial order stripping them of office. As I understand it, they sought to abolish the counselling services at the student health program as *psychiatrie policière* (police psychiatry). Additionally, they sought contact (at considerable cost in telephone bills) with the most radical elements of the Japanese student movement.

They did make a contribution to national and international discussion by publishing a brilliant and witty pamphlet, *De la Misère en Milieu Étudiant*, in part a complaint about economic and sexual deprivation, in part a demand for more attention from their teachers, in part a derisive rejection of our pedagogy as fraudulent—inauthentic preparation for an incomprehensible world.

They moved, shortly thereafter, to the suburban Parisian university at Nanterre (to which Lefebvre had moved in the fall of 1965) and in March 1968 launched the campaign which led to the revolt of May at the Sorbonne. When, in New York in 1967, I read solemn accounts in *The New York Times* of their success at Strasbourg (the entire attention of France was concentrated on their antics), I asked friends in Strasbourg whether the docility of most Strasbourg students had been succeeded by zeal not seen in the city since the 1790s. Not at all, was the response; the *Situationnistes* were a vanguard without anyone behind them—a judgment, in the event, rather too hasty.

My own teaching at Strasbourg consisted of a *cours magistral* (a lecture course, given once a week for two hours), seminars of my own, some work with the teachers of American studies, and participation in Lefebvre's seminars for advanced students.

The *cours magistral* was a serious matter, quite formal. I gave the first on modern social thought and followed it by one on modern industrial society. As I began the first lecture, I thought of my high school French teacher and his low opinion of my abilities and performance in his class. He would have been deeply shocked at the thought of one of his more mediocre pupils entrusted with a major French cultural responsibility. Somehow I managed, and my imperfect French became less imperfect as time went on.

That had been a theme when I first met the senior philosopher at Strasbourg, the learned and sardonic George Gusdorf. He had to approve of my appointment, and I called on him in his office down the street (Rue Goethe) from the old villa housing our department. He began, frankly enough, with the observation that my French was quite inelegant. All the more reason, I said, to hope that he would sympathize with my candidacy for a teaching post. Too old to obtain a scholarship from the Alliance Française, it would give me a chance to practice. Gusdorf then tried another tack: I suppose, he mused, that you are one of the great thinkers in *le monde Anglophone*. No, I said; I would prefer to be thought of as having a more modest status—rather like his in France. That did it: he came around from his desk, extended his hand, and welcomed me to Strasbourg.

Gusdorf came from an Alsatian family that moved to Bordeaux in 1871 rather than live under the Germans. His total devotion to the life of the mind had as a corollary a low evaluation of the rest of existence, as if it were intrinsically disappointing. Bald, short, dressed in conventional dullness, curt and precise of address, he looked like someone in a satiric film about French academic life. He seemed thoroughly secular, yet was motivated by a great passion—the belief that thought could seize existence and perhaps one day master it. If he had been asked about Freud's remark that religion was subject to disproof and that the scientific pursuit of truth was the only road to integrity, he would have disparaged Freud's certainty—but he was very close to that view himself. He did not admit a principled distinction between natural scientific and philosophical enquiry—all of existence was his laboratory. Rooted in his milieu (a professor Unrat who, unlike the character in *Der Blaue Engel*, would not dream of visiting a nightclub), he was quite adventurous in thought.

Fixed provincial rhythms marked life in Strasbourg, but some of the university's teachers were adventurers of the intellect. The others were certainly at a very high European level. Alsace's experience as a historical crossroads—an experience which, given four shifts from France to Germany and back (1871, 1918, 1940, 1944), which many of its inhabitants would have been glad to have been spared—imparted more than local interest to its peculiarities. The university was certainly at least as open to the world as Oxford—if only in its own way.

We had plenty of visitors. I recall George Lichtheim, on his way back to London from a visit to Habermas in Frankfurt, as more than usually open about his habitual melancholy. He had written a very positive—justly positive—review of some of Habermas's work in the *Times Literary Supplement*, and not neglected to regret the narrow and local limits of contemporary British social thought. That was not all he regretted, and perhaps not the main thing. He talked more openly than he had in England about his own fate. Had matters been different, he said, I too would have been a professor in Germany with an institute, junior colleagues, and students. George had also visited in Bonn, whose restricted politics he regarded with patronizing distaste. He did not think the neutralization of Germany was possible, but thought that the Bonn republic for all of its strengths (its younger people and newer intellectuals) exhibited a peculiar combination of whining self-pity and subservience to the "West." George knew, of course, of the CIA funding of the Congress for Cultural Freedom and had benefited from some of it himself. I did not challenge him about it, but he could have defended himself: no amount of money would make him alter his judgement of the amateurishness of American politics, particularly after the murder of Kennedy, whom he admired. George spent some time at Columbia University in 1965 writing a book on French Marxism—and was duly grateful for the books I sent him and general ideological reportage I provided. He was a critical but admiring observer of de Gaulle, in whom he found a European authenticity.

Other visitors included the Habermas family. I do not recall what deep themes we discussed. I do recall a walk through the monumental parts of the city, and Jürgen's response to it: "Beautiful, but I could never live here; it is too close to Germany." With much of his German generation, in fact, he preferred New York to Paris, and it was only relatively late in his life that he realized that he, Foucault, and Ricœur had more in common than divided them.

I made any number of trips. I recall one into the Soviet bloc to give talks in 1965. I began in Budapest, where Ágnes Heller, Ferenc Fehér, and Ivan Varga were my hosts. The revolt and the Soviet invasion were not quite a decade in the past, but were not directly talked about.

The leader installed by the Soviet Union, Janos Kadar, had pro-

With Jürgen Habermas.

claimed his version of openness ("those who are not against us are with us"). That entailed encouragement of the pursuit of private purposes, and Budapest in its shabby/genteel décor was strikingly different from East Berlin with its iconography and slogans. While the Opera Café in East Berlin was at the time stolid and grey, for example, the old Gerbaud Café on Vörösmarty Square in Budapest animated. The waiters were quite like those in Vienna; in their deliberate pace they seemed to be thinking of the departed glories of the Austro-Hungarian monarchy.

My friends in Budapest constituted a circle, allowed to write and think differently about philosophy and even a bit of meta-history, as long as they did not challenge the existence of the regime. They still sought an ideal Communism; the purged party wanted to increase the production of consumer goods. So Ágnes Heller wrote about ideal needs while the party, much undisturbed, set about satisfying the actual ones. In these trying circumstances, I was taken to call on the iconic figure of unorthodox orthodox Marxism, György Lukács.

He had been minister of culture in the short lived independent government of Imre Nagy in 1956, then taken to Romania, and was allowed to return to Hungary a year later, but was not for a long while published in Hungary. His long—very long—works were published instead in the Federal German Republic. It is striking that he was spared the fate of Nagy, who was executed (or murdered) by the restored pro-Soviet Hungarian regime in 1957: Lukács's extinction would have caused an uproar among western intellectuals. As to whether the decision to spare him was taken after consultation with the Soviet regime, it is difficult to reach a firm conclusion. Presumably, they feared the political consequences of eliminating him. By letting him continue to work, if in exceedingly abstract terms, they kept open the possibility (and, as importantly, the impression) of preparing an alternative dogma in case a major change were needed. More prosaically, however, they might have decided that his exceedingly dense prose would bring no one onto the streets.

I did not use the visit to ask him about his repudiation of his own masterpiece, *History and Class Consciousness*, attacked by the Soviet party when it appeared in 1923. I also left his course thereafter unchallenged, and did not even ask how he had managed to stay alive and out of jail during the purges of the thirties in Moscow. I'm now sorry I was so hesitant. He was insistent that I give him my view of Western Europe and the US. In the ensuing discussion, it was clear that he had much ground to make up: he was under the impression that *Partisan Review* was as committed to social revolution as it had been (and even then with plenty of reservations) in the thirties. He had some knowledge of the Frankfurt School, of Sartre, but entire areas of Western thought were either outside his ken or reduced to their own caricatures. He was very appreciative of the visit, and gave the impression of serenity rather than resignation: he was devoting his final energies, the world having been so disappointing, to describing the essence of a better one. I now see that I responded to the opportunity with too much reverence. There would have been no point in asking him why he did not emigrate to the West, or publish critical works of much more historical specificity, since official restrictions and censorship were evident—although I regret not asking him what unpublished writing was in his files.

A small group of younger persons had organized itself around him. One of them was András Hegedüs, unlike the others not Jewish, a recruit to the revived Communist Party after the arrival of the Soviet Army in 1945. By 1956 he was prime minister, and was sent by the Soviet embassy to Moscow along with the senior leaders of the party when the Nagy government was formed. I recollect his saying that in the airplane, Rákosi and the others declared the rising against them the work of "fascists." He said the moment marked the beginning of his own journey from Stalinism: if so many "fascists" remained in socialist Hungary, there was something wrong with their model of socialism. He studied social sciences at the Soviet Academy of Sciences and returned to Hungary as deputy director of the official office of social statistics. In fact, he became quite an acute sociologist, concentrating on questions of labor and (within limits) citizenship. His work exemplified the uses of empirical inquiry in a situation in which reigning dogma denied the obvious: domination and exploitation in state socialist relationships of production. The philosophers and theorists emigrated, eventually; Hegedüs remained to experience a considerable loosening of party controls and the beginnings of the transition to electoral democracy.

I went on to Warsaw. By contrast with the official tediousness of Budapest, Warsaw was in permanent ebullience. The party had to share influence and some power with the Catholic Church, and the uneasy co-existence of the mutually suspicious hierarchies produced a certain amount of free space in the assortment of journals, publishing houses, research institutes, and universities which marked Poland's intellectual life.

I was told, many times, the story of the day in 1956 when Gomulka was visited in prison by his party comrades. There was, they said, good news and bad news: the good news was that he was to be released; the bad news was that he was now general secretary of the party. Gomułka in his turn promptly released Cardinal Wyszyński from confined residence in a village, asked him to resume command of the Polish Church, and conferred with him about the economic and social crisis of the nation. The Warsaw intellectuals, Catholic, Communist and other, frequented the café of the Hotel Bristol in those days, where the coffee was good, Carpe Juive better, and foreign newspapers available. A Communist burst in on the group, asked if they had heard the news of the meeting, and provoked a response from a Catholic friend. "They have met? How terrible; now everything will be forbidden." I found that sardonic atmosphere, not at all concealed, nearly everywhere I went.

My hosts were the sociologists, fully in touch by then with work in other countries, and engaged in a range of projects on Poland's actual institutions. They did not hesitate to employ a class analysis of Polish society, and found support or at least tolerance for this from Adam Schaff, the party's more or less official philosopher. When I was there, he was less so, since the Polish edition of his book on Marxism and the individual had been published after first being published in West Germany. There was a public discussion of the book and Gomułka himself had been heard to complain. When the party threw him in jail for seeking a more open course, he said, Schaff joined in condemning him. Now that Poland had that course, Schaff found that there were large amounts of alienation in Poland. Not a profound thinker, Gomułka found that unfair. Schaff was neither sent to jail or dismissed from the Academy of Sciences, where he had a major role in the social sciences—but was subjected to a good deal of criticism. When I arrived one night at the Kołakowskis' for dinner (they lived near the truly hideous Palace of Culture given by the USSR), Leszek showed me the Polish literary weekly, with a long article on the book. "Who wrote it," I asked. "A great thinker," replied Leszek. "Great thinkers were rare," I objected. "No," he said, "the man thinks all the time—as to how he can keep his job as head of state radio."

I wondered to what extent, as an adaptation to Poland's position as a Soviet satellite, the sardonic voice I found in 1965 Warsaw was a continuation of the defense against total anguish by a nation always beleaguered. I experienced another kind of cultural continuity: the Baumans took me to the opera, and the public and their manners were far more reminiscent of La Scala or Covent Garden than of some *Proletkult* performance—and that dread seriousness and organizational hypertrophy which marked East Berlin was totally missing.

I walked around what had been the Ghetto and its monuments, of course, and drove to my grandfather's city, Radom, on empty highways. At the municipal records office, there was a card on a Birnbaum family which had emigrated to Sweden at the end of the war, but no indication of how they had survived it. I knew who they were—distant relatives who had then moved on to Israel. There was not a trace of Jewish life in the town otherwise: no synagogue, no Jewish merchants. Leszek Kołakowski had grown up there, and had recalled it as full of orthodox Jews.

As with the rest of my intellectual and political life, the search for roots, the concern with Jewishness, the fascination with anti-Semitism and the Holocaust, was there—but subordinated (perhaps I should say sublimated). What was central was my attention not to the past but to present and future, a critical approach to real existing society, a search for the way to transcend it.

My Polish friend Jan Szczepański (who was not a Marxist) had declared that if political interference were eliminated, the scientists and applied scientists would move humanity forward. There were resemblances, in his approach, to the work of the Western thinkers who under a miscellany of names were saying much the same thing. The new working class, the knowledge elite, would not only take control of the processes of production; they would extend that to the governance of society entire. The widespread diffusion of education and a general rise in the educational level would do the rest, as an enlightened body politic would control those with specialized knowledge. Just how the obdurate refusal of the Communist parties in the East, and the political class in the West, backed by citizens skeptical of a knowledge elite, could be overcome no one quite knew. A new agency of liberation, or rather progress, had been imagined to replace a revolutionary working class which shirked its historic duty. Old or new working class, liberation or even substantial progress toward it, still lay over a perpetually receding horizon.

Poland, two years later, was to suffer the consequences of the 1967 war in the Middle East. A nationalist faction of the Communist Party denounced "Zionists," by which they meant the socially integrated and highly educated Jews who had influential positions in government, the party and the professions. It was a convenient way to combine Polish nationalism with the appearance of service to the Soviet Union, where Brezhnev and his regime were themselves hostile to intellectuals, Jewish or not, whom they suspected of excessive interest in a larger world. Many Polish Jews left the country (the Catholic Kołakowski did so in general disgust, and because his wife was Jewish). Ideological troublemakers were removed from the nation. Their posts, however, went to politically conformist careerists incapable of dealing with the many problems of the society. Their short-term success led to a heightening of the tensions which, little over a decade later, engendered the movement of Solidarity (*Solidarność*) and all that followed.

There were almost no Jews to expel from the German Democratic Republic, but it managed dissent by brutal repression—or by expelling dissenters, often against their will, to West Germany. Still, the regime insisted on the appearance of contact with the West. I was invited to visit colleagues at the University of Jena who worked on the sociology of religion. My host, Olof Klohr, met me at the rail station in Leipzig and explained that the drive to Jena would be slow. The Warsaw Pact was engaged in maneuvers, and the party daily *Neues Deutschland* was extremely proud of one German general—described as commanding a multi-national force at "the front." We encountered a Polish airborne unit, if in trucks, and a tank column from the Soviet Army itself, many of the crews obviously from the Asian republics. Klohr was from an old Communist family that had moved to Communist Germany from Hamburg, and his wife was the daughter of state Defense Minister General Hofmann (who, as General Gomez, had defended Madrid as an International Brigade commander thirty years earlier). Klohr and his colleagues did not use their protected situation to try intellectual experiments.

Their sociology of religion was a schematic view of secularization, as a necessary consequence of the triumph of instrumental reason. It was an orthodox Marxist version of Western modernization doctrine. Since alienation was ending with the development of socialism, it was only a matter of time before its residues, such as religious belief, also disappeared. What was not explained, or even confronted, was the existence in the Democratic Republic of an intellectually and socially (and in the end, politically) active Protestant church. Part of it had a positive relationship to the regime (*Kirche im Sozialismus*, or Church in Socialism). Another, smaller segment, was carefully and selectively oppositional. The entire church cultivated relations with the church in West Germany (the two had not institutionally divided until the erection of the Berlin Wall in 1961). The regime had a minister who dealt with the church, and the Ministry of State Security certainly had it under observation. The Jena group, however, appeared to keep its distance from the church.

The Protestants who certainly did not limit themselves to attendance at Sunday service, but who worked in the church's institutions of education and solidarity, were not culturally backward. Despite large obstacles to admission to universities put in their way at different times in the history of the Communist German state, they were very well educated, frequently in science (such as Angela Merkel) or the professions. Their spiritual cousins in the Federal Republic opposed the total rationalization of life in capitalism— and the Protestant vanguard and no small part of the main body on the other side of the Wall were engaged in a similar effort in state socialism. Asked about it, their usual reply was that they sought to construct a different sort of social space—and to be ready for history's unexpected ruptures. The collapse of the regime twenty-four years after I visited Jena in 1965 showed how right they were—and how obtuse my Jena colleagues.

Back in France, I made regular visits to the weekly seminars directed by Henri Desroche. The seminar themes included issues of community development in the Third World to resistance to cultural homogenization in the First, studies of the most varied secular and social movements, and inquiries into the persistence and transformation of religious belief and practice in different historical settings. Desroche was immensely sensitive to cultural and psychological nuance, but insisted nonetheless on returning to his own beginning point: the liberty of spirit in a world of constraint.

His institute occupied the top floors of a building on a cul-de-sac in Paris Seven, not far from the Seine. The attic had been converted into an apartment for the family. As always, Henri was a totally devoted and loyal friend—which, he thought, entailed the duty of speaking frankly to those he considered close. In my case, he argued that I should write more, noted that I seemed more at ease in spontaneously developing ideas than in formally presenting them, and regretted that I was missing opportunities to join a larger dialogue. His admonitions did not add to my misery, since I had long since made their obvious truth my own. They did not stir me to immediate devotion to larger projects, but as marks of friendship they were invaluable. Henri lived to experience what was, much later, more creativity on my part. I think he appreciated that as a delayed tribute to our friendship.

Another friend of the period in Paris was Lucien Goldmann, who was at the same institution with a chair in cultural studies. Lucien had come to France from Romania, managed to flee to Switzerland during the war (and to evade the Swiss border police, so that he was not sent back to certain death), and studied there with Jean Piaget in Geneva.

He developed his own version of Piaget's *structuralisme génétique*, a version he thought a contribution to Marxism but which in many ways was quite original and in any case entirely un-dogmatic. He studied the inner development, psychological emphasis, and intellectual structure of ideas in historical contexts. His masterpiece was a book on Pascal, Racine, and their situation in seventeenth-century France, *Le Dieu Caché* (*The Hidden God*). In his essay, "Juif et Anti-Sémite," written years before Goldmann's work appeared, Sartre mocked the French anti-Semite who believed that no one with a Jewish origin could understand French culture, and named Racine as a totemic figure. I wonder if that, in part, spurred Lucien to choice of theme. He was a large person, direct, even at times obstreperous, with firm conviction that he had great talents precisely where they were not immediately evident even to benign observers—in the analysis of the larger movement of politics and in the conduct of smaller campaigns in the French academy.

He was generous and sympathetic, and I owe to him my introduction to Henri Lefebvre and the support from Georges Gurvitch that opened the way for my appointment to Strasbourg. He and his wife, Annie, who studied film, had an apartment on the Rue de Rennes some few blocks from Saint-Germain-des-Prés and Les Deux Magots. Lucien at times wondered, absurdly, whether he was too far from the action. Any number of foreign and French visitors were always at their table. Lucien had a struggle to be appointed to the École, but the excellence of his book and the discussion it stimulated made it impossible for his detractors to block his ascent. Nothing so pleased him as his international recognition, and I recall his triumphal visits to the Free University of Berlin and to the United States. It was cruel that he died relatively young—with much unsaid and unwritten.

As all of these events were occurring, and as Nina and Anna and Antonia so visibly enjoyed Strasbourg, I struggled to find an answer to the question: what next? My Oxford appointment was to terminate in 1966; there did not seem to be any plausible openings in the small world of Great Britain; I was considered for chairs in Germany but had no offers. I could have remained in Strasbourg as a visitor for another year, and that could have become permanent at some point—perhaps. My sense of floating in cultural space was acute, drew upon a deeply rooted conviction of rootlessness. There were good reasons why I was so attracted to the problem of alienation in modern culture. It was unclear what would overcome, or lessen, my own. I had to admit to myself that I was suffering from homesickness. News from the United States, visits from American friends, correspondence with others, had a poignancy I did not experience in other connections. I was very glad to have been asked to review Christopher Lasch's *The New Radicalism in America* by *Partisan Review,* and the new *New York Review of Books* asked me to review Brzezinski's and Huntington's book comparing the United States and the Soviet Union.

What complicated the situation was a very acute sense of failure. The Oxford matter weighed upon me and, far worse, I felt intellectually sterile. I did not revise my thesis and make it into a book. I did not make my own contribution (aside from brief papers) to the discussions of industrial society or secularization. I was intellectually productive in discussion, but could not (or did not) discipline myself to produce a sustained piece of written work. That was, clearly, a disadvantage in my search for a post in two senses. It weakened my bargaining position, and my lack of self-esteem narrowed and indeed distorted my capacity to make realistic assessments of the situation as I negotiated with several institutions. Even without a good deal of written work, my international experience and capacity as a teacher were very large assets. What I had written, meanwhile, was mostly quite good and some of it very good or even excellent. Colleagues were sure of that much; I was not, and some or much of that must have been communicated to my interlocutors.

I visited the University of California at Santa Cruz the year before it opened, and Wesleyan. Santa Cruz offered me a visitorship; Wesleyan, nothing. I finally settled for a three-year appointment to the graduate faculty of the New School for Social Research, accompanied by vague (and worthless) assurances of a tenured appointment at some point. At least we could live in New York.

Nina was emphatically unenthusiastic about moving to the United States, and I was distressed that she did not understand why I thought it necessary to return home. My distress was real, but her understanding might have been greater had I confided in her more. In that, as in other things, I did her an injustice. Mostly however, I did myself an injustice, shrouding myself in self-recrimination. Nina complained of having to live with a severely depressed person, and her complaint was thoroughly justified. The one thing worse was my having to live with myself.

Somehow, I staggered through the year. I was helped by returning to London for a month to work with my original psychoanalyst there, Dr. Walter Joffe. My initial analysis with him, begun in 1954, had gone well, and seemed quite promising when he left in early 1956 to return to South Africa. A month or so isn't a long time in a lifetime of inner conflict, but I gained an indispensable minimum of clarity.

My search for a post had one entertaining consequence: somehow, my name appeared on the list of candidates for a chair at the new German university at Konstanz, and the founding committee wrote to Henri Lefebvre asking for his views of the matter. Henri was busy and suggested that I draft the letter—which, as I wrote it, could not be described as balanced. *"Mon cher Norman,"* said Henri, *"ce n'est pas précisément un chef d'oeuvre de modestie"* ("it is not exactly a masterpiece of modesty"). I responded that I did not see the point of ignoring the advantages presented by an unusual opportunity. Henri may or may not have sent substantially the text I gave him; for whatever reason, the appointment was not offered. Looking back, I note that quite apart from my not wishing to renew the Strasbourg appointment, I made no very systematic efforts to generate possibilities in the UK or in Germany.

As Nina intuited, I had decided to return to the US with as much inner finality as I could muster: reaching that decision took such strength as I had, and dealing with multiple possibilities was beyond my capacity. I could have been more flexible about the US, but treated the process as an experiment in validation, not a test of the job market. Actually, the job market was very much to the advantage of plausible applicants, and much of my anxiety was self-generated.

I visited New York with Anna and Antonia in the spring of 1966. We stayed with my parents in New Rochelle and looked at schools. The girls, as always, treated the trip and the impending changes as a promising occasion. I owe a very great deal to the love and spontaneous enjoyment of life they showed in those uncertain and troubled months. They were my connections to the happier dimensions of existence, and I regret that I did not allow them to teach me more about it.

One final academic engagement in Europe remained—the 1966 International Congress of Sociology at Evian. In contrast to the ideological tensions of the three previous meetings (1956, 1959, 1962), this one was quite routinized. The presence of the sociologists from the Soviet bloc was a matter of course; little energy and time was expended on familiar conflicts, as if a wind of sobriety were blowing in constantly from Lake Geneva.

Considerable attention was given to the common structures of the advanced societies, as if many of the participants were either tired of political argument—or, not quite the same thing, seeking a different way to express it. The turbulence in Germany and the US did not bother the German and American sociologists too much. As it would soon turn out, these events were far from local. What the next years would actually bring, few prophesied—least of all those of us looking for a secular substitute for socialism.

PART II

11

Return to New York

I RETURNED with the family to New York in the fall of 1966. The city, then, was an offshore island, close to the rest of the North American continent but different. When on Lyndon Johnson's staff, the political scientist John Roche allegedly told the president that to end the war in Vietnam he should not bomb Hanoi but attack the Upper West Side of Manhattan. That is, indeed, where we went—to a spacious apartment on West End Avenue, a decided step up from my native Bronx, which had been long since abandoned by my mother and father and most of the prosperous Jewish population.

My move to the graduate faculty of the New School for Social Research was less a step up than a step into no man's land. Its most interesting period, when peopled by European expatriates, was behind it. Some had returned to Europe; a few remained, joined by their own American students. The institution was adrift in mid-Atlantic, not quite connected to a changing Europe and yet defiantly different from the American universities in its (admirable) insistence on a critical and historical social science. The trouble was that its critical ideas did not connect with the new (or old) American social criticism and its historiography was an archaeology collecting the shards of the early twentieth-century European past.

I was no longer an academic apprentice, but still felt errant. I had written some well-received articles, was widely and correctly credited with considerable knowledge of the transatlantic debate on modern society and politics—but I thought of myself as permanently on trial. The Oxford rejection was a wound from which I had not recovered. Faced with a cultural and personal and professional situation so very different from the one I had mastered at Harvard when much younger, I was beset by doubts as to whether I could survive.

Indeed, envisaging the situation was itself difficult. I wanted very much to join the New York intellectuals. My ambition to secure a place in the American academy was not appreciably smaller. I sought to keep and even deepen my European ties. I did not have the inner conviction of a right to success, and its absence made my struggles for success more obsessive and more tormenting.

There were compensations. My children treated the move as an adventure—evidence that Nina and I were reassuring parents. The trip over on the *Queen Mary* was something they enjoyed; the novelties of the big city were fascinating, the attentions of our friends who liked them welcome. Their curiosity, directness, spontaneity, and love were constant sources of spiritual replenishment to me, and, alas, a form of continual rebuke: I envied their spontaneity and delight.

Nina had been very skeptical of our move to the US, and had argued at one point that it broke a compact I had agreed upon to remain in Europe. She did try to make the best of it once we came, but her homesickness and lack of sympathy for much of American and New York culture made it difficult for her. I was so absorbed in my own inner and outer problems that I was not of much help—and so each of us parted inwardly from one another before we separated outwardly.

We did make friends, who counted for a good deal. I had met Barbara Probst Solomon, whose acutely intelligent writings I had read with admiration before, in Chicago in 1962.

Her husband had since died, and she was living with her two daughters in a large apartment on Central Park West when we arrived. Barbara had lived as a very young woman in Paris, had close ties to the Spanish opposition, and was critical of the provincialism of some of the more prominent New York intellectuals. She was generous with her time and very hospitable to us, in ways far deeper than making us members of the permanent salon over which she presided with discernment, tact and style.

There were others, such as Richard Sennett and Caroline Herron, who were then married, and who were especially taken with the children. Richard was beginning his splendid career, had a young person's eyes for the spiritual encrustation of the old and a considerable sense of wonderment that society could function at all. He has kept a freshness of vision, a remarkable achievement in a city in which knowingness was thought all, the rest naïveté. Caroline was then managing editor of *Partisan Review*, which entailed a good deal more than managing its agitated flow of paper: she had also to deal with the permanent inner agitation of the New York intellectuals, against which most defended themselves by plunging into endless quarrels. When I later met Caroline's mother, I realized how much intelligence and toughness she had inherited.

Steven Marcus and his wife, Gertrud Lenzer, were also welcoming—and sympathetic with my difficulties of re-entry and Nina's ambivalence. Gertrud was from Bavaria; Steve, a New Yorker with innate cosmopolitanism and a fine sense of the absurd. Gertrud and I had collaborated in editing a set of texts on religion and society, a project begun at Oxford and which came out in 1968. They and we shared any number of European friends. Steve's large talents and acute eye for the depths of American culture were markers of quality and steadiness in a near-chaotic scene.

Meanwhile, Norman Podhoretz did me the honor of treating me as a serious intellectual as I struggled for a place. Norman was then in the midst of his own struggles, not the least over the reception of his memoir, *Making It*. His early mentor, Lionel Trilling, advised him not to publish it: Norman's avowal of ambition struck Trilling as spiritual nudity. About his own career, Trilling was hardly Franciscan, and he constantly recurred to ambition as central in his depiction of nineteenth-century British culture. Why then was it so dubious in one of his students from Brooklyn—and a remarkably successful one? Much subsequently separated Norman and me, but I am glad to think that I was of some help to him at the time. In his bluffness, he resembled an especially pugnacious boxer—but when he spoke of his troubles, he exhibited the inner indecision of the ambivalent Jews who frequented *Commentary*'s short stories and its contributors' list.

I saw some older friends and classmates, and dully realized that whatever my doubts about my own capacities, they thought well of me—even in realms in which I was deficient: those of empathy. My own large capacities for self-destructive behavior came into play.

Robert Silvers, for whom I had written from Europe, gave me a book to review for the *New York Review of Books*, and I managed not to give him a text. I had had some discussion with Wesleyan, which was looking for a sociologist, and as part of their somewhat cumbersome selection process they invited me to teach a course in their Honors College of Social Science. I drove up once a week, but underperformed.

Above all, however, I made an unsatisfactory situation at the New School even more unsatisfactory.

The graduate faculty was not, collectively, resigned to its marginal place in the American academy, but could do little about it. It could no longer claim to be the primary custodian in North America of a European tradition of historical and philosophical social science. The erstwhile immigrants had spread out across the country, and a newer generation of Americans, their students, were well situated in institutions from Berkeley to Princeton. The graduate faculty was justly proud of its past, but also worried about its future. What would happen when the last of the Europeans retired? Meanwhile, lively American students could experience Europe unalloyed—and encounter a newer Europe hardly represented at the graduate faculty. We attracted some very interesting and talented students, most of them unsettled (and unsettling) in their own outsider roles. We could not compete, generally, with more prosperous American universities for established faculty talents. The rest of the faculty had some interesting figures, especially the philosopher Hans Jonas—whose personal culture in every inflection bespoke twentieth-century Europe. He was also a person of great decency and magnanimity.

We had one thing in common with the faculties at Berkeley and Harvard, Chicago and Wisconsin, MIT and Princeton: our arguments about progress and history, Europe and the US, modernity and tradition, empirical social science and interpretation, increasingly struck our students as remote at best, irrelevant at worst. They were nakedly ignorant of much that would have profited them to know. They were immersed in a culture in which a generation aged in five years, and they let us know that even, or above all, if we had Greek and Latin, we were quite unable to read the signs of the times. They achieved a very considerable feat: the graduate faculty was financially weak, devoid of academic or cultural influence, and supplied not a single faculty member to the government. They imagined, and depicted it, as an agency of oppressive power.

Nowhere did the symbolic dimensions of the American student revolt appear so clearly as in our niche, occupied as it was by permanent transients. The difficulty was that it did not appear so very clearly to me. I had become convinced in Europe that the analysis of the new class structure (in which an educated professional and scientific elite constituted a cultural and political vanguard) was correct. This was the group that was open to new ideas and a broader culture, and that would seek the democratization of society by at least severely reducing the powers of capital—and, in tyrannical socialism, of the party and state. The student revolt in the US certainly enlisted adult fellow travelers from this stratum—but, however inchoately, designated it as the revolution's principal adversary.

The American revolt against the Democratic Party and its "corporate liberalism" was our version of the European student revolt against British Labour, the Communists in Italy, the French Socialists, the German Social Democrats. The Europeans claimed inspiration from Berkeley and the American opposition to the Vietnam War, but drew upon traditions missing or minimally represented in the US. The European protesters sought to renew socialist (and, sometimes, social Christian) legacies. The Americans supposed that they were writing on a blank page, and so with considerable rapidity, mobilized large numbers to march resolutely into intellectual and political dead ends.

The American situation was complicated by the central place of racial conflict. Parts of our student movement equated this to anti-colonial and anti-imperial struggles elsewhere, but that entailed a simplistic condensation of American history. I had had almost no contact with the US movement for racial equality, had a schematic understanding of our past, and uncritically imagined that the persistent discontinuities of American history could be resolved in a large coalition for social change. The actual coalition in the Democratic Party was broken and disintegrating, its segments pursuing different ends with different tactics. I apprehended this dimly and regretted that the US and its labor movement (and working class) had been demobilized. With dogmatic blindness, I ignored the continuing electoral and legislative influence of the movement on local, state and federal government. I became a very ambivalent faculty fellow traveler of the student movement, especially doubtful of its compulsive antinomianism and its philistine attitude to high culture.

I spoke at an SDS meeting in Princeton, and my talk was noted both by the FBI informant present (I read his or her account of what I said) and by the subsequent Columbia student protest leader Mark Rudd. Mark later told me that he had been impressed by my inserting the protest into historical and international context. Had the movement attended to context, it might have developed different tactics and understood itself in decidedly less heroic terms. That would have required what was conspicuously missing—experienced and adult leadership. Maurice Isserman and Michael Kazin, among others, have studied the connections between the New Deal coalition and its post-war incarnations and the protest movements of the sixties. The lines of influence were dense, and intertwined with Christian social, pacifist, sectarian Marxist traditions. Achieving a clear view was made more difficult by the obdurate defense of the war in Vietnam by much of the union movement, initially echoed in the pages of *Dissent* by as formidable a figure as Irving Howe. The defenders of Johnson considered that they owed him a good deal for his legislative triumphs on civil rights and the welfare state. They were, moreover, strenuous anti-Communists—and quite ignorant of the history of Vietnam, where the Communists had appropriated a great deal of that nation's resistance to foreign domination.

The New York City school strike, opposing a Jewish-led teachers' union to local school boards which were frequently African-American or Latino, added to the confusion. Norman Podhoretz assured me, and anyone else who would listen, that McGeorge Bundy, president of the Ford Foundation, was setting African-Americans against Jews to maintain the primacy of the white Protestant ruling class. I heard a less exalted argument for the union from my father, then an assistant principal at a Bronx junior high school, who suddenly took a benign view of the union and its leader, Albert Shanker, on grounds of the defense of professionalism in education. Then came the 1967 war in the Mideast, the Israel victory, and the initial criticism of Israel's occupation of the West Bank of the Jordan River by American supporters of the Palestinians (some of the African-American leadership and some in the churches). The American Jewish community was deeply divided on the Vietnam War, but some were inclined to support Johnson in Vietnam as their end of a bargain: he would back Israel. The amalgam of the Palestinian cause with a global anti-imperial movement was a further disincentive to some Jewish liberals and their allies to criticize the war in Vietnam: they disdained the company they would have kept.

These currents and counter-currents were difficult to grasp, taken singly. It was even more difficult to understand how the cultural and political demiurge that was the US in 1966 and 1967 functioned—what was fundamental and what was not. Occasional trips to the American mainland did not decrease my bewilderment. Above all, I sought a group to join, a circle of the (approximately) like-minded that I could be at home with. Here and there the long coastline opened into welcoming harbors. Once I left one of these (let us say, a friendly and lively dinner party), I was again on my own.

The New York intellectuals might have taken me in, but they were in the throes of angry argument themselves: new recruits were expected to join old cliques. Their pasts weighed heavily upon older figures such as the Trillings and William Phillips, who could not escape the ideas and alignments of the thirties and forties. They saw anti-Semitism, philistinism and Stalinism everywhere, and insisted on proprietary rights to what, in a very felicitous phrase, Harold Rosenberg termed "the tradition of the new." I was reminded more than a bit of the Oxford conviction that an idea which did not evoke attention at the university merited none anywhere else.

Trilling was later to characterize the student revolt and the sixties movements generally as "modernism in the streets," but that may have reflected the understandable self-absorption of an academic committed to his own ideas. It was and remains unclear that the student leaders so prominent in those years were bearers of a modernist culture: what they had not read could (and did) fill entire libraries. No doubt, they were influenced at their colleges by modernist ideas. These came to them, however, in mass-produced popular culture, with its open sexuality and reduction of dissent to a loud and continuous jeer.

Paradoxically, two European trips after I returned to the US helped me to see the nation more clearly. The first, in December 1966, was to Prague for a meeting of sociologists of religion. Our Czech hosts, led by the future state official for religious affairs in Dubček's 1968 government, were, well before the open proclamation of "socialism with a human face," clearly finished with Stalinist dogmatism. They had no one substitute, and were ready to begin from the beginning in their search for moral authenticity. One of the influences on them was the open Catholicism of the Second Vatican Council. Another was the critical Marxism of Western Europe. Yet another was the relentless pluralism and perpetual ideological conflict they read into the American situation. They were impressed by the energy drawn on by the young to defy authority. Some knew more than a bit about Martin Luther King and his spiritual antecedents. The Berkeley revolt and the civil rights movement struck the Europeans, east and west, as convincing evidence for the vitality of American democracy.

The CIA's very substantial investments in culture were by contrast unimaginative interventions in the European debate, which in the end embarrassed those who took its money. Bundy must have thought that, since no sooner did he assume the presidency of the Ford Foundation in 1966 than he dismissed the person in charge of its work in Europe, Shepard Stone, who had collaborated with the CIA in supporting the Congress for Cultural Freedom and much else. He moved to Paris as executive officer of the congress, the eminent leaders of which responded to public discussion of their servitude to the US by disowning their erstwhile colleagues in its administration. My 1959 open letter to then-General Secretary Nicolas Nabokov, asking about the funding of the congress, preceded the 1967 revelations. No one who had so bitterly denounced me for asking a simple question then bothered years later to recall my impiety: they were busy inventing excuses for their venality. Stone remembered, and had blocked my application to the foundation for a grant to study university reform in Western Europe. His departure prompted the foundation to reconsider.

Secondly, in the summer of 1967 I returned to Europe to speak with administrators, civil servants, students, and teachers in the Federal German Republic, France, and the United Kingdom. There were some signs—widespread in Germany, more sporadic in France, politely infrequent in the UK—of large student discontent and a good deal of self-criticism among their teachers, not least the scientists. The complaints were many and contradictory. The students thought instruction deficient, often authoritarian, always remote, insufficiently contemporary. The teachers were institutionally radical: they could not advance knowledge in the conditions they had inherited, and they sought new forms of university organization, with many citing the US as a model. The civil servants and politicians did not think society was getting its money's worth from the universities. The administrators complained that they had to run harder to stay in one place—and doubted that in the end it was worth the effort. The unease was general, but there was little sense (Germany perhaps excepted) of an imminent disruption. The Germans who feared conflict were stern defenders of the institutional continuity of their universities. Those resolutely turned to the past were in some cases rather acute diagnosticians of the immediate future. They trusted their instincts, but had little by way of a new historical concept to contribute.

In fact, there were no clear lines of division. Criticism of the insufficiency of resources came from proponents of more democratization of access to higher education but also from technocratic elitists. Demands for "relevance" (to their culture and careers) came from student leaders and social planners. The conviction that the universities had failed society was widespread; the proposals for new forms of integration with public purpose were quite diverse. National situations were different. Some critical Germans remembered the enthusiastic cooperation of their senior colleagues with the Third Reich; the French recalled the role of the university as a vanguard of opposition to the Algerian war (and as a stronghold of secular republicanism); the British were still struggling with the consequences of Labour's expansion of access to higher education. Opposition to the technocratic rationalization of the universities united traditionalists who considered themselves custodians of Western culture and radicals who sought to define culture anew.

In France, I saw Denis Sauvageot, who was president of the national union of students, and Alain Geismar, a scientist who was general secretary of the largest of the teachers' unions, representing the secular Left. Each had all the time in the world to talk—not the case a year later when I saw them after they'd had large roles in the events of May 1968. In 1967 they were given to reflection on the contrast between the changes they half saw, half guessed at, in the society and in the turgidity of academic culture. They were aware of the obsolescence of fixed descriptions of a class society, unsure of what images and ideas could describe a situation in which some part of modern culture legitimated power and much of the rest undermined it.

I did not encounter one group, *Les Situationnistes*, the extremely vocal conventicle which had no doubts at all. Some had come to Strasbourg to study with Henri Lefebvre when I was there, and had listened to me with respectful skepticism: their knowledge of the US was conspicuous by its total absence. *Les Situationnistes*, influenced by a variety of eccentric authors, some inspired, some a good deal less so, depicted mass culture as the symbolic unifier of a society increasingly centrifugal. It followed that mockery, satire, chaotic acting out, could reinforce latent revolutionary tendencies. Later that year, the Strasbourg group won election as the university's student government and preceded to wreak havoc—provoking the authorities to go to court to evict them from office. The judge's denunciation of their immaturity and irreverence read like one of their satires. They produced the pamphlet "De La Misère au Milieu Étudiant," which had a large readership, and moved from Strasbourg to Nanterre, where in March 1968 they staged a dress rehearsal of the May revolt. In my lack of prescience about their influence I was joined by the lucid Lefebvre.

The conventional defenders of order who saw in these youthful jesters a danger had insights we lacked. We (the adults) were so many Hamlets sicklied over with the pale cast of our thoughts, looking for a revolutionary agency when the revolution had begun before our unseeing eyes. One thinker who had very good eyesight was Alain Touraine, who before the May revolt predicted that student discontent would erupt and function as a detonator of wider protest. Ordinary French institutions did not, he thought, have enough flexibility to meet and contain accumulations of frustration. France had never been so prosperous, the comfortable middle reaches of society never so open, but a psycho-cultural demand for change was far more powerful than the weighing of material advantage.

Touraine had begun as a historian, and he was fully aware of the French custom described decades later by the historian Danielle Tartakowsky—*le pouvoir est dans la rue* (power is in the streets). In crises, large segments of French society trusted only themselves and took to the streets. I heard hints of what could be coming in 1967 in talks with Lefebvre, Morin, and Touraine. The Catholics such as Desroche and others, preoccupied with making the conquests of Vatican II permanent, had a decided sense of the deceptiveness of appearances of historical closure: church history taught them that continuity was at times fragile. In March 1968, Pierre Viansson-Ponté, echoing a theme from de Gaulle's New Year address, in *Le Monde* declared *La France s'ennuie*—France was bored.

These and my other impressions of Europe (as of generational warfare in Germany), I brought back with me in the fall of 1967—imperfectly reflected upon. The main advantage of the trip was to reinforce my conviction of the obvious: the US was different, and the way to understand it was to look again at its history. This was like a New Year's resolution that would require a decade to enact. In the European nations, I had met not only university administrators and teachers, but their interlocutors in government and politics. These were precisely the persons I did not at first meet in the United States. I met colleagues and students, journalists and writers, and some few persons who had been in government (the emigrants from the Kennedy Administration at the Institute for Policy Studies in Washington). I had a passing acquaintance with persons from the growing ranks of political activists, met some from the sacerdotal ranks of the foundations, often rather more pious about their tasks than the theologians I encountered.

My derision gives me a bad conscience: Ford Foundation executives did me the favor of financing my trips to Europe. I knew almost no one in business and finance, an occasional meeting with a college classmate or former Harvard student excepted. John Lindsay was then the mayor of New York, and his press officer had the apartment down the hall—but I did not manage to ask him about his work. In short, I adapted with great rapidity to the hermetic life of a New York intellectual—for whom reality was less interesting than arguments about it. Twenty-four years after leaving New York for Williamstown, I still looked upon the nation with the surprised and uncertain gaze of an outsider who supposed that, somehow, distance was a virtue—but who wondered whether he was right.

    I struggled with my return in several dimensions. Our move to New York made it impossible to avoid the tensions in our marriage, our mutual reproaches of lack of support. Nina was certainly right to feel that I was insufficiently solicitous of her difficulties in a milieu which many Americans found problematic. I was obsessed with the thought that it was now or never: I had to establish myself, finally, as a major intellectual or resign myself to existence on the periphery. My inner resources, of which I was extremely uncertain, had been depleted by the years at Oxford and Strasbourg, where I had adapted for better or worse to the role of an outsider. I was quite incapable of sitting down to a long-term project of historical analysis, and the revolving public stage on which immediate debates took place was already occupied by any number of brilliant performers. The external pressures were considerable, and to these I brought little conviction that I could construct my future. I responded in two ways.

    One involved a great deal of activity, some of it useful, a lot of it for activity's sake. It was surely right, in a period of turbulence in all of the Western universities, to use my international experience to provide running commentary few could match. In the end, it added up, and I could write, in 1972, a very substantial monograph for the Carnegie Commission on Higher Education—and join to it a widely read series of articles in *Change, The Journal of Higher Education*. It was equally right, given my participation in the British New Left and my perspectives on social movements on the Continent, to develop a different view of American social conflict than that available to those who were less traveled. Finally, I could and did bring to the analysis of industrial society, and social thinking generally, a historical and philosophical framework very different from the one standard in the American academy. I had difficulty in bringing these strands together—not only due to the complexity of doing so but also due to my own low capacity for intellectual persistence. Not so long ago, I derided those I considered superficial commentators on contemporary culture and politics by saying that they had great gifts for getting to the surface of events—and remaining there. I was hardly deficient in this regard, and my capacity for avoiding the deep and unresolved problems which limited my creativity was considerable. Consider the lines just written: I began by referring to the difficulties between Nina and me, and as quickly shifted to the problems of my career.

I did seek help, from the psychoanalyst I had seen twenty-three years earlier for two years, Dr. David Beres. He attempted to draw my attention to the inner problems I had with family, my feeling of being insufficiently appreciated. Given the insatiable nature of my need for reassurance, no earthly family could provide it. I preferred to dwell on my crisis of adaptation and work. Indeed, in many years of analysis with different therapists, my defenses against recognizing some very painful truths about myself proved very strong. I claimed to be a profound student of psyche and society—but managed to leave much of my own life out. It was this that accounted for the agitation I felt on my return: I feared being overwhelmed. The graduate faculty of the New School, the groups and persons around the older New York intellectuals, the inchoate, new American Left, were in 1966 hardly settings which encouraged serenity.

The graduate faculty was struggling with several problems. Now that many of the émigrés had returned to Europe or retired, how could it retain its ties to the Old World and find a way to implant itself in the US—at a time when the American universities had considerable direct access to Europe? The students we attracted were often interestingly eccentric and frequently talented, but so few were entering the national teaching ranks that we hardly had a constituency there. The place was a very large raft in mid-ocean, drifting now toward one coast and then another, boarded from time to time by uncertain travelers who regarded the crew with suspicion while thinking of distant shores.

The separate departments were each integrated very differently in their disciplines in the United States. The philosophers were ostentatiously "Continental," given to studying the history of philosophy and the larger themes of history, human nature and politics.

The economists, political scientists and social psychologists were closer in their preoccupations to the American versions of their disciplines. The Americans in these fields included some very talented persons who wished to move, intellectually, across boundaries—and who were especially skeptical about the distinction between "facts" and "values" prevalent in American social science.

The sociologists were a very mixed group. There was one survivor of the émigré generation, the reflective Carl Mayer, who possessed a German culture become rare in post-war Germany. He had an inner core of empathy armored by impeccable manners, and the wisdom of a calm old age. I am sorry that I did not know him better. My Harvard Graduate School classmate Arthur Vidich was the representative of an Americanized sociology, since he had worked on American communities. Arthur, however, had studied at Wisconsin with Hans Gerth, a radical Prussian who was C. Wright Mills's teacher, and brought to his own work the critical and at times disabused eye of an ethnic critic of the nation. Peter Berger came from Austria as a boy, was a Lutheran, and had a large cultural sensibility. He was happily equidistant from the cultures of contemporary Europeans and Americans both, was at home with the Protestant theologians—providing that they shared his distrust of large projects of social transformation. His conservatism put him at a distance from American proponents of order, since he did not see the US as an orderly place. Finally, there was Benjamin Nelson, an authentic polymath who knew so much that he could not write it down, and divided his energies between low feuds and high criticism. Ben had written a very good book on the idea of usury in his early period as a medievalist. He was one of those intellectuals who had left the Talmud behind to read the world (resembling my later friend William Phillips). They could not, however, restrain their huge ambitions and so wrote little but occasional commentary—hardly desultory, invariably acute, but always fragments of a forever uncompleted larger work. I saw in Ben a warning figure: I was on the way, I feared, to a similar fate.

Our students had the large advantage of youth and an accompanying disadvantage—a decided lack of a sense of time, a concentration on the immediate moment.

Some knew that they were participating in a revival of a major strand in American politics, but most did not know much about even the recent past—the post-war years from 1945. My memory for detail is still quite good and I have looked at my own correspondence, notes and some of the writings of the Graduate School protesters. It is at this distance impossible to say what their specific grievances were. They wanted a share in the governance of the department and the graduate faculty, but to what end? The value of the very persons at the graduate faculty whom they regarded as out of touch was, precisely, that they had a certain distance and (if listened to) could communicate a larger view of history. I write that now; at the time, I was torn between my own identification with rebelliousness and my knowing better. To identify the graduate faculty, miserably endowed financially and an institution not noticed by those at the commanding heights of culture and politics, as a fortress defending the established order was preposterous. I especially regret my not having been firm enough to suggest to the students that they distinguish between the actual institutions of power and the very ordinariness of our own circumstances.

In one tragic case, it might have done some good. In one of my seminars, three students wrote a very good term paper on the new middle class, so good that I cited it later in the introduction to *The Crisis of Industrial Society*. One of them was David Gilbert, who had been an undergraduate at Columbia. David, as I now recall, was inwardly driven, a young man with little patience for life's more mundane things. He eventually joined the Weatherman faction of Students for a Democratic Society, as it was writing off most of our reformist history as futile or derisory. In the end, he was sentenced to life imprisonment for his involvement in the attempted robbery of an armored car in Nyack, NY, by African-American militants—an incident in which police officers were killed. It is very unclear that I could have dissuaded David from the course he took, but whatever generalities I advanced on democratic possibilities were clearly unconvincing. We are not responsible for our students' fates, but we are responsible for a certain clarity and directness, which at the time I lacked.

The problem, clearly, was one of connection. I found it very difficult to situate the American mainstream, the more so as it was dividing into separate currents, breaking once-fixed banks and altering the American landscape. Where in the ensuing turbulence could I find a place? I wondered what, in any event, I had to offer, and found it immensely difficult to connect my European experience to the broken sequences of American culture. When I left the country in 1952, it was with an unarticulated sense that there must be some other way to live than the constant striving of Cambridge and New York, their conviction that the only possible direction was up. Even much of psychoanalysis, as I remember it, was given to overcoming inner obstacles to outer success. Now, in a large and rapid reversal, we were instructed that these concerns were contemptible (think of the extremely negative response by some to Norman Podhoretz's panegyric to his own ambition). I found myself with very little capacity for developing a project for the new age, since I shared some essential experiences and language with so few. I cannot, then, say that I ran into locked doors; rather, I stumbled through half-open ones.

My friends, old and new, and most of the other persons I met were helpful and hospitable. They were not overly concerned about, since I did not wish to disclose, my own doubts, which at times became inner turmoil. I went from one group to another, gave myself insufficient time and applied insufficient energy to achieve durable relationships and develop new attitudes and ideas, and so early intimations of the thrill of return were replaced by an aching sense that I was nowhere at home.

The New York intellectuals around *Commentary* and *Partisan Review* were generationally divided. I sympathized with the older ones, despite what I thought of as their obsession with Communism, because of their cultural affinity for Europe. Their fragile sense of Americanization also made them appealing: they did not pretend. There, however, they were often unable to see what was happening in those large segments of American culture they did not know and certainly did not understand. The US, on account of the Protestant character of its older elites and the Catholicism of many of the newly risen ethnic groups, was inhospitable to their version of Jewish intellectuality, reading the world as a book. The Second Vatican Council and its considerable reverberations in American Catholicism did not interest them. They still thought of the nation as dominated by the celebrated Saving Remnant of Protestantism, and the iconic significance of the Kennedys escaped them. The function of Hollywood as maker of instant myths was hardly unknown to them, but they thought of themselves as contemporaries of Chaplin and not James Dean. (Christopher Lasch, whom I had as yet to meet, termed the Kennedy administration a union of Café Society and Route 128, the Boston circumferential highway where Harvard and MIT professors sited their ancillary enterprises.) They had difficulty (Dwight Macdonald excepted, but he had the saving grace of the capacity to laugh) understanding how figures such as Abbie Hoffman and Jerry Rubin were able to speak to much of the nation. They dismissed them as creatures of the media, without realizing how the media (and especially television) had rendered American culture at once more transparent and more national. That so many writers were transcribing reality as if it were on film did not induce them to revise their aesthetic, with its heavy emphasis on moral conflict. They thought of life as a *Bildungsroman*; a newer generation experienced it as an endless tourist trip, in which discontinuity was the only certainty.

A younger generation caught on. However different, Steven Marcus, Richard Poirier, Susan Sontag, and Peter Brooks knew that older distinctions between form and content, art and politics, were dissolving. Imagery and language, notions of character and time, were changing. When I was much younger, Clement Greenberg instructed me to think of myself as a highbrow. Now Norman Mailer, and not only he, mocked the idea. Intellectuals aspired to be prophets, not priests—and not infrequently strove for celebrity status.

The 1967 Arab-Israeli War may have awakened Jewish pride in many American Jews, but it did not figure largely in the lives of the people I knew. They did not, by and large, belong to synagogues, possess much Jewish culture, or concern themselves with the issues that moved persons who were, ethnically, far more preoccupied with the Jewish situation.

Yet they had, especially the elder generation, the very developed consciousness of those who saw their lives as a struggle to move from Jewish distinctiveness to a more inclusive tradition of secularization. I do not use the term "secularism" since it was not for them (or rather, us) a fixed state, nor one defined by boundaries between religion and the rest of life. It was instead an idea of joining a very mixed community, speaking a cacophony of languages, and with a great many different and frequently antithetical ends. I suppose we could term it the Great Church of Modernism, in fact divided into mutually repellent denominations and sects. A great deal of passion had been invoked not by the Eichmann trial directly, but by Hannah Arendt's reporting of it from Jerusalem in 1962, and her criticism of European Jewry for not doing enough to defend itself. With a Democratic government in Washington, and the obvious accession to the American elite of plenty of Jews, she induced maximum discomfort in her readers—increased by her obdurate refusal to offer spiritual compensation of any kind. The episode had no obvious end; debate was suspended as attention returned to life in the US. Assassinations, civil conflicts and war provided enough to argue about for those for whom moving to Israel was simply unthinkable. Those who visited, meanwhile, did spend much time with persons very like themselves.

I did not even visit. I was struck, upon looking around the US in 1966, how much was now taken for granted. In the early sixties, Isaiah Berlin talked (to me) about the possibility of Jewishness being a barrier to a career at Oxford. It was not something spoken about in American universities a couple of years later, because it would not have occurred to anyone as very likely. Presidencies at elite institutions were still, largely, in the hands of Protestants—but that, too, was on the verge of changing. Nathan Glazer and Daniel Patrick Moynihan had published *Beyond the Melting Pot*, on the new politics of ethnicity in New York, in 1963. No wonder the older Protestant elites turned to depicting their past triumphs in literary form. Obliged to compete in the classroom and, increasingly, in the board room, professional firms and partnerships, and everywhere else, they also did battle with the Jewish memoir and novel in the literary marketplace.

In the late sixties memory, the news from the Middle East, and the many possibilities of existence in the US reinforced among Jews the old antitheses. Many were determined to take advantage of American possibility, and so identified themselves as here for our nation's uncertain duration. Others took the space provided by the new ethnicity and concentrated on their Jewishness, commuting actually and spiritually to Israel. Actually, the US was very generous toward its immigrants, allowing them to fashion any number of life courses. My own was still, in many respects, where it had been in adolescence: I sought to join the mainstream. The trouble was, of course, that it had become a torrent, full of undertows and whirlpools—and if one climbed on to a rock in the middle, there was little certainty that one could easily get off it. That, actually, made plunging in seem all the more authentic.

The newly levelling playing field did not yet allow Afro-Americans (as the term was then) and women equal status. The Afro-American segment of the larger movement for social change shrugged off calls to unity of action and purpose as deceptive or worse. The many women joining in the movement quickly realized that its male leaders and activists were indifferent to their emancipatory project, if not hostile to it. These were problems not only for the political process; they affected much of daily life. It was very difficult, reflectively, to separate past, present, and future. A New Journalism, often involving direct participation and first-person narrative, was one way to picture the currents carrying us—by making the moment transparent. The older quarterlies and monthlies and even weeklies still supposed that time moved in a regular sequence; the New Journalism stopped the clock. It superimposed film on the modern novel to construct a rough aesthetic, and its perspective sometimes reminded me of a large blinking eye in a surrealist montage.

I clung to my own notion of a history of the present, but saw that the new journalists were very lively witnesses about events and persons I would otherwise have ignored. I did meet some of them, thanks again to Barbara Solomon. *Harper's* under Willy Morris was a major voice of the New Journalism, its writers combining commentary and reporting in original ways. My recollection of reading in the late thirties reminded me of their dependence upon the culture of the New Deal, the kind of work James Agee and Edmund Wilson did. They preferred to think of themselves as innovators, and given the linearity of ordinary American journalism in the decades before they appeared, they were. In any event, Morris, David Halberstam, Tom Wolfe, and contemporaries were good company and did what they could to enlarge my absurdly narrow view.

One set of major changes was impossible to ignore. The New

School had its own peculiarities, but I was in touch with colleagues and friends at other institutions.

Higher education had expanded, and divided into different communities and hierarchies. Many, especially younger faculty, did not allow themselves to be instructed on their vocations by Ivy League reformers or administrators at the large public systems. They had to deal with different sorts of students, not likely to enter the nation's elites but unwilling to accept that they were eligible only for seats in coach class. The newer emphasis on ethnicity, the rise of an unapologetic Afro-American consciousness, were aspects of a general problem.

What did the universities owe the nation—and what did the nation owe to its teachers and students?

I found it difficult to call for the democratization of higher education, since the phrase was entirely ambiguous. Did it mean equality of access to the acquisition of a higher culture—or a newer conception of culture? Many calling for this last had not troubled to read John Dewey, who had some thoughts on the matter—and were not familiar with the history of educational argument in the nation. I returned from Europe convinced of the possibility that educated segments of the elite could unite with others as vanguards of social transformation, but suppose the publics in the democracies were resolutely opposed to according the educated vanguard functions?

In the decade that followed, I developed a position that held its conflicting elements in uncertain equilibrium. Higher education was higher; it dealt with complex matter that required an arduous and long apprenticeship to master. It needed, as well, the critical reconstruction of a tradition lest our universities were to be abandoned to hypertrophy and sclerosis. Teachers, however, were very vulnerable, since they incurred two major spiritual hazards: they could think of themselves as priests, and were prey to arrogance; they could also think of themselves as servants of society, and incur the dangers of corruption in the selection of their masters.

I eventually formulated an idea of public responsibility, which left the scholars free to choose those segments of the public they served—but which imposed on them the obligation of dialogue. In emotive sympathy with the rebellion of the young, I did not propose to allow them to devise the syllabi of the courses I taught. I did not even think them, after a while, very qualified rebels. It took me an academic year or two to formulate all of this, and the process was complicated by my immersion in matters European. I was aware of the self-absorbed provincialism of much American discussion, sensed that some of it was the consequence of our "newness," and quickly learned that my transatlantic wisdom rarely evoked paroxysms of enthusiasm in those who might have profited from it. All of this took time, stretching from my 1968 article in *The Nation* to my lengthy article (in effect a monograph) "Students, Professors and Philosopher Kings" for the Carnegie Commission on Higher Education, written in 1972 and published a year later. In writing, now, the two comprise a much more coherent and sequential process than the one I experienced in my first two years of return to the United States.

I was in conflict. I wished to participate in revolution, but doubted the qualifications and judgment of my fellow revolutionaries considered many of our fellow citizens quite resistant to major changes. I thought that the structures of learning should be reconstructed, but wished to secure a fixed place before the work of demolition began. I writhed at the smallness of the disputes at the graduate faculty, but had no immediate access to a more centrally located platform. Some of this was due to my situation as a returning emigrant; more owed to an inner unsteadiness, a lack of clarity, so inexpungible that I did not recognize it as such. In fact, I did make my way in two years to a chair at Amherst College and to contributing regularly to *Commentary*, *The Nation*, and *Partisan Review*. The problem was that I could not believe in my own capacity to achieve good fortune.

The situation at the graduate faculty was rent by tensions, and I did not maintain the dignified distance which would have been appropriate—and possibly even rewarding.

I had a three-year appointment as a full professor, and my colleagues in 1967 decided not to make it permanent, postponing decision until the next academic year—the last one of the contract. In the midst of a very large expansion in American higher education, I wondered whether I faced a hand-to-mouth existence. I had not yet, my colleagues informed me, written a book. The manuscript of the Trinity College lectures was half-finished; the article on "The

Crisis of Marxist Sociology," which was later to be much cited, was awaiting publication in the graduate faculty's own journal, *Social Research*. In fact, I did not finish the larger text until after my Amherst appointment, repeating an old pattern: I responded with self-defeating defiance to demands for performance—even, or perhaps above all, when the interlocutors were friendly.

A larger instance of confused self-destructiveness in the period was my leaving my wife and daughters at the end of 1967, sixteen months after we made the difficult journey to New York. No doubt, my marriage to Nina was full of strains, mutual incomprehension, no small amount of ambivalence and anger. Still, I treasured my children and they loved me, and—whatever might have been decided in the end—another *modus vivendi* could have been found. It is incorrect to use the language of decision. It was, instead, as if I were pressed, no rushed, by an impulse to flee. Some of my motives were base—revenge for the criticism and humiliation I thought (again, exaggeratedly) I had had to endure from Nina. Some were distorted—the impression that even the children cared little for me or had little appreciation for the care and love (insofar as I was capable of it) they were receiving. The more lurid the story, the less presumable my own guilt. I concocted a narrative of liberation—but in the end did not feel free.

There were effective reasons for that. I had an attachment to Edith Kurzweil, whom I met at the graduate faculty. Edith had come to the US at sixteen from Vichy France, after leaving Vienna in 1939 with her parents and spending some time in Bruxelles. The parents had left Edith and her younger brother in Bruxelles when they went to the US, intending to send for them. The German invasion of Belgium and the occupation of France made escape problematical. Edith and her brother were sent by a Jewish organization in a group of Jewish children to a house near Toulouse. From there, having been sent their entry visas to the US, Edith managed a trip out of France and across Spain and Portugal—no easy matter. When we met she had had two marriages, both to other emigrants from Jewish Vienna. The first ended in divorce (and two children). The second was in her memory decidedly more positive. Her husband was an engineer and went to Milan to work on Italian economic reconstruction with the Marshall Plan, and remained there as a consultant. Edith enjoyed Italy, but returned to the US (with a third child) when her husband became ill. Upon his death, she completed her college degree, which she had abandoned, and then decided to study further. Having lived in very different milieux, she decided against joining her parents in the family business. The academy, and New York's intellectual life, interested her.

That is where I came in. I found Edith very interested in the sociability of the city, and in my career. That seemed the antipode of Nina's concerns, which I misinterpreted as indifference to my situation. That did serious injustice to Nina's values, which placed the children, friendship and a very high standard of human integrity first, even if these entailed an existence which disregarded much of the conventional success I sought. I can write about these matters now. Then, they were hardly accessible. Edith and I were together, not easily and with occasional separations, from the beginning of 1968 to the fall of 1972. Like any human relationship, it had its own shifting balance of mutual discontent and satisfaction. Suffice it to say that it was not the great emotional step forward I initially sought. For a considerable part of the period, I lived in Amherst and Edith in New York, which reflected rather than caused our problems. We did a certain amount of travelling together, especially to Europe, and spent half the year 1971-1972 in Turin. I'm glad that Edith's youngest child, the novelist Alan Kurzweil, retains a positive memory of our time together. Her daughter, Vivien Schmidt, is a respected scholar in European politics, and a good friend. Not for the only time, a younger generation has helped its seniors retrieve something positive from their lives.

Amidst familial turmoil and its attendant pain, dealing with my professional situation was, almost, a relief. Whatever my colleagues at the graduate faculty might have done in the academic year 1968-1969, in the year 1967-1968 they had been very reluctant to honor the many assurances I had been given of a permanent appointment. Now Fortuna appeared, not for the first time in my life, in New England. Amherst College had no sociologists on its faculty, and I learned from Ely Chinoy, who taught at nearby Smith College, that it wished to appoint a senior sociologist.

Amherst's decision begs the recounting of a tale of academic history. Nietzsche once declared that the father of German philosophy was a Protestant pastor. The same could be said of much of American sociology, with its moral earnestness, connection to social reform, and imperfectly secularized account of social causation—in which persons were important as bearers of values. Indeed, the Harvard Department of Sociology had been formed in 1931 to supersede a previous Department of Social Ethics, and Yale's much older department owed much to William Graham Sumner's appropriation of Spencer's view of progress. The most influential of American sites of sociology was the University of Chicago, where Robert Park was a Protestant clergyman struggling with urban civilization. No doubt, there was an older cleavage in American sociology between proponents of state action and those who favored the voluntarism of independent social groups, but this matched no simple scheme of division between left and right. At Columbia, Robert and Helen Lynd conducted their very critical study of Middletown (Muncie, Indiana) as a community study. At Columbia, too, Robert MacIver brought from Scotland, Great Britain, and Europe his view of community as a sub-stratum of politics. Much of the material of sociology was taught by anthropologists, economists, historians, political scientists and psychologists—and by the law schools. As the disciplines were formed at the end of the nineteenth and beginning of the twentieth centuries, sociology frequently suffered from its interstitial character: it was everywhere in general and nowhere in particular.

To this was added several prejudices. One was that sociology implied, and therefore taught, a disintegrative moral relativism. Another was that it was not only an ancillary of movements for social reform, but opened the way for radical views of the social order.

University presidents, trustees, and watchful alumni already had their hands full with the radicals who populated other disciplines: why bring new troublemakers to campus? Despite these hindrances, sociology was by and large well established in many institutions between the wars. Its status was raised by the fact that in many fields, émigré scholars from Europe depicted classical European sociology as an indispensable part of their intellectual legacies.

At the end of the Second World War, sociology was swept

along in the boom, resulting from increased enrollments, from the demand by society's agencies of power and wealth for reliable accounts of a rapidly changing nation, and by the literate public's quest for knowledge of our new historical circumstances. This led to a striking dualism within sociology, in which colorful social critics and commentators (Daniel Bell, C. Wright Mills and David Riesman) contrasted with drab colleagues who counted—literally. Meanwhile, interesting studies of institutions were done by those who took all of industrial society as their province of inquiry. True, they referred to class in anodyne fashion, by terming it "social stratification," and insisted that Marx was out of date—but no one was fooled. They were dealing with a new class society. Parsons persisted in what was a philosophical argument on the nature of society and the ways it could be thought about. It was impolite to say so, and no one wished to be disrespectful of a scholarly gentleman with considerable intellectual power, but his concern with a grand theory left many colleagues unmoved. His attention to the consensual processes in society led him, a liberal Midwestern Protestant, to be accused of furthering ideological conformity, when he was doing nothing more or less than the other social scientists at Harvard—describing American society, accurately, as being run from the top down. The increased attention to "area studies" was a response to the imperatives of the Cold War, but did lead to fitful challenges to the myth of our nation's direct descent from Magna Carta.

It was in this setting that the liberal arts colleges which had, somehow, not offered instruction in sociology decided to do so. The simultaneous if dissimilar decisions by Cambridge and Oxford to introduce sociology, at the beginning of the sixties, had an effect difficult to describe precisely, because a rather vague matter of atmosphere and influence. The first college to move was Swarthmore (in 1962), whose president was in close touch with Oxford as the American administrator of the Rhodes Scholarships.

Wesleyan bestirred itself in 1965, finally making a permanent appointment in 1967; Amherst followed in 1968. Williams waited somewhat, and by the time it decided to move, I was at Amherst and asked to advise on the process.

When in the spring of 1968 I talked with colleagues at Amherst, they had a clear idea of what they wanted. They were less interested in the development of a master science of society than in finding someone with a grasp of the present. Talcott Parsons was an Amherst alumnus (he had studied biology and originally intended to become a physician) and was consulted. I did not have the impression that he had been listened to with very great attention. Lewis Coser, then at Brandeis, was asked to come but decided against it. The institution that chose Lewis, the founding editor of *Dissent* along with Irving Howe, from Berlin and then Paris, was clearly open to thinking of me as an alternate. Ely Chinoy, the senior sociologist at Smith College; and the Harvard historian Stuart Hughes, who was an Amherst alumnus, helped a great deal by giving very positive opinions. The colleagues on the committee entrusted with the matter, when I visited them in the spring of 1968, were welcoming. One, Leo Marx (whom I had known somewhat at graduate school) asked whether I really wished to leave New York. I sensed, but of course did not say, that a post at Amherst would make it easier to obtain access to Manhattan's commanding cultural heights.

My faculty colleagues did not make appointments; Amherst's president did: Calvin Plimpton, an internist who had been a dean at Columbia University's medical school, had attended Amherst, and, when he served on a committee to search for a new Amherst president, decided that he was interested in the post. He was half-brother of Francis Plimpton, a New York lawyer and Amherst trustee. When one spoke with Francis, it was clear that he thought himself an owner of the United States, the rest of us figuring variously as day laborers or candidates for entry-level managerial jobs. Calvin was a good deal more subtle, sympathetic to the new diversity in higher education but very skeptical about faculty claims to participate in institutional governance. He was a constitutional monarch in minor questions and an absolute ruler in major ones.

We met at the Century Club, in New York. Cal took notes throughout, a reminder of his earlier calling. He appreciated my scoffing at the scientific pretensions of the social sciences, my disdain for the rigidity of disciplinary boundaries. He had gone from medical school to service as an army physician in Europe, and was interested in my account of the travails of the European universities. He asked almost nothing about my years at London and Oxford, was more attentive to my recollections of general education at Harvard (where he had studied medicine). He said nothing at the end of our talk—except that he hoped I would enjoy meeting with his professors. That visit went well, and one person remained to be seen.

Benjamin DeMott taught English at Amherst, but tackled any subject that interested him. For much of his life, that was American character, culture and society. He was a supremely acute observer of the nation, with a singular combination of insight and reserve about persons. He and I arranged to meet for breakfast at the old Fifth Avenue Hotel, and like Leo Marx, Ben wanted to know whether I really intended to leave New York. "After all," he said, "you know that New York literary crowd." "I would not say that," I replied; "I'd say that I was one of them." That ended whatever internal debate he had, and the job was mine in a few days.

Until Cal called, I did not appreciate what an inner difference the change would make. I felt variously, redeemed, liberated, and secure. To add to my pleasure, New School president John Everett invited me to lunch, asked whether I really wished to leave for Amherst, and said that if tenure was what I wanted, he would instruct my then-colleagues to award it. I declined, with thanks, and turned to other matters.

For one, I worked seriously on the manuscript of what was to become *The Crisis of Industrial Society*. For another, I asked myself what connection, writing apart, I could give with the historical tumult around us: the Columbia student revolt uptown in Manhattan; the murder of Martin Luther King and the urban protests that followed; the French student protest and its immediate sequel; the occupation of offices, factories, and ministries by a large segment of the French labor force; protest in Germany (which set students and a segment of the working class against each other), and finally, the murder of Robert Kennedy. In the meantime, I could indulge nostalgia for a Great Britain I had not quite known: there were conflicts at both the LSE and Oxford.

Despite what I knew of history, and a disinclination dating from my high school days to believe that the normal social condition was order, I was surprised. The rigidified structures that two generations, pre-war and post-war, had railed against were giving way. Chaos and no small amount of violence were evident—but was there any ground for hope? Whatever the long-term aspects of the situation, in the United States the problems of the Vietnam War, of the civil rights movement, of the new feminism, of cultural and social protest in forms in which the exotic and the everyday merged, were elements of an agitated collage. Meanwhile, the impending presidential election and the primary contests drew attention to the political refraction of our cultural and social conflicts.

In March I had gone to a New Universities Conference in Chicago. Some of the participants (uninvited undergraduates, some of the graduate students on the organizing committee) thought that a new beginning required the supersession of the professorial elite. The few professors there objected, and the lines of cleavage became clear. The older participants, and some of the younger ones, voiced a severe critique of the established university and college system's servitudes, but supposed that fidelity to the liberal tradition correctly understood would liberate academic energies for radical education. That, we thought, was true education—an unimpeded critical view of society. The rest were skeptical, argued that notions of higher culture or access to reserved traditions poorly concealed authoritarian attitudes. What were needed were totally new institutions, in which older role distinctions were erased and service to social needs replaced the hermetic routines of scholarship. Few natural scientists were there, but the demands for the priority of practice came from scholars and students in literature as well as in the social sciences. I objected that the priority of practice had brought us universities serving the existing institutions of power: perhaps we could make a contribution to American democracy by thinking about new ways to exercise power, about democratization. The idea of the universities as primary agencies of social change was unsustainable if the rest of society did not move. It was curious that those with the greatest disdain for the university in its actual form thought of it Platonically, as a site where philosophers, kings, guardians, would be joined.

The conference ended with brave resolutions to expand our work to a national network of the like-minded—despite the fact of our profound disagreement. Those years were marked by innumerable projects for groups which would somehow fuse action and thought, ad hoc committees to found journals, newsletters, regional and local meetings, conferences. Much of the rhetoric voiced at these gatherings and in the pages of the literature they produced had to do with immediacy and relevance. The search for connection for a time replaced the intellectuals' classical pre-occupation, the search for meaning. It was a trans-valuation of the old values, detachment and irony making a shamefaced exit, partisanship and passion at the center of the stage.

The new recourse to reality was thoroughly academic. In the New Deal years, academics in large numbers went to the Congress and its staffs, to government agencies, to the courts, engaged in advocacy for interest groups large and small. Their heirs in government and public life were now, precisely, the targets of the sixties academic generation's enmity: they were seen as servants of power. The Great Society project was a last attempt to recruit for government a reform party in the universities, and I encountered its survivors on my infrequent visits to Washington. John Kenneth Galbraith, although actively antagonistic to Johnson as war-maker, at the same time tried to convince Michael Harrington that he should abandon his marginal role as an independent socialist and join the Democratic Party. Harrington considered that his influence depended upon his maintaining distance.

The actual movements for social change were themselves increasingly fragmented, and separate from one another. The revival of feminism was a matter mainly not of a direct legacy but of the independent experience of a new generation, which then discovered its own history. The Afro-American movement was itself culturally, geographically, generationally divided—but separate from its white contemporaries. The consequence of our institutions of racial segregation, perhaps above all in the parts of the country where they were not legal and state enforced, was that black and white persons lacked the experience of working together. Some segments of the political spectrum, and the trade union movement, were exceptions—but division was strong even in the churches. Black and white leaders, when they met, often negotiated with one another as representatives of very different parts of the nation, or more brutally, separate nations. The work of James Baldwin and Ralph Ellison, like that of Richard Wright before them, was widely read by whites—but the social worlds they described were known only through these works. To the tenuous and tortured relationship of blacks to whites were now added the new demands of Latinos.

The black civil rights movement was part of a heightened group consciousness across the nation's cultural and political spectrum. In the Jewish community, the impact of the Eichmann trial was recent. The new Jewish consciousness, contrasting with the assimilationist strivings of an earlier generation, insisted on the uniqueness of the Holocaust, the virtues of the state of Israel, and the rights of American Jews to good seats at the national table with equal fervor. Others, such as Italian-Americans and Southern whites, made themselves known with considerable assertiveness and often no small amount of rancor. I was not prepared for this; I had taken American ethnicity as one of those disturbing facts of life one sought to escape by acting as if a new universalism were possible. It was not the same thing as the nationalisms from which the Europeans were supposedly recovering in my years with them. That is a very condensed way to put a complex European phenomenon—and a striking narrowness of vision in myself after so many years of life in a nation which remained obdurately British, or English.

My language of social description and rhetoric of engagement were resolutely classical. Individuals defined themselves in terms of social categories of a very general kind: nation, class, generation. A very large gap had opened between what I experienced concretely in daily life, from the Bronx to New England, Germany, old England, and France, and the ways in which I thought of history. It enabled me to rise above the enduring accidents of existence. No wonder I was so enthused about Sartre's *Critique de la Raison Dialectique* when I read it shortly after he published it in 1962. It was a theology, complete with soteriology and eschatology—a worthy offspring of Marxism, suitably enlivened by a sense of the duties of the person to humanity which Sartre may have owed to his Alsatian Protestant antecedents.

In any event, the news of the outbreak of revolt in France in May caused me to hurry across the Atlantic to familiar ground. By the time I arrived, events had attained a crescendo and then crashed toward normalcy. With not only universities and schools but factories, firms, and entire government offices occupied, the authority of the state had temporarily collapsed. De Gaulle was isolated in the Élysée Palace but struck back on two fronts. First, he flew to Germany to ascertain the loyalty of General Massu, the commander of French forces there (who as a colonel in Algiers was an accomplished torturer). Massu assured him that he would not hesitate to send troops back to France to suppress civil disorder. (De Gaulle's brief trip occasioned rumors that he had resigned or fled the country.) Secondly, he enlisted the army in France to make its contribution to counter-revolution by ensuring the delivery of gas to closed service stations: M. Dupont, the French Everyman, could drive again and saw no reason, in the circumstances, to think that the government had totally lost its efficacy.

De Gaulle's Prime Minister, Georges Pompidou, called upon another ally of de Gaulle, if one pretending to adversary status, the French Communist Party. The Soviet Union's leaders thought of de Gaulle as a valued if tacit ally in Western Europe, who could be relied upon to do what he could to block excessive American ambitions. In a remarkable speech in Phnom Penh, Cambodia, in 1967 de Gaulle had called upon the US to terminate its wars in the region.

The French Communist leadership was given clear orders. The major French trade union under its control, the CGT, concluded an agreement the government and employers: occupations and strikes would desist, in return for concessions on wages and conditions of work. With the majority of the unionized returning to work, the students, employees and followers of the Left Christian unions were abandoned to their revolutionary rhetoric. Reality was far more complicated, and included a massive counter-demonstration in Paris by de Gaulle's supporters. The Gaullists won decisively in that June's parliamentary elections.

Many of my friends began writing their books on the May revolt before the barricades were removed. I particularly liked the book by Edgar Morin and Claude Lefort, *Mai 68: La Brèche*, and the work by Alain Touraine, *Le Mouvement de Mai ou le communisme utopique*. The great counter-text, equally intelligent, was Raymond Aron's *La Révolution Introuvable*. In two months in Paris, I talked with a great many of the participants and many of the leaders of the revolt—and with some of its critics. The revolt began with students who thought of themselves as, depending upon their choice of political language and self-image, dispossessed proletarians or the vanguard of a new ascendant class. The distinction was echoed, if in densely elaborated ways, by the revolt's sympathetic chroniclers. Aron and the more reflective sceptics, however, insisted on seeing a large element of play acting (and self-deception) in the response of the students to their grievances with the university system. The rapid appearance and no less rapid exit of much of the industrial working class from the revolutionary stage provided the sceptics with the evidence they needed: there was no general crisis of French society but a coming together of separate grievances, intensified by the traditional arrogance of the French elite and excessively dramatized by the revolutionary or rather pseudo-revolutionary phrases which the French Left substituted for thought. The flights of imagination which considered the clashes between police and students another 1789 were not the work of the stolid Communist Party, careful behind its militant slogans to enlarge bit by bit the share of social product available to the workers and government employees in its unions, the sceptics held but the fervid constructions of intellectuals desperately searching for revolutionary agencies in a society which was actually quite effective at containing discontent.

No doubt—but so summary a judgment left open large questions, all of which persist to this day in the industrial democracies. The expansion of universities, without concomitant investment, created truly miserable conditions of overcrowding, and in many fields students rarely if at all had direct contact with their teachers. The connection between curriculum and the occupational opportunities of the educated labor force was haphazard—and at the same time, the tracks that had to be followed to degrees offered very little access to a general culture. The teachers themselves were overburdened, and, if they were conscientious about their teaching, risked negative judgments on their capacity as researchers and scholars. The charge (not unique to France) that the academic system was a *vas clos*, a closed system, oblivious to a changing world, was true—but the administrators and teachers who sought to alter that complained that they were not listened to. I recall participating in the Fouchet reforms initiated in 1965-1966 (named after the then-Minister of Education) which provided for small group instruction. Given the lack of teachers to make that effective, seminars and tutorials were reserved for the better students—making the rest feel even more excluded.

The university's hermetic disorder was one symptom of a larger one—the distance from ordinary experience of many in France's governing elite. They served the public interest, but insisted on defining it by and for themselves. Again, exclusion rather than exploitation was the problem. The secularization of Marxism achieved by some in the unions and any number of academic thinkers eschewed grand schemes of revolution, preferring smaller steps toward participation and self-governance in firms, public and private—and in institutions regulating daily life. Indeed, my Strasbourg colleague Henri Lefebvre called for a transformation of the ordinary routines of existence, a new city organized around a perpetual *fete* or festival. Lefebvre came from rural France, and he brought with him to Paris its alternation of unremitting toil and joyous release.

No doubt the aging patriarch de Gaulle thought in terms of centuries—but a younger generation sought to live in the present. The themes of cultural liberation, experiment, and defiant resistance to authority motivated the young (including the younger workers). Their parents were sympathetic: they did not consider that their prosperity entitled them only to sit in front of their television sets. The revolt of the French younger generation had much in common with the culture of the early sixties in Great Britain and the mocking appropriation of mass culture by the American protesters of the late sixties—across all cultural boundaries.

France's May 1968 drew on national traditions of protest—but the heterogeneous bloc which took to the streets and occupied workplaces lacked the organizational capacity to sustain it. The announcement by Mendès France and Mitterrand that they were ready to assume their responsibilities (in other words, succeed de Gaulle) evoked derision: how could the exponents of routine politics suppose that they had the capacity to lead a national rupture with routine? They interpreted the protest as a rejection of de Gaulle's theatrical recreation of Bonapartism, but it was precisely the technocratic aspect of Gaullism that was under attack.

The events of four decades ago are now matter for historians, and sober reflection is much easier now than then. I went to Paris on my own initiative and when I arrived, I enjoyed the excitement of the meetings, their enchanting spontaneity—but it was clear that politically, the movement was disoriented. Increasing numbers of citizens wanted a return to routine: the perpetual *Kermesse* (popular festival) did not strike them as a suitable mode of governance. The revolutionaries returned to routine themselves, but in an altered world. As the memory of rupture faded, so did conflicting accounts of what had happened. The political camps agreed on the Left's lack of organizational preparedness, but the separate parties to the adventures of May did not suppose that improved or perfected organization was what they needed.

It became clear to the more reflective that they were living in an unknown country. The changes in French society since 1945 were so profound that neither skilled opposition nor coherent governance were possible. Even de Gaulle's return to power in 1958, his retention of it ten years later, owed as much to opportunity as to his great flair for seizing control of events. De Gaulle, with his instinct for national historical continuities, was freed by that for the ruthless exercise of power. No wonder he enjoyed the loyalty of an otherwise disordered coalition, in which embittered traditionalists and aggressive modernizers shared power. Indeed, some of the leading Gaullists were both.

What bothered the 1968 revolutionaries was a profound perception that they could admit only with difficulty and, if they did, were usually unable to work through it: the people in their several forms and segments, were not revolutionary.

They were attached to the revolutionary tradition as an adornment of the past, were even ready to participate in modern versions of the never-ending series of French *Jacqueries* (sudden risings by the peasants over particular grievances, dissipating as quickly as they had come). The French still, then, referred to political divisions as matters of *familles politiques* (political families). They were not alone advocates and defenders of particular social interests; they were repositories of memories and cultures.

De Gaulle's strength was that he combined traditions, across class and regional and religious boundaries. He understood governance. He had been an early advocate of a technological conception of warfare despite the resistance of his superiors. He knew how to lead a nation largely *petite bourgeois* into adventures—and when to lead them out. His distance, infuriating to the protesters of 1968, was not an expression of contempt for the citizenry but an acknowledgement that they understood the division of political labor. They would vote and the government would do much of the rest. That contradicted the Left's conviction of the enlargement of possibilities for institutional participation in the new economy. One of the editors of the vanguard publication *Socialisme ou Barbarie* said that the streets full of demonstrators made him wish to convene the editorial board to tell them, *c'est tout vrai* (it is all true).

It was not, and the long march through the institutions that awaited the generation of 1968 has by now exhausted many of them. There were distinct and lasting changes made under the Mitterrand presidency (1981-1995) and the Jospin prime ministership (1997-2002). The persons who brought these about, and their party, have since been submerged by the crisis of capitalism they always evoked—but are unable to confront with hope and vision.

In 1968, I also crossed the Rhine into Germany, where protest was concentrated in the universities. Its aims and messages were mixed. The Social Democrats under Willy Brandt had accepted a subordinate position in a coalition with the Christian Democratic Union and its Bavarian sister party, the Christian Social Union, under the chancellorship of a former Nazi official, Kurt Georg Kiesinger. The working-class Social Democratic voters sought no cultural revolution, and were more concerned (some of the trade unionists excepted) with higher incomes, lifetime employment and secure retirement than with the democratization of German society. The active intelligentsia, led by Brandt's friend Günter Grass, wanted democratization, and some of the new Social Democratic Ministers with the most pronounced critical profiles (Horst Ehmke, Erhard Eppler, Hans Matthöfer) were struggling for it. Another group led by Helmut Schmidt favored a systematic compromise with capitalism, a model with nineteenth-century origins, and considered the Federal German Republic's adherence to the alliance with the US a priority.

Many reflective Protestants (and some of the beleaguered adherents of the ecclesiastical and theological innovations of the Second Vatican Council in a resolutely immobile German Catholic Church) held that expiation for the past imposed upon Germany a very different role in Europe, and an obligation to pursue co-existence with the Soviet Union and the Eastern European Communist states, above all Czechoslovakia and Poland. Meanwhile, the German Communist state, unapologetic about its authoritarianism and repressiveness, insisted that it was the legitimate heir of resistance to Nazism and ceaselessly demanded of the West German government what it refused to concede—recognition of its sovereignty. The inextricable connection of domestic to foreign policy in a West German state that was still occupied, but which possessed the North Atlantic Treaty Organization's most formidable army, converted every argument over NATO and foreign policy into a debate on Germany's past, present, and future. Conducted with much more discretion and often in coded language, a similar debate was being held in the Communist German state. To refer to it was, in the West, an expression of dissidence since it denied a central element in its (increasingly uncertain) consensus—the impossibility of change from within in the other German state.

Youth revolt characterized the movements of the sixties everywhere—and accounted for the huge demands, the mocking gestures, the driven intensity of much of the protest. In every country, however, a senior contingent gave a different voice to the movement. In Germany, however, generational protest was most acute. Jürgen Habermas declared that the rhetoric and tactics of the student revolt were decidedly not "generationally neutral." The matter was deeper than the construction of a temporary stage set to be changed when the cast grew older. In the United States, the Democrats were charged with brutal betrayal of the New Deal legacy; in the United Kingdom, Labour was accused of a loss of the will to reform; in France, the Communists and the Socialists were charged with allying themselves with the technocratic elite. When in 1969 Italy's *l'autunno caldo* (hot autumn) erupted, the Communists were denounced for their explicit elaboration of the "historical compromise" proposed by their sagacious leader, Enrico Berlinguer. In Germany, two ascendant generations were accused: the grandparents (and many of the parents) were criticized for collaborating with varying degrees of intensity with Nazism, with refusal to confront their collective and individual pasts, and with hypocritical adherence to the forms and not the substance of democracy.

The post-war generation in Germany was rejected for its defects of passion. It had installed itself too comfortably in state and social institutions reconstructed, with moral slovenliness, on older lines. The evocation of academic robes by the critical students was telling: "Beneath the robes, the musty odor of a thousand years" was their slogan. Some of their seniors, the very few authentic anti-Nazis and a number of the returned émigrés, were given certificates of authenticity, the others condemned *en masse*. Clashes with the trade union leadership and the many Social Democrats were inevitable: they declined to distance themselves from a working class which was extremely disinclined to criticize a state in which it enjoyed prosperity. The protest generation was especially concerned with the narcotic effects, the distracting infantilism, of consumer culture — without being able to say what could or should replace it.

In Germany, I visited protest meetings and universities, gave interviews, and wrote for a few of the newspapers. My interlocutors were generally the more intellectual leaders of the movement, not street activists such as the younger Joschka Fischer. At a symposium in New York in 1968, Habermas spoke and Arendt commented, at length. I had the honor of serving as chair. Arendt declared that the movement in Germany had something new, a decided spontaneity and impulsiveness, even humor. She cited a demonstration on the *Kurfürstendamm* in West Berlin in which the students had carried a coffin from which a skeleton emerged to protest the possibility of nuclear war. The older German movements, with their endless dogmatic quarrels and wearying writings, would never have been capable, she said, of so direct a statement. In the audience, someone insistently demanded the floor, eventually gaining it and introducing himself as a member of the committee that had prepared the Berlin event. "I can assure Professor Arendt," he said, "that the coffin and skeleton were the results of three days of systematic theoretic discussion." In Germany it struck me that no one had time for that sort of exercise: everyone seemed to be in a hurry, everywhere on the political spectrum. Yet the hard outlines of Germany's geopolitical situation, the balance of internal social forces, were set. Much of the debate was about how to define a condition that could not be wished away.

I spoke at Helmut Schelsky's Institute of Sociology, at the University of Munster, on the American and European movements and earned the master's praise: I had called things by their name. Actually, I cast much doubt on the revolutionary, as opposed to the disruptive, potential of the movements, and argued that sooner or later the protesters with all their energy and some of their ideas would be struggling to re-join in some way the regular political processes they spurned. It was a period in which I had little direct contact with Labour, the French Socialists, the Italian Communists and Socialists, or the German Social Democrats. That was to change, very emphatically, in the decade ahead. In the fall of 1968, when I wrote a longish essay on these matters for *The Nation*, I emphasized the ways in which the movements would change, or had changed, regular politics by raising doubts about the legitimacy and viability of the post-war welfare state settlement in Western Europe and the US.

I wrote that the Western movements had quite independent counterparts in the Soviet bloc, and that the possibilities of change there were as least as great. That was an extremely free translation of a strain of analysis which was not suppressed in the Soviet bloc, being framed in the language of the immanent development of the relations of production under socialism. What our colleagues and comrades there said more openly in conversation was that the several Communist parties' domination could not last. They called upon them to use their advantages, such as a view of politics which began with economic and social analysis in a way that would maximize the opportunities for their citizens of developing their cultural and social development. Instead, the parties insisted that their revolutions were already achieved, pronounced themselves those revolutions' only possible guardians, and refused to discuss what was obvious not only to the well-educated and well-traveled scholars in their academies but to many of their citizens (or subjects): their revolutionary rhetoric was used to justify their privileges. During the most conflictual phase of the West Berlin protests, the German Communist officials dealing with the west insisted that it was West Berlin's obligation to stop the demonstrations since these were a threat to order in the entire city.

Writing about these problems now lends my thoughts a balanced and ordered sequence they did not have then. In August

1968 I traveled with my daughters to the island of Korčula, between Split and Dubrovnik. The occasion was the annual conference organized by the Croatian Society of Philosophy. The island was full of Czech tourists, enjoying the freedom of travel instituted by the new Communist regime, intent on giving substance to Dubcek's slogan, "Socialism with a Human Face." The conference that year attracted some interesting thinkers, quite apart from our Yugoslav hosts: Ernst Bloch, Tom Bottomore, Iring Fetscher, Lucien Goldmann, Jürgen Habermas, Ágnes Heller, and Herbert Marcuse were among them. The students who came had participated in protests in France, Germany, and Yugoslavia itself.

The Yugoslavs were divided. *Vjesnik*, the newspaper published in Zagreb by the Croatian Communist Party, did a sympathetic interview with Marcuse; *Borba*, published in Belgrade by the Serbian party, criticized him severely. The event apparently impressed someone in Washington as important, since a younger Foreign Service officer from the consulate in Zagreb turned up. If he was a CIA officer, he deserved high marks for disguise, since his conversation suggested a quite extraordinary naïveté and rather little knowledge of the conflicts in the Marxist camp.

There was a certain amount of local color. Korčula was also a resort much used by West Germans, and one morning after the overnight boat from Rijeka had discharged its passengers, they made their way to the beach of the Hotel Park. I heard one of them, who had the bearing of a minor civil servant, announce with considerable emphasis to his wife, *Endlich sind wir den Studentrummel los* ("Finally, we are free of all that student noise"). She had obviously seen Marcuse on German TV, or recognized him from the front covers of *Spiegel* and *Stern*: "Isn't that Marcuse over there?" Indeed it was; she had pointed to Marcuse being listened to by a group of students.

One of that group told me that when they protested at Belgrade University, Tito had sent a message to the effect that he was in solidarity with them. It did not take much time, he said, before they realized that as president of the Republic, he proposed to do nothing about their university grievances or more general critique of the limits of expression imposed by the regime. The students told their French counterparts that the security forces had been sent to the factories to prevent their getting in to speak with the workers. "Just the function taken over by the Communist unions in our country," was a French response. With no evident help from their foreign visitors, the Yugoslav students one night literally painted the town red. "Revolution!" and a pointed "Down with the Red Bourgeoisie!" were to be seen as we made our way to the town cafe for mid-morning coffee. The mayor, a rotund Dalmatian, was beside himself. I knew him from previous visits and offered modest consolation. "After all, Mr. Mayor, everyone knows that Yugoslavia is a socialist country." "Yes, but think of the tourists: why remind them?"

It was intelligent of the regime to allow the event. Its position between the blocs had clearly convinced its political rulers that there was little danger in allowing intellectuals to talk with one another, and some prestige to be gained from ostentatious openness. When in the midst of our discussions we learned of the Warsaw Pact's invasion of Czechoslovakia, we were sober, indeed somber. Our hastily formulated declaration of solidarity with the Czechs did not force the Soviet tanks to evacuate Prague—and Johnson's respect for the rules of the Cold War, which precluded intervention, was something we had to accept: no one wished for nuclear confrontation in Europe.

We were brutally returned to all of our doubts. Did our values matter in a world of iron facts? The professorial sympathizers with the student revolt, everywhere, were afraid of losing something precious—a direct and honest view of things untarnished by cynicism and tiredness. The critics thought that we were deficient in our intellectual duty, which was to insist on the newer generation's many illusions. The difficulty was, it was easy to do that when one refrained from criticizing one's own. The assumption of the indefinite continuation of the exquisite stalemate that defined the Western political equilibrium was one illusion; ferocious anti-Communism was another. The West was threatened neither militarily nor politically by the Soviet bloc, and its inner tensions (on the very arguments of the anti-Communists) would in the end prove insurmountable. That left us in a large historical space which we did not know how to occupy. Still, the Warsaw Pact occupation of Czechoslovakia, and television images of the Chicago police attack on protesters at the Democratic National Convention, reminded us of the frailty of ideas.

At ten and eight, my daughters were not ready to worry about these matters at Korčula. They enjoyed talking with my friends, were humorous and insightful about their more obvious failings, and made other friends readily at the beach. They were also excellent travel companions—always curious about new surroundings, and able to extract from almost any situation some measure of pleasure as well as a bit of instruction. We went to Zürich, where their mother met them, and I traveled back to Paris. It was returning to an unsteady normalcy, in which old routines and new doubts competed bitterly. The victors did not trust their good fortune; the disappointed revolutionaries sought new strategies, and the struggles migrated from the streets to endless meetings, symposia and thousands of pages of print. One sardonic critic of the protest movement, Raymond Aron, in his book about the episode termed it *La Révolution Introuvable* (*The Revolution That Could Not Be Found*). In emphasizing the role of memory (the re-enactment of the French revolutionary tradition) and imagination (the demand for a real utopia), he was in unintended agreement with some of the May movement's most ardent voices. It was a revolution in the superstructure, in a society in which the received Marxist notion of base and superstructure no longer applied. It was in this superstructure—the culture of daily life, and primary social relationships, and in the inner lives of persons—that class relations took actual form. The humans tending the machinery of production and administration could not be defined solely by their occupational tasks; they sought to construct (or move to) social spaces in which they were at home.

The European movements of the sixties put an end to the analysis of the "Americanization" of Europe—if "Americanization" meant a society of consumption in which class domination was discreetly modified and as discreetly accepted. The Europeans, apparently, had rediscovered their own traditions of criticism and protest. They also discovered that there was something positive to be learned from the United States—the idea of citizenship which descended from the English Revolution of the seventeenth century and the Country Party of the eighteenth, the notion of freedom from strict obedience to hierarchy and fixed canons of order.

My first two years back in the United States were full, and no little confused, and spent struggling to move from the margins of events and society. The difficulty, as I now see, is that in the agitated collage of American culture it was increasingly unclear what was central, what peripheral. When I returned in the fall of 1968, it was to an ostensibly much more integrated position. Faculty at Amherst were *ex officio* members of the ruling intellectual elite—if one which was torn by the conflict of clans and gnawing ideological and moral doubts.

Before leaving New York, once again, for New England I spoke at the Socialist Scholars Conference. George Fischer had been instrumental in reviving it and it attracted a broad group of participants (many natural scientists and some physicians too), many of them not only talented but accomplished and well known. Where, however, could we go with our newly awakened or reawakened great expectations? The murders of King and Kennedy, the violence of the Chicago police, extreme racial polarization everywhere, were evidence for the destruction of normal politics. The system, to use the language of the time, could not contain its inner contradictions. No doubt, but we were paid to go to our classrooms—and quite free to say what we liked to the young and a larger public. Our more stolid colleagues insisted that we were responsible for much of the turmoil. They attributed a great deal more certainty to us (and more influence) than we thought we possessed. It was unfortunate that we were so strenuously opposed: it provided us with what we had good reason to doubt—a sense that we counted for something.

12

Amherst

I WENT to Amherst in the fall of 1968 with a large and pleasant sense of anticipation, and my early years there justified it. Administration, faculty and students were welcoming; I experienced for the first time in a long while a sense of connection. The Five College setting lent density and variety to daily life. It was a period in which, in any case, national and even international concerns drew the college out of itself. New York was not far, and a steady stream of academic, cultural and political visitors traveled to what was anything but a traditional college town. Ours was a privileged enclave within a town occupied by a large state university. In western Massachusetts, we thought of ourselves as an outer suburb of Cambridge, or even New York, and free to exercise vanguard functions.

Ten years later, at the end of my time there, I felt differently. The excitements of the sixties and early seventies had gone, and the college had returned to routine. Routine meant a certain insistence on the uniqueness of our educational mission, and a great deal of attention to the details of curricular and extracurricular college life. The younger faculty who had come in the sixties was certainly critical, and were a remarkably interesting set of people - including, for the first time, a number of women. However, each of them had to pay attention to their careers, and so they formed a latent rather than active faculty bloc.

I now see how I was regarded as sympathetic elder brother, or maybe, even if it's painful to say, aging uncle. My obstreperous sallies at faculty meetings, and even more at my parties with interesting visitors, were greatly appreciated by the young. That made life at Amherst bearable - no, pleasant. It did not compensate, however, for my increasing sense that I was living in a distant suburb with poor transportation facilities to the metropolis. In the end, my decision to leave Amherst was not a rupture, and certainly not accompanied by resentment; it was rather a regretful matter, like the end of a marriage that had exhausted its possibilities.

Much has been written on the nation's liberal arts colleges. Amherst was distinctive in its institutional conviction, internalized by our students with unquestioning intensity in their very first weeks of residence, that it was a very important place. We were joined to Harvard, Princeton, and Yale in the belief that we had the responsibilities of leadership. That consisted, in Amherst's self-depiction, of a mixture of critical detachment and commitment to *res publicae*, a fusion of devotion to higher things and responsiveness to national needs (as interpreted by Amherst, prepared to delegate nothing to other moral authorities in the nation). This was of course a legacy of the theological tradition of a Calvinist college, founded in 1821 by teachers and students who left Williams in a doctrinal dispute. Amherst at the time favored a very energetic missionary policy. It has indeed graduated many educators, public servants, pastors who thought of their callings in Biblical terms. Much of that stringency, if in secular form, was in the air still when I arrived.

That posed a problem. Many Amherst graduates went into business and the professions. They may have done good, but they certainly did well. An inexpungible tension marked the history of the college—between a very positive attitude to the goods of this world, and attempts, small and large, to change it. By the time I came, the college's religion was the diffuse secular humanism of critical inquiry, embedded in an historical account of the nation which greatly flattered Amherst. Its destiny was to serve. That included the pedagogues, professionals and theologians among its graduates, but also the entrepreneurs and politicians. Calvin Coolidge was the one Amherst graduate who had occupied the White House. The most prominent public figure among its alumni in 1968 was the chair of the board of trustees, John J. McCloy—frequently thought of as general secretary of our power elite.

The Amherst graduates I knew best before joining it were friends at Harvard. One was my teacher, Talcott Parsons, especially generous with me despite my own rebelliousness. Talcott was the

In my study in Amherst, wearing a favorite Italian shirt I purchased when consulting with the Italian trade unions and the Communist Party. I always got myself stylish shirts in Italy, which were much-envied by my then-friend, Norman Podhoretz.

son of a Calvinist missionary to Japan who later became the president of a small Ohio college, Marietta. Another was a fellow tutor at Adams House, the poet Richard Wilbur. The third was the critical historian of Europe H. Stuart Hughes. Leo Marx, whom I had known slightly at Harvard, was on the faculty. I recalled his rejection of a Fulbright professorship in the UK to protest the Vietnam War, and recalled too as I was considering the appointment, a much publicized demonstration against Robert McNamara by teachers and students when he was awarded an honorary degree in 1966.

Amherst had known academic and political controversy well before the 1960s. In 1924, Alexander Meiklejohn was forced out of the presidency and went to Chicago with his great books program. Alumni and faculty conservatism, trustee dismay at his independence, and a large measure of student discontent combined to nullify his attempted curricular reforms. His opponents were defending a muscularly Christian college, where one could achieve enough intellectually to merit gentlemanly status but not so much as to raise too many questions, against innovations which promised only unknown troubles. Perhaps, however, these were not so unknown: the cultural turbulence of the US after World War I threatened received cultural conventions and thought patterns.

The American colleges and universities of the twenties, thirties, and early forties did not have a uniform culture. The larger state universities, the urban institutions, and privileged places such as Amherst all responded differently to the changes in American society brought about by mass culture and consumption, the presence of Catholic and Jewish immigrants, and the social turmoil engendered by the Great Depression. Amherst adhered to a canon of American culture derived from Calvinistic New England, socialized its students in an ethos of personal advancement, character and social responsibility—and allowed some faculty to introduce carefully measured dosages of the newer American realities. Williams, especially in the social sciences but in literature as well, was more open to the New Deal.

That changed after the war, when Charles Cole became president. He was an Amherst graduate, a historian of French political economy who had taught at Columbia. With the manners of a gentleman, he brought to Amherst some of the intellectual drive of Columbia, its creative alternation of the cultural intensity of New York with the patrician traditions of what had been founded as King's College. (I was about to write "immigrant New York," but then recalled that much of New York's vitality came from persons from elsewhere in the US seeking their futures in the city.) The academic icon of the university when Cole left it was certainly the Vermonter John Dewey. He was followed by Richard Hofstadter of Buffalo and C. Wright Mills from Texas, whose contemporaries were indeed two New Yorkers of recent immigrant descent, Meyer Schapiro and Lionel Trilling. Cole brought different sorts of teachers to Amherst. They were no doubt scholars and gentlemen, but they valued scholarship (and scientific research) as something more than a gentlemanly pursuit. Living by their own wits (true not only of the new Jewish contingent in the faculty but of their colleagues) they thought their task as educators was to form reflective citizens. The genteel tradition at Amherst was resolutely transformed, and became itself the object of inquiry. A new building reflected the nationalization of the scientific disciplines, a closer relationship between the larger centers of research and their graduates on our faculty. Resident artists, musicians, theatrical creators, writers, and a well-endowed visiting program enabled the college to move out of aesthetic appreciation into artistic production itself.

Inherited forms of curricular organization could not contain or convey these energies. A new curriculum was devised which required of students some very rigorous introductory courses in the basic fields of inquiry. As these changed, however, the new curriculum itself was deemed old. It was replaced by requiring students to take inter-disciplinary introductions in the clusters of learning, termed "Problems of Inquiry." The relentless self-interrogation of contemporary learning was common to an intellectually diverse faculty. They were freer of disciplinary constraints, by and large, than their teachers in the graduate schools—and free to innovate pedagogically in deciding what our students would do well to learn. The students accepted the preceptorial role of the faculty with as much grace as they could muster. Doing well at college entailed, not least, claiming junior membership in the fraternity of learning. Doing well meant access to the straight if narrow road to graduate and professional schools, or to starred entry-level posts in business. There were Amherst undergraduates who experimented after college with occupational eccentricity, but it was not until the late sixties that they found themselves—to the astonishment of their elder siblings and their teachers—serving as role models.

Meanwhile, the New England colleges were considering what to do about sociology. The discipline was well established at the larger Ivy institutions, but for a variety of reasons the Little Three - Amherst, Wesleyan and Williams - had been reluctant to invite sociologists to their faculties. Some traditionalists feared the discipline's supposed moral relativism, although at Amherst they could have been reassured by the notion of consensus fundamental to the theory of society propounded by their distinguished graduate, Talcott Parsons. Some modernists thought the opposite: sociology's search for invariant laws ignored what was conflictual, creative, in human existence.

Many scholars in history and some in political science thought of sociologists as high priests of the obvious, rephrasing banalities as if they were profundities. Others considered that they took account of what was useful to them in the writing of the sociologists and they did not need reinforcement. When I arrived at Amherst, the library certainly did have a great many of the discipline's important texts. In the end, however, what Harvard, Princeton and Yale failed to do, Cambridge and Oxford accomplished: their example impelled the Little Three to institute departments of sociology. Once the ancient British universities put sociology into their undergraduate curricula, New England concluded that it ought not to lag behind the mother country. What we actually did at Oxford, and indeed my adventure and misadventure there, interested my Amherst colleagues rather little. They were clear that they wanted a colleague able to converse across the disciplines, not someone who would tell them that they were methodologically deficient. My first public performance at Amherst, a talk to the daily college assembly at chapel in the late spring, guaranteed a friendly reception: I spoke of sociology as historical commentary and political philosophy.

Amherst had a Department of Anthropology, headed by Donald Pitkin, and I agreed that sociology should be incorporated in a renamed Department of Anthropology and Sociology. Donald was a Harvard graduate of the wartime Class of 1944, a descendant of both a Bunker Hill combatant and the Harvard progressivism of the late New Deal years. He had resided in and studied an Italian village which, as it became more prosperous, voted ever more Communist. He was not only a shrewd and helpful colleague but a discerning and warm human being, a widower and the devoted father of two small children. Another anthropologist was Alan Babb, who had studied an Indian village and was especially interested in the extraordinary complexity of Hinduism. He had a detached and ironic eye for the foibles of our own academic village with its religion of rationality. The third anthropologist was Fred Errington, who left the department to return in the enviable role of husband of his successor, Deborah Gewertz. Deborah was one of the early women recruits to the Amherst faculty, and brought to the male student body and mainly male faculty a superb self-confidence and a knowing eye. No one could intimidate her because no one dared try.

Daughter Anna reading the paper in our kitchen in Amherst.

Daughters Anna (standing) and Antonia, Amherst 1976

I owed and owe much to many colleagues at Amherst, but to no one more than Jan Dizard. Jan was teaching at Berkeley when I met him and was in charge of placing graduate students in jobs. I was there searching for a promising candidate for an assistant professorship and gathered that he wished to place himself at Amherst - a promising idea which appears even better nearly fifty years later. Jan had been an undergraduate at the Duluth campus of the University of Minnesota, and studied for a doctorate at the University of Chicago. He raised dogs and hunted, snowshoed, had environmental passions and knew the American working class. Talking about our decision to invite him to Amherst, President Plimpton was very complimentary. "It is very broad of you, as a New York intellectual with European ties, to suggest this authentic Midwesterner as your first appointment." I ascertained that the President had indeed mailed his offer, before telling him that his parents had been such stalwarts of the Communist Party in Minnesota that they attracted the enmity of Hubert Humphrey, who in pursuit of the presidency voiced an anti-Communism undistinguishable from that of the least reflective of politicians. That, too, was a moment in our national history it profited our students to learn of.

I was right, even in the open atmosphere of the sixties, to exercise a bit of caution. As the turbulence of the decade reached Amherst, some alumni who clearly had not profited fully from their educations blamed faculty radicalism for disturbing a college which otherwise would have remained tranquil. One Trustee, Eustace Seligman, a lawyer from Cromwell and Sullivan, the firm that had been graced by John Foster Dulles, was said to have described Leo Marx and myself as "Communists" despite lacking the format to speak with us directly. The chair of the board, the formidable John J. McCloy, was not so hesitant: in a public statement he deplored the protection tenure gave to Amherst's professors, above all the "dead wood" among them. My colleagues were exceedingly vexed; President William Ward publicly differed with the chairman, and I published my own reply. The American ruling class, I wrote, whose actual general secretary was McCloy, was conspicuous for three things. It was incompetent: who else could win an empire and set about, as in Vietnam, losing it? It was murderously hypocritical. And finally, unlike its British counterparts, it lacked manners and style: one did not usually insult those one wished to have as diligent servants. McCloy was furious, asked Ward to obtain an apology from me, was told that the President was sure that that would be impossible—and resigned as chair a bit later on.

In fact, Amherst's teachers were very devoted to their calling, and often very good scholars. Many helped their students grow up. McCloy's seedy arrogance was the mark of a striver who did not quite manage to become a gentleman. Other trustees, in this respect, were better and finer. I enjoyed the company of my colleagues. With some, I felt a special affinity. Tom Yost was a politically engaged biologist. Later president of the American Association of University Professors, he had maintained contacts with Soviet colleagues to help them in the terrible years in which the Stalinist fraud Lysenko ruled Soviet biology. I recall a meeting between faculty and students at which the faculty radicals were charged with systematic dishonesty. We had tenure, lived in comfortable college houses, and had no revolutionary credibility. I suspect that the fact that we were parents did not improve our images, but that was unsaid. Tom listened and then declared, "You should know that Professor Birnbaum and I have been thrown out of better places than you could get into." Tom was right, since my experience at Oxford was paralleled by his at Johns Hopkins.

Lot of persons come to mind when I think of my Amherst colleagues, who tolerated my overly developed egocentricity, I suppose, since they felt I connected them with realms (from Berlin to New York) they did not know. The faculty's other striking characters, however, stand out. Benjamin DeMott did not need me to introduce him to national intellectual life, in which he was a prominent participant. Leo Marx bridged, with very great elegance and even more sobriety, the forties and the sixties; George Kateb was a political philosopher of great erudition, with a baseball fan's appreciation of the finer points of the game of politics. Bill and Jane Taubman, travelers to the USSR, were searching for the red thread that would lead from the Soviet present to a more open future. Lewis Mudge and I had Europe in common, as he had been a theologian at the World Presbyterian Alliance in Geneva. Younger colleagues appreciated my rebelliousness, and I certainly appreciated their support and company—and what they taught me of the American generation that had matured when I was in Europe.

Generational succession and its inevitable accompaniment, antagonism, has concerned historians for some time. Now it has been supplanted by inquiry into memory. What do I recall of our students as they were when I arrived? The oldest had been born when I graduated from college in 1947, the youngest during the Korean War. They had been children under Eisenhower and adolescents under Kennedy. They brought to Amherst, when asked about it, a good deal of familial experience. Some were children or grandchildren of immigrants; others had endured the strains of internal migration across class and ethnic barriers. They were not often asked about it, although as themes of class became more salient in national discussion in the late sixties and early seventies, more and more seemed to be thinking about their origins—and how to reconcile acknowledging their families' pasts with their own futures.

The Amherst I recalled from my own days at Williams seemed to be a rather monotone place, peopled by polite young men earnestly seeking to meet their elders' expectations. Whether preparing for business or the professions, they were spiritually content to occupy the better seats in the national stadium—and did so with a visible sense of entitlement made possible by an ostentatious lack of self-consciousness. Their successors (including their own sons) were much more worried. They need not have been, with respect to careers. True, they were about to enter a competitive marketplace and face challenges from women, African-Americans, and Latinos, that their fathers had not faced—although the fathers (unlike their grandfathers) had had to deal with the newly unrestricted energies of Jewish contemporaries. Admission to Amherst was *prima facie* evidence that one was a good candidate for advancement.

Our students had every reason to believe that they would do very well, but they were beset by anxiety regardless. A great many had the need to justify themselves; others felt the need to fulfill themselves. Lionel Trilling has described the revolts of the sixties as "modernism in the streets," and while Amherst lacked New York's streets, the students had difficult inner landscapes to traverse. I'm reminded of one who told me he disliked coming to speak with me in office hours, since that made him feel he was not unique. Our students wanted recognition—somewhat before treatises on it were staples of political philosophy. That had an effect which greatly increased the inner and outer workloads of faculty. We were surrogates for not only parents but for much of the rest of the world. Ignoring how little we counted for in the national elite (we were not Harvard or MIT professors with Washington connections), our students were eager for our approval.

Since we lived, or claimed to live, by our scholarly swords, the students thought it necessary to develop devotion to scholarly combat. Our departments of the arts, the theater, and writing provided space for the aesthetic, the laboratories for the scientific, and the rest of us were confronted by the passions, however temporary, of aspirants to the status of intellectuals. I am uncertain of the numbers, but I suppose that at least six of ten of our students at least temporarily joined the church of culture. The others were autonomous enough, for whatever reasons, to keep their distances—and presented us with much easier pedagogic tasks. For them, we had only to present a defined body of knowledge or a set of texts, provide some modest help in dealing with it, and move on. For the others, we were engaged in the much more difficult business of the cure of souls, a project with no limits and one made the more difficult by our own inner struggles. We had good reason to fear that the more we revealed of these, the less authority we would have. Yet if we did not act as if we were revealing something of ourselves, we were likely to be taxed with snobbish indifference or even disdain for our students. No wonder our faculty included large number of involuntary thespians, trying not to have to pour out their hearts entirely in the classroom or during office hours, but constructing plausible roles they could adopt before leaving the campus for a well-earned drink.

It is rather simple to write in this way this many years later, but the insights are rather late ones. At the time, I was quite prepared to accept ordination from my students and, indeed, my colleagues. I presented myself as a missionary from Europe and New York and the higher spheres of culture generally, who would provide them with a sophisticated and multi-colored equivalent of Mao's little red book, a manual for high-toned revolution—unwritten but to be found between the lines of my course syllabi.

In fact, I had to design a two-course introductory sequence. The first was an introduction to modern sociological thought intended to be consonant with what the students would later learn in studying the history of political philosophy. I had an inspiration which I still like: some years later, I set them, at the beginning, to reading Daniel Bell's book *The Coming of Post-Industrial Society* and its ostensible antipode, Herbert Marcuse's *One-Dimensional Man*. We then began to read in the history of sociological thought. We began with Rousseau's *The Social Contract*, and continued with Saint-Simon, Marx, Maine, Spencer, Tönnies, Weber, and Durkheim. I argued, rightly, that sociology was a commentary on industrial society and not a project encompassing all of human existence. One question was: if Bell and Marcuse were so new, how come so many of their ideas were anticipated by their nineteenth- and early twentieth-century predecessors. (Later, I experimented by putting Nietzsche's *The Genealogy of Morals* and Freud's *Civilization and Its Discontents* on the list. It was difficult to integrate Freud in the sequence. Most likely, the fusion of genres of description of western civilization and criticism of it posed problems that stretched the resources even of our very intelligent students. The effort certainly stretched mine, even if I could not admit it at the time.)

The second course dealt with the current problems of industrial society, and I emphasized class division and class conflict. Initially, I thought that I would take an international view—including Western Europe and perhaps something on the state socialist societies. I decided to be more cautious, in view of the fact that most students had little knowledge or experience of Europe. I concentrated on the United States, and that was difficult enough: the more uncritical students were unable to accept that exploitation was a permanent element in the American experience; the radical ones could not understand why it had not been swept away. I made a point at the beginning by noting that some of the students were offspring of alumni and that might have made it easier for the college to have found reasons to admit them. The class, I continued, should understand that I welcomed a conflict of views in discussion and each and every student was free to express himself. However, I would appreciate it if those who had been especially privileged in this way would think twice before strenuous advocacy of the position that we were a meritocratic society. I may have done them an injustice: in the new American meritocracy, social inheritance brought many to the starting line, but thereafter, they had to fight for advancement.

To these introductory courses I added more advanced ones on matters such as the politics of industrial society, modern social thought, and Marxism. This last attracted under the Five College arrangement quite a few students from Hampshire, Mount Holyoke, and Smith, and a few from the University of Massachusetts. The university had lots of first-generation college students, and most were reluctant to take advantage of the possibility of taking courses with us—or the other private institutions. Our students were quite friendly to these visitors from another social world—but obvious differences in language and manners inhibited both sides. As for the visitors from the women's colleges, they were generally reticent in class discussion, but at the end produced course and examination papers at least as good and often better than those of the more vocal young men. Reticence was hardly the most visible characteristic of the Hampshire students, men and women. They were inveterately outspoken, often critical, demanding of their teachers' time—and frequently mercurial.

Hampshire opened in 1969. One of its students was Arthur Samuelson, who campaigned for academic work on the Holocaust when the field was, if not dormant, at a very early stage. Arthur became a prominent publisher. Arthur frequently dropped by to talk and we became friends. He enrolled in one of my courses, dropped it, and came back at the end. Months later he asked me to give him a "Pass" grade for what he described, with considerable exaggeration, as his "work" in the course. I responded that Amherst did not use that grade, but that if we did, I would definitely have to give him a "Fail" on account of his very intermittent attendance. Not at all discouraged, Arthur asked for a letter to be put in his file, since Hampshire also assembled student dossiers. I offered to let him see the letter, then decide whether he wanted it. The text ran, roughly, as follows:

> Mr. Samuelson was initially a student in my seminar, 'Ideas and History.' After a few weeks, he informed me that the reading did not 'speak' to him and suggested that I change it. Since the reading included Aristotle, Plato, and Augus-

tine, I suggested that it might profit him to persist and noted that I saw no reason to alter the list. He promptly withdrew, to return without formality for the last few meetings. He spent much of that time whispering to a very good student from Smith College but I am glad to report that he did not interfere with her successful completion of the course. He now tells me that the course was 'a great intellectual experience.' I am unable to evaluate what is, in the circumstances, an astonishing assertion and pass this note on to Hampshire College for such use as can be made of it.

Arthur pronounced the letter "much better than nothing" and took it for his dossier.

My pedagogic goals at Amherst were shaped by European example. I used sociology as a bridge to modern social thought and presented social research in its selection of theme and language as a form of political commentary. I invited a variety of guests to Amherst: Zygmunt Bauman, Hans Peter Dreitzel, Iring Fetscher, Wilhelm Hennis, Henri Lefebvre, Ernest Mandel, Marcus Raskin, Richard Sennett, Rudi Supek, Paul Sweezy, Alain Touraine. The Five College setting was cosmopolitan enough to enjoy the visitors. As for any change I may have wrought at Amherst College itself, I recall a question by a colleague at Berkeley, who wished to know how sociology was progressing on what had been its last frontier. Splendidly, I told him: the English Department was doing a field study of Springfield and I was teaching Matthew Arnold. It was a division of intellectual labor matching that of the older British universities, where in fact similar things happened.

I learned a good deal, in my first years at Amherst, from our American historians and scholars in American culture. They gave me a sense of the currents and depths of our New England and national traditions which was all the more affecting for my nostalgia for Europe. Ostensibly casual remarks by historians Theodore Green and Hugh Hawkins were worth entire book chapters. Leo Marx, however, conveyed a vision of a struggle with the national past which distilled much of the Widener Library. Leo had grown up in New Deal New York, studied at Harvard with F. O. Matthiessen in the epoch of Harvard progressivism, had commanded a minesweeper in the Pacific War, and returned to Harvard to write a doctoral thesis which became a major book. *The Machine in the Garden* depicted the cultural consequences of nineteenth-century industrialization, and writing it sharpened Leo's attentiveness to the nuance and substance of contemporary changes. Years later, when I published *The Radical Renewal: The Politics of Ideas in Modern America* (1988), Leo expressed his pleased surprise at how much of the work done in American studies I had appropriated. I replied that the credit was largely his.

William J. Ward was another friend who helped in a large way. Bill's father was a surgeon, and I recall Bill himself referring to the "Lace Curtain Irish" of Brookline, where he grew up and from whence he went to Harvard. He had also been in the wartime Marines and survived their deathly island battles. Bill's imagery of the US was saturated with conflict between virtue and crookedness, a mosaic in which margin and center were increasingly indistinguishable. After listening to him, I understood the Kennedys better. He had an American version of the Catholic social realism I had come to know in Europe.

Theodore Green and Hugh Hawkins were historians with great knowledge of American higher education. Green's excursions into the past were especially instructive when he ironized on the similarity between religious revivalism on the campus in the nineteenth century and our own students' response to the nation's afflictions. Ted did not hesitate to point to the coincidence, earlier and later, of a sense of urgency about the failings of the outer world, demanding instant action, and the tedious banality of approaching examinations. Hugh had a fine grasp of the larger sweep of events.

In the spring of 1969, the college found that routine was insufficient to contain the waves of tension breaking upon us. The Afro-American students (the preferred term at the time) were restive and announced a strike of indefinite length to obtain a larger presence: a program in Afro-American studies, more Afro-American students, more Afro-American teachers. The white radicals wished to confront the war machine, difficult to do directly at Amherst where, divisions of opinion apart, no faculty member commuted to Washington. There were also some demands, not very precise ones, for more "relevant" instruction. The search for "relevance" was to dominate argument for the next two years. The traditional liberal arts curriculum in its Amherst incarnation had to be given some credit: at the least, it provided the students with a language of protest.

Or did it? Much of our campus turmoil was a struggle, waged with (and within) ourselves to find a language of connectedness. The practice was difficult. We were not in the armed services or the government, and could not disobey orders since we had none. Few of our students were threatened with the draft and paths to avoid it quite legally were plentiful. We were certainly in no position to make changes in the American racial situation, apart from increasing the numbers of Afro-Americans at the college and paying more attention to what had been (but was no longer) a disregarded aspect of our history. The Afro-American students at Amherst sensed that they were caught in a contradiction. They had been invited to join the privileged, but what was their responsibility to those left behind?

I am struck by a possible parallel, which I do not recollect anyone raising at the time in public or private discussion at Amherst. The offspring of the newly prosperous Jewish middle class were at Amherst as a way station, or transfer point, to careers in business, government, the professions. They were ambitious, disciplined and even relentless recruits to the rational and secular culture exemplified by their teachers. I recall a course on religion and modern society I taught with Lewis Mudge, who had a doctorate from Princeton Theological Seminary. I do not recall much difference of intellectual emphasis between us.

Some years later, the Department of Religion brought a congenial pair of Jewish scholars of Jewish tradition to the campus. Neither I nor, as far as I could see, any of the other Jewish Amherst professors were challenged to reconsider our cultural and familial roots. Of course, there was a large difference between coming from the disadvantaged Afro-American community and the Jewish one. Some of Amherst's Afro-American students came from educated and established families in Atlanta and Washington. Their response to the racial crisis in the nation was one of full engagement and identification with the rest of the community. A certain number of Jewish faculty and students were stirred by the Yom Kippur war of

1973 to declare their solidarity with Israel. I signed the statement of support circulating at the college without any critical reflection, and did not take my distance from Zionism until decades later. I took, however, no active steps toward it. It was as if there were no serious problem. We had arrived in America and were free to pitch our tents wherever and however we liked. Even the choice of supporting Israel (by gesture since Nixon and Kissinger were active in other spheres) had an un-coerced quality. I certainly took the war as an episode in the conflict between the US and the USSR, and was much more concerned with the fate of Chile.

The years 1969-1970 were those of four Amherst College moratoria. The term moratorium itself spoke volumes. We thought our educational tasks sufficiently important to render time off a very special occasion. It was defined as a pause, an interruption in the normal sequence of events. In these, our studying, teaching, writing, were central. Some of the students thought differently and for them, the interruption was proof that they had conquered and were holding terrain far different from that they were (in their view) coerced into tending in ordinary existence. The moratoria had, in part, aspects of a *kermesse*, a *fête*, a release from everyday bonds — but their ambitious aims, to rethink the entire relationship of our institution to society, made them very sober affairs.

The first one anticipated a student occupation of a building in April 1969. At a small college, denunciations of the authoritarian remoteness of faculty or even administration could hardly convince. Having heard of the intention of some students to protest, sympathetic faculty prevailed on the rest of our colleagues to suspend classes for two days to consider our situation. A spectrum of themes was evoked and discussed in an impromptu general assembly of the college in the baseball cage of the gymnasium. I found myself, with an energetic student named Steve Nagler, chairing one of these sessions. (Steve had been dismissed some years earlier for poor academic performance, a considerable achievement in view of his many talents, immediately received letters requesting that as an alumnus he contribute, and had made his way back.) It was not a debate; it had some attributes of a revivalist event with personal confessions, and wound on for many hours. The main complaints were two: a large majority of faculty and students (staff were there but not very audible) were deeply troubled by the Vietnam War and wished to see it end at once. The second was that the college, as an institution, was somehow failing its members by not responding to their deepest concerns. There, our divisions began to multiply.

Some wished for direct engagement with the body politic, even if they were quite unclear as to how this was to be done. Others wanted, alternately and sometimes simultaneously, recognition of their personal qualities and assistance in developing these. The college was repeatedly described as deficient in parenting, or brothering — in any case in its supposed familial tasks. Those discussing the learning process wished to see it profoundly altered in method and substance. The cleavages were not between teachers and students, although the younger teachers were less skeptical about some of the students' complaints and demands. One very visible contrast separated those seeking what they termed experiential content in education from those more interested in its intellectual dimensions. That in turn was connected to differences between those primarily interested in the inner life of the college and those concerned with the larger society. A great deal had come into motion (or become unstuck) in a very short time. The actual alignments were provisional, experimental and tentative. A good many students and no small number of faculty confessed that they had been brought, very quickly, to confront assumptions they had not questioned. That accounted for the atmosphere of holiday, of respite from routine, which was enchanting to many and quite disturbing to others.

Years later, I appeared at the Wellfleet Psychohistory Conference with, or rather in, a pair of striped jeans. "That marks your transition," Bob Lifton said, "from the old to the New Left." I did not find changing or discovering attitudes as simple as acquiring new clothes, and defended myself against inner confusion (little of which I acknowledged or admitted to consciousness) by interpreting new events in familiar terms. I concentrated on the antiauthoritarian components of the protest, and thought of authority in its familiar forms, as exercised by the groups cited in texts like C. Wright Mills's *The Power Elite*. I knew, as a matter of theory, that a good deal of inner psychological transformation would have to precede large-scale experiments with new forms of governance and participation. I knew myself well enough to conclude that enthusiastic participation in a movement for democratization was a matter of my seeking a place for myself at the top. It was not an insight I chose, at the time, to dwell upon; I was, however, quite attentive to the intellectual vulgarities of parts of the movement. That accounted for my refusal to think its iconoclasm authentic or likely to endure. Iconoclasm in its most effective forms presupposed creative alternatives: few were evident in the shallow egalitarianism of the movement.

There was something to the criticism by some of our students of the middle-aged radicals on the faculty. We had conquered (I'll let the bravura term stand) space in the cultural super-structure and could speak freely in politics. The students were derisive. Much of the nation cared nothing for our version of culture, and the precondition of our freedom to speak was the certainty in the ruling elite that few would listen. It did not follow that the acting out of youthful rebelliousness was an adequate response to these difficulties. It was regressive. Jürgen Habermas put it more distantly when he said of the German student revolt that its tactics were not generationally neutral.

That much said, the generations united sufficiently at Amherst to agree on a letter to be sent to President Nixon, despite the reasonable supposition that he was not waiting for it. The text, signed by President Plimpton on behalf of administrators, faculty, and students, said that the Vietnam War and domestic problems of racial discrimination and poverty required systematic attention, and that the nation in its pursuit of war and rejection of dissent was on the wrong course. (I write as the 2012 presidential campaign sets the tone of public discourse—not exceedingly elevated. Laments about reaching new depths do seem exaggerated, when one recalls the invective directed at rather polite expressions of dissent like the Amherst letter.)

The first moratorium was followed by another, initiated by Afro-American students, devoted to questions of race—in the nation and at the college. A year later, a program in black studies was instituted. Amherst had a long tradition of enrolling students from what Franklin Frazier termed the "black bourgeoisie"—the better situated Afro-Americans of Atlanta, Washington, New York. Our two best known Afro-American graduates at the time were Judge

Hastie, who for many years was the highest ranking Afro-American in the judicial system, and Benjamin Davis. When I was young, Davis was on the New York City Council, elected from Harlem. He was also a leader of the American Communist Party and was tried and jailed in the infamous Smith Act case of 1948-1949. At one point, Amherst organized an American Black History Week and issued a brochure about its distinguished Afro-American graduates. Davis was not left out, but was described as having had "a career in public service."

The Afro-American students at the college (who worked closely with others at the neighboring places) saw little need for, and less value in, the college's sort of discretion. They were right, but their militancy posed problems. Their white fellow students, and faculty, were decidedly sympathetic to the civil rights movement. Expanding opportunities for Afro-Americans to study at Amherst, enlarging the curriculum to include black studies, were obvious steps to begin reversing a miserable legacy of racism—in its genteel New England academic version, which consisted of ignoring or under-emphasizing the problem. There were, after all, great New England traditions to call upon—conspicuously dormant when I attended post-war Harvard. One problem was that there was little else the college could do. It was neither chartered nor organized as an agency of direct social action, however much that distressed our militant undergraduates.

The Afro-American students were not content with anodyne analyses of this sort. They persisted with demonstrative campaigns, which continued on and off after the rest of the sixties' movements had become memories. The campaigns had two not entirely separate aspects: one was an insistence on Afro-American presence. They had views about, or interests in, a great many issues on campus and in the college's relationship to the larger society. It followed that there should be Afro-American participation in the decision-making process—which otherwise could be or would be regarded as illegitimate by the Amherst Afro-American community (and by implication, the larger one to which it was connected). There were plenty of difficulties with their demand, which in its most literal form required recognition of the Afro-Americans as a unique community with unique rights, justified by the need for compensating them for systematic neglect, or worse, in the recent past. That is, inclusion in the larger community as citizens would not suffice.

The second, more diffuse, Afro-American demand was for recognition of the specificity of Afro-American culture. This was a demand directed as much to Afro-Americans as (if not more than) to anyone else. Recall the scene from Ralph Ellison's *Invisible Man* in which the narrator is confronted by a street merchant selling candied sweet potatoes and asked whether he knew his interlocutor. It was a criticism of zealous assimilation to an American norm (in fact a fictive one, since the rest of the nation was quite fragmented) and in its barest and most bitter terms, a rejection of "whiteness" — which again, ignored the fact that whites were not identical.

The Afro-American rising confronted every segment of our society with serious challenges. We were forced to think about our own sorts of historical specificity, about what we had or could have in common, about the several dimensions of citizenship and the practice of solidarity. We were also obliged to think about how to achieve social change, about the limits on government and the rule of law. It was and is difficult to construct specific programs in a situation marked not only by openness but by ambiguity.

At the time, I was skeptical of the Afro-American insistence on the separateness of their struggle. Unless there were prosperity for a broad cross section of the nation, much of the populace would be functionally deaf to appeals to right economic wrongs done to Afro-Americans—as flagrant as these were. The New Deal coalition worked economically even when its constituent ethnic groups were far from friendly, but these groups generally had equal starting points. It was true that large segments of white America profited, economically, from racial discrimination, if only in the minimization or elimination of Afro-American competition. The large pedagogic efforts and psychological transformations required by the project of the reduction of racism could not be separated from the larger tasks of constructing a more egalitarian society. I did not share the outrage experienced by some when Daniel Patrick Moynihan, as White House advisor on social issues, suggested "benign neglect" of race and emphasis on economic problems. It was not because I attributed great insight to Moynihan, whom I sadly and somewhat shabbily underestimated. (I also misconstrued Nixon, not appreciating the social dimensions of his imperialism—or the magnitude of his achievements in relationships to China and the USSR.) I was a captive of a narrative in which class struggle claimed exclusive attention, in which the New Deal was resumed and completed. I do not think that was due to excessive reliance on Western European models of social transformation: only when I had achieved a more exacting if sobered view of Europe did I begin to appreciate the exceptionality of the US.

I'd now say that was far too little place for time and place in my narrative, that I had insufficiently learned the lessons taught by my colleagues on *Past and Present* and the *Annales* historians, as well as a newer German generation struggling with its nation's past. I had been betrayed by what was otherwise an advantage—large powers of synthesis. My use of these was so effective that it frequently cut me off from specificity of experience. My present became past and future with equal speed.

For the duration of my appointment at Amherst, I had good, even comradely, relations to Afro-American students and to the distinguished historian Asa Davis when we were fortunate enough to induce him to join us. They counted on me as someone who could be relied upon in a crisis, as on their side—but we rarely discussed the different modes of an alliance between them and radicals of other backgrounds. I abjured the philistine self-congratulation of Jewish figures such as Norman Podhoretz. We made it in the US without affirmative action, was their assertion, and the Afro-Americans would do well to follow our example. But the Afro-Americans came to the US without the benefit of what Jews truthfully claimed: a written tradition of no few millennia, and the collective experience of living under or with strange Gods. Actually, affirmative Action owes much to the incessant legal campaigns of American Jewish organizations in the thirties and forties against discrimination in education, employment, and housing. As for the complaint that Afro-Americans were insufficiently attentive to the common aspects of American citizenship, that came with ill grace from those who made the defense of Israel a very high priority.

The paragraph above is history, reconstructed. In the flux of actual events, I was by no means as clear or as steady in judgment. The pressure of history as experienced was so unrelenting that I hardly achieved a vantage point before it was flooded with new impressions and I had to flee in search of higher ground somewhere else. Amherst's own moratorium of the spring of 1969 was followed by a nationally organized day of protest in the fall. The term may be an exaggeration. Campuses, large and small, across the spectrum of higher education, were so open to stimuli from outside that a contact or a letter or a visit was hardly required to move local groups to action. They had only to read about other places in the newspaper, or glimpse a demonstration on television.

Amherst had a much-awaited visit, from Mark Rudd, the leader of the Columbia occupation of the spring of 1968, in the fall of that year. I was asked to speak with him at the meeting, held in our chapel. I made an arch reference to differences in age, noting that if my generation was not over the hill we could be said to be cresting. To my surprise, Mark recalled hearing me at a Princeton conference of Students for a Democratic Society in 1967 and said that I had been "inspiring." That did a great deal for my standing in Amherst, but to the best of my recollection, in 1967 I warned against a politics of gesture in favor of one of long-term organizing. I could not effectively convey much of what I had learned in Europe, or recalled from my days as political apprentice in the forties (which terminated in a long latency period during my stay at Cold War Harvard).

Others expressed differently their discomfiture with the younger generation's apparent belief that it was at the beginning of historical time. Irving Howe was a stern patriarch, a custodian of a threatened tradition of reflection. Mike Harrington was avuncular, a sympathetic elder brother, occasionally confessing sorrow at the ineptness of younger siblings. Dwight Macdonald thought it splendid that the young had bestirred themselves, and waited with his criticism: the important thing was to demonstrate solidarity. Marcuse wrote and acted as if he wished he were forty years younger, and there was something compelling in his depiction of the new march of the spirit.

Nuances of experience and perspective divided the faculty friends with whom I shared the wish to be helpful to the students. Donald Pitkin and Leo Marx were older than I, had been at late New Deal Harvard, and were heirs of the determined Progressivism which had retreated by the time I arrived in 1947. Tom Yost was the only Amherst faculty member to have admitted a connection to the Communist Party, and had performed no small service for his Soviet colleagues by keeping in touch with them through the period of intellectual disaster that was marked by the doctrines of the Stalinist biologist (and charlatan) Lysenko. Tom had the additional virtue of a direct sense of what the American working class, not infrequently mythicized by the middle class young, was about. George Kateb had the advantages of Arab descent (he was a Syrian Christian, from one of Christianity's oldest churches). In moving from Brooklyn to Columbia and Harvard, he developed a persona as political philosopher with a clear sense of the limitations imposed on thought by history, working through ordinary motives and ambitions, not least ambition and pride. Jan Dizard's parents had spent their lives in the trade union movement which shaped a segment of Minnesota political activism, and he too had a familiarity with the working class unusual at Amherst.

We each thought it important to let our students know of our solidarity with them—but what did that mean in specific terms? I was struck by how many in the movements of the sixties and early seventies hoped to join a church of salvation—or a political party which would also have familial functions. These wishes were not openly acknowledged, but a certain moral absolutism and a register of psychological demands made their unspoken agendas clear. The students often ignored their historical descent: they frequently supposed that they had invented protest, even revolution.

The college joined the nationwide student strike of 1970 which followed the attack into Cambodia. After a certain amount of wavering, the faculty voted to end classes for the semester at once. Free to demonstrate and remonstrate, our position was clear: we were floating in historical space. A good deal of the nation agreed with our opposition to the intensification of the war, and that no doubt included a substantial number of those serving in the military. (It was only later that we realized how much disobedience and dissent there was in the armed forces, although we could draw only one conclusion from the Pacific Fleet's inability to move some of its vessels from southern California to Vietnam.) Any number of legislators, nationally and in state governments, sought a very early end to the war. Much of the public, however, backed the calculated ambiguities of Kissinger and Nixon. By threatening to extend the war, even to use nuclear weapons, they thought that they could compel the Communist Vietnamese state and the somewhat more diffusely composed armed opposition in South Vietnam to make major concessions. Later research showed that the Communist leadership considered time on its side, not least because of the US anti-war movement, which it followed closely. Kissinger and Nixon were able to mobilize not only the primitivism of American chauvinism, but to neutralize a good deal of the opposition by appealing to their sense of what passed for political realism. The student movement was speaking to the already converted in a very polarized nation. It could not relent, since that would encourage the president's adventurism. It could not, however, expand its public, since that was already at its maximum. As for the long-term tasks of reducing American militarism, it was precisely that—a project which would take years.

A large college contingent went to Washington in April 1970 to join some 600,000 other citizens in a very large protest march. The students and some faculty went in chartered buses. Characteristically, Leo and Jane Marx joined the students for the eight-hour overnight drive. I chose to stay in New York and fly to the capital the day of the event on a shuttle plane whose captain announced that he was making no comment on what he thought many of his passengers would do in Washington—comment enough. Bob Silvers, the perpetual editor of *The New York Review of Books*, was on the flight. I did not ask him, to my regret, with what group he was marching. The discipline and numbers of the demonstrators were impressive. It was later reported that Nixon had stationed armored forces around and in the city to repress disturbances, but there were none sufficient to justify their use. I talked with students from a number of very different states and social settings. Their sense of the futility of the war had been transmuted into one of its evil by the murders at Kent State, and this in turn expressed a very generalized sense of remoteness from, hostility to, the nation's dominant institutions. Very few, however, had a sense of a long-term project for change—or much of an idea of what the march represented in American history.

One major Amherst protest somewhat later attracted national

attention. President William Ward, faculty, and students in 1972 trespassed at Westover Air Force Base near Springfield and were arrested. In a moving article in *The New York Times*, Ward voiced the despairing uncertainty of the movement. He supposed that little could be changed, which made the protest even more necessary. The demonstration, and others like it, followed the mining of Hanoi Harbor by the government. That was an element in a strategy of compelling Communist Vietnam to concessions in negotiations. Kissinger and Nixon had already been to China, successfully used the opening to China to impress the American public, and so presented in contrast to the peace movement a long-term project of foreign policy realism which also included a new balance of relations with the Soviet Union. Against that, we had projects for international development, hints of a nascent human rights campaign, a vision of a more domesticated, saner world—but little prospect of convincing the nation to follow us. Quite a few of Amherst's scholars in modern history and politics had known Kissinger in his academic role. The president's son-in-law, David Eisenhower, was one of our students. These connections increased, if anything, our sense that we were indeed outsiders.

My own response to that was to construct a world, or worlds, in which I could be at home. Amherst in welcoming me did a good deal to convince me that I belonged to a family worth joining. So obvious an explanation of such felicity as I was then capable of enjoying was difficult for me to acknowledge: it had to be part of a larger and more systematic world view. I took this in some measure from the larger creed of a liberal arts education, in part from the belief in the critical task of intellectuals, and finally from a new appreciation of the openness (in part real, in part imaginary) of American history.

What was the larger creed of a liberal arts education? I realized, without allowing the disturbing inequality of the situation to intrude overmuch, that the ideas and techniques, the objects, of pedagogy we pursued were rare social goods. The lower one descended in the exceedingly stratified hierarchy of American higher education, the less accessible the realm of spirit. That did not render my colleagues and myself less enthusiastic about our tasks as custodians of a tradition, but flattered our self-importance. We could portray ourselves as a vanguard acting in a general interest as yet to be recognized by those who would eventually profit from it. What was, more specifically, our creed? I adhered quite unequivocally to the view that the curriculum had to comprise "the best that has been thought and said." My one emendation was to argue for a radically or thoroughly historical approach to the great texts. These reflected their times, all right, but that implied that they expressed a great deal of conflict. Now, I would say that their greatness frequently consisted in the struggles to fully grasp those conflicts, struggles which exhausted their creators.

I took my idea of the critical task of intellectuals from the thoughts of Antonio Gramsci (a founder of the Italian Communist Party in the twenties and a strikingly original thinker who died in a Fascist jail) on the implicit democratization of thought in modern societies. However, Gramsci's evocation of democratic possibility was just that—evocation. Plenty of his countrymen remained quasi-literate and certainly intellectually passive. Fascism (in Northern and Eastern Europe too) conquered the universities in some places before it conquered the streets. That was true of Germany. And in France in the thirties, the maintenance of parliamentary democracy was a narrow escape rather than a great victory. My thought at the time was wrung from a good deal of experience and observation—beginning with my father's colleagues in 1930s New York and continuing through the other groups I encountered, from *Partisan Review* and the New York intellectuals to Britain's politically engaged thinkers and then on to the not-quite-captive scholars of the Soviet-bloc states.

In the first article I published, a text taken from a discussion of the general education program at Harvard in 1952 and published in the *Journal of General Education*, I depicted even, or above all, intellectuals integrated in social tasks as "underground men" (our sisters will have to forgive my abject conventionality). They bored from within. By 1966, I gave us rather more daylight—we could use our socially legitimated functions as guardians of tradition to alter it. When I came to Amherst I published some ruminations on intellectuals as a vanguard in *Partisan Review*. Steven Marcus, invariably acute, said that the essay lacked my usual clarity. He was right, and its formal defects were caused by a substantive one: if the educated could assume a vanguard role in movements for social change, the ties that bound them to the social order could not be all that onerous. I did not propose that we were running through open doors, but assigned us a role which combined the permitted insolence of the court jester with the harder convictions of a social critic. That left a large space for manoeuver—and in any case justified my teaching at Amherst.

I owed much to two rather different groups. I had always noticed something freer about natural scientists, in that they seemed to choose their politics with a different kind of attention. They lacked the obdurate dogmatism of some of the social scientists. Natural scientists joined the protests of the sixties in large numbers. I recall the measured words of the physicist Victor Weisskopf about the "Research Strike" at MIT and other universities in March 1969. Weisskopf had been at Gymnasium in Vienna with the Austrian Socialist leader and Chancellor Bruno Kreisky, and they shared a pluralistic approach to politics. There were different ways, Weisskopf told the strikers, of exercising influence and it was impossible to ascribe moral superiority to any one of them.

There was something else: the social sciences entailed large amounts of interpretation. A good many natural scientific findings, and their technological derivatives, involved linear reasoning. One could put the products of natural scientific research at the disposition of those with power—or not. Social science constructed or reconstructed social worlds directly, were parts of the observable universe. We were tied to our works in ways different from the natural scientists. Medicine and psychiatry were on border territory. At the time, I knew rather a lot about psychoanalysis and little about anything else among the natural sciences, and it would have been rewarding to extend and deepen my knowledge. I concentrated on conveying to others matters I was surer about (or so I thought).

What I was sure about was that I was, decidedly, with it. Just as decidedly, I was wrong. I did take Western Europe (with occasional glances at its easternmost outposts, held by the dissenting intelligentsia of the Soviet bloc) as well as the US as my point of reference. I prided myself on not being provincial—all the while ignoring large parts of the world and some very substantial segments of the US. Franklin County, to the north of Hampshire County where

I lived, was one of the poorest in the country—but my weekends were spent in Manhattan. What I was wrong about, however, was not a matter of geopolitical attention but much of the history we were already experiencing. I was wrong in attributing to it much larger possibilities of positive transformation (toward more inner and outer freedom, more justice, more authentic spirituality) than was the case. I grossly, even grotesquely, over-estimated the influence of our own progressive intelligentsia on American life.

It is no consolation to note that our European cousins had similar illusions, in their idioms. Sartre for a while supported a French Maoist sect, and the German conservatives actually feared the German students and urban bohemians. More confident of continuity, a British diplomat described a visiting president of the National Union of Students as "scruffy." That student was Jack Straw, who later became foreign secretary. When I came to Washington in 1979, I was invited to lunch by a former student already on his way up in the State Department. Two classmates joined—one a newly appointed partner in a prestigious law firm, the other a senior staff member of an influential senator. They took pains to recall my course on Marxism as a high point of their Amherst experience.

I did not primarily cast myself as an academic advocate of Marxism. What I sought was an open approach to the Western tradition of social thought, which would rule out neither Marxism nor the many responses (some of them quite profound) it evoked. I did insist on the central place of Marxism in the Western intellectual tradition. That I had learned, in some measure, from the French Catholic theologians who wrote on Marxism in the fifties, such as my friends the Jesuit Jean-Yves Calvez and the former Dominican but inexpugnably Catholic Henri Desroche. I also learned it from the Protestant laypersons and theologians who contributed to *MarximusStudien* when many in West German academic and intellectual life were careful to mark their distance from what was a large part of their own tradition. These persons did not invariably take the same precautions with the legacies that had influenced Nazism. I had assimilated a good deal of Anglo-Marxism, with its British skepticism about schematism, in the United Kingdom. Thanks to Leo Marx, the intricate paths of Marxist influence on American Progressivism, which I partly knew and partly sensed when young, came back to me in broader and deeper ways.

I was able to enter into alliances—sometimes implicit, sometimes negotiated in conversation, with both cultural traditionalists and those who thought of themselves as modernists. The traditionalists were strong on New England tradition, so they had already taken large steps in a modernist direction by acknowledging the specificity of place and time. The modernists insisted, above all, on interpretation—not for them isolated texts. When they had finished, however, they were likely to find themselves on unexpected ground: the traditionalist insistence on the connection between character, comportment, and value, in which purpose itself was the result of history shaping a person. That was not impossibly remote from the many versions of the Marxist theory of ideology omnipresent in modern thought.

It was impossible to convey to students the centuries of struggle, the religious conflicts, the agonies of spirit and intellect, which went into the twentieth century. All that we could do was to suggest that a great many acts had preceded our own, and that the drama was unending. As a pedagogue returning to New England, I contradicted, once again but much more openly, the shallow scientism with which I had been confronted twenty-one years earlier at Harvard. I was sure that I was right to tell colleagues and students that social science was interpretive and open to cultural and political influences. It would have been even more of a service to them had I been more rigorous in situating my own ideas, and those I encouraged them to consider, in our own time-bound context. I exaggerated the qualities of independence required to voice my uncertain synthesis of Marxism and modernism, and did not provide much preparation for the next decades in American intellectual life. That I inflicted the same unwilled blindness on myself is not consolation. I was swimming on a tide of enthusiastic recognition I had not experienced before—from the academic world and its public in the higher journalism, even politics.

At Amherst, that led to my appointment as chair of the Committee on Educational Policy of the faculty, charged with revising our curriculum in the light of new cultural and social demands. A lot of the students chafed at what they thought of as the restrictions on their liberty inherent in requirements and others thought that matters of the present moment (empire and war, poverty and race) should have more attention and still others wanted closer contact, often undefined or little specified, with large parts of American society beyond the classroom. Younger faculty portrayed themselves as recalcitrant heirs of local academic traditions they wished to alter. A good deal of energy at Amherst at the time was free-floating, and some of it eruptive. Many, younger and older, wiser and less so, wished to change the larger society and chose the college, *faute de mieux*, as the place to begin. The two other faculty members on the committee—John Ratté, a Catholic historian of Europe, and Tom Yost, a socially critical biologist who knew a great many things—agreed with me on points we thought essential. The college was integrated in the larger society and in many ways expressed its flaws and illusions, its arrogance and cruelty. Amherst especially, however, was a college, and not a research university very integrated in the routine maintenance of power. We had the possibility, at least, of constituting an enclave in which cultural dissidence could be cultivated, alternative national narratives written, ideas of another world (or worlds) considered. We anticipated what now has become more desperate: the struggle of much of American higher education against the baseness of economic rationalization, stupid populism, and deformed realism.

One difficulty was that we had to struggle against many of our most articulate and energetic students. No few of them were true believers in simplified notions of equality and democracy. If teachers and students were equal, they argued, then our prescriptive rights, our claims to know more, had to be rethought and indeed denied. (If they had known more, they would have charged us with claiming, like the bewhiskered clergy who taught at an earlier Amherst, a sort of scriptural authority.) We were excessively conciliatory and used phrases which intimated that we were equal, but that we simply knew different things. The students on the committee were much more reticent to make grandiose claims of intellectual autonomy. They concentrated on the services faculty could render students precisely by drawing upon our greater knowledge and life experience - the most important of which being to recount our struggles to gain a truer view of the world.

Our proposals included retaining requirements in two ways. For one, new students at Amherst were to take seminars in small groups of fifteen. These were to serve as introductions to college work and were not to be standardized as to form or content. There, reflection and decision on the rest of the student's career would begin. Secondly, students would take three introductory courses in the humanities, natural sciences, and social sciences—courses specifically designed as introductions. This was not in principle a break with the intentions of the introductory courses then in place, termed "Problems of Inquiry." We left it to those teaching these courses to broaden them to include new foci of knowledge and new social concerns.

Asian civilizations were an instance of the former; problems of cultural pluralism in the US constituted the latter. (As far as I recollect, the Arab cultures and Muslim world did not interest Amherst in 1971. At larger places, there were specialized departments and institutes to deal with it. After Edward Said published *Orientalism* in 1978, there were some stirrings—rather more than followed the Yom Kippur War in 1973. China, perhaps owing to the college's missionary legacy, was never totally ignored at Amherst.) The paths from Chaucer's Canterbury and the Puritans' New England wilderness and the Ohio River frontier were many, but there was no collective college effort to privilege a few. It was very clear what we were leaving behind—the last remnants of the genteel tradition—much less so what lay ahead. Fortunately for the college, some of the very best teaching and writing of faculty involved re-evaluations of that tradition, a consequence of the college's early commitment to making American studies central. Much depended upon the accidents of appointment policies over the past decades, or the codified conventions of New England's version of academic culture.

At the time, some talked of a "movement" for political and social change—and, with quite varying degrees of enthusiasm (in the case of many of our alumni and most of our trustees, none at all), thought of academic reform as part of it. In fact, there were any number of movements with quite different aims, social composition and patterns of recruitment. Moreover, one large division marked much that we did, especially at the college.

One segment of the movement sought changes in social institutions and practices: relations between races and sexes, parents and children, physicians and patients, government and citizen, the US and the rest of the world, producer and consumer, employer and worker (and of course, teacher and student). Another sought inner transformation, the release of repressed energies, a new sense of self. The two were obviously connected. The revival of the older American notion of the commune, where new lives could supposedly be lived in new circumstances, attested to that. Still, the currents were different.

Our committee responded by recourse to a perennial New England trope. Persons were responsible for their own salvation and had large amounts of inner freedom, but recognition of the authority of the congregation was the indispensable condition of attaining that freedom. We accepted that the college was a learning community, but allowed its senior members a very large share in its governance and program. We asked for a thorough critical examination of the departmental system and proposed, in effect, its extreme attenuation by allowing students to construct their own inter-departmental majors. In our new design for undergraduate voyages, each and every college teacher had to serve as a guide through much uncharted territory.

Previously, curricular changes reflected what there was of consensus in the learned community. The expectation that most Amherst teachers would spend their lives there made possible a decent gradualism, punctuated by occasions in which the slow work of accumulating new perspectives quickened into a larger revision. The senior members of faculty most definitely did not adhere to ideas and methods they had acquired thirty years previously in graduate schools. Frequent sabbaticals, a library up to date in scholarly and scientific research and the addition to the departments of younger members all meant that senior faculty did not have live from intellectual capital alone. Most had no wish to do so and valued Amherst because they could renew their scholarship in their own time and in their own way, free of the competition and pressure which sometimes disfigured the graduate schools.

Our curricular proposal earned considerable praise as a contribution to the discussion, but we did not convince a majority of our colleagues to take major steps toward revising the sovereignty of the departments. Some colleagues felt that we were too confident of the average undergraduate's capacity to navigate seas which (for instance) induced caution at Harvard. There, a review of the general education program and the curriculum had brought about some alterations, but no major transformation. Others thought that the arrangements we had, with small modifications, could meet the demand for inter-disciplinary studies in particular. We had at least widened the college's field of vision or view of possibility. The years immediately following were those of an increase in student experimentation with their own programs. At least as importantly, new perspectives were increasingly represented in ordinary course work in the humanities and social sciences.

Thereafter, I concentrated on work in our department and my own courses. I did ask the Committee on Educational Policy, some years later, to consider an experiment: two teachers from different disciplines would assume responsibility for an entire semester or even an entire year of the work of a group of students. As an example, a historian and a teacher of literature could deal with the nineteenth century—hardly a small topic. I regret that I did not try to interest the scientists in a similar venture in the origins and history of modern science: I would have learned a lot. On another occasion, I discussed with our very cultivated dean, Prosser Gifford, a different experiment: a group in an incoming first-year class could devote most or all of its first year to reading great texts. We concluded that the idea was not likely to pass faculty scrutiny and dropped it.

Amherst required all departments to submit new courses to the scrutiny of the entire faculty. It was a very good idea, as it enabled all of us to glimpse what our colleagues thought of as ventures on the frontiers of learning, or new pedagogies. Occasionally, the discussion touched on someone's deepest concerns. The biologist Bill Hexter, a very effective teacher, was a zealous guardian of the border that divided (as he thought) overly specialized graduate school instruction from more fundamental matter needed in the college. A medieval historian and a Chaucer scholar in English proposed a course on the Middle Ages. Bill (whose own work involved generations of fruit flies as laboratory specimens) rose to ask whether this was not a graduate school course. I asked the proposers what centuries were covered by their idea of the Middle Ages, and they responded with the dates 400 to 1400. That gave me a chance to ask Bill whether he would agree that it was somewhat longer than the life of a fruit fly. Not every faculty meeting, then, needed to be tedious.

Gradually, as the excitements of the late sixties and early seventies dissipated in the larger society, the college settled into routine. Some faculty thought that the average student admitted from that period on were less rebellious and less interesting than their immediate predecessors. Perhaps, but as the nation relaxed into what passed for quiescence, one would have had to lack a sense of proportion to expect one college to remain an enclave of excitement. There was excitement enough in the nation. The 1972 election matched an authentic candidate of the American opposition m George McGovern, against Nixon. The only conclusion to be drawn from McGovern's very large defeat was that those seeking major transformations should prepare themselves for a very long struggle. Despite its obviousness, I found it difficult to alter my perspective on work and political engagement. The reconciliation (of sorts) with China, the gradual normalization of relations with the Soviet Union, the *coup d'état* in Chile, the Yom Kippur war, succeeded one another on our television screens and in the newspapers until the curtain rose, bit by bit, on the Watergate drama.

I took a sabbatical in the year 1971-1972 and spent a good deal of it in Italy, mostly at the Agnelli Foundation in Turin. *The Crisis of Industrial Society* was published in 1969, and Oxford University Press followed with a collection of essays which were mainly extended footnotes to the theses of the book, *Toward a Critical Sociology,* in 1971. In the period immediately following I wrote two very long essays or short monographs, "Beyond Marx in the Sociology of Religion" and "Professors, Students and Philosopher Kings." They reflected what I had at the time of creativity. They contained, as well, what I could formulate of persistent interest in a secular path to salvation (which at the time I thought of as the overcoming of a classical condition of alienation in economy and polity)—and, in an unintended sense, an argument to the effect that the path was blocked. My accumulated writings on the universities in the Western world voiced implicit skepticism that the intellectuals and our publics could alter the society around us. I depicted the universities as alternating between technocratic tasks for society's elites and ventures in reflection. These satisfied curiosity and offered aesthetic pleasures. Historical and social philosophical and psychological inquiry might deepen insight.

As a consequence of my own travels, I imperfectly grasped the historically conditioned nature of social thought. I use the term "imperfectly" to describe a problem. If our own ideas were (like everyone else's) bound to a time and a place, how would we know when to modify these, and how? I'd long been convinced that it was false to think of a cumulative social science on the model of the natural sciences. I could think Marxism valuable as a description of a specific historical structure, and had no answer to the questions about the functioning of pre-capitalist social formations. Certainly I could say very little about imaginary post-capitalist ones. At the same time I was convinced that Freud's picture of human nature was right, for all of his dependence on nineteenth-century evolutionary thought, I did not accept the theoretic challenge entailed in these contradictions, and limited myself to dealing with the larger social problems of the Western democracies, with occasional attention to the travails of those imprisoned in the post-Stalinist regimes. I was adept at portraying myself and my intellectual allies as a vanguard, as we resolutely refused to risk moving beyond arguing with contemporaries who might have been even more limited. If so, we merited little credit for taking them as major antagonists.

What would have been entailed by a broader and deeper perspective? I learned a great deal by reading Sulloway's *Freud, Biologist of the Mind*. Sulloway documented Freud's passionate membership in the church of evolutionary thought. It provided him with a culture and a home outside Judaism, including Reformed Judaism. The idea of evolution was more than a methodological precept or even a meta-philosophical assumption. It was the language of those who came from very different starting points on the late nineteenth-century map, and made it possible for them to identify one another as members of an international fraternity. Recall Freud's warm welcome by Clark, James, and Putnam in New England. For them, the idea of evolution was a depiction of the world and a legitimation of their scientific projects, to which it lent moral meaning and historical specificity.

They had Darwin and each other; we had Thomas Kuhn (a very

considerable thinker and a very cultivated sensibility), and an increasingly fragmented intellectual cosmos, in which many disputes were ephemeral. That perhaps was the reason for the adherence of so many to Marxism as a meta-historical belief. It enabled us to attribute coherence to an otherwise disordered historical universe. Kuhn criticized the use of his view of natural scientific revolutions to describe changes in the social sciences, which did not at all deter social scientists from doing so. They were insisting on their autonomy as observers, claiming that they were up to the demands of their times by advancing knowledge. They inhabited a world devoid of inner structure.

Across differences of national culture, religious adherence, intellectual descent, a large number in my academic and intellectual generation thought that we had advanced beyond mere empiricism. Actually, we would have been well served by more immersion in the sheer disorder of ordinary existence. In our protected positions we lamented and at times mocked the imprisonment of others in routine—and did not dwell overly much on our realization that we were modern equivalents of court jesters, allowed to utter inconvenient truths because we were quite unable to do very much to alter things. I had contemporaries and friends who were more able than I to connect with the rawness of our cultural and social life, its discontinuities and frequent senselessness: Ernest Gellner, Clifford Geertz, Alvin Gouldner, Christopher Lasch, Henri Lefebvre, Robert Lifton, Edgar Morin, Richard Sennett, and Edward Thompson were among them. Dwight Macdonald, Norman Mailer, Norman Podhoretz, and Susan Sontag did as well in their own ways. I avoided the problem by adamantly turning away from it.

It was not simply a matter of the disordered vulgarities of mass culture. The sixties and perhaps even more the seventies were a period in which survivors and a newer generation turned again to the horrors of the century's earlier decades, after a period just after the war of looking in any direction but back. My resolute turn to an imagined future was my way of dealing with the Holocaust, Hiroshima and the assorted brutalities I knew a great deal about.

My very large need to escape my own faintly articulated doubts about my own optimism may have made me into a more convincing teacher, since above all, I had to convince myself. What I conveyed to my students was a singular mixture of American Progressivism, Western Marxism, and autobiographical irony. From them, I received no complaints of boredom, though some that I was engaged in indoctrination. I responded in two ways—one was that quite literally no one had complained of being graded unfairly. The other was that if pluralism were to be taken seriously, critical perspectives not voiced in the same way by others on the faculty should be welcomed.

There was a larger difficulty. Amherst's pedagogic tradition had an ideological component: we were preparing young persons for elite careers by giving them access to the culture of which we and they were heirs. Amherst's understanding of itself as a learning community presupposed faculty acceptance of this implicit, but stark, description of our functions, when we preferred to think of ourselves as defenders of liberalism or modernity or secular freedom. Suppose, however, that the content of our teaching was quite secondary to our functions as guardians and monitors of good behavior, understood as convincing our students that they should fit in? It was easier to accept the more implicit aspects of our work as much of elite culture was modern, as ethnic and racial and later gender equality were increasingly accepted by economic and political elites as making their work easier. Thinking of it even now evokes a jab of conscience: I said these things then, but what did I do about them?

I resorted to an evasive stratagem, not entirely honest. I took the view that my lectures, reading lists, provision of the college with interesting lectures from outside, even the incorporation in my teaching of high-level gossip but gossip nonetheless (sometimes disguised as supplying color or giving ideas a human face) were quite enough. I did not see the need to extend myself in a tutorial capacity. I kept a certain distance, outer as well as inner, from the student activists who hoped that in my classroom they would find (or construct) a congregation of the saved. I was true to Amherst's theological tradition, if not always intentionally so. We were all, necessarily, sinners, facing with the frankness (and, let it be said, courage) of New England the disappointments—no, the anguish—an implacable God visited upon us. The translation I favored was that we did not live in progressive times, that the European societies were closer to the Promised Land. Their parties, social movements, thinkers, especially the parliamentary socialists, merited far more attention than they had had from our movements of the sixties. I reminded our revolutionary apprentices of this, with the passage of time increasingly evoked the New Deal and its ideological pluralism.

Omissions spoke loudly. I did not give any attention worth mentioning to the Third World, much less to Cuba and evolutionary movements elsewhere in the impoverished parts of the world. I paid equally little attention to China or India. I attended even less to Israel, or the problems posed by Zionism. I was skeptical of what I thought of as excessive attention to the distinctiveness of Afro-American culture. The new emphasis on human rights struck me as largely a derivative of Cold War strategies to discredit state socialism. I thought the calls for participatory democracy valuable, did not experiment at all in thought or on paper with the construction of new institutions—but did spend some energy on the vanguard functions of intellectuals and the possibility of enlarging these to newer, educated segments of the labor force. That was something, again, I brought back with me from France.

I did ask the question, why so much drift, indeed stagnation, in the transatlantic Left after the turbulences of the sixties? My answer, somewhat vague, had to do with the insufficiency of cultural and psychological preparation for a long-term project. That, in turn, reinforced my positive views of the French Socialists, the German Social Democrats, the Italian Communists. We needed a party in which generational succession was a problem to be solved, not an incentive to fratricidal (or rather patricidal) civil war.

In short, in my mid-forties I began to act rather like the older persons I had derided so vocally: responding to historical newness with the ideas of the past, if of the recent past. One thing I did not do at Amherst was to concern myself with the intellectual and personal development of individual students. I thought, and sometimes said, that it was our task to convey the traditions of learning left to us—and theirs to struggle with what they heard from us and read in the texts, and to join this to their experiences. I interpreted Holy Writ but had no enthusiasm for the cure of souls. It would have been better had I had less worldly ambition and more empathy. Indeed, I might have been more productive in the end. The Amherst Department of Sociology's current website, referring to the history of the discipline at the college, describes me as an "urbane presence." I take that as positive and leave it at that.

One contemporary who most definitely did not leave it at that was my erstwhile faculty colleague and personal friend, William Ward. Bill was the first Catholic president of a Little Three (Amherst, Wesleyan, Williams) college and the first at Amherst to have graduated elsewhere (he went to Harvard). His field was American studies, and he had written some very readable articles, had a very good sense of continuity and discontinuity in our culture and history and a quite audible skepticism about the claims of our elites that they ruled on account of competence. His father was a surgeon and they lived in Brookline, but Bill felt no inner need to part with much of the Boston Irish legacy of combativeness mixed with irony. After Harvard, he studied for a doctorate with Leo Marx and William Nash Smith (the historian of the westward movement and much else besides) and taught for some years at Princeton. Leo Marx arranged for Bill to come to Amherst, where he was much liked by colleagues and students—myself certainly included. We became friends, and spoke occasionally of the similarities of our paths from the Jewish Bronx and Irish Boston to higher academic terrain. We also spoke of the contrasts between Europe and the US—especially the contrasting ideas and fates of American progressivism and European socialism. Bill was interested, even fascinated, by the New York intellectual milieu of which I was a newly countrified cousin, and thought it far less stiff than the Eastern academy.

He was friendly with the exiled Greek-American family, the Papandreous, and it was at his house that I met Andreas and his wife, Margaret (an American). Andreas and I had common friends in the European socialist parties and a common language. He had been saved from death at the hands of the Greek military rulers by American academic colleagues in or close to the US government—as well as by the intervention of the German Social Democrats. He later returned to mixed achievements as prime minister, and his son studied at Amherst and in due course also became prime minister—and then had to endure the adverse winds of the crisis of the Euro in its tragic Greek version.

Bill's friendship with the Papandreous was evidence, if it were needed, of his interest in a larger world. He was drawn, however, to advancing in our distinctly smaller one. He was a faculty member of a committee searching for a new president when Cal Plimpton retired in 1971 to return to medicine. I thought at the time that that was not the entire story. Cal very much enjoyed not administering but ruling Amherst. However obscure or merely subtle his moves, it was clear that he took seriously the notion that the president was indeed *primus inter pares*, first among equals, with the emphasis decidedly not on equality. He conducted his own transition into the epoch of new demands for the sharing of authority and power with shrewdness not unmixed with slyness. At the time I admired his flexibility, or what the French would term *habilité*, a higher form of agility. It served us all well—but he left as soon as he decently could. Years later, when I saw how Tim Healy dominated Georgetown, I thought that the New England patrician and the New York Jesuit had a great deal in common—a certain conviction of one's capacity to deal with the inner demands of the self and the outer demands of the world.

In those days, I didn't pursue my very real doubts, instead insisting on my compensatory certitudes. I only dimly admitted that what I lacked most was that sort of conviction. Bill and I shared the ambition that frequently compensated for a lack of inner serenity. In any event, early in the presidential search he left the nominating committee and declared himself a candidate—after screening some of his competitors. I told him that he could easily obtain a college presidency and return later to Amherst as its head, but that this behavior wasn't entirely in good form. He cordially disagreed and was shortly thereafter named president. Bill might have done better to remain a professor and continue with his writing. He had published a very good essay on Emma Goldman in *The New York Review of Books* shortly before accepting the presidency, and he could have had large influence as a writer—instead of dealing with matters important (co-education at the college) and less so (dogs on campus).

He began his presidency in a blaze of national publicity as he led a group of colleagues and students in the trespass at Westover Air Force Base near Springfield. After they were arrested, Bill was about to assume the role of the nation's most militant academic administrator when he thought better of it. I did not join the Westover expedition, but did go to Washington on my own to participate in a demonstration at the Congress organized by my friend Robert Lifton, the psychiatrist who wrote excellently about culture and politics. He had talked with Bill and was expecting him, but he did not arrive. There was not a participant but an agitated visitor from Amherst, our director of development, John Callahan. He was perplexed not to find Bill, and yet relieved. I gathered that he had come to deliver a message, perhaps an ultimatum of some sort, from the trustees for Bill. Whatever it was, he did not deliver it that afternoon. Bob Lifton, Dick Gregory, Judy Collins and others refused to leave the Capitol when told that it was closing and were arrested. For reasons I cannot now recall, other than generalized cowardice, I did not stay. As I recall it, Bob was exceedingly disappointed that Bill neither came nor excused himself.

Bill's public role thereafter consisted of the kinds of statements other administrators made without engaging in symbolic politics I did not discuss the matter with Bill, but he could have rationalized his withdrawal from militancy by concluding that keeping the college on the path of reform was an onerous public duty in itself. That was certainly true, but did he keep it moving forward or was he responsible for some years of an academic stalemate?

Particularly after the defeat of George McGovern in the 1972 election, the cultural and social climate was not encouraging of innovation. At the college, faculty settled in for the long run, pursuing ideas and projects that they knew would take years to come to fruition. Strong commitments to a common educational enterprise persisted, but this was now defined in more individualistic terms. In curricular matters, the departments and not the faculty as a whole became, once again, arbiters. To this was added another element— a certain conventionality in many of the students we admitted. The eccentric and idiosyncratic students who lit up the landscape when I arrived in 1968 were far fewer in number four years later. The students we did admit were certainly dutiful, their eyes on the prizes of careers—but they were incapable of the frequently vexing, often exaggerated, but sometimes creative disorder of their immediate predecessors. Yet Bill Ward had been installed by the trustees in part as a concession to the aggressive militancy of faculty and students. He became, very rapidly, a man adrift.

Himself an anti-authoritarian, humorously critical in ways which possibly drew upon deeper resentments, he had considerable difficulty in dealing with the authority that was now his. In particular, the demands of a role that gave him some influence (setting salaries, for instance) on matters important to friends appeared at times to trouble him. Looking for a larger theme for his presidency and finding none, he took a number of misguided initiatives. McCloy with his philistinism was gone from the board of trustees, but others inflicted themselves on the college. Tenure and its drawbacks was one of their themes, and Bill did not quite achieve the tone of tolerant bemusement with which he could have dismissed it. Instead, he attempted a compromise that satisfied no one: he devised a scheme for the re-evaluation of tenured faculty at intervals of five years. Left open was the essential question: what was to be done if the re-evaluation concluded that the person in question was not up to standards? Indeed, the standards were not specified in the initial proposal, and a vague reference to judgment by peers was quite unspecific. Were colleagues outside the college to be called upon? Were departments to be responsible for their own members? What roles would fall to the president and the dean of faculty? Bill had the excellent good sense to bring the matter to faculty for discussion, and critical questions and strenuous skepticism characterized the first responses. In the discussion, I noted that the president was very firm on the beneficial effects of scrutiny for the colleagues enjoying it. Why deny these benefits to our president and dean, I asked, and proposed a quinquennial review by faculty of their performances. I may have evoked the possibility of faculty also scrutinizing the trustees. The re-evaluation scheme disappeared rather rapidly.

Much more serious was the struggle over co-education. Other places were making the change from all male institutions to co-education, and by the time Amherst came around to discussing it Princeton, Williams, Wesleyan and Yale had done so. Harvard had terminated the remnants of Radcliffe's distinctiveness. The Five Colleges systems allowed women students from Hampshire College, the University of Massachusetts. Mount Holyoke, and Smith to take our courses and many (especially from the two women's colleges) did. There were exchange arrangements which allowed women from other colleges to spend a year at Amherst. We did not, then, live entirely in an all-male enclave. Still, it was not the equivalent for either faculty or students to having women students with us from the beginning to the end of their undergraduate careers.

The arguments for co-education were two. One was that we were missing something important; the second, that we were denying women a privilege accorded to their fathers and brothers. The continued refusal of Amherst to change to co-education, moreover, made it more difficult to recruit women teachers.

The college made a mess of the matter. After much discussion and no little agitation among alumni and students (and a minority of teachers) opposed to the change, Bill Ward recommended it to the trustees. They blocked the initiative and proposed that an Amherst committee of inquiry visit institutions newly co-educational to see what could be learned from them. The sub-text was that co-education might have damaged Princeton, Williams, and Yale. Colleagues at these places treated Amherst's obduracy with ironic disdain. Bill might have stopped the foolishness by mobilizing that considerable faculty majority which was behind him on the issue—and threatening to resign. He did not do so, acceded to the trustees' delaying tactics, and undermined his authority with nearly everyone.

What accounted for the recalcitrance of alumni and trustees? Some acknowledged openly that, faced with the new demands for equality by their daughters, sisters, wives, and workplace colleagues, they wished to keep the college of their imagination intact—a men's club of their thoroughly sentimentalized recollections of their adolescence. Others were worried lest clever women edge out their rather slower sons in the admissions process. Still others, alienated by the obvious sympathy of a faculty majority for the movements of the sixties, thought this an occasion to draw a line. Perhaps it isn't entirely coincidental that the final decision to admit women was taken in the year in which Saigon fell.

The young women admitted, either as first-year students or transfers, were in many respects remarkably liked the young men we were used to. They came from generally prosperous families and good schools, and were not reticent about their goals in life: success. Some had more complex and more humane values. Some spoke in what Carol Gilligan had termed "another voice," but those who did were generally older and had not come directly from secondary schools or other colleges. One of the unexpected benefits of co-education was the arrival of quite a few older women who were local residents, whose college educations had been interrupted, and who (often after raising families) were a great help to us in encouraging the other students to grow up. Some faculty spouses had been a bit anxious about the presence on campus of so many twenty-year-olds: they had not reckoned with the attractiveness of students much nearer their own ages.

Throughout these years, my interest in and attachment to the college diminished, partly due to my disbelief that in the long run, our students would take seriously what we had to say. Some few did and would; the others went on to decent and useful lives—no small achievement on their part—as exemplary citizens. The difficulty was in the reigning criteria of citizenship. My problem was quite another one, and had to do with two things. One was my unhealthy tendency to limit my attachment to persons, places, and everything else. Yes, it made me an interplanetary traveler in our cultural galaxy, but it would take decades before I began to count the costs of what was a compulsion. The other was ambition for a larger role in a wider world. I did not satisfy that in an obvious if challenging way—by sitting down and writing two or three interesting books. Instead, I fragmented my interests, wrote for different publics. No doubt what I wrote was evidence for a larger project but a direct statement about it at some length was continuously postponed. I knew this, however much I turned away from the insight. That made my ambition even more frenzied: I lacked the serenity of inner clarity.

Bill Ward, himself so obviously ambivalent about his new office, certainly intuited this. We had several confrontations. When I requested his assent in the academic year 1972-1973 to teach one day a week at Yale, he suggested that I limit myself to one semester—and was not pleased when I recalled that some years previously, he had been at Yale one day a week for two semesters. Students had complained to him of some of my absences when I went to Italy on the project on contemporary industrial society I was doing for the Fondazione Agnelli—but he had not spoken with me about the matter, and clearly retained the correspondence for use in another argument. When I returned from my year at the Institute for Advanced Study (1975-76), I found that my annual increase in salary was very nominal.

I asked Bill about it, and it was then that he produced the correspondence with the students—three years after the event. Without telling me, he wrote to the faculty asking for their evaluation of my contribution to the college. He asked me for a list of colleagues elsewhere he could write to about my scholarship. There was no provision in the faculty handbook, which governed the conditions of our employment, for steps of this sort. Discreet soundings were always possible, but Bill was using a megaphone. He agreed to my request not to write to scholars at other places, and in the meantime nearly all the Amherst colleagues he had written to communicated their dismay or unease to him. I asked a lawyer with experience of academic issues to represent me. In due course, Bill circulated a letter to faculty explaining that he did not wish to be misunderstood, that there was no one for whom he had higher esteem. By then it was November, and the lawyer remarked that the president at Thanksgiving would certainly be glad to enjoy turkey rather than crow.

Looking back, I regret that the two of us allowed the matter to go that far. I was not the only faculty member at odds with Bill. His approach was uncongenial, even offensive, to others. Ben DeMott, George Kateb, and I took turns at faculty meetings in making our discontent clear. Since Bill was so obviously struggling with the burdens of office, it would have been far more decent and generous of us to have tried to help him.

My final three years at Amherst passed without very much new about them. The Department of Anthropology and Sociology ran itself, not least when I was chair. I varied my courses, without introducing large new approaches in subject matter or pedagogy. By then, in Europe, what there was of social experimentation was living off the intellectual capital of the sixties. The continental Marxists were repeating themselves, with the exception of the patient inquiries and occasional brilliant reconstructions of the historians, figures as different as Edward Thompson and François Furet. Structuralism, then the new perspectives of Foucault, occupied much of the French intellectual landscape. The "New Philosophers," neither very new nor very philosophical, purveyed their commonplaces about the Soviet Union as if they were new. My perspective remained remarkably Eurocentric, as if I had just moved to Manhattan from the Bronx in the forties. The revolutions in the Third World and their striking failures did not interest me, and I was very slow to appreciate the implications of the convulsions in China around Deng's return. The one new threshold I crossed led to the American past, as a new generation of cultural and social historians revised Progressivism by showing how shallow much of it had been.

The ashes of the late sixties and early seventies cooled. I recollect one student who complained to me one Friday afternoon of the rural tranquility of Amherst. I noted that he was from New York, and that he probably lived near the Madison Delicatessen and its superb corned beef sandwiches. He was surprised that I had guessed right. In that case, I told him his path out of Amherst's version of what Marx termed the idiocy of rural life was simple: all he had to do was to go to the registrar's office, collect his transcript, withdraw from the college, and after a weekend with family enroll at City College on Monday morning. I advised against walking up through Saint Nicholas Park to get to the City campus: that might bring him too much urban stimulation. The proposal reduced him to astonished silence, until he came up with an objection. "If I do not stay at Amherst, how can I be sure to get into Harvard Law School?"

More serious was the episode of the search for a new president. Bill Ward resigned in the late fall of 1978. Without consulting faculty, the trustees advertised for his successor, and declared that preference would be given to a graduate of the college. That excluded women and a few faculty members who had served devotedly for decades and were obviously very promising candidates for the post. Amidst the general anger and dismay, I wrote to the *Chronicle of Higher Education*. A liberal arts college, I said, was an institution of learning and not a country club. The distinction had escaped the trustees. If the faculty were to be convinced that the successful candidate owed appointment mainly to the accident of college choice by an eighteen-year-old, we could certainly guarantee him an interesting, if possibly brief, resumption of his Amherst education. In the event, the trustees agreed to appoint faculty and students to the search committee but reserved the decision to themselves.

The final contenders were Julian Gibb, who taught chemistry at Brown and was an Amherst graduate of 1946, and Neil Rudenstine, who was then Provost at Princeton and later President of Harvard. Gibb was chosen, and, realizing that he would encounter some skepticism, arranged in the spring to meet with some of us. Ben DeMott, George Kateb and I were honored as his first dinner guests at the Lord Jeffrey Inn. Gibb was cordiality itself and began by saying that he presumed that I attributed his appointment to his Amherst background. "No, Mr. President," I replied; "I am sure that it also helped that you were not Jewish." He took it in good grace. When, some months later, I asked to be allowed to take leave on short notice for a visiting appointment at Georgetown, he was eager to be of help.

13

The US Again

MY PERIOD at Amherst was full of activities outside it—a large source of stimulation for my teaching and writing at the college. In a vertiginously fragmented American cosmos, I sought terra firma on a couple of planets—to find, eventually, that they too spun off into space. I indulged my penchant for variety by moving into and out of several worlds. No doubt, I would have done better and been more creative had I settled on one. Perhaps I was quite unintendedly parodying a New England example—the moral migration across New York into the west, into what was called by historians the conscience belt. Ohio's small colleges with their abolitionist traditions were spiritual colonies of the New England states. The simile breaks down on the fact that I had no fixed vision, but was seeking to construct one out of the very mixed materials of my existence. Shortly after I came to Amherst, Norman Mailer instructed the members of the Modern Language Association that they ought to leave their classrooms to find American reality in the streets. That did not fit my powers—and I had, after all, become a scholar in order to escape the streets.

It would be more accurate to say that I was not seeking a new vision but obliged by the discontinuity and shock of experience to defend the one I had. Some of Mailer's openness would have helped me to form a truer one, but it took a long time for me to learn that. (Later, I had the good fortune to know Norman, and he rather enjoyed the visions I produced.) Upon arriving at Amherst, I sought out groups, movements, persons beyond the college who would legitimate what I thought that I was doing in it—educating apprentices to a critical vanguard. Who better to do that but the critical vanguard itself, the New York intellectuals, their (or our) publics on the mainland, and the thinkers (and as time went on, some of the actors) who were working at renewing progressivism. Many or most were fellow teachers. There were continuing battles enough in the colleges and universities, and on important matters (class, empire, ethnicity, gender, race). I tried to avoid being drawn into these, to keep to the task of constructing a new view of the whole. That gave my writings on higher education in *Change* a somewhat distant, frequently ironic, tone—as if I were in possession of truths my readers did not entirely possess. My past was a journey through very different milieu and I was not shy about mentioning it, but I did use it to good advantage.

In Amherst itself, public education on a very large scale at the University of Massachusetts offered a contrast to our artisanal culture at the college. University of Massachusetts faculty were drawn from a wider range of educational and social backgrounds than those at the college. The student body had a large number of first-generation college students. They were entitled to take our courses under the Five Colleges exchange arrangements, but very few did so. One young woman who had been advised to enroll in one of my courses by a faculty member came to see me and voiced her ambivalence: she felt as if she was being disloyal by crossing class lines. I responded that if the ruling class allowed a radical social scientist to teach at the college, and herself to listen, without additional payment, perhaps she should take advantage of their mistake. This proved convincing, and she did well in the course. There seemed to be little social intercourse between Amherst students and their contemporaries at the university. That was true to a large degree of my colleagues at the college, too. I was reminded of what I had been told of the Oxford of the thirties and forties Oxford: there were two Communist Party groups, one for the workers in the automobile factory in the city suburb of Cowley, and one for the dons.

The University published the *Massachusetts Review*, which gathered a lively group of contributors and editors. Occasionally, I wrote for it and better still, came to know the colleagues involved. They gave me a view of the nation's problems not covered with ivy. The figure who stood out was a gifted and productive Jewish fellow traveler of the African-American intellectual elite, Jules Chametzky, who had mastered large segments of American experience I did not know of, even from books. It was Jules who suggested the books, and occasionally introduced me to the persons, who were recreating our past and aware of aspects of the present even the nation had difficulty in grasping.

The university had a sociology department with some interesting and productive scholars in it. Long-time friends Alice and Peter Rossi joined it from Chicago. The university sociologists did make me a very substantial gift. A graduate student, Alan Sica, sought me out as intellectual mentor. Alan, son of a north Italian musician, defined himself as an intellectual, not as an apprentice technician working on (an entirely imaginary) social scientific equivalent of a cyclotron. He was for many years the editor of *Contemporary Sociology* and, along with Kai Erikson and Immanuel Wallerstein, one of my few connections to what was once my discipline. The Smith College sociologists Ely Chinoy, Charles Page, Peter Rose, and I shared a common language. We had been brought to sociology by our interest in politics, in the possibilities of a common life; we situated ourselves in American progressivism, and we ignored the narrow and pseudo-empirical borders others drew around the discipline.

Page had taught at City College and an entire generation of scholars were among his students, including Alvin Gouldner and Martin Lipset. He was himself a student of my early mentor Robert MacIver. Ely and Peter brought a Jewish pathos I belatedly recognized to their work, a sense of moral struggle and human connection that echoed, however distantly, centuries of questioning. In those years, however, I was only subliminally aware of the chains of experience behind us.

My year as chair of the Amherst Committee on Educational Policy gave me a seat on a Five Colleges committee dealing with the theme—and some insight into how the other institutions in what was termed the Pioneer Valley dealt with their curricular and pedagogic problems. If I were asked to characterize their response, I would say that it differed from Amherst's in that our neighbors had less ostentatious bravado and were more inclined to admit their confusion, which we all shared. The student members from each of the institutions brought enthusiastic certainty to counter balance what they instantly read as the tired wariness of faculty. Their reading was wrong and we should have been wary of the belief that we were like the earlier residents of our towns, pioneers. The original white inhabitants of the region carried the cultural ethos of Boston and the earlier settlements of the Massachusetts Bay Colony with them. Some Five Colleges faculty looked, though sometimes pretending not to, toward Harvard, then engaged in an entirely unconvincing curricular reform of its own. I am reminded of the old line about the Lowells speaking only to the Cabots and they in turn speaking only to God, but the Lord in those years had other priorities. What theological or meta-historical roots we had were unacknowledged; we shared a vague American progressivism and a secularized and doubting sense of educational mission.

I traveled to other colleges and universities rather often in my initial years at Amherst. Sometimes, I was enlisted to serve on tenure committees, since those on the left thought of me as comrade or first cousin, while the others were reassured by what they knew of my academic traditionalism. In some cases Oxford, about which they knew very little, figured in their minds as a supremely validating credential. American votaries of the Oxford tutorial system were unaware of how much tutoring was done by cheap graduate student labor, or by tenured dons teaching in fields other than their own. They certainly did not know how much of Oxford's energies were devoted to the insistence that pedagogy at Oxford needed neither doctrinal nor practical revision since its longevity was proof of its value.

I wrote quite a lot on higher education in those years for the journal *Change*. I tried to bring the distinctiveness and immediacy of university conflicts in Western Europe to American readers who viewed these as somehow folklore, or unique to the Old World. The phase I used to describe the entire student movement—an anticipatory strike by the labor force of tomorrow—does not now appear to have had much predictive power. The student generation of the sixties has been integrated in the stratified society it sought to make more equal. Indeed, there has been levelling—a levelling of subjugation to a market gravely altered by the global enlargement of production. The veterans of student protest are to be found all over the social map, in posts of command and high income as well as in the ranks of the culturally creative, in the helping professions, public service occupations or successor political movements. There, many have joined the reformist formations they disdained as younger persons; others have animated civic and human rights, educational, environmental, ethnic, feminist, medical, or urban activism. The World Social Forum and its internationalism of solidarity is a spiritually legitimate offspring of the sixties. The colleges and universities criticized then as having been crippled by intellectual traditionalism and corrupted by service to power now appear to have served as schools of public conscience. They did so by providing intellectual and social space for groups of students and teachers who were determined to confront larger questions of the direction of the polity and society. The failure of parts of the protest movement to convert universities into equivalents of churches of salvation or political parties was inevitable. Their accomplishment was in precisely what their more militant voices scorned—consciousness-raising. It could also have been termed broadening the content of education.

I also wrote about the situation in colleges and universities in the United States. I wrote ironically of the protest movement's efforts to convert institutions of learning into centers of revolutionary action: the rest of society was obdurately unresponsive when not extremely hostile. My message was certainly painted in chiaroscuro. In "Students, Professors and Philosopher Kings," I did allow faculties and entire academic communities the right, even the duty, to issue pronouncements on major political issues. That was rather gratuitous, as the occasions on which sufficient internal agreement could be reached to justify an institutional declaration were exceedingly rare. The major point of the most substantial of my contributions to the debate of the seventies was that the continuing tension between serving the existing social order and taking critical distance from it was the source of such creativity as we could produce.

The Rockefeller Foundation in the early seventies sponsored a *Change* symposium, which I organized, on the liberal arts. I did expend a considerable amount of energy in those years on discussions of higher education. I ask myself now, if I had moved very much from evoking an "underground man" of exceptional critical profundity as an academic prototype, the rhetoric of my very first article, published in *The Journal of General Education* in 1952 from a talk I had given at a discussion of the Harvard program. The difficulty with the simile in the seventies was that I was anything but underground, enjoying a readership beyond the academy, and a participant in national and international debate. That was true of many of the contemporaries I came to know, older and younger: we were well situated academically or in the literary marketplace, materially prosperous—and yet we relentlessly cultivated our own unease, even alienation. Our publics took this as evidence of our legitimacy; we insisted on it as evidence of our authenticity.

I moved in several circles. In some cases, it was a circle of one, and that was emphatically true of Herbert Marcuse. By the time I came to Amherst, he had retired from Brandeis University on the outskirts of Boston and moved to the much warmer city of La Jolla to teach at the University of California. I visited the Marcuses there in the winter of 1969, driving from Amherst to Hartford Airport in a snowstorm on an icy highway to fly there. When Herbert and I walked to the campus the next morning, the temperature was at seventy, the sun of course shining, and the campus dotted with palm trees. Herbert with his white hair and finely chiseled features was an icon, and of course he was greeted by "good morning" salutations as we made our way to his office. I recall that his well-mannered responses were perhaps a bit more emphatic when the greeting came from one of the many young women on the way. I observed that the setting was a striking contrast to New England. "Norman, I have always told you: winter is a bourgeois ideology."

Herbert's irony, not unmixed with a sardonic undertone, was a measure of his mood. In a series of writings beginning with *One-Dimensional Man* in 1964, he had given the international protest movement its philosophical marching orders by sketching the dimensions of a revolution in the superstructure. Engels and Marx and their direct descendants in Western European socialism, Lenin and Mao and the Marxists of the impoverished nations, agreed on the imperative of socializing the means of production. Marcuse (with a contemporary such as Henri Lefebvre) called for a revolution of consciousness. His *Eros and Civilization*, in 1951, was a masterpiece in its depiction of "surplus repression" and provided a substructure for his later work. It was also a brilliant Western response, perhaps the definitive one, to Stalinism. Stalin's perversion of revolution (repeated with grotesque exaggeration by Mao) entailed the use of state and party to create a society that would function as a machine. There was little question of liberating human nature since this was infinitely plastic. For Marcuse and the Western Marxists he exemplified, the problem was, precisely, to set humans free to struggle—against economic exploitation, to be sure, but also against cultural deformation. Marcuse, no less than Social Democrats such as Crosland and Galbraith thought the problem of abundance could be solved: the question was the qualitative development of the citizenry.

Marcuse provided the ideas of Adorno and Horkheimer in *The Dialectic of Enlightenment* (the steady enlargement of servitude as new scientific and technical powers took on a life or lives of their own) with a revivalist élan. It is a question to what extent Marcuse and his colleagues were influenced by the culture they so ostentatiously disdained: American mass culture. It defined Americans' daily lives as much as their workplace experiences. The masters of the *Institut für Sozialforschung* did not look for the critical messages buried in the productions of mass culture, which came to the surface with increasing frequency on the eve of the eruptions of the sixties. They had generally ignored the New Deal narratives and the political content in films such as *The Grapes of Wrath* and *Casablanca*, and were deaf to jazz and popular balladry and openly political folk music. The contrast with Brecht was striking, but Brecht as a younger man in Weimar Germany was much more interested in and sympathetic to German popular culture—some of it very deeply rooted—than they. Marcuse's closest American friends were the patricians H. Stuart Hughes and Barrington Moore, combative and elegant inner exiles during the Cold War.

Like many without his genius, Marcuse lived in the shadow of the failed revolution. In his case, it was not only the Soviet Revolution that brought its full measure of disappointment but the unfulfilled promise of liberation of psychoanalysis, and the uprightness of character required by the liberal idea of citizenship. Historical abstraction was for Marcuse the only possible mode of survival, theory making sense of a world of devastating facts. His works can be understood as commentary on a fallen world, and an attack on it for the sake of alternatives most were compelled or enjoined not to imagine. His personal defiance made his words tangible. There was indeed something prophetic about him. There was also something sad, something I had glimpsed in his younger fellow exile, George Lichtheim—homesickness for Germany before 1933.

David Riesman at this time was at the height of his influence. He was eleven years younger than Marcuse, born into American prosperity, and had begun a promising career in the law by clerking with Justice Brandeis. Brandeis had a large vision of the scope of law and considerable moral generosity, which Riesman admired and shared. Riesman took seriously even the most contrarian of opinions in matters ostensibly decided by consensus, was relentless in his pursuit of evidence. He had an acute sense of the multiplicity of the nation's cultural and social worlds and a directness of description rather like that of a novelist. I had first met him as a graduate student, had written the essay on his political views in a volume of the series *Continuities in Social Research* given to his work. He objected, in gentlemanly fashion—a contrast with the bitter anger and vengefulness which was Edward Shils's response to my critical article on one of his papers. It would be too simple to say that Riesman had an inner security born of both personal self-respect and inherited social position and that Shils had neither—though not untrue. They had been colleagues at Chicago, and Shils could not contain his hostility when Riesman's *The Lonely Crowd* became one of those books (like those of Galbraith and Mills) both widely read and discussed. Dave and his remarkably acute wife, Evey, made me welcome in Cambridge when I visited. Their house was the site of a perpetual salon (quite like that of Catherine and John Kenneth Galbraith). Academics of all countries, lawyers of all kinds, artists, journalists, writers, students came in and out. The Riesmans were particularly attentive to younger people, junior faculty and students, and served them well by exposing them to a quite striking range of their seniors.

I had known him for some time, had been a correspondent in the newsletter and discussion circle termed *Committees of Correspondence*, had experienced him as an engaged critic of the Cold War apparatus. He had been more favorable to Eisenhower than to Kennedy, considering that Eisenhower's resistance to the inertia of the

Cold War apparatus and its ideology was a difficult achievement. David had an acute sense of the fear, ignorance and philistinism of much of American politics. His initial criticism of Kennedy and the colleagues who had joined him was that they were in effect too clever by half. They knew how dangerously reckless the Cold Warriors were, but sought legitimation by claiming to be even more committed antagonists of China and the USSR than their predecessors, as in Kennedy's campaign fiction of a "missile gap" which rendered the US inferior to the USSR in striking power, and so denied themselves the chance to begin a necessarily difficult and slow process of public re-education. Bundy some months into office in 1961 asked Riesman to suggest someone to serve as the voice of criticism in the White House. He suggested Marcus Raskin, who as a congressional staff member and organizer of the Congressional Liberal Caucus with Congressman Kastenmeier, knew how tortuous were Washington's paths. When Raskin in 1962 decided that the White House was no place for someone interested in changing American politics, Riesman was a collaborator in the foundation of the Institute for Policy Studies.

Riesman's view of the late sixties and early seventies could be condensed in the French phrase *il ne faut pas exagérer*: it does not pay to exaggerate. He saw much of the student movement, the movements of protest in general, as self-indulgent and intellectually slovenly, devoid of an accurate sense of political possibility, and oblivious of its most obvious defect: its lack of a common language with ordinary citizens. In particular, he decried its attack on the university as undermining the institution of critical sensibility and thought which, instead of functioning as the intellectual vanguard of a new project of reform, had to defend itself against its internal proletariat. He chronicled much of the epoch of possibility in his 1968 book *The Academic Revolution*, with revolution defined as the nationalization of what had been a university culture restricted to a relatively small number of elite private and public universities.

By the time I returned to New England, Riesman had reconsidered his role. His irenic criticism of American society, set down in *The Lonely Crowd* and continued in the essay volumes *Individualism Reconsidered* and *Abundance for What?* had become sharper in the political criticism that joined him to scientists in calling for nuclear arms control. He did not think that serving power was the highest privilege of the universities. I recall with pleasure his remark that American intellectuals were of more use to their country when they had less use for it. In his short volume on Thorstein Veblen (carrying that title), he portrayed his iconoclasm as less effective because he was so adamantly disrespectful of reigning codes of behavior — but found Veblen's independence admirable. David as time went on concentrated on higher education, with its multiple functions of educating an elite, preparing an enlarged middle class for private responsibilities and public careers, and (occasionally) producing critical ideas. He served as a sage, dispensing counsel freely to the many who asked for it. He had favorites, however, in the more independent and outspoken of his younger colleagues, was profoundly engaged as a founder of the Institute for Policy Studies — and joined no one's court. Certainly, he enjoyed his national status as part prophet, part sympathetic chronicler of much in our culture. He was exasperated by prejudice and provincialism, did not despair of the eventual conversion of the ignorant, even of the haters, to civic manners.

In *The Lonely Crowd* he had contrasted inner- and outer-directed persons, attributing the difference to cultural and social changes. He had an account of American history which drew upon Weber and Freud to limit the triumphalism of American progressivism by exploring both the less-frequented byways and the sometimes obscure depths of the national experience. He liked the movies, chided intellectuals who derided "Hollywood," and did not disdain what many thought of as "middlebrow culture." He had considerable sympathy with ordinary Americans struggling with material and moral problems, but was increasingly disappointed and then angered by what he perceived as the egocentric impatience of younger and older critics of the nation. His original participation and enthusiasm for the Institute for Policy Studies, which for the half-century since its founding in 1963 has maintained some of the critical perspectives otherwise difficult to find in Washington, gave way rather rapidly to a benign distance. I was struck by how elegantly he assumed the role of elder statesman, behaving very differently from those who interpreted their having to deal with newer rhetorics and sensibilities as affronts, violations of the moral order. He had every reason to take pride in three major achievements. One was to have shaped with his writing a substantial part of the nation's reflections about itself for more than a generation. The second was to have joined the natural scientists and many who were religiously engaged in opposing the nuclearization of foreign policy, depicting it as a mortal threat not only to human existence but to the quality of our national culture. The third was to have encouraged, by example and precept, those younger than himself to temper their energy with reflectiveness. His inner acceptance of his achievements made it possible for him to age gracefully. I recall meeting him at an Eastern Sociological Society annual conference in 1983 and being struck by his curiosity and generosity. If anyone merited the phrase "a gentleman and a scholar," it was David.

Sometimes, generosity isn't enough. Christopher Lasch, certainly one of our major national prophets, kept a certain intellectual and personal distance from contemporaries, although he was recollected in gratitude by his students, with whom he took endless pains. Christopher's parents were large presences in his life. His father was an editorialist for the *St. Louis Post-Dispatch* and later the *Chicago Daily News*, a devout American liberal with a litany of enemies and friends right out of the New Deal's prayer book. His mother was a free spirit from the plains. Christopher had been an undergraduate at Harvard when I was there, but we did not meet. By the time we did, he had developed a quietly acerbic voice, a very fine sensitivity to moral and political contradictions, and a capacity to grasp history in movement that reduced the cautious generalizations of most historians and the inflated concepts of most sociologists to their true dimension—small. He combined these with large hopes for American social transformation, and when these were disappointed, did not burden the nation with recriminations but embarked on an intellectual quest to find out why. That in the end brought him a certain amount of loneliness, but also the consolation of realizing that he was very much his own master.

Christopher began his career with a book on an ultimately unhappy affair—the relationship of the American liberals to the Soviet Revolution. It was followed in 1965 by the ambitious text *The New Radicalism in America: The Intellectual as a Social Type, 1889-1963*, in which he situated his contemporaries and seniors in their ancestral setting—one often ignored by and unknown to themselves. I reviewed it for *Partisan Review,* reading and writing in Strasbourg in Gaullist Alsace, in a Europe looking across the ocean in wonderment at the new American social protests. Christopher's point was that they were not all that new, if one took the excitements of the turn of the last century into account, and that the themes of the social thinkers of the late 1890s and early 1900s were remarkably similar to those of their intellectual grandchildren: the brutality and remoteness of power under capitalism, the illusions and costs of empire, the struggle for personal liberation, the mistaken notion of the nation as an achieved community.

I first met Christopher in 1969. He and his family (and dog and horse) spent summers in South Newfane, Vermont, not all that far from Amherst. My children delighted to visit and Anna, my eldest daughter, was especially admiring of their domestic closeness. The Lasch children, in turn, regarded their new European friends as bringing something different (I think of the French phrase *je ne sais quoi*) into their lives. Nell, Christopher's wife, was the daughter of my colleague Henry Steele Commager, so they occasionally visited Amherst. Nell was determined, lucid and splendidly honest. Once, Christopher and I recorded in their Vermont kitchen a conversation we later published in *Partisan Review.* After listening closely, Nell had a large compliment for me: "You know, Norman, I think you may be intelligent after all."

Christopher and I planned to join forces with others on the board of a new journal to be titled *Phoenix.* Planning went forward in Rochester (where he was a professor at the University of Rochester), at my house in Amherst, and in Cambridge. We assembled an interesting group of editors and potential contributors, united in increasing dismay at the fragmentation and sectarianism of the movements of the sixties and in a refusal to abandon what we thought of as intellectual and political standards. We situated ourselves between the defenders of a "revolution" which existed mainly in their dogmas, and their embittered critics attached to the very liberal pieties thought implausible by so many in the younger generation. It is too simple to portray the matter as primarily conflict between generations. Rather, choices in modes of historical analysis and political values were at stake. Had the American experiment (in itself

My daughter Antonia riding the Lasch family horse.

a positive choice of words) turned out so badly that we had to begin anew? Were there legacies worth honoring, even following? The tension between Christopher and his Rochester colleague Eugene Genovese, then robustly attached to uncompromising rhetoric, was a factor in slowing and then terminating the project. Somewhere, perhaps in Christopher's papers at Rochester University, the documents are preserved: sketches for thematic issues and a list of persons we definitely did not wish to write for us.

In the end, Christopher's series of intellectually and morally exacting books spoke more loudly and consistently than any journal. On mythicized medieval battlefields, kings and knights rode out between the opposing armies to challenge one another. Christopher never hesitated to get between the lines, and then found that he had enemies front and back. His awareness of the connection between a radical politics and culture impelled him to explore the history of the family, to reconsider the nature of authority, and above all to question an American progressivism (and its European origins) become ossified—as its exponents denied their plight by seeking ever more frenetically for new paths to redemption. The revolutions of the sixties, to which he was so drawn, had failed and had made possible a worse politics than the one which originally evoked opposition. Christopher began a search for explanations, and for very different political alternatives.

I kept in close touch with Christopher until I left Amherst for Georgetown in 1979. Even then, I invited him to a conference on liberal education and the law schools at which he was his usual critical self, unwilling to accept prevailing agendas. I deeply regret that I did not maintain our comradeship as I succumbed to the ephemeral charms of involvement in politics (much of it without any positive consequences, as Christopher would have observed had I given him the chance). He withstood the acclaim that works such as *The Culture of Narcissism* brought him with the inward resolution with which he met later charges that he had abandoned the radical faith. His radicalism was one of a commitment to inquiry. His stoicism when facing a terminal illness in his early sixties was admirable. He preferred keeping his lucidity to write to enduring the consequences of chemotherapy. Having opposed the substitution of therapeutic nostrums for moral decision, he was consistent. Looking back, I see how much I could have learned from him, had I been less addicted to a spurious present.

One realm of American experience was impossible to escape in Amherst—the tumultuous reconstruction of relationships between the sexes. I had the good fortune to be able to see through the open eyes of some very unsparing women: my colleague Deborah Gewertz, my neighbor Mary Heath, and my friend Faythe Turner. Faythe was member of a women's discussion group to whose meetings I was emphatically not invited, but she told me about their themes, and her pointed remarks about the vicissitudes of sisterhood were very instructive. Looking back, I cannot decide whether the extreme tolerance I enjoyed on their part was due to the consideration that I was regarded as open to change or the conviction that I was so rooted in a rigid conception of gender that time and history had to be left to do their work. It helped that I was often visited by my daughters: they were much liked by these women friends, who apparently concluded that I was a good father.

Some friends are marked in memory by very special characteristics—intelligence, empathy, humor, helpfulness, in different degrees of saliency. There is the Yiddish word *mensch*, identical to the German term for human—meaning an emphatic sort of humanity. I had the good fortune to become friendly with Lewis and Rose Coser before I went to Europe, when they were rather senior graduate students at Columbia. Lew came from a wealthy Berlin family, grew up initially in Charlottenburg and went to a school on the Knesebeckstrasse, opposite an apartment building in which my daughter Anna later lived. His family prospered and moved to Grünewald—which was indeed green. Lew fled to Paris from the Nazis, was interned in the south of France at war's outbreak, and arrived in the United States just in time. The organization helping immigrants like himself assigned Rose, an earlier arrival from Belgium, to guide him. Her guidance proved so indispensable that Lewis persuaded her to marry him.

Each had exemplary careers in sociology. The one Rose undertook was more difficult in years in which intellectually superior and outspoken women posed difficulties for male colleagues unable to free themselves of male prejudice. Since Rose was exceedingly talented and hardly shy, she certainly counts as an early protagonist of women's emancipation in American sociology, the more so as she worked in the sociology of medicine and had the unalloyed chauvinism of many physicians to deal with as well. Actually, Rose had large maternal capacities and was much loved not only by her own children but by my daughters. Lew had studied literature in Paris and turned to sociology when his teachers there proved resistant to the obvious inquiry into the social setting and functions of literature. Lew had a considerable amount of intellectual elegance, a cosmopolitan grasp of the distinctiveness of American culture and a lively appreciation of the authenticity of American democracy. He rapidly established contact with the heirs of a living American radicalism. In due course, he and Irving Howe joined forces to found *Dissent* in 1954 with some financial help from Norman Mailer and support from a group of intellectuals themselves surprised that they had money as well as energy to expend on a good cause. Irving's background in the Jewish East Bronx and his education at City College were different from Lew's initial immersion in German and French culture. In fact, in the decades of fascism, Nazism, Stalinism, the Spanish Civil War and finally the general conflagration, the desperate attempts of many to construct a humanistic socialism brought them together. The fabled arguments in the City College lunchroom and in Parisian cafes were not, in the end, all that different.

Lew began his academic career by publishing his Columbia dissertation as the book *The Functions of Social Conflict*. At the time, Talcott Parsons dominated American sociology with a complex theory which depicted consensual processes as indispensable to social existence. That led many, including those who did not come from earlier adherence to Marxism, to criticize Parsons for implicit conservatism. That was over simplified and overdone. I am unsure that Parsons understood what a service Lew performed for him with a rigorous argument that societies were also constituted around conflicts. The book was published in Great Britain, and the *Times Literary Supplement* asked me to review it. At the time, Lew was being considered for tenure at Brandeis University. It was the epoch of the Cold War and Brandeis, as a newly founded institution sponsored by the American Jewish community, did not wish to call attention to the fact that a good many faculty had radical pasts. The *TLS* at the time published anonymous reviews. As mentioned previously, I wrote mine in a fairly good imitation of a British voice, terming the book one of the most interesting contributions "that had come to us from across the Atlantic" in some time. I did not know it, but the dean, a humanities scholar, was a reader of *TLS*. He called Lew in and declared, in effect, that if Lew and his work were good enough for the British he was good enough for Brandeis.

The Cosers and I remained friends. They had a house on Great Pond in Wellfleet which my daughters as well as I knew as a place of warmth. Lew was certainly a sympathetic friend but also a critical one—with the sympathy rendering the criticism even more effective. There was one respect in which I was of some help to Lew: He followed European politics and thought closely, went to France from time to time, and confessed in the early years after the war a large inner resistance to re-visiting Germany. I urged on him that there was a new German academic, intellectual, and political generation, and that they merited our respect and support in their struggle with the past. In the end, he did re-visit the nation and city of his birth—and enjoyed his welcome. Indeed, toward the end of his life he was given an honorary degree by the Humboldt University, where some senior teachers could rightly claim to have performed critically and honorably under Communist rule. Lew's historical sense about Berlin was in any event infallible. Before he could bring himself to go, I described Charlottenburg, site of his childhood, as an intellectually thriving center of cultural life in what was then West Berlin. He asked whether the practitioners of a very old profession were still at their posts at Savignyplatz and was reassured that continuity had prevailed.

Lew's boyhood, as I envisage it from his recollections in conversations, was very much shaped by the febrility of Weimar Berlin. It is difficult to imagine, given the close identification of the city for centuries with German Jewish life, that only four percent of the population was Jewish in 1933. Berlin's Jews were by no means homogenous; they practiced several varieties of Judaism—or none at all. Gershom Scholem's father, the proprietor of a successful printing plant, was indignant, no shocked, when his son declared an interest in Judaism. Little wonder that so many Berlin Jews, having fled to this country, found New York so congenial. The city in the thirties and forties had every variety of Jewish belief and practice, and its secular Jews made their lives in their own worlds, marked by differences no less striking than the ones which divided the religious from those who did not belong to synagogues.

When after my taking up residence in Amherst I visited New York, it was to a city obviously divided on economic, ethnic, racial, and religious lines—if rather different ones those of my boyhood. The divisions were cultural, too: I recollect Barbara Fisher, daughter of my friends Charles and Betty Fisher, recounting that many of her students in English at Lehman College in the Bronx did not habitually read *The New York Times*. I prided myself on having joined the New York intellectuals—a group quite unknown to most New Yorkers.

First, however, I needed something less recondite and more elementary—a family. My familial connection to New York was an adoptive one. Years previously, when visiting from the UK in 1957, I explored the possibility of obtaining the approval of the New York Psychoanalytic Institute for a training analysis in London. The London Freudians did accept social scientists as candidates, but foreigners needed the consent of their colleagues in their own country. I called on two analysts in charge of training and research in New York. One was Heinz Hartmann, who had come from Vienna and told me that he had taken courses with Max Weber as a young man. He was a formidable figure, questioned me on my conceptions of social scientific method, seemed reassured by my intellectual agility and familiarity with the work in ego psychology he had done so very much to develop. He asked nothing about more personal matters. At the time, I was experiencing a good deal of relief at having finished my Harvard dissertation and felt free from that peculiar combination of anxious ambition and dread of failure which I date from very early adolescence, if not before, and which has haunted me since. The other person I had to see was an American, in fact a Californian by origin, Charles Fisher. I had a quite clear recollection of having met him in 1945 at a large social gathering, when he was in the uniform of the US Public Health Service—but none of what we talked about. Twelve years later, I told him of my British and European adventures, gathered that he found these evidence for venturesomeness. I could not declare that I was fleeing something (most evident to myself, the challenges of a career at home) since I was not inclined to be that honest with myself. Somehow, Fisher in the brief hour we spent together so reduced my usual combination of aggressive intellectuality and personal reticence that I felt more than a bit of warmth. In the event, when I returned to London I abandoned the idea, resumed my personal or therapeutic analysis with Dr. Hilda Abraham (which did not afford me a sense of inner accomplishment) and concentrated on other matters. Going out in New York with Edith Kurzweil after I parted from Nina, we met the Fishers. He and I both recalled my visit, and he surprised me by saying that he and Hartmann had been very ready to approve my candidacy, and that he was sorry that I had not pursued it. I told him what I had done, omitting its considerable inner costs, and he responded in a way that conveyed active acceptance, or empathy. There began a very rewarding friendship. He was eighteen years older, but I was more a younger brother, even accomplice, when it came to talking about the foibles and weaknesses of others, than older son. Rather, my role varied depending on the context, giving several dimensions to the dyad. On matters intellectual and political, I was listened to, on matters personal, I tried to listen to him—and did so when I could tolerate what was invariably good advice. Betty felt glad to be included, especially when we entered the realm of what we thought of as very relentless analysis of others' beliefs and character, but which she correctly interpreted as gossip.

Charles (Chuck) and Betty were influenced by the Depression, in which they came to maturity, by their nearness to the Eastern European Jewish emigrant community in which they grew up, and by their origins in California and Chicago. They occupied a large (and I think rent-controlled) apartment on Lexington Avenue at 88th Street; Chuck had a chair at Mount Sinai Medical School and a private practice and was a former president of the New York Psychoanalytic Society and Institute. They lived sparingly. In the summers they rented a small cottage in the East End of Provincetown, opposite the large house of Chuck's psychoanalytic colleague Buddy Meyers, down the street from Mailer's place on the water. Winters, they took a one-week trip to London with friends. Betty complained to me once that one could no longer get a good men's shirt for eighteen dollars, and Chuck had the air of a man indulging himself when, once a year, he bought a new suit at Saks.

Betty cooked herself, excellently, for their dinner parties. If something was lacking at the last moment, I was sent out to buy it. I recall procuring salt, after being instructed not to buy at Gristedes at the corner but to make the three-block walk to another supermarket, where it was two or three cents cheaper. (I allowed Amherst College to cover the Gristedes price.) There were also interminable discussions of renewing the carpets, and fearless questioning of fate: in their sixties and certain to pass away before too long, should they really throw the money away?

They were, however, big spenders of feeling. They still lavished attention, concern, and love on their two daughters and were enthusiastic grandparents. I once visited with Faythe Turner and her three children—who were made, instantly, to feel welcome in the apartment. My own daughters were treated as virtual grandchildren and were delighted to visit them. I recall one Sunday afternoon in 1973 when the girls were scheduled to fly back to Europe. Antonia, thirteen at the time, was not feeling well. Chuck offered to examine her. "But you are an analyst," Antonia objected. "I have a regular MD and a diploma to prove it; there it is on the wall." They went off and I heard Chuck say, "As your physician, I advise you against crossing the Atlantic tonight." Antonia: "I feel better already." Friends relied on the Fishers for understanding and support. Certainly, I did.

The Fishers, however, had decided reservations about dogs. They came to Amherst for one of my birthday parties. My daughters were there; so were the Lasches, and Faythe was there with her three children and their amiable golden retriever, whom the Fishers regarded with considerable distrust. It was on this occasion that the day after the birthday itself, as I was making breakfast for the crowd, the phone rang. It was my mother, to complain that I had not phoned her on my birthday. Chuck said that we could file the episode in the archive of Jewish mother stories: "Perhaps she will disinherit me." "No, she will leave you the money so that you will feel guilty." He had, not quite hidden behind an open and welcoming manner, a wit sharpened by the unfailing acuity of his perceptions. He told me of a prospective patient who expressed surprise at Chuck's intimation of an hourly fee: "Is that all?" Chuck's response: "How much more should I charge you to make you feel better?"

The milieu in which he felt at home—other analysts and their friends from culture, business, journalism, the professions (an occasional writer was always welcome)—was largely Jewish. Physicians of the soul, heirs to Freud's universalism, Chuck's contemporaries remembered the tenements they had come from as they enjoyed their mastery of Manhattan, East and West Side, north of 59th Street. The younger analysts had not wrestled with Americanization, since they took that for granted. The Europeans frequently looked on the entire scene from *haut en bas*, elegant manners not quite concealing a certain distance. I was a puzzle to some of them, if a welcome interlocutor: I knew the new Europe. Conversation at the Fisher dinner parties entailed a component of professional politics (not discernibly different from the academic kind), comment on public events, and very little direct personal matter. The women, professional or not, struck me as more free, more open, and even adventurous in what they said. Freud wrote of the irreducible misery of living, but the dinner guests treated their evenings as periods of licensed release. Cold War, Watergate, the women's movement, all evoked little that I recall as new insight. The analysts seemed as bewildered by history as the rest of us.

Infrequently, on the way from Amherst to regular weekends at the Fishers, I stopped in New Rochelle to visit with my father and mother, or my sister and her family, who lived nearby. I had transferred familial allegiances to the Fishers, to the point of treating Betty with the sort of condescension I reserved for my own mother. Perhaps I ought to modify the description of Chuck as adopted elder brother; there was something paternal in his behavior to me, a combination of rigor and tolerance. He urged me to more creativity, more discipline, more maturity. Perhaps he should have been more insistent, and I should certainly have been more attentive, more grateful. Chuck died in 1988, and saw his last patient just days before he departed. I was settled in Washington by then, visited New York and the Fishers much less often. I was one of those he wished to speak at the funeral. For once, I wrote out my remarks. I recalled his great gifts of friendship, his large understanding of the human situation. We were all, I said, thought by Chuck to be in need. There, his response was certain: "A friend in need is a friend indeed." That struck many nerves, and quite a few of the mourners told me that they appreciated my words. They were small enough recompense for much unbought grace.

In the talk, I recalled the convivial climate of the Fisher dinner parties, with Chuck presiding imperturbably. I drew a contrast with Chuck's critical, sometimes amused, presence at a different sort of regular event, the annual weekends of the Wellfleet Psychohistory Conference. These were annual gatherings organized by Robert Lifton at his house on the cliff above the Atlantic at Cape Cod. They were very long intellectual weekends at which academics and therapists, writers and thinkers, gathered to talk—and, occasionally, to listen. I joined the group in 1970. One had to be approved by Lifton's own mentor, Erik Erikson. I had not met him at the time, but he told Bob that he had read a very good article of

Wellfleet, Robert Lifton's house, with a terrace looking over the ocean.

mine in the *American Sociological Review*. The one article I published there was a very positive review of Erikson's *Young Man Luther*, which indeed was a masterpiece of historical interpretation. There was a certain division of roles between Bob and Erikson, who with David Riesman had been an early sponsor of Lifton's at Harvard.

Bob did the conceptual digging, arranged the intellectual landscape for the meetings. Erik's was a not quite brooding but decidedly authoritative presence, so that his contributions (usually on the second or third and final day of the meeting) were secular consecrations of the entire enterprise. We were occasionally fortunate enough to hear Erik reminisce about his own life on two continents and in three nations: Germany, Austria, and the US. More, he gave us rather direct accounts of the Vienna psychoanalytical milieu, and of Berkeley as a cultural antipode to Harvard. He wrote about Germany (in the unforgettable essay "Hitler's Imagery and German Youth") but he spoke sparingly of his youth there, of his attachment to the youth movement, and left it to us to imagine why he had gone to Austria years before the Nazis seized power in 1933. I now wonder whether it was a deliberate if unavowed way to deal with the scrutiny of younger persons, all accomplished life historians, an injunction that there were matters one was entitled to keep for oneself.

For years the routine was the same (and is to this day): We met late in August (many of the participants were regular summer residents of Wellfleet) beginning on a Friday—and the Liftons offered us a splendid celebratory dinner on Friday nights, which quickly became occasions for the reunion of friends ordinarily separated by distance. Chosen guests, academic or from public culture, opened the proceedings. Bob set the annual theme, with an eye to current events and his own projects. The one permanent current event was the threat of nuclear war; in one form or another, it pervaded our discussions until the end of the Cold War. The Vietnam War and its domestic consequences occupied us until its ignominious and inevitable end in 1975. The threat of nuclear extirpation involved issues of science and governance, protest and resistance, human destructiveness, nationalism, and universalism. Two of our regular members, George Kistiakowsky and Philip Morrison, had actually worked on the Hiroshima bomb, and Kistiakowsky had been Eisen-

At Welfleet in more recent days, with Dan Ellsberg. Robert Lifton is at the back left, in the plaid shirt.

hower's scientific advisor. Dan Ellsberg came regularly. Alexander Mitscherlich visited us from Germany, and he had been jailed by the Nazis. Everyone's experience involved some encounters with history. We were not, then, academically remote.

Bob was quite right to enlist us in the development of his own thought. He wrote two masterful works over the decades of our common work. One was *The Broken Connection*, on the psyche in culture. His inquiry into the Nazi doctors was based on actual interviews with some of them, as well as with their involuntary assistants in concentration camp clinics, inmate physicians—and their victims. Our group was quite productive. Some of us wrote individual essays for a volume edited by Bob and Eric Olsen titled *The Wellfleet Papers*. I did one on Marx and Freud, and returned to the charge when years later we presented Bob on his seventieth birthday with a two-volume Festschrift. I wrote on socialism and the psyche, opening doors to corridors I did not then dare to enter. Whatever we presented or said in discussions, which were invariably dense and instructive, all of us came away from the meetings with the conviction that we had touched the nerves of the present.

Not only because many of our participants were Jewish, the Holocaust weighed on us. There were regular members from Israel. One chided me for referring to Begin and Shamir as terrorists. My remarks, she said, could be "misunderstood." I denied that, declaring that my meaning was clear: the Zionists arrogated to themselves attitudes and behavior they reproved in the Palestinians. Most of the Jewish participants in the conference did not make Israel the center of their existence. They were not resigned to the problematic morality of the occupation and Israelis practice of apartheid, and admired the occasional conscientious objector from the Israel armed forces who joined our sessions, but did not seek serious engagement with the matter.

Another great tragedy of the twentieth century, the deformation of the Chinese and Soviet Revolutions, did not burden a group mostly too young to have experienced the political torments of the thirties. The physicist Phillip Morrison and the psychoanalyst Margaret Brenman had political stories from the thirties and forties, some of which they told. The larger group was mostly concerned with the fate of the American Revolution, which many of us regarded as the beginning of our history. We gave it a redemptive function, even if few of us had ancestors on American soil that far back. The first meetings followed the passage of the Civil Rights Act. Political immediacy in the early years was the opposition to the Vietnam War and the social movements which many of us encountered on our campuses.

Each of us had and used many opportunities to attend interesting meetings, join national and sometimes international debates, and to situate our ideas and work in larger settings. Why did the Wellfleet meetings become so important for many of us? In my own case, it was the occasion for developing lasting friendships with persons who had much to teach. There were Erikson and Lifton, of course, but also Peter Balakian, Margaret Brenman, Peter Brooks, Harvey Cox, Carol Gilligan, Kai Erikson, Kenneth Keniston, Norman Mailer, Phillip Morrison, Charles Strozier, Daniel Yankelovich. Most of all, however, it was Erik Erikson in the background and Bob Lifton in the foreground whose dogged and inspired engagements with the world had model functions for the rest of us.

Just there, problems begin. As I understand, the early history of the group (from 1965) entailed a very self-conscious effort to apply the ideas and techniques of psychohistory to the national experience. As time went on, however, experience overwhelmed our capacity to explain much less shape the nation. We began to rush after history, hoping to touch Minerva's gown.

It was as if two of the most cited modern references to history haunted us, although neither was much cited at the meetings: James Joyce's "History is a nightmare from which I am trying to awake," from *Ulysses;* and Walter Benjamin's parable of the Angel of History—"His face is turned toward the past. Where we perceive a chain of events, he sees one single catastrophe which keeps piling wreckage upon wreckage and hurls it in front of his feet." was equally unmentioned. Immersed in the dark matter of our social universe, the Wellfleet participants resolutely denied the possibility that they could disappear in a black hole and tried to fly toward what they thought of as the light. Icarus comes to mind—but what, specifically, melted our wings?

The journey embarked on by the group was not intended as a flight from history but an attempt to create a new one, an inquiry into the possibility of liberation. No sooner had we advanced tentatively onto cleared terrain than older life forms reclaimed it. We were wary of elder colleagues, such as Margaret Brenman and Phillip Morrison, who had come to political awareness when Soviet communism and several varieties of fascism set the historical agenda. For all of our preoccupation with life histories, the extraordinary patrician Franklin Roosevelt did not interest us. Robert Lifton had worked on *Chinese Communism*, in an inquiry into what he termed Mao's search for revolutionary immortality. That depicted in predominantly clinical terms a titanic effort to alter the course of the world's largest nation and oldest state. Erikson chose to write on Gandhi, on the other side of the world, and Luther, five centuries distant. We understood ourselves as part of the larger critical community of the American intellectual elite, but ignored those who had renounced criticism to join what was for the indefinite future the winning side, the heterogeneous party of American empire.

Occasionally in our discussions I reminded the group of Europeans such as Berlinguer, Brandt and Mitterrand, whose politics did bring past and present together. Richard Barnet came from

Washington several times to talk in larger terms of the Cold War. We did not ask Senator Kennedy, his summer house at Hyannisport an hour away, to drop in—even if he was the leader of the American opposition with which we identified. The meetings had crossroad functions for us—a place to meet other travelers, occasionally to reflect on alternatives. At its best we experienced creative disquiet, a sufficient reward for returning year after year. To be sure, we also allowed ourselves the pleasure of belonging to an exclusive club. That posed a delicate problem in intellectual diplomacy. We wanted recognition, but the more obvious the demand, the more resistance to it from the uninvited. A certain amount of self-preoccupation had its uses. Given our view that we were on top of things, we had to justify it by sustained productivity. Membership in the group brought, then, demands impossible to escape.

The claims of the Wellfleet group, explicit and implicit, were exercises of moral asceticism when contrasted with those of the journal *Partisan Review*, which insisted that its readings of the world, despite some vertiginous changes, were definitive. *Partisan Review* had a long history. Begun in 1934 by William Phillips and Phillip Rahv, connected to the John Reed Club and the American Communist Party, it transformed itself in 1936. Instead of finding revolutionary potential in the American working class of the early New Deal years, it found redemptive energy in struggles yet to come. Its editors and writers disdained the social realism, the concessions to popular taste, of the New Deal narrative. They found an American modernism worthy of its European models. Aesthetic and cultural and social experimentation, biographical daring, were necessary to achieve the authentic revolution—one that would destroy routine. Trotsky influenced its politics, the European avant-garde its view of art. Trotsky found the ultimate revolution possible, if over the historical horizon. The avant-garde, however, brooked no delay; its time scale fused past, present and future. The indefinite postponement of revolution and the immediacy of experimentation in art and literature were compelling to those who dreaded nothing so much as incorporation in routine. *Partisan Review* was written by and for outsiders who claimed permanent rights to dissidence, whatever the issues. Its public in the thirties included many in the genteel reaches of the cultural industry. The very brashness of *Partisan Review* struck them as evidence for its authenticity.

I have written of the journal's iconic role in my own life, as a port of entry into a wide and fascinating, if unknown, bewildering and challenging world of culture. When I moved to Amherst in 1968, I kept in touch with William Phillips. By then, Phillip Rahv had left the journal. William did not think of modifying, much less relinquishing, his belief that the journal (and he as its champion and steward) stood at the apex of Western culture. When, after the Congress for Cultural Freedom's connection to the CIA became known in 1967, the Ford Foundation for a while gave money to *Encounter*. William indignantly declared that American cultural enterprises merited priority. William gave the impression that he lived primarily in the realm of spirit, but was hardly naive about the importance of less sublime constraints. The exact details of his relationship to the CIA, in the form of backing for *Partisan Review* from the American Committee for Cultural Freedom, are difficult to trace. William did tell me of being asked to distribute CIA money to French citizens in Paris, expressing considerable skepticism about the proceeding and indicating that he had not complied with the request. My guess is that he saw the dangers in subsidization, not least in terms of the autonomy of the editors. In the end, he housed *Partisan Review* first at Rutgers and then at Boston University, keeping matters in his own hands.

William had a great deal of ambivalence about the movements of the sixties—even if these ostensibly shared his view that much of academic culture was ossified and remote. The radical American cultural critics, he thought, were often victims of self-deception about the popular culture some of them espoused. They rejected academic canons which they saw as too remote from ordinary experience. William thought much academic work not remote enough, and adamantly refused to find hitherto hidden virtues in the mass culture *Partisan Review* writers had routinely, and sometimes, ritually, rejected. The British recourse to the tradition of popular wisdom, whether uttered by the Marxist historians such as Edward Thompson, Labour cultural critics such as Raymond Williams, or younger theorists such as Stuart Hall, was indeed situated 4,000 miles from Manhattan. Graduates of City College such as William (and many who came from state universities as well) were quite aware of what they were leaving behind and devoid of sentimentalism about it.

Still, the breakdown in the American consensus which had impelled the 1953 symposium on "Our Country and our Culture" was obvious. William had been chair of the committee of artists and writers backing Robert Kennedy in 1968, and Kennedy's was indeed a radical candidacy. Recalls to order had little charm for someone who prided himself on his iconoclasm. William in 1962 had published a symposium, with some very critical contributions, on the Cold War—as well as an article of which I remain proud, "The Coming End of Anti-Communism." The symposium was consonant with the effort by John Kennedy and some of his advisors to escape the constraints of Cold War rigidity. My article did predict, if in no very precise way, the US opposition to the Vietnam War and the European attempt (in West Germany, Poland and the Vatican) to develop alternatives to the permanent confrontation of superpower blocs. William was not a systematic thinker and did not claim to be one, but he did have the capacity to ask questions before they were on everyone's mind. In the case of the New Left, he often in conversation regretted that the questions were old questions, reminding him of the pieties of the thirties. He was somewhat more diffident about the British New Left, since he recognized that it was embedded in the experience of modern British history, so very different from our own. About France, he did leave the *Partisan Review* treatment of the May 1968 movement to an American sympathizer with great knowledge of France, Peter Brooks. Briefly put, William was ready by the end of the sixties to rethink the dogmas of both Cold War and post-New Deal acceptance of a supposedly reformed capitalism. The contrast with Norman Podhoretz, much younger, was striking. Podhoretz as new editor of *Commentary* in 1960 was one of the founders of the New Left, from which he disengaged with considerable energy within less than a decade. William's course was much more hesitant but quite authentic in its very unevenness.

One evening in 1971, William convened a group to discuss the situation of culture and politics. I recollect Peter Brooks, James Gilbert, Robert Lifton, Steven Marcus, Richard Poirier, and Susan Sontag as participants. William was insistent in a certain skepticism: what was new about the New Left, and what would become of the sensibilities it entailed? The use of the plural form suggested that William had another question. The New Left was an incoherent assemblage of groups, movements, thinkers, with different experiences, aims, vocabularies—and no obvious capacity to renew itself, the excitements of the present passed. It wasn't even clear that its segments agreed on a list of antagonists, much less one of cultural and political priorities. It was, he implied, everywhere and nowhere. What he wanted was not something for an editorial stance but a program for editorial inquiry.

That was William's very great talent: he asked questions which at first seemed obvious, next had to be accepted as fundamental, and then with the alchemy of time and thought, had to be understood as original. The meeting was the prelude to a decade of interesting writing from both within and without the New Left. Like the universe, it was breaking into distinct constellations, galaxies, systems as it aged. Unlike it, however, it was not expanding. For a long time, I jested about the meeting and its sequel, saying that William was always intent on catching up with the spirit of the times, but that he had caught up with the New Left only when it was on the way down—or out. Yet he was right to intuit that it would leave an altered consciousness, a somewhat different way of seeing the relationships between art, culture, and politics. William's approach was his tribute to the *Partisan Review* legacy, the intellectual pride of a vanguard journal critical of the very idea of a vanguard.

It is amusing to recount William's foibles. He was very sparing with money. Contributors receiving their decidedly modest checks from the journal were sent a letter which declared that he was sorry that he could not pay more, but that while the journal's expenses were incurred in the affluent society, its income was garnered in the other America. Once, when I received the letter, I pointed out to William that in fact he had paid me more than he had on the last occasion, and for a shorter article. He promptly suggested that as family (I had been elevated to the editorial board), I might wish to return the difference.

He was adamantly self-centered. We talked frequently on the phone when I was in Amherst. One day he told me that he had decided to rejuvenate the editorial board by appointing three promising younger persons: Christopher Lasch, Susan Sontag and me. I thanked him for putting me in such good company, but did suggest that perhaps in our thirties and forties, and not entirely unknown, we were no longer just promising younger figures. "Well," he replied, "you are younger than I am."

William did have a decidedly purposeful view of the past. In his telling, it served as morality tale, as an inexhaustible font of reminders of the sovereignty of illusion. It was also a reminder: there was (almost) nothing new under the sun. At times, however, the past could be stored away. In 1982 I asked him what he intended to do about the fiftieth anniversary of the journal, coming up in 1984. "We really began in 1936," he replied, "when we were entirely modernist and took Trotsky's ideas seriously." I pointed out that libraries the world over had back series of *Partisan Review* dating from 1934, that large numbers of dissertations had been written in several languages on its history, and that there were plenty of books and memoirs on its early years, in and out of print. Everyone, then, knew of its early intellectual and political travails. He said, "Why remind them?" In the end, he did agree to celebrate the fiftieth anniversary in 1984. I was no longer on the board then, and was not invited to the occasion. I remain very much in William's debt, first for what I experienced and learned on the board, secondly for the rewards of my dismissal from it—unfailingly entertaining matter at dinner parties and evidence that in some ways, ideas were important.

The seventies were years which did not add up, or lend themselves to clear ideological characterization. I write in 2014, decidedly a generation later. The politics of the decade were initially marked by a linear continuation of the anti-war movement and its temporary appropriation of the national Democratic Party with the nomination of George McGovern in 1972. McGovern as an air force officer in World War Two had flown some very dangerous missions (from Italy to bomb the Romanian oil fields) and had saved his crew by landing his damaged plane on the Adriatic island Vis, held by Tito's partisans. That did not prevent his antagonists from inventing the term "McGovernite" to designate a lack of resolve to defend the nation. The term was especially favored by those who themselves had known no combat more strenuous than the struggle for fellowships at centers of research or space on editorial pages. The long war in Vietnam had terrible human costs in the country and for the Americans obliged to go there. It also institutionalized a mode of political discourse in which moral strength and weakness were political categories associated with endorsing the use of force—or, rather, the readiness to do so. Reagan, who had served in uniform but never left Hollywood, declared as he took office early in the new decade that "America is standing tall again." Presumably the anatomical reference was dual, an expression of the limitless potency anxieties of many American men.

Whatever changes the founding generation of *Partisan Review* experienced, William and his contemporaries took for granted a dominant role for men. They lacked an emotive vocabulary to consider the claims of the women's movement. They were if anything even more baffled by African-American protest and its cultural claims, which were quite far from the thought of the black theorists of their generation, such as Du Bois and C. L. R. James. William's notions of revolution and class referred to a very schematic 1917, modified substantially by the American sit-down strikes of 1936. Reconciled to the post-war American welfare state, he dimly realized that Nixon found it an ideal field for a new class politics, in which the motto "divide and conquer" allowed a new ruling elite to legitimate itself as judge, jury, plaintiff, defendant and public.

He counted on Lasch and myself, and older thinkers such as Galbraith and Schlesinger, to keep him up to date. Christopher and I, however, found it difficult enough to read modern history in the light of our concerns for democratic citizenship. William did not share these, since he thought in the categories of the thirties and forties, in which new masses confronted old exploiters. The modern forms of exploitation, the conversion of nation into supermarket, had been formally intuited by Mills, sorrowfully recorded by Hofstadter, and celebrated as the new politics by Mailer in his Kennedy election essay. William kept looking for the plot behind these phenomena, a quest especially agitated when the Watergate affair broke. Christopher and I doubted that there was anything behind the agitation on the Washington stage, but had some difficulty in convincing ourselves that the new lack of substance of American politics was in fact as much substantiality as we could in the circumstances hope for. We were not quite convinced by our own minor prophecy.

No doubt, the Vietnam War and the domestic political alignments and realignments it provoked dominated politics until the fall of Saigon in 1975. Some of us noticed but did not dwell upon Nixon's abstention from reversing the Great Society, indeed his half-stealthy, half-loud, series of incremental improvements to it. The most significant of these, the Earned Income Tax Credit, went far beyond the McGovern redistribution proposals of the 1972 campaign, for which the candidate was made to pay with crude and vulgar stereotypes by the Republicans and anxious repudiations by his own party. The measure was introduced by Ford, but of course had been prepared by Nixon and his advisors before his resignation in 1974. It was a remarkable instance of American government using the tax system to provide income minima.

William inhabited a meta-historical cosmos in which events of this sort passed largely unnoticed. A certain amount of blindness was induced in myself and Christopher by our disdain for Nixon. He abandoned Vietnam with all too deliberate slowness, but the visit to China and arms control agreements with the Soviet Union were evidence for nothing less than a continuation of Kennedyite diplomacy. The Harvardians serving Kennedy and later Johnson had no very great use for their colleague Kissinger, He was the person he wished to become—a ruthlessly realistic manager of an imperfect but workable international order—and had no hesitation about making his own the policies of those who had snubbed him. In the early seventies, however, a singular coalition opposed detente and did so with considerable energy and skill.

The coalition was a bipartisan enterprise. It insisted on making human rights a major element in American diplomacy, and was especially interested in demanding of the Soviet Union that it allow Jewish emigration. That was, at the time, an unrealizable demand, since the Soviet Union was unlikely to brusque its Arab client states. It also put the Soviet Jewish community in some danger by casting it as devoid of primary loyalty to the Soviet state. However, it served to maintain tension between the US and the USSR, which was in the interest of Israel as its political elite largely defined it. The mobilization on behalf of Soviet Jewry in the Jewish community was considerable. The antagonists of détente also included vocal groups among the Cuban immigrants and entailed a revival of "captive nation" ideology among Eastern European lobbies. Of course, economically and ideologically motivated proponents of "strength," as well as those in the foreign policy apparatus who had made careers in the Cold War and could not conceive of a world with alternative policies, also opposed Nixon and later Ford and Kissinger.

In the spring of 1976 Norman Podhoretz published in *Commentary* his essay "Making the World Safe for Communism," in which Ford and Kissinger were bitterly attacked for their failure of nerve. William phoned me, said that "we" ought to respond, and agreed when I interpreted that as an invitation to write a commentary. I did so, and then phoned Norman to tell him that I would send him an advance copy—and added that I trusted that he would treat it as a criticism of his views and not his person. Norman replied expressing doubt on that score and read me a quote from Chaim Weizmann denouncing socialists as hypocrites in very brutal terms. I was for once speechless, mumbled something about waiting, and the conversation ended. It was a year I was at the Institute for Advanced Study. The Podhoretzes had previously invited me to a book party at their West End Avenue apartment for our mutual friend and their neighbor, the gifted and outspoken literary psychiatrist Leslie Farber. Midge Decter, Norman's wife, was in fact his editor. I had planned a literary day, with a stop for lunch at New Brunswick with William and his executive editor, Edith Kurzweil (my second wife, from whom I was by then divorced), to be followed by the party in New York. I was about to leave my Princeton office on that day to meet a friend who was to accompany me, when Midge telephoned. Direct and not invariably soft-spoken, she hardly needed a landline. "I am tired of these attacks on us," she said—and told me that I was not welcome at the party. I decided to go to New York anyhow, collected my friend and we stopped at *Partisan Review*'s office where I recounted the episode. "What an outrage," William declared—and added that since he had not been invited, he felt left out since he could not be uninvited. I suspect that Norman had not been told of Midge's initiative, since I did have one final invitation to write for *Commentary* subsequently, for a symposium on liberalism. Many years before, my London neighbor George Lichtheim returned from a year at *Commentary* and when I asked him his view of New York intellectual life, the elegant European gentleman replied that it reminded him of an especially quarrelsome Eastern European Jewish family. One sees what he meant.

There was, however, a real world, and for a while William did me the honor of relying on my views of it in political and social commentary. I could report in the journal on my own intellectual and geopolitical travels, suggest contributors—and, above all, enjoy William's insistence on sticking to basic questions. These arose from his formative years, and the years in which the journal truly spoke for and to a vanguard. That it spoke in several tongues at once made it all the more exciting. About politics, William never quite relinquished his regret at the failure of the Soviet Revolution. Of course, he adhered to welfare capitalism. Beneath the commonplace ideas he unenthusiastically espoused, there were unspoken wells of disappointment and discontent. He received my reports on modernizing actions in the Vatican, of an authentic German conversion to parliamentary democracy and negotiated co-existence, of the quite acute political thinking of the American trade unionists and Congress members I came to know, as if they came from a distant planet.

William's more fundamental concerns were different. Perhaps these were secularized reflections of the Judaism that had been imparted to him as a boy, of which he never spoke to me. I regret that I did not ask him. He sought to read the book of the world, which he understood as a linear narrative. Cultural modernism for him was a deepened, truer, reading. He frequently declared that new and profound works were always difficult of access. *Partisan Review* almost never discussed issues arising from inquiry in the natural sciences and ignored a great deal of modern philosophy and theology. William thought of "culture" as an individual acquisition, which in the best case enabled well-formed persons to withstand the entirely inevitable injuries and insults of history. For him, much academic, cultural, intellectual work was so much noise. What counted was the capacity to understand the moment in its setting. That accounted for his admiration for Susan Sontag, who thought historically and whose daring he liked.

William had great gifts for seizing the moment and its cultural imperatives and no small capacity to take his distance from ideas and sensibilities he intuited (often correctly) as ephemeral and shallow. This was the period of my maximal activity with *The Nation*. I wrote for it often and was appointed to the newly formed editorial board, producing a crisis between myself and William. *Partisan Review* and *The Nation* represented very different cultural and political responses to our century. It was mainly *The Nation*'s past that so disturbed William - its sometimes-sentimental American populism and its lack of critical distance from the Soviet Union.

Founded in 1865, *The Nation* evolved from conventional support of continental expansion, of the supposed identity of national interest, and that of the new capitalism that emerged triumphant from the Civil War. Fifty years later, it was at the vortex of the debate on imperialism and war, on economic and social rights, In short, it joined the new American progressivism—the trade union movement, agrarian and urban protests often motivated by Christian social doctrines, and an unsteady alliance of modernist secularists with the defenders of ethnic and local solidarities. By the twenties, as the offspring of the emigration from Eastern Europe confronted an America vastly more open than the European societies of their parents and grandparents, it became one of the fixed points on the intellectual compass of a new Jewish intelligentsia. New York, however, was a cosmopolitan place, a magnet attracting the ambitious from all over the country. *The Nation* was written for and by the new American cultural elite—with close connections to brothers and sisters (the language of the unions) engaged in actual social struggles.

The Nation I first read was edited by Freda Kirchwey, a protagonist of the generation of women which included Frances Perkins. Editor throughout the New Deal, the Second World War and the trying years of the beginning of the Cold War, she was adamantly attached to her vision of a more just and egalitarian United States. That *The Nation* supported the New Deal was clear, but it also reported on and advanced the claims of the social movements which made the New Deal possible and sought to go beyond it. *The Nation* also gave considerable attention to the arts and literature, and when I first met Clement Greenberg in 1945, he was its art critic.

In the thirties and more intensely in the forties and after the war, *The Nation* was criticized for its refusal to voice the anti-communism that became, in Cold War America, our national substitute for thought. I had been immunized against a belief in the USSR as a nation incorporating mankind's most sublime hopes by reading the Dewey Commission report on the treason trials, as well as by reading novels, autobiographies and biographies which depicted Stalinism in all of its terrible nakedness. That left the problem, in the thirties and forties, of the impossibility of defeating Nazism and fascism without the Soviet Union. There were plenty of scholars and writers whose time in the communist movement either left them with much to expiate, or who chose permanent expiation by joining one of the Marxist sects arguing interminably about the failure of revolution. I was quite frightened, like many others, of the possibility of nuclear war, and thought that avoiding it by establishing some stability in the form of co-existence was a pre-condition of internal change in the USSR. Moreover, the often virulent intensity of anti-communism diverted energy and capacity from the tasks of constructing better Western societies.

When I went to Europe, my skepticism about making anti-communism the central theme of our time grew. In Germany, I met many who had been stringent anti-communists in the years 1933 to 1945 and were now fervent defenders of Western civilization. The moral opportunism of these ex-Nazis was total. For the Europeans, the problem of the Soviet Union and of the communist movement was not a matter of dogmatics, the Soviet Union was present in Central Europe; there were large communist parties in France and Italy, and there were, too, acute memories of common struggles in the Resistance. There were also far more open policies of détente—and a general thickness of historical experience which excluded the reductionism of, let us say, the Dulles brothers. The novel *1984* is indeed a classic of anti-communism, but the UK it depicted was (with occasional attacks by missiles to keep the populace alarmed about external threats) an advanced American air base—which was indeed the case of the UK I lived in from 1953 to 1964.

In Berlin, it was possible to take the subway through the Iron Curtain—at least until the Wall went up in August 1961. Moreover, once Stalin died in 1953, the Iron Curtain became much more transparent and even occasionally porous. In my years in Britain I traveled to communist Germany, Hungary, and Poland. I met lots of academics and writers from the Soviet bloc on their visits to the UK.

The French and Italian communists I encountered in their countries struck me as French and Italian. In the UK, I came to know Edward Thompson and Christopher Hill—Marxist historians who did not leave the Communist Party until 1956. I knew Eric Hobsbawm, who did not leave the party, although he was rather open in his distaste for the Soviet Union. I had been dismayed in the US before I left for Europe in 1952 by the fusion of anti-communism with American triumphalism. I was, therefore, not receptive to charges that *The Nation* was morally blackened by its depiction of the Soviet Union and the early Cold War.

In the event, *The Nation* I wrote for occasionally in the fifties and early sixties from Europe was edited by Carey McWilliams, who brought to it a national perspective shaped by his years as a Californian. When I returned to the US, Carey was very hospitable to my writing about the newer social movements in a larger perspective than that of many of their exponents. I recall a long essay on the events of 1968, at home and abroad, which anticipated in its excessive optimism about the imminence of a large transformation the book I published in 1969, *The Crisis of Industrial Society*. It also had the virtues of the larger text: a certain amount of nuance and a clear view of the historical specificity of the movements in different nations, as well as a warning, which should have been more insistent, that intellectuals, teachers, and students by themselves were incapable of sustaining a long-term movement for social change.

Carey was succeeded by Blair Clark, who had had a quite extraordinary journalistic and public career. A Harvard classmate and friend of Ben Bradlee and John Kennedy, he covered the beginning of the Algerian revolution for *The New York Times*. He had also managed Averill Harriman's short-lived presidential campaign in 1952, and directed the CBS radio news organization. He brought to *The Nation* his patrician disdain for the corruption and lies of the Nixon years, and a quite extraordinary hostility to Henry Kissinger on account of his cynicism. Blair rather liked the plain-spokenness of Jimmy Carter, and thought of him as a genuine republican—but feared, rightly that the Washington apparatus would overwhelm him. I saw rather a lot of Blair in the year 1975-1976, when I was at the Institute for Advanced Study at Princeton, where he had a house. Blair lived in a permanent inner emigration from a nation he wished to be able to think better of. My long years in Europe had given me a distance I could not dispense with, even if I had wished to do so. That brought us together.

Blair was succeeded by Victor Navasky in 1978. Victor was a lawyer with plenty of immersion in politics. He had won a National Book Award for a book on the McCarthy era, *Naming Names*, and was at home in the culture of critical journalism, which he correctly understood as a form for writing history. With Victor as with Blair, I did a good deal of reporting on Western Europe, a certain amount of commentary on current American politics. Victor was an encouraging and generous editor and let me choose my own themes. He had a good sense of the reach of the weekly, had a woodsman's instinctive sense of the thick forest of American culture. It is customary to categorize *The Nation* as a quintessential product of New York City. No doubt true, but New York is a national metropolis and attracted ambitious and creative migrants from the rest of the country—and from the several continents.

The Nation had an interesting annual rotation of interns, many going on to substantial journalistic careers. My daughter Anna was

With daughter Anna as a teenager.

there for a while, much liked by the editors because of her European manners and ideas. The interns who rose highest in politics were Ed Miliband and Nick Clegg. Our successes in the House of Commons were not quite matched in the Congress, where we had readers and some graduates on staffs but hardly persons at the commanding heights. A common criticism of *The Nation* is that its radicalism was simply a derivative of the century's progressivism, tinged by the past. That is in many ways high praise: we kept a tradition alive, and were a point of inquiry for those outside that tradition (or questioning it) who wanted to know its contemporary condition.

The Nation had a cadre of editors who remained with it for long periods, even entire careers. Under Carey McWilliams, Robert Hatch was the managing editor and I learned a good deal from his exacting and humorous editing. The same was true of Richard Lingeman, still at it, who occasionally interrupted his *Nation* travails to write excellent biographies (on Dreiser and Lewis among others). For some years, Elizabeth Pochoda was literary editor. Formerly a teacher of medieval English literature, she found in modern America a new pilgrimage to Canterbury, the cathedral city forever receding over the horizon. She was succeeded by Elsa Dixler, who had taught American history and had large gifts for reminding contributors that we were all heirs of a very complicated past. Visiting the office to talk with these colleagues made the trip from Massachusetts to New York worthwhile. Unlike *Partisan Review*, *The Nation* was not a one-man show. William demanded a high price for admission to the charmed inner circle of the journal, that we make his agenda a priority; Victor actually asked for advice and did so throughout his tenure.

I also acquired readers. The *Partisan Review* readership was concentrated in colleges and university faculties, and literary and intellectual circles in New York. With the departure of the Kennedyites, the aging of officials and journalists who had experienced the thirties, its numbers in Washington diminished. Perhaps there were some 10,000 readers of each issue nationally. *The Nation* in those last decades of the age of print had ten times that many and at times more. Its range was broader, from trade unionists and politicians to politically curious and engaged citizens to metropolitan and university publishing and the makers of opinion. Writing from Amherst about the contenders for appointment as Carter's secretary of state, I was invited to discuss the matter on the *MacNeil/Lehrer NewsHour* at the height of its influence. I still meet readers who recall my articles on the Cold War—senior citizens or about to join our ranks. The quarter-century since the fall of the Berlin Wall seems very long, as if another Wall had been erected in our memory and sensibility to block off the previous epoch and give us a sense of living in some endless present.

With all of these activities, I remained a university teacher. I have described my years at Amherst, but there were trips on the side. I taught at Yale one day a week in 1972-1973. Yale had a program of college seminars, and I gave one at the college headed by my friend Kai Erikson. I found the twenty or so students who signed on for an inquiry into Marxism in the late twentieth century exceedingly diligent, very intelligent, and quite eager to hear new ideas. What I gave them was certainly new to them even if they could have heard much the same from Wolfgang Leonard and Peter Gay, among others on the Yale faculty. The question I did not share with them was whether I was repeating myself, drawing down intellectual capital that I did not sufficiently renew. The identical problem arose with a graduate seminar I gave in the second semester of my visit, on the politics of the Western industrial democracies. The graduate students came not only from sociology but from American studies, history, and political science. There were two visitors from Spain who became firm friends over the subsequent decades— the sociology professor Miguel Beltran, who had a very instructive sense of Spain's place in European history, and the sociologist and the constitutional lawyer Julian Santamaria, who later participated in writing the new Spanish Constitution. During his visit, Julian was in touch with a group of Spanish academics and publicists already preparing the transition to democracy. Two decades later he came to the US again, as ambassador of Spain. In the seminar, I learned a good deal from the dialogue between the Spaniards and a political philosopher, Seyla Benhabib, whose ancestors had had to leave Spain in 1492 and who had grown up in Istanbul. Seyla spoke Ladino, the Spanish of the Sephardic Jews. With her sense of the struggle to impose meaning on the senselessness of history, she became an acute and influential political thinker.

A visit to UCLA in the summer of 1977 was to a much different world. The students included any number of mature school teachers, who did not need me to tell them of the nation's social troubles and cultural disturbances. The undergraduates were friendly, not at all hostile to ideas new to them and socially critical, but determined to let nothing disturb their sense of entitlement to pleasure in life. The Westwood campus of UCLA was verdant but free of ivy and the anxieties that marked it in the East. I saw something of the city's very mixed society. I visited with a Jewish congregation, politically progressive, and one of its pillars, a *Nation* reader, invited me to his box at Dodger Stadium. He took me to his supermarkets in Watts, the impoverished African-American and Latino segment of the city, and introduced me to some of the community leaders and pastors with whom he constantly negotiated. I met a family from the film industry, was struck at their Brentwood dinner parties by their circle's rapid conversational alternation between cosmopolitanism and parochialism. These directors and writers were quite aware that they were addressing the nation, but seemed to think that the nation had some sort of obligation to listen to them.

As for my academic colleagues, many had come to the Pacific coast to seek a different sort of personal autonomy than that afforded by successful academic careers elsewhere. Were they freer than the rest of us east of the Rockies—or bound by different sorts of chains? By the time I could formulate the question, I was on my way home. A serious answer had been given by Leo Rangell, a medical psychoanalyst who was especially hospitable during my stay. The fluidity of West Coast America, he thought, made life especially difficult for some and encouraged a therapeutic optimism for which there was no evidence in practice. A great many Europeans liked southern California. Those I met welcomed its lack of European constraints. Western Europe, however, was by then hardly classical in its culture. Perhaps the Europeans brought illusions of renewal with them. The Californians were profanely indifferent, for the most part, to the spiritual dramas of their visitors.

It was a large if condensed contrast with the year I spent 1975-1976 at the Institute for Advanced Study. It began when the director, my old friend Carl Kaysen, telephoned rather late in the spring to invite me to the Institute for the next academic year. Tell your president, he instructed me, that you are the first Amherst professor invited. I refrained from remarking that that was precisely what Bill Ward would not like to hear, since his ambivalence about having exchanged a career of writing for the life of an administrator was considerable. Bill graciously made no objection to my going and was, presumably, glad to be unburdened of my excessively aggressive presence for a year. I did ask Carl why, after eight years at the Institute, he had suddenly reminded himself of an old friend. I have had complaints, he said, that we never invite Marxists—and you are the best of a bad lot. For Carl, that statement was high praise. I left the question of what it meant to be a Marxist to my ruminations at the Institute—where the authentically Marxist figure was the French mathematician André Weil, who lived in a Left Bank of the imagination.

When the Institute was founded in the early thirties, it was unique in American higher education as a site of scholarship free of the burdens of teaching. Nearly a half-century later, the American university landscape was replete with centers of research; many senior academic figures had positions enabling them to pursue their scholarly or scientific work all the time. The Institute had the aura of its past (Einstein spent his last decades there), but its professors knew they lived in an uncertain present and were facing a very open future. The permanent faculty of some twenty-five scholars were divided into schools of natural sciences, mathematics, historical studies and social science. This last was new, founded on Carl Kaysen's initiative, and its first two professors were Clifford Geertz and Albert Hirschman. Some years before I came, Kaysen and Geertz had attempted to name Robert Bellah to a professorship. A *fronde* formed in opposition, some of it expressing other resentments of Carl (he had named himself a professor of social sciences, and some of the old guard saw that as illegitimate). Others thought Bellah's work on religion to be poorly disguised theology. The ensuing struggle resembled a novel; disagreements turned to permanent enmity. Some who opposed Bellah did so because they suspected Kaysen of intending to make of the School of Social Sciences a public policy institution like the Kennedy School. That was preposterous: if Bellah were a precursor of policy studies, it only remained for the Kennedy School to offer a chair to Susan Sontag. In any event, the institutional climate was tense, unpleasantly so.

However, a visitor who made clear his distance from these quarrels could count on a cordial welcome, and I was fortunate enough to be assigned to this category. I learned something from the physicists, if only a firm impression of the arcane aesthetics of their thought. John Bahcall, who worked on black holes, was a brilliant expositor of matter utterly remote from what historians and social scientists did. With André Weil I talked of European politics. George Kennan was a distant presence, seemed interested in my knowledge of Germany, and actually talked with me at tea. I recall his persistent fulminations about ethnic lobbying in American foreign policy. With me, he chose to dwell on the Ukrainians—very possibly because he was not sure whether I was a Zionist and did not wish to ask directly. It should have been clear to him and perhaps was (he was remarkably reticent) that a younger American Jew with my intellectual and political interests was unlikely to have been drawn to Zionism, whatever the culture of earlier generations.

The name of the school I belonged to, School of Social Science, implied that there was a unitary social science, or that one was possible—despite the considerable variety of assumptions, perspectives, and methods of its visitors. Clifford Geertz and Albert Hirschman did not spend interminable hours, as did too many of my Harvard teachers, worrying about a unitary social science. Geertz, with a large debt to the *Annales* group in France, concentrated on "thick description" in his inquiries, and Hirschman drew upon much of twentieth-century European thought and combined it with his own lucidity and rigor.

Geertz was a contemporary of mine at Harvard in the Department of Social Relations, and took his degree in social anthropology, but studied historical Islamic societies; that is, societies with written traditions. Along the way, he contracted an alliance with a newer generation of cultural and social historians, some inspired by the British Marxists of the *Past and Present* group, some inspired by the obvious exceptionalism of American history. Geertz's method was pre-eminently historical, with groups, institutions, and persons struggling to deal with past, present, and future. He did not explicitly refer much to Freud, but there was a certain resemblance to interpretation in Freud's later ego psychology. That is, modal cultural behavior was the often conflicted result of drive and defense against it, constituted by institutions and the precarious norms they constructed.

The other permanent member of the School of Social Science was Albert Hirschman. Driven out of his native Berlin as a young man, he studied in Paris and Trieste (before the Fascist anti-Semitic laws of 1938, any number of German Jewish students and scholars found Italy somewhat hospitable); he fought in the army of the Spanish Republic, and joined Varian Fry in arranging for the escape from Europe of a significant group of European artists and intellectuals. He was a political economist of the broadest sort of experience, did not expend much energy on refuting the quantitative obsessions and narrow conceptions of human nature of routinized economics, but kept probing for new ideas. He had invited my next-door neighbor in Institute housing, Enrique Cardozo, for the year and was clearly at home in what for other scholars were distinct milieu. He had a quiet irony about him, amusement at human folly which contrasted with the obvious impatience of Geertz. Together, they were splendid hosts.

The School held weekly seminars. I gave an all-too-predictable talk on European socialism, quite failing to see that its innovative capacity was nearly exhausted. I had sufficient insight to connect its fate with that of American social reform—but here too I missed the discomforting signs of the times. A moment of consolation was offered by my old friend from Manchester, the anthropologist Victor Turner, who opened at the University of Chicago a brief campaign to bring me to the Committee on Social Thought as Hannah Arendt's successor. The antagonism of Edward Shils precluded that, but Vic's enthusiasm implied that I had something to offer my colleagues. What was it? Colleagues saw me as seeking a larger view, as defining our scholarly responsibilities as public, and as (beneath an urbane, voluble and witty view of things) very serious about understanding our place in history.

Perhaps that accounted for an episode not without entertainment value: Carl Kaysen decided to leave the directorship to take up a chair at MIT, and the institute trustees advertised to invite letters of application. My experience of academic administration was limited to the chairmanship of Amherst's Department of Anthropology and Sociology, comprising six teachers and a secretary.

(In the six or so years in which I was chair, we had semi-annual meetings; for the rest, I encouraged them to administer themselves. To this day, former colleagues express their gratitude.) I certainly would have liked to remain at the institute as a professor, but that was not on anyone's agenda. To my surprise, André Weil and my dear Harvard friend, Morton White, invited me to a good meal at Princeton's major temple of European cuisine, a Belgian restaurant with rather heavy entrees. They talked in general terms, at first, of the search for a new director and I observed that the new incumbent would have his trials, like having to deal with them. Then they came to the heart of the matter: why did I not apply, since the scientists had a very good opinion of me (presumably, for confessing my deep and systematic ignorance of what they did).

I slept on their flattering suggestion and decided, why not? I typed out a letter to the trustees, suggesting that the new director should have a brief term and make it his principal task to lead a self-study of the Institute. The colleagues to whom I showed the letter liked the idea. The trustees may or may not have been interested in the proposal, but wisely entrusted the post to a former provost at Johns Hopkins. In the meantime, Weil and White had told me that perhaps their backing was as much handicap as anything else, that perhaps I should recruit other supporters while they maintained a benign discretion. *Sic transit gloria mundi*. Actually, a series of directors since then have revived the institute, expanded into fields such as biology which it had absurdly ignored, and shown a good deal of imagination in appointments. The last two directors have been British and Dutch, so the institute's internationalism continues.

The year at the institute also brought contacts with Princeton faculty and students. A lively group of undergraduates sought my help in keeping the spirit of the sixties alive in the seventies. I was torn between the political impulse to encourage them and a pedagogic one—to ask them to reflect on an altered historical situation. Perhaps my ambivalence was instructive. I also had some glimpses of an excellent university at work. I do recall the younger colleague who told me what a Princeton assistant professor's life was like: "You have to publish as if you were at Harvard and teach as if you were at Amherst." In the end, he and many others found the effort worthwhile. Not everyone could have Victor Brombert and Carl Schorske as colleagues.

Of course, the institute was at the very center of the universe of scholarship and science. Its professors had good reason to think of themselves as high priests of the temple of learning. In my ten months there I read, thought, wrote. I completed no major work, experienced no new insights, and was hardly critical of the assumptions about human nature and society I brought with me. Scholarship in the social sciences and humanities is indeed the work of groups worrying about specific cultural and historical sequences. Contemporaneity is more important than ideology in shaping their views. Explicit or implicit, acknowledged or not, political themes and sometimes political argument unite the most fundamental social group in the university, the generation. My generation of political sociologists, joined by political scientists and social historians and anthropologists, asked whether the sources of enduring social power could be found in the class structure—and then disagreed on what the class structure was. We were motivated by the ideal of an educated democratic nation (a theme which joined post-New Deal Americans to post-authoritarian Europeans). The more we experienced and thought, the more difficult and remote the ideal became.

In my own case, I found plausible and even useful diversions. After publishing *The Crisis of Industrial Society* in 1969 (translated into French, German, Italian, Portuguese, Spanish, and Turkish) I thought of larger works—and wrote none of them. One was to be on the Marxist legacy; another, on the elements of social structure. Some of the ideas that could have been used in these unwritten texts did find their way into print in the form of essays and monographs. In 1971 I assembled some of the essays in *Toward a Critical Sociology*. I published "Beyond Marx in the Sociology of Religion," a lengthy explication of the Marxist theory of religion in that year, in a contribution to a volume on the sociology of religion. In 1973's essay "Professors, Students and Philosopher Kings: The University as Critic and Defender of the Social Order," I drew upon British, French, German experience as well as our own and sought to redeem the sixties by arguing that protest and reform were responses to problems definitely not limited to our own decades. So much history did not please those who thought themselves radical innovators but also discountenanced conservatives claiming exclusive possession of past and future alike. They did not enjoy my portrait of some of them as lost in the present, the more so as I spoke for a radical traditionalism.

No doubt, a continuing stream of articles and reviews in different fora constituted a substantial contribution to public debate far beyond the confines of the academy. What I did not do, however, bothers me still. I did not follow the critical beginnings of a deeper view of our history by constructing a larger and more systematic account of the present. In very different ways, quite a few of my contemporaries (Avineri, Bottomore, Brooks, Calvez, Habermas, Lasch, Lifton, Sennett, Touraine, and Morin among them) made this their major project, and I regret not having joined them more fully. Older friends, too (Hughes, Lefebvre, Marcuse) had a right to expect more. Still, what I did do was interesting enough—and had more than a hint of originality.

14

Transatlantic Politics

BETTER LATE than never. From adolescence on, I avidly followed politics, read newspapers, magazines, autobiographies and biographies, histories and journalistic reportage. I listened to the news programs on radio, went to the newsreel theatres. I read the report on the Soviet trials by the commission presided by John Dewey by the time I entered high school, of course knew Edgar Snow's *Red Star Over China* as well. I can still hear Hitler's high-pitched voice, and fully recall Churchill's somber and passionate BBC talk the afternoon of the German attack on the Soviet Union. There was plenty of matter I am still struggling to understand, such as the European nationalisms. I understood Marxism in outline, but could not see how the world of colonialism, fascism, imperialism could be explained. On New York street corners, rival sellers offered Father Coughlin's *Social Justice* and the Communist Party's *New Masses*—but on my father's bookshelves, Beard and Parrington told different, more reassuring, American stories.

As time went on, I participated in student politics, never faltered in my political curiosity and a passion for justice—but I had great, practically insuperable, difficulty in imagining a role for myself in ordinary politics. I recall my surprise when I learned that Malraux had joined de Gaulle as his minister of information. It was much later that I recognized that de Gaulle himself was an intellectual. I knew of New Deal intellectuals, Ickes and Wallace and the economists, lawyers, writers in the government agencies and departments. When Labour won in 1945, I found the names of authors I had read, such as John Strachey and Richard Crossman, in the list of newly elected parliamentarians—but that was in another, near-mythic, country. I never considered studying law, had in any event no talent for economics with its quantitative rigor, and for all of my fascination with immersion in the news of political conflicts here, there, everywhere, hoped that I would eventually write books that would be taken seriously.

I also was rebellious, hostile to authority, and deeply attached to a sense of authenticity I could not entirely analyze or articulate. For a large part of my childhood and youth I thought of ordinary activities as too ordinary. That this was joined in no very clear way to inordinate ambition complicated life for me. In the realm of culture, I insisted on the value of high culture—which distilled the traditions of the great books and major ideas I taught and simultaneously appeared in the works of artistic and intellectual vanguards opposing tradition. By the time I arrived at Amherst in 1968, I was quite aware of the historical specificity of the American protest movements, was not surprised at the diffuse and spasmodic nature of their influence, and intuited that a path to electoral politics had to be found—or beaten out. My writings on immediate politics became increasingly ironic but I was rather reticent, initially, about suggesting realignments and the tactical compromises these entailed. The long essay on the political tasks of colleges and universities was an exception, but there I was on ground I knew very well.

The 1970s began with my taking the short-lived New University Conference as a platform and ended with my working on the Edward Kennedy presidential campaign. In Europe, it began with my attachment to the students and generally younger faculty of the protest movements in France and Germany and ended with my advising Brandt, Berlinguer, and Mitterrand. I began the decade close to Hughes and Marcuse, ended with Galbraith and Harrington. I do not think that I was repudiating a past, but rather seeking a more ample and productive future.

The New University Conference was a case in point. In a political landscape in which there were books, journals, and organizations aplenty given to changing the structures which governed our lives, university teachers and their graduate-student apprentices had to march under other banners. The American Association of University Professors was consistent and noble in its defense of a broad conception of academic freedom, but it did not take political stands as such. Its moral energies, moreover, were defensive and guild-like, and its modes of activity were deliberate and measured. A group of predominantly younger scholars, natural scientists in a distinct minority, came together to see whether they could make a contribution, emphatically generational, to their own futures. They (or we) saw ourselves as speaking for and within the system of higher education—but also as an intermittently loyal opposition.

One difficulty was, of course, that the system consisted of a few thousand separate jurisdictions, public and private, with very different traditions of political expression and participation. For all of the pluralism of American higher education, organizational models were quite similar—but institutions were formally and substantively independent. The German protesters could confront the Conference of Rectors and the Conference of Ministers of Higher Education; the French teacher and student unions had the Ministry of Education to deal with; our American interlocutors were dispersed, plethoric, and quite unanimous in their large indifference to outside opinions they preferred to ignore.

The New University Conference met in Chicago in the spring of 1968, issued bold manifestos after intensive discussion, and by 1972 dissolved itself, broke, and turned its archives over to the University of Wisconsin. With campuses as vanguard strongpoints in the newer social struggles, its journey into history was remarkably rapid. There were several causes. The group supposed that its good intentions went a long way toward defining its tasks, when in fact these were no substitutes for a critical scrutiny of its organizational possibilities. It could serve as a periodic place of contact and support for pre-existing groups on separate campuses, but its initial ambitions were larger. As I recall the discussions at the University of Chicago campus, many participants argued for a vanguard role for the group. In an exceedingly schematic reconstruction, we can say that they thought of themselves as already in possession of the knowledge needed to change society for the better.

There was another source of controversy: did the group propose to concentrate on the democratization of higher education, and of what would democratization consist? Was it a matter of widened access to higher education or of more faculty and student participation in governance? In a period of the widening of curricula to include matters previously ignored or relegated to the margins (women's studies and the spectrum of scholarship which encompassed African-American and Latino cultures and histories), how were scarce educational resources to be allocated? The New University Conference was predominantly white, recruited from public universities, and composed mainly of junior faculty. The rest of the turbulent, indeed shaken, academic world ignored its claims and continued to speak in many tongues.

There was a further difficulty. I have mentioned the minimal representation of the sciences at the meetings. Scientific careers and scientific research had rather different patterns than work in the humanities and social sciences. The natural sciences were prime examples of funding by the academic-military complex — in the standard demonology of the critical social movements of the period. That was, however, not the case and much scientific research was relatively disinterested, There were real questions of the misallocation of resources, of the underfunding of what were then relatively new concerns about the environment, and (then as now) of the corrupting influence of industry in the medical sciences. In the discussion, themes from the fifties and early sixties were given insufficient attention: in a scientific and technological world, higher education had an obligation to prepare citizens to deal intelligently with the political and social consequences of constant change. That was quite distant from discussions of higher education as a path to the experience of personal psychological fulfilment or group liberation.

Scientists had large publics and direct access to elites. In the seventies, the counteroffensive of the Biblical literalists was just beginning, their influence limited to corners of the nation bound (or so we thought) sooner rather than later to become modern and secular. Intellectual high fliers in the sciences allied themselves with the political progressives on issues as diverse as the necessity of arms control agreements with the USSR and increased funding for education and research. At the very beginning of the decade, some on scientific faculties advocated a "research strike" as a way to dramatize their antagonism to the integration of science in the apparatus of wartime empire — or its enlistment in the corporate search for profits. In March 1969 there was a day of discussion at MIT which was termed a research strike. Reading accounts of it, I was struck by the words of the physicist Victor Weisskopf that there were several ways to influence policy, not all of them involving direct conflict. He later was advisor to the Vatican on nuclear arms. The Vatican entrusted a substantial amount of its foreign policy, especially relations with the Soviet Union, to Cardinal König of Vienna, in turn a friend of the Austrian political leader Bruno Kreisky—a schoolmate of Weisskopf.

In the forties and fifties, the party of reform in the US conceived of an alliance of politics and science. It certainly was not entirely missing from the Eisenhower government, the president relying on his scientific advisors to back his disinclination to follow his former military colleagues into confrontation with the USSR and China. The Kennedy White House mobilized more of the nation's reserve of brainpower—but was slow to develop the larger projects Kennedy might have favored had he been allowed to live. In the rest of the decade, politics drew upon an uncertain alternation of accumulated intellectual capital and improvisation in immediate crises. The more radical the books that were written, the more remote from influence their authors and readers (however numerous) became.

There were parallel developments in Western Europe and even in the Soviet bloc. Historically, societies which had large and powerful bureaucracies were hospitable to the politics of educated elites. A significant discussion among Western socialists emphasized the democratic potential, rather than the possible authoritarianism, of an economy and polity dependent on knowledge. Increased possibilities of upward mobility were evoked. Since a new working class required more education, newer sorts of administration and production would entail more participation in administration and planning. That proved illusory. The newer sorts of privileged occupational groups, in welfare capitalism and state socialism, did not think of themselves as vanguards of democratization—but insisted on their privileges. Meanwhile, competition from Asia was lowering employment and income of the Western industrial working class. A long period of stagnation (which has not yet ended) was beginning, while some of us otherwise known for acuteness were still looking for new possibilities on the assumption of continuing economic growth.

Nixon's 1972 victory over George McGovern ended the very temporary ascent of the New Left in the Democratic Party. Nixon baffled his antagonists with his opening to China, his pursuit of arms control agreements with the Soviet Union, the 1973 truce in the Vietnam War, and the expansion of the welfare state. His departure before formal ouster over the Watergate affair was largely interpreted in terms of the abuse of power. The disaster in Vietnam certainly slowed the imperial apparatus but did not stop it. In Europe, the situation was decidedly mixed. Wilson's Labour government was succeeded by the irresolute Toryism of Heath. In France, Mitterrand's reform coalition advanced, but decidedly slowly. In Italy, the communists steadily gained votes and entered into a covert coalition with the Christian Democrats—but altered little. In Germany, by contrast, Brandt and the Social Democrats in 1972 won the largest electoral triumph in the party's history, only to have it followed two years later by Brandt's resignation, ostensibly over a security scandal.

I followed these events, trying to find an opening for an American program of radical reform. It was clear that the American white working class, even its unionized segment, was not available for a new social project. The voting statistics spoke plainly, and so did episodes such as the attack on student protesters by unionists in 1970 in New York. Sometimes, a larger view (President Bill Clinton's remarks at Nixon's funeral asking us to consider the whole Nixon) induces spiritual slowness. There was at the time of Watergate good reason to fear what the besieged president could do. The traditions of American liberalism and pluralism were strong enough to save our republic—but where were the forces that could change it?

American history is marked by eruptions of political and spiritual passion which, after long latency periods, engage in struggles which change our culture, only to retreat to the realms of memory. The New Deal was sustained by social movements of the most varied kind, not least religious. That was equally true of the Great Society project, including the Civil Rights Act. The movements subsided, sometimes leaving organizations as their legacies, sometimes not. Some groups—the American Civil Liberties Union, the National Association for the Advancement of Colored People—survived all of our late twentieth-century storms, while some, such as the New University Conference, the Southern Tenant Farms Union, and the American Socialist Party led by Norman Thomas, did not. We had nothing like the European socialist parties, spanning two centuries in their persistent projects of transformation.

My friend Michael Harrington was formed by two institutions. He studied with the Jesuits at Holy Cross University, then joined the uncompromising Dorothy Day in the Catholic Worker movement. Later, he apprenticed himself to the democratic American socialist tradition, working with Norman Thomas himself (heir to the moral rigor of American social Protestantism). The Catholic Worker movement was a sect calling upon the larger Catholic Church to repent of its accommodation to the world and to revive the egalitarianism of the New Testament. The Socialist Party was caught in the turbulence generated by Soviet communism, by the divisions of American working-class politics, by the limitless quarrelsomeness of the very limited numbers of American socialists, including intellectuals who came from every stratum of our society, old family and new immigrants. Mike learned patience and the long view from the Church, learned to deal with vagaries of American life by enjoying so much of it. He was eminently capable of thinking in systemic terms, but left much of that to others and wrote *The Other America*, calling the nation's attention to the poverty many of our citizens preferred not to see. Dwight Macdonald wrote favorably of the book at length in *The New Yorker*; President Kennedy read the review, and Mike was invited to the White House to discuss an anti-poverty campaign,

That confirmed Mike's great sense of American possibility. Mike knew Europe and understood its politics, and Europeans such as Willy Brandt thought very well of him. He had a sense of time and its implacable demands. By 1973, it was more than clear that the energies and hopes of the sixties were dissipated. It was morally unacceptable to tell an entire generation to construct its own normalcy. Whatever the quarrels of the recent past (Mike was notably unenthusiastic about the founding of Students for a Democratic Society and with Irving Howe had said so in *Dissent* and elsewhere), the new order of the day was recuperation. We had to recover from a very large series of defeats, great and small, and we had to abandon the old and new quarrels of the Left to find some common ground. Mike surely had the Fabians in mind, as well as European groups such as Rocard's Parti Socialiste Unifié, which had contributed to the revitalization of the French Socialist Party. He also wished to join forces with the considerable number of trade union activists, some older but some younger, who thought in larger terms of social reconstruction.

By the time we met in Chicago in the fall of 1973, terming ourselves The Democratic Socialist Organizing Committee, we had achieved a commendable degree of modesty. We would continue with our other affiliations and also envisaged participating in the politics of the Democratic Party. Ronald Dellums, the congressman from Oakland and Berkeley, was a founding member—and we had any number of persons on congressional staffs. With Irving Howe as one of our founders, of course there were connections to *Dissent*. Giving organizational backing to Mike was not the least of our tasks—and the Socialist International recognized us, allowing Mike to attend its meetings. That gave the US a rather unique situation in the Socialist International. Social Democrats USA was still part of the organization. They were backed by the AFL-CIO and had with whatever degree of reluctance supported the war in Vietnam, thus inducing Mike and others to leave it some years earlier. It was grotesque that the United States, with no discernible popular socialist movement whatsoever, had two separate members of the International.

The Democratic Socialist Organizing Committee included some very intelligent persons who thought that democratic socialists should unite with others to contain, and wherever possible, vanquish the communism of the Soviet bloc. Many came from the Jewish labor movement, and had profound ties to Israel and especially the Israel Labor Party. Some, indeed, were somewhat suspicious of the German Social Democrats' project of co-existence with the Soviet Union and the Soviet bloc, including communist Germany. Their preferred ally in the Democratic Party was Senator Henry Jackson, of Washington, who indeed came from that state's strong union movement. Our political allies in Congress were members of the Black Congressional Caucus and the Progressive Caucus—and Senators such as Church and Kennedy who favored an American version of co-existence. They feared nuclear war, and were aware of the deformations in American democracy that permanent mobilization entailed.

I was elected to the executive committee and served several terms, deriving a good deal from the experience. My academic comrades came mostly from public universities, and the pedagogic problems they talked about were very different from those we faced in leafier settings. They were empirical of necessity. I also found the trade unionists very good company and very good at conveying what life in and out of work entailed for their members. There were New Yorkers in the group from Jewish socialist milieus I had only slightly known when growing up. The differences with the AFL-CIO on foreign policy set me to reading on aspects of American history I knew only schematically. I was glad to meet younger persons committed to careers defined by authentic idealism. Most of all, I learned a good deal from Mike with his great gifts of humor and proportion. In part founded to give Mike organizational backing, by the time Mike died too young in 1989, the group was largely sustained by his leadership. In 1982 it merged with what had been the New American Movement and was renamed Democratic Socialists of America. It had a small group of devoted senior members, served to educate a small if steady contingent of younger persons. One of its most significant achievements was an ecumenical one.

Mike and some members of Congress, their staffs, and some unionists formed a group, Progressive Agenda, to challenge the Democratic Party's increasingly insistent denial of its own reformist past. I went to a mid-term Democratic Party meeting in Philadelphia in 1982 with *The Nation*'s new Washington correspondent, Christopher Hitchens, who at the time would have been at home at a Labor Party Conference, but found the Democratic gathering *terra incognita*. (With a bit of help from me, he rather quickly made it his own.) I recall Mike observing that we were the only group at the meeting with a cash bar: we had no corporate sponsors. That asceticism served us rather well—conventional careers had to be made elsewhere. Those who stuck with DSA could enjoy the pleasures of imagining a better world while liberating themselves of illusions about this one. Meanwhile, learning to live with moral complexity was useful.

I was not of any use to my comrades organizationally, left the executive board, kept my membership and inner sense of attachment to a socialist tradition. It provided me with something quite precious—a standard by which to judge an unredeemed world. I never thought that Mike had fully left Catholicism; he retained a sense of the need to make provisional arrangements while awaiting better. That could induce the despair of the nineteenth-century declaration: "We expected the Kingdom of Heaven and got the Roman Catholic Church." That brought him close to his Jewish friends, who like Irving Howe knew the value of (delayed) Messianic expectation: it could generate resignation, but also provided perspective. Irving, for example, entitled his memoir *Steady Work*, and cited the story of the impoverished and unattached Eastern European Jew who was finally offered employment as *shamus*, custodian, of a synagogue. The elders instructed him that he would keep things in order, and otherwise post himself at the Gate of the Ghetto, to tell the community if the Messiah arrived. He protested at what he considered too small a wage, but was told not to complain: "It is steady work." Like any number of other Jewish scholars, Irving was at home in American and British literature written by those who had grown up with the Old Testament. That brought the working-class Bronx, the American Midwest, and the British Midlands closer.

Suppose, however, that there were an American group intent on change which used for the most part rhetoric of Main Street, manifested continuous optimism, eschewed irony, and insisted that there was but one possible ending to the American narrative— an achieved democracy constructed by an educated and egalitarian people. It was not extraordinary that in the culture of American politics in the Kennedy years, a group of this sort emerged: The Institute for Policy Studies. What was extraordinary is that its founders, whatever affinities they developed, could not claim apprenticeships in the American grass roots. Two of them had worked in the Kennedy administration, one in the government during the New Deal. One Kennedy official was Marcus Raskin, born in Milwaukee, a graduate of the University of Chicago and its Law School (and a very accomplished pianist who had initially prepared for a musical career by studying in Paris). He worked for Representative Kastenmeier in the Congress (descended from the Farmer-Labor tradition in Wisconsin) and organized a caucus of young and relatively radical congressmen and congresswomen. The other was Richard Barnet, born in Boston, who had studied at both Harvard College and Harvard Law School, knew Russian, and, after military service in Europe joined the law firm of Ropes and Gray, at the top of all the Boston hierarchies. Under Kennedy, he joined the Arms Control and Disarmament Agency, while Raskin worked closely with the president's scientific advisor, the physicist Jerome Wiesner from MIT, and went with him to Geneva to negotiate the Atmospheric Test Ban Treaty. The third founder, functioning at a distance as guide and sponsor, was David Riesman, whose writings had made him an ecumenical national spiritual advisor. I've already written of the work of his *Committees of Correspondence* and its effectively relentless criticism of the Cold War, and of his relationship with the Kennedy government: Riesman did not join the government, as he was thought too independent and too distinguished), but it was he who, asked by McGeorge Bundy to suggest a critical voice for the National Security Council staff, named Raskin—not least because Raskin knew how Washington worked.

In the late sixties, the institute considered offering permanent posts to Hannah Arendt, Herbert Marcuse and me. By then, however, other voices were audible. The institute's assistants and secretaries considered that each should have a day of the week free of regular duties to pursue self-development. The idea was admirable, but it threatened to leave the telephone switchboard unattended. The solution was the assignment to the switchboard of the senior staff. I can testify that it actually happened, as I can recall days when the institute was incommunicado: someone like Raskin or Barnet was clearly at work and no less clearly unequal to the task. I do not believe that Arendt and Marcuse were ever asked whether they would accept switchboard duty as part of an appointment: the responses would have been enlightening.

At the beginning, the institute took the promise of the New Frontier seriously. The great productivity of the economy was to be used for qualitative growth, science and technology were to be made politically and socially responsible, a culture of democracy was to be combined with an ethos of personal development. The ideas of the critical thinkers of the fifties were to be taken from the bookshelves and seminar rooms and brought into politics. The institute sought the modernization of American populism. Abroad, it reinterpreted strategies such as the Alliance for Progress to emphasize national and regional experimentation with ideas of economic growth. The dangers of the nuclearization of politics were to be met by exchanges between peoples, whilst an international community of scientists would devise in international agreements ways to stop mutual assured destruction before it could start.

The origins of the project were in the New Deal, in the continuous activity of the trade unions and the broadly reformist groups in the Democratic Party. The institute in this perspective could be depicted as a Brookings Institution of a more adventurous kind. Indeed, in the sixties Brookings itself was sufficiently critical for Nixon to have thought of having it firebombed, even if its president was Johnson's former director of management and budget, Kermit Gordon. The institute's integration in the processes of national opinion formation was certainly a major priority of David Riesman.

In the initial years of the institute, I was at Oxford and Strasbourg. I visited with Dick Barnet (I knew him from his undergraduate days) and Raskin (whom I had met in 1961 when he was at the White House) when I visited to the US, and we corresponded when I was in Europe. By the time I returned from Europe in 1966, the idea of the institute as a new fixture in a regularly functioning Washington was a sentimental mirage. Public culture and private passions were joined in a series of spasms. Class, gender, generation, race, region, religion were so many points of conflict. The intensified war in Vietnam made the home front an imperial field of battle. Riesman had long since left the project, warning that calling the spirits from the American dark involved incalculable risks—evident in Nixon's mobilization of the party of *ressentiment*.

The institute responded in several ways. Barnet and others (including Raskin) persisted in developing a larger set of ideas about our historical situation. Their major question was whether democracy could be reformed, or better yet, revitalized. The militarization of public life produced by the Cold War might be reduced or at some hypothetical future fate eliminated. Capitalism would remain in all of its effective control not only of politics but of mass consciousness. The institute sought out some of the political movements which struggled to construct a counter politics. It developed close ties to the Congressional Black Caucus and the Congressional Progressive Caucus. Many of these were matters of personal relationships, exemplified in Raskin's close friendship with Reps. Kastenmeier and Conyers. Dick and Marcus had extremely dense networks of personal influence (as with Paul Warnke, a consistently dissident insider).

Others at the institute worked in other ways. It was a very early exponent of environmental politics. The prominent role of women at the Institute gave it a vanguard role in women's issues, especially in employment. An egalitarian and open atmosphere made it a place in which the young felt at home. Literally hundreds of assistants at the institute became senior figures in the academy, in government, in foundations, in all kinds of social movements. The institute's openness, meanwhile, resulted in firm connections to Washington's African-American intelligentsia.

There were other, more problematic aspects of the institute's work. It was right for them to establish relations with the Castro regime, but it did so uncritically: it might have been more rewarding to open the institute to the dissidents who considered that the Cuban Revolution had become too bureaucratic and authoritarian. Relations with the Soviet bloc were largely confined to the official Institute for the USA and Canada at the Soviet Academy of Sciences, which was also a personal vehicle for the influential Georgy Arbatov, who actually sat on the Central Committee of the Soviet Communist Party and his own network. Arbatov did have connections to the most critical elements of the Soviet intelligentsia, but the institute did not spend much energy on these groups. It remained without significant contact with their counterparts elsewhere in Soviet Europe.

What I found most troubling in the institute's priorities was its political misjudgment about marginal groups everywhere. I am sure that some at the institute were put off by the propaganda success of the Mexican Zapatistas. To qualify for the attention of some of the younger persons at the institute, a totally marginal position in a (small) Third World society was exceedingly helpful. Groups and persons of this sort were invited for awards, celebrated—and as promptly dropped. Dick, with his work on globalization (assisted by the younger John Cavanagh), did not indulge in this sort of sentimentalism.

It was a perspective which resulted in distance from the active elements of critical socialism and social democracy in Western Europe. After all, it was Willy Brandt, then president of the Socialist International, who was asked by Robert McNamara when he was at the World Bank to head an international commission to report on poverty. A familiar question was involved, one certainly known to many at the institute from their studies. Radical movements for social change are slowed and stopped, sooner rather than later, by the many resistances of the world. There are then, at times, possibilities which do not entail a choice between resigned adaptation to the world as it is and obdurate and even sectarian resistance to it. Certainly, the institute, in working for decades with the Congressional Progressive Caucus and Black Congressional Caucus, testified to the belief that the world was not entirely unredeemable. Dick and Marcus had friendly contacts with former colleagues in the Kennedy government. One especially effective institute director, Robert Borosage, insisted on close collaboration with many public interest groups, unions, and members of Congress. The institute rendered the public sphere great services in serving as a way station for apprentices who later went on to Congressional staffs, government, and the organizations which had their roots in the sixties—or for that matter, in the thirties.

Were my reservations, then, unjustified—a not-so-oblique expression of academic and political snobbery? Possibly, but more likely they were born of disappointment at the lack of a new view of the whole, a new conception of politics. Why the institute, and especially its younger figures, should be blamed for this when we all bear responsibility is unclear. I first hoped for a new project from the radical vanguard in the academy and culture, then supposed that the very deep experience of Marcus and Richard would somehow both inspire and educate their younger colleagues, The inspiration was there; the education was much more difficult as we had first to educate ourselves—and we did so very imperfectly. I wonder whether I have been living off intellectual capital for decades and eased the struggle for new ideas when I had completed my reintegration in the United States a decade after returning.

My affiliation with the institute in the years before I moved from New England to Washington in 1979 was very much a matter of personal relationship to Marcus and Richard, maintained by letter, telephone, visits. Marcus, whom I thought of in these years as increasingly utopian (a cheap criticism in view of the academicism of my literary politics) was in the end the gatekeeper who made it possible for me to come closer to real politics.

First, however, I had an interesting encounter with the judicial system—and with the CIA. I've recounted the warmth of my welcome to the UK in 1953 when I was mistakenly identified as fleeing from McCarthyite persecution. In 1976, just returned to Amherst from the Institute for Advanced Study, I confronted the CIA directly. Under the Freedom of Information Act, my lawyer, Leonard Boudin, had asked the CIA and FBI for whatever material about me was in their files. The FBI file conformed my suspicion that an earlier home visitation in Amherst by the IRS was in fact an FBI visit. The FBI agent, poorly disguised as an IRS official from Greenfield, appeared in my driveway in a Porsche and was entirely interested in one thing: was I in receipt of foreign funding and if so, from where? The files suggested a broader perspective in which my activity as a speaker was at issue. In particular, I found a quite good account of a talk I had given to a meeting of Students for a Democratic Society early in 1967 at Princeton. It was a meeting at which Mark Rudd later told me (and a large public in Amherst) that he found my words inspiring. I do not recall what they were exactly but I do not think that I called for student revolt and occupation of campuses, but rather pointed out that the European movements I knew were most effective when they influenced the established political parties. To my regret, I did not follow up the FBI file disclosure but decided, with Boudin, to sue the CIA for violation of my Fourth Amendment right to privacy.

The CIA file we obtained contained one item: a copy of a letter I had written in 1971 to a colleague and friend, Dmitri Ugrinovitsch, at Moscow University, where he had a chair of Scientific Atheism. Dmitri was about my age, we met when I was secretary and then chair of the International Sociological Association's Research Committee on the Sociology of Religion. Dmitri was a person of depth and reflectiveness, who had a large capacity for conveying agreement, skepticism, and dissent with a brief and seemingly casual turn of phrase or movement of hands or head. I suppose this was a skill one learned in repressive regimes. I experienced other persons responding this way in Czechoslovakia, and the German Democratic Republic. Poland and Yugoslavia were much more open in providing a large spectrum of forms for criticism. A comparison with the freer societies of the West is difficult or even beside the point. The political and social institutions in which we act in the Western democracies are organized differently; the rewards of assent and the punishments for dissent function differently, then as now. Dmitri had chosen a career in philosophy with a specialization in official anti-religiosity, since he was a fervent Orthodox believer. He grew up under Stalin, and his academic specialty was a way to provide access to the barred collection of books on religion in the Lenin Library. He had not joined the Orthodox Church as a priest, since he abjured its collaboration with the regime. Other friends in the USSR let me know when I was preparing visits that they would wish me to smuggle in the works of Trotsky or texts such as Deutscher and Souveraine on Stalin. I did not have the courage to do so. Dmitri, *per contra,* wanted me to bring in Karl Barth or Russian thinkers such as Berdyaev and Florensky. There, too, I lacked the courage, although on one trip, Soviet Customs looked at but did not confiscate Niebuhr's *Moral Man and Immoral Society,* which I gave to Dmitri.

The letter opened by the CIA discussed arrangements for a future meeting of the research committee. In 1971, when it was written, the CIA had a program at Kennedy Airport's international mail facility, and opened letters to official Soviet institutions, to and from American Fulbright scholars in the USSR, and those sent to a watch list of Soviet persons interesting to the CIA. Boudin chose the Federal District Court in Brooklyn, and the case went to Judge Weinstein. He empowered an advisory jury and joined my case to two others by plaintiffs represented by other attorneys: one plaintiff was the father of a Fulbright Scholar in the USSR who claimed damages for the opening of correspondence with his son; the other was a woman who had written to a Soviet citizen she had met when he was visiting the US, and her view was that the government had probed into her personal sphere with no justification. Leonard

Boudin designated one of his younger colleagues, Herbert Jordan, to manage the case, and I greatly enjoyed working with him.

The proceedings at the district court took two days. Herbert Jordan in his statement of the case referred to the bills of attainder which had provoked, among other things, the subjects of the Crown to revolt in the American colonies. To dramatize his rhetoric, he pointed to the bench on which the government attorneys sat and pronounced them latter-day descendants of George III. Some of the attorneys wore skullcaps and were obviously observant Orthodox Jews, but the likeness stuck. Sitting in the courtroom, I chatted with an Ivy Leaguer who was the CIA counsel. My own testimony had to do with the anguish I had suffered as a result of the discovery. The government in its defense did not use my writings on authoritarianism and the Cold War to suggest, as it might have, that I was unlikely to have been surprised by what occurred.

As I recollect, the government did do its best to exclude as members of the advisory panel anyone likely to be a regular reader of *The New York Times*, and the jury represented a cross section of ethnic Brooklyn. The advice they gave to the judge was certainly not supportive of the government. I am sorry that I did not get the chance to talk with these fellow citizens, certainly not descended from subjects of George III in a familial sense but rooted in our traditions of freedom nonetheless. That could also be said of the judge.

The times were different, and when the court heard the case, there was considerable media attention. Watergate was more than a distant memory, and a variety of House and Senate inquiries into what were still considered abuses of power by the government, and especially the CIA, were very much on the public mind. Indeed, it was possible in the late seventies to speak of a public and not be taken for a hopelessly nostalgic senior citizen who knew nothing of the social media. CBS sent its legal reporter, Fred Graham, to cover the hearing, and since filming in the court was impermissible, an accompanying artist sketched me. The hearing, complete with sketch, was the opening story on that evening's CBS News. The court adjourned early in the afternoon and I drove back to Amherst for the monthly faculty meeting, which began at 7 p.m. At 6:30 the local CBS station, in Hartford, put on the news—so that when I took a seat at the faculty gathering, a good many colleagues had seen the sketch. Indeed, President Ward had something gracious to say about my contribution to public life. Often enough, Amherst faculty were well able to restrain their enthusiasm about the public achievements of colleagues. On this occasion, they showed authentic solidarity.

The case took time, but in due course, the judge ruled in favor of all three plaintiffs. The CIA was ordered to issue an apology and a cash award of $1,000 to each of us. The CIA appealed, and the appeals court ruled 2 to 1 to uphold Judge Weinstein in 1979. No further appeal was made.

Later, I had the chance to speak of the matter with President Carter's solicitor general, Harry Edwards, after he had returned to his chair at the University of Michigan Law School. Edwards told me that he had decided against an appeal since he was sure that the Supreme Court would not reverse the original decision. The letter had been opened when Richard Helms was CIA director and, by the time the apology was issued, Carter's CIA director, Admiral Stansfield Turner, signed it. Later in 1979, Turner and I appeared once together on a panel at the University of Rhode Island, and since I was then for a very brief interval a consultant to the National Security Council—if a systematically unconsulted one—Turner enjoyed depicting me as an outsider who had finally volunteered for insider status. I trust that I am right when I say that was not quite the case.

One great insider who transcended the usual categories was John Kenneth Galbraith. I had the pleasure and profit of getting to know him when he was most at home, as sovereign of his family's kingdom in Townshend, Vermont, near Brattleboro. I admired the needlepoint at the entrance to the separate study he had built for himself a bit down the road from the original farm house, which read "Modesty Is a Vastly Overrated Virtue." Ken's Scots Calvinist background might have pushed him toward a censorious temper. In fact, he enjoyed contributing to the more colorful aspects of our common life—and was merciless about the foibles of friends. I recall walking with the Galbraiths and my Amherst friend Faythe Turner toward their swimming pond. Ken explained that they had tried for years to dam a creek on their property, with no success. Then a beaver family arrived and they had a pond overnight. What Ken declared as peaceful co-existence with the beavers allowed them to swim in it. On the way, a horse they were keeping for a daughter-in-law came to the fence of his field, to greet us. I like horses and stroked its head and neck. Ken observed that had I grown up where he did, on a farm in Ontario, rather than where I did, on the streets of the Bronx, I would have been distinctly less enthusiastic about horses. On another occasion we had lunch at the Newfane Inn and at the end of the meal, I was given clear instructions. "Do not pretend to fumble for the check, Norman; I am the best-paid author in the US who does not pay alimony." His wife, Catherine, was multilingual, read widely, and was very glad to hear my reports from Europe. She grasped the nuances at once.

Ken telephoned one day from Cambridge and asked me to send him some thoughts on bureaucratization. The ensuing letter was at least as good as most of my articles, and I am proud that he responded by assuring me that he would appropriate my ideas. Ken towered over his contemporaries not only in height but in historical judgment and political acuity. As a friend of his youngest son, Jamie, I like to think of myself as member of the extended family. His memorial service at Harvard had a festive rather than somber air—no doubt, just as he planned. One of the speakers, George McGovern, told me that Ken expressed interest in editing, if not writing, the comments of the mourners. Ken's assault on what he termed the conventional wisdom was connected to a larger project, born of his joining the New Deal legacy and the modern European experience to the prairie radicalism he inherited in Canada. He was of course a student of Keynes, but he was also much more—a fierce advocate of politics as civic education, a scholar who conceived of the world as his classroom. The fluency of his writing did not disguise the exceptional quality of his works, ornaments of a great tradition of historically and philosophically tempered economic analysis with deep roots in his ancestral Scotland.

In 1976, the United Automobile Workers and their president, Leonard Woodcock, were strong supporters of Jimmy Carter's presidential campaign. The union's representative in Washington and general counsel was Stephen Schlossberg. He asked Marcus to suggest a scholar who could assist with preparing position papers. The union had a very competent research department, but apparently a different emphasis was desired. Marcus introduced me to Steve; I met with him several times, and gave him a draft paper on a matter in which I was definitely not an expert: international economic relations. At the time, the countries selling raw materials to the industrial world sought to have their products' prices indexed to the price of manufactured goods. No less a figure than Helmut Schmidt pronounced this "confiscation." The point was that Carter promised to bring to the White House, if elected, the experience of the economically dominated South. He had talked of childhood memories of electrification coming to his family farm on account of the New Deal. Perhaps, I suggested to Steve, we could have another president like Lyndon Johnson, risen from impoverished circumstances and with a large measure of empathy for what Franklin Roosevelt had termed "the forgotten man." Transposing this to the global stage, with Robert McNamara as a conscience-stricken head of the World Bank, could prove an alternative route to loosening the rigidities of the Cold War. After all, we were only three years distant from the destruction of Allende's Chilean model of development.

Carter most definitely did not campaign on themes like this, but did promise a new morality in national affairs. Ford suffered from his pardoning of Nixon, which I thought reasonable and even just. Why prolong the agony, I asked, and considered that Nixon had been sufficiently punished by having to leave the White House. Through Steve and the UAW, and somewhat on my own, I did what I could for the issues group working for Carter under the direction of the theologian Joseph Duffy. My contributions were hardly critical, though may have contributed bit to the construction of a public impression of a potential president at home with the nation's brainpower. I met Carter during the campaign, and had a good impression of his intellectual openness. We talked about European socialism, publicly owned banks and industry in Western Europe and why experiments of this sort might be useful in the US. The future president's interest in the theme did not surface in electoral debate. Subtly conveyed, it might not have proven fatal. The election, clearly, hinged on a familiar American trope: time for a change.

Carter elected, the profound divisions within the Democratic

Party became very audible in the formation of the new administration. In foreign policy, the appointment of Brzezinski as national security advisor was balanced by the naming of Cyrus Vance as secretary of state. I had written a *Nation* article in early summer about the competition for the secretaryship, and had not mentioned Vance. He was described somewhat patronizingly by Hamilton Jordan, Carter's chief of staff, as "the best of that WASP New York crowd." What Hamilton may have known, but did not say, was that the crowd did have experienced and instincts for keeping power. Nixon half appeased, half opposed them and attributed his misfortunes to their antagonism. The most persistent opposition to Vance in his period of office came from the Democratic protagonists of the Cold War led by Senator Henry Jackson. For some of them, pressure on the Soviet Union to allow Jewish emigration was a way to maintain national mobilization for permanent confrontation with the USSR. For others, permanent confrontation was necessary to support Soviet Jewry. For both segments of the Cold War Democratic camp, it was also a career. It was a period in which I wrote frequently for *The Nation* on domestic and foreign policy. I underestimated my own influence, neglected to follow through with a critical book and was convinced of what was not the case—that I was at home in *The Nation* and *Partisan Review*, but otherwise an outsider. What I did not see was how many engaged citizens and some lawmakers and officials valued my outside advice. Conventionality was readily available; serious criticism was not.

Woodcock, of the UAW, was offered an ambassadorship, and initially opted to go to Moscow. Averill Harriman advised him against it: the Soviet leaders would not be impressed by a trade unionist; they respected true capitalists, bankers and industrialists. Leonard decided to go to Peking. Meanwhile, Steve Schlossberg and Leonard's successor, Douglas Fraser (born in Glasgow, his parents having known Ramsay Macdonald, the UK's first Labour prime minister), on behalf of the UAW backed me for an appointment in the new administration. At first it was suggested that I join the White House as intellectual in residence, a successor to Arthur M. Schlesinger Jr. I was told that Carter was thinking about it, but that the circle of Georgians around him was doubtful that I would fit in. No doubt, they were right. Then I was suggested for an ambassadorship—to the German Democratic Republic. That would have guaranteed my success on the lecture circuit, since I certainly would have been declared *persona non grata* sooner rather than later. At the meeting at which these appointments were considered, Vance (who quite reasonably wanted a professional for so difficult a post) gave proof of patrician elegance by declaring that he did not wish to see so eminent a thinker removed from academic life. Then my name came up for the post of assistant secretary in the Department of Health, Education, and Welfare, dealing with postsecondary education—and quite a few billion dollars of expenditures. Someone from the Carter group called me and said that they knew of my academic distinction but would wish to learn more of my administrative experience. I pointed out that I was chair of a department of six, with one secretary. Asked about the budget I administered, I explained that I did not. Amherst was a very well-endowed college, and department chairs were quite free to spend as they thought best. My interlocutor was not slow to realize that I thought myself destined for other callings and appreciated my candor; we ended an enjoyable conversation.

That did not terminate my involvement in the formation of the new administration. I was phoned one day by George McGovern's office. The senator had learned that Samuel Huntington, of Harvard, was to be nominated as undersecretary of defense for policy, quite an important position. The senator had his doubts, and asked what I thought and whether I could assist him by suggesting that a few colleagues make their doubts known. I recalled Huntington's *Foreign Affairs* article of 1968 in which he described free fire zones, defoliation, and the enforced removal of entire populations from their villages in Vietnam as a particularly successful process of urbanization. *The Washington Post* published my letter of protest. I also wrote an extremely direct letter to the secretary of defense designate, the president of California Institute of Technology, Harold Brown. Brown had been secretary of the air force under Johnson, and I said that if the Huntington nomination became a matter of public controversy, the public would be reminded of his role in the Vietnam disaster. Brown replied with rather emphatic coolness, but the nomination did not proceed.

One did not need to go to Washington to become some part

of the scene, as any number of academic and literary figures had realized well before I did. In the Carter years, thanks to the friendship and support of Steve Schlossberg, I served as a foreign policy advisor to the UAW. The UAW had its own interesting foreign connections: at the beginning of the post-war years, its late and very influential leader Walter Reuther had proposed to the auto manufacturers that they provide seats on their boards of directors for representatives of the union. They emphatically refused. Later, in Germany, Willy Brandt's Social Democratic government instituted *Mitbestimmung* (co-determination), which provided for worker representation on the boards of large firms. Ford and GM had factories in Germany, and the German union Industriegewerkschaft Metall (Metal Workers Union) allowed a UAW representative to occupy one of them. Reuther and his brother Victor were sons of a German Social Democratic immigrant, had themselves worked in Europe and the USSR as younger men, and were thoroughly internationalist in their perspectives.

The UAW's research director was Dan Luria, whose father had fled fascist Italy and who as an MIT biologist had won a Nobel Prize. The UAW membership also included large numbers of internal migrants, to the north from the rural black and white South. The union had experienced severe ideological tensions in the thirties and early forties. By the time I came to know it, no doubt it was ruled by a bureaucratized officialdom. Still, it was a very active heir of the New Deal, and made large contributions to public debate on much of economic and social policy. I went to national meetings and spoke with the rank and file members who were delegates. Lots of them struck me as right out of the New Deal-era films depicting virtuous heads of families acutely aware of the dignity of labor—and of the value of their own contributions to the common good. Many had children in college. A certain amount of bureaucratization was a small price to pay for the lives their unions enabled to be made so much better. It was the golden age of the American welfare state: nostalgia is the inevitable consequence of recalling it.

Nostalgia, however, has a melancholy counterpart. Numbers of auto workers' families voted for George Wallace in Michigan in 1968 and subsequently for Nixon—and later for Reagan. The educative reach of the UAW was large—but not large enough. Families of union members do vote for a larger view of the nation more often than not. The unions' pedagogic tasks, however, have been especially difficult when the economic situation has been constricted.

I followed the UAW's economic and social projects with interest, learned a great deal about the slowness of American politics and (thanks to Steve's indefatigable instruction) also about its rougher sides. My own contribution was to insist that the ultimate security of the US was to be found in co-existence with the USSR— which might in time allow inner openings in what was mistakenly thought of as the monolithic Soviet bloc. The union made it clear that it supported Paul Warnke, who was the director of the Arms Control and Disarmament Agency under Carter and who was an honored guest at meetings of the union's executive committee. There was a paradox: the factory in which the B-1 bomber was built was a UAW plant. The union's researchers had considerable openness to projects for the conversion of the arms industry, but that waited upon larger political decisions which were excruciatingly slow in coming. The UAW was not alone in having to live with the constraints of the present and hopes for the future. Any number of Congress members, senators, and governors had to deal with the presence in their districts and states of factories and military bases which provided employment that often paid rather well.

Senator Kennedy himself assumed the patronage of a not-very-recent Navy airplane produced in Massachusetts. Along with the UAW, his senatorial office was a site I began to visit. Kennedy's internationalism, of course, followed familial tradition. As he gradually assumed the role of leader of the Democratic Party's dispersed forces of change, an international public and their political leaders responded to him as the voice of the radical version of American democracy they favored. (I recall François Mitterrand, visiting Washington before his election to the presidency, commenting favorably on the senator's loss of weight.) Members of his staff often remained for very long periods; others were placed by the senator in the government and the judiciary, foundations and education; some went on to their own political careers. I was struck by the ecumenical qualities of the staff—Irish Catholics out of Frank O'Connor's novels balanced by scholarly Jewish and Protestant colleagues, and women in important, sometimes leading, positions. I was immensely pleased when, in 1978, I was asked to draft a very special text for the senator—the first elections to the European Parliament were about to take place, and *Le Monde* asked the senator and Andrei Sakharov to give their opinions.

Of course, I spoke with the senator from time to time. I had the advantage of frequent contact with three of his foreign policy advisors. The first was Robert Hunter, who like me had taught at the London School of Economics. Bob left to serve first as director for Europe, then for the Mideast, on Carter's National Security Council. He was replaced by Foreign Service officer Jan Kalicki, who mixed Old World manners and a very intelligent wariness. Jan was especially protective of the senator when his support of a freeze in nuclear testing encouraged the West German and European peace movements to adopt the senator as their American voice. Jan was made nervous by the unruliness of the European demonstrations of the late seventies and early eighties. The democratization of foreign policy, Jan intimated, had limits. That was not the view of his successor, Gregory Craig. As president of the Harvard student government, he had invited Bundy and McNamara to explain their policies in Vietnam and a large number of student body presidents to Cambridge to listen to them. It took just one day, Greg told me, for the nationwide student protest movement to come to life: Johnson's authorized spokesmen were convincing, if not as they intended. Greg went back to his law firm and later defended John Hinckley, the disturbed young man who shot Reagan, and represented the Cuban government in the tragicomic affair of Elian Gonzalez, the small boy washed ashore in Florida when the boat carrying his family sank. Greg was also the leading defender of Bill Clinton in his impeachment trial and chief policy planner in the State Department under Madeleine Albright. Later, Greg supported Barack Obama, and expected to be named national security advisor, but was made White House counsel instead. He had the format to argue for closing Guantanamo and repudiating torture. That cost him his job. I hope that a future Democratic president will have the insight to place Greg where he belongs—making foreign policy.

I am struck by the psychological aspects of politics. Hunter, after leaving active politics (he was Ambassador to NATO under Clinton) indulged a sardonic view he had restrained when occupying office. I did not see Kalicki after he left Kennedy's staff to go to Brown University, but he retained the detached realism he communicated in Washington when he began to work in international finance. Greg had several public sides: servant of a higher cause, resigned harvester in damaged fields. I sensed the workings of a buried theological passion—and a persistent sort of empathy. I learned a lot from each about the costs of dealing with power—and also something of the benefits unavailable to unchained reflection.

A third portal to Washington in my Amherst years was opened by Marcus Raskin, again, when he introduced me to Ron Dellums and Bob Brauer. Ron was the congressman from Berkeley-Oakland, and so represented both a world-class university and a depressed population in the harbor city. He had leading roles in both the Black Congressional Caucus and the Progressive Caucus. Bob was his senior advisor—a white Californian steeped in the state's radical tradition, which was decades older than the Berkeley revolt of 1965. There were any number of creative and critical California academics in their orbit, but they clearly thought that I had something to add—I suppose it was my ties to Europe and New York. I certainly learned a lot from them—about the ideological and political intricacies of the making of military policy (Ron was a senior member of the Armed Services Committee and later worked on Intelligence), about California politics, about black politics. I also learned something of the complexity and slowness of legislating—even with a large Democratic majority and a Democratic president.

These were, under Carter as well as under Ford and Nixon, years of obdurate resistance to following through on the social and economic gains of the Johnson presidency. There is a case to be made for the depiction of Nixon as a late New Dealer, if by calculation rather than conviction. After all, he had grown up under Roosevelt. His national career began with a disgusting and successful campaign against the New Deal congresswoman Helen Gahagan Douglas. By the seventies, the immediate beneficiaries of the New Deal and Truman's Fair Deal, including millions who went to college and university under the GI Bill of Rights, profited from federal mortgage assistance, and could retire in some dignity owing to Social Security, were often likely to manifest resentment of citizens unlike themselves profiting from these government programs. No doubt, the economic and social falsehoods so assiduously propagated by dedicated servants of capital such as the ascending Ronald Reagan corrupted what was left of the very different public mind of the thirties and forties. What accounted, however, for the anxiety, the disintegration of what there had been of social solidarity, the readiness to believe the worst of fellow citizens who were different? The very real threat during the Cold War that everything could end in an apocalyptic minute had something to do with it. Yet in Europe, no less menaced by nuclear extinction, the sixties and seventies were still in some nations years of social openness.

I had chosen, then, to join electoral and legislative politics in its American version just when its most promising modern moments were relegated to the past, when ideological rigidity and rhetorical ritualism were rapidly replacing the experimentalism and the passion of the New Deal. The legacy was profound, often a matter of personal and familial memory. Whatever there was of creativity and durability in a second legacy, that of the sixties, was so new that the advantages of critical distance were not to be had. Still, the academic veterans of the sixties and early seventies were responsible for the historical recovery of important aspects of the past—in studies of African-Americans, native Americans, ethnicity, gender, immigration, labor and cultural and social life generally. Generational and ideological conflict could hardly be separated in academic departments. Some of this was for all of its intensity a substitute for politics outside the university. Still, the differences were real enough. In the older generation, as solid an historian as C. Vann Woodward in his capacity as editor of the Oxford University Press series on American history refused to allow Charles Sellers's quite remarkable book, *The Market Revolution*, to appear under his auspices. There were innumerable political conflicts which took the form of disputes over appointments, tenure, and curriculum.

My interest in actual American politics and its possibilities was greatly encouraged by changes in the attitudes of many of my European contemporaries and friends. In 1953, with Germany about to re-arm, a former dissenting minister in Adenauer's first government, Gustav Heinemann, formed the German People's Party. Its platform was the unification of a neutral and demilitarized nation. The party won a derisory one and one-half percent of the vote. Heinemann himself later became justice minister as a Social Democrat and was elected in 1969 the first post-war Social Democratic president. His supporters in 1953 included Johannes Rau, later minister president of North Rhine-Westphalia, West Germany's largest state and a two-term president of the nation. The public philosopher Jürgen Habermas and the later Social Democratic minister and Protestant leader Erhard Eppler were also in Heinemann's original campaign. Günter Grass became an ardent and active supporter of Willy Brandt in the sixties. Many in the protest generation of the German late sixties and early seventies went into local and national politics with the Social Democrats, participated in the development of the Green Party, or worked for the trade unions. There were similar developments in France, Italy, and the UK. Decades later, when I came to know the Spanish socialists with González in office, I learned that the Franco regime had had to endure a rambunctious sixties, not least in the ranks of its own youth and women's organizations.

It has frequently been said that American scholars interested in European culture and politics adopted European socialist and social democratic parties as their own as compensation for their disappointment with American politics. The generally critical bent of the Americans supposedly kept many of them from studying the actually quite interesting formations of the European Christian and conservative political spectrum. In my own case, I hardly required instruction as to the persistence of deep strains of cultural and social conservatism in Western Europe. Christian Democrats in several nations, after all, had essential roles in the formation and extension of the welfare states. West European working-class communities were usually quite conservative culturally, and, as in the United Kingdom, attached to their churches. My decades of direct contact with European Catholics and Protestants rendered me immune to the absurdities of characterizing them as opposed to modernity and social justice. In the course of the seventies, I experienced at first hand the major role of German Protestants in the Green and Social Democratic parties. I witnessed the critical contribution of the Protestant church to an enlarged public space in communist Germany. I was surprised, as the decade went on, to learn how closely the Italian Communist Party and major groups and persons in the Italian Catholic Church collaborated.

At first sight, my political and spiritual return to Europe was explicable by my wish not to allow my years there to become, simply, memories—there were deeper reasons. What better way to learn what really constituted American "exceptionalism" than living and thinking, if possible, in a transatlantic setting? There were also ties of friendship: there was one large exception, to be sure. Despite my eleven years of residence in Great Britain, and all that went with it, I left many of my British ties untouched. Of course, I visited the United Kingdom regularly, but I hardly followed events there intensely. Partly, this was misplaced rancour: somehow, I failed to take the necessary distance from my academic disappointment at Oxford. There was, however, another and more productive if very subtle dimension to the matter—the twenty miles of open water between the Continent and England have indeed made British history unique. Philip the Second, Napoleon the First, Hitler, each failed to clear Customs at Dover. How much I learned of culture and politics, ideology and social movements, the rhythms of ordinary life and the continuities of history, when living in the United Kingdom came to my awareness very slowly, and well after I had left the country. Perhaps a period of distance was necessary to set my acquired knowledge in a usable form. Still, I regret not having taken more advantage in the seventies of what persons I knew (such as Tony Benn, Jim Callaghan, Anthony Crosland, Stuart Hall, Eric Hobsbawm, and Edward Thompson) could have taught me.

Of the new lands I sought to reach, Italy was the newest. Of course I knew some of its acute and civilized intellectuals. I visited from time to time, wrote occasionally for Italian journals. One of my friends was the Italian constitutional lawyer and leader of a small party situated uncertainly between the communists and the socialists, Lelio Basso. Another was the former correspondent of *La Stampa* in Washington, Nicola Caracciolo, from the family which owned the daily *La Repubblica* and the weekly *L'Espresso*. Antonio Gambino, the weekly's illusion-free and insightful international affairs columnist. Then there was the quintessentially Italian Vatican official Monsignor Grumelli. He was the administrator of the Viennese Cardinal König's Vatican Secretariat, bearing the rather anodyne designation of secretariat for non-believers. In fact, strongly backed by Vatican Prime Minister Cardinal Casaroli, it was the channel of communication with the Soviet bloc. Grumelli thought that my own singular position between worlds made me an interesting interlocutor—a flattering compliment I certainly did not refuse. I recall walks with him through the Vatican gardens—and his quite extraordinary knowledge of excellent familial restaurants in a wide radius about the Holy City. To enter one with him, as the proprietary family greeted him warmly, was a celebratory anticipation of a very good meal.

Nonetheless, my bookish knowledge of Italian history, my sense of the culture, were quite stereotyped. I knew little of how Italian familism worked, less of the intricate patterns of its public life, and sensed that there were great depths beneath conventionally depicted surfaces—but did not know how to reach these. In 1971 and early 1972 that changed: I was able to spend some months at the Agnelli Foundation in Turin—and Italian worlds opened, since there were several of them. The Agnelli Foundation, bearing the name of the family that owned Fiat, was situated a few blocks from the River Po in what had been the mansion of the Henry Ford of Italy, Gianni Agnelli. It was also down the street from company headquarters. American foundations (and German ones such as VolkswagenStiftung) do function independently of the company and family which originally supplied their capital: one of the Fords once expressed his dismay at the projects undertaken by the foundation bearing the family name. When McGeorge Bundy arrived at its presidency in 1966, his manner of expiation for Vietnam was to concentrate on the toughest of domestic problems, poverty and race. In Italy, with its artful modes of frankness, no one thought that the Agnelli institution was anything but a subsidiary of the family and its enterprises. That made it a very useful place to meet the nation's economic and political and intellectual elites. Italy had its own history but it was still European: thought and language counted.

Turin was especially European. A gracious and cosmopolitan foundation official told me, "We are not Italians; we are Piemontese." The nearness of France was palpable, and so was the presence of a Jewish community in the city for centuries. The House of Savoy's original capital was Turin, and it was also a founding city of the Italian Communist Party. Italian liberalism, too, was rooted in the city. The liberal post-war president Einaudi came from the city, and the familial publishing house, a portal to the rest of the world for post-fascist Italy, was there. Turin was considered a difficult diocese by the Church, which took care to appoint worldly bishops to head it. In many Italian cities, the business and political elites were Catholic, if routinely so. In Turin (as in Milan) that was not quite the case: a tradition of anti-clericalism was the legacy of past struggles against the papal state. It was also, of course, a consequence of Italy's, and especially northern Italy's, agonizing struggle with modernity. Was the fascist movement a pathogenic case of modernity—or a theatrically regressive defense against it?

All of these questions rose as I worked, day after day, at the Foundation. The wooded banks of the Po were a few streets away. Somewhat more distant was the grimmer neighborhood of Mirafiore, which housed the original and still functioning main Fiat factory. I met some of the local unionists. At the airport, there were frequent landings by large Soviet transport aircraft. Fiat was building a factory at the Volga town of Togliattigrad, and machines and men were sent by air. The planes loaded large vats—pasta for the Italian engineers and workers sent by the firm to supervise the project. I talked with some of them, and even the communists among them were adamantly critical of Soviet industrial organization and labor discipline and skill.

The first months in Turin were a very convincing introduction to Italy's diversity. There were other cities and provinces—and Rome. I did have access to one important if new Italian political group, the Communist Party dissidents around the journal *Il Manifesto*. The title came from a pamphlet issued by these very active intellectuals, some in elective office, in 1969. The year 1968 is remembered in the US for the terrible murders of King and Robert Kennedy, for uprisings in the black ghettos, for the tumultuous Democratic convention and accompanying streets conflicts in Chicago (and the Tet offensive in Vietnam). We refer to the entire period of disturbance and rupture as "the sixties" and to the progenitors as "the movement" or "movements." In France and Germany, the May revolts in Paris and the rest of the country, and the university protests across the Rhine, earned the protagonists the title of Soixante-huitards or Achtundsechzigern. In Italy, schools, universities, and factories erupted a year later in what was termed the hot autumn, *l'autunno caldo*. What made the Italian situation distinctive was a much larger and visible working class participation. The Communist Party and its union CGIL, dominated the horizon of the left, but its omnipresence had called forth for years all kinds of dissidence. Small conventicles of the revolutionary elect, determined sets of critics, occupied the interstices of political space. Nineteen-sixty-nine was their moment, when they came together to express the grievances that had accumulated against the communists' relentless organization of political culture, against the Socialist Party's institutional schizophrenia (in national government with the Christian Democrats, it shared regional and municipal governments with the communists). In the workplace, industrial and otherwise, union shop stewards ruled in ways which would have been instantly recognizable to the most heavy-handed of their American counterparts.

As occurred often, *l'autunno caldo* was set off by a combination of external events with the growth of previously repressed antagonisms and grievances. Certainly, the examples of France and Germany (and the American movements, too) were compelling. Students and teachers returning from these other nations were bearers of new ideas and impulses. A generation rejected the imposition of long apprenticeship on itself. There were, however, specifically Italian causes. The effects of the Second Vatican Council, the *aggiornamento* or opening of the Catholic Church, brought a distinctively Catholic fervor to some of the protests. The other great Italian church, meanwhile, the Communist Party, had indeed under the new leadership of Enrico Berlinguer sought to loosen the bureaucratic rigidities of its version of Stalinism. That was a process, the Party's leadership found, that it could not control. Many communists, older and younger, were inspired by the Czech experiment of "socialism with a human face" and extremely disappointed by what they thought of as the rather tepid response of their party to the occupation of Czechoslovakia by the troops of the Warsaw Pact. There were sufficient numbers of former communists and independent leftists in Italy to make "I told you so" a credible position. Italy, many said, was European, wealthy and self-governing: why do we have to act as if our labor rights and welfare projects are perpetually at risk—instead of deepening these. Movements of a major kind, as the renewal of feminism, and special ones as new models of psychiatry, contributed to an atmosphere in which critical experimentation appeared not only possible but necessary.

It was in this setting that the Manifesto group, not entirely anticipating the resonance it would evoke, issued its first call to renewal. I was one of a set of American social scientists who wrote about it, in 1971, in a special issue of the journal *Politics and Society*. My own article was termed "A New Version of the Socialist Tradition." When I arrived in Italy and contacted the Manifesto group, I found that it had been appreciated. The Manifesto leaders, Rossanda, Pintor, Magri, may well have known other Americans, but they were quite reticent about talking with me. They were of an Italian intellectual generation that had little knowledge of the complexities of American history. The two persons in the group who were much more open were Luciana Castellina and Valentino Parlato.

Luciana had worked as a journalist, had a very striking personal presence. Her mother was Jewish, from Eastern Europe. Luciana had been married to a communist leader of the generation of Berlinguer and Napolitano, Alberto Reichlein, and their daughter is today the chief economist of the European Central Bank. Luciana, and the other leaders in the group, were expelled from the Communist Party shortly after publishing their call for renewal. They began to publish their own newspaper, *Il Manifesto*, of which Valentino was the editor. At different times in the seventies, eighties, nineties, they won election to Parliament as members of their own party, at other times they were reintegrated in the Communist Party and welcomed as prodigal children. In the spheres of culture, education, community organization and unionism, they had large numbers of open activists and many sympathizers. Many of these preferred to remain in the Communist Party, others concentrated their efforts around journals, in informal networks, I noted the similarity to the New Left's relationship to Labour, the German dissidents and the Social Democrats, the groups pressing the French socialists to renew themselves, even to the ambiguities and ambivalence of the fragmented American left's attitudes to the Democratic Party. Larger, often bureaucratized and patronage ridden, and above all traditional parties of the left were mercilessly pilloried—and yet in the end deemed indispensable to larger social projects.

In the early seventies, however, no one thought that the Italian Communist Party would be gone in less than a generation. Criticism of it for being too closely integrated with the economic and political institutions of Italy was also a tribute to its durability, organizational capacity, and to its leaders' ability to retain the loyalties of millions of citizens. The party did have a Stalinist legacy. Persecuted under Fascism, its leaders were jailed and killed, or forced into exile. The Moscow leadership under Togliatti returned to Italy in 1944 to collaborate with the long term supporters of the Fascists in the Badoglio government. As the Cold War became acute in 1947, the US and its west European allies saw themselves confronted with a large and well organized Italian Communist Party, especially strong in the industrialized north and in cultural institutions. Stalin's crimes were distant for the party's Italian supporters: what counted were the party's anti-fascist record and its rootedness in the profane struggles for existence of the citizens of an impoverished nation. Interestingly, the elements of the party closest to the USSR were also those inclined to compromise on cultural issues with the Italian Catholics. With the expulsion of the party from government in 1947 and the Christian Democratic electoral triumph of 1948 the party was consigned for the indefinite future to permanent opposition. That had the consequence of concentrating its electoral efforts in cities and regions, and legitimating it as the major force of alternatives in a nation struggling simultaneously with backwardness and newness.

When I arrived in Italy in the fall of 1971, the party was certainly used to permanent crisis. It had endured a certain amount of Cold War repression, had to deal with the serial crises of the Soviet Union after Stalin's death, and itself had experienced the generational change that brought Enrico Berlinguer to its leadership. The protest movements of the Hot Autumn of 1969 intended to undermine its role as the potential agent of Italian reform. Instead, by opening the party to a great deal of internal debate and dissension, they strengthened it—by making it more representative of the many contradictions of the society. What precisely, for instance, was the use of a notion of party as vanguard when critical social processes occurred outside the state institutions the party aspired to command? How to characterize Italian capitalism when its facet included the familiar corruptions of the south (and not only the south) but also the technocrats, many of them moralizing Catholics, in charge of the state industrial holding, the Italian Institute of Reconstruction? Finally, how to conceive of classes in a nation increasingly marked by the internal differentiation of entire social categories?

The party had participated in the development of an Italo-Marxism which had functions rather like those of the Austro-Marxism of the first half of the twentieth century—to account for the specificity of Italian history. I was invited in October 1971 to two days of discussion of a book by Nicola Badaloni on Italian Marxism in the sixties. Many of the party's leaders, its intellectuals, and some not in its orbit spoke. The older Italian rhetorical style prevailed: the speakers presented set pieces, there was little open discussion. I recall a large challenge by the very gifted Italian philosopher Rusconi, who pointed out that the Germans had had the advantage of the Frankfurt School's challenge to orthodoxy, that a younger German generation had appropriated Weimar thought, and that the PCI had to be wary of intellectual ossification. Some younger thinkers did present challenges—but the Manifesto group and others who were critical of the party (the editors and contributors to *Quaderni Piacentini*) were absent. My Italian at the time was passive rather than active, and I thought of asking for the floor to say something in English about the international context of the discussion—but did not do so. An Italian friend later thanked me for my restraint. Had I spoken, he said, the Soviet academician present would certainly have risen for at least forty five minutes in Russian.

I did speak directly in those months with communist figures such as Giorgio Amendola and Giorgio Napolitano. I had the impression that they appreciated a view of the United States which was unforgiving in its insistence on complexity. From these encounters, and of course meetings with any number of Italian academics and journalists, I certainly learned that Italy was so steeped in its own history that responses to immediate events were frequently exercises in memory—or in the construction of memory. The communists shared the past, then, with their antagonists, who were also at the same time their collaborators, in the Catholic camp. There, too, I began an apprenticeship in contemporary Italy's political culture by talking with figures from the Christian Democratic Party like one of its Roman leaders, Giovanni Galloni. He was an outspoken advocate of a new course for his party, of much greater receptivity to collaboration with the communists—not least to strengthen the reformist elements in the party. Galloni was no isolated figure; he was in very close touch with the urbane groups in the Vatican and the Italian Church which saw in the communists a distinctly Italian phenomenon profoundly marked by Catholicism. Indeed, his closest communist friend was Antonio Tatò who was Berlinguer's chief of staff and had been in the Catholic resistance movement when Nazi Germany occupied much of Italy,

The Italian Socialist Party had been in alliance with the Communist Party and then after 1956 in an unmarked border zone until 1963, when the Kennedy government reversed the previous American veto on its participation in national government. The Socialist Party had a long tradition and both the Communist Party and the Fascist movement were originally the work of socialists. It provided a place for those who despaired of reforming the Communist Party, for many who had never wished to join it, and sought to represent a distinctive secular political culture While the communists claimed that there was an Italian Third Way between social democracy and state socialism, the socialists insisted on the primacy of parliamentary democracy and the autonomy of civil society. Its considerable strength among the educated and the intellectual elite was not matched by a large appeal to the working class. As the communist national vote climbed toward one third, the socialists had to content themselves with less than half that much. There were certain cities and regions in which it was strong, but its political influence depended upon its capacity to make alliances. In the generation after its historic leader, Pietro Nenni, and those who were imprisoned with him by the fascists, there were plenty of persons of great intellectual and moral integrity. There were also socialist trade unionists. I came to know one of them, Enzo Mattina, who was one of the three general secretaries who shared governance of the Metal Workers Union, quite well. I also knew younger figures such as Giorgio Ruffolo and Enrico Manca.

Unfortunately, the socialists were in a position which brought to the fore the qualities described by Pareto as congenial to foxes:

slyness, the ability to move at night. The significant socialist leader of my decades of visiting Italy was Bettino Craxi, the head of the party in Milan. A person of extraordinary political instincts, he had some allies like Giuliano Amato who were great servants of the republic. Craxi and his immediate circle, however, were immersed in the financial corruption that eventually brought down what is termed the First Italian Republic. Craxi ended his years in self-imposed exile in Tunisia. I did not know him, knew one of his principal deputies, Claudio Martelli, who actually went to prison after having been chief of staff to the prime minister, justice minister, and finance minister. Martelli was very intelligent, well read, at his ease in Europe and the US. The loss of gifts like his to the nation was considerable, a pathetic footnote to the self-destruction of a great Italian political tradition. In his defense, Craxi argued that the socialists took money not for themselves but for the party, that he had been singled out for prosecution while other politicians went free. The argument was neither subtle nor convincing.

There was another Italy which exercised its own spiritual sovereignty apart from the cloudy worlds of politics, a group of academics, artists, film makers, journalists, publishers, writers—and no small number of entrepreneurs, in private and state sectors. They were generally secular, if sympathetic to the critical and reformist elements in the Catholic Church. Their numbers included some Protestants and quite a few of Italy's educated Jews. They were pronouncedly European, welcoming every step that tied Italy more closely to its west European neighbors—and they took their distance from the Italian cultural and political bloc which cultivated its ties to the US. I had the impression that some of our diplomats had shallow views of Italy and sometimes mistook feigned friendship for the real thing. Others, to be sure, understood that in Italy surface and depth were quite far apart. No wonder the Communist Party had close ties to the Catholics. It was itself organized as an imperfectly authoritarian church, a community of true believers rather than of the critical citizenship practiced by the post-Stalinists. In time, the true believers developed a good deal of skepticism— and were ready to see the world on its own terms. In Germany, the closeness in the Brandt and Schmidt years of the Social Democrats and many Protestants caused a quite thorough ethicization of public life. In France, the old opposition of Church and Republic gave way to more intricate and reciprocal relations. Europe's secularism was saturated with ecclesiastical legacies. France and Italy in the sixteenth century did not become Protestant nations—but had strong Protestant currents which were inextricably connected to the systematic defiance of the alliance of Catholic Church and authoritarian state.

These not-quite-buried strata of belief expressed themselves in ostensibly mundane matters like the very varied resistance of the Italian political parties to corruption. The Church's toleration of human weakness was certainly evidence for its realism. It did not ask too much of most humans. A certain number of Christian Democratic politicians and officials were relieved to hear it: they held themselves absolved for yielding to temptation. The socialist contribution to Italy's public a-moralism suggested that ecclesiastical legitimation wasn't needed: as in Craxi's case, all that one needed was a convincing rationalization. I recollect a conversation with an Italian minister of justice, Stefano Rodotà, in the nineties. He was in the successor party to the communists, the Party of Democratic Socialism. Our city and regional officials and legislative representatives, he said, are under the most severe of pressures. Their colleagues from other political formations, or a significant number of them, have become wealthy in the Italian building boom—which required the purchase by builders of all sorts of regulatory permits. Stefano, who was Jewish, expressed his admiration for rectitude which he termed Franciscan.

It took many years of visits to Italy to achieve these insights, with the 1971-1972 visit a beginning. The officers of the foundation apparently thought me capable of dealing with Italian complexity. When I returned to the US in the fall of 1972, they sent one of their academic consultants, Gianni Giannotti (who taught sociology in the beautiful if little-visited city of Lecce, but who lived in Florence) to visit me in Amherst. He proposed that I should organize and direct for the Foundation an international study group on the future of the industrial democracies. I agreed and we met in 1973 and 1974 successively in Turin, London, Paris. Subsequently, there was a change of leadership at the Foundation and the project was dropped. The original group I had convened managed on our own

In Italy with the Italian Communist Party. I'm looking at the camera. Far left is Mayor Renato Zangheri of Bologna. Foreground is the Chief of Staff to General Secretary Enrico Berlinguer, Antonino Tatò.

to publish our work as the essay volume *Beyond the Crisis*, in 1977 (it appeared in French and German as well).

The project made it possible for me to travel to Italy frequently in the early seventies, and to connect with colleagues I was very glad to meet. Amongst those who came to our meetings were Leszek Kołakowski, Hans Peter Dreitzel, Jean Ziegler, Tom Bottomore, Richard Sennett, Claus Offe, Marcello De Cecco, Alessandro Pizzorno, Rudi Supek, Alain Touraine, and Serge Moscovici. I had the impression that the foundation and above all its patron, Gianni Agnelli, were certainly interested in the intellectual stimulation provided by these thinkers, while enjoying gaining a reputation for openness.

At our first meeting in April 1973, Agnelli gave a dinner in our honor. I was seated to his left, Alain Touraine to his right. France had just had elections for the National Assembly and the parties of the left had done quite well. Agnelli asked Alain how the results could be explained, and Alain responded that in France, a majority wished to live in a social democratic state. "But that is what we all want," was the comment of the proprietor of Fiat. French elections were not the only item in the news. I had flown overnight from Boston to Rome and at a morning stop in Paris, the newspapers headlined the resignations of Ehrlichman and Haldeman as the Watergate crisis deepened. Agnelli told me that he had been assured by the Italian ambassador to the US that Nixon was in no danger of losing his office. I disagreed and pointed to the resignations as evidence that the president was on his way out. "I'll ask the ambassador for another report," said Agnelli—who rightly supposed that the state apparatus was at his disposition.

Our discussions, and the published contributions that followed, were marked by the themes of the early seventies. The turbulences of the sixties having ended, an intellectual balance sheet had to be drawn. I inadvertently used the language of accountancy—despite our emphatically voiced claim to be concerned with a qualitative politics. Rather different themes were meant by of that phrase. We asked what could increase autonomy in the practice of citizenship, access to culture and education, the exercise of a much larger degree of control in the workplace. We described the existing model of capitalism as technocratic—and we understood that to entail the enlargement of the power of the elites indispensable to a scientific and technological economy. We gave very little attention to the industrialization of Asia, the beginning of the secular decline in income and political power of the western working class. Immigration from the Third World did not engage us, and the revival of nationalism did not trouble us.

We suffered from a variant of the sin of pride. No small part of our project was guided, not always explicitly, by the search for a model of western democracy that could be exported to the Soviet bloc when its ideological borders opened. In that sense, we were paying intellectual tribute to the theorists of the convergence of industrial societies—without confronting them directly. (I think of Bell and Sakharov and ideas like those of the Triple Revolution group in the American sixties.) We certainly had in mind the work of Radovan Richta and the others in the communist dictatorships who saw a way out of them in a potential alliance of technocrats and ordinary citizens which could take power from the intellectually ossified party elites. Alain Touraine, who began as an historian, had an acute eye for the dramaturgy of the Cultural Revolution in China. Even Alain missed what was imminent, an alliance of capital and ruling party in China and a very emphatic rejection of the Cultural Revolution. When André Malraux visited Mao in 1965, the Chinese leader ruminated aloud on the possibility of a younger generation rejecting his version of Chinese communism. Not for the first time, Malraux had seen a future rather different from the one imagined by most of his contemporaries.

In *The Opium of the Intellectuals*, published in 1955 by Raymond Aron when the revolutionary myths he derided were already losing a good deal of their force, he castigated the French intellectuals for their failure to grasp the real politics of administered interest in the western democracies. In fact, France was governed by educated civil servants and quite a few educated political leaders who drew upon a national tradition of state control which made ideas of revolutionary rupture implausible. A revolutionary France, as understood by the French left, would have to scrutinize the effects of governmental programs of investment and redistribution, enlarge and redirect these—but by no means break with national tradition. The Café de Flore and café Les Deux Magots were at the time a long block away from that site of intellectual sobriety, the École Nationale d'Administration. Sartre's journal, *Les Temps Modernes* (the title of a great Chaplin film on the industrial age) propagated the idea of an alternative world—to readers quite aware that their lives were shaped not only by the legacy of the French Revolution, but of its Napoleonic sequel—which gave body to revolutionary spirit.-

I had known the France of the critical Catholics, of the historians, philosophers, sociologists who had left their church, the Communist Party, of a newer generation which did not deign to enter it. It was against this background that vanguard thinkers in France abandoned the old ouvrierism, with its notion of a working class totally alienated from society. New notions of the capacity of the working class to administer the processes of production replaced older ones of all pervasive class conflict. The French Communist Party talked revolution, but was quite careful to attend to the present interests and needs of its voters in factories and government agencies and schools and universities. The authentic party of change in France was constituted by those who, often, were quite integrated in its institutions.

In the decade after 1968, its excitement and promise did not entirely become an exercise in nostalgia. Many of its participants, prominent and less so, devoted themselves to keeping its legacy alive—in small conventicles, cultural creation, the professions, unions and even or above all in the political activity the Movement of May had originally scorned. I was interested in the projects of economic democracy advanced especially by the CFDT, the trade union of Christian provenance (which had not only Catholic but Protestant roots). The work of CERES, the Centre d'Études, de Recherches et d'Éducation Socialiste, sought a connection between parliamentary socialism with projects in the institutions of society. CERES figures like Jean-Pierre Chevènement and Didier Motchane experimented with ideas and projects which envisaged a more responsive state and a freer society constituted by widespread self-governance. On a parallel track Michel Rocard made a modernized and full conception of citizenship the theme of the Parti Socialiste Unifié he had founded in 1964. These intellectual politicians drew upon the works of French thinkers who sought to invent forms of modernity rooted in new social possibilities. More education, more income, more leisure marked an increasingly large segment of the French labor force: they could not be thought of as a classical proletariat. My Strasbourg colleague and friend Henri Lefebvre with his notions of the city as in a permanently festive condition, Serge Mallet with his studies of the new working class, Alain Touraine with his view of history as possibility, were but some of the sources of a new socialist imagination. Patrick Viveret and Pierre Rosanvallon developed a political philosophy of active citizenship. In its matter of fact inquiry into the practice of democracy, it contrasted with Habermas's doubts on the longevity of a public sphere open to deepening and widening, and with Rawls' transposition of Bentham—a new social utilitarianism for speakers of American English who did not wish to be pushed around by history. Two large problems faced the disparate currents of the French left. Even when they added their electoral resources (small socialist groupings, the larger Socialist Party, the obdurately omnipresent Communist Party and the groups descended from the old Radical tradition of the Third Republic) they could not muster the fifty one percent needed to win presidential elections. The second problem was posed by the persistence of the communist electorate. They would indeed follow the party into alliances with other groups—but that would discountenance voters who were dismayed by the party's loyalty to the Soviet Union, and also many who thought its version of socialism out of date. There were Euro-communist currents in the Communist Party, but it was very far from the internal pluralism of the Italian Communist Party.

In 1971 François Mitterrand left the Radical tradition behind him and assumed leadership of the Socialist Party. Mitterrand as a young man had been a quite ordinary adherent of the classical French right, had even worked for the Vichy government after his release from prisoner of war camp. With characteristic aplomb he presented himself after the war as a representative of the Resistance (which indeed he joined a year before France was liberated), was Mendès France's Interior Minister in 1954 when the Algerians revolted. He was deeply rooted in the culture of the Fourth Republic with its high rhetoric and low cunning, somehow discovered a socialist vocation late in life. He owed a great deal to the example of Mendès France, who stood for what was left of a morally rigorous and anti-authoritarian strand of French Republicanism. Mitterrand intuited, correctly, that the communists could be managed. A rather precise common project was agreed to by the socialists and communists in 1973—and Mitterrand made it clear that in any governmental alliance, the socialists would be in command. The rather darker sides of his own career were in this respect an advantage: no one in France could suppose that Mitterrand would be outmaneuvered.

How sincere was his conversion to socialism? Sincerity is a concept difficult to apply with any precision to most human beings and Mitterrand was an unusually complex and discreet figure. I spoke with him on a very few occasions, since I was quite friendly with one of his closest advisors, Claude Estier. Mitterrand was a well-read intellectual and relied in revivifying the Socialist Party on younger figures who were unequivocally committed to change. These included his rival for a time, Michel Rocard, his later Élysée advisor Jacques Attali, and future ministers like Jean-Pierre Cot, Jack Lang, Jean-Pierre Chevènement. I wrote for *La Revue Socialiste*, very occasionally for *Le Monde*, my books had been published in France. This was added to my academic stays in the nation, and my connections to Edward Kennedy and later Willy Brandt. My French was fluent, at times even idiomatic, if always horribly accented. It added up: the new socialists regarded me as *l'ami américain*. Talking with them was often intellectually strenuous, and no small contribution to my own education.

France is the oldest ally of the US and Jefferson exulted when he learned of the French Revolution: we had shown the way. Still, much separated our nations. Even the anti-clerical (and Protestant) French regarded France as a Catholic nation. Its centralized state spoke for itself, whatever its pronounced regional differences. There was no large stream of French emigration to the US (or to the British colonies before our statehood). In the post-war period, hopes and fears about Americanization were not particularly central in French debate. The country's elites knew the US, but periods of study in our universities were much less frequent than for their British, German, and other European counterparts. There were exceptions: Jean-Pierre Cot had grown up in Washington since his father was the wartime Gaullist ambassador. I knew the determined Atlanticist Raymond Aron, did not have the impression that he insisted that his students study in the US. My interlocutors on the French left were often curious about the US, but had no very clear views of our history—for all of the popularity in France of American films, literature and jazz. They were quite surprised to be told of the traditions of American progressivism—as if the New Deal, the Vietnam protests, the civil rights movement, were historical oddities. Perhaps they had extrapolated too much from de Tocqueville's sketch of the early nineteenth-century nation. Few had paused to reflect on what Marx saw when he predicted a rapid advance to socialism for the US.

In 1954, the Swiss historian Herbert Lüthy published *Frankreichs Uhren Gehen Anders*, mistranslated as *France Against Herself*. A more accurate translation would have been more literal: *French Clocks Run to Their Own Time*. Everyone in France was Gaullist, in that they insisted on their own exceptionalism. Perhaps that was why the Algerians and the Vietnamese, to fight the French, had to develop their own nationalism and why it was a group of Francophonique Africans who developed the notion of the distinctiveness of "Négritude" as a codex for their struggle against French colonialism. The first Congress of African Artists and Writers met in Paris. The nation which espoused universalism, which traced much of its modern politics to *The Declaration of the Rights of Man and of the Citizen* of 1789 also insisted that its hexagonal world was culturally and morally self-sufficient. The British with their singular habits presented as common sense, mocked the abstraction of French thought. The more perceptive of them realized that it was not abstract at all, but a very French dialect. No doubt, France was in the vanguard of that complex and diffuse process we term modernity—even in matters theological, Catholic and Protestant. The Eiffel Tower still serves as a national symbol, even if farmers sometimes come to protest insufficient governmental subsidies by bringing their cows to its base. The French socialists and that extraordinary grouping the French term *les Catholiques de Gauche* (Delors was one) have something distinctive, inimitable about them. I have seen enough of the other half of France (when I taught at Strasbourg de Gaulle was at the zenith of his power) to sense that it was shared across cultural boundaries. The French use the term *famille politique* to describe political affinities—but there is also, often in argument and difference, a *famille nationale*, brought together by the very persistence of their conflicts. It is interesting that much of the modern historiography of memory began in France, where competing versions of national history took root before the French Revolution.

Even the French Communist Party, which unlike its Italian sister party, did not provide much space for those within it seeking to take their distance from Stalinism, was imprisoned in its own version of French history. It depicted itself as the heir to a revolutionary tradition which had inspired the Bolsheviks—and so found strong analogies between the Jacobins and themselves. There was a de facto alliance with the Gaullists, since they each thought of politics as the mastery of a very centralized, indeed implacable, state. By the sixties, and especially after the USSR terminated the Czech experiment of 1968, the communists failed to attract the most original and even the most routinely competent of intellectuals. There were exceptions, like the party economist Guy Herzog, and some of the leaders allowed themselves moments of critical lucidity. The one I knew was the party's expert on higher education, himself a graduate of the École Normale Supérieure and an *agrégé* in German. The *agrégation* was a French degree making its holder eligible to teach the highest courses in Lycées, those preparing students for the elite Grandes Écoles, His name was Pierre Juquin and in a couple of conversations, he vaunted the party's opening to a more ordered and transparent constitutional democracy. I reported on one of our talks in *Partisan Review* and fear that I did not do him justice. I recall our talking about Watergate (Nixon had just left office). He expressed what was a very general French attitude: "On ne peut pas se défaire d'un bon President pour une histoire banale des écoutes." Large segments of French opinion viewed Nixon positively, not least on account of the opening to China. The communists were no exception, and Juquin and his colleagues suspected that Nixon had been the victim of a plot.

The most orthodox of Marxist parties in Western Europe was the most devoid of the intellectual inspiration that so many other groups found in their interpretations of Marxism. The old Communist Party was a textbook instance of the interest representation of the standard interpretations of western politics as pluralistic. Its electorates in state service, especially in the educational system, in the factories, certainly adhered to a Jacobin idea of the state as the embodiment of the general will. By the sixties, they left revolutionary exaltation to others and concentrated on wages and hours—while asking of the state not that it construct a new society but that it lift them with an entire series of benefits, to the privileges of the bourgeoisie. Mitterrand and his colleagues, denounced as betraying western freedom for their electoral alliance with the communists, were supremely realistic: the communist threat to civic order was non-existent.

How different was (and is) Germany. In the twentieth century it experienced the Empire, the Weimar Republic, the Third Reich, occupation and two separate states, a unified state if not a unified nation—and the material and moral devastation of two wars. As I look back on my conversations with Germans from the day I arrived in September of 1952, most of my interlocutors insisted on the authenticity and intensity of their own experience of discontinuity in the nation and their own lives. Those who preferred not to dwell on their recent pasts emphasized their beginning anew. There were some claims to disinter elements of continuity ignored or erased 1933-1945, by older persons, but I mostly heard praise for rupture.

I became over the years an active American friend of the German opposition. From the group around Abendroth, my contacts extended to a spectrum of critical academics, journalists, writers (Grass, Habermas, Kogon), some critical theologians (Huber and Moltmann). After some of the tumult of the sixties had subsided, many found themselves confronted with an unexpected challenge. From 1966 with the SPD's entry into government to the Chancellorship of Willy Brandt and the succession by Schmidt, many who had begun as antagonists of the institutions of the Federal Republic found themselves in charge of these. In national, state, municipal governments they occupied major posts. Not only in the universities but in public radio and television, and the more important weeklies and dailies, they had platforms. The trade unions provided yet another sort of opportunity. At the beginning of the seventies, I was in some danger of continuing to fight the battles of the previous decade, as Germany most emphatically changed.

I took the via regis to the new Germany with my typewriter, began to write for the Social Democratic weekly, *Vorwärts*. The articles were reports on a United States many of our embassies abroad (and especially the one in Bonn although at times the US Mission in West Berlin took a more open approach) were at some pains not to represent. It was the US of the New Deal legacy, of continuing struggles for Civil Rights, of the movement against the war in Vietnam transformed into a broader peace movement after the fall of Saigon. For many younger Germans of the immediate post-war decades, the US was familiar: many had spent semesters in our colleges and universities, some through church and familial connections had even attended American high schools. The contrast with the continuing rigidity of German culture had quite enchanted them. John Kennedy was a hero for many Germans because of his averting catastrophe in the Cuban missile crisis. Later Robert Kennedy and after him Edward were depicted like their elder brother as exemplar of a politics fit for the young. Joined to the memories of the Berkeley revolt and all that followed, the Kennedy imagery gave us a pro-American generation. The American trade unions meanwhile—the vanguard in American social reform—had contact at several levels with their German counterparts.

The brothers Reuther, Victor and Walter, were sons of a German working-class immigrant, and explicitly and implicitly supportive of the deepening and extension of an American version the German welfare state. Their union, the United Auto Workers, with its nearly three million members, had failed in discussions after the end of the war to obtain worker representation on the boards of directors of the large American auto manufacturers. Under the Co-Determination arrangement instituted by the Brandt government, the YAW sister union the German metal workers, named a United Auto Workers official to the board of General Motors with the votes of the workers at Opel, the General Motors German subsidiary. Hans Matthöfer, later Labor and Finance Minister, had actually worked in an American auto factory when studying at the University of Wisconsin and Ulrich Klose, later Mayor of Hamburg and Chair of the Social Democratic Parliamentary group, had attended high school in Ohio.

What I could give to German readers was an historical perspective on American politics—on national traditions of social protest simply not conveyed by the day to day reporting of the German media. I was also able, even before I came to Washington in 1979, to describe the immense difficulty of achieving change in so complex and diverse a society. In my interest in and relationships with Germany I was hardly alone. Quite a few persons born in the US (many Jewish, without familial connections to German Jewry) had studied with the émigré generation or worked with the émigrés in government agencies during the war. Nowhere else, not in the UK despite the presence of figures as different as Karl Mannheim and Michael Polanyi, was the influence of German thought as pervasive. I suppose that I was also able to address a German public because of years of reading German history, literature, and political and social thought. The seventies were also the years in which I joined *Partisan Review*, which had brought modernist European culture to New York and its intellectual provinces in the American colleges and universities. Many Americans were very knowledgeable about Germany, but I had a rather unique combination of intellectual and political knowledge, as well as plenty of personal experience of the country.

When Carter took office in 1977, the United Auto Workers were confident of access to the White House and to the New Deal's Congressional and Senatorial descendants: Edward Kennedy foremost among them. Former UAW President Leonard Woodcock went to Peking as Ambassador and Douglas Fraser succeeded him. Doug had been born in Scotland and his international interests were large. With Mike Harrington, I persuaded Doug that the UAW should sponsor an event in the US at which the leaders of European socialism could present their ideas to Americans, especially Democrats, who had no map of the new European intellectual and political landscape. While Democrats insistent on observing the rigid exclusions and taboos, the permanent hostility, of the Cold War harassed Carter, a much smaller group was aware that in Europe itself, much had changed. The German policy of opening toward and collaboration with the USSR and the Soviet bloc had been accepted by Nixon and Kissinger and later Ford. Senator Jackson organized opposition to it, supported of course by allies in the permanent government—not least at the CIA, State and the Pentagon. Jackson was every bit as attached to the New Deal tradition as Kennedy and a long-time ally of the labor movement and the same was true of Senator Moynihan. Their opposition to the European predilection for detente was a consequence of a political culture which marked the American labor movement—the long struggle between social democrats (and followers of Trotsky) with American Communists, This was joined to the alliance between the labor movement and the Israel lobby, a consequence of the large presence of Jewish leaders and members in the unions. As the offspring of the Jewish working class joined the American middle class, and often the government, their sympathies for an Israel still led by its own Labour Party resulted in the seventies in a campaign to persuade the USSR to allow Jewish emigration. The strategists of the campaign in the US were hardly naïve, and they could not have believed that the USSR would allow a highly educated segment of its population to leave when denying the same privilege to others—or that it would put at risk its own alliances in the Mideast with Muslim nations. The campaign served the general interest of the Cold War party in American politics by blocking progress toward long term détente: arms control treaties were actually not proceeded with in the Congress. It also engendered rifts in the bloc which would otherwise have been more energetically supporting co-existence. In the setting, collaboration with Europeans on their own paths to reducing Cold War tensions was difficult.

Nonetheless, the UAW leadership, the Black and Progressive Caucuses in the Congress, decided to move ahead to closer collaboration with our friends and comrades in Europe. Europe at the time was the object of quite extraordinary American ambivalence. The Europeans were suspected of a profound reluctance to fight, amply demonstrated by their refusal to send troops to Viet-Nam and the generally hostile response of European populations to the war in Viet-Nam. European prosperity was hard to disguise, and a large number of Americans were perplexed by phenomena like long vacations, frequent holidays, shorter working weeks—and the strong political position of the labor movements, with large redistributive and regulatory functions performed by states. The considerable contribution to the welfare state tradition in Europe of Catholic political and social movements was known to American historians of Europe and to American Catholics who had studied or worked in Europe, but Protestant America (some theologians apart) did not know it. Condensed or deformed versions of Reinhold Niebuhr's thought were in circulation, but few recalled that he had begun as a pastor close to the labor movement in Detroit. For some Americans, encounters with Europe were beginning points on a long trip of discovery of an American past which was, actually, quite recent.

As the seventies proceeded, a positive view of Western Europe was deemed eccentric—or evidence for hopeless ideological nostalgia. Some years later, "European" became a term of abuse for some. The celebration of supposedly common values was a constant theme of Transatlantic groups, and there were plenty of Europeans ready to join Americans critical of Europe by suggesting that their fellow Europeans should show more courage in the face of the Soviet bloc, or more entrepreneurial spirit in dealing with the global economy, more willingness to reconsider the welfare state. In 1972, to mark the twenty fifth anniversary of Secretary of State George Marshall's announcement at Harvard of an American recovery project for Europe, the Marshall Plan, the German government announced the gift of an endowment for a foundation, the German Marshall Fund of the US. The foundation was to inquire into the common problems of the industrial democracies, but it was to be American led. The German Chancellor who announced the gift at Harvard was Willy Brandt. His policy of détente in central

Europe, of economic and political engagement with the Soviet bloc nations was viewed with skepticism and even hostility by influential segments of the American elite, seconded by the political opponents of Brandt, the Social Democrats and the Free Democrats in Germany. Brandt and his advisors knew the American political landscape, were not hesitant to challenge American political philistinism, and were attentive to American groups and persons with a positive view of their projects for Europe.

There was not, clearly, a large socialist movement in the US and memories of the late nineteenth century and early twentieth century American socialist groups were largely cultivated by academics. That Bellamy's *Looking Backward* had been a best seller in 1888, that clubs had sprung up to discuss and propagate his ideas, were, equally, recollections of an historic oddity. Brandt as a young man in the early German resistance and then in the exile community had not only followed the New Deal, he had considered emigrating to the US. He was as president of the Socialist International following his 1974 departure from the Chancellorship aware of the Cold War divisions in the Democratic Party, had developed considerable affection and respect for Harrington and Edward Kennedy, both. I first met Brandt on the occasion of another of his visits to Harvard, in the spring of 1977. My daughter Anna, on spring vacation from her first university year at Tübingen, was with me and especially delighted to talk with Brandt.

I found him in manner and substance, to have the rigor and restraint of Protestant Prussia. He also had its directness. I understood him as a citizen of the world who had learned not to expect gifts from history. I was struck by the exactness of his political judgments, his emphasis on timing, on the frequently slow movement of events until ruptures occurred. Above all, I was fascinated by his appreciation of the varieties and vagaries of psychological engagement in politics, his sense of soul. Especially in our first meetings (after Boston I saw him over the next years regularly in Bonn) he preferred to listen as I recounted my impressions of the American situation, He sometimes questioned me about my life and he was quite taken with two matters. One was my leaving the Bronx for New England, the other was the summer spent at Campobello. I had an intuition, speaking with him at our first meeting, of his capacity to cross many cultural boundaries in Germany and the rest of the world. Perhaps it was nostalgic reminiscence for the society in which he grew up and its diversity: he had not only Jewish friends from that period and his subsequent experience of the emigration, but a persistent attachment to Jews throughout his life. At the memorial service in the German Embassy in Washington I ventured the view that he saw Jews as Protestants with hearts.

Before and after: Campobello July 1942, and a reunion in front of Eleanor Roosevelt's house

Willy was especially interested in younger persons and had a way of attracting their loyalty while imparting the lessons of his life. Speaking to Malraux in Peking, Mao after having encouraged the Cultural Revolution and its terrible ravages said that he did not know if a younger generation would wish to pursue the Chinese revolutionary project to which he had devoted his life. Brandt was incapable of that sort of detachment, feigned or real. He regarded passing on his experience as a primary task. His own elder friend when he was a very young man was the Social Democrat Julius Leber, who was subsequently executed for his role in the 1944 conspiracy to terminate Nazism. I recall Brandt remarking of the plotters that their lives showed that not ideological correctness but an irreducible element of character was necessary if nations were to achieve civil dignity. He gave the younger Social Democrats he educated (Gerhard Schröder, Karl-Heinz Klär, Thomas Mirow, Albrecht Müller, and many others) a sense of the moral reflectiveness impelling his political commitments. Many who did not know him personally, but heard him at meetings or on television seemed to apprehend the same thing.

I have mentioned what in Germany is known as the generation of his "grandchildren"—but there were also somewhat older figures, many survivors of the armed forces at the end of the war, When I met Willy in Boston one of them was along, his former chief of staff in the Chancellor's office, and also a former Minister of Justice, the colorful, educated and thoroughly enjoyable Horst Ehmke. He was the son of a physician, managed to make an early departure from Soviet captivity by working for a while for Soviet army doctors, was an early post-war visitor to the US (Princeton) and was a determined adversary of political cowardice. Eventually becoming the senior Social Democratic spokesperson in foreign affairs, he delighted in describing the most nightmarish situation for the American foreign policy elite—the possibility that he could become German Foreign Minister. He was hyper-active, so much so that a Bonn story about him had him jumping into his official car to be asked by the driver: "Where to, Herr Professor?" "It doesn't matter, I am needed everywhere." Actually, Horst combined a thoroughly realistic view of world politics with an acute sense of human limitation. He depicted himself as a modern Diogenes, but was quite prepared to admit that there were others who could carry the lantern. He was a brilliant parliamentary orator and a marvelous raconteur. Had he remained in the university, he might well have become the equivalent of Carl Schmitt for the German party of enlightenment. In the course of many years working with him, I was struck by a contrast. He made American officialdom uncomfortable but in the Soviet bloc, he was a valued interlocutor. Very possibility, he was acting out their fantasies of independence.

From 1977 to the summer of 1979, I continued to live in Amherst, visited New York very often and Washington occasionally, and went to Europe several times a year. My daughters were in Strasbourg but visits to Paris (occasionally Rome) and Bonn were invariable parts of my itinerary. The project of a transatlantic conference in Washington was slow to materialize, but I gradually constructed a network of academic, journalistic and political interlocutors which widened the group I had formed when working on the Industrial Society project. In Washington, I visited the Institute for Policy Studies, where Richard Barnet, Robert Borosage, Marcus Raskin were my hosts, with the Congressional Progressive Caucus, and especially Congressman Dellums and his staff and Congressman John Conyers, who is now the senior member of the House. I talked at length with Steve Schlossberg and the UAW (and with the Machinists as well). No one needed advice from western Massachusetts as to what they were experiencing day by day, the hesitant politics of the Carter government and the gathering Republican resurgence. I was writing regularly at the time for *The Nation* and *Partisan Review* and I was received as a favored cousin from out of town. It was assumed that I had a long view, that at the intersection of the American academy, New York intellectual life, and European socialist politics I could favor my friends with insights so profound as to illuminate the hidden depths of their own world. Of course, I could not, since the narrative I employed could have been joined to any number of accounts of current events. My themes concerned a new class structure in which managerial and intellectual skills were as important as the possession of monetary wealth, a secular decline in the autonomy of citizens, the interaction of global and domestic politics, the counter attack on a broad front by capital's political agents in a determined effort to limit, reduce and eventually terminate the welfare state I also spoke with the government, that is, with Robert Hunter as the official in charge of Europe at the National Security Council, with Paul Warnke at the Arms Control and Disarmament Agency. From time to time, too, I visited with Senator Kennedy.

The inability of Jimmy Carter to use Democratic majorities in House and Senate to renew the Democratic legislative legacy bothered Kennedy. He had learned how political moments had to be seized, how demoralizing were periods of enforced repose for the activists and volunteers needed in serious political struggles, Carter was a child of the New Deal, and his family had profited from the New Deal's agricultural programs, as rural electrification. He was obdurately insensitive to the problems of disinvestment and stagnation in the industrial economy. He had some economic advisors like the Secretary of the Treasury, Michael Blumenthal, and the Chair of the Council of Economic Advisors, Charles Schultze, with political imagination. He listened, however, to the faceless budget cutters who inhabited the artificial worlds of conventionalized national accounting. In foreign policy, Carter was in Kennedy's view overly deferential to the proponents of maximal armament. The Brezhnev years were hardly ones of steps to a more open Soviet future, but alongside the ritualized complacency of the party apparatus, a Soviet civil society was eager for experiment—and (as I learned in visits in the USSR and elsewhere) hoped for American gestures so as to be able to press for a diminution of Cold War blockages in the psychic economies of the nations of the Warsaw Pact.

Kennedy decided to challenge Carter in the Democratic primaries, and ran into two major difficulties. A president collects political creditors, and Carter had major ones like the National Education Association. Secondly, Kennedy seriously under estimated the damage done to his reputation by the terrible accident at Chappaquiddick, Martha's Vineyard, in which in 1969 he drove a car off a bridge and a young woman on his staff who was with him drowned. His many antagonists, within and without the party, were unrelenting in raising the issue. The Senator would present himself for a television interview in a city in which factories had been shuttered, only to find that he could not talk about the economy since the local interviewer at once raised the question of the accident. Even had Kennedy won the nomination, he might well have lost to Reagan in the actual election. As it was, a seriously divided party did not mobilize behind Carter and the loss was his. For Kennedy, it was in the long run liberating. From then onward he concentrated on his extraordinarily productive legislative work and his role as active custodian of the party's New Deal legacy.

Of course, *The Nation* supported Kennedy and I wrote in its pages in the same vein. When Kennedy withdrew, after a very moving speech at the convention in New York, some of us made a gesture. We nominated Ronald Dellums, the African-American Congressman from Oakland and Berkeley, as president. The convention managers refused to accept the nominating petition but after the threat of legal action to stop the convention proceeding, relented. Dellums made a very good speech. I wrote the original draft, upon which he improvised, was pleased that he used some of it. The national media did not bother to allow the public to hear it, and many of the delegates had little enthusiasm for an exercise in symbolic politics. With time, I have become increasingly skeptical about the excessive emphasis on symbolic politics in the segments of US opinion with which I sympathize. Still, there are periods of discouragement and retreat in which symbolic acts devoid of immediate consequences still are useful. Something is stored in memory, some hint of possibility draws back for a moment the leaden curtain of discouragement. In any event, our small group (organized by Ron's staff member Bob Brauer) was astonished to be rewarded with convention credentials which allowed us to enjoy the drink and food available in the lounge reserved for the candidates' staff. I am quite unable to say how many of those who gathered around us recall the incident. To be sure, there were not that many.

That winter, after quite complicated and laborious preparations, a somewhat ecumenical group hosted in December what was for Washington a quite extraordinary gathering. Mike Harrington, myself and some other American intellectuals, the UAW, Democratic Socialists of America, the Congressional Black and Progressive Caucuses, joined to welcome to Washington a set of European socialist leaders. Willy Brandt, François Mitterrand, Olof Palme were there, so was the former Netherlands Prime Minister Joop den Uyl and two future French Prime Ministers, Édith Cresson and Michel Rocard, as well as Felipe González and Tony Benn. Jacques Attali and Claude Estier added to the European presence The Italian Socialist Party sent no one, but a very knowledgeable and sophisticated official of CGIL, the Italian Communist-Socialist union, Giacinto Militello, came. Giacinto was later head of the industrial department of his union and after that in charge of Social Security in Italy. We became friends.

Support was provided by the German Marshall Fund of America and thereby hangs a sad tale. Steve Schlossberg of the UAW and I spoke with the AFL-CIO president, Lane Kirkland, on possible participation by his union. We had made it ideologically easier for him by not inviting the Italian or any other western European communist party. He still objected without quite saying so directly: Palme's antagonism to the Cold War and Brandt's pursuit of engagement with the Soviet bloc were not to his liking. Kirkland was courteous as always, but as a board member of the Marshall Fund he arranged for the dismissal of its very competent president, Gerald Livingston. Gerry was a retired Foreign Service Officer and went on to found the Johns Hopkins American Institute of Contemporary German Studies. Kirkland's behavior lacked class, and was even more regrettable since Kirkland could hardly complain of a want of opportunities to promote his own foreign policy agenda. The rigidification of the defense of western pluralism in the Cold War tended to reduce serious matters to street fights. Abe Rosenthal, then the editor of *The New York Times*, was adept in the matter. He refused to publish anything about the meeting at all, since his sympathies were with the Social Democrats USA, the other American group in the Socialist International and one decidedly cool to European criticism of the Cold War, We lacked a large scale socialist movement, but we had its usual accompaniment, profound political feuds.

The event did enthuse a large number of teachers and graduate students in colleges and universities near and far, a considerable number of Congressional and Senatorial staff, and many from the very varied spectrum of public interest groups in Washington. I cannot say that the Europeans walked off the pages of our newspapers or out of our television studios to present themselves in person. Mostly, despite their importance in Europe, they were absent from our media. Occasionally, they made appearances to be asked in the most vulgar terms about their attitudes to the US. Dellums gave the welcoming address for the hosts, stressing the inevitable internationalization of American politics. Brandt made a keynote speech in which he anticipated many of the events of the decades to come, from ruptures in the state socialist societies to climate change, the universalization of human rights to the necessity to rethink socialist political economy in the light of globalization. There were any number of panels: what the American public took away was an indelible impression of the directness and openness of our guests. I have an image of Mitterrand, hardly a Gallic equivalent of a glad handing American politician, talking at some length with a group of younger Americans asking what he would do as president. They must have intuited something. When I asked Brzezinski, who was still at the White House in Carter's last weeks, and David Albright, who was in charge of the foreign policy transition group for President-elect Reagan, if they wished to meet Mitterrand, I had identical answers. Did I really believe that he was going to defeat d'Estaing in the imminent French election? Credit where credit is due: I later learned that an entire team of CIA analysts of Europe had descended on the conference and followed every word. They did not, however, identify themselves.

We were about to enter the epoch of Reagan, the Bush interim, and Clinton years made murkier by Bill Clinton's resolute opportunism, Reagan had voted four times for Franklin Roosevelt, but preferred not to dwell on that in his vacuous tirades against "government." González was twenty two months away from assuming the Spanish Prime Ministership for fourteen years that brought Spain into the twentieth century. Mitterrand was about to become president for a very mixed fourteen years, in which he maneuvered to keep alive the possibility of reform—only to be reduced to practicing the art of political survival. Brandt had already been Chancellor, with international and national legacies of very large dimensions. Benn was to serve as guardian of Labour's reformist heritage in the arid and brutal Thatcher years. The European socialists were about to continue the Washington discussion for decades at home: what was, actually, socialism at the end of the twentieth century in nations with working welfare states?

The next decade was to be one of challenge. I moved to Washington, where much discussion began on the surface of events—and remained there. The nation's elites were convinced that they had our own society firmly in view and in hand, and thought the same of much of the rest of the world. In fact, they expended considerable energy fabricating the conventional wisdom—only to be surprised repeatedly by discontinuities and ruptures they could not explain. Washington's intellectual landscape was ostensibly dominated by the centers of research, government agencies, independent projects which allowed an academic army to occupy the city. Suppose, however, that the newcomers were so influenced by the by the older inhabitants of the city interested in money and power, that their clarity and originality shrank when it did not entirely dissolve. A stranger come to the capital, I was to remain one—but did not quite know it at the time.

15

Germans to a Different Front

WHEN IN 1900 European forces were sent to Peking to repress the Boxer Rising, the British officer in command occasioned great enthusiasm in Germany with his order: "Germans to the front." Since then, military ardor in the German public (and, indeed, in the present German army) is difficult to find. When I came to Germany in 1952, the debate on re-armament was bringing with it as thorough a national self-examination as the Germans in the new Federal Republic could afford—replete with cultural, generational, political conflict. I knew the outlines of the conflicted history of the Social Democratic Party in its relationship to German preparation for war and war itself. I was surprised neither by the party's opposition to re-armament in those years or by its dutiful acceptance of the new German army. The Social Democrats I first encountered in the early fifties were (many in the trade unions) ardent advocates of economic citizenship, of a (parliamentary and peaceful) transition to democratic control of and participation in the economy. They and the unions were, however, loyal partners of the restored economic and political elites in the reconstruction of German capitalism—if of a capitalism with a decent component of redistribution and regulation. The actual political and social behavior of the Social Democrats, in contrast to their ideological fixity, was the ground for the rhetorical reassessment in the Bad Godesberg program of 1959. The Social Democrats accepted German membership in NATO, accepted what the Christian Democrats termed a social market economy, renounced the role of permanent opposition and assumed the full consequences of their actual participation in the governance of the Federal Republic and its states.

The sixties were a long march toward Social Democratic participation in national government as junior partner to the Christian Democrats in 1966, followed by Brandt's Chancellorships in 1969 and 1972. It was marked by the extraordinary achievement of Brandt's Ostpolitik, large beginnings of reconciliation with the USSR and Poland and a measured but widening opening of relations with the communist German state. The indispensable cultural and social element in the often untidy politics of the period was the maturing of the post-war generation. It reckoned with the burden of the past by assiduously reviving Germany's democratic traditions, and it confronted the future with a new internationalism—in part a sense of belonging to a larger European community and in part a positive view of democracy in the United States. The beginnings of the Green movement and engagement on behalf of the Third World were also parts of a new German consciousness. Not quite silenced peers in communist Germany, knew or intuited what was happening on the other side of the Wall, which went up in 1961, and many envied what they saw.

I have noted how closely I worked with the European protest movements of the late fifties and sixties. I regret that my own turn to the politics of the Democratic Party in the US was belated. The German generation with which I came into close contact in the seventies had already concluded that they would have to speak in electoral prose rather than revolutionary poetry. They often began in local and state politics and remained there, as permanent representatives of their party—and insistent voices at party fora for their constituents. Others were in public service, many in the several branches of education, many others in health and the social services. There were cineastes, theatre people, writers. Günter Grass campaigned for and with Willy Brandt and he was joined by other writers, by figures from pop culture, by sports stars. I was impressed by the extent and depth of the trade union presence in the party, by the unionists who had senior ministries. Most of all, I think, I was impressed by the integration of the [party with German society: in large areas of Germany, the younger Social Democrats could hardly complain of the "Establishment"—term taken over from British political discourse of the fifties and used with increasing imprecision to describe an effective elite in command of culture, society, state. Henry Fairlie coined it, obviously drawing on the relationship of state to the Anglican Church. The Social Democrats, could hardly claim to be outsiders, I knew them as insiders troubled by a sense of having embarked on a journey far from completed—and not without doubts as to some of their fellow travelers, even or especially some in high places.

There were few entrepreneurs or managers or business proprietors among the Social Democrats. There were, however, politicians who insisted that the party had to cultivate them. Klaus von Dohnányi (whose father died in the 1944 plot against Hitler) was one and he was Mayor of Hamburg, with its mixture of patrician, proletarian and middle class traditions. Helmut Schmidt was another. He came from the Hamburg skilled working class, was an officer during the war, made his way upward by his combination of hardness and technocratic intelligence. The German economic elite liked Schmidt—but so did many of the party's working-class voters. Brandt had impassioned them, Schmidt impressed them with his assured, perhaps overly assured, competence. Schmidt inherited Brandt's foreign policy and (in alliance with the party of both business and civic liberalism, the Free Democrats) extended it. Brandt incarnated, led, the moral and political forces which revivified Germany's democratic heritage and confronted its recent murderous past. Schmidt, like Brandt a Protestant, concentrated on the demands of routine. Germany's situation, even after the normalization of relations with the smaller communist German state and the Soviet Union and its satellites, was extraordinary. Its division threatened to lengthen indefinitely. In case of nuclear war between the superpowers, both parts of the nation risked nuclear extirpation. In the circumstances, routine was a very approximate synonym for crisis management.

The crises were many. In culture and politics, and in everyday existence, Germany's past was present. The churches, especially the Protestant Church, had assigned themselves the tasks of confrontation and repentance—but much of the nation struck one as a very large congregation listening with very different degrees of willingness to a ceaseless succession of preachers. Some of the younger protesters had marched or slid into terrorism. The party of aggrieved normality took this as evidence for the danger of excessive attention to flaws in the recent past. One Bruno Heck, an official of the Christian Democratic Union, pronounced the legacy of 1968 worse than that of 1933. These fissures apart, there was widespread agreement that the "German model" of welfare capitalism provided the indispensable economic and social preconditions of democratization and civility itself. However, with economic growth slowing, and inequality increasing, the debate on the near future intensified.

As I came to know the Social Democrats, I realized that they were divided on these questions, divisions reflected in the distinctive emphases of Brandt as Party Chairman and of Schmidt as Chancellor. Schmidt has been widely cited as regretting that when he succeeded Brandt in 1974 he did not also assume the chairmanship. Actually, their disagreements would have been significant in any case. Some schematic depictions of the conflict are overly schematic. Schmidt had the loyalty of the trade unions and the approval of the economic elite. The support of those who thought that a Germany which had come a very long way to stability needed a disciplinarian. For some of them, disruption was always a possibility and Schmidt's distance an asset. Brandt had indeed altered the Federal Republic and had his own public in the DDR and beyond. There was a time for everything, and the time for Schmidt's dramatic calm had come. Brandt's most enthusiastic followers among the young, and the critical intelligentsia thought Schmidt was deliberately slowing the pace and limiting the extent of change—or ignoring the imperatives for it. In an Irenic view, the ensuing conflicts were positive. They provided persons of different social characteristics and of varied temperaments, with shares in a common enterprise. The two leaders, and their closest collaborators, were careful about avoiding irreparable rupture. The drama lent interest to the Social Democrats. The rival formations, the Christian Democratic Union and the Christian Social Union in Bavaria, had their own differences but seemed duller by comparison.

Actually, one of my earliest friends in the Social Democratic Party worked for Schmidt as Director of Policy Planning. Albrecht Müller held that post under Brandt and Schmidt, who admired his many talents and thought it best to make the gesture of keeping him. Albrecht was the electoral strategist who brought Brandt and the party forty five percent of the vote in the 1972 elections, a quite extraordinary result in Germany. He had studied economics, had a large intellectual curiosity, a great deal of empathy and generosity—connected to a large suspicion of ordinary human motives and a considerable capacity to speak his mind,

He lived in the seventies in a large house on an agreeable plot of land in the center of Bonn, with his young family. At the back of the large garden he kept chickens, and a neighbor sued because the cock's crowing disturbed his sleep. The case went through several judicial instances, accumulating ever thicker dossiers. Albrecht's argument, that his chickens represented a salutary presence of the countryside in the city eventually carried the day and Albrecht has identified himself as an early father of the German Green movement. The large house did not escape Schmidt's attention and at a meeting with his staff right after a very large rally in Bonn to protest the stationing of newer American missiles in Germany, he told Albrecht that he supposed that he had housed ten of the demonstrators. "Twenty four, Herr Bundeskanzler" was his widely quoted reply. Albrecht had large views of political possibility and convinced Schmidt to consider a television free Sunday as a family friendly project. It came to naught but even those who dismissed it acknowledged its cultural seriousness. It was a singularly German fusion of Lutheran traditionalism and rejection of the omnipotence of the market.

Albrecht later served in the Bundestag as representative of the vineyard region of the state of Rheinland-Pfalz, north of Alsace. The trip to visit him from Strasbourg was an experience of old Europe (the bunkers of the Maginot and Siegfried lines) and the new (the absence of controls at the border). Albrecht in parliament was notably independent in forming and expressing his opinion and both the lobbyists for German business and the punctilious advocates of party discipline came to fear him. He had a national following and when he retired, he started what has become a widely read online journal, *NachDenkSeiten*, the Reflective Pages. Americans of a certain age can think of it as reminiscent of the newspaper *PM*, or Dwight Macdonald's *Politics* magazine. Albrecht in its pages himself takes on current German clichés in economic and foreign policy with sovereign contempt. I had the honor of speaking at his seventy-fifth birthday celebration, to which many of his former colleagues in the Chancellor's office and some from the Bundestag came. The house in Bonn had been exchanged for a small water castle, its moat filled in. I have very good memories of my visits over the years, not least of the Müller cat, who came in and out of the upstairs window of the combined living room and kitchen on a steep ladder. I also have memories of being treated by the human inhabitants as family—attitudes which somehow were transmitted to the cat.

Albert's deputy, Stefan Pelny, was closer to Schmidt. Here I recall a cat and a dog. The family cat, in their house in Rhöndorf and later near Kiel, was extremely indignant about my occupying his territory, the guest room and a chair in front of TV during the evening news, which he watched with the family. The Pelnys also had a very large dog, extremely friendly, but (he was a Newfoundland dog) if he was enthused about a visitor he could easily push one over. In manner, Pelny was skeptical of all-encompassing projects, gave the impression of thinking twice or even thrice about any political move, did refer with something like British off handedness to the characterological flaws of major figures. He had begun his career by working with Horst Ehmke, whose ebullience was certainly a contrast with Schmidt's dourness. Schmidt clearly profited from Albrecht's large ideas and Pelny's tactical refinement. The presence in his office of these younger figures who fused conviction with their skills was a considerable asset in his relationship to the party.

Stefan had a Master's in Law from Yale and was surprised by nothing that happened in the US. After the Social Democrats left government in 1982 he was appointed vice president of the Office for the Defense of the Constitution—the German intelligence agency which dealt with internal threats. He was invited to the US by the CIA, which offered Stefan and his wife Enkelin their choice of Washington's better hotels. They chose to stay with me, which the CIA took in ecumenical good spirits and was gracious enough to invite me to their farewell dinner for the Pelnys, at the Four Seasons. There is much to be said about the CIA contra and pro—but the good taste of its senior officers in wine was convincing evidence that their years of service abroad had indeed taught them much.

Enkelin Pelny was a Gymnasium teacher of history. When Richard Burt was Ambassador, he had the inspired idea of visiting a

Gymnasium to discuss American history. Enkelin's class was chosen, and I was chosen—without coordination with the Embassy—to supply background reading and suggest themes for discussion. The Ambassador apparently found it an educational experience.

Stefan in due course left the intelligence agency in a public breach: he did not think it appropriate that the Green Party, in its first term in the Parliament, was an object of scrutiny. His subsequent career demonstrated the vagaries of political fortune. He worked with Gerhard Schröder in his first campaign for the Minister Presidency of Lower Saxony, which he very narrowly lost. Had he won, Stefan would have become his State Secretary and presumably moved with him later to the Federal Chancellor's office. Instead, he became State Secretary to the Schleswig-Holstein Minister President, Björn Engholm, who for a time was leader of the national party. Engholm's ascent was abruptly ended by a very untransparent episode, and Stefan shortly thereafter left public service. The loss was the party's and the nation's.

I learned a good deal from Albrecht and Stefan. Rather like the persons I knew in the Kennedy White House and those who worked with Carter, they knew how difficult the transformation of good ideas into everyday politics, how constricting the routines and rituals of office were, and how difficult especially to keep envisaging larger ends.

Albrecht and Stefan were caught, as I came to know them, in an extraordinary German crisis, the national debate over the installation of medium range nuclear missiles following the NATO decision of late 1979 to proceed with deployment. Other NATO states experienced similar divisions—the United Kingdom, the Low Countries, Italy. The pathos of the German argument was not a matter of questioning the effectiveness of the missiles as a deterrent to hypothetical Soviet aggression. There were questions, by the officers' corps of the German army and its ordinary, conscripted, soldiers. (In Italy, the commanding officer of the nation's armed forces resigned after refusing to comply with the decision.) The citizenry of the Federal Republic conceived of the problem in terms of their conceptions of nationhood—on both sides of a very complex debate.

The NATO decision to install the medium range missiles was

not the consequence of an informed and open debate. German academics, journalists, officials, politicians and of course military commanders, had been integrated in an Atlanticist consensus. That consensus rested only propositions which were not supposed to be questioned. One was the indispensability and competence of American leadership. Another was the immutability of the Russian (then Soviet) drive to expand westward. A third was the efficacy of nuclear deterrence. A fourth, an unacknowledged contradiction was that preparation for the failure of deterrence was necessary.

Actually, in the decade preceding 1979, détente had been expanded and consolidated. There were arms control treaties between the US and the USSR, the Helsinki accords and Germany's Ostpolitik had stabilized the situation in Central Europe and allowed larger ranges of freedoms for the citizens of the Soviet bloc. The Cold War, however, had generated, in each bloc, a self-renewing apparatus which legitimated its demands on policy and resources by claiming that it alone was the guarantor of security. The development by the Soviet Union of intermediate range missiles and its plans to station these in Central Europe provided an opening for the Atlanticist maximalists. Threatening the Soviet Union in case it sought to move into Western Europe with nuclear destruction of Russia itself meant that the defense of Europe put the US homeland at risk. The Euro-missiles, as they were termed, opened the possibility of engaging and stopping the Soviet Union in central Europe, that is, in Czechoslovakia, Poland, and the two German states. De Gaulle had envisaged one Europe, from the Atlantic to the Urals. The Euro-missiles anticipated one Hiroshima, from the Rhine to the Vistula.

The period was one of the most contradictory happenings. The turbulences of 1968 in the west had echoes in the east. The Prague spring was extirpated by the Warsaw Pact, at large cost to the communist regimes which sent troops to Czechoslovakia. The DDR contingents had to be recalled, the sullen conscripts were deemed unreliable. (A Czech witness recounted a DDR soldier saying to a café waiter at first unwilling to serve him: "Come on, it is the first time occupied countries occupy another.") The leaders of the DDR alternately cajoled, expelled, jailed successive waves of dissenters, only to face new ones. The Hungarian communists took a discreet path to openness ("whoever is not against us is with us") Solidarity in Poland emerged in 1980, and its subsequent repression was a half acknowledged communist recognition of bankruptcy. In the USSR itself, the cultural and political legacy of the earlier post-Stalin thaw was too deeply and widely rooted to be dug up. Gorbachev's project was entirely audible and visible before the reformer himself took charge, among the intelligentsia and in official institutions, as well as in critical attitudes in Soviet civil society.

The Euro-missile crisis was an unintendedly cooperative project of the Cold War bureaucracies and ideologues of both blocs. In place of politics, even in their halting Soviet bloc form, it put arms and preparation for their use at the center of the several nations' lives. Had each side refrained from installing the new arms, discontent in the east and protest in the west might have seriously altered the relations of the blocs well before 1989. I am reminded of a cartoon in a Munich newspaper, showing two heavily armed DDR border guards atop the Wall. One is peering in the distance with binoculars, "Get a load of that bearded demonstrator over there. Is he on their side, and a courageous friend of peace? Or is he on ours, and a dangerous enemy of the state?"

Deeply engraved in short term political memory, the protest movement in the Federal Republic altered both political consciousness and political structure permanently. It brought the Green Party sufficient profile and sufficient votes to enter the Bundestag in 1983. It made all but the most rigid of Atlanticists acutely aware of the actual fragilities of the alliance with the US and obliged many officers to rethink their ideas of warfare itself. (Decades later I heard Helmut Schmidt refer to his "comprehension" of the German officers who told him that they would never fire nuclear weapons at the DDR.) When Foreign Minister Genscher withdrew the Free Democratic Party in 1982 from the thirteen year old alliance with the Social Democrats, it was not to abandon the policy of reconciliation with the Soviet bloc and the East German state, but to conserve his capacity to pursue these ends by constructing a new consensus with a changed Christian Democratic Union In a few years, Chancellor Kohl emerged as practitioner of rapprochement with the other half of Europe.

The chronology of events does not convey the density and passions, fears and hopes, of those years, the infusion of political decision with sober Calculation and eschatological imagery, not infrequently alternating vertiginously. In 1979 NATO approved the installation of the Euro-missiles and the opening of negotiations with the Soviet Union on alternative measures. In 1981, negotiations began. In 1983, the Bundestag approved the Federal Republic's participation in the plan, and the USSR stopped the negotiations. By 1987, however, the two superpowers negotiated a treaty removing the weapons. In 1985 Gorbachev took office and begun his reforms. In 1986 Gorbachev and Reagan met in Iceland and actually discussed the abolition of nuclear weaponry. The ensuing consternation among Cold War officialdom and their supporting groups in the NATO nations ebbed when the superpowers did not reach agreement on a cessation of the US Strategic Defensive Initiative. It is unclear to me how much of the "Star Wars" project was a serious technological design and how much was simply fraudulent.

Political events in the Soviet bloc commanded attention. In June of 1989 the communist military dictatorship imposed in 1981 in Poland collapsed and allowed free elections. In July the Hungarian regime opened its borders, and refused to stop DDR citizens from travelling to the west. In September, DDR citizens occupied the grounds of the Federal Republic's embassy in Prague and demanded to be allowed to travel to the west. With some help from his Soviet colleague, Genscher negotiated a solution which allowed them to travel, but required that they pass through the DDR. DDR citizens in the thousands came to the railway stations en route and sought to board the trains. Large scale demonstrations against the regime began in Leipzig, organized largely by the Protestant Church. They were also responses to a letter to the government from a small group of dissidents in Berlin who asked under the DDR constitution to be allowed to activate a new forum for discussion with party and state. The request by the Neues Forum group was denied but evoked widespread adherence in the country. The ruling party itself began to split openly on the issue of reform, with a large demonstration in Berlin on 4 November organized by cultural and political figures associated with the regime, like the novelist Christa Wolf and the retired intelligence official Markus Wolf. By this time, the opening of the Wall was a foregone conclusion, as the state party was reduced to operating on the principle "sauve qui peut" ("every man for himself"). Gorbachev had personally contributed to the supersession of the aging Stalinists in the DDR half of Berlin by declaring, as their guest at the fortieth anniversary celebration of the founding of their state, that history punished those who came too late. Even (or perhaps above all) school children in the DDR got the point.

There are plenty of different ways to interpret history, particularly the history of times which the chronicler has personally experienced. Historians argue about the ways in which they tell their stories—history as past politics, as an account of decisions by those in power and their immediate antagonists, or history as a social tableau, perhaps archaeology, in which larger currents and institutions dictate the choices of those who think they rule—but are creatures of larger circumstances they may or may not see. I participated in politics in the eighties as commentator in several languages in different sorts of journalism, as occasional advisor to those in office (mostly, themselves critical outsiders), as very informal and often self-appointed liaison officer between groups separated by the ocean. I sought my interlocutors in churches, parties, civic action groups, editorial rooms and government offices. I was greatly aided by students and my own daughters in reaching a younger generation, by sympathetic officials approaching middle age in speaking to those who had (or thought they had) real power. In small gatherings in homes in Berlin and Bonn, especially, I glimpsed a society come alive, a culture of citizens educating themselves. That was supposed to be a proprietary fixture of American politics, but the acutely disappointed American activists of the sixties and seventies in the eighties professionalized themselves—or left the work of education and lobbying to organizations which functioned from the top down. Norman Mailer's marvelous depiction of the march on the Pentagon in his *Armies of the Night* had echoes in Bonn more than a decade later, even if only a few grasped the exact parallel. The sense of participating in an international enterprise was not only conveyed but exemplified in writers like Böll, Grass, Mailer, with very large publics.

Much of the work that led to public challenges to the uncommunicative Cold War apparatus of the Federal Republic was done at the level of local congregations of the Protestant Church. Congregants formed study groups, invited public officials and military officers and academic experts and journalists to discussions. A Cardinal sent by the Medici Pope to Germany to deal with the uproar occasioned by the pamphlets of the hitherto unknown monk, Martin Luther, wrote to Rome that Germany was indeed strange: "Every fishwife quotes the Bible." The denigration of dissent by referring to women daring to speak out was not peculiar to the Reformation. In Bonn, in particular, the wives (and children) of senior officials challenged patriarchy in the larger society by making it impossible in the household. There were plenty of instances of a political division of labor. Children and wives joined the peace movement; husbands and fathers continued with their governmental duties but were not invariably immune to serious doubts.

The national venues for the political expression of the views of the church—in the form of intensive discussion with public figures—were the Kirchentagen, National Assemblies of the Church. The first had taken place right after the war, and they continued, increasingly serving as national fora. They were organized by a permanent group connected to but independent of the other institutions of the church, and led by laypersons. During the intense periods of strife over the Euro-missiles, I attended and spoke at the meetings of 1981 in Hamburg and 1983 in Hannover. I spoke for myself, describing the views of the heterogeneous American peace movement. The events brought me into contact with laypersons and church persons who struck me as being motivated by beliefs quite different from political ideologies. Some needed to bear witness, others to listen to those who were so moved, others were struggling with Biblical texts on peace (the Old Testament, especially difficult in this respect, also claimed attention). I was especially impressed by the interaction of generations. There were some rather courageous officers of the Bundeswehr. In uniform, come to defend the view that they belonged to an organization that preserved peace. There were others, not in uniform, who did not take that position and had clearly come to listen. There were participants from the DDR, as far as I could determine few in number and voicing the view of party and state: the Warsaw Pact's nuclear weapons were defensive. One Bishop from the DDR was challenged on the absence of representatives of the protest groups within his church and in effect shrugged his shoulders—whether a gesture of realism or of resignation or a mixture of each, it was difficult to say. One participant from the DDR I met at the 1986 Kirchentag in Düsseldorf was Manfred Stolpe, then as a lawyer executive officer of the Protestant Church in the DDR. He later was a Social Democratic Minister of Transport and Minister President of Brandenburg. He did not figure more prominently in the SPD since he was for many years criticized, sometimes bitterly, for collaborating with the state in the DDR. I found him, from the first, a person of considerable capacity for dealing with complexity, historically and intellectually curious, someone inclined to do the work of the world. He was, after all, the Church's first lawyer and not its first theologian. There were dissenters in the DDR who objected to what they regarded as a shallow approach to its past in the period after unification when memories (and injuries) were still quite vivid. It is impossible to compare the situation with that of the Third Reich, in which much of the population was complicit with a regime that was not imposed on the nation by a foreign occupier—and the crimes of which were far more horrible. Yet, the decision to reintegrate Germany in the west having been taken (and not least the decision to arm the Federal Republic) the de-Nazification project was extremely attenuated when it was not simply dropped.

Two figures who were leaders of the National Assembly became enduring friends. One was Wolfgang Huber, then a Professor of Theology at the Protestant Faculty of the University of Heidelberg, later Bishop of Berlin-Brandenburg just after the joining of what had been the West Berlin Church with the neighboring ones in the very early period of unification. Wolfgang was originally a scholar in the area of social ethics, and had a large view of society by no means confined to Germany. He had to deal with a particularly sensitive and no doubt painful familial situation: his father, a student of Carl Schmitt, was a very prominent Nazi as legal scholar and advisor to the government of the Third Reich. It was the situation which prevailed, if in a less striking way, in millions of German families. Wolfgang did not burden me with the story, and I note that he had considerable curiosity as to what moved an American Jewish intellectual to engagement. Like many Germans who admired

American democracy, he was interested by our own phenomena of racism and ethnic and religious prejudice, as well as our variants of chauvinism and militarism, In Germany, as a theologian and church leader, he was a very audible voice for a new German internationalism, with large elements of social solidarity and pacifism. The conflict over the Euro-missiles was not the first which divided the Protestant Church. Decades before, Church commissions had rejected nuclear armament for the Federal Republic and anticipated Brandt's Ostpolitik. The senior ranks of the Church were peopled by prominent laypersons and theologians who, with very differing perspectives, were caught up in their nation's history. Wolfgang spoke for the peace movement when Germany could claim a unique contribution to the domestication of the Cold War, the Ostpolitik — as well as disposing of the single largest NATO military force in Europe. Previous German interventions in world politics were somewhat tentative. The German opposition to the Vietnam War, little noticed by an American public absorbed by our own conflicts, was the bridge from the restiveness of an occupied nation to the demand for sovereignty of a new one.

It was in this sense that Wolfgang spoke when he came to the US in the early eighties to meet with the American churches. On one visit, he was my house guest and I introduced him to a set of Washington policy makers. Those who knew Germany, like Gerald Livingston of the Marshall Fund and the American Institute for Contemporary German Studies, were aware of the importance of the Church in a nation with a very concentrated ecclesiastical life, very different from our own dispersed pluralism. It was a period in which large German demonstrations had so puzzled President Reagan that he asked his foreign policy advisors for a report. Eventually, the CIA's experts on Germany presented their Director with a paper refuting the easy answer, that the peace movement was a consequence of manipulation by the German communist state. The Director, William Casey, reportedly thought that he could not take this report to the president and asked for another one emphasizing Soviet bloc influence. I was definitely not privy to the inner workings of the CIA but gathered that a crisis of morale followed.

Huber in conversation and dialogue had a refined, even delicate, manner. His interlocutors were immediately assured that he took them seriously, knew of their background and wished to learn more. That served him on his American visits as when he had to administer a Bishopric with two populations of different historical experiences. Wolfgang's quiet presence did not quite conceal his insistence on knowing other persons' needs, and that made him a formidable leader—ostensibly unobtrusive, actually at the heart of the matter. I had the good fortune to keep in touch with him through the years, recall an episode when we were panelists at a conference on international peace organized by the German section of the International organization, Physicians Against Nuclear War. It was during the American destruction of Iraq, I recounted a visit by then opposition leader Angela Merkel to Georgetown University. In her fluent English, she had criticized the Social Democratic-Green coalition's refusal to join the US and the UK in Baghdad. I asked her about what seemed to be a paradox. She was the leader of a coalition of two parties proclaiming their Christian identities, and yet both the German Catholic Bishops' Conference and the Protestant Church had quite formally criticized the course taken by Blair and Bush. "They do theology, we do politics," was her reply, exactly consonant with Luther's doctrine of the two realms. Huber's comment was: "Because I do theology, I have to do politics." In 1524, he would not have been against the urban artisans and small peasants who rose against their masters and lords. It is much to be regretted that he did not become president of Germany when the Social Democrats backed his candidacy, in 2013. (The Greens insisted on their candidate, the former DDR dissenting pastor, Joachim Gauck. They thought that on issues like the legal and social status of homosexuals, he was to be preferred. Some, I gather, have been surprised to learn the obvious, that the president is an unremitting moralist with some opinions that can hardly be deemed unconventional. His advocacy of highly unspecific policies of "strength" with regard to Russia does not bespeak much reflectiveness.)

Bishop Huber remains a person of quite extraordinary tact and empathy—qualities which served the peace movement very well as it legitimated itself as an expression of public concern insufficiently addressed by government and parliament. He was very effective with American church groups not invariably aware of the historical roots of German protest. There were, of course, an entire gallery of visitors from Germany in the turbulent late seventies and early eighties. One had prophetic qualities and hardly hid these. Erhard Eppler had been a soldier and Nazi party member during the war, and like any number of influential figures in the subsequent years of the Federal Republic, a participant in Gustav Heinemann's All-German People's Party in its extremely unsuccessful electoral campaign of 1953. Heinemann opposed rearmament, favored considering Stalin's offer to allow the unification of a demilitarized and neutral Germany, and had less than two percent of the vote. Sixteen years later as a Social Democrat he became president of Germany. The younger figures who were originally with him included Johannes Rau, himself later president, and the philosopher Jürgen Habermas, whose political engagement put his academic career in jeopardy. Eppler taught English in a Gymnasium, joined the Social Democrats, and by 1966 was Minister of Development. He was a very outspoken ally of Brandt and a major contributor to Germany's modern environmental movement. He left Schmidt's government in disagreement on the budgetary allocation for developmental assistance, could hardly have remained in it on account of his determined opposition to the Euro-missile decision.

President of the National Assembly of the Protestant Church, a widely read author, a frequent speaker on television and at local meetings, his public presence was considerable. He also had a good deal of influence on younger Social Democrats, and for some years was leader of the party in his home state, Baden-Wuerttemberg, but lost successive state elections when he ran as candidate for the Minister Presidency. He occasionally spoke, within the Social Democratic Party, in terms unavailable to Brandt, who was its Chair and bound by a certain discretion. Eppler had a good deal of Brandt's combination of larger designs and tactical political capacity. His critics frequently derided what they saw a schoolmasterish manner—a confession of their inability to deal with his consequential thinking. Eppler's career demonstrated that some criteria of political success are too narrow. Well past formal retirement, he remains a public figure.

His American visits were characterized by directness. As Development Minister, he had worked with Robert McNamara when he was at the World Bank. Eppler understood the ambiguities and intricacies of American politics, grasped the irreducible Protestantism of much of our public life. I recall his holding the attention of a mixed audience at The Washington National Cathedral, religious outsiders and official insiders alike. I also recall an exchange with Richard Pipes, then in charge of Soviet bloc affairs at the National Security Council, in which Pipes rather reluctantly acknowledged that NATO's nuclear tactics might well devastate the eastern European nations otherwise described as candidates for liberation. I particularly enjoyed a conversation between Eppler and the then German Ambassador, Peter Hermes. Hermes was a pronouncedly conservative Catholic, who had expressed his incomprehension of his own children's Catholic engagement in a movement termed "the basis of the Church." Hermes asked Eppler if he had any impressions of the meeting of the National Assembly of the Catholic Church, which he had attended as president of the Protestant Assembly. Eppler's reply: "Ambassador, I heard much that was enlightening and sympathetic, but in the end, I said to myself, perhaps Luther was not so wrong after all."

Perhaps I had not been wrong, years before that, in studying the Reformation as my own introduction to modern German history. Some of the Americans dealing with Germany, as academics, journalists, officials, politicians, were acutely aware of the ecclesiastical and religious undercurrents of the Federal Republic (and of the DDR). The movement for the development of European institutions was also the work of the Churches—and of European figures with personal religious engagements.

Huber and Eppler connected the peace movement in German civil society to the center of German public space, where government, parliament, the parties and the media constituted a moving tableau. In cities and townships, larger and smaller, the parishes were organizing points—and so were the local branches of the Social Democratic Party. I met their representatives in Bonn, as parliamentarians, or at national meetings of the party, as delegates or officials. I had begun at the top, with Brandt and Ehmke and Schmidt's staff—but came to know the quite extraordinary persons who labored day by day at uncelebrated but indispensable tasks.

One set of friends were the Social Democratic Bundestag members from Schleswig Holstein who occupied a corner of a high floor of a tall building (Lange Eugen) in the governmental complex around the chamber. The views of the Rhine and countryside were good, the nearness to the top floor café and restaurant with its memorable pastries and excellent roasts even better. Norbert Gansel and Heide Simonis remained friends to this day. Norbert was from Kiel, worked in the shipyards there summers, combined political rigor with an intuitive grasp of popular concerns. He eschewed party office, had large moral influence on the rest of the parliamentary group, was Mayor of Kiel in his final years of public service. An observer said of him that his career showed how much influence one could gain by renouncing the pursuit of parliamentary or governmental offices. Heidi had studied economics and was a particularly critical analyst of the Defense Ministry budget much feared by generals and civil servants in that labyrinthine institution. She later became the first woman Minister President of a German state, renowned for her splendid hats and direct speech.

The social origins of the Social Democratic activists traced recent changes in the Federal Republic, their educational biographies the success of Social Democratic programs which made university education accessible for the first time to children of the working class. The predominantly working-class party, with strong representation from trade unionists expanded to incorporate another milieu. By the time I came to know it, university graduates were increasingly prevalent in its ranks—as were women. Many came from the working class, especially its artisanal; and skilled ranks, but there were exceptions.

First, there were a certain number of persons termed in German grossbürgerliche—a term difficult to translate and certainly not translatable by the American notion of an upper-middle class. The term conveyed (and more importantly the persons designated by it do) a certain sense of belonging, an acquired or inherited right to be listened to and at the same time a somewhat open view of the world's inner divisions. The one Social Democrat I knew who matched this description was Horst Ehmke. He had lots of energy and self-confidence. Witness an Ehmke anecdote very widely cited. He rushes out of the Bundestag and into his car, and the driver asks, "Where to, Herr Professor?" "It doesn't matter; I'm needed everywhere." Some worked hard to learn to behave in this way, others were born to it.

There were also Social Democratic aristocrats. I knew three. One was an academic colleague, Peter von Oertzen who at one point was Minister of Higher Education in Lower Saxony and who throughout his academic and political career seemed to disdain pettiness. Peter was as a younger man attracted by the legacy of Trotsky. Maturing by a certain age, Peter cannot have thought that elections in Lower Saxony were preliminaries to world revolution—but he let one know that he kept the possibility in mind. Another aristocrat was Andreas von Bülow, who was Minister for Science and at one point a Deputy Minister of Defense. The Ministry of Science had a very tall building in Bonn with his office at the top. Andreas had a very competent personal assistant, Peer Steinbrück, who brought us coffee, later when he was Minister of Finance told me that he had learned from Andreas to think in the long term. Andreas, explaining why he was at home in the Defense post, was succinct: his ancestors were responsible for any number of major German military disasters. He had what I understood as inner certainty.

That quality was very evident in yet another noble Social Democrat, Klaus von Dohnányi, a Mayor of Hamburg, Minister of Education, Deputy Foreign Minister. Klaus had seen too much of German history: his father, a civil servant, was executed for his participation in the 1944 plot. I had the pleasure and profit of serving with him on the Executive Committee of the International Institute of Peace in Vienna, of which he was vice president. Klaus had a great deal of access to the elites of Germany and the world, struck me as above condescension: he did not need to stoop to it. When (to be sure in cashmere coat) he appeared at a factory gate at six in the morning to campaign, his citizens listened. Inevitably, I was reminded of our Bostonians or New Yorkers of the Roosevelt vintage. Klaus knew the US, where he worked as a younger man, thought our divisions too deep and our changes too rapid for older American traditions to count.

The Social Democrats have had and have plenty of persons who know the US quite well—having studied or worked in the US, having read our literature and experienced our art and films. Marx never got here but his congratulatory letter to Lincoln on his reelection remains one of the more moving documents of a long relationship. There were very large numbers of Social Democrats who

With Erwin Lanc at the International Institute of Peace in Vienna.

The scholarly advisory board of The International Institute of Peace in Vienna, of which I was the chair.

migrated to the US and contributed to the long struggle that led to the New Deal—and returning émigrés who brought their American experiences to the post-war revival of German democracy. Before he joined Nixon in the White House, Henry Kissinger as a Harvard professor administered a CIA funded international seminar at our ancient university. It brought younger citizens of other countries who had begun interesting careers to Harvard for brief but intense immersions in our culture and politics. In 1962, the visitors included Günter Gaus, later editor of *Der Spiegel*, advisor to Brandt, and first representative of the Federal Republic in the DDR, and Eppler. They and Kissinger maintained friendly relations throughout the subsequent decades, despite the turbulence of the development of the Ostpolitik. I was struck years later by the fact that when the German Historical Institute in Washington unveiled a portrait of Brandt, with an accompanying talk by Egon Bahr, Kissinger traveled from New York for the event, .On more than one occasion, he intimated his skepticism about the egalitarianism and efficiency of socialism, but he did respect and collaborate with the Social Democrats. We talked at the unveiling and he recollected our time as graduate students and teaching assistants at Harvard. I certainly did not expect to become Secretary of State, and you surely did not expect to become so close a friend of the Social Democrats, he said. I ventured to point out that even then, his contemporaries thought of him as intending to play a major role in the world—while our own ambitions were more academic. I was rewarded with the observation that he always found me perceptive.

My acquaintance with the Social Democrats was extensive, but two figures stand out. I met Gerhard Schröder when he was chair of the party's youth organization, It was at a party congress in Berlin in 1979 and one night we went out for dinner at the West Berlin temple of Indonesian food, Bali—with my two daughters, both at the time students at the Free University of Berlin. Gerd's human instincts led him to remark thereafter on our familial closeness. In the many conversations we have had since I am reminded of his account of beginning university, with the help of a Social Democratic project to broaden university access. For much of his life he had to rise on most days very early and report for work, when he began his studies he was for the first time free to dispose of his schedule.

With Gerhard Schröder, on one of his recent trips to Washington, DC.

The detail was telling, if small, and suggests something of his appeal to many who like himself came from the bottom of a society which, despite the welfare state, remained profoundly stratified. There is another aspect of the national experience Schröder shared with many: he never knew his father, who did not return from fighting the Soviet Army.

I visited with Gerd in the Bundestag, in Lower Saxony and then in the Chancellor's office and of course saw him in his visits to the US. He had gifts of rapport with his citizens rather like those of Bill Clinton, and it was not surprising that they became close. His American counterpart also came from very modest circumstances. With Blair, they evoked a Third Way—a political project between the inherited canons of Social Democracy and an opportunistic utilization of the market. The project rested on neutralizing the managers of large scale concentrations of capital by making them partners of government, while curtailing government's alliance with the trade unions and its functions as an agency of redistribution and social investment. It also entrusted large amounts of decision making to technocratic elites and elevated entrepreneurship (whatever its economic and social content) to an honorific social function.

In Germany this took the form of the Agenda 2010 and reforms which reduced payments to the unemployed, required them to accept alternative jobs at lower levels of income and security. Conceptually, an additive idea of the public good began to replace the practice of social solidarity—which became a residual and diffuse aim of social policy. Gerd kept in close touch with the party's indispensable allies, the trade unions—themselves struggling with the fragmentation of the labor force and large scale exports of investment capital. Gerd's greatest single political asset, his capacity to read public moods, clearly told him that a defense of a social model conceived for an earlier phase of German capitalism would render the party even more ideologically disoriented than it was already. Long term investments in education and science were ventures in the future, but the present generation would have to pay for these with curtailed current compensation.

Gerd fended off criticism in ways reminiscent of arguments by Democrats around Clinton (and by Clinton himself) that given the balance of forces in economy and society, and the readiness of capital's political representatives to proceed even more brutally with the dismantlement of the German welfare state, the public would have to rely on the Chancellor as guardian of its long term interests. In one major area, he was clearly right-and widely seen to be so. In close contact with Chirac in France, and supported by his Green Foreign Minister Joschka Fischer, he refused to allow Germany to be drawn into the Anglo-American disaster in Iraq. The experience of Ostpolitik, of the peace movement, the political recomposition of a unified Germany, contributed to the decision and it was reinforced by the increasingly visible deceit and incompetence of the Anglo-Americans.

When I saw Gerd in the course of his years as Chancellor, it was a welcome occasion to renew acquaintance with Frank-Walter Steinmeier, who had been with him in Hannover. His admirers are right to see in him the sort of German civil servant apostrophized by Max Weber, attentive to the demands of office, the limits of authority, the consequences of decision. That overlooks the man of feeling and humor, the passionate partisan of a special German responsibility in Europe, the custodian of memory. I was particularly struck, as well, by Steinmeier's chief of staff, now himself a State

Secretary, Stephan Steinlein. Stephan was one of the few DDR diplomats taken into the Foreign Ministry at reunification, had served in France. In fact, he had done a doctoral dissertation with the critical DDR theologian Ullman and had written on the French Catholic ideas of renewal which had eventually led to Vatican II. Pope John XXIII as Papal Nuncio had served in Paris and come to know the persons and writings of the French Dominicans who were in extreme disfavor at the time in the Vatican of Pius XII. I came to know their writings and then their persons through my French friend Henri Desroche, a former Dominican. This was clearly not what Stephan expected of a Jewish intellectual from New York. Stephan and I agreed: large centralized systems had to find paths to renewal or they would ossify and break.

Gerd Schröder has a contemporary, friend and erstwhile rival for party leadership, Oskar Lafontaine. I first met Oskar when he was Mayor of Saarbrücken and very active in the movement against the stationing of the Euro-missiles. Oskar had studied physics, was not given to doubt, and was an unrelenting polemicist. His strength was plain and hard speech. I helped him to a more differentiated view of the functioning of American democracy than the one which he derived from the epoch of Vietnam. I recollect a meeting with the citizens of Saarbrücken at which he, Eppler, Grass, and the editor and writer Johano Strasser spoke. It fell to me to insist that the early Reagan government did not command total unanimity in American opinion.

Oskar's subsequent career reflected his singular alteration of impetuousness and reflective decisiveness. He can certainly claim a significant share of the credit for the SPD electoral triumph of 1998—after, as party Chair, he had systematically reorganized the party. His unexpected and total exit from government, party (and for a while) politics shortly thereafter bespoke either uncompromising honesty or a pervasive lack of realism. No one explanation will suffice. We had kept in touch during the long years of his ascent, and I saw him again occasionally when he moved to the Left Party. Given the ordered sequence of most German public careers, it is unsurprising that his idiosyncrasy shocked and disappointed many who had placed their hopes in him, confirmed the negative judgment of his critics.

There was something else about the SPD of the late seventies and eighties, its cultural resonance. A great many artists, teachers, writers as well as a considerable segment of the educated public recognized itself in the SPD's larger design, its critical view of the German past, its visionary one for the future. These cultural figures were often well situated economically, or at least in stable and secure circumstances. The party nationally and locally protected them in several ways—by public support for culture, education, science and by active intervention when organized philistinism (and nostalgic Nazism) threatened artistic and intellectual freedom.

The SPD could also rely on active sympathy in critical segments of the media. In the public television chains, the principle of proportionality gave it a voice. In the print media, the situation was mixed. I was struck by how much support there was for the SPD in daily and weekly journalism. I wrote myself, occasionally, for *Der Spiegel*, *Stern* and *Die Zeit*, and did radio and television interviews. I came to know a generation of journalists in addition to my academic contemporaries. Of many, four became especial friends. The first was Valeska von Roques, who was in Washington for *Spiegel* when I arrived in 1979. Valeska was from a Berlin Huguenot family, had that particular sense of self the Calvinists developed the better to serve God, and had lived in New York for some time at the center of the American fringes. She read American history and literature, was surprised by nothing and not much impressed by anyone, made trips into the heartland and had a very considerable grasp of the heights and depths of the American experience. Another German correspondent in the US was the television reporter from ARD, Fritz Pleitgen, who had been in Moscow and would later return to serve in East Berlin. Fritz was not boastful but he could claim in the end to have irritated officialdom everywhere he went. In the US, he took little time to learn that both our foreign guests and the home team were judged by their exhibiting team spirit—that is, not contradicting a coherent and omnipresent political line. Contradiction, however, was precisely his notion of journalism. In Bonn itself, I had the good fortune to come to know two journalists with very open eyes and large intellectual curiosity. One had grown up in Austria, was indeed a graduate of the famous Benedictine Monastery school at Cloister Melk, and came to Germany originally for *Die Neue Presse*. He moved to the *Allgemeine Sonntagsblatt*, the Protestant weekly, that gave me the chance to support ecclesiastical journalism in Germany, since its budget did not provide for Werner's hotel expenses in Washington when accompanying the Foreign Minister and occasionally the Chancellor on trips to our capital. My guest room, where the bookshelves at the time housed my edition of the complete works of Marx and Engels, was used by Werner in an ecumenical spirit. He had grown up in post-war Vienna and experienced its political vicissitudes first hand in his family, later became quite friendly with Bruno Kreisky. He eventually became a senior editor and political correspondent at *Die Zeit*. It was a long way from his Catholic boyhood but a direct entry into the new Europe. The fourth friend was Günter Hoffman of *Die Zeit*, where he exemplified a traditional kind of European journalism. Günter wrote of everyday politics *sub specie aeternitatis*, in an enduring search for the long view. His subsequent book length portraits of political leaders anticipated the work of historians. His articles were essays in philosophy and politics, reports on nascent conflicts that might have otherwise escaped his readers' attention—especially as they were the protagonists.

I learned a great deal from my journalistic friends, not only about Germany and Europe. Their questions about the United States often made me think again about my views of American history. The late seventies and early eighties were years in which a new American academic generation, students or younger faculty in the turbulence of the late sixties and early seventies, came of academic age. They quite literally rewrote much of our received history, by examining the institutions that framed the lives of African-Americans, children, immigrants, women, workers. Intellectual exchange between the new American academic generation and its German counterparts was frequent. My own German academic friends were pillars of integrity and insight: Margherita von Brentano, Iring Fetscher, Jürgen Habermas and somewhat younger ones like Bernd Greiner and Ekkehart Krippendorff. I also knew figures like Peter Glotz, who moved with relentless purpose between academic and political arenas. I also knew somewhat later Helmut Kohl's speechwriter and resident intellectual in his office, Michael Mertes. Finally I had the good fortune to know Kurt Biedenkopf, university reformer before he became General Secretary of the Christian Democratic Union and its intellectual conscience and gatekeeper to the second half of the twentieth century.

Political fictions are long lived. One is that universities are, or ought to be, politically neutral. Perhaps there is a nation of which that is true. My experience consists only of teaching in the US, the UK and for shorter periods in France and Germany and Italy. Each nation had its distinctive modes of joining academic inquiry and thought to politics, but the connections were enduring and often open. No set of academic administrators and teachers is as bound to unexamined assumptions and ossified intellectual habits as those proclaiming (in whatever language) their strict objectivity.

Its version of political culture, the enlistment of the party of the modern in the ranks of the Social Democrats, intensified one of the party's serious problems. It was difficult enough to incorporate distinctive generations with specific historical experiences. The task was more arduous when the generations had not only different memories but distinctive languages. It was a commonplace of discussion about the SPD in the seventies and eighties that it was divided between a stolid and incremental political approach, taking the world as it was and renouncing eschatological rhetoric, and a much more visionary project, seeking a large social transformation. Schmidt was the leader of the earthbound group (a phrase which reflected his decidedly positive self-portrayal), Brandt the voice of those who wished to live on an altered planet. There were in fact rival conventicles within the party, the "Seeheim Circle" (*Seeheimer Kreis*) around Schmidt, the "Charlottenburger Circle" around Brandt. The older working-class members of the party, and the electoral groups for which they spoke, were wary of the cultural experimentation practiced by the SPD's younger and university educated newcomers. The schematic antithesis can be carried too far. In fact, these very different groups were quite aware that they needed each other. The boundaries between them were by no means fixed, battles had to be fought and were fought side by side, and any number of the party's leaders made a point of travelling between the cultures. Brandt was extremely popular with the working class, Schmidt was at pains to present himself as a serious intellectual (which of course he was).

The internal tensions within the SPD were appreciably reduced by the apparition of a new Green Party. The group made the environment a central issue, but also raised questions of decentralization, participatory democracy, women's rights, immigration, assistance to the Third World, and of foreign and military policy. With some roots in the movement against the Viet-Nam war, the nascent Greens were extremely critical of Germany's membership in NATO. The Greens presented a large paradox which bedeviled their political adversaries, who loudly denounced them as affording gratuitous support to the Soviet bloc. The Greens championed human rights and were extremely outspoken about their denial in the state socialist nations and especially in the DDR. They gave the DDR dissidents explicit support, were quite unmoved by arguments as to the long term benefits of the Ostpolitik. In the political turbulence of the time, a troubled theologian in the Federal Republic thought that he had identified a major difficulty. He had co-religionists, he said, who were so naïve and unthinking that they expected to put the words of the Gospel into immediate effect. The Greens were in their early years consistently and widely criticized for their utopianism. Yet it was they who provided a revivification of politics in Germany, with their influenced extending into the DDR where their campaigns in the west excited interest and a certain amount of imitation.

The early Green leaders were recruited, or rather recruited themselves, from urban and regional protest groups with a variety of themes. Artists, writers, students, research and teaching assistants were prominent in their ranks—and so were women. Many lived cheaply, in shared apartments. The distinctly unconventional views and tactics of the Greens constituted a strategy: we are already living differently. There was a very audible and visible contingent of the purposely unemployed, living off welfare payments, to the insistently expressed criticism of antagonists in politics and the press who succeeded in mobilizing a good deal of public resentment at those who were permanent disturbers of the peace. Any number of quite solid citizens in conventional circumstances were, however, drawn by the Greens' ideas. Environmental degradation, the threat of nuclear war, global inequality and women's rights were matters of concern even to those who did not spend much time, or any time at all, demonstrating.

In the US, knowledge of, much less acquaintance with, the Greens was, until their parliamentary victory of 1983, very limited. A handful of academic, official, journalistic experts on Europe and Germany had an accurate picture of the group and its possibilities. Others dismissed them as eccentric, or as isolated survivors of the movements of the sixties, some identified them with the German groups practicing violence. I recollect being asked by a colleague at the Brookings Institution to give an opinion on a text about the Greens written by the Princeton scholar, Klaus Knorr. He did not locate them in German political tradition, could not fathom their criticism of industrial capitalism, and argued that they would rapidly disappear. Brookings did Knorr a favor and did not publish the text. When in the elections of March 1983 they won parliamentary seats, American commentators were surprised, and some shocked. I was invited to participate in what was then the MacNeil/Lehrer News Hour on Public Television, and Jim Lehrer had a question for me: "Isn't their Parliamentary success very bad news?" I persuaded him to reformulate it.

In fact the first generation of Greens had been visiting the US since the end of the seventies. They spoke at colleges and universities, met with American environmentalists and advocates of nuclear disarmament, introduced themselves to the American churches. I was able to put them in touch with Congressman Dellums, Senator Kennedy, the Congressional Progressive Caucus and the organizations supporting it. Some of the visitors had been to the USA before as students. Petra Kelly's stepfather was an American military officer. She was part of a group that included Gert Bastian, Otto Schily and Michael Vesper. While visiting political allies in the US, they also talked to the centers of research around Dupont Circle—and the Washington universities.

In 1983, the Ebert Foundation invited to Bonn an American group which included then Congresswoman Jane Harman, the former White House economic advisor William Nordhaus, Senator Dale Bumpers and former Governor Jerry Brown. Our Social Democratic hosts arranged a meeting with some members of the new Green Bundestag group, Joschka Fischer among them. I was pleased that Joschka had read my writings, impressed by how much he knew of Brown's environmental policy in his period as

Governor. Brown was surprised by Joschka's understanding of the working of American state politics. It was free of stereotypes. Joschka himself explained that even a limited amount of time in Bonn had taught him that lobbying was a considerable American export model.

Of course, I continued and deepened my contacts with SPD and Greens in the seemingly interminable years of Helmut Kohl. I also had the good fortune to be able to free myself of stereotypes by coming to now any number of Christian Democrats and some from the Christian Social Union—including figures other Americans who treated the SPD and Greens as ideological siblings did not ordinarily meet: Alfred Dregger and Franz Josef Strauss. It was this set of conversations (as well as a certain proclivity for reading below the headlines) along with rather regular visits to the Adenauer Foundation that enabled me to follow with a mixture of awe and admiration the initially (and for a long time) silent process sometimes described as the Social Democratization of the CDU-CSU. In the Federal Republic in the Adenauer years, the path from academic thinkers and bureaucrats like Müller-Armack to Norbert Blüm, Kohl's very effective Labor Minister and a trade unionist, was made possible by two groups producing social ideas. One consisted of the Catholic and Protestant Churches, often exerting influence through their academies, insistently exploring the questions of the moral values of a very modern capitalism. The other was comprised of the German trade unions, which assumed not only a representative function but a pedagogic one—a pedagogy directed not only at their members but also at their interlocutors, the employers and the public. Terms like social climate are vague, sometimes usefully so. There is no way to understand the construction of a German social consensus on the limits of the market without referring to the continuous weighing of measurable interest and tangible values in the very language of negotiations.

One of the most famous lines in German literature is uttered in Goethe's *Faust* by the troubled protagonist: "Oh, two souls dwell in my breast." Goethe was a very great poet but he has been outdone by the modern German Free Democratic Party. It has three souls: a foreign policy of realism and restraint, a commitment to civil rights, and a decided penchant for deregulating markets and reducing state organized redistribution. (There was at times in the coalition with the Social Democrats a small and modestly vocal social fraction, espousing a capitalism with less sharp edges, but not much of it has survived.) I came to know Genscher's perpetual Parliamentary Minister, Helmut Schäfer, quite well. I recall a visit by Schäfer to Washington in June of 1989, when he was asked by an American auditor for his view of prospects of German reunification. My constituents in Mainz, he replied, simply assume that it is not on the immediate historical agenda, and they are rather more concerned with problems like the ecological damage to the Amazon rain forests. Schäfer was, despite his closeness to the historically shrewd Genscher, not the only well informed German to have misread the moment.

Appendix to Chapter Fifteen
My DDR Adventure:
Walled Out—Or, Why I Could Not
Visit Stalinism by Subway

I WAS NOT surprised when the Berlin Wall was opened on 9 November of 1989. The disintegrating regime of the Stalinists ruling the German Democratic Republic had already announced that its citizens could travel to the west. The offhand remark by one of its leaders at a press conference, to the effect that he supposed that they could cross at any time, was characteristic of a political group in bondage to illusion, and panic in equal measure. After demonstrating for two months without stringent reprisal, the citizenry knew that it had the communist bosses by their throats—the more so as the rulers were openly divided.

I was not in Berlin when the Wall fell, but did spend much time there before and after. I knew many of the dramatis personae— Walter Momper, the West Berlin Mayor at the time, Willy Brandt, his great predecessor, the ostensibly marginalized dissidents in east Berlin who in their rundown apartments in a neighborhood had defied the state for years. I also knew theologians and pastors and active laypersons in the Protestant churches on both sides of the Wall, who for years kept hopes of a more open German future alive. I knew West German parliamentarians and officials across the spectrum of parties, as well as academic colleagues, editors, journalists, writers. In communist Germany, I went often to party and state institutes. My official interlocutors, older and younger, had quite clear and accurate notions of the culture, politics, society of the Federal Republic. They had visited the west, had family members who visited them, read West German books, journals, newspapers—and of course like all citizens of the DDR were (without talking too much about it) daily viewers of western television.

Knowledge of the other western European nations was much more fortuitous. I thought that I detected an undercurrent of envy, particularly among party intellectuals, of the Italian sister party and the liberties its leaders and members took with the post-Stalinist rigidities advanced in Moscow. A very evident confusion prevailed as to the USA. Some had actually visited, others knew something of our history. Wide stretches of US terrain were simply terra incognita for otherwise rather sophisticated DDR minds. They grasped our historical uniqueness, could not describe in any serious way what constituted it.

I recollect a visit to the party institute of philosophy. I gave a talk on American social protest (I termed it "dissidence" to bring matters closer to home for my hosts.) We went for lunch afterwards to the restaurant next to the Staatsoper, now considerably improved, then providing standardized fare for guests most of whom were wearing party buttons in their lapels or on their dresses. Otto Reinhold, the institute director, was courtesy itself. He said that they understood that I knew a good deal about Europe. But where had I learned so much about Marxism? I explained that I had had a typical New York adolescence, making the transition from uncritical Stalinism to critical Trotskyism at twelve — and proceeded to supplement my formal talk by describing the continuous intellectual torments of the American Communist Party even in its years of greatest influence, the thirties. The group simply did not know how to talk about these matters and their silence spoke volumes. My daughter Antonia, then studying philosophy at the Free University in West Berlin but before that a versed militant of the Ligue Communiste Révolutionnaire in Paris, as we traveled home on the underground, was exceedingly impressed. "I never was prouder of you."

In the turbulent eighties, my two daughters lived in West Berlin. My late elder daughter, a journalist who had interned at *The Nation*, at WETA in Washington and Channel Thirteen in New York, was a permanent resident, an early participant in the environmental and peace movements. My younger daughter Antonia came from Paris in 1985 to study for five years in West Berlin. She was active in a French initiative termed Alternatives, which joined Christians and anti-Stalinist leftists in supporting the oppositional movements within the Soviet bloc. They visited East Berlin often. When a group of East Berlin women organized a "peace kindergarten" to oppose the regime's enthusiastic imitation of Prussian militarism, they were promptly jailed. My daughters were in the daily protests of West Berlin women at Checkpoint Charlie which shamed the regime into letting the pacifist miscreants free.

1986 was a very active year for us, as I went to West Berlin for twelve months at two of its scholarly centers. I visited in East Berlin regularly, often going from official institutes to see my dissident friends. Sometime in the spring, the KGB officer on my case invited me to dinner in East Berlin with colleagues from the Soviet bloc. I had written a biting commentary in *Der Spiegel* on the Reagan air attack on Gadhafi and they wished to honor an American dissenter. (Sakharov was still in enforced inner exile in Gorki.) I accepted but asked that a car be sent for me, as the border formalities were tedious. He agreed but turned up unannounced as always at my office and said that there was a problem. The DDR authorities had told him that I was barred from entering their territory. He said not to worry, the USSR had a special entrance at one of the crossings. I did not wish to be in East Berlin under its auspices (a regular crossing was covered by American protection) so the event did not take place. The visits by the officer continued, as he went shopping at West Berlin's Bloomingdales, KDW at the end of each. The officer in question knew German, and even some German history, was more provincial than the FBI and CIA people I knew. I had been passed on to him by a KGB officer in Washington. He was visibly anxious to please not only his superiors but also his wife, a physician of familial standing—quite important in the class ridden classless society.

I tested the matter by taking the S-Bahn, elevated railway, to the main crossing point at Friedrichstrasse. My name came up on the computer (IBM) and I was asked to wait. An officer appeared, looking like a minor character in Hogan's Heroes, informed me brusquely that my visit was "unerwünscht" ("not wanted") and suggested that I return to West Berlin without delay. I asked him if he could tell me why I could not visit and he drew himself up to his not very impressive full height: they were not obliged to answer such questions. I excused myself fulsomely, declaring that of course I should have realized that his own rank was not high enough for him to have the answer. That brought several colors to his face and he was clearly on the point of shouting. We were, however, in an open area and other visitors were beginning to observe our conversation. He regained control of himself and changed his tone. "Bitte." ("Please.") It did seem a good idea to seize the moment and turn away.

Later that year Sidney Blumenthal visited West Berlin, asked me to accompany him to East Berlin to visit with dissidents. I gave him instructions on visiting the Poppe residence (no phoning in advance) and a verbal message which would reassure them that he was not working for State Security. Sidney did have a good visit with them, but at the Friedrichstrasse station on his way back to West Berlin was asked to step into a room with an officer. He was asked to empty his pockets and presented his White House press card, identifying him as a reporter for *The Washington Post*. The interrogator had no less presence of mind, instantly opened the door, declared that there had been a regrettable error, and wished Sidney a safe journey back to West Berlin. Sidney produced a very full account of his adventure for the Style section of the *Washington Post* some days later. He recounted our dinner that evening in a West Berlin's restaurant much favored by the cognoscenti, Exile, in the mixed artistic, student, working-class and Turkish quarter, Kreuzberg. He quoted Antonia who, joining us after a university seminar, declared it a "post-structuralist" institution. Four years later, on the occasion of the first and last free elections in the German Democratic Republic, I had dinner there with Senator Paul Sarbanes and his wife. He had come as an election observer. He asked me where the Berlin Turks lived and I said that they were all around us. There was a café down the street full of older and younger Turks, and I was sure that they would be interested to meet the head of the Greek lobby in the US Congress. Paul decided to postpone the pleasure.

I returned to Washington, protested his government's lack of hospitality to the GDR Ambassador—who stolidly and repeatedly termed the matter "a technical difficulty" which would be rectified in very short order. Rectification did follow, a couple of weeks after the Wall opened. I visited Potsdam in the GDR on trip to Berlin a month after the change. Potsdam was not available for day trips as was East Berlin and some visibly uncertain GDR border officers still presided at the checkpoint between Berlin and its famed suburb. My passport now had a GDR visa in it, but it was clear from the officer's initial confusion that in the regime computer, I was still an unwanted visitor. I am unable to say whether he was being discreet or valorous but he did let me through.

Actually, the regime had done me a favor by barring me. In 1987, after my return from West Berlin, the Ambassador invited me to a reception at his residence for a group of visiting scholars. The residence was quite spacious, it was a warm day in suburban Chevy Chase, and conversation was lively. Still, the Ambassador had a Prussian sense of duty and asked the guests to assemble for an orderly discussion. He called upon a State Department official to speak on the situation in central Europe and then, to my surprise, asked me to comment. I began by asking the Ambassador, an international lawyer, if in his residence we were legally on the territory of the GDR. He replied affirmatively and I said that in that case, I wished to express my pleasure at being able to visit at least one part of his country, since I was barred from the rest. The US government officials present later told me that they were prepared for a time to forgive my other transgressions.

A major one was my very insistent support of the West German Social Democrats in a project which entailed discussions between their party and the ruling party in the GDR (the Socialist Unity Party, originally a forced fusion of the communists with the Social Democrats). These discussions eventually resulted in a joint declaration endorsing a culture of "political conflict"—thereafter cited by the GDR churches and any and all dissenting groups as legitimation. The Central Committee of the party was, reportedly, furious at the theoreticians who had formulated the document with the West Germans. I knew the GDR representatives and was struck by their rather mixed motives. They may have thought the matter harmless, since few in the GDR at that point were inclined to believe anything the regime said. One more or less overtly and two others covertly—as I gathered in talks after the collapse of the regime—hoped for an opening for themselves. They (Erich Hahn, Otto Reinhold, Ralf Reissig) were in charge of the Institute of Social

Sciences of the GDR Academy of Sciences under the direct control of the Central Committee.

The last meeting of the joint project was in the West German countryside near Bonn in December of 1988. Each delegation invited foreign friends. The West German Social Democrats, under Erhard Eppler, invited outspoken Netherlands colleagues who raised the question of civic and human rights in the DDR. That evoked from Erich Hahn a resigned confession: there, he said, we have to admit that we have ground to recover. The French socialists were also there but their representative was at pains to criticize the entire proceeding. An Italian socialist arrived late, read a paper with little relation to the central themes, distributed very large visiting cards, promised that we would all be invited to a follow up conference at Taormina or some such enchanting site—and disappeared, not to be heard from again. The GDR invited a Bulgarian group, whose members asked me to help them get to the US, and Czechs who spent a great deal of time denouncing their internal opposition in the most sordid way. The USSR sent Yuri Krasin, close to Gorbachev and director of their party's Institute of Social Sciences. I was there, representing no one but myself. Krasin sided with the West German participants on every issue. The GDR group exuded resignation. They had come to the end of the road, knew it, but could not quite say so. Their remarks in formal sessions had a tired and ritualized quality and in private, they shrugged their shoulders, spoke elliptically of unspecified things to come, and seemed very glad to be out of East Berlin.

It was winter and I took a brisk walk one day with Krasin. I told him that I was glad to have had the opportunity to meet him and he reminded me that we had met briefly once before. I had come to his institute in Moscow in 1973, long before he was Director and given a talk on "western Marxism." "What did you think?" I asked. His reply was unhesitating: "I thought what we all thought: he can talk, he lives in Massachusetts."

Some years later, I obtained the file kept on myself by the GDR Ministry of State Security. Some of it was entertaining, like a serious exchange among several bureaus of the Ministry on the question, did I have one daughter with two passports or two. One element was flattering: a fifty page analysis of my writing by an anonymous

Moscow 1973. I joined Doris Kearns Goodwin and others in this meeting with Soviet hosts.

GDR scholar with intellectual access to the western European and American world. He took a long time to reach the conclusion that my response to the Soviet Revolution (curiously, in the eighties he still wrote of it as revolutionary) was negative. He noted, correctly, that I seemed as disappointed with the results of the "bourgeois" revolutions of 1641, 1776, 1789. The author was clearly a GDR social scientist who had met me or heard me talk. If he were one of those I had hosted or helped on visits to the United Kingdom or United States, that was well disguised. Once, on a flight to Europe, I talked with a GDR scholar who had been in the US to work on the former socialist journal, *The Masses*, become *The New Masses* under the Communist Party. He was quite aware of the complex history of the US left, and it might have been he.

My writings apart, the Ministry had a network of informers in West Berlin and West Germany who provided a rather exact account of my connections there. The depiction of my location in the US was no less exact, the author quite able to distinguish between *Commentary* and *The Nation*. The file contained several exchanges of letters between the Ministry and the GDR Foreign Ministry. The latter relayed the urgent and repeated request of the GDR Embassy in Washington that the ban on my entry be lifted. I was known, it argued, as an American dissident, I was loudly outspoken about being barred, and they wished to terminate their embarrassment. The responses, one from the Deputy Minister, were adamant: I was conspiring with very dangerous enemies of the state—my friends from what was then the rundown neighborhood of Prenzlauer Berg.

The Pastor and congregation of the nearby Zionskirche under the legend of environmental discussion) provided them with what was for the GDDR a public forum—that is, an occasional closely watched gathering. My friends sought an open and democratic GDR, rejected joining the Federal Republic, and intended the new German state to join West Germany in a nuclear free and ultimately disarmed and neutral zone of central Europe. They were in touch with groups of similar views elsewhere in the Soviet bloc and had some conversational partners in Leningrad and Moscow. Their most consistent and helpful foreign supporters were, however, in the West German peace movement and the West German Green party as well as in the West German Protestant Church. The West German Social Democrats officially kept a distance, but did tell their interlocutors in the GDR that by intermittently arresting members of the group, they had certainly raised its profile in the west and made more difficulty the Social Democrats' project of normalization of relations between the states. The dissident artist Bärbel Bohley exasperated her GDR prosecutors, after she was arrested for demonstrating against the regime, by declaring the proceedings incompatible with the Helsinki agreements signed by the government—and described herself as a dutiful citizen seeking to help the government meet its international obligations. When she was sent out of the GDR in 1988, she went to Bonn to ask government and opposition to arrange for her repatriation.

Other members of the group included Gerd Poppe, who afterwards served in the Parliament as a Green member and was Human Rights Director at the Foreign Ministry of the unified nation, and Katja Havemann, the widow of a dissident scientist the regime was 'unable to jail, since he had been in Nazi concentration camps. There was in fact a certain amount of locally organized dissidence, often using the Protestant Church as a protecting instance. The dissidents, however, could not establish regular contacts with groups other than their own: State Security was as omnipresent as its depiction in the film, *The Lives of Others*. Those who were tried and sentenced to harsh treatment in the regime's prisons were frequently released and expelled to West Germany. The West German government ransomed as many of them as it could. One former prisoner, the novelist Erich Loest, in a work of fiction and film script *Nikolaikirche* wrote about the final breakdown of the regime as in part the work of a faction in the ruling party inspired and indeed steered by the Soviet party.

My visits in the GDR before I was barred gave me the impression of a political collage. I had glimpses of critical views beneath conformist surfaces. I could usually tell which academic, church person, official, party leader, writer, had doubts and reservations. Some, like the novelists Monika Maron and Christa Wulff were quasi-official if restrained regime critics. The singer Wolf Biermann pushed his role as the GDR's Bob Dylan to the limits—and beyond, since he was finally told not to return from a trip to the west. In the work of the research institutes, and occasional publications by individuals, there was a substantial amount of implicit criticism. The explicit discussion of alternative social projects (often presented as obedient responses to party ideological directives) was pursued in protected spaces. When the regime took as a slogan "the educated nation," the way was open for any number of formulations of new dimensions of citizenship freer of tutelage. Some had much more courage than others. In 1977 Rudolf Bahro published his book *The Alternative*, calling for the total transformation of the GDR, in the west, was interviewed by *Der Spiegel*—and promptly arrested, tried and jailed and then expelled to the west. His fate impelled others not to cease thinking, but to find modes of communication less likely to draw the attention of the thought police. Bahro himself reappeared in the GDR in December of 1989 to address the reformed Communist Party which had renamed itself, Party of Democratic Socialism. The rapidity with which he was invited suggested that his prosecution had provided him with a waiting public in the GDR, not least in the ruling party itself.

The opening of the Wall was indeed dramatic, but the decisive change had come on 18 October, when the ruling party in desperation and decomposition ousted Erich Honecker as its General Secretary. That was in response to insistent demonstrations, but was followed by more of these—including one on 4 November in which the inner party opposition (including the legendary spymaster, the retired General Markus Wolf side by side with the novelist Christa Wulff) demanded a very different GDR. An entire series of changes followed.

The situation was temporarily stabilized later in November when the Communist Mayor of Dresden, Hans Modrow, became Prime Minister of an all-party government including representatives of citizens' groups. The one and only elected government of the GDR, led by a Berlin Huguenot, Lothar de Maizière, whose cousins included a former commander of the West German Army and his son, the present Minister of the Interior, took office in March of 1990 and then dissolved itself as the union with West Germany was completed in October. Much occurred in the year between Honecker's ouster and the end of the state. There were, initially, attacks by the citizens on the offices of the internal security forces, stopped by newly emergent oppositional groups which successfully called for order. The calls were heeded not least because prosecutions of some of the old regime's leading figures had begun. (West Berlin Mayor Momper told me a month after the opening of the Wall that he feared nothing so much as a flight to West Berlin by Honecker.)

What was clear was that the great majority of the GDR population wished to live not in a separate if free socialist German state, but in West Germany's welfare capitalism. In the March 1990 GDR election, which the Social Democrats expected to win, the Christian Democrats triumphed, reaping a harvest that had been sown by the Social Democrats, with the policies of "Change through Closeness" initiated by Brandt in 1966 as Foreign Minister, These were bitterly opposed by the Christian Democrats—until Kohl, Chancellor from 1982 to 1998, reversed his party's course, even inviting Honecker to visit West Germany in 1987. Kohl's indispensable coalition partner, the Free Democrats, had abandoned their alliance with the Social Democrats in 1982 for two quite openly acknowledged reasons. One was the slowdown in West German economic growth, a declining share of national income for the majority of households. The sponsors of the Free Democrats in large and small German business considered that limits on redistribution were necessary and that the Social Democrats would not impose these. The second factor was perpetual Foreign Minister Genscher's entirely correct intuition that he could bring Kohl and the Christian Democrats, however reluctantly, to pursue reconciliation with the Soviet bloc, and economic assistance to the GDR. Genscher was Foreign Minister with the Social Democrats from 1974 until 1982 and then with the Christian Democrats until 1992. A former citizen of the GDR himself, he feared nothing so much as destabilization in the GDR and the ensuing possibility of nuclear conflict by the occupying powers on German soil.

In 1990, Georgetown University awarded Genscher an honorary degree. Genscher and Kohl had indeed ignored the German peace movement and agreed to the stationing of medium range nuclear missiles in West Germany. However, they refused some years later newer missiles to "modernize" the NATO arsenal. Genscher declared, "Let us modernize our ideas and not our weapons" and, especially after Gorbachev took power in the USSR pursued active co-existence. The Georgetown honorary degree citation quoted the Genscher phrase, which was not to the liking of some of his interlocutors in the US. The German press declared the degree and the citation evidence for a reconciliation of the US establishment with Genscher. No doubt—but I wrote it.

What brought us to the opening of the Wall, the unification of Germany, and the incorporation of the legacy of the GDR in the new German state? The most obvious answer is that the Soviet Union could not hold on to its conquests indefinitely. Its surrogates in the Soviet bloc gave way one by one to the constraints of their nations' own histories and geopolitical circumstances. The Gorbachev reforms in the Soviet Union completed a process begun with Khrushchev's 1956 speech repudiating Stalin. The academics, journalists, officials, party leaders, writers who surfaced in the Soviet Union as Gorbachev's supporters had their own networks of likeminded critics of Stalinism in the GDR. Five days before the Wall fell, reformist critics of the GDR ruling party and regime from within its own privileged elites spoke at a meeting in East Berlin to demand fundamental changes in their state. When Gorbachev visited the GDR to participate in the ceremonies marking the fortieth anniversary of the state early in October of 1989, he issued a public admonition: history punished those who came too late. Berlin crowds demonstrated against the regime to shouts of "Gorby" and a fortnight later, Honecker was forced to resign and the open dissolution of party power began. The Soviet Union had already told the GDR leadership that it would not commit the Soviet garrison to intervening against GDR citizens protesting against their government. The inner party resistance did not form spontaneously overnight; it was long in the making.

The increasingly dense contacts of the GDR with western Germany had considerable effects. Western relatives visited their relations in the GDR, and senior GDR citizens could travel to West Germany. The Protestant Churches in the nation's two halves had very close ties. I recall a discussion of the control of nuclear weapons at a study center of the West German church near Hannover, in June of 1983. The American Ambassador Arthur Burns was there, so were the commanding general of the German army, von Ondarza, and the Soviet arms control negotiator Kvitsinsky as well as academics, journalists, parliamentarians and citizens from West Germany and the US including a youngish professor of Soviet politics, Condoleezza Rice. The presiding pastor asked each of the participants to identify themselves. Finally, a rather dignified gentleman stood up and declared that he was Friedrich Schoenherr, Church Superintendent in Berlin, "capital of the GDR." The West Germans applauded quite strongly. I was seated behind the general, who I knew from his time as military attaché in Washington. "Das fehlte uns noch," he said to his adjutant. ("That is all we need.") Ambassador Burns's pained expression suggested that he knew that the applause was also a message to himself.

Censorship and strict inspections at the borders did not alter the access by the educated elites of the GDR to West German books, journals and magazines, newspapers. Somehow, they got across. Visiting the homes of friends in the DDR, or official institutes, I was struck by how up to date they were on West German discussions. Those who did not have printed matter had television: West German television had no more devoted public than in the DDR. There were difficulties in reception in Dresden, on account of the topography. The rest of the GDR began to refer to the region as "the Valley of Those Who Are Not With It" and the regime installed towers to enable the Dresdeners to look west.

The policies of recognition and closeness that eventually became consensual in the west had a very large impact, The DDR regime had constantly to look over its shoulder lest internal repression bring open condemnation by the government and opinion in the west. Funding to cover the deficits of the DDR economy came from the west. One very large source was the state banking system in Bavaria, where the Minister President, strongman Franz Josef Strauss, took time off occasionally from his strident anti-communism to fly in his own plane to the DDR and talk with its leaders. Later there were hints of covert dealing between the Bavarians and a singular GDR figure, the official in charge of procuring foreign currency, one Schalck-Golodkowski. There were rumors of arms sales in the Third World, of speculation. The official was sought by GDR prosecutors in the months that followed the fall of the Wall, fled to an estate behind its own walls in Bavaria, and was never tried. Most of all, however, West Germany influenced the GDR by its authentic practice of democracy. On the frequent occasions on which demonstrations in West Berlin flared up, its officials and city councilmen told me, there invariably followed remonstrances from their East Berlin colleagues. I am reminded of a cartoon showing two GDR border guards, armed to the teeth, in a watch tower atop the Wall. One, with binoculars, addresses the other. "Get a load of that bearded demonstrator over there. Is he on their side—and a courageous friend of peace? Or is he on ours—and a dangerous enemy of the state?"

The events of 1989 in the GDR owe, equally, to the larger setting. A friend at a Moscow Institute who spoke no German occasionally visited the GDR where the schools provided obligatory years of instruction in Russian. Ordinary citizens, asked for directions, responded in English or German. Gorbachev's advent, he recalled, was marked by their recalling their language lessons at school. The Soviet leader's policies, obviously, had a cumulative effect—but the release of Sakharov from internal exile and his return to Moscow in 1986 was particularly striking to the cultural and scientific elite in the GDR.

Three events in June of 1989 shook the regime. The massacre of student protesters in Tiananmen Square by the Chinese army was known instantly. When party leader Egon Krenz visited Peking shortly thereafter, he publicly congratulated the Chinese regime on its defense of "socialism." Krenz briefly "succeeded Honecker as head of the Party and Prime Minister but the revulsion induced by his performance in Peking made him a detested figure who was chased from office in two months with what was left of the regime. Repression in China coincided with the openings of its borders to Austria by Hungary, and the Hungarian government's refusal to restrain GDR citizens from using the new crossings. The GDR government openly rebuked the Hungarians, and barred its citizens from travelling to the country. Meanwhile, the communist and nationalist military dictatorship in Poland agreed to hold elections in which the Communist Party did not win a single Parliamentary seat. Poland became a people's democracy in a literal sense, The Polish elections were all the more sharply etched in GDR public consciousness, since their own municipal elections earlier in the year were thought to have been fraudulent.

In September, the Neues Forum group issued its call to national dialogue—immediately refused by the regime which initially declared the group subversive and illegal. Thousands adhered to the appeal. In Leipzig, under the sponsorship of the Protestant Church, Monday demonstrations began. They were followed and imitated throughout the nation. One of the interesting questions of the history of the GDR is how and why the local authorities did not use force to stop the demonstrations, which grew to massive size. They were accompanied by another blunder by a regime which had lost all sense of reality. Early in September GDR visitors to Prague occupied the grounds of the West German embassy and insisted on being given exit visas and transportation to West Germany. The Czechoslovak government, alarmed at the response of its citizens (they brought food and drink to the occupiers) told the GDR that it wanted the situation ended. The West Germans, with some help from the USSR, persuaded the GDR government to allow the occupiers to leave for the west. With an unfailing instinct for making matters worse, the GDR regime insisted that its citizens travel through the GDR—occasioning rioting at rail stations as thousands sought to board the trains or to express solidarity with those who were leaving.

Many in West Germany, in western Europe, in the United States (and as best they could, in the states of the Soviet bloc) helped the citizens of the GDR in their struggle with their regime. There was no one clear line of resistance and the modes of dissent were extremely varied. My friends in Neues Forum had a moment of great influence, but they had made a large contribution to what they did not seek, the unification of the two German states. At least, they finally achieved the political freedom denied them previously—and used it to continue under unforeseen circumstances their own projects. I am glad to have helped somewhat by conveying my sense of the world beyond their borders. I did the same for the dissidents' much more cautious fellow citizens in the institutions of the regime. Upon reflection, the Ministry of State Security was right. They, the dissidents, were dangerous enemies of their state and in connecting them to a larger world, I became one too. I am reminded of the scene in *The Lives of Others* in which, the regime gone, its literary antagonist looks up his file. The attendant, wheeling in a cartload of documents, voiced his response: "Compliments." I'll permit myself to a modest note of self-congratulation.

An event in June of 1983 reproduced much of the tension of the relationship between the two German states—and yet anticipated the end of the division. The study center of the Protestant Church in Lower Saxony, the Evangelische Akademie at Loccum not far from Hannover, arranged a conference on the situation after two major developments. Helmut Kohl replaced Helmut Schmidt as Bundeskanzler in the fall of 1982 and he and his party won a convincing electoral victory in the early spring elections. The two superpowers had installed their dreadful intermediate range weapons, but had begun negotiations to avoid some of the dangers inherent in the situation.

Each of the West German churches had these academies, located in most of the Federal states. These were sites where cultural, economic and political figures discussed the issues of the day with Church members, ordained and lay. One of my first experiences of the life of the Academies lay far back in Berlin before the Wall went up. The director of the academy of the Protestant Church in the east was a remarkable figure named Bassarak, extremely disliked by the then Bishop of a still united Berlin Church, Bishop Dibelius. Dibelius (a fellow traveler of the Nazis) was a strenuous antagonist of the Communist state, and Bassarack, a realist if ever there was one, took a much more nuanced position. His opposite number in West Berlin was Wolf-Dieter Marsch, a theologian who had written a book on Lincoln which taught me a good deal—and was the friend who called my attention to a newly published novel, which he thought was rather readable, *The Tin Drum*.

By 1983 those initial encounters seemed epochs past. I was accompanied to the Loccum meeting by my late daughter. Anna, a very committed activist for détente and social justice in West Berlin and my friend from Virginia, Sally Guthrie, who as she said was delighted to experience something other than the legacy of our Civil War. There were German and US lay persons present, but also the Soviet diplomat Kvitinsky and the US Ambassador Arthur Burns, a group of West German officers led by General von Ondarza, who commanded the West German army, and a full spectrum of West German academics, journalists, politicians. One of the American academics present was a young professor from Stanford, Condoleezza Rice. I gathered from talking with her that she knew a good deal about the USSR, pronouncedly less about Germany.

There was one high point of the meeting. The Director of the Academy asked each participant to rise and identify himself or herself. It took some time but was interesting. It was especially interesting when a distinguished looking gentleman rose to declare that he was Friedrich Schoenherr, Superintendent of the Church in Berlin, DDR. Most of the West Germans broke into quite prolonged applause (the Superintendent was the only person from the DDR present.) I was seated behind the General, who turned to his adjutant and said, *Das fehlte uns noch* ("That is all that we need"). Ambassador Burns looked vexed: he had gotten the message. Condi Rice later asked me what I thought that was all about and I told her that it was a message to both the Americans and the Soviet diplomat: there was one Germany and sooner rather than later it would reassert itself, whatever the present system of alliances and entanglements.

In 1985 I wrote an opinion article for *The New York Times* declaring that it was time for the superpowers to leave Germany and for the Germans to take their history in their own hands. I was promptly invited to Berlin by the Evangelische Akademie West and did come and speak at several places in the city. I was asked to talk at official institutes in East Berlin, but there was no question of my addressing a general public. No matter, I had been interviewed by West Berlin television and was quite sure that no small number of DDR citizens had accessed the telecast. I recall a white Volkswagen parked in front of the Hotel Savoy, where I stayed, which then turned up (I had noted the West Berlin license plate) wherever I spoke or met friends for dinner. To this day I do not know whether it belonged to the West German, US or East German or Soviet intelligence services. I was flattered to be followed — and it took only four more years for anticipation to become reality.

Finally, one small episode gave any number of people in both German states a measure of pleasure. A couple of years before the end of the DDR, the US government thought it was time to try to influence it. The American Institute of Contemporary German Studies was allowed, or encouraged, to invite the senior ideologue of the ruling party to Washington. His name was Hermann Axen and he had been a prisoner in Buchenwald and claimed to have participated in a prisoners' revolt shortly before the US Army arrived in Weimar and liberated the camp, on the city's outskirts. Axen's public talk at the Institute was filmed by East German television. Questions were taken and I asked when party and state in the DDR would recall the emancipatory legacy of Marxism and concentrate on that instead of pursuing the construction of a rigid Prussian state. Axen did not appreciate the question but somehow, it was heard in the DDR. Some who recalled it sometime later told me that I had read their minds.

16

A Routine-ization of History

TIME DOES ITS WORK. The nearer I draw to the present, the less full, less lively, less compelling my own memories become, and the effort to recount them becomes heavier. I suffer from disappointment in the telling. As a psychoanalytic friend put it with admirable bluntness: "You did not change the world." I came to Washington to leave what I thought of as a form of imprisonment, confinement to the tasks of a professor in a liberal arts college. Amherst was at the time certainly an urbane institution, but it was not in an urban setting. One of my most admired colleagues, Ben DeMott, moved miles away to the real country (Worthington) and devoted himself to writing. Another, George Kateb, bided his time and then went to Princeton. Others of great talent remained and were exceedingly productive. I need not have left Amherst to accomplish a good deal, but clearly thought I did. What, specifically, had I in mind?

I had two beliefs. One was that the proximity to national politics would add a dimension of reality to my socio-political thinking. The other was that I would find a different public among serious and sympathetic political actors and so gain influence. The first proposition was roughly true, but a couple of years in Washington might well have sufficed. As for the second, in The Nation and elsewhere I already had a public in Washington. Its more critical members did respond to new and serious, or new or serious, ideas—but they did not first inspect their postmarks. Any number of major American thinkers managed quite well without Washington experience, or with little of it.

I sought contact, excitement, and reassurance. As with my restless probing of the limits of dissent as an Amherst teacher, I was driven and surely insufficiently reflective on the optimal uses of energy and time. As it turned out, there was no coherent political movement I could join, no stairway to climb to historic heights. The escalator, like the one at the Q Street entrance of the Metro at Dupont Circle, often needed repair—and in any case brought one to the same place with boring regularity.

In Goethe's *Faust*, Mephistopheles mocks academic life: "Where ideas are absent, words replace them" is a rough but accurate translation. Where history presents difficult problems, and concepts are worn, it is unwise to assign our difficulties to personal failings. Indeed, these may be seen as consequences of times out of joint. When I arrived in Washington in 1979, a good many radical pieties required revision. Was it only ten years ago that I had published, in English, French, German, Italian, Spanish, Portuguese, *The Crisis of Industrial Society*, noting with approval Malraux's remark that the alliance of workers and students, not seen before, promised much? He was wrong: it had been experienced before, and it did not as it intended transform society.

I was indeed at one of the centers of world power, had daily contacts with those who were managing it, and began to experience a problem which, a third of a century later, remains one, "Where, and how, to fit in?" Many of my colleagues at the Georgetown University Law faculty were using their legal knowledge in different parts of government, or working for public interest groups, or educating the next generation in the classroom and challenging the inertia of the system by publishing new perspectives in the law reviews. *The Washington Post* (its Watergate pathos intact still) and *The New York Times*, television and radio, wanted short, current and simple narratives. The denser intellectual world of the serious journals did not, by and large, interest Washington. Again, there is a necessary qualification: it was interested in serious ideas, if presented in forms directly connected to current events. As the Carter years neared their end, our politics were living off inherited intellectual capital. There was not much local interest, even from those who sympathized, with rebellious intellectual heirs. They were given the attention accorded to the four questions at Orthodox Seders—a very decided brush off.

Less than a decade had passed since the movements of the sixties and early seventies claimed attention but the activist and intellectual veterans of those days had to struggle to recall to their publics what had bothered them. There is a narrative which declares that on the contrary, new ideas and attitudes had become the stuff of everyday encounters. A new generation of women in politics, the arrival in Washington of many educated Afro-Americans and Latinos in public interest groups, journalism, legislative and governmental positions, were often cited as evidence for the institutionalization of protest—or, rather, its transformation into legitimated social practice. That was certainly true where some Democrats had influence, in many cultural institutions, in some segments of organized religion. In large parts of society (and in the public sphere, that is in the offices of Congress and state and municipal governments, in much of the media) the decade past was depicted, variously, as a dangerous or preposterous period in which arrogant excess and systematic illusions nearly carried a generation away. Worse was avoided, or so it was said, by the sound common sense of ordinary citizens who had every reason to be distrustful of their own children and, above all, of many of their teachers—as well as of artists, writers, film makers, journalists who despite their defiance of what had been convention were quite audible and visible.

The success of the neo-conservatives is now matter for the historians. They did not create a political climate, they exploited existing opportunity. A good many citizens were hostile to the ideas of emancipation and solidarity of the sixties movements. Many regarded opposition to the Vietnam War as unpatriotic and were convinced that the Soviet Union threatened the US. They had no realistic view of the economy and believed that much of government (the police were generally thought of favorably) was intrinsically inefficient, wasteful and often intrusive if not authoritarian. The impoverished suffered from their own defects. Unashamed racism and ethnic and social self-satisfaction were difficult to distinguish. These last two were woven into a triumphalist narrative in which the phrase, "the greatest nation on earth" was actually uttered without embarrassment.

There were serious figures in the background, like Freedman and Hayek (rather more favorable to the welfare state than many of his readers noticed.) The neo-conservatives were not original thinkers but publicists. They occupied the crowded terrain of American narcissism—just when the energies that might have impelled a critical re-evaluation of the New Deal legacy, of progressivism in general, were diminished among their protagonists. I wrote about this, ambivalently, in my 1988 book, *The Radical Renewal*. It was a fair description of American intellectual life from 1945 onward, but I did underestimate the contradictions and silences of the radical position I defended. Portraying American citizens as complacently ignorant, morally inert, and organized into smaller familial, neighborhood, class and ethnic circles had some claims to accuracy. Why, however, demand of these persons that they join a near heroic project of national self-transformation? A segment of the American left has frequently suffered from a shallow populism, attributing innate virtue to citizens of null reflectiveness and limitless impulsiveness. (I am aware of Noam Chomsky's argument about their obdurate independence in matters of professional sport.) The neo-conservatives, uninhibited in their cynicism, had their own version of the idea of deeply rooted national virtues—very much like those expressed in the television program, "All In The Family."

What the Neo-Conservatives did not dwell upon was the acceleration in the decline of American living standards, the increasingly visible effects of low wage competition in Asia and Latin America. This was surprising not least in the light of their foreign policy alliance with the AFL-CIO. The alliance concentrated on one dimensional depictions of the Soviet Union, ignored all the national and political differences in the Soviet bloc, and required unquestioning support of permanent confrontation with Stalin's heirs. It is difficult to say, looking back, what the new anti-Communism abjured the most. There were plenty of thinkers, in the universities and government, who held that co-existence would enable the party of reform to develop in the post-Stalinist regimes. The neo-conservatives rejected the notion of post-Stalinism, argued for the unchanging nature of the Soviet bloc's institutions of repression and advanced a remarkably vague prediction of ultimate collapse under maximal western pressure. The refusal of large and influential groups in the citizenries and political elites of the NATO nations to accept these beliefs occasioned constant denunciations of their alleged moral deficiencies. West Germany, in particular drew a great deal of opprobrium. Much of public opinion there had been critical of the Vietnam War and especially reluctant to envisage nuclear Armageddon on German soil. Brandt in particular was derided as naïve and his successor Schmidt fared only marginally better, despite his much more positive attitude to Germany's role in the western military configuration. They allowed themselves to be flattered by the Christian Democrats under Kohl, who continued the policies of Brandt and Schmidt without saying so too loudly. A large amount of ignorance of German history and society was the indispensable precondition of these attitudes: in these respects, the Neo-Conservatives were peerless.

They fought an ideological war regarding foreign policy, on two fronts. I have already described their enmity to Kissinger. He was a particularly disturbing figure since he could hardly be depicted as a moralizing sentimentalist. They could not acknowledge, publicly and possibly privately, their own cynicism. It was a considerable feat to depict the US as universal guardian of democracy and human rights when our nation had either installed or otherwise supported authoritarian and repressive regimes in Brazil, Chile, Indonesia, Iran, Pakistan, Portugal, South Africa, South Korea, Spain, Turkey and any number of other nations. Kissinger's openness, the aura of cosmopolitan knowingness he wore, discomfited them. Very possibly, it reminded them of the extreme effort they had had to make to escape (or obscure) their own provincialism. There was a paradox about this: Kissinger himself asked about what would have become of his life had Germany not succumbed to Nazism, was unhesitating. He would have become an accountant in the small German city of Fürth. Kissinger's high standing with many of the senior figures of the German elite paralleled his conquest of the American elite.

There, too, the neo-conservatives were discountenanced. Kissinger was originally a protégé of Nelson Rockefeller, who recommended him to Nixon. The neo-conservatives in their first three decades, the sixties, seventies, eighties, prided themselves on their success as social climbers in a supposedly open society. Their self-depiction did not emphasize the services they rendered to established elites who used their scurrying. (The CIA's cultural operations embodied this relationship earlier. The Ivy graduates running the Agency were quite astute in exploiting the aptitude and eagerness of the New York Jewish intellectuals to be of service. It is quite true that the neo-conservatives were by no means entirely Jewish. Daniel Patrick Moynihan was a charter member who gradually, especially on American economic and social policy, took his distance. Jeane Kirkpatrick was as a Midwestern Methodist another charter member of the neo-conservative group not pre-selected for success.

Neo-Conservatism had a decided if not entirely dominant Jewish pathos. It was largely the work of descendants of the traditions of the Jewish labor movement in central and eastern Europe, which had a very pronounced and justified revulsion for Stalinism. The Jewish labor movement's emigrants to the US and their offspring found cultural and political homes in the New Deal and in the American labor movement. When their offspring praised the US for its openness, they knew whereof they spoke. Post World War Two the US was a hitherto unimaginable promised land for them, with large opportunities in the realms of culture, business and finance, education, government and the professions. Support for Israel, meanwhile, was at first unproblematic: for decades, the Jewish state belonged to the Zionist component of the Jewish labor movement.

The Neo-Conservatives found an ecumenical cause in the campaign to obtain for Soviet Jewry the right to emigrate. Of course, the Soviet leadership could not easily accede to the demand, Anti-Semitic or not, the Russian masters of the Soviet state did not wish to lose an educated segment of its labor force. Allowing Jews to emigrate while denying the privilege to others would certainly increase domestic tensions. The Arab client states of the Soviet Union would have grounds for loud complaint: plenty of the emigrants would inevitably end in Israel, strengthening its economic and military capacities. That is what happened. What happened as well, however, was a rapprochement of Israel and Russia after the end of the Soviet Union as the successor Russian state confronted its own Islamist enemies.

The Neo-Conservatives came to their self-assigned function as defenders of western civilization against Islam rather late—after having concentrated their energies on the specter of Communism as embodied in the Soviet bloc. Since that bloc, in the eighties, was hardly compelling in its ideological appeal to the western nations, a rather complicated dramaturgy was invented. Western weakness did not reside in the belief that there were major positive elements in the Communist nations. It was to be found, rather, in a certain complacency about Communism's historical course. Earlier, the critical concept was "Finlandization." The western nations would purchase security by weakening their NATO commitment, with the ultimate end of abandoning the alliance with the US and openly accepting permanent Soviet domination in central and Eastern Europe. The Federal German Republic, or rather significant segments of its elites and publics, was suspected of planning to become a larger Finland. The argument moved rapidly from geopolitics to cultural and moral criticism. Did the western nations, including the US, where the ideas and sensibilities of the sixties were dominant in large sectors of culture, especially higher education, believe sufficiently in western values to actually defend these?

In the Neo-Conservative depiction of American society, hardworking, religiously engaged, and above all, ordinary citizens were the ethically reliable custodians of the nation—and quite right to be wary of the assorted charlatans and illusionists who had seized much of what passed for high culture. A sub-group, to be sure, concentrated on the vendors of moral laxity, allied themselves with the Christians and Jews opposed to sexual openness and, of course, homosexual rights. The neo-conservatives called for a moral reversal which would have put Sinclair Lewis on its index, Most of those so vehemently defended by the Neo-Conservatives were unaware of the transcendent role assigned to them in the national drama. The conflict did not, of course alter the serial vulgarities and popular prejudices which continued to dominate much of everyday life. It was fought over the command of imagery. One text that contrasted imagery with actuality was written by a figure who prided himself on not allowing himself to be fooled, Daniel Bell in his Cultural Contradictions of Capitalism. He was a personal friend of the Neo-Conservatives and did them the favor of not publishing his book until they had reached their apogee. Actually, Christopher Lasch years earlier anticipated Bell's arguments on the destructive consequences of market embedded individualism—while stripping it of its claim to embody a moral national tradition.

Ideas requiring historical depth and a decent minimum of intellectual rigor were not the neo-conservatives' strongest points. Their imagined nation did not have a working class beset by rapidly increasing deindustrialization, declining incomes, shrunken or missing pensions, and an obvious inability to provide economic and social resources for the future of their children. Meanwhile, cuts in public expenditure for education restricted the opportunity available to their offspring. The lurid picture painted by the neo-conservatives of much of higher education, depicted alternately as a site of formless self-indulgence and a recruiting ground for organized assault on western civilization was certainly not intended to enthuse private and public funders about the uses of their money. In the previous decade at Amherst, the younger alumni and trustees viewed the attacks of elderly gentlemen like John J. McCloy and Eustace Seligman on the supposed radicalism of the faculty as a clinical phenomenon. The neo-conservatives were far more effective, and their success was not entirely due to the volume at which they spoke. Their own mixed but critical beginnings were important: they voiced, however crudely, an authentic disappointment. The neo-conservatives themselves termed it a learning experience.

How deep, how original, how conservative were the neo-conservatives? It is not especially illuminating to suggest that they were careerists. I have not encountered, in the American and West European left, many candidates for sainthood. The biographical and historical literature on modern movements for change in both church and state give evidence for a large set of personal and political ambition. Hill writing on the origins of the English Revolution, Bailyn on the American one, Mornet on the French one, tell us a good deal about the formation of intellectual climates in which new projects rapidly appear feasible. I once had the privilege of discussing the relationship of intellectuals to social movements with a serious student of the matter, György Lukács. The date was 1965 and the place Budapest. He suggested that much of the dogmatism disfiguring modern Marxism, in the Soviet bloc and outside it, was due to limitations on social possibility. The neo-conservatives certainly seized upon the social possibilities of the late twentieth century in the US. They declared the American experiment—a phrase by then not much in use—an achieved revolution. Their ideas were largely to be found in many of the writings assembled in the Partisan Review symposium, our Country and our Culture, in 1952. The US offered, they argued, larger degrees of economic security and personal and political freedom than anywhere else (Western Europe was, apparently, deemed a place for vacations or home to malevolent purveyors of error like Sartre).

Critical progressivism was simply out of date, its advocates obdurately refusing to recognize their own triumphs. The midcentury authors had begun their lives in the years of Depression and New Deal, their neoconservative children knew post—war prosperity. They also knew the War on Poverty and the limits it encountered in the nation's several cultures of failure. A frequent, and especially vulgar comparison, was to contrast the European immigrant with their ethos of familial solidarity, their churches, to the Afro-Americans and their problems of cultural disintegration in the north. Many Jewish families at Seders had to endure the harangues of an obsessed uncle, denouncing the Afro—Americans for their lack of the initiative and persistence shown by Jews. There was indeed a contrast to be drawn—between a people with several thousand years of literacy and urban existence and one wrenched from tribal existence in Africa and brought to the US as slaves forbidden literacy and the development of skills, their families constantly threatened by owners who sold their human chattels at will. For all of their problems, the Slavic, Italian, Irish immigrants enjoyed enormous advantages over the African-Americans.

I knew the rising or risen neo-conservatives. Allen Weinstein had been a colleague at Smith, moved to Washington and actually alerted me to the availability of the house I bought in 1981, attached to his.in Cathedral Heights. The lively Weinstein family had an especially neighborly member, a terrier, and I was sometimes asked to host him over weekends or vacations. The animal missed its family but was quite obviously free of ideological prejudice. He enjoyed the company of Jürgen and Ute Habermas when they visited, despite their sympathies for the German peace movement. The members of the group were more rather than less good company, despite an ineradicable tendency to attempt to save my soul by harangues on the errors and sins of an (absurdly depicted) "left." Coming from the Jewish neo-conservatives, these exercises were strikingly reminiscent of attempts to reclaim errant souls — let us say, converts to Ethical Culture.

The neo-conservatives, however, were not all Jewish. There was Daniel Patrick Moynihan, with whom I very occasionally talked. He remembered my father, Dean at Benjamin Franklin High School and one of the teachers who encouraged him to attend City College. Moynihan had spent a post-war year at the London School of Economics, worked for Governor Averell Harriman, knew American urban and party politics inside out. He was free of the eschatological yearnings which sometimes impelled others to metahistorical visions. Perhaps (he hinted at this himself) his own experience of the New York Irish working class and its troubles gave him a different view of reality. Beaten and mauled for his misinterpreted report on the Afro-American family, he seemed to find it easier than most to go beyond stereotypes — or to keep quiet when everyone else was shouting. He did convince Nixon to introduce the Earned Income Tax Credit, encouraged him to resist the Republicans who wished to use his Presidency for a grand reversal of the New Deal. Moynihan clearly, had learned something from the empiricism of British Labour — if rather distant from the continental European versions of social policy, even the Christian ones.

A differentiated view of reality did not mark Moynihan's approach to foreign policy. Like so many adherents of a triumphalist notion of American Exceptionalism, he saw it as an agency for the realization of universal human values. In that case, we were hardly that exceptional — a problem he was not the only one to overlook. Strident defiance of the Soviet Union and unequivocal support for Israel at the UN, the beginning of the campaign for the emigration of Soviet Jewry, helped him to win r nomination as Democratic candidate for the Senate in New York in 1976. Israel helped with a timely honorary doctorate from the Hebrew University. I wrote a note of protest at this intervention in an American election to the Israel UN Ambassador, Isaac Herzog, who replied with asperity that I had misinterpreted a gesture which was entirely in the competence of the university.

In American politics, conflicts, projects, groups, persons move on and off center stage with very great regularity — but much of the real movement remains unseen. The stage eventually darkens, the very measurement of time changes, and issues as well as figures commanding attention often fade quite quickly. Was Moynihan a child or grandchild of the New Deal? In any event, he began to take a much longer view once he arrived at the Senate and acted as if elder statesman status was what he sought. His model might have been Edward Kennedy, already in the Senate for fourteen years when Moynihan arrived. Actually, Moynihan had in mind an entire set of historic legislators who learned to make their way in the procedural labyrinth that was the Senate. Lifelong projects did not come to fruition at once required immense patience and the willingness to endure recurrent setbacks. Sometimes their progenitors waited for sudden breaks in political continuity, sometimes they counted on the weight of accumulation. Moynihan had studied in London when Labour in the Spartan circumstances of post-war Britain (cold and hungry) moved ahead with measures it had envisaged for a generation, if not two. His New York Senatorial predecessors included Robert Wagner, who used the New Deal to advance the interests of organized labor over decades. Moynihan was interestingly perplexing, since he seemed to have two political personae. In foreign affairs, he spoke in terms of an ecumenical apocalypse, in which all the forces of good had to combat the concentrated powers of evil. Geopolitical realists and democrats envisaging gradual changes in the Soviet bloc alike earned his scorn. In matters of economic and social policy (and their connections to race relations) he was the champion of incrementalism.) In due course (perhaps he had some intimation of how little time the Soviet model would last, some knowledge of its internal changes) his foreign policy fervor diminished. No New York Senator at the time was able to evade the importunities of Israel's supporters, but Moynihan's voice and votes became more routinized. He drew away from the Podhoretz family, closer to its cautious and technocratic adversaries in the foreign policy apparatus. Clearly, like Daniel Bell, he was not a neoconservative but a skeptical and reflective reformer.

I regret that I did not grasp more of this and talk more often with Moynihan in the eighties and nineties. These were decades in which the political culture of Washington was changing. I did not know the city in its previous phases. I knew enough not to believe that it was actually dominated by persons living in Georgetown, or that "comity" ruled as senior legislators took their national responsibilities seriously. I was certainly aware of all kinds of lobbying, even if I recall my surprise at the openness of certain relationships. Les Aspin of Wisconsin, as Chair of the House Armed Services Committee, received friends at the beginning of a term—and firms dealing with the Pentagon served as hosts. I do recall a conversation with William Fulbright in which I evoked my admiration for his long dissent during the Vietnam War, How right he had been. Yes, he said, that is why I am a former Senator. Washington resembled nothing so much as a Tanguy construction, and I kept thinking of it as a Pollock painting. I published continuously in *The Nation* and in Europe, began to construct the tale that eventually became my 1987 book, *The Radical Renewal*. What I realized but did not sufficiently reflect upon was that no single narrative would serve. Events in the world beyond our borders definitely were not controlled by the US. The obsessive triumphalism of the imperial party and the compulsory moralism of those of us who opposed it were each increasingly beyond the point. No doubt, a rather self-selected grouping within the American population opposed the capitalist elite—some of the unions, the Congressional Progressive Caucus, the thematically mixed public interest groups. A majority of citizens asked what government could do for them, affirmed its positive functions or complained of its intrusiveness and inefficiency while ignoring its real working, its distortion and dysfunctions of interest representation.

Dialogue in Washington was becoming a cacophony. I went to one of the last of the old school meeting places, Joseph Pechman's Brookings Friday lunches. The Brookings researchers, then far fewer in number than today, came—and so did a faithful set of academics, journalists, officials, and some active politicians. Joe chose a theme, asked someone to open the discussion—and we enjoyed an hour and a half of serious debate. I sometimes assumed an ambassadorial role for the European left, which I was at pains to depict as much part of European culture as anything else. After an Italian election and words from myself on the Italian Communist Party, I had the gratifying experience of hearing the former NATO Commander in the Mediterranean seconding my view that the Italian Communists were not a revolutionary threat. There were other sites of discussion—for Europe, the Center for Strategic and International Studies, still attached to Georgetown, the German Marshall Fund, the Carnegie Endowment. Rather small sets of regular participants came to know each other. Occasionally, chiefly on matters of foreign policy, discreet figures appeared to describe themselves as from the "Executive Branch." The CIA, clearly, intended that its staffs should not be denied the intellectual benefits of an open Washington culture.

The newer elements in that culture were openly subsidized to produce the right intellectual results—in several senses. First the American Enterprise Institute and then the Heritage Foundation, the Center for Strategic and International Studies after it parted from our university, were advocacy groups as well as centers of research. In matters economic, the AFL-CIO defended itself by sponsoring the Economic Policy Institute. There were occasional visitors from the universities, but staff profiles involved assignments in government and, in the newly formed institute, concentration on the issues of the day. Brookings, with Henry Aaron, Charles Schulze, Arthur Okun and Joe Pechman, began to resemble a Keynesian La Rochelle. The Woodrow Wilson International Center for Scholars, headed by the learned historian of Russia with large intellectual range, James Billington, provided the capital with the presence of original thinkers, many from abroad. I met Bronisław Geremek there in his capacity as historian of the middle ages, before the Solidarność movement made him a political figure. Interestingly, he studied medieval social movements, rebellions and revolts in pre-modern settings. Zeev Sternhell, who commanded knowledge of the intellectual origins of European fascisms, was there as well.

My own introduction to Washington was a summer at the Wilson Center. I had sought an invitation for a year with a project on redefining the public interest which was, to be sure, rather thin. Jim Billington was good enough to compensate me for not receiving a one-year fellowship with a summer's stay. Jim explained in praiseworthy candor that it was easier for him to invite Marxist scholars from the Communist nations than from New England. Whatever I had retained of Marxism was at the time in extreme flux—but treating the Marxist tradition as alive was very rare in the capital. Jim himself had written a splendid book on nineteenth-century revolutionary thought in Europe (*Fire in the Minds of Men*) and saw to it that the Wilson Center habitually took a larger view—or rather provided space for thinkers not consumed by very immediate issues. The nation's elites were taken by total surprise by events after 1989 (some were even surprised by the rapid return of China to importance.) A longer view would have been of use. In the division of intellectual labor that prevailed during the Cold War, even the longer view was one academic specialty among many. The common historical understanding was a singular mixture in which somehow the US was the culmination of evolution (a tale I had encountered at Harvard decades earlier in the form of theories of "modernization"). Theology was kept in the attic, to be called upon when in crises prayers were needed. It was widely agreed that God had blessed the US and to a lesser extent on account of the presence of too many doubters Europe, especially Western Europe. Just how and why He had done so was, again, a matter for the theologians to debate in some secluded space. The large number of our fellow citizens who were literal readers of the Bible, the interest in Orthodoxy of many Jews ostensibly integrated in a secular world, the diverse movements in Catholicism that had given us first John XXIII and then John Paul were thought interesting and even occasionally important, but caused little or no perplexity. At Amherst, we were aware that Cambridge, New York, Paris, maybe Los Angeles, were the centers of cultural production to which we had no choice but to look. I am now struck by the casualness with which Washington took everything except the day's newspapers.

Max Weber declared that privileged strata celebrate what they are, negatively privileged groups what they will become. In the US of the eighties, that observation was stood on its head. The many and mixed voices of a triumphant capitalism looked forward to the expansion of their advantages and incomes and property. Ordinary people, threatened by unemployment, a decline in public services, a generalized uncertainty clung to the private and public goods still in their possession. Some of this was white and masculine self-congratulation, some was in the form of public assistance and subsidy. The conservatives and their eloquent leader, Ronald Reagan, continuously referred to widened realms of individual and familial choice. The heirs of the New Deal warned of imminent loss, acted to defend institutions and programs marked for reduction and even termination. The unions and the progressive politicians in Congress, the state houses and the cities could rightly claim that they spoke for the large American majority benefiting from the legacies of New Deal and Great Society (and even Nixon's creeping and unavowed use of the New Deal.) In the eighties, the cultural innovations and shocks of the seventies were absorbed. No new cultural language emerged, the conflicts of the sixties and seventies were seemingly bound to continue indefinitely. Reagan and his adherents constantly evoked new horizons, which kept receding from view, which made it easy for their opponents to paint darkening landscapes.

I saw something of the union milieu—the United Auto Workers and the Machinists. Don Stillman and Steve Schlossberg were my friends at the UAW. I knew Leonard Woodcock slightly but he left for his Ambassadorial post in Peking. I enjoyed talking with his successor, Douglas Fraser, who had a Scots heritage and followed events in the UK. Not only on account of the very mixed ethnic and racial situation in the working class in the UAW's home territory, the Midwest, the group was singularly internationalist in outlook. German law required large firms to put representatives of the work force on their boards of directors. Ford and GM defeated, at the end of the Second World War, Walter Reuther's project of introducing a similar practice in the auto industry. The UAW sister union in Germany, Industriegewerkschaft Metall, invited the UAW to name one of the labor directors at German Ford and German GM. That apart, the UAW had a very comprehensive health insurance plan—and campaigned continuously for a national health insurance system. It was also in the front line on the entire complex of issues involving poverty and race. The union leadership won legitimation by what it did in the workplace and its successes in obtaining benefits and wages. It did a considerable amount of educational work, some of it in courses at night, some of it in more diffuse ways. It was a partner of the state's public universities in developing institutes in economic and social policy and industrial relations.

Much of the more populated southern part of the state was as a consequence reliably Democratic in its vote—but not always. In 1968 the racist governor of Alabama, George Wallace, made considerable inroads on the votes of union households in his campaign for the Presidency. There was a certain amount of racial tension in the factories, mirroring that in some urban and suburban neighborhoods. There was certainly an African-American proletariat in the Detroit area and southern Michigan, but that could hardly designate the skilled and well paid Afro-American auto workers, and their usually quite stable families. The UAW in long years of negotiation with the manufacturers and their sub-contractors had constructed a separate but quite identifiable welfare state. However productive of high wages and benefits over the years of post-war prosperity, it was threatened by the competition of cars manufactured by cheaper labor—mainly in Asia but also in the American south, where unions had not taken root. A threat to living standard and employment began to pre-occupy UAW members, and no matter how trusted the union, its inability to stave off the threat became increasingly clear. Racial antagonism was hardly buried in American culture, and that these surfaced at a socio-economic breaking point was not surprising. What was surprising that after all the years of united struggle in the factories, and in state politics, the alliance of African-Americans and whites fell apart so quickly, The workers who voted for Wallace became Reagan Democrats in subsequent elections. The matter was not limited to Michigan and not confined to one union. In my early years in Washington I also knew the Machinists, who later merged with the UAW. The Machinists' President, William Winpisinger, was a burly figure who had the prescience to write a book on rebuilding the US. It was, substantially, the same project as the one Obama vainly argues for investment in new infra-structure to expand and modernize the economy, Like their colleagues at UAW, the Machinist officials were exceedingly articulate politically, could situate their problems at once in a larger context—and had totally admirable personal qualities of moral staying power.

    I listened to my union friends, learned a lot about the daily workings of union politics, was with them in the last Carter year and the traumatic beginning of the Reagan presidency. I was of direct help to the UAW in explaining the European situation. I also worked with Paul Warnke, who headed the Arms Control and Disarmament Agency and counted on the UAW to back his projects in the Congress. My close friend at the UAW was Steve Schlossberg, who opened family and house to me and made my initial years in Washington familial. Steve had a clear sense of comradeship. I know he admired my travels through several worlds and my writings. I retain a sense of gratitude for his generosity and loyalty. For the rest, to him and my friends at the Machinists, I could only offer something like Pastoral or Rabbinical counsel: things might be bad but viewed in the long run, they could be worse. I did not realize how much worse.

Like the unionists, my friends in the Congress, and their staffs, and those in the large spectrum of organizations which had each appropriated some part of the New Deal tradition were taken with the detailed work of the day. They had to deal with legislation, with regulation and administrative and judicial rulings, with the specific interests of their clients and supporters. They drew upon an effectively codified set of assumptions about political possibility and did not generally think it their task to revise these in any explicit way. Ideas and projects deriving from them that appeared increasingly remote were dropped, new language and perspectives introduced in no very systematic way—or subject to much debate. The liberal weeklies and monthlies covered the process, sometimes in reports from the capital or critical parts of the country, sometimes in book reviews, sometimes in essays. The opinion makers were divided between those following the electoral calendar and the groups and persons figuring on it, and those thinking in shorter or longer intervals. The difference between academic reflection and serious journalism was often exaggerated by the practitioners of each.

The proliferation of centers of research which were (and are) openly political was the response of factions within the political parties to the need to define themselves as intellectually relevant. It was also a response to the expansion of the educated labor force in public and private sectors alike. It was also a way to balance the freedoms accorded to themselves by independent academics: protected by tenure, they could think as they wished. I was much struck, five years before coming to Washington, by being asked by the then MacNeil/Lehrer Report to appear on a program about foreign policy in the Carter campaign for the Presidency after I wrote about the theme in *The Nation*. Washington's regular journalists, I was told, were rather tactful: who knew who would be in government if Carter won, and what doors would open and shut? In my own case, a certain lack of tact was an asset in what was later to be a Washington career. Ferocious and unbending critic or tolerated and legitimated court jester? It is often difficult to distinguish. I had a public, in effect, in the centers of research I visited. They appreciated what they thought of as learning and lucidity combined with a disregard for mannered conventionalism. The fact that I was a tenured university teacher made my independence possible.

In the years from 1979 until 2001 I of course had my academic duties (and pleasures) at Georgetown Law Center. That was a source of identity, legitimation, home and club. Since it was up to me to define my academic tasks, set the content of my teaching, design my own presence at the Law Center, it was an experience of academic freedom in a quite literal sense. I will write a chapter about it when I finish my account of Washington. For the moment I envisage a climber on a rocky cliff face, trying pathway after pathway to the top, never quite getting there or falling off—experiencing a lasting sense of hope marred by permanent frustration. That is quite an accurate description of the inner aspect of my many political connections. My witty friend Ernest Gellner once observed that great ideas in ethics were always saved for the next chapter. Enduring and solid contacts bringing a sense of embeddedness were always promised by the next group, There were people I knew who spent much of their working political lives with one or another Congress member or Senator. Ted Kennedy was famous for assembling and keeping generations of very devoted and talented staff. My political journeys always seemed to end in my own living room often with familiar casts of characters, sometimes with new friends.

In the turbulence of the sixties, a group or rather groups of activists formed a New Democratic Coalition. As I understood from Marcus Raskin, he and others intended to integrate the several streams of protest of the late sixties (against the war in Vietnam, the civil rights movement, a revived feminism, renewal in education) in a cohesive and large segment of the Democratic Party. At the 1968 Democratic Convention in Chicago the movement reached its high point—and promptly fell apart. The newer African-American leaders, veterans of the confrontations in the American south, anxious to recruit a following that could be used politically in the north, had no inclination to begin the arduous process of organizational fusion with white comrades with their own agendas. The segments of what was termed "the movement" were in fact sects ostensibly looking for a larger church to join, but actually working on their own. They did come together later, in the McGovern Presidential campaign—and its electoral result made clear that the Movement, however defined, had but a third of the nation behind its aspirations to transform the nation. The Movement remained a visible and even effective political presence in the early Nixon years—precisely because its distinct components could focus their energies on their own projects. A very different process was occurring in Europe, where in France, Germany, Italy, a large party (the French Socialists, the German Social Democrats, the Italian Communists) brought the previously dispersed fragments of their nations' oppositions into political discipline. Labour, on the other hand, was splitting—in part on the question of how far and fast to alter institutions, that is to seek some control of the financial industry, in part on the UK's subordinate role in the alliance with the US. In our imperial homeland, the Democratic Party was deeply divided on adherence to the doctrine and practice of the Cold War. (I write just after President Obama has presented the argument for negotiated co-existence with Iran. The skepticism of the Democrats does not derive alone from the influence of Israel's supporters, it expresses the incapacity of the nation to renounce hegemony.)

The Nixon and Ford years, the Carter Presidency, was a period in which the separate elements of the original New Democratic Coalition became ever more separate—and then institutionalized themselves to present a ragged front as the progressive part of the Democratic Party. Court rulings and the emerge4nce of nodes of African-American power in the states (especially the southern states) allowed a sizeable Black Caucus to emerge in the Congress. Old union traditions, active memories of Bob Kennedy's and later George McGovern's campaigns. The concentrated forces of several single issue groups, the need to defend Social Security, Medicare, the newer welfare state legislation, mobilized white legislators. They constituted half of the Progressive Caucus, the Afro-Americans the other half. There was no set of priorities, the battles were fought as conflicts came up and inconclusiveness was permanent.

There is a psychoanalytic phrase, the narcissism of small differences. At first sight, the burgeoning conflicts within the Democratic Party on extending the scope of government, redistribution, even the Cold War seemed small in comparison with the full Republican program of deregulation, Welfare State retrenchment, Cold War maximalism. In fact, there was no majority support for that entire program and the skirmishes and battles around the edges were important in years and even decades in which totalizing confrontation was not possible—even if rhetorical bellicosity on both sides greatly exaggerated the significance of the moment. A good deal of American politics consisted of symbolic conflicts. My friend Ron Dellums was an authentic adversary of Cold War—and for periods Chair of both the House Armed Services Committee and the Intelligence Committee. We all lived with or in a considerable amount of ambiguity. There is another way to describe it. Our [political ideas correctly depicted a permanent contest, between welfare state and free market, social mobilization and individuation, between the American Revolution as still to be achieved or as accomplished. The structures of society, however, were quite rigidified. Ideas rang hollow and a considerable personalization occurred: Reagan and Kennedy, Buckley and Vidal, Jesse Jackson and Billy Graham, Phyllis Schlafly and Gloria Steinem.

I met any number of interesting and committed persons in Washington, had glimpses at very different milieux (Christian social activists for instance), noted the distance between thinkers and writers outside Washington and those immersed or imprisoned in it. As time went on I did not integrate the past or my past with an increasingly indifferent present—just took it that distance was unbridgeable. Two younger friends had the reassuring gifts of making me welcome in the present. The first was Christopher Hitchens. Christopher came to Oxford as an undergraduate four years after I left it, and his tutor, Steven Lukes, had studied with me. Christopher did not wish for an academic career, eventually became Foreign Editor of the venerable but relentlessly contemporary *New Statesman*, knew an entire political generation mot only in Europe but across the continents. An earlier trip to the US had given him a sense of possibility he missed in Great Britain and he was very happy when as *New Statesman* editor he could spend three months at *The Nation* on an exchange. In 1981 he decided to join us for the indefinite future, and Victor Navasky in a quite inspired moment thought he should write for *The Nation* from Washington. He turned up on my doorstep and I did my best to introduce him to a Washington I was just getting to know. Christopher, sometimes not overly punctilious about convention and form, fulsomely praised me as mentor in his memoir, wrote another generous line or two about my internationalism—and left it at that,

I found it both amusing and instructive, perhaps instructive because amusing, to introduce Christopher to a spectrum of Washingtonians, from my Jesuit friends to the younger KGB agent assigned to my case. Christopher had extraordinary instincts for situating persons in their own settings, for rapidly calculating what he could learn from them (or gain from them) the while giving them the impression that they were being taken very seriously. He was in other words a very accomplished social adventurer, using his directness to persuade the most well-placed Americans, some of them actually formidable, that he was honoring them with his attention.

I do not use the term "social climber" since Christopher rather successfully conveyed the notion that he had no need to scale heights: he was already on top of things. Much was written about Christopher on our side of the Atlantic after his terribly early death. I was struck by how casual or shallow even admirers and friends were about his Britishness. My years in the UK were, in understanding him, not wasted, Christopher's father had been a warrant officer in the pre-war Royal Navy, an officer during the war, and quite unwillingly retired after it. He became an administrator at a small public which is to say private school—and Christopher's mother determined on successful careers for her sons. (His brother Peter was a very Tory journalist, audibly at a loss what to say when Christopher rather suddenly began to agree with him on the virtues of empire. Before that, Christopher had to deal with the discovery by his mother that she was Jewish. There was a complicated story about that, embedded in the social changes experienced by the British during Depression, war, and thereafter, To what extent did his mother, father, and the brothers subliminally know something?

The extent of British anti-Semitism is greatly exaggerated in the US—but clearly, a family integrated in a monotone or rather monotonous Anglican normality would find the discovery troubling.

Christopher, however, did not need the discovery to devise his own version of that integration. Britain's critics and rebels were as indispensable to it as its most stolid citizens. Christopher spoke with some e emotion of his father's disappointment at not being able to remain in the Royal Navy. Christopher himself amassed quite a lot of knowledge of the Navy, its contribution to the British process of democratization—a rather pronounced replacement of old hierarchies by new ones, with new places for new men (and even women.) Christopher at Oxford was a very vocal leader of the British version of the protests of the decade—one that did not disown a British past but imagined a much more radical one. My colleague and friend Chelly Halsey did meticulous work on Oxford's social history. Christopher arrived when its function as a preparatory school for an economic and political elite that required active intelligence had replaced the gentlemanly dilettantism of fiction and memoir. A comparative study of Harvard and Oxford in the sixties would show more similarities than differences in both conformity and revolt.

Christopher read widely, was acutely aware of the ways in which literary and intellectual argument was familial—and decided early against an academic career. Perhaps he disliked its sedentary aspects as well as the deference expected of beginners. His darting intelligence and waspish temperament were hardly unique in British journalism. There is no reason to doubt his truthfulness when he said that in the US he felt freer. A great many intellectuals from the United Kingdom found the US in the second half of the last century irresistible, Christopher had good instincts for marketing, and clearly realized that his own alternation between the poses of weary disdain and enthusiastic knowingness would impress American editors and readers alike. His choice of Lady Diana and Mother Teresa as objects of scathing scrutiny suggested that he was quite content not to cast himself as Gibbon. The description of the modern age was a project hinted at, but proceeded with in fragments.

When I first met Christopher, he was married to Eleni, a Greek

Cypriot of much substance. They had two sons, taken back to London when he and Eleni parted. His second wife was Carol, the daughter of a Stanford scientist, They lived in the Wyoming and their lunches and dinners were all arranged at the last moment—or perhaps that was simply the category of my invitations. I did not and could not complain, the company was always interesting, enabled me to keep up somewhat with Britain without flying to London. The sequencing of the guests over the years refracted Christopher's changes of political position. The event in honor of Edward Said was followed only a few years later by assemblages of supporters of the war on Iraq. There was hardly an intervening phase.

Christopher was tireless in his denunciations of what he saw as the authoritarianism and barbarism of Islam. He threw away the knowledge of Mideast complexity available to educated Britons, ignored the zealotry of the Christians and Jews making of Islam a caricature to justify their attacks on it—and emerged as a person he would have abjured but a few years earlier. Nuance was a nuisance, limitless aggressivity a virtue. Christopher's change, from scourge of all constituted authority to volunteer in the ideological striking force behind Bush. Cheney, Rumsfeld, has no simple explanation. A phrase like "opportunism" tells us nothing: he renounced much of the public which admired his iconoclasm and the defenders of a fictive reversion to western civilization did not disguise their suspicion of anything he did or said. Christopher certainly knew the cash value of doing or saying nothing by halves and maintained his intransigence, now turned against erstwhile friends. There are plenty of British instances of cultural careers in which the chapters had no obvious coherence. That was a consequence of the large certitude of British thinkers and writers: they belonged to the ages, even if their own age was regrettably indifferent to what they had to offer. It was part of that continuity which marked the English and their Celtic cousins. My Oxford colleagues, I recall, agreed on little or nothing—but did assume that they were at the center and everyone and everything else at the periphery.

Christopher insistently proclaimed his admiration for the US— and behaved as if he had never left England. He wrote on Jefferson, had considerable knowledge of our history, but did not expend much energy in the labyrinth of our culture. He studied with revolutionary British Calvinism's great apologist, Christopher Hill, but did not interest himself in American Puritanism. He remained a visitor who, left to the natives or other long-term residents, issues of ethnicity, race, religion—even many of the peculiarities of our class system, with its remarkable collusions and hidden conflicts.

To my regret, I saw rather little of Christopher toward the end of his life. He refused denial, wrote bravely and helpfully for others of his illness—and died as a gentleman who did not complain.

I was involved in an episode in which Christopher did not behave as a gentleman. He had a considerable dislike of Bill Clinton, whom he knew slightly at Oxford. Christopher was quite friendly, even closely so, with Sidney Blumenthal. Sidney eventually worked at the White House, and was there as the Republicans were attempting to impeach the President. Christopher accused Sidney of what might have been illegal behavior in allegedly defaming persons whose testimony might have been used in the proceedings. Sidney was promptly cited by the Republican-led investigative committee—and had to defend himself at large cost. The entire atmosphere of the capital at the time was sordid, and a personal betrayal of this sort not unusual. What made it painful to experience was the fact that Christopher and Sidney had been close friends ever since Sidney came to Washington in 1985. I promptly wrote to Christopher declaring his behavior terrible. Christopher thanked me for not denouncing him publicly: there was so much condemnation that it is unclear that any one voice would be heard.

Sidney Blumenthal grew up in Chicago, studied at Brandeis, began a journalistic career in the marginal media of Boston, and came to Washington to write for the *Post* in 1985. Sidney had a cinematic imagination possibly shaped by Talmudic story telling. In his reportage, persons could not escape judgment—they were constantly reminded of their own contributions to their fortunes. Perhaps Nixon and the Watergate drama had as much literary influence on him as Singer or his fellow Chicagoan Bellow. At this moment Sidney is working on a Lincoln biography, whilst awaiting a possible return to duty in a Clinton White House. Lincoln's mournfulness perhaps appeal to him as balancing his own tendency to depict politics as a carousel.

When Sidney joined Bill Clinton's staff, he was given a large assignment. He was responsible for arranging a series of international discussions on the so-called Third Way. The term the Third Way was intended to describe a set of policies which would somehow reconcile social democracy with its reliance on state intervention with a new sort of social entrepreneurship using the discipline and innovative capacity of the market.

The Third Way gained in plausibility owing to the expansion everywhere in the industrial nations made possible by the rapid development of electronic communication. Third Way arguments seized on this as evidence for the functional necessity of decentralization and individuation—despite the obvious concentrations of capital required for the new technologies and the centralized controls they entailed. Third Way doctrine was in fact quite independent of electronic innovation, since it insisted on the efficacy of the market and the intrinsic inefficiency of public institutions unconstrained by market discipline. There were a number of meetings at which social democratic and socialist heads of government from Europe (France, Germany, Italy, Netherlands, Sweden, the United Kingdom) discussed these matters in very general terms. The meetings coincided with a general decline in the values of solidarity, in the belief in the efficacy of the state as mediating social interests, and in the capacity of welfare states to respond to changes in the global economic system and in civic culture. Some of this was contrived to justify lowered social costs to meet competition from low wage economies. Some of it was the result of decades of ceaseless economic argument depicting solidarity as too costly. Some of it used familiar notions of freedom for "individuals," abstracted of course from their actual economic and social constraints. (Addressing the French National Assembly, Tony Blair cited the selfish behavior of fellow workers at a Parisian café as convincing evidence for the unrealistic nature of socialist ideals.) Clinton presented himself, of course, as seeking the path to prosperity free of dogma. His welfare reforms, which required single mothers to go to work irrespective of their ability to care for dependent children is hardly a matter of empirically verified social policy. In Clinton's years, long established regulation of the larger banks, put in place by the New Deal, was nullified. That gave the Bush government an opening for allowing the financial industry degrees of freedom it had not enjoyed since before the Presidency of Theodore Roosevelt.

Why did experienced European political leaders, certainly not economically and socially unsophisticated, and aware of the long roads their nations had taken to achieve welfare states, allow Blair and Clinton to enlist them in disparaging the European social model? Why did Clinton himself as a grandchild of the New Deal and son of the Great Society treat his party's heritage with casual disregard? Personal histories are not irrelevant, but they refract a larger history, too. In the US, the defenders of the New Deal and the Great Society legacies suffered from two large problems, The first was (and is) that they are precisely that—defenders. They lacked and lack a large and comprehensible idea of the future. Their primary references are to the impact of economic and social policies on individual fates—fates invariably described in terms of personal aspiration. True, frequent references to families and even communities reduce the starkness of the imagery, but the notion of personhood as autonomous remains dominant. Democrats rather more than Republicans (Clinton and Obama) often express the afterthought that united, Americans can do much, but it is a rhetorical afterthought.

Their second problem is the additive and disparate quality of the projects of Franklin Roosevelt's and Lyndon Johnson's heirs. Entirely new groups occupied or contended for center stage: African-Americans struggling against the conjoint burdens of discrimination and poverty, women contesting patriarchal domination and rigid notions of domesticity. When Johnson signed the Medicare bill in 1965 he spoke with justified pride of offering dignity to eighteen million citizens over sixty-five and described most of them as poor. The working class as such has by now disappeared, divided ethnically, racially, religiously, regionally as well as by age and education. The abstractions of demographers and political economists do not translate into a language of politics, as a concept of citizenship disintegrates. When Romney as Presidential candidate in 2012 disparaged the "forty-seven percent": who in his view were insufficiently industrious and productive, he voiced the contempt and distance many Americans experience when they think of those unlike themselves, particularly when they are less prosperous.

When to this are added the divisions of culture and religion the recourse to additive politics seems inevitable. A common project is very difficult if not impossible even to formulate. To reinforce the general fragmentation, the electoral system makes its own contribution. States and Congressional districts have very different economic and social compositions. Governors, Senators, Representatives have primary responsibilities to their own constituencies. Historically, national legislative figures could count on continuity in support by their own electorates: Edward Kennedy in Massachusetts and before him Taft in Ohio were examples—as were some of the Southerners when the South was regularly Democratic. Humphrey for years before he lost the Presidential nomination to the younger John Kennedy was convener rather than leader of the New Deal segment of the Democrats while the masterful Senatorial tactician Johnson waited until he was President to pursue unhindered his deepest social convictions.

By the eighties, the inner division within the Democratic Party on economy and state, on state intervention in issues on which the nation was culturally and racially divided rigidified. The continuation of the Cold War with the Soviet Union was another cause of division, with the group recognizing complexity and asking for historical patience permanently on the defensive. The inexorable realists, Kissinger and Nixon, won considerable freedom of maneuver due to their brutality and absence of scruple. Reagan and the first Bush and their extremely acute Secretaries of State, Shultz and Baker, appropriated the support of the Democrats skeptical of the Cold War to negotiate armistices on some fronts, but these were often not spoken of as consequences of compromise. Rather, like the entire Gorbachev phenomenon, they were interpreted in triumphalist terms: due to our supposed steadfastness, the USSR was retreating. The Republicans could recall, after all, Dean Rusk's simplistic response to the end of the Cuban missile crisis, his words to the effect that the USSR had blinked.

In the centers of research and universities, opinion pages, in testimony before Congressional committees, much argument was if not ritualized, repetitive. The progressives in the public interest groups and in the Congress (and under Clinton occasionally in government itself) struggled to defend what their parents and grandparents had won, and did battle on no long front but in an unending series of smaller and disconnected engagements. There was one large triumph: Medicare, to some extent Medicaid, and

Social Security were untouched. It was not obvious that they would remain so. Large numbers of citizens believed that the nation could not afford what were termed by their antagonists entitlements. The stabilizing and even expansive economic functions of these expenditures escaped the attention of ordinary citizens whose primitive economic thinking was a parody of the returned neo-classical economics in the universities. The university economists did not, of course, suppose that there was a fixed quantity of money in the possession of the state and that it was being drained away They did nothing, however, to educate the public about larger economic processes and public goods. Millions of citizens who bought houses with mortgages were open to fulminations about public debt. The Clinton White House was ready for what was termed a grand bargain, in which Medicare and Social Security would be cut but retained as entire other areas of government spending were reduced. The project came to a stop as Clinton had to rely on the Democrats to retain his Presidency when impeached. The Republicans' corporate funders were unable to impose a long term economic strategy on Republican politicians seeking above all to delegitimize the Democrats and driven by the obsessions and hatreds of their voters. Of course, Medicare and Social Security were increasingly thought of in positive terms as demographic change increased the proportion of elder Americans—whose children were relieved of paying for their parents' final years. Programs of social welfare for the impoverished were, however, ejected because they supposedly rewarded the incompetent and lazy—and the racially inferior. A rhetoric of individual and familial responsibility generated an ideal image of a nation in which personal autonomy was a virtue.

For years, political economists like Milton Friedman and their wealthy sponsors pursued the idea of a deregulated economy. They could not for all of the legislators they subsidized, academic and pseudo-academic institutions they founded, media imagery they bought, achieve the total re-privatization of the nation. They succeeded, if that is the term, in engendering frustration and resentment which had consequences they could not control. Meanwhile, there was an increase in governmental functions they could not stop. In the maintenance of old infrastructure and the provision of new goods and services, the federal government could not be eliminated or even reduced without grave and visible damage to the society. Decades ago, fluoride in water supplies caused hysteria. Now it is the turn of compulsory vaccination to evoke resistance. The abolition of the Centers for Disease Control and Prevention or the National Institutes of Health is not on the agenda of any but the clinically deranged. Entire levels of education from advanced research universities to kindergartens receive federal subsidies. Disaster assistance is a governmental function. The advocates or prophets of the superiority of the market have reduced the efficiency of government by casting doubt on it, limiting its resources, and then complaining that it is incapable of performing well. Governmental employment in the US hardly carries the authority and prestige it has in the other advanced nations, including Great Britain.

There was recurrent attention to a third sector — to non-profit organizations, to welfare projects embedded in the churches, to the organization of a broad spectrum of activities which do not privilege motives of immediate gain or the accumulation of property. It is a theme which has as a complement the notions of decentralization, smallness, localized self-government (even in the economy), the virtues of a distinctively American practice of grassroots democracy. The large foundations certainly had their apogee in the projects of the Great Society. Bundy's assumption of the presidency of the Ford Foundation was plausibly interpreted as penance for the systematic destructiveness of the foreign policy he administered in the White House as National Security Advisor to Kennedy and then for some years to Johnson. Johnson had sent McNamara to the World Bank as President when he sensed, in 1968, that he was considering public disavowal of the Vietnam War he was so instrumental in devising. By the time I arrived in Washington, McNamara was in his last years as World Bank president and had commissioned a report on global development by an international committee chaired by Willy Brandt. None of these ideas, projects, sensibilities were at the center of attention of the Carter government, overwhelmed by immediate problems: domestic inflation and unemployment, the Soviet Afghan invasion and the intensification of the Cold War caused by the conflict over new nuclear missiles in Europe. Carter in his post-presidential years is a noble and far-seeing figure, but was unable in the White House to use his intelligence and moral vision. Washington was, increasingly, dominated by those who bought and lied their way to influence and a share of power—which was all they required to stop anything like an enduring project for social reconstruction. The progressives were resigned to indefinite deferral of major projects. Their concentration on saving governmental programs indispensable to the survival of large numbers of citizens who might otherwise have lacked the necessities of life was a responsible choice: the impoverished and unskilled had few other allies.

Out of sight of those who wrote headlines, and ignored by those who thought of themselves as thinking in large terms, significant battles were fought in matters of the rights of children, of women, of homosexuals, over access to facilities previously reserved for prosperous whites (indeed for prosperous white males). Educational institutions were a particular focus of these conflicts, and so was the provision of health care. Federal and state courts, local government, federal rule-making, legislative supervision of the executive, ostensibly arcane items in the federal budget and those of the states were sites of redefinitions of both citizenship and personhood.

Much of this was very far from the recondite discussions of democratic renewal, of the economic and social dimensions of citizenship still dominating the transatlantic intellectual conversations in which I was a participant. There were similar phenomena in Western Europe, where poverty and social helplessness was indeed on a much smaller scale. There too, however, the vanguard functions of the socialist parties (and the Christian social parties which shared their views of general welfare) shrank as the defense of the acquired advantages of post-war politics took priority.

Cultural and social changes, planned, improvised and over determined altered the texture of daily life. Defenders of what they thought of as Christian traditionalism were right to blame the colleges and universities to which their children went for alienating them from parental and local values. However, the production of pieties had long since ceased to pay in the cultural industry. Not just the campuses and a few larger cities, but much of the country was a cultural danger zone for traditionalists. The American churches, always at internal odds, were more divided than ever.

There were even large and vocal differences within Catholicism, with those formed by the Second Vatican Council facing determined counter reformers led by Pope John Paul II. The impulsion to work for social justice did not subside in American Protestantism, but expressed itself in multiple currents. American Jews did not become less liberal or modern (the guitar had long since replaced the ram's horn in many congregations) but concentrated their energies on defining themselves in the light of demands from Israel that Jerusalem had claims which Cambridge, Los Angeles and New York could not deny.

I was struck in this period by the constancy of social commitment of persons who had been formed by the churches, some of them moving back to work in them after periods elsewhere, some who had never left. I caught glimpses of inner qualities (hope, patience, serenity) which I did not possess. I was aware of a certain febrility, even a shortness of view despite my historical knowledge, which I could not transcend. I certainly was not trying to do so, but chose allies and friends who were inwardly different. I recall being honored by a rather long and personal criticism in *Contentions*, the broadsheet of the Committee for a Free World, The author was Neal Kozodoy. Years earlier I had tried to assist his search for academic employment and the episode reminds me of the New York adage, "Why are you so hostile, I haven't done anything for you recently." Neal was scornful of my use of English expressions and especially indignant about a reference I had made to Jewishness. He did not think that I had any right to claim it.

Let Jehovah judge. I had reached a rather too-simple solution to the problem with which so many contemporaries struggled so openly. I was heir to a Jewish tradition of learning and moral reflection, much of which I claimed rather peremptorily. I could not say how I acquired it, and a good deal had come to me indirectly through studying and living with Protestantism. I recurred frequently to Irving Howe's favored story, about the impoverished Jew in Eastern Europe who was offered a custodial job at a village synagogue, and told that he was also to sit at the gate of the Ghetto and watch the horizon for the coming of the Messiah. He protested that the salary was too low and was silenced with the retort, it is a lifetime job. I do not think that it was the analogy to academic tenure that accounted for my attachment to the tale. Justice, social reform, a new society, were clearly unavailable in my lifetime. I knew the Freudian legacy had a sense of his burden of unbelief. There was something I was not quite facing, involving tradition and contemporaneity, familial legacy and personal choices. What I did under its yoke had a considerable charge of brilliance. What there was of staying power was forced upon me: a world without God could become a large black hole at any moment. It was best to rush, there were no guarantees about time, inner and outer.

Much of significance was happening out of my sight—the daily struggle by electoral and judicial means for the extension and codification of voting rights in the south, where action had been shifted from the streets to legislatures, the Congress, and the courts. I knew of creeping deindustrialization, of the lowering of living standards in what had been thriving working-class communities, where the younger generation did not go into factories but to state colleges and universities. The decline in city and state revenues (intensified by redistribution upward when progressive energy diminished and market ideologies prevailed) made education a commodity and not a public good. My own students complained of their burdens, found it restricted their choice of careers and made commitment to public service difficult. Possibilities were changing and shrinking. I did not alter my narrative very much, found it harder to maintain hope, and harder still to develop a new longer view. Many of those on offer were derived from the trauma of failed democratic revolution and successful fascist and state socialist ones. Many contemporaries thought of our very imperfections and failures as reassuring: at least, we were not engaged in utopian politics.

The Christians I knew had rather different moral temperaments. The Catholics were struggling with the flattening of the landscape promised by Vatican II as the Polish Pope pursued his version of Counter Reformation. The Protestants had an extraordinary variety of doctrinal paths, social forms and personal choices open to them. In the sixties, some Protestant theologians had seized upon Bloch's *Das Prinzip Hoffnung, The Principle of Hope,* actually written in exile in the US in the late thirties and early forties and published to a great deal of praise and rather less comprehension in Germany in the mid-fifties. Bloch was then a citizen of the DDR and teaching at Leipzig. Stalin was dead when he was finally allowed to publish an exceedingly unorthodox text drawing upon religious figures of thought, including Jewish mysticism, it was met by incomprehension in much of Soviet Europe and embarrassment among western Marxists. Some of the critical Lutherans, like Jürgen Moltmann, saw the point. The actual movement of capitalism did not provide convincing evidence of its own immanent transcendence. We could hope, however and hope was indispensable: it made us aware of the possibility of transformation which everything in ordinary existence denied, Henri Lefebvre in his critical writings on everyday life depicted it as, simultaneously, a prison and a place where a new future could be rehearsed.

Jesse Jackson is a Pastor, with pulpit serving as stage. In the critical writing on the movements of the sixties and early seventies, considerable attention is given to the project as an enlarged form of street theater. What about the ways it took ritual out of circumscribed Sunday practice and sent it to politics. I knew Jesse and appreciated his shrewdness, sense of the moment, eye for paradox. I do not think he read Bloch but he did know of Jürgen Moltmann and his theology of hope. Let us say that Jesse's familiar slogan, "Keep Hope Alive," came from the African-American church as so central a part of the Civil Rights movement. Jesse, well before his Presidential campaigns of 1984 and 1988, regarded himself as ministering to the exploited, the impoverished, the morally traduced, well beyond the African-American community. He was quite clear on the necessity of comradeship (not just communication) with the white working class, and journeyed regularly to the sites of strikes to seek direct contact with the rank and file—not always to the enthusiasm of union officialdom.

It was regrettable when in the course of his 1988 campaign he was overheard describing New York as "Hymietown." That evoked paroxysms of condemnation from Jewish Democrats already hostile on account of his sympathy for the Palestinians. He apologized and I wrote in *The Nation* that reading him out of the Democratic Party was unwise as well as unjust. The Jewish community had to learn to live with our African-American fellow citizens in terms rather different from the past. In the event, in the 1988 New York state Democratic primary, Jesse did have a majority in New York

City—on account of a door-to-door mobilization that anticipated Barack Obama's national tactics twenty years later.

1996, trade unions in the person of John Sweeney, the President of the AFL-CIO, and a lively group of older and younger academics organized by Nelson Lichtenstein, responded to the sense of drift and discouragement of the Clinton years by forming a group to connect campus and the unions. Sweeney, the son of a motorman on the New York subway who emigrated from Ireland, had a large grasp of Catholic social thought. He also had an acute sense of what was and was not possible in a situation in which the New Deal and the Great Society were "history" in the idiomatic American sense— relegated to a past without much connection with the present. The academic-union group had some success in interesting students in union careers, sponsored symposia in which students learned something of the role of unions in the recent American past, encouraged younger academics to bring work into their inquiries. It did not last in its original form, but renewed a legacy and -if haltingly and indirectly—encouraged a newer one. At the inaugural meeting at Columbia University I met an old friend, Carl Schorske, eleven years in fact older than myself, climbing the steps of Low Library to listen to the talks. It takes me, said Carl, back to the thirties.

I will not rewrite the chapter, or recant what I said about the defensiveness and fragmentation of the reformist project. There are dimensions I should have emphasized. Younger persons did seek careers in the offices of critical members of Congress, or with government officials attempting to extend a reformist franchise. Others joined public interest groups, or began academic careers marked by a search for social responsibility. A large movement could not be found, but a great many smaller ones were started—and continued. Above all, some of our politics had pedagogic functions for those who engaged themselves—and purposely or not, passed commitment, energy and ideas onto younger persons. The absence of great projects had compensatory consequences in many smaller ones.

In the meantime, I was teaching full time, and that too was a political vocation—one which, looking back, may have been considerable.

17

Georgetown Law Center: A Welcoming Academic Home

THE INCESSANTLY cited words of Tolstoy that all happy families are alike, unhappy ones different, are untrue. Happy families are happy in different ways and therefore unalike. I consider Georgetown University Law Center in the years in which I was on faculty (1979-2001) to have been an exemplary institution. Students were cared for, staff were treated with appreciation. Deans actually listened to colleagues thought to merit respect despite, or perhaps because of, their foibles. I had come from Amherst, which at the time alternated between exaggerated complacency and acute institutional doubt, with ensuing short tempers. (There were good practices and persons I did not appreciate, and in any event, matters are now much improved.) Before that I had been at institutions of very proprietary sorts of conflict and melancholy.

What made Georgetown so welcoming, not only to myself but to others? The faculty experienced a sense of triumph as it realized that it was mastering a difficult task, transforming a somewhat local and culturally specific institution into a multi-faceted national one. Georgetown kept its Jesuit identity as best it could (there were fewer and fewer Jesuits educated in the law) and certainly retained its connections to Congress and government. The contingent of teachers in ascendance when I arrived came, often, from other law schools, had frequently clerked at the high levels of the judiciary, and took the entire world of legal scholarship for their province.

I had a premonition of this in my first talk with the first Dean I served under, the affable, shrewd and warm David McCarthy. Dave was from Hartford and perfectly able to locate Amherst on the cultural map. You are coming from Presbyterian Amherst, he told me, but do not be put off by what you might think of as Catholic and Jesuit conventions: the essential divisions in our faculty are Orthodox, Conservative, Reformed. I told him that Amherst insofar as it was anything was decidedly post-Presbyterian, that I had had instructive, no, illuminating, collaborations with Catholic theologians and lay persons, and welcomed the opportunity to experience more of Catholicism at Georgetown. David told me that Father Timothy Healy had urged on him that the Law Center was about to meet an authentic New York Jewish intellectual, he hadn't expected my Catholic connections. I instructed Dave that the successfully marketed mythos of the New York intellectuals used Jewishness (most were quite remote from Judaism) as something exciting, arcane. Still, there was a problem: James Burnham, Dwight Macdonald, Mary McCarthy, Edmund Wilson, were definitely not Jewish—and not converts in culture or manners, either.

Dave was encouraging and supportive throughout our years together, tolerant of my considerable residue of narcissism. Musing at his farewell dinner, he recollected the arrival of myself as a "super-star." That was just what I wanted to hear, but I interjected: "star will do." Dave asked if there was a physician at the dinner: I might be unwell. He retired not only from the Deanship but rather early from his professorship and went to live in Charlottesville. It is pleasant to salute a person of discernment and sympathy, by no means lacking the toughness that leaders had to have. With a certain quiet persistence, Dave urged those who were our stars to think of what they owed the institution, tolerated eccentricity when it served the institution, and asked everyone to consider if he or she were doing their best. He was acutely aware that those who were students would carry their memories of the Law Center into their professional lives, and convinced cohorts of students that he was on their side. When I came, there were loud student complaints of the indifference of faculty. In a few years, Dave marshalled his professors' better natures and students actually said that they had been made to feel welcome.

The newer and younger faculty joined a very flexible group of old timers in an enterprise of reconstruction, perhaps re-foundation is a more precise term. As I glimpsed it in the accounts of older colleagues, Georgetown had been pronouncedly Catholic, and a resource for those working in Washington (frequently in government) who sought law degrees to advance their careers. A distinguished Catholic philosopher of Natural Law, Father Lacey, in the thirties argued that legal positivism and realism had opened the way for sinister developments in other nations. If legal institutions were self-legitimating, there could be no standpoint from which to judge their morality. His was hardly a lost voice, but in the thirties, forties, fifties, legal thought moved in other directions, insisting with earlier thinkers on its cultural and social contexts and consequences. I was struck by the way awareness of generation after generation of legal thinkers informed the critical rhetoric the younger faculty members used. They had pronounced historical views of their own situation and that gave them intellectual and personal depth. I noted a contrast with the social science disciplines, where entire generations eschewed the experience of their elders to proclaim themselves a vanguard, triumphant victors over the illusions of the past. I am still somewhat perplexed as to what accounts for the historical sophistication evident in contemporary jurisprudence. I know that some of my colleagues would dispute my conclusion as too flattering, and point to the sharpness and sometimes bitterness of conflicts in the legal academy. Equally, I recall the remark of Daniel Ernst, that Supreme Court decisions invariably incorporated historical scholarship long since refuted by the historians. Dan's irreverence was compelling evidence for the intellectual quality of his generation at the Law Center.

Whether as clerks to judges or younger practitioners, my colleagues had a sense of the tangled and stubborn ways in which conflicts of interest and values in matters large and small provided the stuff law sought to master. By contrast with many in the academy, they had had experience of diversity—or, more exactly, of the large cultural and social divisions of our society. (A municipal shelter for the homeless is on the next block, not the sort of edifice that was part of the topography of Harvard Square.) They also possessed, I realized, a sense of the varieties of human conduct, somewhat reminiscent of what the very senior psychoanalysts in the Fisher circle had but not especially evident in their younger colleagues. Of course, there were cultural differences in the faculty which were not only those of age. The younger cohort included more women and Latinos and African-Americans and Asians. There were foreign visitors, and a fixed connection to Heidelberg brought German jurisprudence and its terrible past and expiatory present to us. Some colleagues had governmental positions, advisory and active. Quite a few took occasional leaves to work in government.

Father Robert Drinan had been in Congress for the Brookline-Newton district of Massachusetts, with many Jewish and Protestant constituents. Before that he had been dean at Boston College's law faculty. The Pope had instructed him to leave the Congress and Bob, so obviously attached to his order and his priestly role, agreed—but the hurt sat deep. Bob learned that I was a frequent traveler at the time to Rome, and when I returned was no little ironic. "No doubt, the Holy Father was asking after me." Bob's former colleagues in the Congress, persons like Paul Simon of Illinois, were extremely devoted to him and he remained part of a circle which included their families. On any given day of the week, there was a television crew or two in the hall seeking him out, sometimes from Latin America ("Il Padre Drinan, por favor?"). Bob's complex relationship to the Church, his commitment to issues of human rights, his iconic standing among American progressives, his quite extraordinary energy and knowledge combined with personal generosity re his energy and time made him valuable to colleagues and students alike. I was particularly struck by his reminiscences of a Boston boyhood in an Irish Catholic milieu, and his time as a novice in what was then the Jesuit seminary in Lenox in the Berkshires. The seminary was long gone, but the move into Protestant New England clearly succeeded.

How did the Law Center keep its Catholic traditions intact as faculty and student body diversified—and as the leadership of the Roman Catholic Church in the US increasingly defined its specificity by militant opposition to (in alliance with Protestant Fundamentalists and a small but vocal group of Orthodox Jews) abortion and rights for homosexuals, as well as a very decided rejection of a broad feminist agenda. Our long-term Catholic chaplains, Fathers Malley and Michalenko and Sister Dorinda Young certainly did not comport themselves as representatives of Church authority. Rather, they cultivated dialogue in many forms, were ever present in the entire spectrum of Law Center activities, ministered to the larger community as well as to Catholic faculty, staff, students. "Law is the means, justice is the end" was the motto of the Law Center. The chaplains—joined by Protestant and Jewish and later Muslim colleagues—continually reminded the rest of us of a larger vision in a larger world. That is, they took Catholicism as an opening to the several possibilities of history. Catholicism was represented at the Law Center by contending versions of itself. There was a small but vocal remnant which thought of the faculty's completed journey into modernity as perdition—but gallantly kept its sense of humor and courtesy I was struck, yet again, by the force of integration in American society. It is difficult to find a metaphor for it—but an unexpected comparison comes to mind. The twenty miles separating England from France are decisive in British history. William and his Normans made it across, but Philip II, Napoleon, Hitler, never did clear Customs at Dover. The US by contrast has been open to the world, but it has managed to impose its peculiarity upon a constant stream of the most different newcomers.

The student body intake drew upon Georgetown and other Catholic institutions. Very rarely did I encounter students who objected (politely) to what they thought of as the excessively pluralistic atmosphere of the Law Center. By comparison, I had far more encounters at Amherst with students objecting to what they thought of as the unbalanced radicalism of faculty. For a while, indeed, one of the Jesuit members of our Board of Directors (and the committee dealing with the Law Center) was my French friend, Father Jean-Yves Calvez. He had been the Jesuit charged at their Curia in Rome with administering Europe and with his American colleague, Father Vincent O'Keefe, was barred by Pope John Paul II in no uncertain terms from candidacy for the Jesuit Generalship in succession to Father Arrupe. When Father Calvez came to us, he was back in France and advising Cardinal Lustiger of Paris on many matters. (I first knew Calvez when I learned about the opening to the world of the French Church which preceded John XXIII's reforms. Calvez at the beginning of his career wrote a remarkably acute and deep book, *La Pensée de Karl Marx*.)

When Pope John Paul II admonished Catholic universities in the US to emphasize Catholicism more, a certain number of non-Catholic colleagues wondered aloud if the Pope's injunction portended restrictions on their academic freedom. Our Jesuit colleagues offered reassurance: they had been fending off the Vatican for centuries and they would certainly do so in this case. I recollect that Father Healy, in one of his annual speeches to the university, spoke of his pleasure and profit at meeting with His Holiness in the company of other American Catholic university presidents. As far as I can remember, Father Tim declared that when His Holiness spoke of the duties of Catholic universities in the US, he was impressed yet again with his rootedness in Poland.

I knew colleagues at the Main Campus, in Georgetown itself and in many ways a world away. When I came as a visitor, it was proposed to the Government department that I be invited to give a seminar. I did so, on the politics of the industrial societies with attention to Western Europe—but not before my sponsors overcame the objection of Jeane Kirkpatrick, who declared that I was not a scholar but an ideologue. She was not listened to and some little time later, I found her very critical and intelligent son in one of my courses, He must have convinced his mother that I was in some respects a very conventional figure, a university teacher with critical views of society that were very unlikely to be immediately implemented—and in no case someone with a conspicuous taste for the martyrdom of marginalization.

My most intensive connections to the main campus were two. One was to the Woodstock Theological Center, then directed by my old friend Father Thomas Gannon. I went there often for seminars and meals, developed a sense of the struggles within the Church to retain a social ethic of solidarity. When the American Catholic Bishops published a pastoral letter in the Reagan years calling for a preferential option for the poor, the Woodstock group convened a set of thinkers to talk about it and write about it. My article, "The Bishops in the Iron Cage," may or may not have graced the volume, but it was there, black on white, and was widely read. It brought me welcome contact with the America of the Catholic social reformers—a milieu rather different from the penumbras of *The Nation, Partisan Review*, or even the academic ecumene of political economists and political philosophers. It was a period in which Rawls' work on justice was much discussed, and the Catholic project was a convincing case of what Max Weber once termed "exemplary prophecy." (The volume we produced was edited by Father Gannon and given the brief title, *The Catholic Challenge to the American Economy*, 1987.)

Many Catholic trade unionists, members of Congress and elected and appointed public officials, college and university teachers across the spectrum of humanities and the social sciences were active witnesses with values they refused to forget or flatten in the resurgence of the market. The long-term effects were considerable: a cadre of activists, intellectuals, citizens able to think against the current. Their commitment was certainly tested in the following years, as Reagan was succeeded by the elder Bush in 1989 and he in turn in 1993 by Bill Clinton, intent on demonstrating his distance from the social welfare traditions of the Democratic Party. Had it not been for, among others, the Catholic remnant in the party and among its Representatives, Senators, Governors and Mayors, the group around Clinton might have entered into what was termed "the grand bargain." That was the project of curtailing "entitlements" (itself a phrase with purposively negative implications, as if the recipients of Social Security and Medicare were getting something for nothing) to reduce the projected federal deficit. The matter was pursued with obsessive determination by, among others, a Wall Street figure named Peter Peterson. The boom in the new information technology in the Clinton years brought money to the Treasury and the budget was for the time being balanced—a quite unplanned and unintended undermining of the project typified by Peterson's absurdist rhetoric. Clinton, aided by a Sidney Blumenthal in the final years of his presidency joined Blair, Schröder, the Netherlands Prime Minister Wim Kok, the French Prime Minister Jospin and the Italian D'Alema as well as the Swedish Prime Minister Göran Persson in an informal but ideologically effective Third Way alliance.

They could have spared themselves the frequent self-congratulation that accompanied their meetings and the pronouncements of their intellectual supporters. Their main theme was that by collaborating with the forces of the market they were steering their nations into new but entirely safe territory, in which entrepreneurship and especially technological innovation would bring about a self-sustaining prosperity. They ignored or more accurately underestimated the universality of technology, which enabled the Asian nations to become very effective industrial competitors in a very short time. They did not ignore but surely under estimated the large cultural and social deficits in their own nations—in the availability and quality of education, in civic participation, in the situation of women, perhaps above all in planning.

In the thirties and forties and the fifties the planning functions of government were emphasized by an (unplanned) alliance of technocrats and socialists. The erstwhile follower of Leon Trotsky, James Burnham, in his *The Managerial Revolution* secularized what had been his faith in the seizure of power by a socialist vanguard. Now the vanguard was composed of managers, using science and technology to advance their own interests but serving the larger society precisely by developing canons of productivity which enabled shared increase in wealth. Later, in the US, the Triple Revolution group re-attached these ideas to notions of commonwealth. By the sixties a state socialist variant appeared in the report of the Czech Academy of Sciences on the scientific-technological revolution. Reading between the lines was not difficult: an educated labor force led by administrators and scientists attuned to public needs would in the end make the role of parties monopolizing political power redundant. Sakharov had been treated as heretic for anticipating these themes. In the west, they proliferated in several conceptual languages. In Germany in 1971 the Max Planck Society—the central body of German scholarship across the disciplines—invited Jürgen Habermas as sociologist and social philosopher to join Carl Friedrich von Weizsäcker as physicist and philosopher in a new institute on the future of a technological-scientific civilization. The financing and no little of the impulse came from a government led by the Social Democrats, and the dissolution of the institute occurred just after the party left government. In Italy the Communist Party and the unions responded to the demands for renewal of a younger generation with a thorough-going modernization of the Marxist legacy and a rapprochement of a very explicit sort with Catholic and social democratic thought. (The book by the philosopher Nicola Badaloni on Marxism in Italy in the sixties was the theme of a conference I attended in Rome in 1971.)

I mention this intellectual setting, in which party lines were frequently crossed or ignored, in which social Christians and secular liberals and socialists were united, argumentatively, in the effort to develop new concepts for a modern welfare state, in which the quantitative successes of the New Deal and the post-war European welfare state governments were critically scrutinized for possible openings for a qualitative social doctrine. The Third Way dismissed or minimized much of this inheritance and concentrated on narrowing the focus of government, consigned the emergence of new social movements and initiatives to a grey zone —which it largely ignored as well.

It was against this background that the intellectual and moral steadfastness of my Catholic friends stood out. They were joined, of course, by any number of serious Protestant thinkers (Harvey Cox in the USA, Jürgen Moltmann in Germany, Christopher Lasch with his wide ecumenical vision too). Their works included major treatises and attempts at systematizing our bewilderingly fragmented experience—or more simply what I term presence. They showed up, frequently uninvited, on behalf of any number of causes and groups. Jesse Jackson was there continuously, taking the role of intermediary between a world of Christian conceptions and the daily business of politics. That was also characteristic of many African-American pastors. Barack Obama was savagely attacked for his early discipleship with the Reverend Wright, but he clearly learned something from the Reverend Wright and any number of other pastors in Chicago that was not entirely overlaid by the intelligent circumspection he absorbed at Harvard Law School later. The Jewish moral energies which earlier flowed so unremittingly into American social reform were no longer so conspicuous, even if protest movements and agencies and organizations working for reform had a very large Jewish presence. Some of this was due to the diversionary moral effect of adherence to the state of Israel, some of it to a very different cause, the success of assimilation to the upper middle and commanding segments of American society. I grasped some of these developments intuitively, saw no point in indulging in self-romanticization, reserved large amounts of energy and some insights for myself when they could have been put to public use. In any event, it was a complicated response to an unequivocal moral message. Years ago, in Henry Murray's *Explorations in Personality*, he distinguished between the conflicted inwardness of the Jewish subjects of the Harvard inquiry and the uncomplicated clarity of the Catholic ones. There may have been elements of envy in the construction, as Murray himself struggled with the academic and medical worlds of Harvard in the thirties and forties. For my part, the Catholic moral imprint represented something I sensed I lacked, a certain serenity. I did not then open the chapter of Jewish legacy, knew all along that somehow I had brought something essential from childhood and boyhood into my adult life, my distance from the synagogue notwithstanding.

The other connection to Georgetown was through German studies. The Georgetown University BMW Center for German and European Studies celebrated (October 2015) its twenty-fifth year. It began with a grant from the German government. Father Healy had made the acquaintance of then Chancellor Kohl. The German government provided money for three centers, at Berkeley, Harvard, and Georgetown. Later, the BMW Foundation gave the university a very substantial ten million dollars. The program included an annual visiting professorship occupied by a German scholar. Research support was available to Georgetown faculty, and just as important, a location and program enabled those working on Germany to come together. The first Director was Sam Barnes, a political scientist from Michigan and the second (now finishing his term), Jeffrey Anderson, who came from Brown. One of our stars was and is Angela Stent, who grew up in the UK in a German Jewish family that had fled the Third Reich, studied at Cambridge, and was also a fluent Russian speaker. Like myself, Angela knew many German academics, journalists, politicians.

The major German parties, CDU, CSU, SPD, Free Democrats and later Greens maintained offices in Washington through their foundations, and no week passed without a visitor from Bonn or one of the regional governments or large cities. The Ambassadors frequently groaned as minor German political figures demanded major attention: the diplomats found it difficult to arrange appointments for the visitors with American legislators and governmental officials who considered that they had been hospitable enough. In any event, no one at Georgetown could complain that direct contact with Germany was rare. I would have wished for more trade unionists, writers, social activists—and a larger attention to Germany's own struggles with its past. I followed at a distance the Harvard program at its Center for European Studies and conclude that Georgetown did at least as well in making contemporary Germany come alive.

I occasionally brought figures like then Professor of Theology at Heidelberg Wolfgang Huber and former Minister of Development Erhard Eppler (each President of the National Assembly of the Protestant Church during the turbulence of the German debate on the installation of Euromissiles in the late seventies and early eighties) to the center. On one occasion, I delivered an annual lecture in an endowed series, I spoke on the legacy and actuality of the Social Democratic Party and the socialist project. A retired CIA officer with long experience of Germany was (he thought) complimentary. I always depicted you, he said, as an apologist for the German left, now I see that you are a serious scholar. I responded with surprised thanks.

The CIA officer evoked a real problem. I came to Georgetown well after the conflicts of the sixties had been routinized. In academic jurisprudence, Critical Legal Theory accounted for debate—although some of its antagonists caricatured it by ignoring its obvious descent from Legal Realism. Across the political spectrum, all of us teaching in universities (especially in the humanities and social sciences) had somehow to reconcile our political preferences with our intellectual obligations to colleagues and, above all, students. At Georgetown, nearly every course I taught was elective, and a certain number of my students sought me out precisely because of my political views. They, or their parents, had read my *Nation* articles—or read my books in college. Others regarded signing up for a course with me as an adventure, imagined that they were entering dangerous territory. I was no different from many of my colleagues in the law, and in other disciplines. I made it clear that I had certain moral and social preferences, acknowledged that these accounted for my rhetoric, for my choice of problems, for my interest in certain authors. I told the students that I would appreciate criticism, dissent, opposition—and some were good enough to comply.

Since I could determine my own course matter, I usually chose themes on which I was working. I used the history of American

Progressivism (and, of course, its European counterparts) as a general source—and found that the older I became, the more useful the past. Some of the students were struck by comparing course matter to their parents' (or grandparents') experience. Occasionally, the elder generation visited in class—and were surprised and pleased (and usually not at all reluctant) to be drawn into the discussion. One of the tasks I assigned at the beginning of every course was the writing of an intellectual and social autobiography. That enchanted any number of students who were glad that their individuality was taken into account. Quite a few used the opportunity to do some familial research; quite a few said that it brought the Great Depression, or World War Two, out of film and fiction and history texts and made these periods alive. I found that for my part, I was proprietor of an unending object of curiosity—a boyhood in the Bronx of the New Deal. There I could draw on family history, my father's accounts of his adventures as a public school teacher in the city.

The pedagogic challenges of teaching at Georgetown Law were very different from those at Amherst. In age, class, ethnicity, race and religion the law students were far more diverse. I recall a seminar in which an MA in Classics from Yale sat next to a student who had studied business at the University of Oklahoma—to their mutual profit. The presence of older students, attending after other careers or working full time were of considerable value to those who came directly from undergraduate studies—and to myself. It was often a matter of perspective, of their capacity to recollect their own experience. One episode is imprinted on my memory. In a seminar on "Class, Ethnicity, Race" I had assigned the classic text by W. E. B. Du Bois, *The Souls of Black Folk* and described the authors to the class. A white student asked why Du Bois had a Huguenot name, and I observed that mixed ancestry was extremely common among our African-American fellow citizens. For whatever reason, that surprised the student: "So he was in part white?" One of the other students was a very self-possessed and intelligent government official, an African-American lady of a certain age. "So are we all, young man," was her observation: I am sure that the entire class learned something from it.

My own favorite memory concerns gender. I gave a lecture course on texts in social thought and asked the students to read

Mary Wollstonecraft's *A Vindication of the Rights of Woman*. That evoked a certain discussion, not least on account of her contemporaneity. One student, a former Georgetown undergraduate of considerable amiability and intelligence was, clearly, struggling with rather traditionalist notions of women's roles. He accepted, he said, that there were different cultural and social interpretations of biological difference—but surely, the difference remained critical. Perhaps, I suggested, we should ask Dr. Lucey. She was a NASA astronaut, a scientist, about to depart for six months on the International Space Station. NASA had given her a good deal of television time, the more so as she was a grandmother. She had told the public of a discussion in her primary school, when the children were asked what they envisaged as occupations. She had stated her intention of becoming an explorer, to be derided by one of the boys: "Girls don't become explorers." Now, I said, she was about to travel to the Mir Space Station from Cape Kennedy, but no doubt the boy in question was also flying, presumably, the loan desk at the local bank. Afterward, a student I did not know, who appeared to be a Midwesterner young woman of firm social convictions and correspondingly straightforward appearance stopped on her way out. "Professor, I know that I should not say this, but I could hug you."

I did not expect or receive this sort of response from every student I taught. I do think that I generally succeeded in encouraging them to think about their historical and social assumptions—and in calling their attention to aspects of our academic and intellectual culture they had not encountered in college. My coming to the Law Center did coincide with a general extension of the reach of legal education. Georgetown remains known for the excellence of its clinical programs. Its present teachers, additionally, have a very large range of intellectual competence and interest which goes beyond earlier conceptions of the reach of the law. My contemporaries, when I arrived in 1979, were anything but legal technicians. They were men (and, increasingly, women) of the world at home in our entire culture.

I did a certain amount of collaborative teaching with colleagues. The main campus philosopher Terry Pinkard and I gave a seminar on the philosophy of law at the very beginning of my sojourn at Georgetown. A third of a century later, the very learned Jesuit Father Ladislas Orsy was medically incapacitated halfway through his course on the Philosophy of Law. He had worked through Plato, Aristotle and Aquinas (with a glance at the Old Testament.) Locke, Rousseau, Kant, Marx and the modern Realists remained. Father suggested that I could fill in. After all, I was younger. He was ninety-three and I was only eighty nine and some months. I took on the task at, literally, a day's notice, re-read the assigned parts of the classics—and learned a good deal while doing so.

The first thing I learned was hardly new: our students came from undergraduate education with no shared background in the history of ideas—or the history of anything else. I had experienced that before retiring in 2001, but my 2015 experience suggested that the cultural black hole in which the students lived had increased its retaining powers. A couple of the students had read the classics as undergraduates, others were at first puzzled by the notion that the texts were classics. (I use T.S. Eliot's definition of a classic text as one which alters our reading of the past.) I took an improvised survey. None had read Dostoyevsky's *Notes From Underground* or Freud's *Civilization and its Discontents* or Dos Passos's *U.S.A*. None could identify André Malraux. Nearly all, per contra, had read *1984* but none knew of Orwell's *Homage to Catalonia*. We read Locke, but the British seventeenth century, despite its importance for our own origins, was *terra incognita*. Father Orsy had emphasized the enduring problems of historical and moral existence in his months with the students. They clearly appreciated his insights, and no less clearly struggled to relate these ideas to the world in which they thought they lived.

I was much taken with Father's intention of depicting fundamental philosophies of existence (humans as part of nature) in their effects on political and social ideas. Marx, he insisted, should be interpreted in the light of the doctrines of permanent change he found on the Greek philosophers the sage examined for his doctoral dissertation. Our students' fundamental notions were unreflectively put together—or a set of rigidly conventional ideas which blocked what they feared—a view of the abyss, the systematic indeterminacy of our existence. In the few weeks and sparse hours I had with them, I thought it most helpful to them to give them a sense of the history that enveloped and disturbed the texts. Holmes left the Supreme Court in 1932 in a very different nation than the one in which we now live. The students hardly had a deep grasp of American history in the interval.

I was reminded of a constant theme in my teaching at the Law Center—a marathon to make up ground for both the students and myself. The recurring problems of class culture, gender, psyche, and race I dealt with in seminar after seminar drove me further back into our past, deeper into segments of our national life not covered with ivy. I had a device for encouraging the students to think about a larger context: I asked them to write autobiographies, with attention to their families and their histories. The students usually reported that they had not been asked to do this before and most took it as an interesting challenge and not a professorial idiosyncrasy. Occasionally, I offered encouragement by recounting my own early life. The sketches I received certainly were evidence for the diversity of our student body. I was struck by many accounts of growing up in families themselves diverse. A contrast comes to mind—the rather homogenous milieu in Emilia-Romagna from which my students came when I met them as a Fulbright Professor at Bologna in 1998. Most were offspring of civil servants, entrepreneurs, proprietors of the small firms which had made the area one of the wealthiest in Europe. There, the autobiographies dealt with migration to the city from the countryside in earlier generations, with political affiliation across the generations (not least, in the Communist Party), with reminiscences of grandparental enlistment in the resistance to Fascism and German occupation. A consistent secularism marked many of these younger Europeans. They were not anti-clerical, took the Catholic Church and its works, good, bad, indifferent for granted—again a contrast with the wide spectrum of religious choice by our students.

I greatly enjoyed the opportunities I had for teaching with colleagues. One venture brought me onto entirely new territory. Georgetown had a large clinical program in which students could gain direct experience of legal practice. Philip Schrag gave a course on representing claimants before the administrative tribunals of Social Security and Small Claims Court. His very effective pedagogical approach was entirely non-directive, and from the beginning of the course students had to take charge of every aspect of the process. In one rehearsal for an actual hearing, I played a very aggressive lawyer and was extremely pleased when Phil suggested that I could have become a useful member of the Bar.

I taught on the Philosophy of Law with Terry Pinkard and Sherman Cohn, gave a seminar in interpretation with Mark Tushnet, joined Judith Areen and an historian in a seminar on the family, and had an unusual colleagueship with Warren Schwartz in a course we termed "Theories of Justice." Warren and I had similar social backgrounds—but disagreed on nearly everything about social order. Warren was an enthusiastic and skilled proponent of the Economic Theory of the Law, then (in the very early eighties) the contentious intellectual sibling of Critical Legal Theory. Neither was as textured, as close to the actual working of legal institutions as earlier streams of thought grouped in the movement of Legal Realism. The Economic Theory of Law (Warren induced me to read Posner) struck me as reductionist and shallow, Critical Legal Theory a re-edition of the social criticism of Progressivism. I do recollect one episode from the seminar with Warren. We met at eleven and he turned up one day in an elegiac mood. He explained to the class that, not for the first time, he was very glad to have chosen a career as a teacher. One could drive in after rush hour, one worked on interesting matters, the vacations were long. "Beats working" was his conclusion. Unfortunately, he had chosen the day on which a tuition rise was announced: the students responded accordingly.

One of the most rewarding pedagogic experiences I owe to Michael Seidman. He and others had devised a different sort of introductory legal curriculum for the first year. It combined a classic introduction to law with philosophical and social analysis. I took responsibility for a section in the course on justice. The self-selected students in what was termed the new curriculum were committed to continuing, at law school, the inquiries into the humanities and social sciences they had known at college.

The new curriculum was introduced some years after I had been host, in my first year at the Law Center, to a conference on legal and undergraduate education. I convinced my Amherst colleague Ben DeMott and Christopher Lasch to come, as well as Charles Stevens, the British barrister who taught at Yale and then became President of Haverford College. Michael Dirda, *The Washington Post's* literary columnist, was also there, as well as Father Healy. We considered the disjunction between the way the world was represented in undergraduate curricula and the rhetoric and ritual of legal education. Life is also a matter of the accumulation of regrets, and I regret that I did not follow the event, attended by quite a few of Law Center faculty, with soundings at the main campus on joining the Law Center in a program which would prepare undergraduates for legal studies by directing them to historical and philosophical courses they would find useful. I'll console myself with the thought that I was of use to the Law Center by my presence. I did serve on a long-term planning committee. Perhaps it can be summed up by noting that my presence reinforced a larger change. More of the younger Law Center teachers came with degrees in other fields of the social sciences as well as their legal ones. More importantly still, they (and their seniors) were self-conscious citizens of a wide republic of learning as well as participants in the extremely complex and demanding tasks of the law.

What, precisely, did I teach when on my own? I did one lecture course which attracted some forty students when I first gave it and then repeated it. It was textual: we read classics of social thought in chronological order, from Rousseau to Freud. Some of the students had studied political philosophy as undergraduates, others were interested in matter they had not encountered. Upon talking to the newcomers to the history of social thought, I found that perplexity about contemporary issues of social justice, and about the larger movement of society, impelled them to join me in looking at our recent past. For myself, it was also a return to beginnings—to ideas and texts I had begun to consider in college and at graduate school. Indeed, I'd draw a line from the readings I did as a high school student stimulated by our history teachers to the books we taught in General Education at Harvard to the historical sensibility of the British scholars I met in the UK. I attribute large pedagogic gifts to my colleagues teaching in the several fields of the law. Somehow, they made matters phrased in the rhetoric and using the techniques of legal analysis evoke larger intellectual perspectives among their students.

Mostly, however, I taught seminars of about twenty students. In selecting reading, I took on some texts and themes I was unfamiliar with—or knew only in a very general way. There was no requirement that the pleasures (and difficulties) of intellectual travel be reserved for student tourists. There were some problems to which I recurred during my entire twenty-two years at the Law Center. The social role and moral responsibility of the educated was one, the American class system another, the varieties of American religious life a third. Of course, I brought in Europe, but there was a difficulty. Most American scholars studying the Old World wrote for each other and it was often difficult to find texts for intelligent readers with large curiosity and little knowledge. On the Holocaust and Fascism and Nazism, as well as on Communism and its history, there was much to choose from. On the postwar welfare states of Western Europe there was a large scholarly literature but few general texts. Looking back, I have to acknowledge a sin of omission. I could have used novels (and films) to good effect. Students whose grandparents had experienced the Great Depression might have understood more had they read Dos Passos, Victor Serge on *The Case of Comrade Tulayev* might have made the Soviet Revolution and its failure easier to understand, and *The Tin Drum* answered some of the questions of those perplexed by Nazism.

Those who took my seminars were self-selected, some had a considerable amount of experience after college—but all had to be urged to trust that most uncertain, often deceptive and yet indispensable human attribute, the imagination. As we moved from electronic pre-history to the age of internet, another problem became salient. My course reading lists usually consisted of books, excerpts from books or other printed texts. Some students preferred to do research for their term papers by using the internet rather than the texts I suggested as beginning points for their research. I did not give examinations, but asked the students to do seminar papers on themes they selected which required a preliminary discussion with me. That gave me a welcome opportunity to learn more about them, insofar as they wished to talk I was struck by the very disparate and large spectrum of motives which had led them to legal studies, and the decidedly varied career objectives they had, in legal practice, government, or the private and non-profit sectors.

I was at the Law Center long enough to meet very different cultural and political cohorts. Identifying the ways in which my students situated themselves in history was not simple, the more so as their ages varied. When I arrived in 1979, the turbulence of the late sixties and early seventies were not quite faded memories—and in any event, the younger students had studied with veterans of the protest movements. Norman Mailer once observed that the character of a president is what shapes the culture of his period in office. That was a characteristically dogmatic pronouncement by our national sage—but like most of his obiter dicta, true. The Reagan years brought in students with very different mind sets, whatever their views of the President and his projects. Few thought of changing the world in major ways, quite a few had specific social problems in mind. Civil rights, the environment, criminal justice reform, the rights of children and women, were recurrent foci of student interest. A considerable number had been abroad for longer periods, some as offspring of American business, diplomatic and military families, some in the Peace Corps, others on their own. The beginnings of human rights jurisprudence attracted some. I had quite a few students from the newer Asian and Latino immigrant groups—and no small number who had come from very different nations to study with us for a year or two before returning.

Of course, the elective status of my courses skewed the distribution of cultural and political profiles among my students. There were quite a few, however, who if determinedly conventional, took my courses for relief from the pursuit of credentials or because they had heard that they promised interesting hours. I think that I succeeded in making them feel welcome. About some, I was reminded of Freud's remark on the contrast between the bright and spontaneous spirits of young children and the dreary ordinariness of so many adults. On the way to success, many of our students were ironing a good deal of spontaneity, and perhaps creativity, out of their souls. It is easy enough for me to have wished something else for them. A university teacher's career offers, still, an astonishing range of freedoms compared with most other occupations—as novels about the academy have testified for generations. Hamlet's injunction to Horatio, that there were more things under heaven and earth than dreamed of in his philosophy, was my pedagogic motto. When I encounter former students, I often have the impression that they profited from it.

Professors at the Law Center were provided with research assistants, students who were at their disposition for fifteen hours of work a week. I had a very helpful and interesting succession of assistants with a variety of academic and intellectual and social backgrounds. They were very talented men and women, and I am sorry that I did not stay in touch with more of them. That is an aspect of a larger complex of nostalgia about my Georgetown years. I wish, equally, that I had spent more time, paid more attention, to my students. I was quite determined about what I had to transmit to them—a trait I acquired, almost certainly, from the New York intellectuals of an older generation, as my friends Clement Greenberg and William Phillips. If they had doubts, they were very good at concealing these: the frontier of western culture, as they understood it, was their own front doors—and their most recent articles had to be thought of as defining the situation for those in search of history. Put in another way, I was so focused on imparting what I thought of as the real story that my listening capacity was underused. I do not think that I derived much of this from my teaching apprenticeships at Harvard and in the United Kingdom. There, one thought less of students and more of one's colleagues—even or above all when ruling one's seminar room with no apparent challenges to one's sovereignty. Somehow, in a day or less one's colleagues would know what one had said.

My Georgetown colleagues were under no obligation to listen to my anecdotes, cultural and political musings, high-toned gossip. They were busy constructing their own universes. We recognized, however, the necessity of sharing whatever of space and time bounded our small part of existence on New Jersey Avenue. I listened to them—and was much the better for it. I was particularly struck by their capacity for making sense of the chaotic discontinuity of our national life by explicating paradigmatic cases. Teachers of law were often thought of as rigorous, even obsessive, chroniclers of the most routine sequences of life. In fact, in unwritten footnotes to exceedingly well-footnoted law review articles, many employ a good novelist's sense of persons, places and time. That is why a visit I arranged at the beginning of my appointment by Clifford Geertz was considered significant and why a later visit by Peter Brooks turned into a continuing connection between Peter and the Law Center.

I wish that I had been more aware of, and therefore more able to use, the quite profound undercurrents of lived jurisprudence. Their effect on my thought, teaching, writing, was considerable—if largely implicit. That continued a pattern I had set much earlier. I moved through very different cultures, within and without the United States, keeping my distance, sometimes ironically, sometimes respectfully—and when I joined, the attachment inevitably ran its course without my agonizing over the ensuing breaks and ruptures. Somewhat uncertainly, I would liken my learning experience at the Law Center to my apprenticeship in Great Britain. It was only afterward that I realized how much I had acquired—and what, specifically, it was. Of course, this was inner price I paid for an obdurate kind of independence. I have titled this memoir, *From The Bronx to Oxford—And Not Quite Back*. I now see, years after the choice of title, that in major and positive ways I did not leave the Bronx—or, rather, that I still am the bookish child who imagined his way into other worlds.

In one of those worlds, the academy, I learned rather belatedly that leadership counts for a great deal. When I was at Williams, the President, James Phinney Baxter III, was a born insider, old but not rich New England family, very attentive to nuances of status and the depths and eddies of reigning opinion in the partially public, partially restricted culture shared by the institutions of learning and those of power. Yet he was ferociously attached to the liberal ideals of higher education and insisted—through the Cold War—on academic freedom at his college. At Harvard, I was impressed by the commitment to intellectual independence and quality of the historian, David Owen, who chaired the Committee on General Education and kept avaricious university politicians at a distance. At the LSE, the Director, Sir Alexander Carr-Saunders, made it clear that nothing was as much contemporary use as what I would term administered liberalism, with himself as the administrator. In a bleak and constricted intellectual climate he kept a decent minimum of freedom alive—and the LSE well ahead of the ancient universities in relevance. At Oxford, per contra, the Warden of my college, Norman Chester, was a son of Manchester who did not see the point of overmuch subtlety. He repeatedly mastered the refined intriguers of university committees by presenting them with *faits accom-*

pli, stacked sub-committees, and threats of carrying business into hours reserved for sherry and small talk. He ran the college, aided by a band of acolytes, in the same way. I was there in the years of nuclear deterrence, and conclude in retrospect that the Warden must have learned a good deal from the Cold War strategists. Finally, at Amherst, I had the very contrasting experience of two presidents. The first, Calvin Plimpton, was a physician who treated the institution as a place for the cure of souls. Those inclined to disruption found that their causes were treated as recognized and indeed honored affiliations. Somehow, however, they ended up accepting the good doctor's cures, often disguised as concessions to the patients' wishes. I have already written the sad story of his professorial successor's incumbency. It coincided with the presidency, in France, of Giscard d'Estaing. M. le President was rumored to be consulting a psychiatrist. The weekly *Le Canard Enchaîné* published a cartoon showing the president on the couch, telling his physician, "Docteur, j'ai eu un cauchemar. J'ai rêvé que j'étais Président de la République." Bill Ward was an excellent colleague and friend, but his large talents were different from those required by the presidency of a small college with a very independent faculty.

Our Deans offered interesting contrasts in background and personal approach, but the three I served with had in common a very acute understanding of faculty sensibility, near perfect judgment as to the timing of their own interventions in debates on institutional policy, and an amused appreciation of human weakness not invariably kept to themselves. Each could draw upon a personal history well matched to the period in which he or she led the institution to wider fields. David McCarthy took his law degrees at Georgetown after undergraduate studies at the Jesuit university Fairfield in his native Connecticut. He was attuned to the inevitable reticence of the traditionalists on faculty and among alumni to the substance and rapidity of changes they had not envisaged. His successor, Robert Pitofsky, was not much younger—but represented a wider sort of professionalism in legal education and the practice of law itself. Chairman of the Federal Trade Commission under President Clinton, when he returned to the Law faculty he worked with the iconic Washington law firm, Arnold and Porter, as Counsel. I admired in Bob his ability to connect the rigors of legal scholarship with the demands of practice in a politically charged setting. It was a tribute to his own breadth that in his Deanship, the faculty's expansion into new areas of inter-disciplinary inquiry and public engagement continued. His successor was Judith Areen. She had been at Yale Law School in one of its most intellectually innovative periods, had indeed studied with Anna Freud. As Georgetown Law Center's first woman Dean, she was of course sensitive to the issues of gender, ethnicity, race. I taught a seminar with her on the American family and family law, historically viewed, and later offered help (mainly bibliographical, in an old fashioned way) when she worked on the early Protestantism and the family. I was continuously impressed by her capacity to encourage others to take long intellectual strides. As the Law Center expanded, academic and professional fragmentation was a danger. Judith brought her own considerable resources of curiosity and openness to make sure that we understood ourselves as sharing a large, if complex, pedagogic vision.

Behind every successful Dean there is a supportive President. My own debt to my friend Timothy Healy is immeasurable. I could make a token payment of recognition by filling pages with Healy anecdotes, and his priceless sayings. When I came to Georgetown, Tim told me that he had instructed his Vice Presidents not to come to him with problems unless they also brought solutions. With what results, I asked. Tim's reply was unhesitant: he did not see very much of them. I especially liked his remark at our celebratory dinner after he had appointed me to a University Professorship: "Now Norman, I have had to read your illusory thoughts (he used somewhat stronger language) on academic democracy for some time. Now is the time admit it—if I had relied on our university tenure committee, you would not have had the job, you are too smart for them." I was not the only person on faculty to profit from his humor, vast enjoyment of human possibility, and luminous intellectual power. We were each New Yorkers who had come to admire the British. I think that our shared debt to our native city and its culture was primary: I regretted that my father did not live long enough to meet Tim as they, too, would have found common ground, very possibly in comparing notes on teaching in New York high schools.

It would be ungracious to conclude without mentioning my appreciation of Tim's successors, first Father Leo O'Donovan and then John DeGioia, who actually took a seminar with me when studying for his degrees in Law and Philosophy. Jack DeGioia worked for years with Tim, which meant that we thought of ourselves as part of a family. In the coldness and hardness of much of life, that is an aspect of Georgetown that makes me grateful to belong. Somehow, despite its concentration on mastering a very perplexing and often unforgiving world, Georgetown has been a home to many of us.

18

The End of a Century

IN THE TWENTY-FIRST CENTURY, I think of myself as a stranger from very far away. Passing ninety I am aware of the obvious, that my time has come and gone. When I dealt with themes like alienation, about which I taught and wrote, I was on familiar ground—at home in imagined homelessness. It is difficult, now, to disentangle my need for a decent minimum of attention to these matters from my carefully constructed defenses against being overwhelmed. What did my pre-occupation with Germany mean if not a search for both explanation of its crimes and relief at its redemption? My initial outer and inner self-exile from the United States (after I had at Harvard climbed several rungs of the ladder to the top) changed into a decidedly non-ironic patriotism, expressed as a question: who else had done better? Modernism, in its American form, had I thought freed me—or, at least, given me a place. It took some years into this century and into my eighties for me to realize that I had entered into a bargain with an implacable creditor who disregarded my impeccable record of punctual payment. I had to take out a new mortgage in a dwelling of strange dimensions, with indifferent neighbors, and no available transportation to any place I knew. I was not making a new beginning, I was marooned in historical space.

My sense of bewildered disconnectedness is not all-consuming. There are blessed moments of relief, often when I am asked about the past. I am deemed by others capable of establishing continuities they are searching for, or at least recalling matters they think important but which they find baffling. The most apt sporting analogy is of the veteran quarterback who is third in rotation, grateful that he is not on the practice squad, and requiring no special instructions when sent into the game. A rather convincing analogy, but now we learn that an entire generation of retired players has reason to fear for its health. My inner travail is not a matter of analogy, more or less appropriate, but of real existence. I'll return to the problem at the end: there is more to write about how I got to the end of the last century and began this one.

Teaching at Yale in 1972-3, I had two visiting Spanish scholars in a seminar on the politics of industrial society. One was Miguel Beltran and the other Julian Santamaria. Both returned to Spain to make distinguished careers. Julian was one of the authors, after the end of the Franco regime, of the new constitution that in 1978 provided restored Spanish democracy with an institutional framework. He returned to the US in 1986 as Ambassador. He brought with him as media advisor Helga Diekhoff Soto, and the two of them introduced me to the new Spain. I knew Felipe González, who became Prime Minister in 1982 and remained in office until 1996, but had experienced the Spanish transition from afar. Julian and Helga introduced me to a Spain very different from the one I had known from reading about the Civil War and its aftermath, the Franco dictatorship, as well as its origins in a very distinctive past. Spain had had a severe Counter-Reformation, but no Reformation, a stringently anti-modern and illiberal response to the Enlightenment and its western European derivatives but a tormented reception of western European ideas.

Helga was born in Kiel in Germany in 1940, had memories of bombing attacks and of the serial traumas of the immediate post war period. Her father was away in the German army and did not return to the family after the war. Her mother moved with Helga and her brother to the vicinity of Bremerhaven. Families in her restricted economic circumstances did not send their children to academic high schools, much less universities. Helga studied to become a commercial secretary, learned English and went to Spain in 1960 to learn Spanish. The rhythms of Spanish life enchanted her, despite her aversion to the Franco dictatorship. She married, had two sons, and with her educated husband Jorge (a successful businessman) plunged into the cultural and political turbulence of the Spanish sixties. The aging Franco's denunciations of Communists

Helga and I at Venice's Caffè Florian.

and Freemasons became ever shriller as much of the nation, led by a singular alliance of older and younger democrats, secular modernists and social Catholics, and a newly self-conscious generation of women, Europeanized itself. The cultural certainties of Spanish fascism were clung to by an aging and pious bourgeoisie, the rest of the nation lived as if the regime had the tedious irrelevance of aging relatives insisting on authority the young refused to accept. There were conflicts enough, and repressive violence as protest increasingly took to the streets. Younger (and some reflective older) figures in the regime began negotiations for the restoration of democracy years before Franco's death in 1975.

Christopher Mayer, a senior British diplomat, told me that his first posting was to Madrid in the early seventies. The Ambassador (Christopher's description placed him squarely between the covers of a novel by Waugh) instructed him that it was his task to follow an opposition he, the Ambassador, scoffed at. "Bunch of chaps talking at a restaurant, nothing to it." Christopher asked about the succession: Franco was no longer young. "They will find someone." Christopher came to know González, Polanco who later founded *El País*, the Falangist youth leader Adolfo Suarez who was a friend of the future King and later his reformist Prime Minister, and the writers of the new Constitution, as they negotiated a post-Franco settlement before the Generalissimo's death. I asked Helga about the months in which Franco was known to be mortally ill: "What you need to know is that it was impossible, in all of Spain, to buy a bottle of Champagne."

Listening to Helga and her friends, I learned that the post-Franco transition had begun well before the Generalissimo was buried alongside the Falangist dead of the Civil War. Spanish young women of the bourgeoisie had long ceased to marry upon leaving convent schools run by devout nuns. They went to universities and pursued careers. (Some of the nuns were adherents of Vatican II and aligned themselves with churchmen who found the regime an embarrassment and an offense.) The Falangists thought to contain the possibility of revolution in their own households by enlisting women in a special organization. It was promptly taken over by women antagonists of the sclerotic patriarchalism of traditionalist Spain. The regime sought to control an increasingly restive working class, aware of its power as Spain modernized its economy. Many workers returned from prolonged stays in France and Germany and saw themselves as, potentially, citizens as well as workers. The Workers' Commissions were the regime's device for allowing the workers representation while denying them classical trade unions. The opposition, Communists and Socialists, took command of the Commissions. In Franco's last years, the ruling party found that its censors were powerless to stop the torrent of books and film bringing ideas of an open culture from the rest of Europe. Latin America, and the US. Particularly in urban Spain, the regime was culturally defeated before Franco's death.

González assumed leadership of the Socialist Party, its headquarters in Toulouse. He moved it to Spain, but spent only one night in prison. The political police was in continual conflict with the groups organizing demonstrations—but the negotiations for a different Spain were unimpeded. I learned about this period, in which light and shadow alternated vertiginously, from Helga. She was press officer of the Socialist Party, registered as a business consulting firm. Press conferences were often held in the passenger terminal at the airport in Madrid, where police intervention would be limited. When Franco died in 1975, there followed a period of great turbulence and a good deal of violent repression and mass protest. In the end, elections were held in 1977 and civic and political stability achieved. The idea of normalcy in democratic politics is very imprecise and whatever its Spanish version was, a great rupture occurred in 1981 when groups in the armed forces attempted a *coup d'état* to terminate parliamentary rule. Helga was in the Parliament when it was seized by the national police, managed to phone the offices of the party in Madrid, later found her name on a list of persons pre-sentenced to be killed. The king, the permanent officials of the ministries, ended the episode in hours: it marked public consciousness for years thereafter. American forces in Spain were, reportedly, instructed before the occupation of Parliament to remain on their bases that day. Then Secretary of State Haig issued a statement to the effect that the matter was an internal Spanish one. In that, of course, he was correct.

I collected accounts of those years from Helga and her friends a decade afterward. I had no extensive knowledge of Spain, even if for me the Civil War was an unforgettable event. I learned a great deal from the experience of the generations which reconstructed Spain. They comprised different age cohorts, returned Republican exiles and those who had worked with the regime as well as those who had opposed it. The last decades of the regime involved increasing cultural integration with western Europe as well as more open dissidence, some of it within the Falangist movement and government, and disorganized, even incoherent, but increasingly pervasive resistance. The most relevant frame of reference was the most difficult one, the history of modern Spain itself, with its ethnic and regional peculiarities, its relations to Europe, Latin America, North Africa, its archaic and modern Catholicism and militant secularism. Not least, it was a matter of life histories, of persons struggling for self-definition by seeking to create a new public sphere.

Helga, her sons, her contemporaries in the Socialist Party, her former husband and his quite conservative family, were guides on my trip into Spanish life. She was at the center of a group of engaged and independent women who were proud of their cultural conquests and quite vocal about them. Apart from her comrades in the leadership of the party (when Helga returned to Spain she became press spokeswoman of the Socialist Parliamentary group before returning to her original post in charge of media for the entire party), there were ordinary members and voters. Helga was a familiar visage in Spain, and in cafes, restaurants, shops, she was greeted by many with a mixture of affection and familiarity, and as promptly called to account for the party's failings. I particularly liked the proprietor of a wine shop in her village on the northern outskirts of the city, whose favorite vintages were political anecdotes. Spain, like Italy and France, had a restaurant culture that could be termed familial. Owners and waiters treated their guests as friends, but also as fortunate beneficiaries of their hospitality: there was a certain distance dictated by their clear mastery of the rituals of their art and a meal in the circumstances was both formal and familiar, even a privilege. Some restaurants were, along with some cafes, cultural monuments and political gathering places. El Espejo, a restaurant in Madrid with belle époque decor, was a meeting ground across political boundaries. I went one evening with Helga and Joaquín Almunia, newly elected leader of the Socialist Party after González. We were seated next to a group of senior citizens who had obviously walked over from Salamanca, a Madrid neighborhood not all of whose residents were at home in the new Spain. Indeed, they looked like figures in a film about the Spanish fifties. They nodded, stiffly, to Joaquín and opened no conversation. "Not our voters," he declared.

Where I did find openness was at *El País*. I wrote occasionally for its opinion pages in the early nineties. Then the American Ambassador to Spain, Professor Richard Gardner of Columbia University Law School, did me an unintended favor. Gardner had been Ambassador to Italy in the Carter government. Those were difficult years in the nation, with a certain amount of terror by the Red Brigades — which may or may not have been authentically Red but certainly attempted the destabilization of Italian politics. Friends across the political spectrum in Italy, including some at the Vatican) and Germans with access to their own intelligence sources were unanimous: not everything was as was as it seemed to be. On a visit to Italy I was interviewed by the weekly *Panorama*, and asked about the CIA in Italy, I replied that I had no privileged information and that anything was possible. An angered Gardner summoned me to the Embassy to tell me that I had endangered his life. Not so many years later, at an event at the Italian Embassy in Washington after he had returned to his Columbia chair, he returned to the attack—surprising, as I recall it, our fellow guest Governor Mario Cuomo—and the Ambassador himself. Gardner had gone to Harvard, was a former Rhodes Scholar, had married into the Italian Jewish elite, and had a very successful public career—yet he behaved without what is conventionally termed "class." Indeed, the next day he wrote to the President of Georgetown expressing surprise that I was on the faculty. Father Healy showed me the letter and his own expressively understated reply, to the effect that the CIA was to blame for the frequency with which it was suspected of malfeasance, and, thanking our colleague for his interest in Georgetown's appointments policy.

Gardner was Clinton's Ambassador to Spain and so could read my columns in *El País*. He wrote to the editors, describing me as a person of unreliability and no standing in the US, and contravening their description of myself as a former consultant to the National Security Council. Gardner sent me a copy of the letter. I sent no reply but did send *El País* an item of correspondence from the NSC which confirmed the connection. *El País* responded by suggesting that we make my contributions more frequent. These continued quite regularly until 2010. Amongst other benefits, I became friendly with the opinion page editor, the very intelligent Catalan, Lluís Bassets. *El País* was widely read in Latin America, and my columns were sometimes republished by *La Stampa* and *Le Monde* as well as elsewhere in Europe. They also produced a number of invitations to conferences in Spain and elsewhere in Europe. I retained my ties to France, Germany, Italy, the UK, appreciated the intellectual subtlety and personal warmth of my new Spanish friends.

Two occasions at the summer school of the Madrid university, Complutense, remain in memory. Helga and I organized a conference on the US in 1991, persuaded Donna Shalala, then Chancellor of the Madison campus of the University of Wisconsin, Orlando Patterson of Harvard, and Robert and Peggy Boyers, the editors of the cultural political journal *Salmagundi*, as well as Walter Russell Mead to come. The Spaniards who drove out to El Escorial for the sessions declared that they were rewarded by views of our culture and society they had not encountered. A decade later, the Summer School organized a conference on the Third Way, and Felipe González and Anthony Giddens came. I recall Giddens talking at length of the necessity of socialists respecting the workings of the market: it was before 2008. González was his usual self, combining a larger vision of progress with an artisanal attention to political detail. Tony, like many academics seeking to escape the pale cast of thought, joined strategy and tactics, portrayed our moment as though it would last indefinitely. González, an intellectual with a quite extraordinary experience, was more tentative, more aware of the possibility of being surprised. González delivered the eulogy at Willy Brandt's funeral, a role assigned by Willy, and the Austrian Socialists asked him to speak when they celebrated the one hundredth anniversary of Bruno Kreisky's birth. Kreisky had a cottage on Majorca, where he regularly saw another summer visitor, King Juan Carlos. Brandt and Kreisky each had narrowly escaped Nazi concentration camps, and they clearly saw in González a member of the next generation who was not only an heir to socialism but someone who could rejuvenate it. Felipe himself thought his major accomplishment as Prime Minister from 1982 to 1996 the consolidation of Spanish parliamentary democracy and the integration of Spain in Europe. He was beset by the violent nationalism of a small party of Basques, by the Catalan insistence on autonomy, by the refusal of a substantial segment of Spanish Catholicism to accept that a Spanish majority sought cultural pluralism. He was opposed within his own party by those dissatisfied with his compromises with European and Spanish capital.

Felipe, who had obdurately led the party away from self-depiction as Marxist before winning the 1982 election, could have defended himself by a Marxist argument. A Spanish path to socialism would presuppose a very large development of the nation's productive forces, and that was possible only by accepting the European mixed economy—regulated-capitalism and the welfare state—for the indefinite future. Meanwhile, the Socialists had increased social benefits directly and its larger projects (from superhighways and high-speed trains to increased investment in education and health care) ended some of Spain's backwardness. Many citizens and plenty of Socialist voters were dubious about Spain joining NATO, but responded in a referendum to the argument that membership gave Spain a voice and a vote in decisions which would otherwise be taken without it. NATO membership also provided for the education of a new officer corps, one less likely to be tempted by the armed forces' self-assigned role in the past as authoritarian guardian of the entire national legacy.

I added Spain, then, to the nations I learned to know in a familial way—with actual family (daughters and grandson) in Germany and later France, and friends who were close. The Spanish transition to democracy and cultural freedom was quite unlike that in Germany and Italy since for some decades it entailed deliberate restraint in dealing with the past. No one term is accurate in describing the circumspection with which Civil War and Franco's regime were treated. A younger Spanish generation was, initially, enlisted in an organized truce. Integration in Europe and a larger world was a priority, the immediate Spanish past left to mainly foreign historians. Uncomfortable truths were, however, voiced by the disconsolate—families, for instance, whose older members had disappeared in Civil War and subsequent repression. I was asked, with increasing frequency, to recount my memories of the impact of the Civil War on the United States, to explain why there was so little resistance to the incorporation of the Franco regime in the western alliance. Occasionally, the near total lack of self-criticism of our officialdom provided an opportunity to make a point. Visiting Spain as Secretary of State, Condoleezza Rice at a joint press conference with her Spanish colleague rebuked him for having traveled to Havana and met with Castro, but not with the Cuban dissidents. *El País* published a letter from me the next day, explaining that as a senior citizen I appeared to be suffering from memory loss, and that I would welcome being reminded of the name of the US Secretary of State who had visited Franco in Madrid and then met with antagonists of Spanish fascism.

Helga passed away in 2007. She had retired from the Socialist Party but was called upon by a citizens' group concerned with environment and human rights (in effect a Spanish Green movement)

With Helga Soto at Wellfleet.

to take on major responsibilities. Hers was an exceptional European journey—at one point the German Social Democrats considered asking her to return to become their press officer—and a tribute to both her Spanish comrades and the larger public which treated her as one of their own. I kept my valued ties to Spain. When I presented the book I wrote in the nineties, *After Progress*, at the Politics and Prose bookstore in 2001, the Spanish Ambassador agreed to serve as commentator, a gracious gesture from a representative of a Spanish government formed by the Popular Party and not my Socialist friends.

My relations with *El País* changed abruptly in 2010. The holding company which owned the newspaper was in financial difficulty, and the American investor Nicolas Berggruen came to the rescue with a large investment. Journalists of long years of service, often from the inception of the newspaper in 1976, were dismissed with miserable compensation. Nothing was said to me, but my articles, submitted in the usual way and at the usual intervals, were not published. I did notice a new American contributor, a Mr. David Harris, Executive Director of the American Jewish Committee, and a proponent of the Israel government's views of the world. Enough said.

The nineties and the years thereafter, however, were years in which I published continuously in Europe. Reviewing the German edition of my book in *Die Zeit*, Werner Perger detected—correctly—a note of nostalgia for the New Deal. The nostalgia in many of my articles, and in the larger book, was less for the New Deal than for its transatlantic legacy. I've referred to the defensiveness of the groups in the Democratic Party to which I was and am close—the stubborn refusal of many to accept reductions in the welfare state, diminish governmental functions as regulator and investor, exchange ideas of social solidarity for a fictive society of opportunity to which an increasingly undisguised social Darwinism returned. In other philosophical accents and languages, the same processes were at work in Europe. The Green movement and the Green parties seized newness from the socialists and social democrats, were especially intransigent on cultural and social issues. Their most effective formation, the German Greens, took only a decade and a half from initially entering the German parliament in 1983 to join a government in 1998. The custody of the earth, questions of gender, extended and intensified ideas of human rights, were not the property of one political sensibility. Reflective conservatives, especially social Christians, responded to what began as insurgency on the left by reconsidering their own response to change.

The book I wrote in the nineties, *After Progress*, did not live up to its title. I was right to point out that the proponents of the Third Way, subtly and less so, avoided facing the question of choice of society, of the development of new forms of sociability, of new sequences of career, of amplifying choice in (indeed, of new forms of choice) in life history. As intelligent a figure as Blair, politically astute ones (Clinton, Schröder, Wok), serious intellectuals (Jospin), said or made it clear in other ways that they supposed that major currents in modern culture and society would provide models of conduct, values, alternatives—from which citizens could construct their own life worlds. Quite apart from the inherited and new conflicts of modern culture, I was skeptical that there was that amount of choice. The familiar lessons of those who described the attack on moral autonomy constituted by mass culture still bothered me.

I was unconvinced that the citizens of our democracies were as sovereign as the younger post-socialists thought. It was decidedly premature to reduce the functions of politics, to declare that older visions were out of date, that the very idea of visionary politics was something grand-paternal and grand-maternal, or represented nostalgia for a past well behind us. I read some Catholic, Jewish, Protestant theology in those years, was struck by the fact that the theologians had not ceased to worry.

In 1998 I spent three months in Bologna as a Fulbright Professor of American Studies. It was the legendary city of the civic triumph of the Italian Communist Party (I recollect Midge Decter telling me in the seventies that she was tired of hearing about Bologna). My friends in Rome referred me to a few older comrades, but the city was run by technocrats in alliance with local capital. A group of Catholic thinkers who edited the journal *Il Regno* were glad to talk with me. "Believe us, Professore, we are the only ones left in the city who worry about the moral problems of capitalism."

Italy in the late eighties and nineties had something to teach us, a disturbing lesson. The Italian Communist Party was conspicuous in the last decades of the Cold War for taking its distance from the Soviet Union. Forming municipal and regional governments, usually with the Socialist Party, it was an explicit partner of the Christian Democratic Party in national and international affairs. There were no Communist ministers, but in every other respect (including the presence of Communists in high offices in justice and state administration) it had a major role in governance. What, however, was the society it shared in governing? The cultural and socio-economic division between north and south did not lessen. The south, recipient of first Italian and then European funds for development, evolved its singular fusion of state capitalism with small enterprise. Corruption was not an alternative economy, it was essential to the economy itself. A determined corps of honest civil servants and magistrates could not break the system: they constituted the actual opposition. In the north, the unions represented the labor force, in the south they were appreciably weaker. In a quite open bargain, north and south functioned as connected but distinct societies. The Communists, their post-Communist successor parties, and their allies and interlocutors in the financial, industrial and technocratic elite (often committed social Catholics) were resigned to the division of Italy—and worked with others to keep the north from fusing with the south.

The north Italian social model entailed a bargain between unions and employers, large-scale capital and small, familial enterprise, a large state and a regulated market. Churches and parties had deep networks of local associations, independent print media expressed civic consciousness in regions and nationally, state television cultivated a decent minimum of pluralism. On a map extending from north to south, this modern and secular society was concentrated in ever-fewer cities and regions south of Rome, to change to a different system on a line drawn from Naples eastward. That was familistic in a patriarchal manner—obdurately local—but delivering votes and political influence as well as market shares to the northern parties. National unity in Italy rested on a bargain which implied a troubled conscience: the north had to look the other way. Film directors, novelists, some television and print journalists did not. Neither did a segment of the magistracy and police—and some courageous figures paid for their sense of duty with their lives.

Visiting Professorships at Bari in 1997 and Bologna in 1998 brought Italy's very different regionalisms alive. At Bari, the senior permanent official of the region accompanied me on a visit to the old city—with two police officers behind. None of the officials I met in Bologna thought that a visitor needed protection in their city. What I did learn in those years was quite a lot. The students at Bari were looking forward to joining the Italian civil service, those at Bologna had the European Commission in mind and told me that if they did not get to Bruxelles, they would not work for the Italian state but for their family's businesses. I also spent some months in 1997 at the Alcide De Gasperi Foundation in Rome, close to the Christian Democrats and their allies in the Italian Church. Pope John Paul II had a larger world in view, which allowed the conflicting groups in the Italian church a certain openness about their differences. When I visited the Archbishop of Milan, Cardinal Carlo Maria Martini, who had been sent there by the Pope from his post as Rector of the Jesuit university in Rome, the Pontifical Gregorian, he thanked me for coming from Bologna. "My brother Archbishop does not wish me to visit with his clergy and communicants."

Milano was a city in which the elites were decidedly secular, and supported the Liberal or Republican Parties and not the Christian Democrats. The Archbishop was a person of large influence in an ecumenical milieu, which he clearly enjoyed. At the end of my visit he graciously brought me to the door of his suite in the Archiepiscopal Palace, noted that I was rare among his visitors in not having evoked the possibility of his becoming Pope. I said that he certainly had my best wishes, but that was a matter I had to leave to the church. That is it, he said, my Jewish friends are for me—but lack votes in the Conclave.

From the outside, the Roman Catholic Church appears far more monolithic than it is. Significant groups within the Italian church circumvented or ignored the strenuous efforts of John Paul II to limit or nullify the doctrinal and institutional advances of Vatican II. In particular, social activists organized in the parishes worked on behalf of immigrants, to assist the Italian poor. Catholic trade unionists and in the post-1989 fluidity of Italian politics any number of Christian Democratic figures and groups, openly sought alliances on national economic and social policy with the Communists, the Socialists, and the smaller formations of the left in local and regional campaigns. In the larger institutions of the church, the Pope's theological authority, Cardinal Ratzinger, exercised his considerable powers with great strenuousness. In 1984, the Brazilian Franciscan Leonardo Boff was called to Rome to discuss what Ratzinger depicted as errors in the interpretation of the church's mission: Boff was a proponent of Liberation Theology and an increasingly popular figure among the Latin American laity. I was visiting Rome at the time and recollect a conversation with the newly elected Jesuit General, Father Kolvenbach. "We already have a German Luther," he said, "do we really need a Brazilian one?" Boff in due time suspended his obedience to Rome. When Cardinal Ratzinger was elected Pope in 2005, Cardinal Martini received a very small number of votes as the candidate of the party of reform and renewal. Their turn came when Cardinal Ratzinger, as Pope Benedict XVI, took the unusual step of retiring in 2013. The election of the Argentinian Jesuit, Cardinal Bergoglio—son of an Italian immigrant family—again opened the church to the continuation of the work of Vatican II. The new Pope took the name of Saint Francis, in his time an innovator, indeed a spiritual revolutionary. Decades before, my then-new Communist friends of Catholic adherence or sympathy told me in no uncertain terms that we Americans were often too impatient. Change took time, God's ways were not direct (one said that as a Jew, I should know that), and institutions were often resistant to change but when it was possible, established and experienced institutions were needed to seize new opportunities. The present Italian Prime Minister, Matteo Renzi, grew up in Florentine Catholicism and Italy's representative on the European Commission, Federica Mogherini (in charge of European foreign policy) grew up in a Tuscan Communist milieu. In fact, the two cultural and political legacies have been allied since 1945.

It remains to be seen what future the new generation can make. Their party, the Democratici, bears the burden of decades of disappointment. As the rigidities of the Cold War dissolved at the end of the eighties and beginning of the nineties, the entire political system fell apart. The difference between North and South was not as large as the North in perpetual self-congratulation believed. Stringent investigating magistrates brought a great deal of corruption to light. Many Christian Democrats were indicted, among them the iconic leader Andreotti. The Socialist Party had occupied a good deal of the space between the Communists and the Christian Democrats by claiming to be representative of efficiency, reform and social justice—and by emphasizing its kinship with the northern European socialist and social democratic formations and the American Democrats. Its leader, Craxi, was Prime Minister from 1983 to 1987 but in 1994 fled to Tunisia, never to return, rather than accept imprisonment for bribery. I did not know him, but did know his closest associate and former chief of staff in the Prime Minister's office, Claudio Martelli. Claudio seemed to represent much that was promising in an open Italian future. He was young, cosmopolitan, direct in speech and determined (he was later Justice Minister and had a role in initiating serious prosecution of the Mafia) to sweep aside the traditional clutter of Italian politics—perpetual deal making and small changes beclouded by large phrases. He too was caught by accusations of bribery which effectively ended his career. He subsequently rejoined the Catholic church, engaged in local campaigns for social justice.

There were major figures in Italian politics (Amato, Ciampi, Napolitano, Prodi) who for longer or shorter periods were capable of rising above these storms, assuming governmental responsibilities, attempting large scale economic and social reforms in alliance with similar leaders in the other European Union nations. The trade unions were divided between the defense of the immediate interests of their members, and willingness to accept the costs of long term projects. There was an Italian alliance for reform, for civic renewal, for a different sort of politics but it was incapable of maintaining a larger and steady course over time. The civic culture which could back it was conspicuous by its weakness and in some parts of the nation, absence. The obstacles to durable political effectiveness were several, beginning with the domination of much of politics and public life by the struggle for tactical advantages. There were plenty of leaders, some women, ready for national and local leadership, in civic and church associations, the state service, the academy and culture, journalism—and, indeed, in the upper levels of finance and industry.

The Berlusconi phenomenon, which was to burden Italy from his assumption of the Prime Ministership in 1994 until his judicially required departure from public life in 2013, condensed and confirmed many of Italy's enduring pathologies. Silvio Berlusconi began to accumulate wealth as a real estate entrepreneur in Milan, entered into an alliance with the local Socialist Party, was aided by Craxi (the senior Milanese Socialist) to develop holdings in television and mass communication across Europe. He built his own movement and party, Forza Italia, out of the detritus of the party system of what was called the First Italian Republic. Berlusconi's strength was his vulgarity, his scorn for what there was of refinement and tact in Italian public life, his boasting of his own successful avarice, and above all, his direct appeal to the low common denominator of pervasive cynicism. "Andiamo in piazza" ("Let us take to the streets") remained the recourse of the engaged citizens across the spectrum of secular and Catholic groups, often at neighborhood and parish levels, undertaking specific political and social campaigns. Berlusconi, who had become rich by lowering the cultural level of Italian television, made it a point to deride Italy's traditions of activism. He propagated an ideology, indeed a culture, of civic withdrawal, of purposeful privatization. His chosen instrument, Forza Italia, was a political party composed of cliques and gangs emerging from the self-destruction of the system which lived so openly from the varieties of parasitism. His coalition partners were the former Neo-Fascist Party, renamed Alleanza Nazionale, and a separatist formation from the north, Lega Nord. They, like Berlusconi's immediate followers, were relentless exploiters of state funding—and did not hesitate to initiate noisy parliamentary rows, violent public demonstrations, and the threat of prolonged and chaotic aggression to mark their presence. Berlusconi practiced, then, a division of cultural and political labor which converted the public sphere into entertainment. His distance from the moral and pedagogic seriousness of Catholic, liberal, socialist traditions in Italy was something of which he boasted.

When Berlusconi won the Italian election of 1994, there was plenty of evidence of a re-emergence of a cultural and political sensibility across Western Europe which espoused authoritarianism, xenophobic nationalism, and a pseudo-politics of pluralistic representation poorly disguising avarice. These revenants of a terrible if recent past resurfaced as Western Europe was still repairing its wartime bomb damage. They were held in check by democratic conviction, moral and religious shame, and political discretion. What was shocking about the Berlusconi coalition was the participation of a party which had changed its name but openly acknowledged its descent from fascism, the Alleanza Nazionale. I suggested to then Senator Joseph Biden, who was Chair of the Senate Foreign Relations Committee's sub-committee on Europe, to schedule a hearing on the entire development—and traveled to Italy for a week to look at matters first-hand.

The senior permanent official of the Italian Foreign Ministry, Ferdinando Salleo (later a very effective Ambassador to the US) arranged a series of meetings for me. Berlusconi, presumably informed of my previous ties to sectors of Italian opinion opposed to his project, did not make himself available. I did speak with any number of his political allies with a variety of political origins, including the Alleanza Nazionale leader Gianfranco Fini and the head of Lega Nord, Bossi. Of course, I also spoke with others in the academy, church, journalism and politics. I was accompanied on my rounds by a Foreign Ministry official delighted that his time had come: he had been a member of the Alleanza Nazionale predecessor group (the Italian Social Movement).

Eventually, I wrote a report and delivered it at a hearing of the Committee. Much of what I wrote was not particularly original, if correct. The collapse of the old Italian party system had simply laid bare the cultural and political mechanisms the previous Italian state was incapable of transforming. The unions managed, more or less, to protect their members (and were increasingly organizations for the retired.) They could not join the state technocrats in a large scale development plan for the south (where European Union funds arrived and disappeared with great regularity). The south was very difficult to change and the north constantly drew many of the most energetic and intelligent southerners to itself. In some of the northern regions, alliances of the unions and small scale capital—under coalitions of Christian Democrats, Communists, Socialists, sometimes the smaller Liberal and Republican Parties—provided for some enlargement of prosperity, for some improvements in education and infra-structure. The dysfunctional tax system and large scale evasion, as well as flagrantly outright corruption, encouraged the construction of a parallel economy, administered by direct bargaining at local levels. A public sphere was an ad hoc construction when it functioned half well, a bad joke when it was captured by interest groups acting concertedly to circumvent or seize the state. Ordinary citizens relied on familial and local networks, Church intervention, and political patronage when they sought familial or personal advantages. Many thought things would never change, and even those with political resources thought of these as uncertain. Berlusconi depicted himself not as someone who could institute a new, more open and transparent public sphere but as someone who would maximize the opportunities for private initiatives. He was far from the refined Liberalism of the older northern Italian elites, with their deference to law—in effect, he was a Social Darwinist flaunting his contempt for rules: they were for the faint of heart.

In my report, I predicted an abbreviated political future for him, suggested that the social components of the authoritarianism inherited by Fini would carry him farther. The Lega Nord struck me as a patronage party united by a plebian localism. The disunited remnants of the Christian Democrats who joined Berlusconi practiced exactly what they had done before, joining organized rapacity to a familistic ideology. I seriously overestimated the extent and strength of the party of civic resistance, and of the party of social capital, the twin legacies of Italian republicanism and socialism. Having only partially made good their promises in the seventies and eighties, having resorted to interest group protectionism, they lacked a vision of the future. It was not enough to point to Western Europe (France and Germany predominantly) and announce that Italy was sure to become like them. Italy indeed was certain not to become like them, for as long as the destructive derision with which Berlusconi treated the public sphere was shared by large numbers of citizens and for as long as local and regional allegiances excluded national solidarity. Above all, I did not grasp the way in which the Italian welfare state was used not as a path to a wider society but as an instrument to consolidate group advantage.

My Foreign Ministry escort spoke frequently of his attachment to the values of tradition and family. On my last day in Rome, he volunteered to accompany me on a shopping mission—to acquire a stylistic purse for my friend Sally Guthrie. The diplomat said that he knew of two shops. One had goods less expensive, if I were buying for my wife. The other had higher value items, in case I was buying for a lady friend.

On return, I presented the report at a hearing. The Italian Embassy could not send an official to the hearing, asked me for a copy of the report—which had a certain amount of attention in the Italian press. I sent one to the Embassy, but the Ambassador's office for several days complained of not getting it. In fact, it took about four days for it to get to the Ambassador's office from the front door desk. Berlusconi did not appreciate the report and declared, asked about it at a press conference, that I should have remained in Washington, since ignorant of Italy. A reporter asked him if he knew that I was a professor at a Jesuit university. He conferred with staff and came up with a triumphant note: "Our information is that he is not a Jesuit."

In many respects, that was and is a pity. Had I been a Jesuit, I would have been less surprised by the darker ides of human nature. I would also have had a deeper appreciation of historical time (something my British friends of every spiritual family were particularly good at), and a more modest sense of my own possibilities. There are remarks on Jewish melancholy by some of our non-Jewish friends—to the effect that we are mourning the lost Temple, or saddened by the Messiah's conspicuous failure to arrive to redeem us or some of us. Perhaps—but there is an alternative explanation. Cast by history on strange shores, caught up in the general turbulence of the post-Enlightenment age, freed of or stripped of Biblical sequences, we secular Jews had and have nothing to rely on but our interpretive wits. We expect a great deal of ourselves and our colleagues, friends, neighbors, students—and of the countries to which we attach ourselves. That renders us prime candidates to join in the general American nervousness: no wonder Norman Mailer became something of a prophet, a role he greatly enjoyed. In my own case, I kept trying to scale impossibly steep heights of understanding, felt diminished by ending as I thought forever at the bottom of the Tower of Babel.

Berlusconi until his downfall went in and out of the Prime Ministership. Rather competent leaders of the center-left (Amato, D'Alema, Ciampi, Prodi) formed governments of some degree of stability, undertook some reforms, were unable to institutionalize a civic culture of national dimensions. They were respected in Europe, treated dismissively or resignedly by significant sectors of Italian opinion, either attached to the clientelism of their cities and regions or inured to its permanence. The Communist Party had dissolved itself in 1991 to become the Party of Democratic Socialism and join the European socialist and social democratic parties in the European Socialist Party. A third of the party formed its own irredentist group, Rifondazione Comunista. By 1998 the Party of Democratic Socialism abandoned its distinctiveness to join other groups in a party terming itself the Democrats (Democratici), uniting survivors of the Socialist Party and former Christian Democrats in a formation proclaiming its ecumenism and realism.

A singular strength of the old Communist Party had been its local implantations, in which families and neighborhoods were sites of the direct inheritance of political traditions and experience. The dispersion and mobility of modern Italy affected its secular church, the Communist Party, as much as its religious one. Many in Italy were surprised, others shocked and saddened, when in the 1994 election Berlusconi's party won the constituency in Turin. Mirafiori One (next to the Fiat factory) which had long been Communist. Television and the newer media, education and Europeanization, contributed to cultural differentiation which was certainly broadening and even enriching. However, it undermined some of the social continuity on which the Communists had relied. Newer sorts of local activism, a good deal of it organized in Church parishes, some of it quite ecumenical, much of it marked by environmentalism, flowed into the vacuum left by the Communist retreat. One still saw, in city streets, brave and colorful storefronts put up by the former Communist dissidents. Perhaps it would be appropriate to term them survivalists.

Many of my Italian friends refashioned their political commitments, intensified their professional lives, spent entire periods elsewhere in Europe. Others remained in the political sphere. I saw them on visits to Italy, observed a certain melancholy when we talked. A regular guest of the Communists at their annual festival, the Festa dell'Unità, organized in different cities by the Communist daily, I was invited in 1997 to visit for a month by the Demochristian foundation, Fondazione Alcide De Gasperi. It had no very evident program of public activity, seemed to be a discreet disbursing agency for projects conducted by a small inner circle. When in Rome, I rented a small house on a noisy street in what had been the red light district of Republic and Empire. The local shopkeepers and residents recognized me after a very short time, I became part of the landscape. Giorgio Napolitano was at the time Interior Minister and lived some few blocks away, habitually walked to his office down the Via Nazionale, accompanied by a very visible armed escort. I accompanied him occasionally on these morning walks, we had coffee in his office, talked, and he began his official day. He noted that his office had originally served as the Prime Minister's office and that one previous Prime Minister, Benito Mussolini, had combined the post with the Interior Ministership.

There is a quote from the French nineteenth-century thinker Guignebert: we expected the kingdom of heaven, we got the Roman Catholic Church. My Italian friends clearly had their own version. We had the Communist Party, now we have an ordinary modern European experience. Aldo Tortorella bought the rights to the journal *Critica Marxista* from the Party, published it for a while, then dropped the enterprise. Rifondazione Comunista, the Manifesto group, kept an eschatological sensibility alive, but it was experienced as rhetorical, no, ritualized. The efficient agencies of the Italian left were the unions with their attention to economic policy, and a group of leaders with a sense of state. I saw Giuliano Amato a few times, he later had very good words for my book on socialism. Yet even as intelligent and reflective Prime Minister as he was could not organize a permanent coalition to make a beginning in changing Italy's civic culture. As for Andreotti, in a new historical situation he adhered to his attitude of knowing distance. I think that he saw himself as a guardian of the nation—with a paternalistic indulgence of its many flaws.

These were the undercurrents of what for my Italian friends were of course busy days and years. In 1998 in Bologna I had a glimpse of their great gifts of improvisation, their capacity to seize the day every day. My colleagues and the entire Bolognese middle class were very pleased that their airport offered a reliable connection to the rest of Europe—any number of Lufthansa flights a day. Italian academic salaries were pinched, research facilities limited. No one complained—but many did go off every week to teach at universities from Lund to Athens. One colleague asked me to share a seminar with him—and returned once a month from a visiting post at UCLA.

As for the students, I had large numbers of Erasmus students— citizens of other EU nations taking advantage of the EU program which enabled them to study for a semester in another EU nation. I have already written of the calculating shrewdness of the Italian students, contrasted the larger ambitions of the northerners with the emphasis of my southern students on fixing a modest but secure place for themselves. The university building was down an arcaded street from the office of the Mondadori publishing firm—which published academic and commercial products with mechanical efficiency. It had once been part of post-fascist Italian cultural argument, was now another Italian multi-national. A diligent group of colleagues at the university were the editors of a journal of politics, its articles very contemporary, yet weighted with history and certainly acute. I asked if they thought that newspaper editorialists, officials, politicians read the journal and the answer was yes, and they hoped for occasional influence.

In Bologna, I saw old friends and made new ones. Not very far away, in Ferrara, there was a professor of philosophy whose father I had met on my first visit to Italy a half-century earlier. He was a Waldensian, member of a brave and small Protestant sect which had somehow survived the catastrophes of national history and kept to its ecumenical conviction that other Italians would do well to listen to it. I went to Rome to visit with old friends, went to Milan to see the Archbishop. The phrase is clearly exaggerated: the transcendental urgency of the Cold War had gone, a politics of small steps and measured ambitions now seemed irreversible. I was only dimly aware of it at the time, but at age seventy-two, the necessity of drawing accounts was a large challenge I somewhat shirked. The result was the sense of living in a permanent interim, a pause for reflection not directly undertaken.

From Bologna, I went to London for a one-month visit to the London School of Economics as guest of the Director, Tony Giddens. The LSE I knew between 1953 and 1959 was febrile, moral and personal conflicts could not be avoided, thirties, forties, fifties seemed to merge. The one I visited was free of metahistorical ambitions. A small group of former students listened politely to my reminiscences as if I were disinterring an archaeological inscription. At lunch one day in the faculty restaurant, I encountered Raymond Firth—age ninety-seven and a very senior figure at the LSE when I was there. Raymond was glad to see me and with his Methodist directness, complimented me on aging well. The LSE had become an international consulting firm, its politics not for sale but packaged and stored away. Of course there were exceptions like John Gray, an iconoclast grateful for idols to smash but quite aware that he was somehow being indulged. The busyness of the Blair government rendered London an economic and political entrepôt.

Of course, I saw Eric Hobsbawm with his imperturbable patience, insight, and sympathetic humor. I cannot now explain why I did not call on the new *New Left Review* editors. I suspect that I was not ready to ask myself about paths not taken. I did visit with a highly intelligent Labour MP, an editor of *The Political Quarterly*, Tony Wright. He had significant committee assignments in the House of Commons, was never advanced to the ministerial rank his talents merited. I have the impression that made him decidedly proud: he was thought too independent. I visited with some of the Labour Parliamentarians not enthused by Blair's projects, was struck by how little contact they had with the Congressional Progressive Caucus. I called on one of the many Lords Morgan in the House of Lords, the historian of Labour and biographer of Clement Attlee. We had a drink and a good talk, and on my way out, I asked to be directed to the facilities. He pointed to a door. "It says 'Peers,'" I observed. "My dear chap, how much more awkward it would be were it to say, 'Peeresses.'"

I renewed acquaintance with the learned and sharp British journalists Barbara Smith of *The Economist* and Michael White of *The Guardian*, having known them in Washington. They had a quality of intellectual distance which reminded me of the British historians I had known when on the board of *Past and Present*. Of course, I called on *The New Statesman and Tribune*—for which I had written forty years previously. David Goodhart of *Prospect* was hospitable and he revived old insights to accurate if discouraging effect. In both the UK and the US, welfare state benefits for the ethnically and racially distant and immigrants were greeted with skepticism and even hostility by the white working class. Ira Katznelson was later to chronicle how the design and administration of much of the US welfare state institutionalized racial prejudice.

Ralph Miliband was, alas, gone but I visited with his widow Marion and saw his sons, David working for Blair and Ed for Gordon Brown. I did not visit with the (relatively) newly installed Labourites, considering that I could anticipate what they would say. No doubt, but there are matters of speech that are more often than not revealing, and one can learn something and even a good deal by immersion in what presents itself as routine.

In Germany, per contra, as Gerhard Schröder assumed the Chancellorship in 1998, I did visit in the Green and Social Democratic Ministries, as well as the office of the Chancellor himself— run by the calm, tireless and lucidly intelligent Frank-Walter Steinmeier. When my book *After Progress* was published in Germany,

Frank in an interview with *Der Spiegel* declared (rightly) that I had said very little about the future of the socialist tradition whose history I had chronicled. That gave me a chance to reply by recalling Umberto Eco's great work on modern art, *Opera Aperta* (The Open Art Work). Modern art, he declared, consisted of essentially unfinished works which were completed in the imagination of listeners, readers, viewers. Modern socialism, then, was open and to be reformed by its contemporary leaders and voters. The reference was impeccable—but reality was not.

Schröder's government underwent a crisis early in 1999 with the sudden resignation from Parliament and government and party office of the finance minister and party chair, Oskar Lafontaine. He and Schröder had been somewhat friendly rivals for the party leadership and chancellor candidacy until the actual year of the election. As party chair since 1995, Lafontaine had brought the party to effective electoral discipline. When Schröder was re-elected Minister President in his state Lower Saxony, in 1998 by a convincing margin, Lafontaine withdrew his candidacy for the chancellorship. With his openness and presence, Schröder was indeed a plausible candidate: the intellectual Lafontaine with his inexpungable rigor was an object of the derision and hostility of a German media spectrum become ever more mediocre and shallow—and unprincipled.

In fact, the matter was one of policy and not personality. In a situation in which productivity and wage gains were shrinking, the income of the German labor force was declining. Schröder was convinced by his economists and officials that deep cuts in the welfare state were necessary to save it. Lafontaine did not agree, but lacked the political resources in his own party, and in its Green coalition partner, to sustain an alternative entailing planned investment and systematic redistribution. There was no support for him from France, despite its Socialist government under Jospin, much less from the United Kingdom. The International Monetary Fund and the European Central Bank were addicted to market ideology (poorly disguised as economic orthodoxy) and a Clinton government pursuing its own compromise with American finance was no help. Not only the lower segments of the German labor force but groups previously accounted a classical labor aristocracy (the skilled in machine tools and heavy industry) experienced declines in real income, social benefits, retirement.

The Social Democrats and Greens narrowly won the election of 2002, had the good sense to ally themselves with French President Chirac in refusing to join the US in attacking Iraq. German forces were sent to Afghanistan, just as they had participated earlier in the Yugoslav conflicts. Deep skepticism about the moral and political efficacy of armed intervention marked the parties' electorates—joined to a conspicuously unenthusiastic judgment of the statecraft of the Bush presidency. When Bush made his first presidential visit to Berlin in 2002, the Greens were in a quandary. As participants in the ruling coalition, they were hosts and could hardly sponsor demonstrations against the visitor. Their electorate was, however, antagonistic to ideology and reality of the early "war on terror." The party leadership, independently of the parliamentary group, thought it had found a way around protocol and good form. It announced a public forum to be held on Unter den Linden—with speeches by a panel excluding the parliamentarians.

I was invited to speak (not for the first time) for "the other America." I was told that Robert Redford was the alternative, but that since he could not speak German, a rather more routine choice had to be made. My moment arrived—and hardly had I begun when the street platform was stormed by members of an "autonomous" group—street fighters for whom the fight was usually more important than the issue. One of my fellow speakers, the Green Justice Commissioner of the City of Berlin, had foreseen what was coming and rushed me to safety down a ladder placed at the back of the platform, as the Berlin police came on to clear what had become a chaotic scene. We retreated to Green Party headquarters some streets away, gave a press conference, and had the satisfaction of seeing and hearing ourselves as the first item on the evening television news broadcasts.

In those years I was repeatedly invited to Germany to speak. I was not telling the more sophisticated segments of the German public anything they did not know. It was a way of showing the flag—a star-spangled banner of critical American opinion, long since blowing in our cross winds, and behind which there was in the US no very special mobilization. Of course, I talked with friends in politics across the political spectrum. Germany had excellent ambassadors with acute powers of analysis in Washington, there were some very intelligent German journalists here too, and plenty of officials and politicians in Berlin had their own direct experience of the US. It was flattering to be treated as needed—but there was no particular urgency about it.

One somewhat exceptional event comes to mind. The German branch of International Physicians for the Prevention of Nuclear War in 2004 convened a Berlin meeting on the Iraq war and invited me to speak. I traveled to Berlin a few months after hearing the then-leader of the opposition, Angela Merkel, speak at Georgetown. She was very critical of the Schröder government's refusal to join the adventure. In the discussion I remarked that both the German Bishops' Conference and the Protestant Church supported the government. She was the head of a political formation which unhesitatingly designated itself as Christian: what could she say of the divergence? Clearly drawing upon the Lutheran doctrine of the two realms, earthly and spiritual, she was ready with a reply. "They do theology, we do politics." I quoted her and another member of the panel, my friend Wolfgang Huber, at the time Bishop of Berlin-Brandenburg and presiding officer of the Protestant Church, seized the opening: "Because I do theology, I must do politics." Wolfgang's presence on the panel was a reminder of the persistence of the churches' concern for first and last things as elements of German politics.

The event brought another encounter. One of the participants was the Social Democratic Mayor of Lübeck, home town of both Thomas Mann and Willy Brandt. We talked and I told him that I was very glad to meet the successor to the sixteenth-century Mayor, Jürgen Wollenweber, who had led the Reformation in the city. The Mayor was surprised: not many of his Social Democratic contemporaries, he said, would have recalled Wollenweber. My evoking the religious currents which were essential to both American social reform and European socialism in my final book had struck Jürgen Habermas as a significant contribution: he said so on several public occasions.

Frank Kermode had titled his deep essays on modern culture *The Sense of an Ending*. In the final years of the last century and the beginning ones of our own, I had a vague but pervasive feeling that something had ended. It was not just a matter of taking a longer and more complex view of the possibilities of reconstructive social transformation. I no longer had the inner certainty that I was on a road I could recommend, with conviction, to others. I did not experience a negative conversion, a concentrated and enduring moment of doubt. It was a matter, rather, of occasional pointed episodes of skepticism, an increasing indifference to a standard radical narrative, an inclination to return to earlier periods of American and European history for a different sort of evidence—on the more destructive human urges, on fusions of blindness and hatred. Schematically, *Civilization and Its Discontents* or even *Notes From Underground* now offered more reliable ways to read past and present than *The German Ideology*. After all, my very sage friend Robert Lifton, in his choice of themes for the annual meetings of our psychohistory group, had resolutely if somewhat tacitly turned from a universal therapy.

In 2001, just before my retirement from Georgetown, Nuffield College invited me to spend a month as official visitor. The fellows I had known were gone or in retirement, a few made occasional appearances for tea. Few at the university seemed interested in my recounting years past—and as for the present, it was the end of the academic year and I was given to understand that as for messages from the US, sensory overload had done its work Europeans who had read my writings in their countries (France, Germany, Italy, Spain) came to my room (one still did not have anything as business like as an office). The British, some very old friends and a couple of interesting younger ones apart, were politely distant. The College porters and secretaries, per contra, often related to those I had known forty years earlier, were quite welcoming.

I was invited by colleagues at Sheffield to talk on the political and social situation in the US. Some of my listeners recalled hearing me on the same theme a generation ago. "The US seems to be itself, only more so," said one. I made some rounds in London. The British were bored by Bush and as a BBC producer said, were looking elsewhere for both enlightenment and entertainment. It was June 2001. On a day of slight rain, I slipped on college flagstones notorious much earlier for being dangerous—but which the college said it could not alter since the building was a protected monument. I broke my elbow, enjoyed excellent immediate treatment at the gcounty hospital, and flew back to Washington in a large cast regarded with extreme suspicion by the US Customs officers.

Looking back, I was surprised by the indifferent British reception of *After Progress*. The Oxford University Press employees charged with publicity were politesse itself, could not understand why an American would bother himself with socialism when their Labour Prime Minister so openly derided it. They had not the least notions of the British intellectual and political milieu I had known decades before. Months later, in Washington, I was interviewed on an interesting BBC talk show, and my host did have a very defined and quite accurate idea of Britain in the fifties and sixties. He described me as "legendary"—a euphemism expressing admiration for survival. Nuffield's stolid indifference changed with time. At a Washington reunion of Nuffield alumni with the present Warden, I was received with totemic respect. The sardonic Oxford social anthropologists I knew in the sixties would not have been surprised.

Conclusion

I RETIRED from teaching at the end of the academic year 2001; the Law Center at Georgetown has the agreeable custom of arranging farewell dinners to mark these transitions. Mine was scheduled for the evening of 11 September.

My daughters arrived a few days earlier, and so did Helga. I went out in the morning, to return with our breakfast croissants. Helga had turned on the television, and the first airplane had just struck a World Trade Center tower. "You are not," Helga declared, "retiring today."

Not so long thereafter, we went out to watch columns of autos fleeing the city. En route to Washington for the event, Victor Navasky was stopped when Amtrak shut down. My visitors remained until flights resumed. The dinner was held in November. Much of the recent past was evoked, but not that morning: talking about it seemed quite gratuitous—an effort to reach depths still unmeasurable, and certainly unimaginable a few months earlier.

I have published some two hundred articles since, some of them about the past (on *Partisan Review*, Lasch and Mills, reminiscences of Grass and Lessing), but a good deal of political commentary about events on both sides of the Atlantic as well. I have the disturbing conviction that I have lived far too much on intellectual capital. I envisage a serious effort to depict our new world, decidedly not a brave one. As I have passed ninety, I trust that the task will call up the inner resources to continue.

American historians frequently refer to a search for a usable past. I and a few friends and colleagues (Peter Brooks, Harvey Cox, Jürgen Habermas, Stuart Hall, Eric Hobsbawm, Leszek Kołakowski,

Robert Lifton, Pierre Nora, Barbara Probst Solomon, Charles Taylor, Alain Touraine, my daughter Antonia) have or had our own usable past or pasts. We have pondered fascism and imperialism, the contradictions of mass democracy, the persistence of ethnicity, the inexpungable presence of the world religions, the fragility of a pluralistic culture. Yet the authoritarianism, barbarism, militarism, violence of our world has shaken us.

I came to cultural and political awareness in the terrible year 1938. Ideals and illusions have claimed my attention since—in no linear way. I was right to title my last book *After Progress*, hesitant in it to do justice to the title. I will give the theme one last try.

Receiving the Grand Cross of the Order of Merit of the Federal Republic of Germany from German Ambassador Peter Wittig, March 2017. (l-r) Ambassador Wittig makes the presentation at his residence in Washington, DC; standing with my daughter Antonia and Terry Flood after the ceremony.

About the Author

Norman Birnbaum is University Professor Emeritus, Georgetown University Law Center. He was a founding editor of *New Left Review*, on the editorial board of *Partisan Review*, and is the senior member of the editorial board of *The Nation*. He was educated at New York City public schools, Williams College and has a doctorate in sociology from Harvard. He came to the Law Center in 1979 from a Professorship of Sociology at Amherst College. Before returning to New England he taught at the London School of Economics, Oxford University and the University of Strasbourg. He introduced sociology to the undergraduate curriculum at Oxford and Amherst. He was a Fulbright Distinguished Professor at the University of Bologna and is Chair, Scholarly Advisory Board, International Institute of Peace, Vienna.

At Georgetown, Dr. Birnbaum taught courses at the intersection of law, humanities, and politics. His visiting appointments included a year at the Science Center and the Institute of Advanced Studies, Berlin, as well as a year at the Institute for Advanced Studies, Princeton. His most recent book, *After Progress: American Social Reform and European Socialism in the Twentieth Century* (Oxford University Press, 2001), was also published in German and Spanish. Other works include *Searching For The Light: Essays In Thought and Culture* (Oxford University Press, 1993), *The Radical Renewal, The Politics of Ideas in Modern America* (Pantheon, 1988), *Toward a Critical Sociology* (Oxford University Press, 1971), and *The Crisis of Industrial Society* (Oxford University Press, 1969). He continues to publish in US and European journals and newspapers.

Index of Names

Aaron, Henry, 623
Abbe Godin (Henri Godin), 337
Abendroth, Lisa, 156, 276
Abendroth, Wolfgang, 145, 147-150, 156, 189, 276, 547
Abraham, Hilda, 180, 181, 210, 470
Abraham, Karl, 180
Acheson, Dean, 49, 328
Adams, John, 117, 127
Adenauer, Konrad, 152, 157, 160, 183, 276, 278, 279, 329, 527, 590
Adorno, Theodor, 144, 145, 311, 459
Aesop, 310
Agee, James, 381
Agnelli, Gianni, 439, 449, 530, 539, 540
Albright, David, 558
Albright, Madeleine, 525
Alighieri, Dante, 125
Allende, Salvador, 520
Allport, Gordon, 104, 116, 117
Almunia, Joaquín, 674
Amato, Giuliano, 537, 684, 688, 690
Amendola, Giorgio, 535
Ames, Edward, 48
Amis, Kingsley, 176
Anderson, Jeffrey, 654
Anderson, Perry, 239, 240, 298
Andreotti, Giulio, 683, 690
Andreski, Stanislav, 263
Angell, Sir Norman, 62
Antelme, Robert, 338
Apel family, 151, 152
Apel, Gudrun (Nina), 23, 150-152, 156, 161, 166, 181, 182, 184, 203, 210, photo with NB 211, 212, 213, 219, 225, 228, 231, 244, 245, 252, 265, 267-268, 275, 276, 279, 281, 285, 288, 293, 295, 297, 314, 316, 323, 330, 337, 342, 357, 359, 364, 365, 374, 375, 384, 385, 470
Appleman Williams, William, 299
Aquinas, Thomas, 157
Arab-Ogly, Edward, 296
Arbatov, Georgy, 513
Arendt, Hannah, 48, 141, 181, 182, 380, 399, 497, 511
Aristotle, 172, 417, 658
Arnold, Matthew, 52, 125, 218, 219, 233, 418
Aron, Raymond, 183, 189, 198, 206, 290, 311, 324, 339, 340, 393, 394, 403, 541, 544
Arrupe, Pedro, SJ, 649
Aspin, Les, 622
Aston, Trevor, 264
Attali, Jacques, 543, 557
Attlee, Clement, 172, 340, 692
Augustine of Hippo, 125, 417
Aulard, François-Alphonse, 336
Austin, J. L., 259, 341
Ausubel, Isidore, 33
Avineri, Shlomo, 500
Axen, Hermann, 609

Babb, Alan, 410
Backer family, 10
Badaloni, Nicola, 535, 652
Bader, Morton, 72
Bader, Richard, 72
Badoglio, Pietro, 534

Bahcall, John, 496
Bahr, Egon, 581
Bahrdt, Hans Paul, 189
Bahro, Rudolf, 601
Bailyn, Bernard, 123, 128, 618
Bakunin, Mikhail, 29
Balakian, Peter, 477
Baldwin, James, 391
Barnet, Richard, 273, 274, 303, 314, 478, 511-515, 554
Barnet, Vincent, 87
Barraclough, Geoffrey, 184
Barrett, William, 107
Barth, Karl, 98, 516
Barzun, Jacques, 60
Baskin family (fiction), 219
Bassarak, Gerhard, 196, 277, 278, 608
Basso, Lelio, 529
Bastian, Gert, 589
Bauman, Zygmunt, 353, 418
Baxter, James Phinney, III, 67, 665
Bayley, John, 267
Bazelon, David, 75, 77
Beard, Charles, 5, 22, 44, 60, 130, 501
Beaurain, Nicole, 342
Beauvoir, Simone de, 340
Beer, Sam, 122, 124, 127, 129, 138, 165, 212, 220, 271
Begg, Roy, 27
Begin, Menachem, 477
Bell, Daniel, 189, 216, 290, 294, 314, 387, 416, 540, 617, 621
Bellah, Robert, 131, 495
Bellamy, Edward, 551
Bellow, Saul, 634
Beloff, Max, 262, 264
Beltran, Miguel, 493, 670
Bendiner, Robert, 74
Bendix, Reinhard, 189
Benhabib, Seyla, 493

Benjamin, Walter, 52, 182, 478
Benn, Tony, 529, 557, 558
Bentham, Jeremy, 5427
Berdyaev, Nikolai, 516
Beres, David, 73, 74, 77, 81, 375
Berger, Peter, 186, 376
Bergoglio, Jorge Mario, Pope Francis, 682
Berking, Max, 42, 43, 51
Berlin, Isaiah, 164, 178, 201, 210, 213, 252, 262, 263, 269, 283-287, 293, 331, 380
Berlinguer, Enrico, 398, 478, 502, 532-534, 536
Berlusconi, Silvio, 684-689
Berman, Marshall, 283
Bevan, Anuerin, 172, 237
Beveridge, William, 62, 175, 178
Biden, Joseph, 685
Biedenkopf, Kurt, 586
Biermann, Wolf, 601
Billington, James, 623
Binder, David, 129
Birnbaum family, 353
Birnbaum, Anna (daughter) dedication, 210, 244, 245, 265, 268, 275, 281, 297, 301, photo on the Canal Grande in Venice 307, 316, 330, 342, 357, 360, 364, 384, photos 411, 464, 467, 472, photo 491, 551, 554, 594, 595, 608
Birnbaum, Antonia (daughter) dedication, 210, 265, 268, 281, 296, 297, 298, 301, 316, 342, 357, 360, 364, 384, photo 411, 464, photo 465, 472, 554, 594-596, 700, photo 700
Birnbaum, Bernard (uncle), 17, 24
Birnbaum, grandfather, 8-10, 13, 17, 24, 296, 353
Birnbaum, Jean (mother) 10, 11, 13, 14, 17, 24, 43, 61, 71, 74, 228, 360, 363, 473

Birnbaum, Ruth (sister), 4, 12, 13, 24, 35, 228, 473
Birnbaum, Silas Jacob (father), 5, photo 6-17, 19-22, 24-26, 32, 33, 35, 38, 42-46, 51-53, 69, 72-74, 81, 228, 360, 363, 368, 431, 473, 501, 620, 656, 667
Blair, Tony, 575, 582, 635, 636, 651, 679, 691, 692
Bloch, Ernst, 295, 401, 642, 643
Bloch, Marc, 193, 275, 334
Bloom, Solomon (fiction), 71
Blue, Carol, 633
Blüm, Norbert, 590
Blumenthal, Michael, 555
Blumenthal, Sidney, 596, 634, 651
Boff, Leonardo, 682
Bohley, Bärbel, 600
Böll, Heinrich, 571
Bonaparte, Napoleon, 142, 275, 296, 336, 344, 395, 529, 541, 649
Borkenau, Franz, 70
Bornkamm, Heinrich, 158
Borosage, Robert, 514, 554
Bossi, Umberto, 685
Bottomore, Tom, 170, 171, 182, 193, 208, 247, 336, 401, 500, 539
Boudin, Leonard, 515-517
Bourdieu, Pierre, 208, 340
Bowers, Claude, 5
Bowra, Maurice, 294
Boyers, Peggy, 675
Boyers, Robert, 675
Bracher, Karl Dietrich, 290
Bradlee, Ben, 490
Brandeis, Louis, 460
Brandt, Willy, 62, 147, 157, 170, 198, 301, 332, 397, 478, 502, 506, 507, 514, 523, 528, 537, 543, 547, 548, 550, 551, 553, 556-558, 562-564, 574, 576, 577, 581, 587, 593, 602, 615, 639, 676, 695
Braudel, Fernand, 185, 242
Brauer, Bob, 526, 556
Brecht, Bertolt, 459
Brenman, Margaret, 477, 478
Brentano, Margherita von, 278, 279, 586
Brezhnev, Leonid, 295, 354, 555
Briggs, A., 189
Brinkerhoff, Derek, 69
Brinton, Crane, 335
Brombert, Victor, 498
Bronfman, Edgar, 65
Brooks, Peter, 379, 477, 481, 500, 664, 699
Brossard, Chandler, 75
Brown, Gordon, 266, 692
Brown, Harold, 522
Brown, Jerry, 589, 590
Brzezinski, Zbigniew, 358, 521, 558
Buck, Pearl, 20
Buckley, William F., 630
Bülow, Andreas von, 579
Bumpers, Dale, 589
Bundy, McGeorge, 220, 272, 310, 314, 368, 370, 461, 511, 525, 530, 639
Burckhardt, Jacob, 71, 85
Burke, Edmund, 125, 192, 223
Burke, Peter, 283, 288
Burnham, Forbes, 170
Burnham, James, 646, 652
Burns, Arthur, 604, 608
Burt, Richard, 566
Bush, Barbara, 89
Bush, George H. W., 558, 595, 637, 651
Bush, George W., 633, 635, 694, 696
Bushman, Richard, 129
Bütikofer, Reinhard, acknowledgements
Butler, David, 258, 260
Butler, Rab, 237, 259

Butterfield, Victor, 294

Callaghan, James, 255, 529
Callahan, John, 446
Calloway, Wayne, 66
Calvez, Jean-Yves, 190, 340, 433, 500, 649
Calvin, John, 38, 105, 123, 136, 137, 138, 195, 266, 274, 275, 286, 291, 336, 406-408, 518, 585, 634
Camus, Albert, 335
Caracciolo, Nicola, 529
Cardozo, Enrique, 497
Carlyle, Thomas, 10
Carr-Saunders, Alexander, 174, 175, 665
Carr, E. H., 178, 183
Carr, Raymond, 270, 271
Carroll, Lewis, 167
Carter, Jimmy, 490, 493, 518-525, 526, 548, 549, 554, 555, 556, 558, 567, 612, 626, 627, 628, 629, 639, 674
Casaroli, Agostino, Cardinal, 529
Casey, William, 574
Castellina, Luciana, 533
Castro, Fidel, 186, 270, 271, 310, 343, 513, 677
Cavanagh, John, 514
Cecco, Marcello De, 539
Celeste, Richard, 270
Cézanne, Paul, 134
Chamberlain, William Henry, 92
Chametzky, Jules, 454-455
Chaplin, Charlie, 134, 541
Chaucer, Geoffrey, 436, 438
Cheever, John, 228
Cheney, Richard, 633
Chenu, Marie-Dominique, 193, 337
Chertoff, Mordechai, 51
Chester, Norman, 258, 259, 665
Chevalier, Haakon, 76

Chevènement, Jean-Pierre, 542, 543
Chinoy, Ely, 385, 388, 455
Chirac, Jacques, 583, 694
Chomsky, Noam, 614
Chorley, Roger, 2nd Baron Chorley, 173, 174
Chou En-Lai, 200
Church, Frank, 508
Churchill, Winston, 36, 41, 54, 58, 501
Ciampi, Carlo Azeglio, 684, 688
Clair, Louis (pen name), 135
Clark, Blair, 490
Claudel, Paul, 193
Clegg, Hugh, 259
Clegg, Nick, 492
Clinton, Bill, 49, 51, 270, 506, 525, 558, 582, 583, 634-638, 644, 651, 666, 675, 679, 693
Cohen, Eliot, 134, 222, 287, 322
Cohen, Morris Raphael, 5
Cohn, Norman, 179
Cohn, Sherman, 660
Cole, Charles, 408
Coleridge, Samuel Taylor, 28
Collins, Judy, 446
Collison, Peter, 283
Colp, Ralph, 41
Commager, Henry Steele, 464
Steele Commager, Henry, 464
Comte, Auguste, 249
Conant, James Bryant, 124, 125, 201
Congar, Jean-Yves, 193, 337
Conyers, John, 513, 554
Cook, Blanche Wiesen, 58
Coolidge, Calvin, 406
Coser, Lewis, 5, 135, 190, 213, 214, 225, 388, 467-469
Coser, Rose, 135, 225, 467, 468
Cot, Jean-Pierre, 543, 544
Coudert, Frederic René, Jr., 30, 33
Coughlin, Charles, 36, 501

Covello, Leonard, 7
Cowley, Malcolm, 65
Cox, Harvey, 23, 477, 653, 699
Coye, Bob, 64, 70, 72, 89
Craig, Gregory, 525
Craxi, Bettino, 537, 538, 683, 684
Cresson, Édith, 557
Cromwell, Oliver, 37, 179, 239
Crosland, Anthony, 238, 261, 290, 332, 459, 529
Crossman, Richard, 501
Cummings, Nathan, acknowledgements
Cuomo, Mario, 675

D'Alema, Massimo, 651, 688
d'Estaing, Giscard, 558, 666
Dahrendorf, Ralf, 157, 170, 189
Dampierre, Éric de, 298
Dante, 125
Darwin, Charles, 41, 440, 679, 686
Davidoff, Judith, 170
Davis, Asa, 426
Davis, Benjamin J., Jr., 38, 424
Davis, Chandler, 120
Day, Dorothy, 507
Day, John, 74
de Beauvoir, Simone, 340
De Cecco, Marcello, 539
de Dampierre, Éric, 298
de Gaulle, Charles, 62, 78, 183, 201, 226, 269, 275, 290, 315, 328, 332, 337, 339, 343, 345, 349, 373, 393, 395, 396, 501, 545, 568
de Lubac, Henri, SJ, 340
de Maizière, Lothar, 602
De Rouvroy, Claude Henri (comte de Saint-Simon), 284, 416
de Tocqueville, Alexis, 284, 335, 544
Dean, James, 379
Debord, Guy, 346

Decter, Midge, 486, 680
Dedalus, Stephen (fiction), 71, 93
DeGioia, John, acknowledgments, 668
Dellums, Ronald, 508, 526, 554, 556, 558, 589, 630
Delors, Jacques, 545
DeMott, Benjamin, 389, 413, 450, 452, 611, 660
den Uyl, Joop, 556-557
Deng Xiaoping, 451
Dennett, Tyler, 67
Despres, Emile, 88, 89
Desroche, Henri, 190, 193, 194, 240, 312, 336, 340, 356, 373, 433, 574
Deutsch, Babette, 48
Deutscher, Isaac, 133, 149, 173, 183, 272, 291, 295, 516
Deutscher, Tanja, 295
Dewey, John, 11, 22, 60, 79, 83, 85, 130, 189, 190, 213, 341, 382, 408, 489, 501
Diana, Princess of Wales, 632
Dibelius, F. K. Otto, Bishop, 608
Dibelius, Hans, 277
Dichter, Channing, 31
Dickens, Charles, 163, 185, 215, 266, 267
Dicks, H. V., 154
Diogenes, 553
Dirda, Michael, 660
Dixler, Elsa, 492
Dizard, Jan, 412, 428
Dizard, Wilson, 57
Dohnányi, Klaus von, 563, 579
Donahue, Thomas, 7
Dos Passos, John, 15, 29, 38, 53, 60, 163, 658, 662
Dostoyevsky, Fyodor, 48, 125, 139, 658
Douglas-Home, Alec, Lord Home, 330

Douglas, Helen Gahagan, 526
Douglass, Frederick, 128
Dregger, Alfred, 590
Dreiser, Theodore, 492
Dreitzel, Hans Peter, 418, 539
Dreyfus, Alfred, 334, 336
Drinan, Robert, 648
Du Bois, W. E. B., 128, 484, 656
Dubček, Alexander, 370
Dubuffet, Jean, 92
Duffy, Joseph, 520
Dulles, Allen, 270, 489
Dulles, John Foster, 98, 200, 412, 489
Dupont, M. (fiction), 393
Durbin, Evan, 177
Durkheim, Émile, 105, 268, 416
Dylan, Bob, 601

Eden, Anthony, 186, 200
Edwards, Harry, 518
Ehmke, Horst, 397, 553, 566, 577, 578
Ehrlichman, John, 539
Eichmann, Adolf, 380, 392
Einaudi, Luigi, 531
Einstein, Albert, 26, 305, 495
Eisenhower, David, 430
Eisenhower, Dwight, 133, 146, 186-187, 189, 190, 197, 212, 214, 220, 221, 222, 273, 302, 310, 322, 414, 460, 475, 505
Eliot, T. S., 41, 68, 134, 224, 658
Elizabeth I of England, 33, 69, 320
Elizabeth II of England, 191, 210, 243
Ellison, Ralph, 391, 425
Ellsberg, Daniel, photo with NB at Wellfleet, 476
Emerson, Ralph Waldo, 85, 127
En-Lai, Chou, 200
Engels, Friedrich, 282, 458

Engholm, Björn, 567
Enlai, Zhou, 200
Eppler, Erhard, 23, 160, 301, 397, 528, 576, 577, 581, 584, 598, 655
Epstein, Klaus, 130
Erikson, Erik, 10, 23, 95, 134, 207, 230, 473, 475, 477, 478
Erikson, Kai, 455, 477, 493
Ernst, Daniel, 647
Errington, Fred, 410
Estier, Claude, 543, 557
Evans-Pritchard, E. E., 255
Everett, John, 389

Fairlie, Henry, 563
Faison, Lane, 86, 89, 91
Fallada, Hans, 199
Farber, Leslie, 486
Farnsworth, Dana, 81
Faulkner, William, 38
Fay, Sidney, 44
Febvre, Lucien, 193-194
Fehér, Ferenc, 349
Fei Xiaotong, 99
Ferguson, Otis, 43
Fernández Krohn, Juan María, 193
Fetscher, Iring, 401, 418, 586
Feuer, Lewis, 41
Fini, Gianfranco, 685, 686
Firth, Raymond, 171, 691
Fischer, Fritz, 137
Fischer, George, 40, 135, 404
Fischer, Joschka, 399, 583, 589
Fischer, Louis, 40
Fisher family, 13
Fisher, Barbara, 469
Fisher, Betty, 469, 471-473
Fisher, Charles, 227, 469-473, 647
Fisher, John, 173
Fitzgerald, F. Scott, 38, 334
Flom, Joseph, 51
Flood, Terry, acknowledgments,

23, 700
Florensky, Pavel, 516
Floud, Jean, 285, 294
Flynn, Elizabeth Gurley, 38
Foot, Michael, 172, 235
Foot, Paul, 268, 269
Ford family (motors), 530
Ford, Gerald, 485, 486, 520, 526, 549, 629
Forster, E. M., 219
Foucault, Michel, 349, 450
Fouchet, Christian, 394
Franco, Francisco, 5, 68, 186, 329, 528, 670-673, 677
Fraser, Douglas, 521, 549, 625
Frazier, Franklin, 423
Freedman, Maurice, 171
Freud, Anna, 106, 180, 227, 667
Freud, Sigmund, 4, 6, 46, 71-73, 95, 113, 114, 116, 117, 142, 154, 180, 182, 183, 236, 241, 291, 292, 348, 416, 440, 462, 470, 472, 473, 476, 496, 642, 658, 661, 663
Fried, Marc, 107, 114
Friedan, Betty, 309
Friedeburg, Ludwig von, 157
Friedman, Milton, 613, 638
Friedmann, Georges, 340
Fromm, Erich, 207
Fry, Varian, 497
Fulbright, William, 622
Fuller, Margaret, 10
Furet, François, 340, 450

Gadhafi, Muammar, 595
Gaitskell, Hugh, 172, 237, 238, 340
Galbraith, Catherine, 460, 518, 519
Galbraith, Jamie, 519
Galbraith, John Kenneth, 67, 95, 103, 176, 189, 216, 226, 238, 290, 299, 306, 310, 322, 332, 391, 459, 460, 484, 502, 518, 519

Galloni, Giovanni, 536
Gambino, Antonio, 529
Gandhi, Mahatma, 86, 478
Gannon, Thomas, SJ, 650, 651
Gansel, Norbert, 578
Gardner, Richard, 674, 675
Garfield, John, 30
Gauck, Joachim, 575
Gaus, Günter, 301, 581
Gay, Peter, 493
Geertz, Clifford, 441, 495, 496, 497, 664
Geismar, Alain, 372
Gell-Mann, Murray, 320
Gellner, Ernest, 167, 168, 175, 212, 247, 252, 441, 628
Gellner, Susan, 168
Genovese, Eugene, 465
Genscher, Hans-Dietrich, 569, 570, 591, 603
George III, 517
Geremek, Bronisław, 623
Gerth, Hans, 99, 212, 376
Gewertz, Deborah, 410, 466
Giannotti, Gianni, 538
Gibb, Julian, 452
Gibbon, Edward, 632
Giddens, Anthony, 676, 691
Gifford, Prosser, 438
Gilbert, David, 377
Gilbert, James, 481
Gilbert, W. S., 249
Gilligan, Carol, 449, 477
Ginsberg, Morris, 169, 247, 266
Giolitti, Antonio, 198
Glass, David, 169, 247, 263
Glazer, Nathan, 380
Globke, Hans, 279
Glotz, Peter, 586
Godin, Henri (Abbe Godin), 337
Goethe, Johann Wolfgang von, 25, 267, 590, 612

Goldman, Emma, 445
Goldmann, Lucien, 295, 340, 357, 401
Goldschmidt, Dietrich, 278, 279
Goldway, David, 28, 30
Gollwitzer, Helmut, 23, 279, 280
Gomułka, Władysław, 352, 353
Gonzalez, Elian, 525
González, Felipe, 528, 557, 558, 670, 672, 674, 676
Goodhart, Arthur, 270
Goodhart, David, 692
Goodman, Paul, 273, 299, 322
Goodwin, Doris Kearns, photo 599
Goodwin, Richard, 271
Gorbachev, Mikhail, 296, 569-571, 598, 603-605, 637
Gordon, Kermit, 88, 512
Gorz, André, 198
Gould, Julius, 169, 247, 263
Gouldner, Alvin, 190, 441, 455
Grafton, Sam, 68
Graham, Billy, 630
Graham, Fred, 517
Gramsci, Antonio, 431
Grass, Günter, 196, 397, 528, 547, 562, 571, 584, 608, 662, 699
Gray, John, 691
Green, Theodore, 418, 419
Greenbaum, Ed, 12
Greenbaum, Joanne, 12
Greenbaum, Susan, 12
Greenberg, Clement, 41, 79, 91-95, 133, 134, 225, 298, 379, 488, 664
Greenberg, Daniel (disambiguation: childhood friend of NB) 35
Greenberg, Daniel (disambiguation: son of Clement), 91
Greenberg, Hank, 15
Greenberg, Martin, 91
Gregory, Dick, 446
Greiner, Bernd, 586

Griffiths, John, 173
Grumelli, Antonio, Monsignor, 529, 530
Guggenheim, Peggy, 90
Guignebert, Charles, 689
Guillen, Claudio, 68, 70
Gurvitch, Annie, 357
Gurvitch, Georges, 122, 311, 335, 357
Gusdorf, Georges, 346-348
Guterman, Norbert, 341, 342
Guthrie, Sally, 608, 687

Habermas, Jürgen, 157, 160, 183, 189, 208, 349, photo with NB 350, 398, 399, 401, 423, 500, 528, 542, 547, 586, 619, 652, 695, 699
Habermas, Ute, 619
Hacker, Andrew, 300, 317
Hahn, Erich, 597, 598
Haig, Alexander, 673
Hailsham, Lord (Quintin Hogg), 295
Halberstam, David, 115, 381
Halbwachs, Maurice, 194
Haldeman, H. R., 539
Hall, Stuart, 215, 231, 239, 480, 529, 699
Halperin, Stanley, 34, 50, photos with NB 56
Halsey, Chelly, 189, 263, 266, 267, 285, 632
Hamlet (fiction), 372, 663
Harman, Jane, 589
Harriman, Averill, 490, 521, 620
Harrington, Michael, 210, 229, 299, 309, 391, 427, 502, 507-510, 549, 551, 556
Harris, David, 678
Hartmann, Heinz, 73, 227, 470
Hartz, Louis, 189, 212, 305
Hastie, William H., 423, 424

Hatch, Robert, 492
Havemann, Katja, 600
Havens, Leston, 66, 69, 70, 72
Hawkins, Hugh, 418, 419
Hayden, Tom, 318, 319, 322
Hayek, Friedrich, 175, 613
Healy, Timothy, SJ, acknowledgements, 16, 445, 646, 650, 654, 661, 667, 675
Heath, Edward, 255, 506
Heath, Mary, 466
Heck, Bruno, 564
Hegedüs, András, 351, 352
Heidegger, Martin, 278, 328, 336
  Galbraith family, 332
Heinemann, Gustav, 160, 527, 528, 576
Heller, Ágnes, 349, 350, 401
Helms, Richard, 518
Hemingway, Ernest, 334
Henkel, Artur, 294
Hennis, Wilhelm, 136, 418
Henri IV of France, 195
Henry VIII of England, 243
Hermes, Peter, 577
Heron, Caroline, 364, 365
Herron, Caroline, 364
Hershey, John, 95
Herzog, Guy, 545
Herzog, Isaac, 620
Hexter, William, 438
Hill, Christopher, 242, 243, 264, 312, 490, 618
Hilton, Rodney, 217, 242
Hinckley, John, 525
Hirschman, Albert, 495-497
Hiss, Alger, 133
Hitchcock, Alfred, 14, 164
Hitchens, Christopher, 268, 509, 630-634
Hitchens, Peter, 631
Hitler, Adolf, 11, 14, 21, 31, 36, 37, 39, 42, 45, 106, 147, 186, 234, 276, 475, 490, 501, 529, 563, 649
Hobbes, Thomas, 112, 266
Hobhouse, Leonard, 169
Hobsbawm, Eric, 142, 178, 183-185, 217, 231, 232, 236, 242, 245, 490, 529, 691, 699
Hochfeld, Julian, 204, 295, 296
Hoffman, Abbie, 379
Hofstadter, Richard, 141, 189, 408, 484
Hogg, Quintin (Lord Hailsham), 295
Hoggart, Richard, 218, 219
Holmes, Oliver Wendell, 130, 658, 659
Homans, George, 117, 213, 249
Hone, Angus, 268
Honecker, Erich, 602-604, 606
Hook, Sidney, 5
Horkheimer, Max, 311, 459
Howard, Edgerton, 72
Howe, Irving, 5, 213, 214, 224, 298, 368, 388, 427, 467, 468, 507, 508, 510, 641
Hsiu, David, 57
Hu Shih, 56
Huber, Wolfgang, 23, 547, 573-577, 655, 695
Hughes, H. Stuart, 301, 303, 388, 407, 459, 500, 502
Hughes, Thomas, 23
Humphrey, Hubert, 340, 412
Hunter, Robert, 525, 555
Hunter, Sam, 84
Huntington, Samuel, 358, 522
Husserl, Edmund, 336
Hutchins, Robert, 23, 44
Huxley, Aldous, 16, 53, 142, 163

Ickes, Harold, 36, 501
Ifill, Christopher, 217

Isserman, Maurice, 368

Jackson, Andrew, 30
Jackson, Henry, 508, 521, 549
Jackson, Jesse, 630, 643, 653
Jagan, Cheddi, 170
James, C. L. R., 484
James, Henry, 119, 120, 125, 142, 164, 334
James, William, 127, 130, 440
Jefferson, Thomas, 5, 127, 544, 633
Jessup, Philip, 218
Joffe, Walter G., 180, 359
John Paul II, Pope, 641, 642, 648, 649, 681
Johnson, Lyndon, 49, 88, 331-333, 363, 368, 369, 391, 402, 485, 512, 520, 525, 526, 636, 637, 639
Jolas, Eugene, 74, 335
Jolas, Maria, 74, 335
Jonas, Hans, 366
Jordan, Hamilton, 521
Jordan, Herbert, 517
Jospe, Roger, 68, 70
Jospin, Lionel, 397, 651, 679, 693
Joyce, James, 29, 51, 53, 68, 74, 93, 142, 478
Juquin, Pierre, 546

Kadar, Janos, 349
Kafka, Franz, 41, 134, 224
Kaganovitch, Lazar, 226
Kalicki, Jan, 525, 526
Kandel, Eric, 129
Kastenmeier, Robert, 272, 461, 510, 513
Kateb, George, 413, 428, 450, 452, 611
Katznelson, Ira, 692
Kaysen, Annette, 131, 212, 314
Kaysen, Carl, 105, 131, 212, 220, 272, 273, 314, 494, 495, 497

Kazin, Alfred, 223, 271
Kazin, Michael, 368
Keats, John, 267
Kelly, Petra, 589
Keniston, Kenneth, 477
Kennan, George, 95, 96, 316, 496
Kennedy, Edward, 301, 419, 479, 502, 524, 525, 543, 547, 548, 549, 551, 555, 556, 589, 621, 628, 630, 637
Kennedy, John, 49, 88, 95, 131, 183, 221, 226, 255, 269, 270-273, 280, 288, 290, 299, 301-304, 307, 310, 313-316, 312, 318, 330-333, 338, 340, 349, 373, 379, 404, 414, 419, 460, 461, 481, 484, 485, 490, 505, 507, 508, 510, 511, 526, 536, 547, 567, 630, 637, 639
Kennedy, Robert, 389, 419, 481, 531, 547, 629
Kermode, Frank, 695
Kernan, Al, 84
Kerr, Clark, 321
Kesselring, Albert, 152
Keynes, John Maynard, 67, 87, 96, 164, 237, 306, 315, 519, 558, 623
Khrushchev, Nikita, 185, 187, 204, 216, 280, 295, 310, 603
Kiesinger, Kurt Georg, 397
King, Martin Luther, 370, 389, 404, 531
King, Richard, 69
Kirchwey, Freda, 488
Kirkland, Lane, 557
Kirkpatrick, Jeane, 186, 616, 650
Kissinger, Henry, 103, 129, 130, 301, 421, 429, 430, 485, 486, 490, 549, 581, 615, 637
Kistiakowsky, George, 475
Klär, Karl-Heinz, 553
Klein, Melanie, 180
Klohr, Olof, 355

Klonsky, Milton, 75
Klose, Ulrich, 548
Kluckhohn, Clyde, 104, 105, 108, 109
Knorr, Klaus, 589
Kogon, Eugen, 159, 547
Kohl, Helmut, 569, 586, 590, 602, 603, 607, 615, 654
Kok, Wim, 651
Kołakowski, Leszek, 353, 354, 539, 699
König, Franz (Cardinal), 505, 529
König, René, 157
Kosík, Karel, 203, 204
Kozodoy, Neal, 641
Krasin, Yuri, 598
Kraus, Michael, 51, 52
Kreisky, Bruno, 432, 505, 586, 676
Krenz, Egon, 606
Krim, Seymour, 75
Krippendorff, Ekkehart, 586
Kris, Ernst, 73
Kristol, Irving, 182, 191, 232, 245
Krohn, Juan María Fernández, 193
Kuhn, Thomas, 125, 311, 440, 441
Kurzweil, Alan, 385
Kurzweil, Edith, 384-385, 470, 486
Kvitsinsky, Yuli, 604, 608

La Guardia, Fiorello, 7, 53, 74
Lafontaine, Oskar, 584, 693
Lanc, Erwin, photo with NB, 580
Lang, Jack, 543
Langer, Walter, 106
Langer, William, 106
Lasch, Christopher, 304, 358, 379, 441, 463-466, 482, 484-485, 500, 617, 653, 660, 699
Lasch, Nell, 464
Lash, Joseph, 55
Laski, Harold, 60, 163, 172, 175, 177, 178

Lawrence, D. H., 170, 235
Lazarsfeld, Paul, 294
Le Bras, Gabriel, 193, 194
Leach, Edmund, 171
Lederer, Emil, 99, 141
Lefebvre, Armel, 342
Lefebvre, Henri, 149, 189, 336, 341, 342, 346, 347, 357, 359, 372, 373, 395, 418, 441, 458, 500, 542, 643
Lefort, Claude, 338, 393
Lehrer, Jim (MacNeil/Lehrer), 493, 589, 627
Lenin, Vladimir, 99, 154, 289, 291, 296, 458, 516
Lenzer, Gertrud, 365, and on list of books by NB
Leonard, Wolfgang, 493
Lerner, Max, 42, 68
Lessing, Doris, 231, 234, 235, 699
Lévi-Strauss, Claude, 335, 340
Levy, Adele, 73
Levy, David, 73, 74
Lewis, Sinclair, 15, 37, 65, 492, 617
Lichtenstein, Nelson, 644
Lichtheim, George, 182, 183, 222, 293, 349, 460, 486
Lifton, Robert, 23, 422, 441, 446, 473, photos of home in Wellfleet 474, 475, photo with NB and Daniel Ellsberg at Wellfleet 476, 477, 478, 481, 500, 696, 700
Lincoln, Abraham, 30, 39, 196, 579, 608, 634
Lindsay, John, 332, 373
Lingeman, Richard, 492
Lipset, Seymour Martin, 189, 192, 267, 314, 455
Little, David, 123
Litvinov, Maxim, 45
Livingston, Robert Gerald, 557, 574
Lloyd-George, Gwilym, 210
Locke, Alain Leroy, 61

Locke, John, 164, 658
Lockwood, David, 170, 189, 247
Loeb, James, 39
Loest, Erich, 601
Loewenstein, Rudolph, 73
Loper, Janet, 89
Lortz, Joseph, 158, 159
Low, David, 31, 36
Lowell family, 456
Lowell, Abbott Lawrence, 101
Löwith, Karl, 138, 190
Lubac, Henri de, SJ, 340
Lubac, Henri de, 340
Lukács, György, 70, 184, 350, 351, 618
Lukes, Steven, 268, 283, 285, 630
Luria, Dan, 523
Lustiger, Jean-Marie, Cardinal, 649
Luther, Martin, 38, 136-138, 141, 145, 158, 195, 207, 274, 376, 475, 478, 565, 572, 575, 577, 643, 682, 695
Lüthy, Herbert, 544
Lynd, Helen, 99, 386
Lynd, Robert Staughton, 99, 189, 273, 299, 311, 312, 386
Lysenko, Trofim, 413, 428

Maccoby, Michael, 220, 273
Macdonald, Dwight, 41, 47, 48, 77, 90, 92, 95, 98, 135, 197, 216, 224, 232, 245, 246, 299, 335, 379, 427, 441, 507, 565, 646
Macdonald, Ramsay, 177, 521
MacDougall, Donald, 260
MacInnes, Colin, 233
MacIver, Robert, 58, 386, 455
Macmillan, Harold, 237, 328, 331
MacNeil, Robert (MacNeil/Lehrer), 493, 589, 627
Macrae, Donald, 165, 166, 168, 247
Magri, Lucio, 533

Mailer, Norman, 213, 216, 224, 379, 441, 453, 467, 471, 477, 484, 571, 663, 688
Maine de Biran, François-Pierre-Gontier, 416
Maizière, Lothar de, 602
Malinowski, Bronisław, 99
Mallet, Serge, 340, 542
Malley, James B., SJ, 648
Malraux, André, 14, 76, 78, 335, 340, 501, 540, 541, 553, 612, 658
Manca, Enrico, 536
Mandel, Ernest, 418
Mann, Thomas, 14, 20, 29, 142, 695
Mannheim, Karl, 86, 99, 122, 311, 548
Mansfield, Harvey, 129
Mao Zedong, 126, 185, 415, 433, 458, 459, 478, 540, 553
Marcantonio, Vito, 7, 38
Marcus, Steven, 365, 379, 431, 481
Marcuse, Herbert, 109, 149, 182, 183, 189, 216, 291, 303, 306, 322, 324, 327, 401, 416, 458-460, 500, 502, 511
Maron, Monika, 601
Marquand, John, 65, 103
Marsch, Wolf-Dieter, 23, 196, 608
Marshall, George C., 34, 87, 384, 550
Marshall, T. H., 169, 170, 189, 208, 247
Martelli, Claudio, 537, 683
Martini, Cardinal Carlo Maria, 681, 682
Marx, Jane, 429
Marx, Karl, 41, 93, 99, 138, 165, 190, 191, 199, 245, 267, 282-284, 286, 310, 316, 317, 340, 342, 387, 416, 439, 451, 458, 476, 499, 544, 579, 586, 658, 659
Marx, Leo, 388, 389, 407, 412, 413, 418, 419, 427, 429, 433, 444

Masaccio, 87
Mascolo, Denys, 338
Massimo, Rick, acknowledgements
Massu, Jacques, 393
Mathiez, Albert, 336
Matthiessen, F. O., 49, 121, 418
Matthöfer, Hans, 397, 548
Mattina, Enzo, 536
Mayer, Carl, 376
Mayer, Christopher, 671
Maynes, William, 270
McCarthy, David, 645, 666
McCarthy, Joseph, 107, 108, 111, 120, 121, 128, 133, 169, 202, 491, 515
McCarthy, Mary, 57, 80, 90, 129, 646
McCloy, John J., 406, 412, 413, 447, 618
McCormick, John, 123
McGovern, George, 439, 446, 483, 485, 506, 519, 522, 629
McNamara, Robert, 310, 407, 514, 520, 525, 576, 639
McNeil, Kenneth, acknowledgements
McWilliams, Carey, 490, 492
Mead, Walter Russell, 676
Meade, James, 174
Medlicott, W. Norton, 178
Mehl, Roger, 23, 275, 334, 342, 344
Meiklejohn, Alexander, 407
Meleagrou, Eleni, 632, 633
Melville, Herman, 119
Mendès France, Pierre, 176, 290, 340, 395, 543
Merkel, Angela, 356, 575, 695
Merleau-Ponty, Maurice, 335, 336, 340
Mertes, Michael, 586
Merton, Robert, 58
Meyers, Buddy, 471

Michalenko, Alexei, SJ, 648
Miliband, David Wright, 212, 692
Miliband, Ed, 492, 692
Miliband, Marion, 692
Miliband, Ralph, 172, 173, 189, 212, 692
Militello, Giacinto, 557
Mill, John Stuart, 164, 284
Miller, Henry, 334
Miller, Perry, 49, 108
Miller, William, 85, 86
Mills, C. Wright, 48, 99, 137, 141, 189, 208, 210-212, 214, 216, 223, 225, 226, 243, 271, 290, 294, 311, 322, 333, 376, 387, 408, 422, 460, 484, 699
Mirow, Thomas, 553
Mitchell, Juliet, 298
Mitscherlich Alexander, 145, 476
Mitterrand, François, 90, 345, 395, 397, 478, 502, 506, 524, 543, 546, 556, 558
Modrow, Hans, 602
Mogherini, Federica, 683
Moltmann, Jürgen, 547, 643, 653
Momper, Walter, 593, 602
Montefiore, Alan, 9
Montefiore, Moses, 8, 9
Moore, Barrington, 109, 306, 459
Morgan, Kenneth O. (Lord Morgan), 692
Morgan, Lord (Kenneth O. Morgan), 692
Morgenthau, Henry, 36
Morin, Edgar, 171, 189, 205, 240, 331, 338, 373, 393, 441, 500
Mornet, Daniel, 618
Morris, William (disambiguation: 19th-century author and designer), 217, 233, 236
Morris, William (disambiguation, birth name of Lord Nuffield), 256

Morris, Willy, 381
Morrison, Philip, 475, 477, 478
Moscovici, Serge, 539
Mosley, Oswald, 234
Motchane, Didier, 542
Mowrer, Edgar Ansel, 20
Moynihan, Daniel Patrick, 7, 380, 425, 549, 616, 620, 621
Mudge, Lewis, 23, 413, 420
Müller-Armack, Alfred, 157, 590
Müller, Albrecht, 553, 564-567
Murdoch, Iris, 60, 232, 233, 267, 282, 294
Murdoch, Rupert, 10
Murray, Henry, 106, 114, 653, 654
Murray, Pauli, 62
Mussolini, Benito, 47, 689
Myrdal, Gunnar, 189

Nabokov, Nicolas, 370
Nagler, Steve, 421
Nagy, Imre, 185, 350-352
Napoleon (Napoleon Bonaparte), 142, 275, 296, 336, 344, 395, 529, 541, 649
Napolitano, Giorgio, 533, 535, 684, 689
Nash Smith, William, 444
Nasser, Gamal Abdel, 185, 186
Navasky, Victor, 491, 492, 631, 699
Naville, Pierre, 189
Nédoncelle, Maurice, Catholic Monsignor, 344
Nell, Ed, 283
Nell, Oona, 283
Nelson, Benjamin, 376
Nenni, Pietro, 536
Newton, Francis (pen name of Eric Hobsbawm), 184
Niebuhr, Reinhold, 38, 39, 126, 290, 516, 550
Niemöller, Martin, 176

Nietzsche, Friedrich, 128, 312, 385, 416
Nixon, Richard M., 33, 421, 423, 425, 426, 429, 430, 439, 484-486, 490, 506, 512, 520, 521, 523, 526, 540, 546, 549, 581, 615, 620, 625, 629, 637
Nora, Pierre, 700
Nordhaus, William, 589
Nuffield, Lord (William Morris), 256
Nye, Joseph, 269

O'Connor, Frank, 524
O'Dea, Tom, 122
O'Donovan, Leo, SJ, 668
O'Keefe, Vincent, SJ, 649
Oakeshott, Michael, 172, 177, 178
Obama, Barack, 525, 626, 629, 636, 644, 653
Odets, Clifford, 30
Oertzen, Peter von, 189, 208, 579
Offe, Claus, 539
Oistrakh, David, 283
Okun, Arthur, 623
Ollman, Bertell, 283
Olsen, Eric, 476
Ondarza, Henning von, 604, 608
Oppenheimer, Robert, 76, 77, 131, 133, 322
Orsy, Ladislas, SJ, 658
Orwell, George, 22, 41, 163, 165, 199, 238, 489, 658
Osborne, John, 176, 233, 287
Oswald, Lee Harvey, 95, 331, 332
Owen, David, 138, 202, 213, 665
Owen, Robert, 172, 173

Pacelli, Eugenio (Pope Pius XII), 194, 338, 584
Paehler, Karl-Heinz, 156
Page, Charles, 455

Palamountain, Joe, 123
Palme, Olof, 556, 557
Papandreou, Andreas, 444, 445
Papandreou, Margaret, 444, 445
Pareto, Vilfredo, 86, 249, 536
Park, Robert, 312, 386
Parlato, Valentino, 533
Parrington, V. L. (Vernon), 5, 501
Parsons, Talcott, 104, 105, 108, 111, 112, 122, 136, 165, 179, 206, 208, 213, 249, 305, 306, 313, 324, 388, 406, 409, 468
Pascal, Blaise, 340, 357
Patterson, Orlando, 675
Pearson, Gabriel, 215
Pechman, Joseph, 622, 623
Pell, Claiborne, 226
Pelny, Enkelin, 566, 567
Pelny, Stefan, 566, 567
Peretz, Martin, 301
Perger, Werner, 679
Perkins, Frances, 488
Perry, Bliss, 54
Persson, Göran, 651
Peterson, Peter, 651
Philip II of Spain, 529, 649
Phillips, William, 79, 90, 92, 216, 222-224, 293, 294, 298, 316, 369, 376, 479-488, 664
Piaget, Jean, 357
Pinkard, Terry, 657, 660
Pintor, Luigi, 533
Pipes, Richard, 577
Pitkin, Donald, 410, 427
Pitofsky, Robert, 666
Pizzorno, Alessandro, 539
Plamenatz, John, 259
Plato, 125, 172, 253, 390, 417, 658
Pleitgen, Fritz, 585
Plessner, Helmuth, 279
Plimpton, Calvin, 388, 412, 423, 445, 666

Plimpton, Francis, 388
Pochoda, Elizabeth, 492
Podhoretz, Norman, 3, 34, 197, 222, 240, 273, 274, 298, 299, 322, 365, 368, 378, 407, 426, 441, 481, 486, 621
Poincare, Henri, 105
Poirier, Richard, 379, 481
Polanco, Jesús, 672
Polanyi, Michael, 287, 548
Pollock, Jackson, 133, 622
Pompidou, Georges, 393
Pope Benedict XVI, Joseph Ratzinger, 682
Pope Francis, Jorge Mario Bergoglio, 682
Pope John XXIII (Angelo Giuseppe Roncalli), 276, 337, 584, 624, 649
Pope Pius XII (Eugenio Pacelli), 194, 338, 584
Poppe, Gerd, 596, 600
Popper, Karl, 164, 178, 287
Powell, Enoch, 234
Pratt, Trude, 55
Prodi, Romano, 684, 688
Putnam, James Jackson, 440

Racine, Jean, 125, 357
Rahv, Philip, 90, 222, 223, 479, 480
Rákosi, Mátyás, 352
Rangell, Leo, 494
Ranke, Leopold von, 145
Rapp, Herbert A., 30, 33
Raskin, Marcus, 272-274, 303, 314, 418, 461, 510-515, 526, 554, 628
Ratté, John, 435
Ratzinger, Joseph, Pope Benedict XVI, 682
Rau, Johannes, 160, 528, 576
Rawls, John, 542, 650
Reagan, Ronald, 484, 523, 525, 527, 556, 558, 570, 574, 584, 595, 624-626, 630, 637, 650, 651, 663

Redford, Robert, 694
Redlich, Norman, 95, 332
Reich, Wilhelm, 46, 95, 114
Reichlein, Alberto, 533
Reinhold, Otto, 594, 597
Reissig, Ralf, 597
Remington, Thomas, 58
Renzi, Matteo, 683
Reuther, Victor, 523, 547
Reuther, Walter, 80, 523, 547, 625
Rice, Condoleezza, 604, 608, 677
Rice, Eugene, 14
Richta, Radovan, 540
Ricoeur, Paul (Ricœur in text), 340, 349
Rieff, Philip, 223, 237
Riesman, David, 132, 213, 226, 247, 271-273, 290, 303, 306, 322, 323, 327, 328, 387, 460-463, 475, 511, 512
Riesman, Evey, 460
Robbins, Lionel, 173, 174, 212
Roberts, Sally and Dick, acknowledgements
Robinson, Edward G., 30
Rocard, Michel, 508, 542, 543, 557
Roche, John, 363
Rockefeller, Nelson, 615
Rodgers, Daniel, 52
Rodotà, Stefano, 538
Rolland, Romain, 71
Romney, Mitt, 636
Roncalli, Angelo Giuseppe (Pope John XXIII), 276, 337, 584, 624, 649
Roosevelt, Eleanor, 39, 41, photograph 55, 57, 58, 60, 552
Roosevelt, Franklin D., 5, 9, 15, 16, 21, 28, 32, 36, 37, 41, 45, 53, 54, 62, 103, 306, 315, 341, 478, 520, 526, 558, 579, 636
Roosevelt, Theodore, 635

Roques, Valeska von, 585
Rosanvallon, Pierre, 542
Rose, Peter, 455
Rosenberg, Harold, 369
Rosenfeld, Isaac, 75, 77
Rosenthal, A. M., "Abe, " 557
Rossanda, Rossana, 533
Rossi, Alice, 455
Rossi, Paolo, 324
Rossi, Peter, 455
Rostow, Walt, 313
Roth, Philip, 36, 37
Rousseau, Jean-Jacques, 164, 179, 284, 335, 416, 658, 661
Rouvroy, Claude Henri de (comte de Saint-Simon), 284, 416
Rubin, Jerry, 379
Rudd, Mark, 368, 427, 515
Rudenstine, Neil, 452
Ruffolo, Giorgio, 536
Rumsfeld, Donald, 633
Rusk, Dean, 272, 637
Russell, Bertrand, 235
Rustin, Bayard, 236

Said, Edward, 436, 633
Saint-Simon, comte de (Claude Henri de Rouvroy), 284, 416
Sakharov, Andrei, 525, 540, 595, 605, 652
Salleo, Ferdinando, 685
Samuel, Ralph, 214, 215, 240
Samuelson, Arthur, 417
Santamaria, Julian, 493, 670
Sarbanes, Paul, 596
Sargent, Carole, acknowledgements
Sartre, Jean-Paul, 78, 79, 122, 199, 220, 224, 271, 335, 336, 338, 340, 341, 351, 357, 392, 433, 541, 619
Sauvageot, Denis, 372
Saville, John, 216, 217

Sawyer, John, 66, 294
Schäfer, Helmut, 591
Schaff, Adam, 204, 353
Schalck-Golodkowski, Alexander, 605
Schapera, Isaac, 171
Schapiro, Meyer, 48, 408
Schelsky, Helmut, 156, 170, 189, 399-400
Schiller, Friedrich, 282
Schily, Otto, 589
Schink, Bernhard, 158
Schlafly, Phyllis, 630
Schlesinger, Arthur, Jr., 103, 104, 123, 220, 226, 270-273, 299, 310, 484, 521
Schlink, Edmund, 158
Schlossberg, Stephen, 519-524, 554, 557, 625, 627
Schmeling, Max, 15
Schmidt, Helmut, 329, 397, 520, 537, 547, 563-566, 569, 576, 577, 587, 607, 615
Schmidt, Vivien, 385
Schmitt, Carl, 324, 554
Schoenherr, Friedrich, 604, 608
Scholem, Gershom, 181, 182, 312, 469
Schorske, Carl, 498, 644
Schrag, Philip, 659
Schröder, Gerhard, 553, 567, 581, photo with NB 582, 583-584, 651, 679, 692, 693, 695
Schultze, Charles, 555, 623
Schumacher, Kurt, 146
Schuman, Frederick, 86, 93, 94, 99
Schumpeter, Joseph, 119, 120, 306
Schwartz, Warren, 660
Seidman, Michael, 660
Selden, Anna, acknowledgements
Seligman, Eustace, 412, 618
Sellers, Charles, 527

Sennett, Richard, 364, 418, 441, 500, 539
Serge, Victor, 662
Shakespeare, William, 125
Shalala, Donna, 675
Shamir, Yitzhak, 477
Shanker, Albert, 368
Shih, Hu, 56
Shils, Edward, 191, 192, 212, 213, 263, 264, 460, 497
Shultz, George P., 637
Sica, Alan, 455
Sigal, Clancy, 234, 237
Silvers, Robert, 366, 429
Simmel, Georg, 241
Simon, Paul, Senator, 648
Simonis, Heide, 578
Sinatra, Frank, 7
Sinclair, Upton, 15
Singer, Isaac Bashevis, 634
Smelser, Neil, 192
Smith, Al, 16
Smith, Barbara, 692
Smith, Constance, 75
Smith, Hallett, 69, 320
Smith, Virginia, 57
Smith, William Nash, 444
Snow, C. P., 249, 285
Snow, Edgar, 20, 501
Solomon, Barbara Probst, 319, 364, 381, 700
Solomon, Izzy, 19, 21
Sontag, Susan, 379, 441, 481, 482, 487, 495
Sorel, Georges, 86
Sorokin, Pitirim, 109
Soto, Helga Diekhoff, 23, 670, photo with NB in Venice, 671, 672-675, 677, photo with NB at Wellfleet 678, 699
Souveraine, Boris, 516
Spencer, Herbert, 250, 386

Spender, Stephen, 191
Stalin, Joseph, 22, 27, 31, 41, 45, 50, 54, 61, 62, 92, 98, 99, 126, 133, 134, 141, 149, 153, 154, 160, 182, 183, 185, 186, 204, 216, 220, 225, 243, 277, 286, 296, 310, 311, 317, 341, 352, 369, 370, 413, 428, 440, 459, 468, 489, 516, 532, 534, 537, 545, 569, 571, 576, 593, 594, 603, 614, 616, 643
Steinbeck, John, 29
Steinberg, Saul, 91
Steinbrück, Peer, 579
Steinem, Gloria, 630
Steiner, George, 285
Steinlein, Stephan, 584
Steinmeier, Frank-Walter, 583, 692, 693
Stendhal, 142, 335
Stent, Angela, 654
Sterling, Paul, 171
Sternhell, Zeev, 623
Stevens, Charles, 660
Stevenson, Adlai, 218, 340
Stillman, Donald, 625
Stimson, Henry, 36
Stocking, Fred, 69
Stolpe, Manfred, 573
Stoltenberg, Gerhard, 136
Stone, I. F., 272-274
Stone, Lawrence, 243, 264, 265
Stone, Shepard, 370
Strachey, John, 20, 60, 163, 501
Strachey, Lytton, 164
Strasser, Johano, 584
Strauss, Franz-Josef, 329, 590, 605
Straw, Jack, 433
Strout, Cushing, 66, 69, 70, 72
Strozier, Charles, 477
Suhard, Emmanuel Célestin, 194
Sullivan, Arthur, 249
Sulloway, Frank, 440

Sumner, William Graham, 386
Supek, Rudi, 418, 539
Sweeney, John, 644
Sweezy, Alan, 67, 87
Sweezy, Paul, 306, 418
Szczepański, Jan, 204, 354

Taft, William Howard, 637
Talmon, Jacob, 179
Tanguy, Yves, 104, 622
Tartakowsky, Danielle, 373
Tatò, Antonio, 536, photo with NB, 539
Taubes, Jakob, 278
Taubman, Bill, 413
Taubman, Jane, 413
Tawney, Roger H., 163, 177
Taylor, Charles, 215, 700
Tayor, A. J. P., 178
Teresa, Mother, 632
Thatcher, Margaret, 558
Thomas, Norman, 120, 507
Thompson, Edward, 216, 217, 236, 239, 242, 441, 450, 480, 490, 529
Titmuss, Richard, 173
Tito, Josip Broz, 107, 133, 401, 483
Tocqueville, Alexis de, 284, 335, 544
Togliatti, Palmiro, 78, 531, 534
Tolstoy, Leo, 210, 645
Tönnies, Ferdinand, 416
Torrance, John, 267, 268, 283, 285
Tortorella, Aldo, 690
Touraine, Alain, 189, 208, 315, 340, 372, 373, 393, 418, 500, 539, 540, 542, 700
Toynbee, Arnold, 184
Trafford, Abigail, 23
Tresckow, Henning von (father of Mark), 150
Tresckow, Mark von, 150
Trevor-Roper, Hugh, 243

Trilling, Diana, 216, 315, 369
Trilling, Lionel, 120, 224, 300, 315, 316, 365, 369, 408, 414
Troeltsch, Ernst, 138, 207
Trotsky, Leon, 19, 22, 26, 28, 29, 32, 44, 50, 60, 64, 120, 133, 183, 214, 223, 272, 315, 479, 483, 516, 549, 579, 594, 652
Truman, Harry, 39, 80, 94, 96, 120, 121, 526
Turner, Faythe, 23, 466, 471, 472, 518
Turner, Frederick, 135
Turner, Stansfield, 518
Turner, Victor, 497

Ugrinovitsch, Dmitri, 515, 516
Ungerer family, 342
Unrat, Professor (fiction), 348

Vance, Cyrus, 521, 522
Vandenberg, Arthur, 94
Varga, Ivan, 349
Veblen, Thorstein, 130, 175, 462
Vesper, Michael, 589
Viansson-Ponté, Pierre, 373
Vidal, Gore, 630
Vidich, Arthur, 376
Viveret, Patrick, 542
Voltaire, 338
von Brentano, Margherita, 278, 279, 586
von Bülow, Andreas, 579
von Dohnányi, Klaus, 563, 579
von Friedeburg, Ludwig, 157
von Oertzen, Peter, 189, 208, 579
von Oertzen, Peter, 189, 579
von Ondarza, Henning, 604, 608
von Ranke, Leopold, 145
von Roques, Valeska, 585
von Tresckow, Henning (father of Mark von Tresckow), 150
von Tresckow, Mark (son), 150
von Weizsäcker, Carl Friedrich, 652
Vyshinsky, Stefan (also spelled Wyszyński), 352

Walker, Patrick Gordon, 78
Wallace, George, 523, 625, 626
Wallace, Henry, 37, 120, 501
Wallerstein, Immanuel, 455
Walsh, Frances, 265, 266, 297
Walsh, George, 68, 70-72
Walsh, John, 265, 266, 269, 297
Walter, Bruno, 14
Ward, William J., 412, 413, 419, 430, 444, 446-451, 495, 518, 666
Warner, W. Lloyd, 249
Warnke, Paul, 513, 524, 555, 626
Waugh, Evelyn, 256, 671
Webb, Beatrice, 249
Webb, Sidney, 249
Weber, Max, 34, 99, 105, 108, 111, 113, 119, 120, 127, 130, 136, 138, 145, 157, 165, 190, 192, 207, 227, 245, 249, 284, 312, 313, 321, 324, 416, 462, 470, 583, 586, 624, 650
Wechsler, James, 60
Wedderburn, William, 173
Weil, André, 495-498
Weil, Simone, 335
Weinstein, Allen, 619
Weinstein, Jack B., 516, 518
Weisskopf, Victor, 432, 505
Weizmann, Chaim, 486
Weizsäcker, Carl Friedrich von, 652
Wells, H. G. 142, 163
Wertheim, Frederick, 95
West, Charles, 196
White, Lucia, 131, 213, 301
White, Michael, 692
White, Morton, 105, 123, 125, 130, 131, 213, 301, 336, 498

White, Robert, 114
Whitehead, Alfred North, 127
Wiatr, Andrzeg, 204
Wiesen Cook, Blanche, 58
Wiesner, Jerome, 511
Wilbur, Richard, 407
Wilhelm II, Kaiser, 16, 137, 146, 328, 342, 344
William I (William the Conqueror), 649
Williams, Joy, 266
Williams, Phillip, 260
Williams, Raymond, 218, 266, 480
Williams, Roger, 38
Williams, William Appleman, 299
Wilson, Brian, 285
Wilson, Edmund, 29, 53, 68, 99, 381, 646
Wilson, Harold, 172, 506
Winnicott, Donald, 227
Winpisinger, William, 626
Wittig, Peter, 700
Wojtyła, Karol Józef, Pope John Paul II, 624, 641, 642, 648, 649, 681, 682
Wok, Othman, 679
Wolf, Christa, 570
Wolf, Markus, 40, 570, 602
Wolfe, Thomas, 163
Wolfe, Tom, 26, 381
Wollenweber, Jürgen, 695
Wollstonecraft, Mary, 657
Wood, Tom, 44
Woodcock, Leonard, 519, 521, 549, 625
Woodhouse, P. G., 164
Woodward, C. Vann, 527
Wordsworth, William, 28, 133, 287

Wright, Jeremiah, 653
Wright, Richard, 391
Wright, Tony, 692
Wrong, Dennis, 135
Wulff, Christa, 601, 602
Wulff, Hans, 195, 196
Wyszyński, Stefan (also spelled Vyshinsky), 352

Xiaoping, Deng (Deng Xiaoping), 451
Xiaotong, Fei, 99

Yankelovich, Daniel, 477
Yard, Molly, 58
Yarmolinsky, Adam, 48, 49
Yarmolinsky, Avrahm, 48
Yerushalmi, David, 291
Yost, Tom, 413, 427, 428, 435
Young, Dorinda, Sr., 648
Young, Michael, 191

Zamoshkin, Yuri, 313, 314
Zangheri, Renato, photo with NB, 539
Zapata, Emiliano, 513
Zedong, Mao (Mao Zedong), 126, 185, 415, 433, 458, 459, 478, 540, 553
Zhou Enlai, 200
Ziegler, Jean, 539
Zilbach, Jacqueline, 107
Zitner, Sheldon, 33
Zola, Émile, 334
zu Solms, Graf, Count, 155, 156
Zwingli, Huldrych, 137, 138, 145, 207, 240, 274

www.ingramcontent.com/pod-product-compliance
Lightning Source LLC
Chambersburg PA
CBHW021755220426
43662CB00006B/67